ARMY HISTORICAL SERIES

AMERICAN MILITARY HISTORY

Maurice Matloff
General Editor

MILITARY INSTRVCTION

OFFICE OF THE CHIEF OF MILITARY HISTORY

UNITED STATES ARMY

WASHINGTON, D.C., 1969

Library of Congress Catalog Card Number: 76–600410

First Printing

For sale by the Superintendent of Documents, U.S. Government Printing Office
Washington, D.C. 20402 - Price $8.

Foreword

The Department of the Army has long recognized the need for a revised and updated volume on the Army's history to replace the work prepared by Army historians during the 1950's for use in the senior ROTC American Military History course. The present book is designed primarily to meet this need. Like its predecessor, this history is the work of many hands; unlike the earlier work, it appears as a publication of the Office of the Chief of Military History in its Army Historical Series and gives appropriate credit and assignment of responsibility to the scholars who have prepared the volume. In my judgment they have produced a history which will not only serve its primary purpose admirably but which will also appeal to the general reader and be useful in college teaching outside the ROTC course.

The list of contributors which follows indicates the multiple authorship of the volume. Consulting freely with one another, the authors have had as well the benefit of considerable outside review by scholars not associated with this office, the goal throughout being to make the volume as accurate, objective, and well balanced as possible in content and interpretation. In some instances they have corrected myths that have become "facts" over the years—there were no minutemen present as the American Revolution erupted on Lexington Common at dawn on April 19, 1775; and the bulk of Korean War casualties were taken in the first year of fighting, not after the truce negotiations began.

As of the time this manuscript goes to press, the final chapter on the Army's role in Vietnam remains unwritten. It is of course especially difficult to write the history of a war not yet over, but Chapter 28, covering the action through the end of 1967, does reflect the research and on-the-spot observation of several able historians whose personal and professional views of the war are by no means uniform. Yet no historical volume can be made perfect, and the Army's historical office urges readers to bring to its attention any errors in this work that they may discover.

Washington, D.C.
2 December 1968

HAL C. PATTISON
Brigadier General, USA
Chief of Military History

OCMH Contributors

BELL, WILLIAM GARDNER (Chapter 14), a graduate of the Cavalry School and a former editor of the *Cavalry Journal* and *Armor Magazine,* has written frequently on the frontier Army and the American West.

COAKLEY, ROBERT W. (Chapters 2, 3, 4, and 23), Ph. D. (Virginia), Chief, Staff Support Branch, is coauthor of the two *Global Logistics and Strategy* volumes in the Army's World War II Series.

CONN, STETSON (Chapter 19), Ph. D. (Yale), Chief Historian, is coauthor of *The Framework of Hemisphere Defense* and *Guarding the United States and Its Outposts.*

COOLING, BENJAMIN F., III (Chapters 10 and 11 and Bibliography), M.A. (Pennsylvania), after five years of OCMH service began teaching at the Pennsylvania Military College in September 1968.

FRIEDMAN, JOSEPH R. (Editor in Chief), B.A. (Oberlin), OCMH Editor in Chief since 1952, is also Editorial Consultant to the George C. Marshall Research Foundation.

HERMES, WALTER G. (Chapters 26 and 27), Ph. D. (Georgetown), Acting Chief, Current History Branch, is author of *Truce Tent and Fighting Front* in the Army's Korean War Series.

JONES, VINCENT P. (Chapters 15 and 16), Ph. D. (Wisconsin), is preparing the volume on *Manhattan: The Army and the Atomic Bomb.*

LUTTICHAU, CHARLES V. P. VON (Chapter 28), M.A. (American), since 1963 has served as principal specialist on the Army's involvement in Vietnam.

MACGREGOR, MORRIS J., JR. (Chapters 5 and 6), M.A. (Catholic), is preparing a volume on Negro integration into the armed forces since 1945.

MACDONALD, CHARLES B. (Chapters 17, 18, 22, and 28), B.A., Litt.D. (Presbyterian), Deputy Chief Historian, is author of *Company Commander* and of the *Three Battles, Siegfried Line,* and *Last Offensive* volumes in the World War II Series.

MATLOFF, MAURICE (Chapters 1, 20, and 21, General Editor), Ph. D. (Harvard), Chief, General History Branch, is coauthor of *Strategic Planning for Coalition Warfare, 1941–1942* and author of *Strategic Planning for Coalition Warfare, 1943–1944.*

MAYO, LIDA (Chapters 7 and 8), B.A. (Randolph-Macon), is coauthor of a biography of Henry Clay and of *The Ordnance Department: Procurement and Supply* and author of *The Ordnance Department: On Beachhead and Battlefront.*

MOSSMAN, B. C. (Chapters 24 and 25), B.A. (Nebraska State), is preparing the *Ebb and Flow* volume in the Korean War Series.

ROMANUS, CHARLES F. (Chapters 9 and 12), M.A. (Illinois), is coauthor of the three volumes on the China-Burma-India Theater and of *The Quartermaster Corps: Operations in the War Against Germany.*

SCHEIPS, PAUL J. (Chapter 13), Ph. D. (American), is serving as the OCMH historian of the Army's role in controlling domestic disturbances.

Preface

The Office of the Chief of Military History has prepared this historical survey of the organization and accomplishments of the United States Army primarily for use in the American Military History course usually given in the sophomore year of the Reserve Officers' Training Corps program in civilian colleges and universities. The aim has been to present a balanced history of the Army from its beginnings through the year 1967, with appropriate attention to peacetime as well as wartime achievements.

In describing military operations through the Civil War the contributors have pointed out, more than in later chapters, the application (or violation) of the principles of war that are discussed in the introductory chapter. In the interest of getting on with the narrative, they have necessarily omitted many other illustrations that will undoubtedly occur to the thoughtful reader. The century since the Civil War receives greater attention in this text than in its predecessor, both through chronological extension and by the inclusion of additional chapters on the post-Civil War period and World War I. Inevitably the story from World War II onward has a broader perspective than the record of the Army's earlier experiences, since in recent decades the Army's history has become increasingly intermingled with that of the other armed services and with that of the higher echelons of government directing the national defense.

In preparing this work, the contributors used as a point of departure the earlier ROTC text, *American Military History, 1607–1958*; but in the present volume half of the chapters are new or completely rewritten, and the remainder have been extensively revised. It is nevertheless only proper to acknowledge the work of previous contributors who wrote some of the basic texts of chapters used in the revision: Dr. Byron Fairchild, now with the Department of State Historical Office; the late Dr. Kent Roberts Greenfield, former Chief Historian; Dr. Richard M. Leighton, now with the faculty of the Industrial College of the Armed Forces; Dr. Leo J. Meyer, now retired; the late Dr. John Miller, jr., former Deputy Chief Historian; Professor Louis Morton of Dartmouth College; Brig. Gen. Paul McD. Robinett, USA (Ret.); and Mr. Robert R. Smith, recently returned to the OCMH staff. A major change has been the inclusion in the present work of an annotated general bibliography and detailed chapter bibliographies. Quotations have been used more generously than before, but it is hoped with sufficient identification in the text to justify the decision against documentation.

The planning for this work and the preparation of its preliminary draft were carried out under the supervision of Dr. Matloff. The draft was then reviewed by a panel with the undersigned as chairman, and consisting otherwise, in addition to four other contributors, of Professor Stephen E. Ambrose of The Johns Hopkins University; Mr. Detmar Finke, Chief, Reference Branch, OCMH; Maj. James A. Garnett, Assistant Professor of Military Science at the University of Virginia; Mr. Ralph W. Hampton of the United States Continental Army Command; Dr. Leighton; and Col. Wolfred K. White, Chief, Histories Division, OCMH. Additionally, the Continental Army Command circulated a number of copies of the draft to the ROTC departments of representative colleges and universities. Both panel and outside review comments aided materially in the final revision of the volume for publication. The Editor in Chief, Mr. Friedman, worked continuously with the contributors throughout the period of preparation and supervised the final editing of the manuscript by staff members of OCMH's Editorial Branch, including its chief, Mr. David Jaffé, and senior editor, Mrs. Loretto C. Stevens.

The forty-seven maps in this volume include six newly prepared by Mr. Mossman plus forty-one retained from those prepared by Maj. James P. Holly for the 1959 version. The photographs were selected by Miss Ruth A. Phillips, and the index was prepared by Mr. Nicholas J. Anthony.

Although the United States Continental Army Command is charged with setting up the guidelines for the ROTC American Military History course, its officials have gladly accepted the suggestions and comments presented by the historians of this office insofar as preparation of the present work is concerned. The contributors assume full responsibility for what appears in the following pages, including any errors of omission or commission.

Washington, D.C.   STETSON CONN
2 December 1968   Chief Historian

Contents

Maps

Illustrations

All illustrations are from Department of Defense files except the following: the picture on page 36 was obtained from the Wisconsin Historical Society, and the National Archives furnished the pictures on pages 145, 190, 191, 210, 226, 259, 278, 312, 314, 329, 356, 378, 394, 395, and 397.

CHAPTER 1

Introduction

The history of the United States Army lies in the mainstream of modern Western military development. Heir to European traditions, the American Army has both borrowed from and contributed to that main current. Molded by the New World environment, a product of democratic and industrial revolutions, it has at the same time evolved, along with the nation it serves, uniquely. To the present generation of Americans faced by complex challenges to their national security, the role that force and military institutions have played in American history becomes of increasing interest and importance. This volume is an introduction to the story of the U.S. Army, and of American military history, of which that story is an integral part.

What Is Military History?

Narrowly defined, the term *military history* used to connote conflicts in arms—campaigns and battles. In the eighteenth century, when the American Army was born and before the French Revolution introduced the modern concept of the "nation in arms," such eruptions in the Western World usually involved clashes by soldiers of the opposing armies and left the civilian masses largely unaffected. Until the latter part of that century, wars were relatively simple and restricted in area, forces, and objectives. The wars of the French Revolution and of Napoleon became mass conflicts of whole nations in arms. With the spread of the industrial revolution, warfare grew more complex and exerted an ever-increasing influence on society. This new era in warfare coincided with the evolution of the United States as an independent nation. In the first half of the twentieth century the effects of large-scale wars became so pervasive that they were felt not only by the combatant nations but throughout the entire world, now grown more compact. The outcome in those wars was no longer measured in terms of the preservation of national honor or the winning of territory, familiar in eighteenth century warfare, but in terms of national survival. Thus, as warfare in the past two centuries has broadened to involve more and more people and more and more of the energies and resources of society to fight it—or in more recent days, to deter it—the definition has had to be extended to encompass more activities.

Broadly defined, military history lies on the frontier between general history and military art and science. It deals with the confluence and interaction of military affairs with diplomatic, political, social, economic, and intellectual trends in society. To understand it therefore requires some knowledge of both general history and military art. In its American context it represents many interrelated facets. Certainly it involves wars—all kinds of wars. It may surprise Americans, who traditionally have regarded themselves as a peaceable and unmilitary people, to learn that the range of warfare in their national experience has been quite wide, and the incidence quite frequent. Born in a revolution, a violent struggle often considered a prelude to other "peoples' wars," the United States has since endured a bitter Civil War and participated in seven international wars. In American national experience war itself has undergone considerable change and oscillation from one mode to another. The American Revolution was a limited war of the eighteenth century variety; the War of 1812 and the Korean conflict of 1950–53 were two later models of limited conflict. The Civil War introduced the age of total war to which World Wars I and II added their bloody chapters. War cut deeper and deeper into the life of the nation. Since World War II, under the shadow of nuclear weapons that threaten all civilization with annihilation, warfare has returned to earlier forms. Guerrilla wars, foreshadowed in American experience by the long-continuing Indian wars and the Philippine Insurrection of 1899–1902, have come into vogue again and American forces have become engaged in counterinsurgency warfare, notably in Vietnam.

Wars used to be regarded as clearly definable exercises in violence when diplomacy failed and statesmen handed over to soldiers the burden of achieving victory. They were usually marked by formal ceremonies—a declaration at the beginning and a surrender and peace treaty at the end. Since World War II these formalities are no longer the fashion. War and peace have become blurred. Neither in Korea nor in Vietnam was war declared. No peace treaty followed the surrender of Germany in World War II, or the truce in Korea in 1953. While this change in the nature of warfare has affected the conduct of war and the role of the military and society in it, participation in organized violence in all its forms is a component of military history that must be treated. Not only must the traditional three C's of warfare—causes, conduct, and consequences—be studied, but as the line between war and peace becomes more indistinct, the periods between the wars gain in interest to students of military history.

Besides war in the broad sense, there is another major facet that military history must deal with and that military historians of this generation have found more and more integral to their subject. To apply force, armies are organized. Reflecting the national culture and varying in their impact on it, armies are institutions, social entities in themselves. Some armies have close relations with the societies from which they are drawn; others are separate and a class apart. For example, in much of United States history the Army was scattered in frontier posts and physically isolated from the rest of society. But in the period since World War II, as in the founding era, civil-military relations have been close. As institutions, armies take form and character. Their institutional outlines are manifested in a number of ways, some overt, some subtle: their organization and administration, system of training, mode of supply, planning for mobilization and the conduct of war, methods of fighting on the battlefield, weaponry and utilization of technology, system of command and control, selection of manpower and leaders, and relations with the civilian population and authorities. The whole host of policies, doctrines, customs, traditions, values, and practices that have grown up about armies are an important part of the institutional story. All of these facets represent histories in themselves and reflect change in the nature of warfare, technology, the country's internal development, and external responsibilities. A shift in one component will inevitably have impact within the institutional structure. For example, a fundamental change in weaponry, equipment, or technology, be it the adoption of gunpowder, the rifle musket, the airplane, the tank, or the atomic bomb, will affect the traditional modes of fighting and reverberate throughout the institutional framework. The phenomenon of cultural lag evident in other human institutions applies to military organizations too, and some armies have been slower to adopt changes than others, often with fatal results in the test of battle.

While the U.S. Army as a social entity has evolved to meet its primary mission—to fight—in its American institutional context military history must also treat the Army as a social force in peace. From the beginning the Army has played a role in developing the country—in exploring, guarding the frontier, and constructing roads, in engineering, transportation, communication, sanitation, and medicine, and in flood control. At the same time the Army has served as a vehicle for social mobility of certain disadvantaged groups—for example, European immigrants in the 1840's and 1850's and Negroes in the 1950's and 1960's. The mixture of the European legacy, native environment, democratic ideals and values, and national experience in war and peace have combined to mold the Army into a distinct institution in American life—a unique blend of professional and civilian elements. Indeed, as Russell F. Weigley, a student of the Army's institutional history, has well expressed it, the story of the American Army is really a history of "two armies"—"a Regular Army of professional soldiers and a citizen army of various components variously known as militia, National Guards, Organized Reserves, selectees."

It has been said that every generation rewrites its history. Its own needs and problems inevitably make it take fresh looks at its own past for light, understanding, guidance, and alternative courses of action. Nowhere is this necessity more evident than in the field of American military history today— broadly conceived. During most of the national existence of the United States the liberal democratic tradition and geographic isolation combined to subordinate in the public mind the role of force and military institutions in its history. Blessed by relatively weak neighbors on the north and south and safe behind its ocean barriers, the United States could define its security in terms of its own boundaries and frontiers. The military factor in its heritage, birth, and development tended to be discounted. But when scientists began to conquer space and time in the twentieth century, and the European system that had maintained order in the nineteenth century began to crumble under the impact of two world wars, Americans began to find their security bound up with the fate of other countries. The nation that began the twentieth century with a strong sense of security by mid-century began to feel insecure. As George F. Kennan, former director of the Policy Planning Staff of the Department of State, put it, "A country which in 1900 had no thought that its prosperity and way of life could in any way be threatened by the outside world had arrived by 1950 at a point where it seemed to be able to think of little else but this danger." Not since the era of the founding fathers has survival in a dangerous world become such an urgent issue and the foundations of national security of such concern.

Theory and Practice of War

The question of whether warfare should be treated as science or art has long interested students of military affairs. In the eighteenth century, the age of enlightenment, when the systematic study of war began, military theory regarded warfare as "mathematical" and "scientific." A general who knew mathematics and topography, the theorists optimistically maintained, could conduct campaigns with geometrical precision and win wars without bloody battles. The violent shock of Napoleonic warfare put a rude end to the notion of war as a purely scientific or mathematical game. But insofar as the application of physical pressure upon the enemy involves the use of mechanical tools under certain predictable or calculable conditions, it is possible to speak in terms of military science. The systematic application of science to the development of weapons and to technology in general is a comparatively recent development. Since World War II, techniques of research and analysis have been enlisted from scientific fields to make calculations and choices among complex weapon systems and in the management of huge defense programs more exact. Over and above the techniques, the successful conduct of war at all levels of command requires assessing unpredictable variables and taking calculated risks under circumstances for which no precise precedent exists. Since the "fog of war" still holds and wars involve men as well as machines, warfare remains in many ways what it has always been essentially— an art.

Military theorists have long searched for the principles underlying the art of war. They have sought to distill from the great mass of military experience over the centuries simple but fundamental truths to guide commanders through the fog of war. The lists of principles they have evolved have been derived from an analysis of the campaigns and the writings of the great captains of war, such as Caesar, Frederick the Great, Napoleon, von Moltke; occasionally the masters have provided their own set of precepts. Foremost among the analysts have been Jomini, Clausewitz, Ardant duPicq, Mahan, Foch, Douhet, Liddell Hart, and Fuller. Almost 2,500 years ago, in 500 B.C., Sun Tzu, a Chinese general, set down thirteen principles. The axioms range from the Confederate General Nathan B. Forrest's oft-quoted advice, "Git thar fustest with the mostest men," to Napoleon's 115 maxims. The lists differ in emphasis as well as in number. Some theorists have stressed that the battle is all and the defeat of the enemy's armed forces the correct objective; others, that the best path to victory is by indirect methods and approaches, by what has been termed obliquity.

Today, all great nations recognize principles of war and incorporate them in army doctrine. The lists vary from nation to nation. In their modern dress in the Western World, the accepted principles are essentially a post-Napoleonic conception, advanced by Clausewitz, the great Prussian philosopher of war in the early nineteenth century, and his contemporary, Jomini, the well-known French general and theorist. Since the United States shares a common military heritage and a common body of military thought with Europe, American students of war have also sought to reduce the conduct of war to certain essential premises. The United States Army recognizes nine principles and includes them in its *Field Service Regulations*. Their proper application, the Army holds, is essential to the exercise of effective command and to the successful conduct of military operations. The Russians and Chinese have a principle of annihilation and the British a principle of flexibility that do not appear on the American list. Indeed, Mao Tse-tung and his disciples in their philosophy of protracted conflict have given the principles a new twist and have challenged conventional Western doctrine.

Despite differences over their precise number and meaning, principles of war are taught in military schools throughout the world. Some cautions are usually attached to the American Army set. The principles are not absolute and have been successfully violated at times for special reasons that have been carefully considered beforehand. The principles are interrelated. They do not operate with equal force under all circumstances. In particular cases they may reinforce each other or be in conflict. They are applied in combination to specific situations. The combinations will vary according to the factors that influence operations, such as the nature of the terrain, the relative strength of the opposing forces, the effect of weather, and the mission of the command. The art of generalship, consequently, is to be found in the proper application of the principles.

The nine principles are concisely stated as objective, offensive, mass, economy of force, maneuver, unity of command, security, surprise, and simplicity. They are set forth in *Field Manual 100–5* as follows:

Objective. Every military operation must be directed toward a clearly defined, decisive, and attainable objective. The ultimate military objective of war is the destruction of the enemy's armed forces and his will to fight. The objective of each operation must contribute to this ultimate objective. Each intermediate objective must be such that its attainment will most directly, quickly, and economically contribute to the purpose of the operation. The selection of an objective is based upon consideration of the means available, the enemy, and the area of operations. Every commander must understand and clearly define his objective and consider each contemplated action in light thereof.

Offensive. Offensive action is necessary to achieve decisive results and to maintain freedom of action. It permits the commander to exercise initiative and impose his will upon the enemy; to set the pace and determine the course of battle; to exploit enemy weaknesses and rapidly changing situations, and to meet unexpected developments. The defensive may be forced on the commander, but it should be deliberately adopted only as a temporary expedient while awaiting an opportunity for offensive action or for the purpose of economizing forces on a front where a decision is not sought. Even on the defensive the commander seeks every opportunity to seize the initiative and achieve decisive results by offensive action.

Mass. Superior combat power must be concentrated at the critical time and place for a decisive purpose. Superiority results from the proper combination of the elements of combat power. Proper application of the principle of mass, in conjunction with the other principles of war, may permit numerically inferior forces to achieve decisive combat superiority.

Economy of Force. Skillful and prudent use of combat power will enable the commander to accomplish the mission with minimum expenditure of resources. This principle is the corollary of the principle of mass. It does not imply husbanding but rather the measured allocation of available combat power to the primary task as well as secondary tasks such as limited attacks, the defense, deception, or even retrograde action in order to insure sufficient combat power at the point of decision.

Maneuver. Maneuver is an essential ingredient of combat power. It contributes materially in exploiting successes and in preserving freedom of action and reducing vulnerability. The object of maneuver is to dispose a force in such a manner as to place the enemy at a relative disadvantage and thus achieve results which would otherwise be more costly in men and materiel. Successful maneuver requires flexibility in organization, administrative support, and command and control. It is the antithesis of permanence of location and implies avoidance of stereotyped patterns of operation.

Unity of Command. The decisive application of full combat power requires unity of command. Unity of command obtains unity of effort by the coordinated action of all forces toward a common goal. While coordination may be attained by cooperation, it is best achieved by vesting a single commander with the requisite authority.

Security. Security is essential to the preservation of combat power. Security is achieved by measures taken to prevent surprise, preserve freedom of action, and deny the enemy information of friendly forces. Since risk is inherent in war, application of the principle of security does not imply undue caution and the avoidance of calculated risk. Security frequently is enhanced by bold seizure and retention of the initiative, which denies the enemy the opportunity to interfere.

Surprise. Surprise can decisively shift the balance of combat power. By surprise, success out of proportion to the effort expended may be obtained. Surprise results from striking an enemy at a time, place, and in a manner for which he is not prepared. It is not essential that the enemy be taken unaware but only that he becomes aware too late to react effectively. Factors contributing to surprise include speed, deception, application of unexpected combat power, effective intelligence and counterintelligences, to include communication and electronic security, and variations in tactics and methods of operation.

Simplicity. Simplicity contributes to successful operations. Direct, simple plans and clear, concise orders minimize misunderstanding and confusion. If other factors are equal, the simplest plan is preferred.

Many examples of the successful employment or of the violation of these principles can be cited in American military history and illustrations will be given in appropriate places in the text. Each case requires careful study in its own context. Here, we may note briefly that the proper objective has often eluded commanders in war. The British in the American Revolution, for example, were never clear as to what their prime objective was, whether to capture strategic positions, to destroy the Continental Army, or simply to try by an appropriate show of force to woo the Americans back to their allegiance to the Crown. As a result, their victories over Washington's army in the field seldom had much meaning. Not until after many years of fighting the elusive Seminoles in the Florida swamps did Col. William J. Worth realize that the destruction of their villages and sources of supply would end the conflict. In the Civil War the North's infatuation with the "On to Richmond" strategy long obscured what proved to be the real objective, the destruction of the enemy forces and control of the principal lines of communications. In the limited wars since 1945, however, the United States has sought to achieve objectives short of the total destruction of the enemy or his productive capacity. The traditional concept of "victory" and "winning" has taken on a different meaning in the new political context of warfare in the nuclear age. Force has been applied with restraint. Fresh support has been given to Clausewitz' reminder that a successful war is one in which the political objectives for which it is waged are achieved by suitable means and at appropriate cost.

No principle has been more ingrained in American military thinking than the belief that only offensive action can achieve decisive results. Many examples can be cited: Washington's brilliant attacks at Trenton, Princeton, and York-town, Grant's and Sherman's campaigns of 1864–65, Pershing's insistence on attack by American units in France in 1918, and Eisenhower's invasion of Normandy in 1944. But opponents of the principle argue that the defense has in certain cases more advantages than the offensive. In Sir Edward Creasy's *The Fifteen Decisive Battles of the World,* ten were won by the defending commander. Some of the most notable actions in American military history have involved the defense—Jackson's stand at New Orleans, the retreat of Chief Joseph and the Nez Perces, McAuliffe at Bastogne, and Ridgway's spoiling tactics on the stabilized front in Korea.

The principle of mass, often called concentration, probably offers more examples of successful and unsuccessful application than any other. Washington at Trenton and Eisenhower in Normandy are two obvious illustrations of how application resulted in success. Conversely, Lee on the second day at Gettysburg, Custer at the Little Bighorn, the Huertgen Forest battle in Germany in World War II, and the Viet Cong in the Ia Drang valley battle show a failure to apply the proper amount of force at the proper place and time. No principle has been more successfully violated by great generals than that of mass. Lee's division of his army at Chancellorsville is a classic case. However inadvertent, dispersal, not concentration, during American airborne operations in Sicily and Nor-mandy during World War II led to a disruption of German communications and tactics. Indeed, the one airborne landing deemed a virtual failure, in Operation MARKET-GARDEN in the Netherlands in 1944, involved the greatest concentration of troops.

The successful application of economy of force has usually resulted in brilliant gains. Lee's battle at Chancellorsville, MacArthur's bypassing of the Japanese stronghold at Rabaul in World War II, and his decision in Korea not to reinforce in great strength Lt. Gen. Walton H. Walker's troops on the Pusan perimeter in order to conserve forces for the Inch'on landing are notable cases in point. No principle of war is probably more important today, in this era of limited war, than restraint in the use of force.

No one would deny the necessity of maneuver to success in military operations. Brilliant examples have occurred throughout American military history: Morgan at Cowpens, Scott at Cerro Gordo, Grant before Vicksburg, Eisenhower in Normandy, Patton's shift of the Third Army's offensive from an east-west axis into Germany to a north-south axis into Luxembourg during the Battle of the Bulge, and MacArthur at Inch'on. Attempts at direct assault, rather than maneuver, have often led to bloody and indecisive actions: Gage at Bunker Hill, Burnside at Fredericksburg, Hodges in the Huertgen Forest. Even a successful maneuver can be subject to criticism—witness the controversy over Eisenhower's decision to advance across Europe along a continuous broad front rather than permit one of his major forces to thrust deep into Germany.

Unity of command was successfully achieved for the Union under Grant in 1864, for the Allies under Marshal Foch in World War I, and for the Allied forces under General Eisenhower in the European Theater of Operations in World War II. Divided command of British forces in America played an important role in leading to the surrender at Saratoga. The lack of unity of command or even effective co-operation between Admiral Halsey's Third Fleet and MacArthur's landing force in Leyte might have cost American forces dearly in 1944. The interservice conflicts between MacArthur and Nimitz during World War II indicate that this principle can in some respects be violated and military victory gained. For the armchair critic, an interesting case in divided command was MacArthur's failure to place X Corps of the United Nations forces under the command of the Eighth Army in Korea during the fall and early winter of 1950.

Security and surprise are obvious necessities and closely related. The Antietam battle saw security violations on both sides—by Lee whose courier allowed the operations plan to fall into Union hands and by McClellan who failed to reconnoiter the approaches to the battlefield before the action took place. Elaborate security precautions taken by the Allies before the Normandy invasion permitted them to deceive the Germans as to the precise time and place of the attack. The success of the Chinese Communist intervention in Korea resulted both from a United Nations' security failure and from a carefully planned deception by the Communist forces. From the time Washington trapped the Hessians at Trenton to the time MacArthur caught the Koreans unaware at Inch'on the principle of surprise has been an effective weapon of commanders. But there have been occasions when commanders have openly flaunted their power in order to demoralize an enemy. Thus, Henry Bouquet marched into the Ohio country in 1764 with a show of British power to impress the Indians engaged in the Pontiac conspiracy.

Of all the principles of war none is now probably harder to follow above the battalion level than the principle of simplicity. Modern warfare, involving mechanization, electronic equipment, and airborne and seaborne operations, is inherently not simple. Even the ostensibly easy movement of a small tank-infantry-artillery team cannot be termed "simple." In counterinsurgency operations the integration of military with political, economic, sociological, and psychological factors often leads to a high degree of complexity. But operations sometimes can become too complex for the commanders to execute. Washington's plan for the attack on the British at Germantown in 1777, involving convergence of four columns of inexperienced troops moving over different roads at night, proved too complicated for successful execution.

The growing complexity and variety of modern warfare have led students of military affairs to take a fresh look at the principles. Since World War II a debate has been raging in military literature over the precise meaning and application of the principles, a debat fed by the new circumstances of nuclear and counterinsurgency warfare. The discussion revolves around three major questions: Are the present principles too exclusive? Are they too inclusive? Does modern insurgent and nuclear warfare make them obsolete? To some extent this is a debate over semantics. The defenders point out that the principles are as valid in modern as in ancient warfare; that each age must make its own applications of the "fundamental truths." Critics argue that they are not immutable scientific laws of universal applicability; that they require constant re-examination; that no two military situations are ever completely alike; that the principles are merely methods and common-sense procedures adopted by great captains in the past and that changes in the conditions of war alter their relative importance; that the new weapons have destroyed whatever infallibility remained; that the principles are not pat formulas for victories to be followed rigidly. They argue that the new conditions of warfare do not allow for the traditional Napoleonic concepts embodied in the principles; that limited conflicts restrict the principles of the offensive and the objective; that in any future nuclear conflict the principle of mass will be severely limited and that dispersion, not concentration of men and equipment, will become critical on the battlefield. The principles, these critics conclude, are no substitute for imaginative thinking, logical analysis, broad professional knowledge, and highly developed qualities of leadership.

Perhaps the key point to be remembered, whatever the outcome of the present debate among the theorists, is that war remains fundamentally an art. Dennis Hart Mahan, famed West Point professor and teacher of the Civil War generals, put it well: "In war, as in every other art based upon settled principles, there are exceptions to all general rules. It is in discovering these cases that the talent of the general is shown." Even the defenders of the principles stress that the art of war lies in their interpretation and application. Within limits, the principles of war nevertheless remain a useful tool for analysis, a general frame of reference, and a checklist, for examining past campaigns. Themselves an inheritance from the past, these adages offer no substitute for real historical inquiry or for thinking and action on the part of the officer. They represent generalizations and premises rather than fixed immutable rules. They provide general guides to conduct, guides that on the whole have in the past led to military success. Nuclear and counterinsurgency operations undoubtedly will demand a modification or application different from so-called conventional warfare. As in the past, the victorious captain will have to adapt concepts or improvise others most suitable to the particular circumstances facing him.

All theorists agree that, in the final analysis, the art of war is what men make it. To quote Mahan again, "No soldier who has made himself conversant with the resources of his art, will allow himself to be trammelled by an exclusive system." He must be flexible. He must learn to deal with men. Napoleon stated that in war, "The moral is to the physical as three to one." The ability to penetrate the fog of war and make the correct decision is the heart of leadership. Indeed, flexibility and leadership might well be added as tenth and eleventh principles, basic concepts inherent in all the others. It is not surprising therefore that the qualities that make for good leadership have long interested the Army and that a whole body of literature has grown up about the theoretical and practical foundations of this phase of the military art.

The military profession, like other professions, has developed its own language to make for easy communication. Aside from the principles of war, it is useful for the student of military history to become familiar with other terms commonly encountered in the literature. In the theory of warfare, strategy and tactics have usually been put into separate categories. Strategy deals with both the preparation for and the waging of war and has often been defined as the art of projecting and directing campaigns. To tactics, its close partner, military jargon has reserved the art of executing plans and handling troops in battle. Strategy is usually regarded as the prelude to the battlefield; tactics the action on the battlefield. As society and warfare have grown more complex, the term *strategy* has been gradually broadened from its eighteenth century connotation as the "art of the general," far beyond its original, narrow military meaning. In the nineteenth century, and even more in the twentieth, distinctions began to be blurred between strategy as a purely military phenomenon and national strategy of a broader variety involving a combination of political, economic, technological, and psychological factors, along with the military elements, in the management of national policy. As a result, the term *grand strategy* (or *higher strategy*) has come to connote the art of employing all the resources of a nation, or coalition of nations, to achieve the objects of war (and peace). The broad policy decisions governing the over-all conduct of war, or its deterrence, are the prerogative of the chief of state and his principal advisers. The strategist, whether in the narrower or broader sense, deals in many uncertainties and his art is the art of the calculated risk. At the opposite end of the scale are *minor tactics,* the term used to describe the maneuver of small units.

Despite distinctions in theory, strategy and tactics cannot always be easily separated in practice. The language of strategic maneuver—putting one's army into the most favorable position to engage the enemy and depriving the enemy of freedom of movement—is also largely the language of tactics. Thus, *envelopment* is an attack on an enemy's flank and toward his rear, usually accompanied by an attack on his front. A *turning movement* is a wide enveloping maneuver, passing around the side of the enemy's main forces and attacking him from the rear. *Double envelopment* involves an attack on both flanks of the enemy while his center is held in check. A *penetration* is an attack on the enemy's front by driving a wedge into it or piercing it completely. It may be followed by an enveloping attack on one or both flanks. In connection with these four basic forms of attack, two terms often are used: *main effort*—concentrating on the critical point in the enemy's position—and *holding attack*—pinning down the remainder of the enemy. To *refuse* a flank is to draw the flank of a line or command to the rear in order to prevent an envelopment by an enemy.

Linking strategy and tactics and attracting more and more attention among the theorists is a third field, *logistics,* simply defined as the art of planning and carrying out the movement and maintenance of forces. This field too has been greatly broadened as warfare has expanded and grown more technological and complex. Logistics deals with the deployment of military forces and their equipment to the area of war, and with innumerable services, such as feeding, clothing, supplying, transporting, and housing troops. The connecting links, the network of railways, waterways, roads, and air routes by which an armed force in the field is reinforced and supplied from its base of operations in the home or friendly area, are called the *lines of communications.* The *theater of operations* comprises the combat zone as well as the supply and administration area directly connected with military operations.

In modern warfare the major divisions of the military art—strategy, logistics, and tactics—are closely interdependent. One field merges into the other, and changes in one inevitably lead to changes in the others. Sometimes weapons have appeared on the battlefield before military theory and planning have fully absorbed them, and adjustments throughout the art have been slow to follow. In the Civil War, for example, the widespread use of the rifle musket upset the relation among the combat arms; the range and accuracy of these weapons in the hands of defending infantry shattered the effectiveness of the concentrated attack in which Napoleonic strategy culminated. But, as often has been observed in the history of warfare, armaments and weapons are more readily changed than ideas. Napoleon's principles continued to be held, sometimes with disastrous consequences on the battlefield. An oft-cited case of the appalling repercussions of holding concepts too long or rigidly is the French offensive spirit in World War I. It is small wonder in light of the carnage of World Wars I and II that the coming of the atomic bomb has caused strategy in the Western World to focus on the deterrence of war and fostered tactics to seek means of dispersal on the battlefield.

It is clear that in modern warfare theory and practice have not always been the same. Wars, particularly in the great coalition conflicts of the twentieth century, are simply not run by rules or theories. Once joined, modern war has had a way of breeding its own strategy, tactics, and weapons. For successful commanders more than ever flexibility has become the only sure guide. World War I, beginning as a war of mass offensives, was a classic case of arrested strategy requiring new tactics and weapons to dig the war out of the trenches. Anglo-American strategy against Germany in World War II proved a compromise of the theory of mass and concentration upheld by the U.S. Army and Winston Churchill's peripheral theory. Despite attention to "principles," Allied strategy in World War II was a hybrid product hammered out largely on the "anvil of necessity." In war, moreover, military strategy varies with political direction and goals. In this vein Clausewitz had argued that military strategy must respond to national policy and political aims. Perhaps he best summed up the political context of modern war in his assertion, "War is not merely a political act, but also a real political instrument, a continuation of policy carried out by other means." "War," he concluded, "admittedly has its own grammar, but not its own logic."

The American Military System

To organize for national security, each nation adopts the military system most suited to its culture, needs, and policies. Some nations have traditionally tended to concentrate significant segments of their economy on the maintenance of huge military forces and to determine national policies largely in terms of their military implications. While the United States shares with Europe a legacy of military thought and practice, whose roots lie deep in the past, its military system has grown out of its own national experience.

The form of government, the traditions of the people, the nature of the country, and its geographical position in relation to other powers have had a profound influence upon American military institutions. In turn, those institutions are a reflection of the American culture and way of life. Indeed, the Army is essentially an institutional form adapted by American society to meet military requirements. The American military system has been developed so as to place a minimum burden upon the people and give the nation a reasonable defense without sacrificing its fundamental values. From the beginning, the United States has sought to reconcile individual liberty with national security without becoming a nation in arms.

Chief among the characteristics of American culture that have a bearing on its military system are the value placed upon human beings as individuals; life, liberty, and the pursuit of happiness and peace as basic goals; the desire to achieve decisive results quickly; a talent for the design and use of machinery; highly developed productive capacity and managerial skills; and great material wealth. These characteristics underline the American penchant for absolutes—the sharp distinction between war and peace, the insistence on complete victory and on short, decisive, offensive action in warfare. They help account for the traditional American attitude toward war as an aberration in which the bully who disturbed the peace must be soundly and quickly thrashed so that American society can return to normality. They also point to the vital importance of public opinion in a democracy in raising and supporting armed forces and to the reason why wars against disturbers of the peace are apt to take on the character of moral crusades. They help explain the traditional rhythm of sharp expansion of the armed forces in wartime and precipitate contraction immediately thereafter.

In turn, these characteristics and attitudes have shaped the Army in its organizational relationships and in its philosophy of operations. They account also for such distinctive Army features as the development of great mechanical power, the stress on firepower rather than sheer manpower, and the concentration on victory by offensive operations.

Throughout its existence the United States has been compelled to provide for military security. The degree to which the provisions were made has varied with the nature and magnitude of the particular threat. Until technology reduced the distance separating the United States from the Old World, the forces in being could be, and were, small. At the same time the deep-seated American reluctance to devote a large proportion of the national wealth to

the support of a standing military force played an important part in the development of a system based upon a small professional nucleus that could be expanded in time of need by the induction of citizen soldiers. This initial system took advantage of the ocean barriers favoring the United States and the balance of power existing in Europe. In accord with Washington's injunction, it held forth the possibility of acquiring greater strength by temporary alliances in extraordinary emergencies. Since World War II the rise of new foes and the destruction of the balance of power in Europe and the Far East have caused a drastic change in the American military system. Accordingly, the United States now maintains large air, land, and sea forces ready for immediate action and for co-operation with forces of its many allies.

The American Army as it exists today has evolved through a historical process paralleling the social, economic, and political development of the United States. Its evolution may in general be divided into three periods: colonial, continental expansion, and overseas operations. During the colonial period (1607–1775) the militia of the various colonies defended the settlers while they were establishing themselves in America, and helped England eliminate the French from North America. This was the period of roots and origins, of the transplanting of military institutions from abroad, particularly from England, and of their modification in the New World. During the era of continental expansion (1775–1898) the militia and volunteers and the Continental Army and its successor, the Regular Army, played a significant role in bringing the United States into being, in winning important extensions of national territory, in saving the nation from internal destruction, and in exploring, policing, and governing vast regions of the west. This was the period of national independence and consolidation. In the wars of this era, the Army's activities were concentrated on problems vital to the establishment, maintenance, and expansion of a nation based on new concepts of individual freedom and representative government. Only once in this period did the Army fight with the help of allies—during the Revolutionary War—and then on a temporary basis.

The year 1898, which saw the outbreak of the Spanish-American War, the symbol of "looking outward," was an important turning point. It marked the emergence of the United States as a world power. In the third period (1898 to the present) the Army has carried the flag to the four corners of the earth. Its assigned role has been to serve as a principal instrument for promoting American policies and American interests overseas and protecting the nation against the menace of tyrannical power. In the two great world wars of the twentieth century, and in Korea and Vietnam, it has fought alongside associated or allied nations, and in the increasing complexity of modern war its operations have become inseparably intertwined with those of the Navy and the Air Force. In the history of the nation and the Army in the twentieth century, World War II marked an important dividing line whose full implications are still not entirely clear. Since World War II the revolution in the strategic position of the United States, its emergence as leader of the free world and of allies in military combination, the cold war, and the nuclear age, have presented unprecedented challenges to traditional American concepts and institutions in national security. Under the nuclear threat the spectrum of war has broadened and theorists have been engaged in great debate on the future of war and military institutions. Berlin, Korea, Cuba, and Vietnam are symbols of the pressures confronting the nation and its army in the new phase of world power, in which the role of force appears to be taking on new meaning and new functions.

Whatever its future contribution, it is as an instrument of force—the primary mission of an army—that the United States Army has played its major role in American history. From desperate hand-to-hand engagements with savages to vast battles with motorized and armored forces, from revolutionary war to world war, civil to foreign war, guerrilla to counterguerrilla war, from hot to cold war, the Army has figured prominently in the nation's conflicts. And the Army has also made important contributions to the general welfare and to the preservation of domestic order in peacetime.

The leaders of the U.S. Army have consistently adhered to the principle basic in the American military system, that the Army is an instrument of civilian authority. This principle, firmly established in practice by General Washington during the Revolutionary War, was embodied in the Constitution of the United States as a fundamental safeguard of republican institutions. The supremacy of civilian authority is the American solution to the problem of forestalling any possible danger from a standing army. Until recently, American military policy has also been based upon the maintenance of very small Regular forces and reliance on citizen soldiers in case of national emergency. In the colonial period almost every able-bodied man was a member of the militia and could be called out in case of need, and this system continued in force at least theoretically during the first century of national existence. It was usually, nonetheless, the citizen volunteer who swelled the Army's ranks in earlier wars. Both the militia and the volunteer principle gave way in the wars of the twentieth century to the idea of universal obligation for military duty under selective service in time of national emergency.

In an age when forces in being may determine the outcome of a war or an emergency action in peacetime, the principle of reliance on masses of citizen soldiers appears to be giving way to the concept of large, efficient professional forces supported by a selected body of trained reserves. The increasing complications of modern warfare, the great rapidity with which attacks can be launched with modern weapons, and the extensive overseas commitments of the United States have negated the traditional American habit of preparing for wars after they have begun. But whatever the future composition of the Army, it will still have to incorporate the historic principle, ingrained in the nation's military system, of being representative of the people and subject to civilian control.

To be truly progressive, a military system, like most evolving human institutions, must operate in two planes of time, the present and the future. In the field of national security, the choices in the twentieth century have never been easy and in a world in ferment since the end of World War II are likely to be crucial. The citizen and the soldier cannot know what path to follow unless they are aware of the breadth of alternatives that have been accepted or rejected in the past. Santayana's dictum that those who ignore the past are condemned to repeat its mistakes is nowhere more apt than in military history. At the same time the blend of the historical with the military art reinforces the caution that no two periods or operations are precisely alike, that the easy analogy and the false comparison must be avoided, that the past must be interpreted in proper context and depth, and that the soldier must not "be trammelled by any exclusive system." For the fledgling officer, as well as the citizen, American military history provides a laboratory of experience, an accumulation of continuities and disparities, a rich storehouse of courage, sacrifice, and knowledge, and a source of inspiration and wisdom. It is to the multifaceted story of the American Army—how it originated and developed, and what it contributed to the nation in war and peace—that we now turn.

CHAPTER 2

The Beginnings

The United States as a nation was, in its origins, a product of English expansion in the New World in the seventeenth and eighteenth centuries—a part of the general outward thrust of western European peoples in this epoch. British people and institutions, transplanted to a virgin continent and mixed with people of different origins, underwent changes that eventually produced a distinctive American culture. In no area was the interaction of the two influences—European heredity and American environment—more apparent than in the shaping of the military institutions of the new nation.

The European Heritage

The European military heritage reaches far back into the dim recesses of history. Many centuries before the birth of Christ, organized armies under formal discipline and employing definite systems of battlefield tactics appeared in the empires of the Near East, rivaling in numbers and in the scope of their conflicts anything that was to appear in the Western World before the nineteenth century. In the fourth century B.C., Alexander the Great of Macedonia brought all these empires and dominions, in fact most of civilization known to the Western World, under his suzerainty in a series of rapid military conquests. In so doing, he carried to the highest point of development the art of war as it was practiced in the Greek city-states. He utilized the phalanx— a solid mass infantry formation using pikes as its cutting edge—as the Greeks had long done, but put far greater emphasis on heavy cavalry and contingents of archers and slingers to increase the maneuverability of his armies.

The Romans eventually fell heir to most of Alexander's empire and extended their conquests westward and northward to include present-day Spain, France, Belgium, and England, bringing these areas within the pale of Roman civilization. The Romans built on the achievements of Alexander and brought the art of war to its zenith in the ancient world. They perfected, in the legion, a tactical military unit of great maneuverability comparable in some respects to the modern division, performed remarkable feats of military engineering, and developed elaborate systems of fortification and siegecraft.

For all their achievements, the Romans made no real progress in the development of new weapons, and Roman military institutions, like Roman political organization and economy, underwent progressive decay after the second century A.D. The Roman Empire in the west was succeeded first by a congeries of barbarian kingdoms and eventually by a highly decentralized political system known as feudalism, under which a multitude of warring nobles exercised authority over local areas of varying size. The art of war underwent profound change with the armored knight on horseback succeeding to the battlefield supremacy that, under the Greeks and Romans, had belonged to disciplined formations of infantry. Society in the Middle Ages was highly stratified, and a rigid division existed between the knightly or ruling noble class and the great mass of peasants who tilled the soil, most of them as serfs bound to the nobles' estates. Warfare became for the most part a monopoly of the ruling classes, for only men of substance could afford horse and armor. Every knight owed a certain number of days of military service to his lord each year in a hierarchical or pyramid arrangement, the king at the apex and the great mass of lesser knights forming the base. But lords who were strong enough defied their superiors. Fortified castles with moat and drawbridge, built on commanding points of terrain, furnished sanctuaries where lesser lords with inferior forces could defy more powerful opponents.

Wherever freemen were found, nonetheless, in town or countryside, they continued to bear arms on occasion as infantry, often as despised adjuncts to armies composed of heavy cavalry. This yeoman class was always stronger in England than on the Continent, except in such remote or mountainous areas as Switzerland and the Scandinavian countries. Even after the Norman conquest had brought feudal institutions to England, the ancient Saxon tradition of the fyrd that required every freeman between sixteen and sixty to bear arms in defense of his country remained alive. In 1181 the English King Henry II declared in his Assize of Arms that every freeman should keep and "bear these arms in his [the king's] service according to his order and in allegiance to the lord King and his realm."

Vestiges of feudal institutions survived well into the twentieth century, nowhere more prominently than in European military organizations where the old feudal nobility long dominated the officer ranks and continued its traditions of honor and chivalry. At the other end of the scale, the militia system, so prominent in British and American history, owed much to medieval precedents, for the Saxon fyrd and Henry II's Assize of Arms underlay the militia tradition transplanted from England to America.

Between the fourteenth and sixteenth centuries the feudal order as the basic political organization of European society gave way gradually to new national states under the dynastic rule of royal families. The growth of towns with their merchant and artisan classes and the consequent appearance of a money economy enabled ambitious kings to levy taxes and borrow money to raise and support military forces and to unify and rule their kingdoms. The Protestant Reformation shattered the religious unity of Western Christendom. A long series of bloody wars ensued in which the bitter animosity of Protestant and Catholic was inextricably mixed with dynastic and national ambition in provoking conflict.

Changes in military organization, weapons, and tactics went hand in hand with political, social, and economic change. In the later Middle Ages formations of disciplined infantry using longbow, crossbow, pike, and halberd (a long-handled ax with a pike head at the end), reasserted their superiority on the battlefield. The introduction of gunpowder in the fourteenth century began a process of technological change in weapons that was to enhance that superiority; more immediately, gunpowder was used in crude artillery to batter down the walls of medieval castles. The age of the armored knight and the castle gave way to an age of mercenary infantry.

In the religious and dynastic wars of the sixteenth and seventeenth centuries, as mercenary armies came more and more to be national armies, various weapons employing gunpowder gradually replaced pike and halberd as the standard infantry weapons, and armor gradually disappeared from the bodies of both infantry and cavalry soldiers. At first musketeers were employed alongside pikemen in square formations, the pikemen protecting the musketeers while they reloaded. As the wheel lock musket succeeded the harquebus as a shoulder arm and the flintlock in turn supplanted the wheel lock, armies came to rely less and less on the pike, more and more on firepower delivered by muskets. By 1700, with the invention of a socket bayonet that could be fitted onto the end of the flintlock musket without plugging the barrel, the pike disappeared entirely and along with it the helmet and body armor that had primarily been designed for protection against pikes. Meanwhile, commanders learned to maneuver large bodies of troops on the battlefield and to employ infantry, cavalry, and artillery in combination. National armies composed of professional soldiers came once again to resemble the imperial forces that had served Alexander the Great and the Roman emperors.

In the destructive Thirty Years' War in Germany (1618-48), religious passions finally ran their course. European warfare would henceforth be a matter of clashes of dynastic and national rather than local or religious interests.

After the chaos and destruction that had attended the religious wars, rulers and ruling classes in all countries sought stability and order. Beginning with the wars of Louis XIV of France in 1660, dynastic rivalries were to be fought out by professional armies within the framework of an established order which, in its essentials, none sought to disturb. The eighteenth century European military system that resulted constituted an important part of the world environment in the period the United States came into being.

Eighteenth Century European Warfare

In contrast to the great world wars of the twentieth century, eighteenth century warfare was limited in character, fought by rival states for restricted territorial gains and not for the subjugation of whole peoples or nations. It was conducted by professional armies and navies without the mobilization of men, economic resources, and popular opinion of entire nations that has characterized twentieth century war, and without the passion and hatred of the religious wars. Except in areas where military operations took place, the people in the warring nations carried on their everyday life as usual.

The professional armies employed in this "formal" warfare reflected the society from which they sprang. Although Europe's titled nobles no longer exercised political power independent of their kings, they remained the dominant privileged class, proprietors of the great estates and leaders of the national armies. The great masses of people remained for the most part without property or voice in the government, either tilling the soil on the nobles' estates or working in the shops and handicraft industries in the towns. Absolute monarchy was the prevailing form of government in every European country save England and certain smaller states on the Continent. In England, where the constitutional power of Parliament had been successfully established over the king, Parliament was by no means a democratic institution but one controlled by the landed gentry and wealthy merchants.

The military distinction nobles had formerly found in leading their own knights in battle they now sought as officers in the armies of their respective kings. Princes, counts, earls, marquises, and barons, men who held position by hereditary right, royal favor, or purchase, filled the higher commands, while "gentlemen" of lesser rank usually served as captains and lieutenants. Advancement to higher ranks depended as much on wealth and influence at court as on demonstrated merit on the battlefield. Eighteenth century officers were hardly professionals in the modern sense of the word, for they might well first enter the service as mere boys through inheritance or purchase of a commission, and, except for technical specialists in artillery and engineering, they were not required to attend a military school to train for their duties.

As the officers came from the highest classes, so the men in the ranks came from the lowest. They were normally recruited for long terms of service, sometimes by force, from among the peasants and the urban unemployed, and more than a sprinkling of paupers, ne'er-do-wells, convicts, and drifters were in the ranks. Since recruiting extended across international boundaries, foreign mercenaries formed part of every European army. Discipline, not patriotic motivation, was the main reliance for making these men fight. Penalties for even minor offenses ran as high as a thousand lashes, and executions by hanging or firing squad were frequent. The habit of obedience inculcated on the drill ground carried over into battle where, it has often been said, the men advanced because they preferred the uncertainties of combat to the certainty of death if orders were disobeyed.

Most of the significant European wars of the period were fought over terrain that was open, relatively flat, and thickly populated. Normally, fighting took place only during favorable weather and during daylight hours; rain or darkness quickly called a halt to a battle, and by December opposing armies usually retired to winter quarters where they awaited spring to resume hostilities. Road and river transportation systems were, for the time, highly developed, facilitating the movement of men and supplies. Food for men and forage for horses were usually available in the areas of military operations, but all supplies were customarily obtained by systematic and regular procedures, not by indiscriminate plunder. Each nation set up a series of fortresses or magazines along the line of march of its army in which replacement supplies and foodstuffs could be stored.

Eighteenth century armies were composed predominantly of infantry, with cavalry and artillery as supporting elements. Because battles were usually fought in open country, cavalry could be employed to full advantage. As for artillery, it was used in both attack and defense, either in campaigns of maneuver or in siege warfare. Some eighteenth century commanders used the three arms skillfully in combination, but it was the clash of infantry that usually decided the issue. In the eighteenth century infantry was truly the "Queen of Battle."

The standard infantry weapon of the time was the flintlock musket with bayonet. Probably the most famous model was Brown Bess, the one used in the British Army. Brown Bess had a smoothbore barrel 3 feet 8 inches long with a 14-inch bayonet and fired a smooth lead ball about three-quarters of an inch in diameter. The musket was highly inaccurate since the barrel had no rifling and the charge necessarily fitted loosely, permitting the escape of gas and reducing the effect of the propelling charge. It misfired occasionally and was useless when the powder in the priming pan got wet. The rate of fire was, at best, about three rounds per minute. When the ball hit within its effective range, 150 to 200 yards, its impact was terrific, tearing ghastly holes in flesh and shattering bone, but the inaccuracy of the weapon practically precluded its use, even for volley fire, at ranges greater than 50 to 100 yards. The inefficiency of the smoothbore musket as a firearm made its attached bayonet almost as important as its firepower, and infantry relied on the bayonet for shock action against an enemy softened by musketry fire.

Cavalrymen were variously armed with pistol and lance, carbine and sword, depending on the country and the time. Pistol and carbine were discharged at close range against the ranks of opposing infantry or cavalry, while lance and sword were used for close-in shock action.

There were many different kinds of artillery. The larger pieces were mainly for siege warfare and were relatively immobile. Artillery used in the field was lighter and mounted on wheeled carriages pulled by men or horses. Whether siege or field, these artillery pieces were, like the muskets, smoothbore muzzle-loaders, very limited in range and highly inaccurate. Loading and firing were even slower than in the case of the musket, for the cannon barrel had to be swabbed out after each round to prevent any residue of burning powder from causing a premature explosion. There was no traverse and the whole carriage had to be moved to change the direction of fire. Cannon fired mainly solid iron balls, or at shorter ranges, grapeshot and canister. Grapeshot was a cluster of small iron balls attached to a central system (thus resembling a bunch of grapes) and dispersed by the explosion of a propellent charge; canister consisted of loose pellets placed in a can and when fired had even greater dispersion than grape.

The nature of the soldiers, their weapons, and the terrain go far to explain the tactics used. These tactics were usually designated *linear* tactics to distinguish them from earlier mass formations such as the Spanish Square and the column formations employed later by Napoleon. Linear tactics were first used by Gustavus Adolphus, the Swedish king and military innovator, in the Thirty Years' War, and they came into general use in European armies in the later dynastic wars of Louis XIV of France with the invention of the socket bayonet. Frederick the Great of Prussia carried them to their ultimate state of perfection, and his armies were the most methodically ordered in Europe. In the mid-eighteenth century the Frederician system was the model that others imitated.

In the employment of linear tactics, troops marched onto the battlefield in columns and then deployed into line. A line consisted of a number of battalions or regiments—the terms were then practically synonymous—formed three or more ranks deep. In the ranks the men stood shoulder to shoulder and delivered their fire. Loading, firing, and bayonet charge were all performed at command in a drill involving many separate motions. Firing, insofar as officers were able to maintain rigid discipline, was entirely by volley, the purpose being to achieve the greatest mass of firepower over a given area. The goal was always the "perfect volley." Individual, aimed fire, given the characteristics of the flintlock musket, was deemed to be of little value.

Artillery was deployed in the line with the infantry, cavalry on the flanks or in the rear. Usually commanders also kept an infantry force in reserve for use at a critical point in the battle. In the traditional eighteenth century battle, both forces would be drawn up in similar formation, and the battle would be opened by artillery fire from both sides. In the midst of this fire, the attacking infantry would move forward, maintaining the rigid linear formation in which it was trained, stopping as frequently as necessary to dress its lines. At a range of 50 to 100 yards, the attacking line would halt on the command of its officers. At a second command, a volley would be fired and answered by the opposing line; or there might be a great deal of jockeying over who should fire first, for it was considered an advantage to take, not to give, the first volley and to deliver one's own answering volley at closer range. In any case, the exchange of volleys would continue until one side determined to try to carry the field by bayonet or cavalry charge, usually committing its reserves in this action. If either side was able to carry the field, the victorious commander then sought to execute a successful pursuit, destroying the enemy's army; the defeated commander attempted to withdraw his force in a semblance of order to a fortress or other defensive position, there to re-form and fight another day.

Eighteenth century battles were bloody affairs. At Zorndorf in 1758, for instance, the victorious army of Frederick lost 38 percent of its effectives, the defeated Russians about half of theirs. Professional soldiers were difficult to replace for there was no national reservoir of trained manpower to draw on, and it took two years or more to train a recruit properly. Commanders, therefore, sparing of the blood of their soldiers, sought to avoid battle and to overcome the enemy by a successful series of maneuvers against his line of communications. They also tried to take advantage of terrain features and of fortified positions, to strike by surprise or against the flanks of the enemy, forcing him to realign his forces while fighting, and to employ artillery and cavalry to the greatest advantage in paving the way for infantry assault. Fortresses, normally constructed along the frontiers to impede the advance of an invading army, played a vital role in these maneuvers. It was considered axiomatic that no army could leave a fortress in its rear athwart its line of communications, that any major fortified point had to be reduced by siege. By 1700 the arts of both fortification and siegecraft had been reduced to certain geometric principles by Marshal Sebastien Vauban, a distinguished soldier and engineer in the service of Louis XIV of France.

Vauban's fortresses were star-shaped, with walls partially sunk in the earth and covered with earthen ramparts on which cannon could be mounted; projections or bastions with mutually supporting fields of fire jutted forth from the main walls; a ditch was dug around the whole and a second smaller wall erected in front of it, with earth also sloped against it to absorb the shock of cannon balls.

Vauban's system for attacking this or any other type of fortified position was known as an approach by parallel lines. Once a fortress had been surrounded and outside aid cut off, batteries of siege artillery were brought up within about 600 yards of the fortress walls, the guns being so placed as to rake the lengths of the bastions with enfilade fire; behind these guns the first parallel trench was dug to protect the gunners and assault troops. Zigzag approach trenches were then dug forward about 200 yards to the points from which a second parallel was constructed, then the same process was repeated and a third parallel was dug. Infantry and siege artillery were moved forward as each parallel was completed until, in the third, they were beneath the outer wall of the fortress. From this vantage point the artillery could breach the main wall and the infantry could take the fortress by storm, but usually the fortress commander surrendered to avoid further bloodshed. Under Vauban's system the capture of a fortress by a superior besieging force was usually only a matter of time, and the siege was conducted, often in leisurely fashion, along lines as rigidly fixed as those of the formal battle in the open field.

Perhaps the most indelible picture of formal eighteenth century warfare that has survived is one of French and British officers at the Battle of Fontenoy in 1746, bowing politely to each other and each inviting the other side to fire the first volley, thus starting the carnage that was to follow. This picture has a certain ludicrous quality about it, but there was method in their madness as there was in eighteenth century warfare generally. The eighteenth century army was adapted to the European environment of the time, to the political and social climate as well as to the geography and terrain. Men knowledgeable in military matters at the time firmly believed that no body of semitrained citizens, however numerous and inspired, could stand before the disciplined ranks of professionals. If today we can see many of the weaknesses in the eighteenth century military system that were not so obvious to contemporaries—

its basic lack of flexibility, a paucity of true professional leadership, and its failure effectively to mobilize national resources for war—these perceptions result from a vastly different social and political environment.

The Colonial Scene

The environment in the British colonies of North America was different from that of Europe. America was a new continent, heavily forested and sparsely populated. The main enemy with whom the English colonists had first to contend was the primitive and savage Indian, who neither knew the rules of formal warfare nor cared to learn them. Colonial society from its very beginnings developed along more democratic and individualistic lines than society in England or continental Europe. Military institutions and practices, though heavily influenced by English patterns, also evolved in the seventeenth and eighteenth centuries along different lines. It would be a mistake to call the society that took form in the thirteen English colonies in North America a new society, for in most respects it followed the English pattern of social, economic, and political organization. But England itself had stronger democratic traditions than existed on the Continent, and important differences in the environment gave these English traditions much stronger force in America. Here there was no titled nobility exercising a monopoly on governmental office or holding a vested title to most of the land. While an aristocracy of wealth soon appeared, it was never able to exercise the same prerogatives as a titled nobility. Besides, it was far easier to move from the poorer to the wealthier class, since acquisition of landed wealth was easier in a country where land was plentiful and labor to work it scarce. If older settled areas tended to develop something approaching the pattern of European class distinction, new frontiers were constantly opening up where dissatisfied individuals could move and find new opportunities. Life under these conditions bred a spirit of individualism and self-reliance.

In political life, this spirit found expression in the popular assemblies that played an increasingly important part in the government of each of the colonies. Each colony had a government modeled generally on England's. Though there were variations in the pattern, the prevailing form consisted of a royal governor appointed by the British Crown, a council appointed by the governor from the ranks of the colonial aristocracy, and a popular assembly elected by the landholders. Modeled on the British House of Commons, these popular assemblies in the colonies rested on a much broader democratic base, since property ownership—the main qualification for voting in Britain and America in this age—

was far more widespread in the colonies. The colonial assemblies claimed the same prerogatives vis-à-vis the royal governor that the British Parliament exercised in its relations with the Crown, including control of the purse and regulation of the military establishment of the colony.

The Indian method of warfare in the forest, perforce adopted by the white man also, was the most significant influence in developing and preserving the spirit of individualism and self-reliance in the military sphere. When the white man came, the Indian relied on bow and spear, or tomahawk and knife, but he soon learned the value of the white man's muskets and was not long in obtaining them in trade for his valuable furs. With bow or musket, his method of fighting was the same. Indian tribes had no organized system of war; warriors simply formed voluntary bands under war chiefs and took off on the warpath. In battle each Indian fought a separate opponent without regard for his fellows. Indians avoided pitched battle whenever possible, instead seeking victory by surprise and carefully utilizing cover and concealment. Only when they had the advantage did they close in for hand-to-hand combat. In such combat the Indian brave lacked neither skill nor courage. Since he cared little about the rules of civilized warfare, he slaughtered men, women, and children indiscriminately. The favorite Indian tactic was a surprise raid on an isolated settlement. When the settlers organized a pursuit, the Indians lay in wait and ambushed them.

The white man soon adapted his tactics to the Indian's, quickly learning the value of surprise and stealth himself. To avoid ambush he sent out scouts as the Indians did, frequently employing friendly Indians in the role. Instead of fighting in the closed formations of Europe, he too adopted the open formation and fought from behind trees, rocks, and fences. In such fighting more depended on individual initiative and courage than on strict discipline and control.

The white settler learned to benefit from some of the enemy's weaknesses. For all their cunning, the Indians never learned the lesson of proper security and did not post guards at night. Nor did they like to fight in winter. Expeditions into the Indian country used as their favorite technique an attack on an Indian village at dawn and in the winter season. This attack almost invariably came as a surprise, and the white man, imitating the savagery of his opponent, burned the Indian's villages and sometimes slaughtered braves, squaws, and papooses.

The settlers tried to provide some permanent protection for their frontiers by erecting forts along the westernmost line of settlement in each colony, moving them forward as the line of settlement moved. These forts were not the elaborate earth and masonry structures of Europe, but simple rectangular inclosures, their walls constructed of upright pointed logs. Usually there were wooden blockhouses at each corner. These rude frontier forts served as points to which settlers and their families could retreat for protection in time of Indian troubles. Having no artillery, the Indians found the forts hard to take and could rely only on burning arrows to set them afire, on surprise attack, or on direct frontal assault. From the last alternative they almost invariably shrank. Their war chiefs possessed no power to order any group of braves to undertake an assault in which they would suffer heavy casualties for the sake of gaining an objective.

Colonial Militia

For fighting Indians, colonial governments were in no position to form professional armies, even had the nature of Indian warfare lent itself to such a practice. Instead they fell back on the ancient British tradition of the militia. This tradition took on new vitality in America at the same time that it was declining in England where, after Oliver Cromwell's time, England's wars were fought on the sea and in foreign lands. The British Government came to rely on its Regular Army and Navy just as other European states did, despite a continuing tradition of opposition to a standing army. Each of the thirteen colonies, except for Pennsylvania where Quaker influence was dominant, enacted laws providing for a compulsory militia organization, generally based on the principle of the Saxon fyrd that every able-bodied free male from sixteen to sixty should render military service. Each member of the militia was obligated to appear for training at his county or town seat a certain number of days each year, to provide himself with weapons, and to hold himself in readiness for call in case of Indian attack or other emergency.

Each colony maintained its separate militia establishment, and each concentrated on the problems of protecting or extending its own frontiers; co-operation among the militias of the various colonies was confined to specific expeditions in which two or more colonies had an interest. The militia was by and large a local institution, administered in county and town or township under the general militia laws of each colony. It was closely integrated with the social and economic structure of colonial society. Though the royal governors or colonial assemblies appointed the general officers and the colonels who commanded militia districts, the companies in each locality elected their own officers. This practice seemingly put a premium on popularity rather than wealth or ability, but rank in the militia generally corresponded with social station in the community.

Each individual militiaman was expected to provide his own weapon—usually a smoothbore musket—and ammunition, clothing, and food for a short expedition, just as the British knight had been required to provide his own horse, armor, and suitable weapons for feudal warfare. Local authorities maintained reserve supplies of muskets to arm those too poor to buy them and collected stores of ammunition and sometimes small cannon that could be dragged along through the wilderness. For really long campaigns, the colonial government had to take charge, the assembly appropriating the money for supplies and designating the supply officers or contractors to handle purchasing and distribution.

Although the militia was organized into units by county or township, it hardly ever fought that way. Instead the local unit served as a training and mobilization base from which individuals could be selected for active operations. When a particular area of a colony was threatened, the colonial government would direct the local militia commander to call out his men and the commander would mobilize as many as he could or as he thought necessary, selecting the younger and more active men for service. For expeditions into the Indian country, individuals from many localities were usually selected and formed into improvised units for the occasion. Selection was generally by volunteering, but local commanders could draft both men and property if necessary. Drafted men were permitted the option of hiring substitutes, a practice that favored the well to do. Volunteer, drafted man, and substitute alike insisted on the militiaman's prerogative to serve only a short period and return to home and fireside as quickly as possible.

As a part-time citizen army, the militia was naturally not a well-disciplined, cohesive force comparable to the professional army of the age. Moreover, its efficiency, even for Indian fighting, varied from colony to colony and even from locality to locality within the same colony, depending on the ability and determination of commanders and the presence or absence of any threat. When engaged in eliminating an Indian threat to their own community, militiamen might be counted on to make up in enthusiasm what they lacked in discipline and formal training, but when the Indian threat was pushed westward there was a tendency for people along the seaboard to relax. Training days, one a week in the early days of settlement, fell to one a month or even one a year. Festivities rather than military training increasingly became the main purpose of many of the gatherings, and the efficiency of the militia in these regions declined accordingly. In some towns and counties, however, the military tradition was kept alive by volunteers who formed units of their own, purchased distinctive uniforms, and prepared themselves to respond in case of war or emergency. These units became known as the volunteer militia and were the predecessors of the National Guard of the United States. In Pennsylvania, which lacked a militia law until 1755 and then passed one that made militia service voluntary rather than compulsory, all units were composed of volunteers.

On the frontier, where Indian raids were a constant threat, training days were more frequent and militia had to be ready for instant action. Except on the frontier, where proficiency in this sort of warfare was a matter of survival, it is doubtful that colonial militia in general were really adept in forest fighting. Training days were devoted not to the techniques of fighting Indians but to learning the drill and motions required on a European battlefield.

The Colonies in the World Conflict, 1689–1783

While England was colonizing the eastern seaboard from Maine to Georgia, France was extending its control over Canada and Louisiana and asserting its claim to the Great Lakes region and the Mississippi Valley in the rear of the British colonies. (*Map 1*) Spain held Florida, an outpost of its vast colonial domains in Mexico, Central and South America, and the West Indies. England

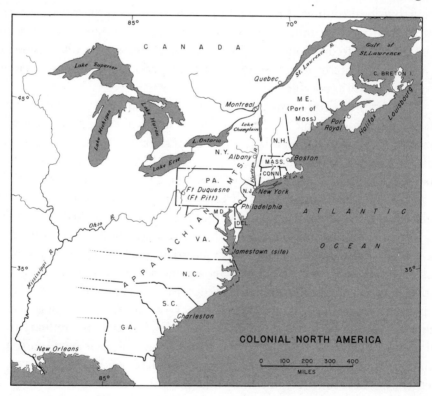

MAP 1

and France were invariably on opposite sides in the four great dynastic coalition wars fought in Europe between 1689 and 1763. Spain was allied with France in the last three of these conflicts. Each of these European wars had its counterpart in a struggle between British and French and Spanish colonists in America, intermingled with a quickening of Indian warfare all along the frontiers as the contestants tried to use the Indian tribes to their advantage. Americans and Europeans called these wars by different names. The War of the League of Augsburg (1689–97) was known in America as King William's War, the War of Spanish Succession (1701–13) as Queen Anne's War, the War of Austrian Succession (1744–48) as King George's War, and the final and decisive conflict, the Seven Years' War (1756–63), as the French and Indian War. In all of these wars one of the matters involved was the control of the North American continent; in the last of them it became the principal point at issue in the eyes of the British Government.

The main centers of French strength were along the St. Lawrence River in Canada—Quebec and Montreal—and the strategic line along which much of the fighting took place in the colonies lay between New York and Quebec, either on the lake and river chain that connects the Hudson with the St. Lawrence in the interior or along the seaways leading from the Atlantic up the St. Lawrence. In the south, the arena of conflict lay in the area between South Carolina and Florida and Louisiana. In 1732 the British Government established the colony of Georgia primarily as a military outpost in this region.

In the struggle for control of North America, the contest between England and France was the vital one, the conflict with Spain, a declining power, important but secondary. This latter conflict reached its height in the "War of Jenkins Ear," a prelude to the War of Austrian Succession, which began in 1739 and pitted the British and their American colonists against the Spanish. In the colonies the war involved a seesaw struggle between the Spanish in Florida and the West Indies and the English colonists in South Carolina and Georgia. Its most notable episode, however, was a British expedition mounted in Jamaica against Cartagena, the main port of the Spanish colony in Colombia. The mainland colonies furnished a regiment to participate in the assault as British Regulars under British command. The expedition ended in disaster, resulting from climate, disease, and the bungling of British commanders, and only about 600 of over 3,000 Americans who participated ever returned to their homes. The net result of the war itself was indecisive.

The first three wars with the French were also indecisive. The nature of the fighting in them was much the same as that in the Indian wars. Although the French maintained garrisons of Regulars in Canada, they were never sufficient to bear the brunt of the fighting. The French Canadians also had their militia, a more centralized and all-embracing system than that in the English colonies, but the population of the French colonies was sparse, scarcely a twentieth of that of the British colonies in 1754. The French relied heavily on Indian allies, whom they equipped with firearms. They were far more successful than the British in influencing the Indians, certainly in part because their sparse population posed little threat to Indian lands. The French could usually count on the support of the Indian tribes in the Great Lakes and Ohio Valley regions, though the British colonists did maintain greater influence with the powerful Iroquois confederacy in New York. The French constructed forts at strategic points and garrisoned them with small numbers of Regulars, a few of whom they usually sent along with militia and Indian raiding parties to supervise operations. Using guerrilla methods, the French gained many local successes and indeed kept the frontiers of the English colonies in a continual state of alarm, but they could achieve no decisive results because of the essential weakness of their position.

The British and their colonists usually took the offensive and sought to strike by land and sea at the citadels of French power in Canada. The British Navy's control of the sea made possible the mounting of sea expeditions against Canada and at the same time made it difficult for the French to reinforce their small Regular garrisons. In 1710 a combined British and colonial expedition captured the French fort at Port Royal on Nova Scotia, and by the treaty of peace in 1713 Nova Scotia became an English possession. In 1745 an all-colonial expedition sponsored by Massachusetts captured Louisbourg on Cape Breton Island in what was perhaps the greatest of colonial military exploits, only to have the stronghold bargained away in 1748 for Madras, a post the French had captured from the British in India.

While militia units played an important part in the colonial wars, colonial governments resorted to a different device to recruit forces for expeditions outside their boundaries such as that against Louisbourg. This was the volunteer force, another institution that was to play an important part in all American wars through the end of the nineteenth century. Unlike the militia units, volunteer forces were built from the top down. The commanding officers were first chosen by one of the colonial governors or assemblies and the men were enlisted by them. The choice of a commander was made with due regard for his popularity in the colony since this was directly related to his ability to persuade officers and men to serve under him. While the militia was the main base for recruitment, and the officers were almost invariably men whose previous experience was in the militia, indentured servants and drifters without military obligation were also enlisted. The enlistment period was only for the duration of a campaign, at best a year or so, not for long periods as in European armies. Colonial assemblies had to vote money for pay and supplies, and assemblies were usually parsimonious as well as unwilling to see volunteer forces assume any of the status of a standing Regular Army. With short enlistments, inexperienced officers, and poor discipline by European standards, even the best of these colonial volunteer units were, like the militia, often held in contempt by British officers.

The only positive British gain up to 1748 was Nova Scotia. The indecisive character of the first three colonial wars was evidence of the inability of the English colonies to unite and muster the necessary military forces for common action, of the inherent difficulty of mounting offensives in unsettled areas, and of a British preoccupation with conflicts in Europe and other areas. Until 1754 the British Government contented itself with maintaining control of the seas and furnishing Regulars for sea expeditions against French and Spanish strongholds; until 1755 no British Regulars took part in the war in the interior, though small "independent companies" of indifferent worth were stationed continuously in New York and occasionally in other colonies. No colony, meanwhile, was usually willing to make any significant contribution to the common cause unless it appeared to be in its own interest. Efforts to form some kind of union, the most notable of which was a plan advanced by Benjamin Franklin in a colonial congress held at Albany in 1754, all came to naught.

Between 1748 and 1754 the French expanded their system of forts around the Great Lakes and moved down into the Ohio Valley, establishing Fort Duquesne at the junction of the Allegheny and Monongahela Rivers in 1753 and staking a claim to the entire region. In so doing, they precipitated the final and decisive conflict which began in America two years before the outbreak of the Seven Years' War in Europe. In 1754 Governor Robert Dinwiddie of Virginia sent young George Washington at the head of a force of Virginia militia to compel the French to withdraw from Fort Duquesne. Washington was driven back and forced to surrender. The British Government then sent over two understrength regiments of Regulars under Maj. Gen. Edward Braddock, a soldier of some forty-five years' experience on continental battlefields, to accomplish the task in which the militia had failed. Accustomed to the parade ground tactics and the open terrain of Europe, Braddock placed all his faith in disciplined Regulars and close order formations. He filled his regiments with American recruits and early in June 1755 set out on the long march through the wilderness to Fort Duquesne with a total force of about

2,200, including a body of Virginia and North Carolina militiamen. (*Map* 2)
George Washington accompanied the expedition, but had no command role.

Braddock's force proceeded westward through the wilderness in traditional
column formation with 300 axmen in front to clear the road and a heavy baggage
train of wagons in the rear. The heavy wagon train so slowed his progress that
about halfway he decided to let it follow as best it could and went ahead with
about 1,300 selected men, a few cannon, wagons, and packhorses. As he approached Fort Duquesne, he crossed the Monongahela twice in order to avoid
a dangerous and narrow passage along the east side where ambush might be
expected. He sent Lt. Col. Thomas Gage with an advance guard to secure the
site of the second crossing, also deemed a most likely spot for an ambush. Gage
found no enemy and the entire force crossed the Monongahela the second
time on the morning of July 9, 1755, then confidently took up the march toward
Fort Duquesne, only seven miles away.

About three quarters of a mile past the Monongahela crossing, Gage's
advance guard suddenly came under fire from a body of French and Indians
concealed in the woods. Actually it was a very inferior force of 70 French

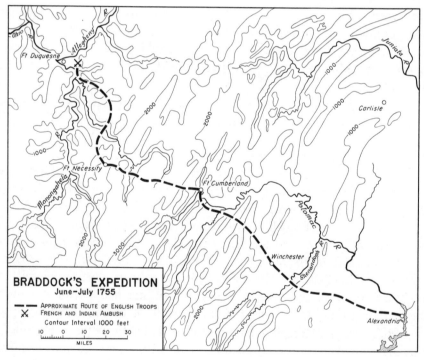

MAP 2

Regulars, 150 Canadian militia (many mere boys), and 650 Indians who had just arrived on the scene after a hasty march from Fort Duquesne. Some authorities think Gage might have changed the whole course of the battle had he pushed forward, forcing the enemy onto the open ground in their rear. Instead he fell back on the main body of Braddock's troops, causing considerable confusion. This confusion was compounded when the French and Indians slipped into the forests on the flanks of the British troops, pouring their fire into a surprised and terrified mass of men who wasted their return volleys on the air. "Scarce an officer or soldier," wrote one of the participants, "can say they ever saw at one time six of the Enemy and the greatest part never saw a single man. . . ."

None of the training or experience of the Regulars had equipped them to cope with this sort of attack, and Braddock could only exhort them to rally in conventional formation. Two-thirds of his officers fell dead or wounded. The militia, following their natural instincts, scattered and took positions behind trees, but there is no evidence they delivered any effective fire, since French and Indian losses for the day totaled only 23 killed and 16 wounded. The few British cannon appear to have been more telling. Braddock, mortally wounded himself, finally attempted to withdraw his force in some semblance of order, but the retreat soon became a disordered flight. The panic-stricken soldiers did not stop even when they reached the baggage wagons many miles to their rear.

Despite the completeness of their victory, the French and Indians made no attempt to follow it up. The few French Regulars had little control over the Indians, who preferred to loot the battlefield and scalp the wounded. The next day the Indians melted back into the forest, and the French commandant at Duquesne noted in his official report: "If the enemy should return with the 1,000 fresh troops that he has in reserve in the rear, at what distance we do not know, we should perhaps be badly embarrassed." The conduct of the battle was not so reprehensible as the precipitate retreat of the entire force back to the safety of the settled frontiers, when no enemy was pursuing it.

Although Braddock had been aware of the possibilities of ambush and had taken what he thought were necessary precautions, in the broader sense he violated the principles of security and maneuver; for when the ambush came he had little idea how to cope with Indian tactics in the forest. As he lay dying on the wagon that transported him from the battlefield, the seemingly inflexible old British general is alleged to have murmured, "Another time we shall know better how to deal with them."

BRADDOCK'S DEFEAT

Braddock could not profit from his appreciation of the lesson but the British Army did. "Over the bones of Braddock," writes Sir John Fortescue, the eminent historian of the British Army, "the British advanced again to the conquest of Canada."

After a series of early reverses, of which Braddock's disastrous defeat was only one, the British Government under the inspired leadership of William Pitt was able to achieve a combination of British and colonial arms that succeeded in overcoming the last French resistance in Canada and in finally removing the French threat from North America. In this combination British Regular troops, the British Navy, British direction, and British financial support were the keys to victory; the colonial effort, though considerable, continued to suffer from lack of unity.

As an immediate reaction to Braddock's defeat, the British Government sought to recruit Regulars in America to fight the war, following the precedent set in the Cartagena expedition. Several American regiments were raised, the most famous among them Col. Henry Bouquet's Royal Americans. On the whole, however, the effort was a failure, for most Americans preferred short service in the militia or provincial volunteer forces to the long-term service and rigid discipline of the British Army. After 1757 the British Government under Pitt, now convinced that America was the area in which the war would be won or lost, dispatched increasing numbers of Regulars from England—a total of 20,000 during the war. The British Regulars were used in conjunction with short-term militia and longer term volunteer forces raised in the service of the various individual colonies. The British never hit upon any effective device to assure the sort of colonial co-operation they desired and the burdens of the war were unequally divided since most colonies did not meet the quotas for troops, services, and supplies the British Government set. Massachusetts, Connecticut, and New York furnished about seven-tenths of the total colonial force employed. The British found it necessary to shoulder the principal financial burden, reimbursing individual colonies for part of their expenses and providing the pay and supply of many of the colonial volunteer units in order to insure their continued service.

Braddock's defeat was not repeated. In no other case in the French and Indian War was an inferior guerrilla force able to overcome any substantial body of Regulars. The lessons of the debacle on the Monongahela, as the British properly understood, were not that Regular forces or European methods were useless in America or that undisciplined American militia were superior to Regular troops. They were rather that tactics and formations had to be adapted to terrain and the nature of the enemy and that Regulars, when employed in the forest, would have to learn to travel faster and lighter and take advantage of cover, concealment, and surprise as their enemies did. Or the British could employ colonial troops and Indian allies versed in this sort of warfare as auxiliaries, something the French had long since learned to do.

The British adopted both methods in the ensuing years of the French and Indian War. Light infantry, trained as scouts and skirmishers, became a permanent part of the British Army organization. When engaged in operations in the forest, these troops were clad in green or brown clothes instead of the traditional red coat of the British soldier, their heads shaved and their skins sometimes painted like the Indians'. Special companies, such as Maj. Robert Rogers' Rangers, were recruited among skilled woodsmen in the colonies and placed in the Regular British establishment.

Despite this employment of light troops as auxiliaries, the British Army did not fundamentally change its tactics and organization in the course of the war in America. The reduction of the French fortress at Louisbourg in 1758 was conducted along the classic lines of European siege warfare. The most decisive single battle of the war was fought in the open field on the Plains of Abraham before the French citadel of Quebec. In a daring move, Maj. Gen. James Wolfe and his men scaled the cliffs leading up to the plain on the night of September 12, 1759, and appeared in traditional line of battle before the city the next morning. Major General the Marquis de Montcalm, the able French commander, accepted the challenge, but his troops, composed partly of militia levies, proved unable to withstand the withering "perfect volleys" of Wolfe's exceptionally well-disciplined regiments.

The ultimate lesson of the colonial wars, then, was that European and American tactics each had its place, and either could be decisive where conditions were best suited to its use. The colonial wars also proved that only troops possessing the organization and discipline of Regulars, whatever their tactics, could actually move in, seize, and hold objectives, and thus achieve decisive results.

Other important lessons lay in the realm of logistics, where American conditions presented difficulties to which European officers were unaccustomed. The impediments to supply and transport in a vast, undeveloped, and sparsely populated country limited both the size and variety of forces employed. The settled portions of the colonies produced enough food, but few manufactured goods. Muskets, cannon, powder, ball, tents, camp kettles, salt, and a variety of other articles necessary for even the simple military operations of the period almost all had to come from Europe. Roads, even in the settled areas, were poor and inadequate; forces penetrating into the interior had to cut their roads as they went, as Braddock did. These logistical problems go far to explain why the fate of America was settled in battles involving hardly one-tenth the size of forces engaged in Europe in the Seven Years' War, and why cavalry was almost never employed and artillery to no great extent except in fixed fortifications and in expeditions by sea when cannon could be transported on board ship. The limited mobility of large Regular forces, whatever the superiority of their organization and tactics, put a premium both on small bodies of trained troops familiar with the terrain and on local forces, not so well trained, already in an area of operations. Commanders operating in America would ignore these logistical limitations at their peril.

The American Rifle

By the end of the French and Indian War, a new weapon had appeared on the frontier in Pennsylvania and to the southward, one far better suited to guerrilla warfare than the musket. This weapon was later to become renowned as the Kentucky rifle. The effects of rifling a gun barrel, that is, of making spiral grooves that imparted a spinning effect to the bullet, giving it greater range and accuracy, had been known for some centuries in Germany and Switzerland. But the early rifles made there were too heavy and slow to load to be of military use. The Germans who settled in Pennsylvania developed, around 1750, a much lighter model, far easier and faster to load. They used a bullet smaller than the bore and a greased patch to keep the fit tight. This early American rifle could, in proper hands, hit a target the size of a man's head at 200 yards.

Despite its superior range and accuracy, the rifle was to undergo almost a hundred years of development before it would supplant the musket as the standard infantry weapon. At first each individual piece was handmade and each required a separate bullet mold. The standard bayonet would fit none of them. The rifle was effective only in the hands of an expert trained in its use. The rate of fire was only about one-third that of the musket, and therefore, without bayonet, the rifle could hardly be used by troops in the line. For the guerrilla tactics of the frontier, where men did not fight in line but from behind trees, bushes, and rocks, it was clearly a superior weapon. Thus, like the tactics of the American forest, it would have its place in any future war fought in America.

The Colonial Heritage

In the Indian wars and the colonial wars with France, Americans gained considerable military experience, albeit much of it in guerrilla warfare that did not require the same degree of organized effort and professional competence as the European style of warfare. The major effort against the French in Canada had, after all, been directed by the British Government. Many colonials later to become famous in the Revolution had served their military apprenticeship as officers of middle rank in the French and Indian War: George Washington, Israel Putnam, Philip Schuyler, and John Stark, for instance, in provincial forces; Charles Lee, Horatio Gates, and Richard Montgomery in the British Army.

Certain traditions had been established that were to influence American military policy and practice right down to the two great world wars of the twentieth century. One of these was primary reliance on the militia for defense and on volunteer forces for special emergencies and expeditions. Another was that relatively permanent volunteer units should be formed within the militia. The fear of a standing army of professionals, an English heritage, had become an even stronger article of faith in America. The colonial experience also established a strong tradition of separatism among the colonies themselves, for each had for a long period of years run its own military establishment. Within each colony, too, the civilian authority represented in the popular assembly had always kept a strict rein on the military, another tradition that was to have marked effect on American military development.

Certain characteristics of the American soldier that were to be fairly constant throughout all future wars had also made their appearance. The American soldier was inclined to be highly individualistic and to resent discipline and the inevitable restrictions of military life; he sought to know why he should do things before he would put his heart into doing them; and if in the end he accepted discipline and order as a stern necessity he did so with the idea of winning victory as quickly as possible so that he could return to his normal civilian pursuits.

These traditions and these characteristics were the product of a society developing along democratic lines. The military strengths and weaknesses they engendered were to be amply demonstrated when the American soldier took up arms against his erstwhile comrade, the British Regular, in the American Revolution.

CHAPTER 3

The American Revolution: First Phase

The American Revolution came about, fundamentally, because by 1763 the English-speaking communities on the far side of the Atlantic had matured to an extent that their interests and goals were distinct from those of the ruling classes in the mother country. British statesmen failed to understand or adjust to the situation. Ironically enough, British victory in the Seven Years' War set the stage for the revolt, for it freed the colonists from the need for British protection against a French threat on their frontiers and gave free play to the forces working for separation.

In 1763 the British Government, reasonably from its point of view, moved to tighten the system of imperial control and to force the colonists to contribute to imperial defense, proposing to station 10,000 soldiers along the American frontiers and to have the Americans pay part of the bill. This imperial defense plan touched off the long controversy about Parliament's right to tax that started with the Stamp and Sugar Acts and ended in December 1773, when a group of Bostonians unceremoniously dumped a cargo of British tea into the city harbor in protest against the latest reminder of the British effort to tax. In this 10-year controversy the several British ministries failed to act either firmly enough to enforce British regulations or wisely enough to develop a more viable form of imperial union, which the colonial leaders, at least until 1776, insisted that they sought. In response to the Boston Tea Party, the king and his ministers blindly pushed through Parliament a series of measures collectively known in America as the Intolerable Acts, closing the port of Boston, placing Massachusetts under the military rule of Maj. Gen. Sir Thomas Gage, and otherwise infringing on what the colonists deemed to be their rights and interests.

Since 1763 the colonial leaders, in holding that only their own popular assemblies, not the British Parliament, had a right to levy taxes on Americans, had raised the specter of an arbitrary British Government collecting taxes in America to support red-coated Regulars who might be used not to protect the frontiers but to suppress American liberties. Placing Massachusetts under military rule gave that specter some substance and led directly to armed revolt.

The Outbreak

The First Continental Congress meeting at Philadelphia on September 5, 1774, addressed respectful petitions to Parliament and king but also adopted nonimportation and nonexportation agreements in an effort to coerce the British Government into repealing the offending measures. To enforce these agreements, committees were formed in almost every county, town, and city throughout the colonies, and in each colony these committees soon became the effective local authorities, the base of a pyramid of revolutionary organizations with revolutionary assemblies, congresses, or conventions, and committees of safety at the top. This loosely knit combination of *de facto* governments super-seded the constituted authorities and established firm control over the whole country before the British were in any position to oppose them. The *de facto* governments took over control of the militia, and out of it began to shape forces that, if the necessity arose, might oppose the British in the field.

In Massachusetts, the seat of the crisis, the Provincial Congress, eyeing Gage's force in Boston, directed the officers in each town to enlist a third of their militia in minutemen organizations to be ready to act at a moment's warn-ing, and began to collect ammunition and other military stores. It established a major depot for these stores at Concord, about twenty miles northwest of Boston.

General Gage learned of the collection of military stores at Concord and determined to send a force of Redcoats to destroy them. His preparations were made with the utmost secrecy. Yet so alert and ubiquitous were the patriot eyes in Boston that when the picked British force of 700 men set out on the night of April 18, 1775, two messengers, Paul Revere and William Dawes, preceded them to spread the alarm throughout the countryside. At dawn on the 19th of April when the British arrived at Lexington, the halfway point to Concord, they found a body of militia drawn up on the village green. Some nervous finger—whether of British Regular or American militiaman is unknown to this day—pressed a trigger. The impatient British Regulars, apparently without any clear orders from their commanding officer, fired a volley, then charged with the bayonet. The militiamen dispersed, leaving eight dead and ten wounded on the ground. The British column went on to Concord, destroyed such of the military stores as the Americans had been unable to remove, and set out on their return journey.

By this time, the alarm had spread far and wide, and both ordinary militia and minutemen had assembled along the British route. From behind walls, rocks, and trees, and from houses they poured their fire into the columns of Redcoats, while the frustrated Regulars found few targets for their accustomed volleys or bayonet charges. Only the arrival of reinforcements sent by Gage enabled the British column to get back to the safety of Boston. At day's end the British counted 273 casualties out of a total of 1,800 men engaged; American casualties numbered 95 men, including the toll at Lexington. What happened was hardly a tribute to the marksmanship of New England farmers—it has been estimated 75,000 shots poured from their muskets that day—but it did testify to a stern determination of the people of Massachusetts to resist any attempt by the British to impose their will by armed force.

The spark lit in Massachusetts soon spread throughout the rest of the colonies. Whatever really may have happened in that misty dawn on Lexington Green, the news that speedy couriers, riding horses to exhaustion, carried through the colonies from New Hampshire to Georgia was of a savage, unprovoked British attack and of farmers rising in the night to protect their lives, their families, and their property. Lexington, like Fort Sumter and Pearl Harbor, furnished an emotional impulse that led all true patriots to gird themselves for battle. From the other New England colonies, militia poured in to join the Massachusetts men and together they soon formed a ring around Boston. Other militia forces under Ethan Allen of Vermont and Benedict Arnold of Connecticut seized the British forts at Ticonderoga and Crown Point, strategic positions on the route between New York and Canada. These posts yielded valuable artillery and other military stores. The Second Continental Congress, which assembled in Philadelphia on May 10, 1775, found itself forced to turn from embargoes and petitions to the problems of organizing, directing, and supplying a military effort.

Before Congress could assume control, the New England forces assembled near Boston fought another battle on their own, the bloodiest single engagement of the entire Revolution. After Lexington and Concord, at the suggestion of Massachusetts, the New England colonies moved to replace the militia gathered before Boston with volunteer forces, constituting what may be loosely called a New England army. Each state raised and administered its own force and appointed a commander for it. Discipline was lax and there was no single chain of command. Though Artemas Ward, the Massachusetts commander, exercised over-all control by informal agreement, it was only because the other commanders chose to co-operate with him, and decisions were made in council. While by mid-June most of the men gathered were volunteers, militia units continued to come and go. The volunteers in the Connecticut service were enlisted until December 10, 1775, those from the other New England states until the end of the year. The men were dressed for the most part in homespun clothes and armed with muskets of varied types; powder and ball were short and only the barest few had bayonets.

Late in May Gage received limited reinforcements from England, bringing his total force to 6,500 rank and file. With the reinforcements came three major generals of reputation—Sir William Howe, Sir Henry Clinton, and Sir John Burgoyne—men destined to play major roles in England's loss of its American colonies. The newcomers all considered that Gage needed more elbowroom and proposed to fortify Dorchester Heights, a dominant position south of Boston previously neglected by both sides. News of the intended move leaked to the Americans, who immediately countered by dispatching a force onto the Charles-town peninsula, where other heights, Bunker Hill and Breed's Hill, overlooked Boston from the north. (*Map 3*) The original intent was to fortify Bunker Hill, the eminence nearest the narrow neck of land connecting the peninsula with the mainland, but the working party sent out on the night of June 16, 1775, decided instead to move closer in and construct works on Breed's Hill—a tacti-cal blunder, for these exposed works could much more easily be cut off by a British landing on the neck in their rear.

The British scorned such a tactic, evidently in the mistaken assumption that the assembled "rabble in arms" would disintegrate in the face of an attack by disciplined British Regulars. On the afternoon of the 17th, Gage sent some 2,200 of his men under Sir William Howe directly against the American posi-tions, by this time manned by perhaps an equal force. Twice the British advanced on the front and flanks of the redoubt on Breed's Hill, and twice the Americans, holding their fire until the compact British lines were at close range, decimated the ranks of the advancing regiments and forced them to fall back and re-form. With reinforcements, Howe carried the hill on the third try but largely because the Americans had run short of ammunition and had no bayonets. The Ameri-can retreat from Breed's Hill was, for inexperienced volunteers and militia, an orderly one and Howe's depleted regiments were unable to prevent the Ameri-cans' escape. British casualties for the day totaled a staggering 1,054, or almost half the force engaged, as opposed to American losses of about 440.

The Battle of Bunker Hill (for it was Bunker that gave its name to a battle actually fought on Breed's Hill) has been aptly characterized as a "tale of great blunders heroically redeemed." The American command structure violated the principle of unity of command from the start, and in moving onto Breed's Hill the patriots exposed an important part of their force in an indefensible position, violating the principles of concentration of force, mass, and maneuver. Gage and Howe, for their parts, sacrificed all the advantages the American blunders gave

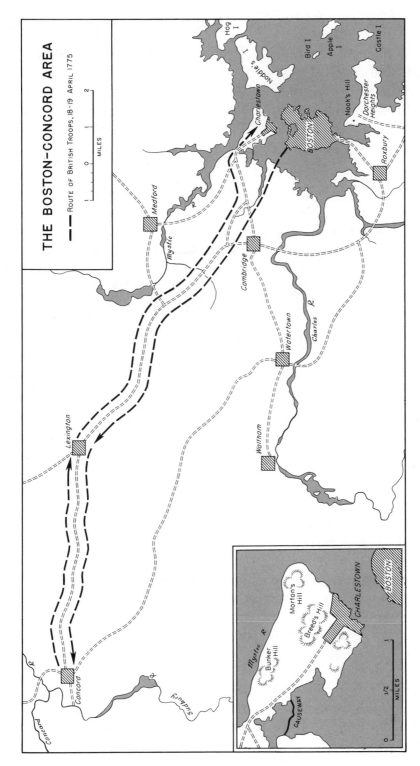

THE BOSTON-CONCORD AREA

▬▬ Route of British Troops, 18-19 April 1775

MILES
1   0   2

Concord
Concord R.
Sudbury R.
Lexington
Waltham
Watertown
Charles R.
Cambridge
Mystic R.
Medford
Charlestown
BOSTON
Roxbury
Nook's Hill
Dorchester Heights
Castle I.
Apple I.
Bird I.
Noddle's I.
Hog I.

Mystic R.
Bunker Hill
Morton's Hill
Breed's Hill
CHARLESTOWN
CAUSEWAY
BOSTON

MILES
1/2   0   1

MAP 3

them, violating the principles of maneuver and surprise by undertaking a suicidal attack on a fortified position.

Bunker Hill was a Pyrrhic victory, its strategic effect practically nil since the two armies remained in virtually the same position they had held before. Its consequences, nevertheless, cannot be ignored. A force of farmers and townsmen, fresh from their fields and shops, with hardly a semblance of orthodox military organization, had met and fought on equal terms with a professional British Army. On the British this astonishing feat had a sobering effect, for it taught them that American resistance was not to be easily overcome; never again would British commanders lightly attempt such an assault on Americans in fortified positions. On the Americans, the effect was hardly sobering, and in the long run was perhaps not salutary. Bunker Hill, along with Lexington and Concord, went far to create the American tradition that the citizen soldier when aroused is more than a match for the trained professional, a tradition that was to be reflected in American military policy for generations afterward.

Formation of the Continental Army

The response of George III and his ministers to the events at Lexington, Concord, and Bunker Hill was a determined effort to subdue the rebellious colonists by force. It took time to mount this effort, and after Bunker Hill the Americans enjoyed a respite lasting almost a year. During most of this period the Second Continental Congress, though forced by events in New England to take on itself the leadership of an armed revolt, proceeded hesitantly, still seeking a formula for reconciliation that would preserve American rights. Military preparations were designed for a short struggle, to endure no longer than the end of the year 1776. Nevertheless the Americans took advantage of the respite to create a national army, to consolidate their hold on the governmental machinery throughout the thirteen colonies, to invade Canada, and finally to force the British to evacuate Boston.

The creation of a Continental Army was in the long run perhaps their most significant achievement. Some time before Bunker Hill the Massachusetts Provincial Congress, aware of the necessity of enlisting the support of all the colonies in the struggle against the British, appealed to the Continental Congress to adopt the New England army. Although there is no formal record of the action, Congress evidently did vote to adopt it on June 14, 1775—the accepted birthday of the U.S. Army. On the same day it voted to raise ten companies of riflemen—the first soldiers to be enlisted directly in the Continental service—in Pennsylvania, Maryland, and Virginia, to march north to join the army before Boston.

The next day, June 15, Congress chose George Washington, a Virginian, to be Commander in Chief. The choice was made for geographical and political as much as for military reasons. The New Englanders felt that in order to enlist the support of the southern colonies, a southerner should be chosen for the post of command. Washington's military experience was perhaps greater than that of any other southerner, and he came from the largest and most important of the southern colonies. His impressive appearance, quiet and confident manner, and good work in the military committees of Congress had impressed all.

The choice proved fortunate. Washington himself recognized, when he accepted the command, that he lacked the requisite experience and knowledge in handling large bodies of men. His whole military experience had been in frontier warfare during the French and Indian War. But experience as a political leader in his native Virginia and in directing the business affairs of his large plantation at Mount Vernon also stood him in good stead. He brought to the task traits of character and abilities as a leader that in the end more than compensated for his lack of professional military experience. Among these qualities were a determination and a steadfastness of purpose rooted in an unshakable conviction of the righteousness of the American cause, a scrupulous sense of honor and duty, and a dignity that inspired respect and confidence in those around him. Conscious of his own defects, he was always willing to profit by experience. From the trials and tribulations of eight years of war he was to learn the essentials of strategy, tactics, and military organization.

Congress also appointed four major generals and eight brigadiers to serve under Washington, set up a series of staff offices closely resembling those in the British Army, prescribed a pay scale and standard ration, and adopted Articles of War to govern the military establishment. The same mixture of geographical, political, and military considerations governed the choice of Washington's sub-ordinates. Two-thirds of them came from New England, in recognition of the fact that the existing army was a New England army. Three others—Charles Lee, Horatio Gates, and Richard Montgomery—were chosen because of their experience in the British Army. Lee, in particular, who had come from England to the colonies in 1773, was in 1775 deemed the foremost military expert in America, and he was for a time to be Washington's first assistant.

The army of which Washington formally took command on July 3, 1775, he described as "a mixed multitude of people . . . under very little discipline, order or government." Out of this "mixed multitude," Washington set out to create an army shaped in large part in the British image. Basing his observations on his experience with British Regulars during the French and Indian War, he wrote: "Discipline is the soul of an army. It makes small numbers formidable;

General Washington (*center*) With Maj. Gen. Artemas Ward (*right*)
and an aide (*left*) *visiting the field, July 1775.*

procures success to the weak and esteem to all." Employing Gates, his experienced adjutant general, to prepare regulations and orders, the Commander in Chief set out to inculcate discipline. A strenuous effort was made to halt the random comings and goings of officers and men and to institute regular roll calls and strength returns. Suspicious of the "leveling" tendencies of the New Englanders, Washington made the distinction between officers and enlisted men more rigid. Various punishments were introduced—lash, pillory, wooden horse, and drumming out of camp—and courts-martial sat almost constantly.

While establishing discipline in the existing army, Washington had at the same time to form a new one enlisted directly in the Continental service. Out of conferences with a Congressional committee that visited camp in September 1775 emerged a plan for such an army, composed of 26 regiments of infantry of 728 men each, plus one regiment of riflemen and one of artillery, 20,372 men in all, to be uniformly paid, supplied, and administered by the Continental Congress and enlisted to the end of the year 1776. Except for the short term of enlistment, it was an excellent plan on paper, but Washington soon found he could not carry it out. Both officers and men resisted a reorganization that cut across the lines of the locally organized units in which they were accustomed to serve. The men saw as their first obligation their families and farms at home, and they were reluctant to re-enlist for another year's service. On December 10, despite pressures and patriotic appeals, most of the Connecticut men went home and militia from New Hampshire and Massachusetts had to be brought in to fill their places in the line. Others, who had jeered and hooted when the Connecticut men left, also went home when their enlistment expired only three weeks later. On January 1, 1776, when the army became "Continental in every respect," Washington found that he had only slightly more than 8,000 enlistments instead of the 20,000 planned. Returns in early March showed only a thousand or so more. "I have often thought how much happier I would have been," wrote a sorely tried commander, "if, instead of accepting a command under such circumstances, I had taken up musket on my shoulder and entered the ranks, or, if I could have justified the measure to posterity and my own conscience, had retired to the back country and lived in a Wigwam."

With enlistments falling short, the only recourse was to continue to use short-term militia to fill the gaps in the lines. A Continental Army had been formed, but it fell far short of the goals Washington and Congress had set for it. This army was enlisted for but a year and the whole troublesome process would have to be repeated at the end of 1776. The short term of enlistment was, of course, a cardinal error, but in 1775 everyone, including Washington, anticipated only a short campaign.

While organizing and disciplining his army, Washington had also to maintain the siege of Boston and overcome his deficiencies in supply. In these efforts he was more successful. Congress and the individual colonies sponsored voyages to the West Indies, where the French and Dutch had conveniently exported quantities of war materials. Washington put some of his troops on board ship and with an improvised navy succeeded in capturing numerous British supply ships. He sent Col. Henry Knox, later to be his Chief of Artillery, to Ticonderoga, and Knox in the winter of 1775–76 brought some fifty pieces of captured cannon to Cambridge over poor or nonexistent roads in icebound New York and New England. By March 1776, despite deficiencies in the number of Continentals, Washington was ready to close in on Boston.

The Invasion of Canada and the Fall of Boston

The major military operations of 1775 and early 1776 were not around Boston but in far-distant Canada, which the Americans tried to add as a fourteenth colony. Canada seemed a tempting and vulnerable target. To take it would eliminate a British base at the head of the familiar invasion route along the lake and river chain connecting the St. Lawrence with the Hudson. Congress, getting no response to an appeal to the Canadians to join in its cause, in late June 1775 instructed Maj. Gen. Philip Schuyler of New York to take possession of Canada if "practicable" and "not disagreeable to the Canadians."

Schuyler managed to get together a force of about 2,000 men from New York and Connecticut, thus forming the nucleus of what was to become known as the Northern Army. In September 1775 Brig. Gen. Richard Montgomery set out with this small army from Ticonderoga with the objective of taking Montreal. To form a second prong to the invasion, Washington detached a force of 1,100 under Col. Benedict Arnold, including a contingent of riflemen under Capt. Daniel Morgan of Virginia, to proceed up the Kennebec River, across the wilds of Maine, and down the Chaudière to join with Montgomery before Quebec. (*Map 4*)

Montgomery, advancing along the route via Lake George, Lake Champlain, and the Richelieu River, was seriously delayed by the British fort at St. Johns but managed to capture Montreal on November 13. Arnold meanwhile had arrived opposite Quebec on November 8, after one of the most rugged marches in history. One part of his force had turned back and others were lost by

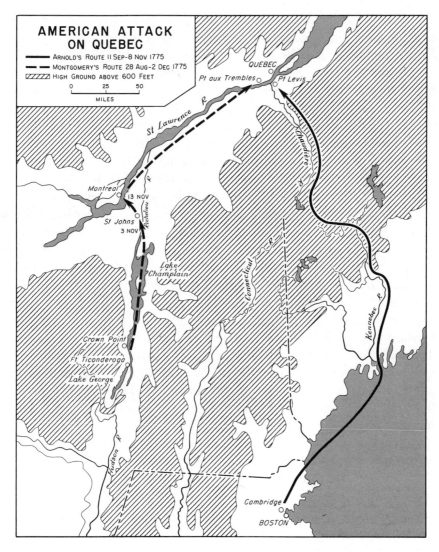

AMERICAN ATTACK ON QUEBEC

—— ARNOLD'S ROUTE 11 SEP–8 NOV 1775
— — MONTGOMERY'S ROUTE 28 AUG–2 DEC 1775
▨▨▨ HIGH GROUND ABOVE 600 FEET

0   25   50
MILES

MAP 4

starvation, sickness, drowning, and desertion. Only 600 men crossed the St. Lawrence on November 13, and in imitation of Wolfe scaled the cliffs and encamped on the Plains of Abraham. It was a magnificent feat, but the force was too small to prevail even against the scattered Canadian militia and British Regulars who, unlike Montcalm, shut themselves up in the city and refused battle in the open. Arnold's men were finally forced to withdraw to Point aux Trembles, where they were joined by Montgomery with all the men he could spare from the defense of Montreal—a total of 300. Nowhere did the Canadians show much inclination to rally to the American cause; the French *habitants* remained indifferent, and the small British population gave its loyalty to the governor general. With the enlistments of about half their men expiring by the new year, Arnold and Montgomery undertook a desperate assault on the city during the night of December 30 in the middle of a raging blizzard. The Americans were outnumbered by the defenders, and the attack was a failure. Montgomery was killed and Arnold wounded.

The wounded Arnold, undaunted, continued to keep up the appearance of a siege with the scattered remnants of his force while he waited for rein-forcements. The reinforcements came—Continental regiments raised in New York, New Jersey, and Pennsylvania—but they came in driblets and there were never enough to build a force capable of again taking the offensive, though a total of 8,000 men were eventually committed to the Canadian campaign. Smallpox and other diseases took their toll and never did the supply line bring in adequate food, clothing, or ammunition. Meanwhile, the British received reinforcements and in June 1776 struck back against a disintegrating American army that retreated before them almost without a fight. By mid-July the Americans were back at Ticonderoga where they had started less than a year earlier, and the initiative on the northern front passed to the British.

While the effort to conquer Canada was moving toward its dismal end, Washington finally took the initiative at Boston. On March 4, 1776, he moved onto Dorchester Heights and emplaced his newly acquired artillery in position to menace the city; a few days later he fortified Nook's Hill, standing still closer in. On March 17 the British moved out. It would be presumptuous to say that their exit was solely a consequence of American pressure. Sir William Howe, who succeeded Gage in command, had concluded long since that Boston was a poor strategic base and intended to stay only until the transports arrived to take his army to Halifax in Nova Scotia to regroup and await reinforcements. Nevertheless, Washington's maneuvers hastened his departure, and the re-occupation of Boston was an important psychological victory for the Americans, balancing the disappointments of the Canadian campaign. The stores of cannon and ammunition the British were forced to leave behind were a welcome addition indeed to the meager American arsenal.

The New Nation

The Declaration of Independence on July 4, 1776, established a new nation and transformed a limited revolt to secure rights within the British empire into a far-reaching one, aimed at complete independence from British control. Since the king and his ministers had determined to restore British rule, the Americans now faced a long, hard struggle for independence requiring a sustained national effort such as they had not expected in 1775.

The new nation was still a weak confederation of thirteen independent states. Such national feeling as existed was a new phenomenon growing out of common opposition to British measures. Colonial tradition, divided loyalties, the nature of the economy, and the spirit of a revolt born in opposition to the use of military force to suppress popular liberties, all worked against the creation of any new strong central authority capable of mobilizing resources effectively for the long struggle that lay ahead.

The thirteen states proclaiming their independence in 1776 possessed a total population of about two and a half million people, but not all the males of military age were part of the military potential. About 20 percent were Negro slaves who except under special circumstances were not eligible for service, though Negroes did serve in the Revolution and not in segregated units. Perhaps one-third of the "politically active" Americans remained loyal to the British Government. As in any society there were also the apathetic and indifferent who swayed with the tide. The genuine patriots still provided a far larger potential of military manpower than the British could possibly transport and supply across the Atlantic, but most of the men of military age were farmers who married young and immediately started large families. Whatever their patriotic sentiments, few were ready to undertake long terms of military service, fearing that if they did their farms and families at home would suffer. Accustomed to the tradition of short-term militia service under local commanders, they infinitely preferred it to long-term service in the Continental Army.

The economy of the thirteen new states was neither self-sufficient nor truly national. The states were essentially a collection of separate agricultural communities, accustomed to exchanging their agricultural surplus for British manufactured goods and West Indian products. Manufacturing was still in its infancy and America produced few of the essentials of military supply. Despite diligent efforts to promote domestic production during the war years, the Continental Army had to rely primarily on captures and imports from Europe and the West Indies, run through a British blockade, for much of its military hardware and even for clothing. While the country produced food-stuffs in ample quantity, transport from one area to another was difficult. The normal avenues of commerce ran up and down the rivers, not overland; roads running north and south were few and inadequate. There was always a shortage of wagons, boats, and other means of transportation. Under these circumstances, it was far easier to support local militia for a few days or weeks than any sizable and continuously operating national army in the field.

The governmental machinery created after the Declaration was character-ized by decentralization and executive weakness. The thirteen new "free and independent states" transformed their existing *de facto* revolutionary govern-ments into legal state governments by adopting constitutions. Almost invariably, these constitutions vested most of the powers of government in the state legis-latures, successors to the popular assemblies of the colonial period, and severely restricted the executive authority of the governors. At the national level, the same general distrust of strong authority was apparent, and the existing Continental Congress, essentially a gathering of delegates chosen by the state legislatures and without either express powers of its own or an executive to carry out its enactments, was continued as the only central governing body. Articles of Confederation stipulating the terms of union and granting Congress specific but limited powers were drawn up shortly after the Declaration, but jealousies among the states prevented ratification until 1781. In the interim, Congress exercised most of the powers granted it under the Articles, but they did not include either the right to levy taxes or the power to raise military forces directly under its auspices. Congress could only determine the Confed-eration's need for troops and money to wage war and set quotas for the states to meet in proportion to their population and wealth. It had no means of insuring that the states met their quotas, and indeed they seldom did.

The decentralized structure provided no adequate means of financing the war. The state legislatures, possessing the power to tax that Congress lacked, hesitated to use it extensively in the face of popular opposition to taxation, and were normally embarrassed to meet even their own expenses. Congress very early took unto itself the power to issue paper money and to negotiate domestic and foreign loans, but it shared these powers with the states, which also printed paper money in profusion and borrowed both at home and abroad to the extent they could. The paper money was a useful expedient in the early part of the war; indeed the Revolution could not have been carried on without it. But successive issues by Congress and the states led to first gradual and then galloping inflation, leaving the phrase "not worth a Con-tinental" as a permanent legacy to the American language. The process of depreciation and the exhaustion of credit gradually robbed both the states and Congress of the power to pay troops, buy supplies, and otherwise meet the multitudinous expenses of war.

Evolution of the Continental Army

Under these circumstances it is not surprising that Washington never got the kind of army, molded in the British image, that he desired. The experience before Boston in 1775 was repeated many times, as local militia had to be called in continually to give the American Army a numerical superiority in the field. The Continental Army, nevertheless, became the center of American resistance, and its commander, Washington, the symbol of the patriot cause. The extent to which militia could be expected to rally to that cause was very largely determined by the Continental Army's success or failure in the field.

Though the militia belonged to the states, the Continental Army was a creation of the Continental Congress. Congress prescribed its size and composition, chose its generals, and governed the system for its administration and supply. Suspicious on principle of a standing army and acutely aware of historic examples of seizure of political power by military leaders, its members kept a watchful eye on the Army's commanders and insisted they defer to civilian authority. Washington countered these suspicions by constantly deferring to Congressional wishes, and he was rewarded by the assiduity with which Congress usually adopted his recommendations.

Lacking an executive, Congress had to rely on committees and boards to carry out its policies—unwieldy devices at best and centers of conflicting interest and discord at worst. In June 1776 it set up a Board of War and Ordnance, consisting of five of its members, the lineal ancestor of the War Department. In 1777 Congress changed the composition of the board, directing that it henceforth be made up of persons outside Congress who could devote full time to their military duties. Neither of these devices really worked well, and Congress continually handled administrative matters by action of the entire membership or by appointment of special committees to go to camp. In 1781 the board was replaced by a single Secretary at War.

Under the Articles of Confederation the states were responsible for raising troops for the Continental Army, for organizing and equipping them, and for appointing officers through the rank of colonel. State authorities called out militia sometimes at the request of Congress and sometimes on their own initiative. When they joined the main army, militia normally shared in its supplies and equipment. The states, however, maintained an interest in supplying and administering the troops of their own "lines" as well as their militia, and the Continental agents had continually to enlist state assistance in their own efforts. Lines of authority crisscrossed at every turn.

It was an inefficient military system for an organized national effort. Washington could never depend on having enough trained men or supplies. He continually inveighed against sending militia to fight his battles and by early 1776 had concluded that he needed an army enlisted for the duration of the war. Congress did not, as has often been charged, ignore his wishes. In October 1776 it voted a new establishment, superseding the plan developed for the army before Boston in 1775 and haphazard arrangements made in the interim for raising Continental regiments in various states. This establishment was to contain 88 battalions of infantry, or about 60,000 men, enlisted to serve three years or "during the present war," with each state assigned a quota in proportion to its population under the system set up in the Articles. After the disastrous retreat across New Jersey in December 1776, Congress went further and authorized an additional 22 battalions to be recruited by Washington's officers directly into the Continental service. These 110 battalions remained the authorized strength of the Continental Army until 1781, when Congress cut it to 59.

Neither the 88 battalions, nor the 110, nor even the 59 ever existed except on paper. The Continental Army never had as many as 30,000 men at any one time, and very rarely was Washington able to muster as many as 15,000 effectives in the field. The states were simply unable to meet their quotas. By the winter of 1777–78, the effort to enlist men for three years or the duration collapsed, and the following spring, with the sanction of Washington, Congress reverted to a system of one-year enlistments and recommended to the states that they institute a system of drafting men from the militia for one year's service. This first American wartime draft was applied irregularly in the various states and succeeded no better than had earlier methods in filling the Continental ranks. Bounties, instituted by both the states and the Congress very early in the war and progressively increased one step behind the pace of inflation, also produced only temporary and irregular results.

The coin did have another side. In reality the shortage of arms and ammunition and of facilities for producing them limited the number of men who could be kept continuously in the field as effectively as did the failure of enlistment drives. The militia system enabled many able-bodied males to perform part-time military service and still remain most of the time in the labor force that kept the economy going. It is doubtful whether the American economy could have sustained such an army as Washington and Congress proposed in 1776, even had there been a central administration with adequate power. As it was, the small Continental Army that did remain in the field intermittently suffered extreme hardship and near starvation. On the other hand, American ability to raise local armies in any threatened region helped to balance the strategic mobility that the British Fleet gave to the British Army. Although militia generally did not perform well in regular warfare, when highly motivated and ably led, they could fight well on terrain suited to their capabilities. Given the conditions under which the Revolution was fought, the American military system was more effective than its critics have recognized, though it failed to provide adequately for a sustained military effort over a period of years.

Perhaps Washington's greatest achievement was simply in maintaining the Continental Army continuously in the field. Despite its many vicissitudes, that army did take shape during the war as the first distinctively American military organization, neither quite a replica of the professional British Army on which it was modeled nor yet the type of national army raised by conscription that was to appear in France after the Revolution of 1789.

The Continental Army operated in three main territorial divisions or departments—the main army under Washington largely in the Middle States, the Northern Army in northern New York, and the Southern Army in the Carolinas and Georgia. Although Washington was Commander in Chief of the whole, the commanders of the Northern and Southern Armies still operated with a considerable measure of independence. Congress, rather than Washington, named their commanders and communicated directly with them. Of the two "separate armies," the Northern Army was by far the most important until 1777 and the Southern Army existed largely on paper; by 1780 the situation was reversed as the British transferred their main effort to the southern states.

The Continental Army was composed mainly of infantry and artillery, with very little cavalry. The basic unit of infantry organization was the regiment or battalion composed of eight companies. Organization above this level was highly flexible. A brigade was usually formed of several regiments and was commanded by a brigadier general; a division consisted of a similar grouping of several brigades commanded by a major general. Artillery was organized into a brigade of four regiments under a Chief of Artillery, Brig. Gen. Henry Knox, but the various companies were distributed among the infantry battalions. There was a small corps of engineers and an even smaller contingent of artificers, who handled the servicing and repair of ordnance.

Washington was provided with a staff generally corresponding to that of the British Army. The most important staff officer was the Quartermaster General, responsible not only for transportation and delivery of supplies but also for arranging the camp, regulating marches, and establishing the order of battle of the army. There were also an Adjutant General, a Judge Advocate

General, a Paymaster General, a Commissary General of Musters, a Commissary General of Provisions, a Clothier General, a Chief Surgeon, and a Chief Engineer. Each of the separate armies also usually had staff officers in these positions, designated as deputies to those of the main army.

All these staff officers had primarily administrative and supply functions. The modern concept of a general staff that acts as a sort of collective brain for the commander had no real counterpart in the eighteenth century. For advice on strategy and operations, Washington relied on a Council of War made up of his principal subordinate commanders, and, conforming to his original instructions from Congress, he usually consulted the council before making major decisions.

Both organization and staff work suffered from the ills that afflicted the whole military system. Regiments were constantly understrength, were organized differently by the various states, and employed varying systems of drill, discipline, and training. In the promotion of officers in the state lines, Continental commanders shared authority with the states, and the confused system gave rise to all sorts of rivalries, jealousies, and resentment, leading to frequent resignations. Staff officers were generally inexperienced, and few had the patience and perseverance to overcome the obstacles posed by divided authority, inadequate means, and poor transportation and communication facilities. The supply and support services of the Continental Army never really functioned efficiently, and with the depreciation in the currency they came close to collapse.

The British Problem

Whatever the American weaknesses, the British Government faced no easy task when it undertook to subdue the revolt by military force. Even though England possessed the central administration, stable financial system, and well-organized Army and Navy that the Americans so sorely lacked, the whole establishment was ill-prepared in 1775 for the struggle in America. A large burden of debt incurred in the wars of the preceding century had forced crippling economies on both Army and Navy. British administrative and supply systems, though far superior to anything the Americans could improvise, were also characterized by division and confusion of authority, and there was much corruption in high places.

To suppress the revolt, Britain had first to raise the necessary forces, then transport and sustain them over 3,000 miles of ocean, and finally use them effectively to regain control of a vast and sparsely populated territory. Recruiting men for an eighteenth century army was most difficult. The British Government had no power to compel service except in the militia in defense of the homeland, and service in the British Army overseas was immensely unpopular. To meet Sir William Howe's request for 50,000 men to conduct the campaign in 1776, the ministry resorted to hiring mercenaries from the small German states, particularly Hesse-Cassell (hence Hessians). These German states were to contribute almost 30,000 men to the British service during the war—complete organizations with their own officers up to the rank of major general and schooled in the system of Frederick the Great. Howe did not get his 50,000 men but by midsummer 1776 his force had passed 30,000 British and Hessians, and additional reinforcements were sent to Canada during the year. Maintaining a force of this size proved to be virtually impossible. The attrition rate in America from battle losses, sickness, disease, and desertion was tremendously high. English jails and poorhouses were drained of able-bodied men, bounties were paid, patriotic appeals were launched throughout England, Scotland, and Ireland, and all the ancient methods of impressment were tried, but the British were never able to recruit enough men to meet the needs of their commanders in America.

Providing adequate support for this army over a long ocean supply line was equally difficult. Even for food and forage, the British Army had to rely primarily on sea lines of supply. Transports were in short supply, the hardships of the 2- to 4-month voyage terrible, and the loss of men and supplies to natural causes heavy. Moreover, though the Americans could muster no navy capable of contesting British control of the seas, their privateers and the ships of their infant navy posed a constant threat to unprotected troop and supply transports. British commanders repeatedly had to delay their operations, awaiting the arrival of men and supplies from England.

Once in America, British armies could find no strategic center or centers whose capture would bring victory. Flat, open country where warfare could be carried on in European style was not common; and woods, hills, and swamps suited to the operations of militia and irregulars were plentiful. A British Army that could win victories in the field over the Continentals had great difficulty in making those victories meaningful. American armies seemed to possess miraculous powers of recuperation, while a British force, once depleted or surrendered, took a tremendous effort to replace.

As long as they controlled the seas, the British could land and establish bases at nearly any point on the long American coast line. The many navigable rivers dotting the coast also provided water avenues of invasion well into the interior. But to crush the revolt the British Army had to cut loose from coastal bases and rivers. When it did so its logistical problems multiplied and its lines of communications became vulnerable to constant harassment. British armies almost inevitably came to grief every time they moved very far from the areas where they could be nurtured by supply ships from the homeland. These difficulties, a British colonel asserted in 1777, had "absolutely prevented us this whole war from going fifteen miles from a navigable river."

The British could not, in any case, ever hope to muster enough strength to occupy with their own troops the vast territory they sought to restore to British rule. Their only real hope of meaningful victory was to use American loyalists as an instrument for controlling the country, as one British general put it, to help "the good Americans to subdue the bad." There were many obstacles to making effective use of the Tories. Patriot organization, weak at the center, was strong at the grass roots, in the local communities throughout America, whereas the Tories were neither well organized nor energetically led. The patriots seized the machinery of local government in most communities at the outset, held it until the British Army appeared in their midst, and then normally regained it after the British departed. Strong local control enabled the patriots to root out the more ardent Tories at the very outset, and by making an example of them to sway the apathetic and indifferent. British commanders were usually disappointed in the number of Tories who flocked to their standards and even more upset by the alacrity with which many of them switched their allegiance when the British Army moved out. They found the Tories a demanding, discordant, and puzzling lot, and they made no really earnest effort to enlist them in British forces until late in the war. By 1781 they had with their armies some 8,000 "provincial rank and file"; perhaps 50,000 in all served the British in some military capacity during the war.

On the frontiers the British could also expect support from the Indian tribes who almost inevitably drifted into the orbit of whatever power controlled Canada. But support of the Indians was a two-edged sword, for nothing could raise frontier enthusiasm for battle like the threat of an Indian attack.

Finally, the British had to fight the war with one eye on their ancient enemies in Europe. France, thirsting for revenge for defeat in the Seven Years' War, stood ready to aid the American cause if for no other purpose than to weaken British power, and by virtue of a Family Compact could almost certainly carry Spain along in any war with England. France and Spain could at the very least provide badly needed money and supplies to sustain the American effort and force the British to divert their forces from the contest in America. At most the combined Franco-Spanish fleet might well prove a match for the British Fleet and neutralize that essential control of the seas needed by the British to carry on the American war.

Of Strategy

The story of the American Revolution can hardly be told in terms of long-term strategy and its success or failure. Neither side ever had any really consistent plan for the conduct of the war. The British, who retained the strategic initiative most of the time, failed to use it to great advantage. They were highly uncertain about their objective; plans were laid from year to year and seldom co-ordinated even for a single year. Blame for this uncertain approach falls in almost equal part on the administration in England and the commanders in America. If King George III, Lord North, his Prime Minister, and Lord George Germain, Secretary of State for the American Department—the three British officials mainly responsible for the conduct of the war—never provided the timely guidance that might have been expected of them, their inability to do so came about in part because the commanders in the field never furnished accurate enough predictions of what to expect and differed so much among themselves as to the proper course to pursue. In assessing blame in this fashion, one must keep in mind the difficulties of logistics and communications under which the British labored, for these difficulties made it virtually impossible to co-ordinate plans over great distances or to assemble men and materials in time to pursue one logical and consistent plan.

American strategy was primarily defensive and consequently had to be shaped largely in terms of countering British moves. Uncertainties as to the supply of both men and materials acted on the American side even more effectively to thwart the development of a consistent plan for winning the war. Yet Washington was never so baffled by the conditions of the war or uncertain of his objective as were the various British commanders. After some early blunders, he soon learned both his own and the enemy's strengths and weaknesses and did his best to exploit them. Though unable to develop a consistent plan, he did try to develop a consistent line of action. He sought to maintain his principal striking force in a central position blocking any British advance into the interior; to be neither too bold nor too timid in seeking battle for limited objectives; to avoid the destruction of his army at all costs; and to find some means of concentrating a sufficient force to strike a decisive offensive blow whenever the British overreached themselves. He showed a better appreciation than the British commanders of the advantages in mobility their Navy gave them, and after 1778, when the French entered the war, he clearly saw that the decisive blow he desired could be struck only by a combined effort of the Continental Army and the French Fleet.

The British Offensive in 1776

If the British ever had a single strategic objective in the war, it was the Hudson River–Lake Champlain line. By taking and holding this line the British believed they could separate New England, considered to be the principal center of the rebellion, from the more malleable colonies to the southward. Howe proposed to make this the main objective of his campaign in 1776 by landing at New York, securing a base of operations there, and then pushing north. He wanted to concentrate the entire British force in America in New York, but the British Government diverted part of it to Canada in early 1776 to repel the American invasion, laying the groundwork for the divided command that was so to plague British operations afterward.

After the evacuation of Boston, Howe stayed at Halifax from March until June, awaiting the arrival of supplies and reinforcements. While he tarried, the British Government ordered another diversion in the south, aimed at encouraging the numerous loyalists who, according to the royal governors watching from their havens on board British warships, were waiting only for the appearance of a British force to rise and overthrow rebel rule. Unfortunately for the British, the naval squadron sent from England under Admiral Sir Peter Parker was delayed and did not arrive off the American coast until late in May. By this time all hopes of effective co-operation with the Tories had been dashed. Loyalist contingents had been completely defeated and dispersed in Virginia, North Carolina, and South Carolina. Parker, undeterred by these developments, determined to attack Charleston, the largest city in the south. There South Carolina militia and newly raised Continentals had prepared and manned defenses under the guidance of Maj. Gen. Charles Lee, whom Washington had dispatched south to assist them. The South Carolinians, contrary to Lee's advice, centered their defenses in Fort Moultrie, a palmetto log fort constructed on Sullivan's Island, commanding the approach to the harbor. It was an unwise decision, somewhat comparable to that at Bunker Hill, but fortunately for the defenders the British had to mount an un-co-ordinated attack in haste. Clinton's troops were landed on nearby Long Island, but on the day the Navy attacked, June 28, the water proved too deep for them to wade across to Sullivan's Island as expected. The British Army consequently sat idly by while the gunners in Fort Moultrie devastated the British warships. Sir Peter Parker suffered the ultimate indignity when his pants were set afire.

The battered British Fleet hastily embarked the British soldiers and sailed northward to join Howe, for it was already behind schedule. For three years following the fiasco at Charleston the British were to leave the south unmolested and the Tories there, who were undoubtedly numerous, without succor.

Howe was meanwhile beset by other delays in the arrival of transports from England, and his attack did not get under way until late August—leaving insufficient time before the advent of winter to carry through the planned advance along the Hudson–Lake Champlain line. He therefore started his invasion of New York with only the limited objective of gaining a foothold for the campaign the following year.

The British commander had, when his force was all assembled, an army of about 32,000 men; it was supported by a powerful fleet under the command of his brother, Admiral Richard Howe. To oppose him Washington had brought most of his army down from Boston, and Congress exerted its utmost efforts to reinforce him by raising Continental regiments in the surrounding states and issuing a general call for the militia. Washington was able to muster a paper strength of roughly 28,500 men, but only about 19,000 were present and fit for duty. As Christopher Ward remarks, "The larger part of them were raw recruits, undisciplined and inexperienced in warfare, and militia, never to be assuredly relied upon."

Washington and Congress made the same decision the South Carolinians had made at Charleston—to defend their territory in the most forward positions—and this time they paid the price for their mistake. The geography of the area gave the side possessing naval supremacy an almost insuperable advantage. The city of New York stood on Manhattan Island, surrounded by the Hudson, Harlem, and East Rivers. (*Map 5*) There was only one connecting link with the mainland, Kingsbridge across the Harlem River at the northern tip of Manhattan. Across the East River on Long Island, Brooklyn Heights stood in a position dominating the southern tip of Manhattan. With the naval forces at their disposal, the Howes could land troops on either Long Island or Manhattan proper and send warships up either the East or Hudson Rivers a considerable distance.

Washington decided he must defend Brooklyn Heights on Long Island if he was to defend Manhattan; he therefore divided his army between the two places—a violation of the principle of mass and the first step toward disaster. For all practical purposes command on Long Island was also divided. Maj. Gen. Nathanael Greene, to whom Washington first entrusted the command, came down with malaria and was replaced by Maj. Gen. John Sullivan. Not completely satisfied with this arrangement, at the last moment Washington placed Maj. Gen. Israel Putnam over Sullivan, but Putnam hardly had time to become acquainted with the situation before the British struck. The forces on Long

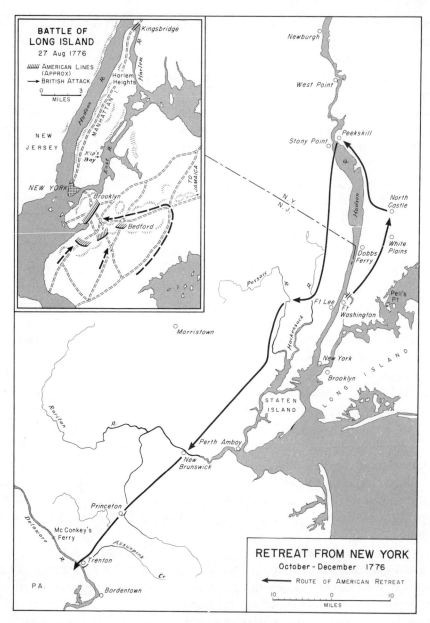

MAP 5

Island, numbering about 10,000, were disposed in fortifications on Brooklyn
Heights and in forward positions back of a line of thickly wooded hills that
ran across the southern end of the island. Sullivan was in command on the left

of the forward line, Brig. Gen. William Alexander (Lord Stirling) on the right. Four roads ran through the hills toward the American positions. (*inset, Map 5*) Unfortunately Sullivan, in violation of the principle of security, left the Jamaica-Bedford road unguarded.

Howe was consequently able to teach the Americans lessons in maneuver and surprise. On August 22 he landed a force of 20,000 on the southwestern tip of Long Island and, in a surprise attack up the Jamaica-Bedford road against the American left flank, crumpled the entire American position. Stirling's valiant fight on the right went for naught, and inexperienced American troops fled in terror before the British and Hessian bayonets, falling back to the fortifications on Brooklyn Heights. It seems clear that had Howe pushed his advantage immediately he could have carried the heights and destroyed half the American Army then and there. Instead he halted at nightfall and began to dig trenches, signaling an intent to take the heights by "regular approaches" in traditional eighteenth century fashion. Washington managed to evacuate his forces across the East River on the night of August 29. According to one theory, wind and weather stopped the British warships from entering the river to prevent the escape; according to another, the Americans had placed impediments in the river that effectively barred their entry. In any case, it was a narrow escape, made possible by the skill, bravery, and perseverance of Col. John Glover's Marblehead Regiment, Massachusetts fishermen who manned the boats.

Washington had two weeks to prepare his defenses on Manhattan before Howe struck again, landing a force at Kip's Bay above the city of New York (now about 34th Street) on September 15. Raw Connecticut militia posted at this point broke and ran "as if the Devil was in them," defying even the efforts of a raging Washington to halt them. Howe once again had an opportunity to split the American Army in two and destroy half, but again he delayed midway across the island to wait until his entire force had landed. General Putnam was able to bring the troops stationed in the city up the west side of Manhattan to join their compatriots in new fortifications on Harlem Heights. There the Americans held out for another month, and even won a skirmish, but this position was also basically untenable.

In mir-October Howe landed again in Washington's rear at Pell's Point. The American commander then finally evacuated the Manhattan trap via Kingsbridge and took up a new position at White Plains, leaving about 6,000 men behind to man two forts, Fort Washington and Fort Lee, on opposite sides of the Hudson. Howe launched a probing attack on the American position at White Plains and was repulsed, but Washington, sensing his inability to meet the British in battle on equal terms, moved away to the north toward the New

York highlands. Again he was outmaneuvered. Howe quickly moved to Dobbs Ferry on the Hudson between Washington's army and the Hudson River forts. On the advice of General Greene (now recovered from his bout with malaria), Washington decided to defend the forts. At the same time he again split his army, moving across the Hudson and into New Jersey with 5,000 men and leaving General Lee and Maj. Gen. William Heath with about 8,000 between them to guard the passes through the New York highlands at Peekskill and North Castle. On November 16 Howe turned against Fort Washington and with the support of British warships on the Hudson stormed it successfully, capturing 3,000 American troops and large quantities of valuable munitions. Greene then hastily evacuated Fort Lee and by the end of November Washington, with mere remnants of his army, was in full retreat across New Jersey with Lord Charles Cornwallis, detached by Howe, pursuing him rapidly from river to river.

While Washington was suffering these disastrous defeats, the army that had been gathered was slowly melting away. Militia left by whole companies and desertion among the Continentals was rife. When Washington finally crossed the Delaware into Pennsylvania in early December, he could muster barely 2,000 men, the hard core of his Continental forces. The 8,000 men in the New York highlands also dwindled away. Even more appalling, most enlistments expired with the end of the year 1776 and a new army would have to be raised for the following year.

Yet neither the unreliability of the militia nor the short period of enlistment fully explained the debacle that had befallen the Continental Army. Washington's generalship was also faulty. Criticism of the Commander in Chief, even among his official family, mounted, centering particularly on his decision to hold Fort Washington. General Lee, the ex-British colonel, ordered by Washington to bring his forces down from New York to join him behind the Delaware, delayed, believing that he might himself salvage the American cause by making incursions into New Jersey. He wrote Horatio Gates, ". . . *entre nous,* a certain great man is most damnably deficient. . . ."

There was only one bright spot in the picture in the autumn of 1776. While Howe was routing Washington around New York City, other British forces under Sir Guy Carleton were attempting to follow up the advantage they had gained in repulsing the attack on Canada earlier in the year. Carleton rather leisurely built a flotilla of boats to carry British forces down Lake Champlain and Lake George, intending at least to reduce the fort at Ticonderoga before winter set in. Benedict Arnold countered by throwing together a much weaker flotilla of American boats with which he contested the British passage. Arnold lost this naval action on the lakes, but he so delayed Carleton's advance that the British commander reached Ticonderoga too late in the year to consider undertaking a siege. He returned his army to winter quarters in Canada, leaving the British with no advance base from which to launch the next year's campaign.

Although its consequences were to be far reaching, this limited victory did little to dispel the gloom that fell on the patriots after Washington's defeats in New York. The British, aware that Continental enlistments expired at the end of the year, had high hopes that the American Army would simply fade away and the rebellion collapse. Howe halted Cornwallis' pursuit of Washington and sent Clinton with a detachment of troops under naval escort to seize Newport, Rhode Island. He then dispersed his troops in winter quarters, establishing a line of posts in New Jersey at Perth Amboy, New Brunswick, Princeton, Trenton, and Bordentown, and retired himself to New York. Howe had gained the object of the 1776 campaign, a strong foothold, and possibly, as he thought at the time, a great deal more.

Trenton and Princeton

While Howe rested comfortably in New York, Washington desperately sought to reconcentrate his forces and redeem the defeat in New York. General Lee had the misfortune to fall into British hands on December 12, and his 2,000 remaining men then made haste to join Washington. Eight decimated regiments were also pulled from the Northern Army, and with some Pennsylvania militia Washington was able to assemble a force totaling about 7,000 by the last week of December 1776. If he was to use this force, he would have to do so before the enlistments expired on December 31. With great boldness, Washington formulated a plan to strike by surprise at the Hessian garrisons at Trenton and Bordentown on Christmas night, when the troops might be expected to relax their guard for holiday revelry. A Continental force of 2,400 men under Washington's personal command was to cross the Delaware at McConkey's Ferry above Trenton and then proceed in two columns by different routes, converging on the opposite ends of the main street of Trenton in the early morning of December 26. (*Map 6*) A second force, mainly militia, under Col. John Cadwalader was to cross below near Bordentown to attack the Hessian garrison there; a third, also militia, under Brig. Gen. James Ewing, was to cross directly opposite Trenton to block the Hessian route of escape across Assunpink Creek.

Christmas night was cold, windy, and snowy and the Delaware River was filled with blocks of ice. Neither Cadwalader nor Ewing was able to fulfill his part of the plan. Driven on by Washington's indomitable will, the main force did cross as planned and the two columns, commanded respectively by Greene and Sullivan, converged on Trenton at eight o'clock in the morning of December 26,

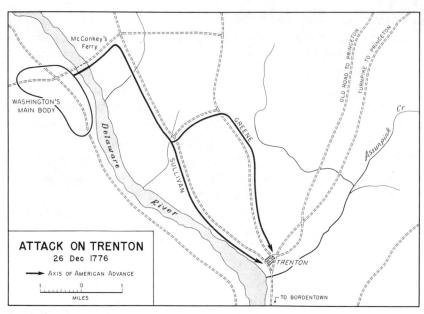

MAP 6

taking the Hessians completely by surprise. A New England private noted in his diary for the 26th: "This morning at 4 a clock we set off with our Field pieces and Marched 8 miles to Trenton whare we ware attacked by a Number of Hushing and we Toock 1000 of them besides killed some. Then we marched back and got to the River at Night and got over all the Hushing." This rather undramatic description of a very dramatic event was not far wrong, except in attributing the attack to the "Hushings." The Hessians surrendered after a fight lasting only an hour and a half. Forty were killed and the prisoner count was 918. Only 400 escaped to Bordentown, and these only because Ewing was not in place to block their escape. The Americans lost only 4 dead and 4 wounded.

Encouraged by this success, Washington determined to make another foray. By an impassioned appeal to the patriotism of the men, supplemented by an offer of a $10 bounty in hard money, he was able to persuade at least part of his old army to remain for six more weeks. With a force of around 5,000 Washington again crossed the Delaware on the night of December 30–31. By this time Cornwallis had hastily gathered together the scattered British garrisons in New Jersey, and took up a position confronting Washington at Trenton on January 2, 1777. Convinced that he had the Americans in a trap, he put off battle until the next day because of the exhausted state of his troops. In the night Washington slipped away, leaving campfires burning brightly to deceive the British. The

ALEXANDER HAMILTON'S ARTILLERY AT TRENTON, *with a 6-pounder brass field gun in the foreground.*

next morning he struck another surprise blow at Princeton, inflicting heavy losses on two British regiments just leaving the town to join Cornwallis. Washington then went into winter quarters in the hills around Morristown, New Jersey. Cornwallis did not pursue. The British had had enough of winter warfare, and Howe drew in his outposts in New Jersey to New Brunswick and Perth Amboy.

Trenton and Princeton not only offset the worst effects of the disastrous defeats in New York but also restored Washington's prestige as a commander with friend and foe alike. In the execution of the two strokes east of the Delaware, Washington had applied the principles of offensive, surprise, and maneuver with great success and finally achieved stature as a military commander. If these victories did not assure him that he could recruit such an army as Congress had voted, they did at least guarantee that he would be able to field a force the following year. Sir William Howe found that, despite his smashing rout of the Americans in New York, he was left with little more than that city, a foothold in New Jersey, and the port of Newport in Rhode Island.

CHAPTER 4

The Winning of Independence
1777–1783

The year 1777 was most critical for the British. The issue, very plainly, was whether they could score such success in putting down the American revolt that the French would not dare enter the war openly to aid the American rebels. Yet it was in this critical year that British plans were most confused and British operations most disjointed. The British campaign of 1777 provides one of the most striking object lessons in military history of the dangers of divided command.

The Campaign of 1777

With secure bases at New York and Newport, Howe had a chance to get the early start that had been denied him the previous year. His first plan, advanced on November 30, 1776, was probably the most comprehensive put forward by any British commander during the war. He proposed to maintain a small force of about 8,000 to contain Washington in New Jersey and 7,000 to garrison New York, while sending one column of 10,000 from Newport into New England and another column of 10,000 from New York up the Hudson to form a junction with a British force moving down from Canada. On the assumption that these moves would be successful by autumn, he would next capture Philadelphia, the rebel capital, and then make the southern provinces the "objects of the winter." For this plan, Howe requested 35,000 men, 15,000 more effective troops than he had left at the end of the 1776 campaign. Sir George Germain, the American Secretary, could promise him only 8,000. Even before receiving this news, but evidently influenced by Trenton and Princeton, Howe changed his plan and proposed to devote his main effort in 1777 to taking Philadelphia. On March 3, 1777, Germain informed Howe that the Philadelphia plan was approved, but that there might be only 5,500 reinforcements. At the same time Germain and the king urged a "warm diversion" against New England.

Meanwhile, Sir John Burgoyne, who had succeeded in obtaining the separate military command in Canada, submitted his plan calling for an advance southward to "a junction with Howe." Germain and the king also approved this plan on March 29, though aware of Howe's intention to go to Philadelphia. They seem to have expected either that Howe would be able to form his junction by the "warm diversion," or else that he would take Philadelphia quickly and then turn north to aid Burgoyne. In any case, Germain approved two separate and un-co-ordinated plans, and Howe and Burgoyne went their separate ways, doing nothing to remedy the situation. Howe's Philadelphia plan did provide for leaving enough force in New York for what its commander, General Clinton, called "a damn'd starved offensive," but Clinton's orders were vague. Quite possibly Burgoyne knew before he left England for Canada that Howe was going to Philadelphia, but ambitious "Gentleman Johnny" was determined to make a reputation in the American war, and evidently believed he could succeed alone. Even when he learned certainly on August 3, 1777, that he could not expect Howe's co-operation, he persisted in his design. As Howe thought Pennsylvania was filled with royalists, Burgoyne cherished the illusion that legions of Tories in New York and western New England were simply awaiting the appearance of the king's troops to rally to the colors.

Again in 1777 the late arrival of Howe's reinforcements and stores ships gave Washington time that he sorely needed. Men to form the new Continental Army came in slowly and not until June did the Americans have a force of 8,000. On the northern line the defenses were even more thinly manned. Supplies for troops in the field were also short, but the arrival of the first three ships bearing secret aid from France vastly improved the situation. They were evidence of the covert support of the French Government; a mission sent by Congress to France was meanwhile working diligently to enlist open aid and to embroil France in a war with England. The French Foreign Minister, the Comte de Vergennes, had already decided to take that risk when and if the American rebels demonstrated their serious purpose and ability to fulfill it by some signal victory in the field.

With the first foreign material aid in 1777, the influx of foreign officers into the American Army began. These officers were no unmixed blessing. Most were adventurers in search of fortune or of reputation with little facility for adjusting themselves to American conditions. Few were willing to accept any but the highest ranks. Nevertheless, they brought with them professional military knowledge and competence that the Continental Army sorely needed. When the misfits were culled out, this knowledge and competence were used to considerable advantage. Louis DuPortail, a Frenchman, and Thaddeus Kosciuszko, a Pole, did much to advance the art of engineering in the Continental Army; Casimir Pulaski, another Pole, organized its first genuine cavalry contingent; Johann de Kalb and Friedrich Wilhelm von Steuben, both Germans, and the Marquis de Lafayette, an influential French nobleman who financed his own way, were all to make valuable contributions as trainers and leaders. On the Continental Army of 1777, however, these foreign volunteers had little effect and it remained much as it had been before, a relatively untrained body of inexperienced enlistees.

When Howe finally began to stir in June 1777, Washington posted his army at Middlebrook, New Jersey, in a position either to bar Howe's overland route to Philadelphia or to move rapidly up the Hudson to oppose an advance northward. Washington confidently expected Howe to move northward to form a junction with Burgoyne, but decided he must stay in front of the main British Army wherever it went. Following the principle of economy of force, he disposed a small part of his army under General Putnam in fortifications guarding the approaches up the Hudson, and at a critical moment detached a small force to aid Schuyler against Burgoyne. The bulk of his army he kept in front of Howe in an effort to defend Philadelphia. Forts were built along the Delaware River and other steps taken to block the approach to the Continental capital by sea.

In the effort to defend Philadelphia Washington again failed, but hardly so ignominiously as he had the year before in New York. After maneuvering in New Jersey for upward of two months, Howe in August put most of his army on board ship and sailed down the coast and up the Chesapeake Bay to Head of Elk (a small town at the head of the Elk River) in Maryland, putting himself even further away from Burgoyne. (*Map 7*) Though surprised by Howe's movement, Washington rapidly shifted his own force south and took up a position at Chad's Ford on Brandywine Creek, blocking the approach to Philadelphia. There on September 11, 1777, Howe executed a flanking movement not dissimilar to that employed on Long Island and again defeated Washington. The American commander had disposed his army in two main parts, one directly opposite Chad's Ford under his personal command and the other under General Sullivan guarding the right flank upstream. While Lt. Gen. Wilhelm von Knyphausen's Hessian troops demonstrated opposite the ford, a larger force under Lord Cornwallis marched upstream, crossed the Brandywine, and moved to take Sullivan from the rear. Washington lacked good cavalry reconnaissance, and did not get positive information on Cornwallis' movement until the eleventh hour. Sullivan was in the process of changing front when

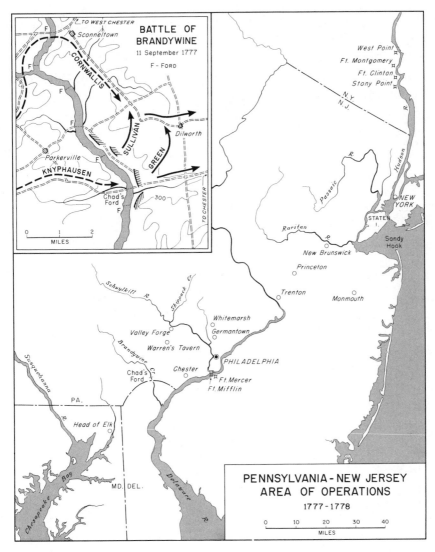

MAP 7

the British struck and his men retreated in confusion. Washington was able to salvage the situation by dispatching General Greene with two brigades to fight a valiant rear-guard action, but the move weakened his front opposite Kynphausen and his forces also had to fall back. Nevertheless, the trap was averted and the Continental Army retired in good order to Chester.

Howe followed with a series of maneuvers comparable to those he had executed in New York, and was able to enter Philadelphia with a minimum of

fighting on September 26. A combined attack of British Army and Navy forces
shortly afterward reduced the forts on the Delaware and opened the river as
a British supply line.

On entering Philadelphia, Howe dispersed his forces, stationing 9,000 men
at Germantown north of the city, 3,000 in New Jersey, and the rest in Philadelphia. As Howe had repeated his performance in New York, Washington
sought to repeat Trenton by a surprise attack on Germantown. The plan was
much like that used at Trenton but involved far more complicated movements
by much larger bodies of troops. Four columns—two of Continentals under
Sullivan and Greene and two of militia—moving at night over different roads
were to converge on Germantown simultaneously at dawn on October 4.
(*Map 8*) The plan violated the principle of simplicity, for such a maneuver was

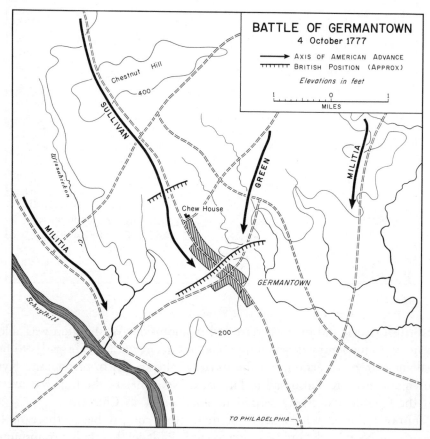

MAP 8

difficult even for well-trained professionals to execute. The two columns of Continentals arrived at different times and fired on each other in an early morning fog. The two militia columns never arrived at all. British fire from a stone house, the Chew Mansion, held up the advance while American generals argued whether they could leave a fortress in their rear. The British, though surprised, had better discipline and cohesion and were able to re-form and send fresh troops into the fray. The Americans retreated about 9:00 a.m., leaving Howe's troops in command of the field.

After Germantown Howe once again concentrated his army and moved to confront Washington at Whitemarsh, but finally withdrew to winter quarters in Philadelphia without giving battle. Washington chose the site for his own winter quarters at a place called Valley Forge, twenty miles northwest of the city. Howe had gained his objective but it proved of no lasting value to him. Congress fled west to York, Pennsylvania. No swarms of loyalists rallied to the British standards. And Howe had left Burgoyne to lose a whole British army in the north.

Burgoyne set out from Canada in June, his object to reach Albany by fall. (*Map 9*) His force was divided into two parts. The first and largest part—7,200 British and Hessian Regulars and 650 Tories, Canadians, and Indians, under his personal command—was to take the route down Lake Champlain to Ticonderoga and thence via Lake George to the Hudson. The second—700 Regulars and 1,000 Tories and Indian braves under Col. Barry St. Leger—was to move via Lake Ontario to Oswego and thence down the Mohawk Valley to join Burgoyne before Albany. In his preparations, Burgoyne evidently forgot the lesson the British had learned in the French and Indian War, that in the wilderness troops had to be prepared to travel light and fight like Indians. He carried 138 pieces of artillery and a heavy load of officers' personal baggage. Numerous ladies of high and low estate accompanied the expedition. When he started down the lakes, Burgoyne did not have enough horses and wagons to transport his artillery and baggage once he had to leave the water and move overland.

At first Burgoyne's American opposition was very weak—only about 2,500 Continentals at Ticonderoga and about 450 at old Fort Stanwix, the sole American bulwark in the Mohawk Valley. Dissension among the Americans was rife, the New Englanders refusing to support Schuyler, the aristocratic New Yorker who commanded the Northern Army, and openly intriguing to replace him with their own favorite, Maj. Gen. Horatio Gates. Ticonderoga fell to Burgoyne on June 27 all too easily. American forces dispersed and Burgoyne pursued the remnants down to Skenesborough. Once that far along, he decided to continue overland to the Hudson instead of returning to Ticonderoga to float his force

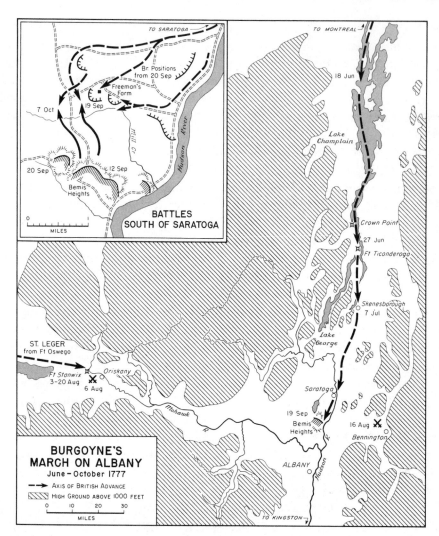

MAP 9

down Lake George, though much of his impedimenta still had to be carried by boat down the lake.

The overland line of advance was already a nightmare, running along wilderness trails, through marshes, and across wide ravines and creeks that had been swollen by abnormally heavy rains. Schuyler adopted the tactic of making it even worse by destroying bridges, cutting trees in Burgoyne's path, and digging trenches to let the waters of swamps onto drier ground. The British were able to move at a rate of little more than a mile a day and took until July 29 to reach Fort Edward on the Hudson. By that time Burgoyne was desperately short of horses, wagons, and oxen. Yet Schuyler, with a unstable force of 4,500 men discouraged by continual retreats, was in no position to give battle.

Washington did what he could to strengthen the Northern Army at this juncture. He first dispatched Maj. Gen. Benedict Arnold, his most aggressive field commander, and Maj. Gen. Benjamin Lincoln, a Massachusetts man noted for his influence with the New England militia. On August 16 he detached Col. Daniel Morgan with 500 riflemen from the main army in Pennsylvania and ordered them along with 750 men from Putnam's force in the New York highlands to join Schuyler. The riflemen were calculated to furnish an antidote for Burgoyne's Indians who, despite his efforts to restrain them, were terrorizing the countryside.

It was the rising militia, rather than Washington, who were to provide the Northern Army with its main reinforcements. Nothing worked more to produce this result than Burgoyne's employment of Indians. The murder and scalping of a beautiful white woman, Jane McCrea, dramatized the Indian threat as nothing else probably could have done. New England militiamen now began to rally to the cause, though they still refused to co-operate with Schuyler. New Hampshire commissioned John Stark, a disgruntled ex-colonel in the Continental Army and a veteran of Bunker Hill and Trenton, as a brigadier general in the state service (a rank denied him by Congress), and Stark quickly recruited 2,000 men. Refusing Schuyler's request that he join the main army, Stark took up a position at Bennington in southern Vermont to guard the New England frontier. On August 11 Burgoyne detached a force of 650 men under Hessian Col. Friedrich Baum to forage for cattle, horses, and transport in the very area Stark was occupying. At Bennington on August 16 Stark nearly annihilated Baum's force, and reinforcements sent by Burgoyne arrived on the field just in time to be soundly thrashed in turn. Burgoyne not only failed to secure his much-needed supplies and transport but also lost about a tenth of his command.

Meanwhile, St. Leger with his Tories and Indians had appeared before Fort Stanwix on August 2. The garrison, fearing massacre by the Indians, determined to hold out to the bitter end. On August 4, the Tryon County militia under Brig. Gen. Nicholas Herkimer set out to relieve the fort but were ambushed by the Indians in a wooded ravine near Oriskany. The militia, under the direction of a mortally wounded Herkimer, scattered in the woods and fought a bloody afternoon's battle in a summer thunderstorm. Both sides suffered heavy losses, and though the militia were unable to relieve Stanwix the losses discouraged St. Leger's Indians, who were already restless in the static siege operation at Stanwix.

Despite his own weak position, when Schuyler learned of the plight of the Stanwix garrison, he courageously detached Benedict Arnold with 950 Continentals to march to its relief. Arnold devised a ruse that took full advantage of the dissatisfaction and natural superstition of the Indians. Employing a half-wit Dutchman, his clothes shot full of holes, and a friendly Oneida Indian as his messengers, Arnold spread the rumor that the Continentals were approaching "as numerous as the leaves on the trees." The Indians, who had special respect for any madman, departed in haste, scalping not a few of their Tory allies as they went, and St. Leger was forced to abandon the siege.

Bennington and Stanwix were serious blows to Burgoyne. By early September he knew he could expect help from neither Howe nor St. Leger. Disillusioned about the Tories, he wrote Germain: "The great bulk of the country is undoubtedly with Congress in principle and zeal; and their measures are executed with a secrecy and dispatch that are not to be equalled. Wherever the King's forces point, militia in the amount of three or four thousand assemble in twenty-four hours; they bring with them their subsistence, etc., and the alarm over, they return to their farms. . . ." Nevertheless, gambler that he was, Burgoyne crossed the Hudson to the west side during September 13 and 14, signaling his intention to get to Albany or lose his army. While his supply problem daily became worse, his Indians, with a natural instinct for sensing approaching disaster, drifted off into the forests, leaving him with little means of gaining intelligence of the American dispositions.

The American forces were meanwhile gathering strength. Congress finally deferred to New England sentiment on August 19 and replaced Schuyler with Gates. Gates was more the beneficiary than the cause of the improved situation, but his appointment helped morale and encouraged the New England militia. Washington's emissary, General Lincoln, also did his part. Gates understood Burgoyne's plight perfectly and adapted his tactics to take full advantage of it. He advanced his forces four miles northward and took up a position, surveyed and prepared by the Polish engineer, Kosciusko, on Bemis Heights, a few miles below Saratoga. Against this position Burgoyne launched his attack on September 19 and was repulsed with heavy losses. In the battle, usually known as Freeman's Farm, Arnold persuaded Gates to let him go forward to counter the British attack, and Colonel Morgan's riflemen, in a wooded terrain well suited to the use of their specialized weapon, took a heavy toll of British officers and men.

After Freeman's Farm, the lines remained stable for three weeks. Burgoyne had heard that Clinton, with the force Howe had left in New York, had started north to relieve him. Clinton, in fact, stormed Forts Clinton and Montgomery on the Hudson on October 6, but, exercising that innate caution characteristic of all his actions, he refused to gamble for high stakes. He simply sent an advance guard on to Kingston and he himself returned to New York.

Burgoyne was left to his fate. Gates strengthened his entrenchments and calmly awaited the attack he was sure Burgoyne would have to make. Militia reinforcements increased his forces to around 10,000 by October 7. Meanwhile Burgoyne's position grew more desperate. Food was running out; the meadows were grazed bare by the animals; and every day more men slipped into the forest, deserting the lost cause. With little intelligence of American strength or dispositions, on October 7 he sent out a "reconnaissance in force" to feel out the American positions. On learning that the British were approaching, Gates sent out a contingent including Morgan's riflemen to meet them, and a second battle developed, usually known as Bemis Heights. The British suffered severe losses, five times those of the Americans, and were driven back to their fortified positions. Arnold, who had been at odds with Gates and was confined to his tent, broke out, rushed into the fray, and again distinguished himself before he was wounded in leading an attack on Breymann's Redoubt.

Two days after the battle, Burgoyne withdrew to a position in the vicinity of Saratoga. Militia soon worked around to his rear and cut his supply lines. His position hopeless, Burgoyne finally capitulated on October 17 at Saratoga. The total prisoner count was nearly 6,000 and great quantities of military stores fell into American hands. The victory at Saratoga brought the Americans out well ahead in the campaign of 1777 despite the loss of Philadelphia. What had been at stake soon became obvious. In February 1778 France negotiated a treaty of alliance with the American states, tantamount to a declaration of war against England.

Valley Forge

The name of Valley Forge has come to stand, and rightly so, as a patriotic symbol of suffering, courage, and perserverance. The hard core of 6,000 Continentals who stayed with Washington during that bitter winter of 1777–78 indeed suffered much. Some men had no shoes, no pants, no blankets. Weeks passed when there was no meat and men were reduced to boiling their shoes and eating them. The wintry winds penetrated the tattered tents that were at first the only shelter.

The symbolism of Valley Forge should not be allowed to obscure the fact that the suffering was largely unnecessary. While the soldiers shivered and went hungry, food rotted and clothing lay unused in depots throughout the country. True, access to Valley Forge was difficult, but little determined effort was made to get supplies into the area. The supply and transport system broke down. In mid-1777, both the Quartermaster and Commissary Generals resigned along with numerous subordinate officials in both departments, mostly merchants who found private trade more lucrative. Congress, in refuge at York, Pennsylvania, and split into factions, found it difficult to find replacements. If there was not, as most historians now believe, an organized cabal seeking to replace Washington with Gates, there were many, both in and out of the Army, who were dissatisfied with the Commander in Chief, and much intrigue went on. Gates was made president of the new Board of War set up in 1777, and at least two of its members were enemies of Washington. In the administrative chaos at the height of the Valley Forge crisis, there was no functioning Quartermaster General at all.

Washington weathered the storm and the Continental Army was to emerge from Valley Forge a more effective force than before. With his advice, Congress instituted reforms in the Quartermaster and Commissary Departments that temporarily restored the effectiveness of both agencies. Washington's ablest subordinate, General Greene, reluctantly accepted the post of Quartermaster General. The Continental Army itself gained a new professional competence from the training given by the Prussian, Friedrich Wilhelm von Steuben.

Steuben appeared at Valley Forge in February 1778 arrayed in such martial splendor that one private thought he had seen Mars, the god of war, himself. He represented himself as a baron, a title he had acquired in the service of a small German state, and as a former lieutenant general on the staff of Frederick the Great, though in reality he had been only a captain. The fraud was harmless, for Steuben had a broad knowledge of military affairs and his remarkable sense of the dramatic was combined with the common touch a true Prussian baron might well have lacked.

Washington had long sensed the need for uniform training and organization, and after a short trial he secured the appointment of Steuben as Inspector General in charge of a training program. Steuben carried out the program during the late winter and early spring of 1778, teaching the Continental Army a simplified but effective version of the drill formations and movements of European armies, proper care of equipment, and the use of the bayonet, a weapon in which British superiority had previously been marked. He attempted to consolidate the understrength regiments and companies and organized light

STEUBEN TRAINING AMERICAN FORCES AT VALLEY FORGE

infantry companies as the elite force of the Army. He constantly sought to impress upon the officers their responsibility for taking care of the men. Steuben never lost sight of the difference between the American citizen soldier and the European professional. He early noted that American soldiers had to be told why they did things before they would do them well, and he applied this philosophy in his training program. His trenchant good humor and vigorous profanity, almost the only English he knew, delighted the Continental soldiers and made the rigorous drill more palatable. After Valley Forge, Continentals would fight on equal terms with British Regulars in the open field.

First Fruits of the French Alliance

While the Continental Army was undergoing its ordeal and transformation at Valley Forge, Howe dallied in Philadelphia, forfeiting whatever remaining chance he had to win a decisive victory before the effects of the French alliance were felt. He had had his fill of the American war and the king accepted his resignation from command, appointing General Clinton as his successor. As Washington prepared to sally forth from Valley Forge, the British Army and the Philadelphia Tories said goodbye to their old commander in one of the most lavish celebrations ever held in America, the *Mischianza,* a veritable Belshazzar's feast. The handwriting on the wall appeared in the form of orders, already in Clinton's hands, to evacuate the American capital. With the French in the war, England had to look to the safety of the long ocean supply line to America and to the protection of its possessions in other parts of the world. Clinton's orders were to detach 5,000 men to the West Indies and 3,000 to Florida, and to return the rest of his army to New York by sea.

As Clinton prepared to depart Philadelphia, Washington had high hopes that the war might be won in 1778 by a co-operative effort between his army and the French Fleet. The Comte d'Estaing with a French naval squadron of eleven ships of the line and transports carrying 4,000 troops left France in May to sail for the American coast. D'Estaing's fleet was considerably more powerful than any Admiral Howe could immediately concentrate in American waters. For a brief period in 1778 the strategic initiative passed from British hands, and Washington hoped to make full use of it.

Clinton had already decided, before he learned of the threat from d'Estaing, to move his army overland to New York prior to making any detachments, largely because he could find no place for 3,000 horses on the transports. On June 18, 1778, he set out with about 10,000 men. Washington, who by that time had gathered about 12,000, immediately occupied Philadelphia and then took up the pursuit of Clinton, undecided as to whether he should risk an attack on the British column while it was on the march. His Council of War was divided, though none of his generals advised a "general action." The boldest, Brig. Gen. Anthony Wayne, and the young major general, the Marquis de Lafayette, urged a "partial attack" to strike at a portion of the British Army while it was strung out on the road; the most cautious, General Lee, who had been exchanged and had rejoined the army at Valley Forge, advised only guerrilla action to harass the British columns. On June 26 Washington decided to take a bold approach, though he issued no orders indicating an intention to bring on a "general action." He sent forward an advance guard composed of almost half his army to strike at the British rear when Clinton moved out of Monmouth Court House on the morning of June 27. Lee, the cautious, claimed the command from Lafayette, the bold, when he learned the detachment would be so large.

In the early morning, Lee advanced over rough ground that had not been reconnoitered and made contact with the British rear, but Clinton reacted quickly and maneuvered to envelop the American right flank. Lee, feeling that his force was in an untenable position, began a retreat that became quite confused. Washington rode up amidst the confusion and, exceedingly irate to find the advance guard in retreat, exchanged harsh words with Lee. He then assumed direction of what had to be a defense against a British counterattack. The battle that followed, involving the bulk of both armies, lasted until nightfall on a hot, sultry day with both sides holding their own. For the first time the Americans fought well with the bayonet as well as with the musket and rifle, and their battlefield behavior generally reflected the Valley Forge training. Nevertheless, Washington failed to strike a telling blow at the British Army, for Clinton slipped away in the night and in a few days completed the retreat to New York. Lee demanded and got a court-martial at which he was judged, perhaps unjustly, guilty of disobedience of orders, poor conduct of the retreat, and disrespect for the Commander in Chief. As a consequence he retired from the Army, though the controversy over his actions at Monmouth was to go on for years.

Washington, meanwhile, sought his victory in co-operation with the French Fleet. D'Estaing arrived off the coast on July 8 and the two commanders at first agreed on a combined land and sea attack on New York, but d'Estaing feared he would be unable to get his deep-draft ships across the bar that extended from Staten Island to Sandy Hook, in order to get at Howe's inferior fleet. They then decided to transfer the attack to the other and weaker British stronghold at Newport, Rhode Island—a city standing on an island with difficult approaches. A plan was agreed on whereby the French Fleet would force the passage on the west side of the island and an American force under General Sullivan would cross over and mount an assault from the east. The whole scheme soon went awry. The French Fleet arrived off Newport on July 29 and successfully forced the passage; Sullivan began crossing on the east on August 8 and d'Estaing began to disembark his troops. Unfortunately at this juncture Admiral Howe appeared with a reinforced British Fleet, forcing d'Estaing to re-embark his troops and put out to sea to meet Howe. As the two fleets maneuvered for advantage, a great gale scattered both on August 12. The British returned to New York to refit, and the French Fleet to Boston, whence d'Estaing decided he must move on to tasks he considered more pressing in the West Indies. Sullivan was left to extricate his forces from an untenable position as best he could, and the first experiment in Franco-American co-operation came to a disappointing end with recriminations on both sides.

The fiasco at Newport ended any hopes for an early victory over the British as a result of the French alliance. By the next year, as the French were forced to devote their major attention to the West Indies, the British regained the initiative on the mainland, and the war entered a new phase.

The New Conditions of the War

After France entered the war in 1778, it rapidly took on the dimensions of a major European as well as an American conflict. In 1779 Spain declared war against England, and in the following year Holland followed suit. The necessity of fighting European enemies in the West Indies and other areas and of standing guard at home against invasion weakened the British effort against the American rebels. Yet the Americans were unable to take full advantage of Britain's embarrassments, for their own effort suffered more and more from war weariness, lack of strong direction, and inadequate finance. Moreover, the interests of European states fighting Britain did not necessarily coincide with American interests. Spain and Holland did not ally themselves with the American states at all, and even France found it expedient to devote its major effort to the West Indies. Finally, the entry of ancient enemies into the fray spurred the British to intensify their effort and evoked some, if not enough, of that characteristic tenacity that has produced victory for England in so many wars. Despite their many new commitments, the British were able to maintain in America an army that was usually superior in numbers to the dwindling Continental Army, though never strong enough to undertake offensives again on the scale of those of 1776 and 1777.

Monmouth was the last general engagement in the north between Washington's and Clinton's armies. In 1779 the situation there became a stalemate and remained so until the end of the war. Washington set up a defense system around New York with its center at West Point, and Clinton made no attempt to attack his main defense line. The British commander did, in late spring 1779, attempt to draw Washington into the open by descending in force on unfinished American outpost fortifications at Verplanck's Point and Stony Point, but Washington refused to take the bait. When Clinton withdrew his main force to New York, the American commander retaliated by sending Maj. Gen. Anthony Wayne on July 15, 1779, with an elite corps of light infantry, on a stealthy night attack on Stony Point, a successful action more notable for demonstrating the proficiency with which the Americans now used the bayonet than for any important strategic gains. Wayne was unable to take Verplanck's, and Clinton rapidly retook Stony Point. Thereafter the war around New York became largely an affair of raids, skirmishes, and constant vigilance on both sides.

Clinton's inaction allowed Washington to attempt to deal with British-inspired Indian attacks. Although Burgoyne's defeat ended the threat of invasion from Canada, the British continued to incite the Indians all along the frontier to bloody raids on American settlements. From Fort Niagara and Detroit they sent out their bands, usually led by Tories, to pillage, scalp, and burn in the Mohawk Valley of New York, the Wyoming Valley of Pennsylvania, and the new American settlements in Kentucky. In August 1779 Washington detached General Sullivan with a force to deal with the Iroquois in Pennsylvania and New York. Sullivan laid waste the Indians' villages and defeated a force of Tories and Indians at Newtown on August 29.

In the winter of 1778–79, the state of Virginia had sponsored an expedition that struck a severe blow at the British and Indians in the northwest. Young Lt. Col. George Rogers Clark with a force of only 175 men, ostensibly recruited for the defense of Kentucky, overran all the British posts in what is today Illinois and Indiana. Neither he nor Sullivan, however, was able to strike at the sources of the trouble—Niagara and Detroit. Indian raids along the frontiers continued, though they were somewhat less frequent and severe.

British Successes in the South

Late in 1778 the British began to turn their main effort to the south. Tory strength was greater in the Carolinas and Georgia and the area was closer to the West Indies, where the British Fleet had to stand guard against the French. The king's ministers hoped to bring the southern states into the fold one by one, and from bases there to strangle the recalcitrant north. A small British force operating from Florida quickly overran thinly populated Georgia in the winter of 1778–79. Alarmed by this development, Congress sent General Benjamin Lincoln south to Charleston in December 1778 to command the Southern Army and organize the southern effort. Lincoln gathered 3,500 Continentals and militiamen, but in May 1779, while he maneuvered along the Georgia border, the British commander, Maj. Gen. Augustine Prevost, slipped around him to lay siege to Charleston. The city barely managed to hold out until Lincoln returned to relieve it. (*Map 10*)

In September 1779 d'Estaing arrived off the coast of Georgia with a strong French Fleet and 6,000 troops. Lincoln then hurried south with 1,350 Americans to join him in a siege of the main British base at Savannah. Unfortunately, the Franco-American force had to hurry its attack because d'Estaing was unwilling to risk his fleet in a position dangerously exposed to autumn storms. The French and Americans mounted a direct assault on Savannah on October 9, abandoning their plan to make a systematic approach by regular parallels. The British in strongly entrenched positions repulsed the attack in what was essentially a Bunker Hill in reverse, the French and Americans suffering

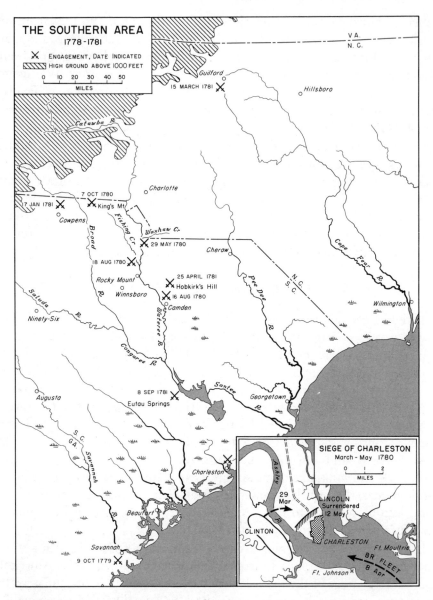

MAP 10

staggering losses. D'Estaing then sailed away to the West Indies, Lincoln returned to Charleston, and the second attempt at Franco-American co-operation ended in much the same atmosphere of bitterness and disillusion as the first.

Meanwhile Clinton, urged on by the British Government, had determined to push the southern campaign in earnest. In October 1779 he withdrew the British garrison from Newport, pulled in his troops from outposts around New York, and prepared to move south against Charleston with a large part of his force. With d'Estaing's withdrawal the British regained control of the sea along the American coast, giving Clinton a mobility that Washington could not match. While Clinton drew forces from New York and Savannah to achieve a decisive concentration of force (14,000 men) at Charleston, Washington was able to send only piecemeal reinforcements to Lincoln over difficult overland routes. Applying the lessons of his experience in 1776, Clinton this time carefully planned a co-ordinated Army-Navy attack. First, he landed his force on John's Island to the south, then moved up to the Ashley River, investing Charleston from the land side. Lincoln, under strong pressure from the South Carolina authorities, concentrated his forces in a citadel defense on the neck of land between the Ashley and Cooper Rivers, leaving Fort Moultrie in the harbor lightly manned. On April 8 British warships successfully forced the passage past Moultrie, investing Charleston from the sea. The siege then proceeded in traditional eighteenth century fashion, and on May 12, 1780, Lincoln surrendered his entire force of 5,466 men, the greatest disaster to befall the American cause during the war. Meanwhile, Col. Abraham Buford with 350 Virginians was moving south to reinforce the garrison. Lt. Col. Banastre Tarleton with a force of British cavalry took Buford by surprise at the Waxhaws, a district near the North Carolina border, and slaughtered most of his men, refusing to honor the white flag Buford displayed.

After the capture of Charleston, Clinton returned to New York with about a third of his force, leaving General Cornwallis with 8,000 men to follow up the victory. Cornwallis established his main seaboard bases at Savannah, Beaufort, Charleston, and Georgetown, and in the interior extended his line of control along the Savannah River westward to Ninety-Six and northward to Camden and Rocky Mount. Cornwallis' force, however, was too small to police so large an area, even with the aid of the numerous Tories who took to the field. Though no organized Continental force remained in the Carolinas and Georgia, American guerrillas, led by Brig. Gens. Thomas Sumter and Andrew Pickens and Lt. Col. Francis Marion, began to harry British posts and lines of communications and to battle the bands of Tories. A bloody, ruthless, and confused civil war ensued, its character determined in no small degree by Tarleton's action at the Waxhaws. In this way, as in the Saratoga campaign, the American grass roots strength began once again to assert itself and to deny the British the fruits of military victory won in the field.

On June 22, 1780, two more understrength Continental brigades from Washington's army arrived at Hillsboro, North Carolina, to form the nucleus of a new Southern Army around which militia could rally and which could serve as the nerve center of guerrilla resistance. In July Congress, without consulting Washington, provided a commander for this army in the person of General Gates, the hero of Saratoga. Gates soon lost his northern laurels. Gathering a force of about 4,000 men, mostly militia, he set out to attack the British post at Camden, South Carolina. Cornwallis hurried north from Charleston with reinforcements and his army of 2,200 British Regulars made contact with Gates outside Camden on the night of August 15. In the battle that ensued the following morning, Gates deployed his militia on the left and the Continentals under Maj. Gen. Johann de Kalb on the right. The militia were still forming in the hazy dawn when Cornwallis struck, and they fled in panic before the British onslaught. De Kalb's outnumbered Continentals put up a valiant but hopeless fight. Tarleton's cavalry pursued the fleeing Americans for 30 miles, killing or making prisoner those who lagged. Gates himself fled too fast for Tarleton, reaching Hillsboro, 160 miles away, in three days. There he was able to gather only about 800 survivors of the Southern Army. To add to the disaster, Tarleton caught up with General Sumter, whom Gates had sent with a detachment to raid a British wagon train, and virtually destroyed his force in a surprise attack at Fishing Creek on August 18. Once more South Carolina seemed safely in British hands.

Nadir of the American Cause

In the summer of 1780 the American cause seemed to be at as low an ebb as it had been after the New York campaign in 1776 or after the defeats at Ticonderoga and Brandywine in 1777. Defeat in the south was not the only discouraging aspect of patriot affairs. In the north a creeping paralysis had set in as the patriotic enthusiasm of the early war years waned. The Continental currency had virtually depreciated out of existence, and Congress was impotent to pay the soldiers or purchase supplies. At Morristown, New Jersey, in the winter of 1779–80 the army suffered worse hardships than at Valley Forge. Congress could do little but attempt to shift its responsibilities onto the states, giving each the task of providing clothing for its own troops and furnishing certain quotas of specific supplies for the entire Army. The system of "specific supplies" worked not at all. Not only were the states laggard in furnishing supplies, but when they did it was seldom at the time or place they were needed. This breakdown in the supply system was more than even General Greene, as Quartermaster General, could cope with, and in early 1780, under heavy criticism in Congress, he resigned his position.

Under such difficulties, Washington had to struggle to hold even a small Army together. Recruiting of Continentals, difficult to begin with, became almost impossible when the troops could neither be paid nor supplied adequately and had to suffer such winters as those at Morristown. Enlistments and drafts from the militia in 1780 produced not quite half as many men for one year's service as had enlisted in 1776 for three years or the duration. While recruiting lagged, morale among those men who had enlisted for the longer terms naturally fell. Mutinies in 1780 and 1781 were suppressed only by measures of great severity.

Germain could write confidently to Clinton: "so very contemptible is the rebel force now . . . that no resistance . . . is to be apprehended that can materially obstruct . . . the speedy suppression of the rebellion . . . the American levies in the King's service are more in number than the whole of the enlisted troops in the service of the Congress." The French were unhappy. In the summer of 1780 they occupied the vacated British base at Newport, moving in a naval squadron and 4,000 troops under the command of Lieutenant General the Comte de Rochambeau. Rochambeau immediately warned his government: "Send us troops, ships and money, but do not count on these people nor on their resources, they have neither money nor credit, their forces exist only momentarily, and when they are about to be attacked in their own homes they assemble . . . to defend themselves." Another French commander thought only one highly placed American traitor was needed to decide the campaign.

Clinton had, in fact, already found his "highly placed traitor" in Benedict Arnold, the hero of the march to Quebec, the naval battle on the lakes, Stanwix, and Saratoga. "Money is this man's God," one of his enemies had said of Arnold earlier, and evidently he was correct. Lucrative rewards promised by the British led to Arnold's treason, though he evidently resented the slights Congress had dealt him, and he justified his act by claiming that the Americans were now fighting for the interests of Catholic France and not their own. Arnold wangled an appointment as commander at West Point and then entered into a plot to deliver this key post to the British. Washington discovered the plot on September 21, 1780, just in time to foil it, though Arnold himself escaped to become a British brigadier.

Arnold's treason in September 1780 marked the nadir of the patriot cause. In the closing months of 1780, the Americans somehow put together the ingredients for a final and decisive burst of energy in 1781. Congress persuaded

Robert Morris, a wealthy Philadelphia merchant, to accept a post as Superintendent of Finance, and Col. Timothy Pickering, an able administrator, to replace Greene as Quartermaster General. Greene, as Washington's choice, was then named to succeed Gates in command of the Southern Army. General Lincoln, exchanged after Charleston, was appointed Secretary at War and the old board was abolished. Morris took over many of the functions previously performed by unwieldy committees. Working closely with Pickering, he abandoned the old paper money entirely and introduced a new policy of supplying the army by private contracts, using his personal credit as eventual guarantee for payment in gold or silver. It was an expedient but, for a time at least, it worked.

Greene's Southern Campaign

It was the frontier militia assembling "when they were about to be attacked in their own homes" who struck the blow that actually marked the turning point in the south. Late in 1780, with Clinton's reluctant consent, Cornwallis set out on the invasion of North Carolina. He sent Maj. Patrick Ferguson, who had successfully organized the Tories in the upcountry of South Carolina, to move north simultaneously with his "American Volunteers," spread the Tory gospel in the North Carolina back country, and join the main army at Charlotte with a maximum number of recruits. Ferguson's advance northward alarmed the "over-mountain men" in western North Carolina, southwest Virginia, and what is now east Tennessee. A picked force of mounted militia riflemen gathered on the Catawba River in western North Carolina, set out to find Ferguson, and brought him to bay at King's Mountain near the border of the two Carolinas on October 7. In a battle of patriot against Tory (Ferguson was the only British soldier present), the patriots' triumph was complete. Ferguson himself was killed and few of his command escaped death or capture. Some got the same "quarter" Tarleton had given Buford's men at the Waxhaws.

King's Mountain was as fatal to Cornwallis' plans as Bennington had been to those of Burgoyne. The North Carolina Tories, cowed by the fate of their compatriots, gave him little support. The British commander on October 14, 1780, began a wretched retreat in the rain back to Winnsboro, South Carolina, with militia harassing his progress. Clinton was forced to divert an expedition of 2,500 men sent to establish a base in Virginia to reinforce Cornwallis.

The frontier militia had turned the tide, but having done so, they returned to their homes. To keep it moving against the British was the task of the new commander, General Greene. When Greene arrived at Charlotte, North Carolina, early in December 1780, he found a command that consisted of 1,500 men fit for duty, only 949 of them Continentals. The army lacked clothing and provisions and had little systematic means of procuring them. Greene decided that he must not engage Cornwallis' army in battle until he had built up his strength, that he must instead pursue delaying tactics to wear down his stronger opponent. The first thing he did was to take the unorthodox step of dividing his army in the face of a superior force, moving part under his personal command to Cheraw Hill, and sending the rest under Brig. Gen. Daniel Morgan west across the Catawba over 100 miles away. It was an intentional violation of the principle of mass. Greene wrote:

I am well satisfied with the movement . . . . It makes the most of my inferior force, for it compels my adversary to divide his, and holds him in doubt as to his own line of conduct. He cannot leave Morgan behind him to come at me, or his posts at Ninety-Six and Augusta would be exposed. And he cannot chase Morgan far, or prosecute his views upon Virginia, while I am here with the whole country open before me. I am as near to Charleston as he is, and as near Hillsborough as I was at Charlotte; so that I am in no danger of being cut off from my reinforcements.

Left unsaid was the fact that divided forces could live off the land much easier than one large force and constitute two rallying points for local militia instead of one. Greene was, in effect, sacrificing mass to enhance maneuver.

Cornwallis, an aggressive commander, had determined to gamble everything on a renewed invasion of North Carolina. Ignoring Clinton's warnings, he depleted his Charleston base by bringing almost all his supplies forward. In the face of Greene's dispositions, Cornwallis divided his army into not two but three parts. He sent a holding force to Camden to contain Green, directed Tarleton with a fast-moving contingent of 1,100 infantry and cavalry to find and crush Morgan, and with the remainder of his army moved cautiously up into North Carolina to cut off any of Morgan's force that escaped Tarleton.

Tarleton caught up with Morgan on January 17, 1781, west of King's Mountain at a place called the Cowpens, an open, sparsely forested area six miles from the Broad River. (*Map 11*) Morgan chose this site to make his stand less by design than necessity, for he had intended to get across the Broad. Nevertheless, on ground seemingly better suited to the action of Regulars, he achieved a little tactical masterpiece, making the most effective use of his heterogeneous force, numerically equal to that of Tarleton but composed of three-fourths militia. Selecting a hill as the center of his position, he placed his Continental infantry on it, deliberately leaving his flanks open. Well out in front of the main line he posted militia riflemen in two lines, instructing the first line to fire two volleys and then fall back on the second, the combined line to fire until the British pressed them, then to fall back to the rear of the Continentals and re-form as a reserve. Behind the hill he placed Lt. Col. William Washing-

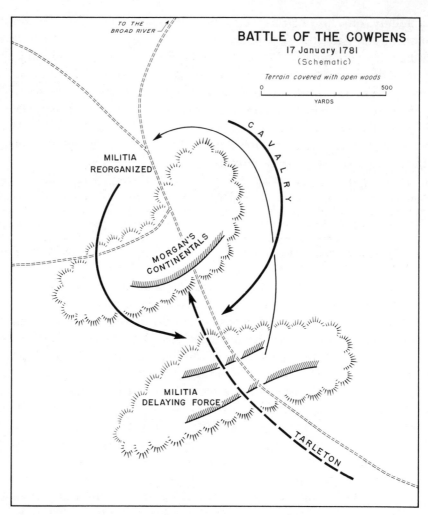

TO THE
BROAD RIVER

BATTLE OF THE COWPENS
17 January 1781
(Schematic)

Terrain covered with open woods

0   500

YARDS

CAVALRY

MILITIA
REORGANIZED

MORGAN'S
CONTINENTALS

MILITIA
DELAYING FORCE

TARLETON

MAP 11

ton's cavalry detachment, ready to charge the attacking enemy at the critical moment. Every man in the ranks was informed of the plan of battle and the part he was expected to play in it.

On finding Morgan, Tarleton ordered an immediate attack. His men moved forward in regular formation, were momentarily checked by the militia rifles, but, taking the retreat of the first two lines to be the beginning of a rout, rushed headlong into the steady fire of the Continentals on the hill. When the British were well advanced, the American cavalry struck them on the right flank and the militia, having re-formed, charged out from behind the hill to hit the British left. Caught in a clever double envelopment, the British surrendered after suffering heavy losses. Tarleton managed to escape with only a small force of cavalry he had held in reserve. It was on a small scale, and with certain significant differences, a repetition of the classic double envelopment of the Romans by a Carthaginian army under Hannibal at Cannae in 216 B.C., an event of which Morgan, no reader of books, probably had not the foggiest notion.

Having struck his fatal blow against Tarleton, Morgan still had to move fast to escape Cornwallis. Covering 100 miles and crossing two rivers in five days, he rejoined Greene early in February. Cornwallis by now was too heavily committed to the campaign in North Carolina to withdraw. Hoping to match the swift movement of the Americans, he destroyed all his superfluous supplies, baggage, and wagons and set forth in pursuit of Greene's army. The American general retreated, through North Carolina, up into southern Virginia, then back into North Carolina again, keeping just far enough in front of his adversary to avoid battle with Cornwallis' superior force. Finally on March 15, 1781, at Guilford Court House in North Carolina, on ground he had himself chosen, Greene halted and gave battle. By this time he had collected 1,500 Continentals and 3,000 militia to the 1,900 Regulars the British could muster. The British held the field after a hard-fought battle, but suffered casualties of about one-fourth of the force engaged. It was, like Bunker Hill, a Pyrrhic victory. His ranks depleted and his supplies exhausted, Cornwallis withdrew to Wilmington on the coast, and then decided to move northward to join the British forces General Clinton had sent to Virginia.

Greene, his army in better condition than six months earlier, pushed quickly into South Carolina to reduce the British posts in the interior. He fought two battles—at Hobkirk's Hill on April 25, and at Eutaw Springs on September 8—losing both but with approximately the same results as at Guilford Court House. One by one the British interior posts fell to Greene's army, or to militia and partisans. By October 1781 the British had been forced to withdraw to their port strongholds along the coast—Charleston and Savannah. Greene had lost battles, but won a campaign. In so doing, he paved the way for the greater victory to follow at Yorktown.

Yorktown: The Final Act

As Howe and Burgoyne went their separate ways in 1777, seemingly determined to satisfy only their personal ambitions, so Clinton and Cornwallis in 1781 paved the road to Yorktown by their disagreements and lack of co-ordination. Clinton was Cornwallis' superior in this case, but the latter enjoyed the confidence of Germain to an extent that Clinton did not. Clinton, believing that without large reinforcements the British could not operate far from coastal bases, had opposed Cornwallis' ventures in the interior of the Carolinas, and when Cornwallis came to Virginia he did so without even informing his superior of his intention.

Since 1779 Clinton had sought to paralyze the state of Virginia by conducting raids up its great rivers, arousing the Tories, and establishing a base in the Chesapeake Bay region. (*Map 12*) He thought this base might eventually be used as a starting point for one arm of a pincers movement against Pennsylvania for which his own idle force in New York would provide the other. A raid conducted in the Hampton Roads area in 1779 was highly successful, but when Clinton sought to follow it up in 1780 the force sent for the purpose had to be diverted to Charleston to bail Cornwallis out after King's Mountain. Finally in 1781 he got an expedition into Virginia, a contingent of 1,600 under the American traitor, Benedict Arnold. In January Arnold conducted a destructive raid up the James River all the way to Richmond. His presence soon proved to be a magnet drawing forces of both sides to Virginia.

In an effort to trap Arnold, Washington dispatched Lafayette to Virginia with 1,200 of his scarce Continentals and persuaded the French to send a naval squadron from Newport to block Arnold's escape by sea. The plan went awry when a British fleet drove the French squadron back to Newport and Clinton sent another 2,600 men to Virginia along with a new commander, Maj. Gen. William Phillips. Phillips and Arnold continued their devastating raids, which Lafayette was too weak to prevent. Then on May 20 Cornwallis arrived from Wilmington and took over from Phillips. With additional reinforcements sent by Clinton he was able to field a force of about 7,000 men, approximately a quarter of the British strength in America. Washington sent down an additional reinforcement of 800 Continentals under General Wayne, but even with Virginia militia Lafayette's force remained greatly outnumbered.

Cornwallis and Clinton were soon working at cross-purposes. Cornwallis proposed to carry out major operations in the interior of Virginia, but Clinton saw as little practical value in this tactic as Cornwallis did in Clinton's plan to establish a base in Virginia for a pincers movement against Pennsylvania. Cornwallis at first turned to the interior and engaged in a fruitless pursuit of Lafayette north of Richmond. Then, on receiving Clinton's positive order to return to the coast, establish a base, and return part of his force to New York, Cornwallis moved back down the Virginia peninsula to take up station at Yorktown, a small tobacco port on the York River just off Chesapeake Bay. In the face of

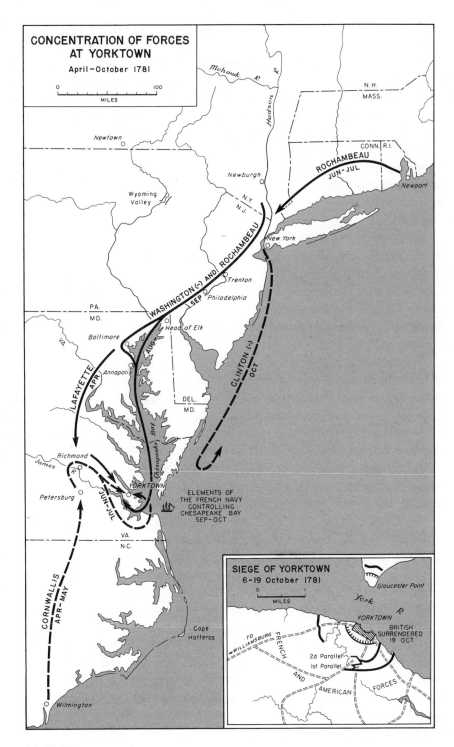

CONCENTRATION OF FORCES
AT YORKTOWN
April–October 1781

SIEGE OF YORKTOWN
6–19 October 1781

ELEMENTS OF
THE FRENCH NAVY
CONTROLLING
CHESAPEAKE BAY
SEP–OCT

MAP 12

Cornwallis' insistence that he must keep all his troops with him, Clinton vacillated, reversing his own orders several times and in the end granting Cornwallis' request. Lafayette and Wayne followed Cornwallis cautiously down the peninsula, lost a skirmish with him at Green Spring near Williamsburg on July 6, and finally took up a position of watchful waiting near Yorktown.

Meanwhile, Washington had been trying to persuade the French to co-operate in a combined land and naval assault on New York in the summer of 1781. Rochambeau brought his 4,000 troops down from Newport in April and placed them under Washington's command. The prospects were still bleak since the combined Franco-American force numbered but 10,000 against Clinton's 17,000 in well-fortified positions. Then on August 14 Washington learned that the French Fleet in the West Indies, commanded by Admiral Francois de Grasse, would not come to New York but would arrive in the Chesapeake later in the month and remain there until October 15. He saw immediately that if he could achieve a superior concentration of force on the land side while de Grasse still held the bay he could destroy the British army at Yorktown before Clinton had a chance to relieve it.

The movements that followed illustrate most effectively a successful application of the principles of the offensive, surprise, objective, mass, and maneuver. Even without unified command of Army and Navy forces, Franco-American co-operation this time was excellent. Admiral Louis, Comte de Barras, immediately put out to sea from Newport to join de Grasse. Washington sent orders to Lafayette to contain Cornwallis at Yorktown and then, after making a feint in the direction of New York to deceive Clinton, on August 21 started the major portion of the Franco-American Army on a rapid secret movement to Virginia, via Chesapeake Bay, leaving only 2,000 Americans behind to watch Clinton.

On August 30, while Washington was on the move southward, de Grasse arrived in the Chesapeake with his entire fleet of twenty-four ships of the line and a few days later debarked 3,000 French troops to join Lafayette. Admiral Thomas Graves, the British naval commander in New York, meanwhile had put out to sea in late August with nineteen ships of the line, hoping either to intercept Barras' squadron or to block de Grasse's entry into the Chesapeake. He failed to find Barras, and when he arrived off Hampton Roads on September 5 he found de Grasse already in the bay. The French admiral sallied forth to meet Graves and the two fleets fought an indecisive action off the Virginia capes. Yet for all practical purposes the victory lay with the French for, while the fleets maneuvered at sea for days following the battle, Barras' squadron slipped into the Chesapeake and the French and American troops got past into the James River. Then de Grasse got back into the bay and joined Barras, con-

SURRENDER OF CORNWALLIS

fronting Graves with so superior a naval force that he decided to return to New York to refit.

When Washington's army arrived on September 26, the French Fleet was in firm control of the bay, blocking Cornwallis' sea route of escape. A decisive concentration had been achieved. Counting 3,000 Virginia militia, Washington had a force of about 9,000 Americans and 6,000 French troops with which to conduct the siege. It proceeded in the best traditions of Vauban under the direction of French engineers. Cornwallis obligingly abandoned his forward position on September 30, and on October 6 the first parallel was begun 600 yards from the main British position. Artillery placed along the trench began its destructive work on October 9. By October 11 the zigzag connecting trench had been dug 200 yards forward, and work on the second parallel had begun. Two British redoubts had to be reduced in order to extend the line to the York River. This accomplished, Cornwallis' only recourse was escape across the river to Gloucester Point where the American line was thinly held. A storm on the night of October 16 frustrated his attempt to do so, leaving him with no hope but relief from New York. Clinton had been considering such relief for days, but he acted too late. On the very day, October 17, that Admiral Graves set sail from New York with a reinforced fleet and 7,000 troops for the relief of Yorktown, Cornwallis began negotiations on terms of surrender. On October 19 his entire army marched out to lay down its arms, the British band playing an old tune called "The World Turned Upside Down."

So far as active campaigning was concerned, Yorktown ended the war. Both Greene and Washington maintained their armies in position near New York and Charleston for nearly two years more, but the only fighting that occurred was some minor skirmishing in the South. Cornwallis' defeat led to the overthrow of the British cabinet and the formation of a new government that decided the war in America was lost. With some success, Britain devoted its energies to trying to salvage what it could in the West Indies and in India. The independence for which Americans had fought thus virtually became a reality when Cornwallis' command marched out of its breached defenses at Yorktown.

The Summing Up: Reasons, Lessons, and Meaning

The American victory in the War of the Revolution was a product of many factors, no one of which can be positively assigned first importance. Washington, looking back on the vicissitudes of eight years, could only explain it as the intervention of "Divine Providence." American historians in the nineteenth century saw that "Divine Providence" as having been manifested primarily in the character and genius of the modest Commander in Chief himself. Washington's leadership was clearly one of the principal factors in American success; it seems fair to say that the Revolution could hardly have succeeded without him. Yet in many of the events that led to victory—Bennington, Saratoga, King's Mountain, and Cowpens, to name but a few—his personal influence was remote.

Today many scholars stress not the astonishment that Washington felt at the victory of a weak and divided confederation of American states over the greatest power of the age, but the practical difficulties the British faced in suppressing the revolt. These were indeed great but they do not appear to have been insuperable if one considers military victory alone and not its political consequences. The British forfeited several chances for military victory in 1776–77, and again in 1780 they might have won had they been able to throw 10,000 fresh troops into the American war. American military leaders were more resourceful and imaginative than the British commanders, and they proved quite capable of profiting from British blunders. In addition to Washington, Nathanael Greene, Henry Knox, Daniel Morgan, and Benedict Arnold showed remarkable military abilities, and of the foreign volunteers Steuben and the young Lafayette were outstanding. The resourcefulness of this extraordinary group of leaders was matched by the dedication of the Continental rank and file to the cause. Only men so dedicated could have endured the hardships of the march to Quebec, the crossing of the Delaware, Valley Forge, Morristown, and Greene's forced marches in the southern campaign. British and Hessian professionals never showed the same spirit; their virtues were exhibited principally in situations where discipline and training counted most.

The militia, the men who fought battles and then went home, also exhibited this spirit on many occasions. The militiamen have been generally maligned as useless by one school of thought, and glorified by another as the true victors in the war. In any balanced view it must be recognized that their contributions were great, though they would have counted for little without a Continental Army to give the American cause that continued sustenance that only a permanent force in being could give it. It was the ubiquity of the militia that made British victories over the Continentals in the field so meaningless. And the success with which the militia did operate derived from the firm political control the patriots had established over the countryside long before the British were in any position to challenge it—the situation that made the British task so difficult in the first place.

For all these American virtues and British difficulties and mistakes, the Americans still required French aid—money, supplies, and in the last phase military force—to win a decisive and clear-cut military victory. Most of the muskets, bayonets, and cannon used by the Continental Army came from France. The French contested the control of the seas that was so vital to the British, and compelled them to divert forces from the American mainland to other areas. The final stroke at Yorktown, though a product of Washington's strategic conception, was possible only because of the temporary predominance of French naval power off the American coast and the presence of a French army.

French aid was doubly necessary because the American war effort lacked strong national direction. The Revolution showed conclusively the need for a central government with power to harness the nation's resources for war. It is not surprising that in 1787 nearly all those who had struggled so long and hard as leaders in the Continental Army or in administrative positions under the Congress were to be found in the ranks of the supporters of a new constitution creating such a central government with a strong executive and the power to "raise armies and navies," call out the militia, and levy taxes directly to support itself.

Strictly military lessons of the Revolution were more equivocal. Tactical innovations were not radical but they did represent a culmination of the trend, which started during the French and Indian War, toward employment of light troops as skirmishers in conjunction with traditional linear formations. By the end of the war both armies were fighting in this fashion. The Americans strove to develop the same proficiency as the British in regular line-of-battle tactics, while the British adapted to the American terrain and tactics by themselves employing skirmishers and fighting when possible from behind cover. Washington was himself a military conservative, and Steuben's training program was designed to equip American troops to fight in European fashion with modifications to provide for the increased use of light infantry. The guerrilla tactics that characterized many actions, principally those of the militia, were no product of the design of Washington or his leading subordinates but of circumstances over which they had little control. The American rifle, most useful in guerrilla actions or in the hands of skirmishers, played no decisive role in the Revolution. It was of great value in wooded areas, as at Saratoga and King's Mountain, but for open-field fighting its slow rate of fire and lack of a bayonet made it inferior to the musket.

Since both militia and Continentals played roles in winning the war, the Revolutionary experience provided ammunition for two diametrically opposed schools of thought on American military policy: the one advocating a large Regular Army, the other reliance on the militia as the bulwark of national defense. The real issue, as Washington fully recognized, was less militia versus Regulars—for he never believed the infant republic needed a large standing army—than the extent to which militia could be trained and organized to form a reliable national reserve. The lesson Washington drew from the Revolution was that the militia should be "well regulated," that is, trained and organized under a uniform national system in all the states and subject to call into national service in war or emergency.

The lesson had far greater implications for the future than any of the tactical changes wrought by the American Revolution. It balanced the rights of freedom and equality, proclaimed in the Declaration of Independence, with a corresponding obligation of all citizens for military service to the nation. This concept, which was to find explicit expression in the "nation in arms" during the French Revolution, was also implicit in the American, and it portended the end of eighteenth century limited war, fought by professional armies officered by an aristocratic class. As Steuben so well recognized, American Continentals were not professional soldiers in the European sense, and militia even less so. They were, instead, a people's army fighting for a cause. In this sense then, the American Revolution began the "democratization of war," a process that was eventually to lead to national conscription and a new concept of total war for total victory.

CHAPTER 5

The Formative Years, 1783–1812

On September 24, 1783, four days after the signing of the Treaty of Paris formally ended the war, Congress directed General Washington to discharge "such parts of the Federal Army now in Service as he shall deem proper and expedient." For the time being Washington retained the force facing the British at New York, discharging the rest of the Continentals. After the British quit New York, he kept only one infantry regiment and a battalion of artillery, 600 men in all, to guard the military supplies at West Point and other posts.

The period leading up to this demobilization was a stormy one for the Congress. During the winter of 1782 the Army had grown impatient, and rumors that it would take matters into its own hands gained credence when several anonymous addresses were circulated among the officers at Newburgh urging them not to fight if the war continued or not to lay down their arms if peace were declared and their pay accounts left unsettled. In an emotional speech to his old comrades, Washington disarmed this threat. He promised to intercede for them, and in the end, Congress did give in to the officers' demands, agreeing to award the men their back pay and to grant the officers full pay for five years in lieu of half pay for life. Demobilization then proceeded peacefully, but it was against the background of these demands and threats that Congress wrestled with a major postwar problem, the size and character of the peacetime military establishment. In the way of most governments, Congress turned the problem over to a committee, this one under Alexander Hamilton, to study the facts and make recommendations for a military establishment.

The Question of a Peacetime Army

Congress subscribed to the prevailing view that the first line of defense should be a "well-regulated and disciplined militia sufficiently armed and accoutered." Its reluctance to create a standing army was understandable; a permanent army would be a heavy expense, and it would complicate the struggle between those who wanted a strong national government and those who preferred the existing loose federation of states. Further, the recent threats of the

Continental officers strengthened the popular fear that a standing army might be used to coerce the states or become an instrument of despotism.

General Washington, to whom Hamilton's committee turned first for advice, echoed the prevailing view. He pointed out that a large standing army in time of peace had always been considered "dangerous to the liberties of a country" and that the nation was "too poor to maintain a standing army adequate to our defense." The question might also be considered, he continued, whether any surplus funds that became available should not better be applied to "building and equipping a Navy without which, in case of War we could neither protect our Commerce, nor yield that assistance to each other which, on such an extent of seacoast, our mutual safety would require." He believed that America should rely ultimately on an improved version of the historic citizens' militia, a force enrolling all males between 18 and 50 liable for service to the nation in emergencies. He also recommended a volunteer militia, recruited in units, periodically trained, and subject to United States rather than state control. At the same time Washington did suggest the creation of a small Regular Army "to awe the Indians, protect our Trade, prevent the encroachment of our Neighbors of Canada and the Floridas, and guard us at least from surprises; also for security of our magazines." He recommended a force of four regiments of infantry and one of artillery, totaling 2,630 officers and men.

Hamilton's committee also listened to suggestions made by General von Steuben, Major General Louis le Bèque Du Portail, Chief Engineer of the Army, and Benjamin Lincoln, Secretary at War. On June 18, 1783, it submitted a plan to Congress similar to Washington's, but with a more ambitious militia program. Congress, however, rejected the proposal. Sectional rivalries, constitutional questions, and, above all, economic objections were too strong to be overcome.

The committee thereupon revised its plan, recommending an even larger army that it hoped to provide at less expense by decreasing the pay of the regimental staff officers and subalterns. Washington when asked admitted that detached service along the frontiers and coasts would probably require more men than he had proposed, but he disagreed that a larger establishment could be provided more economically than the one he had recommended. A considerable number of the delegates to Congress had similar misgivings, and when the committee presented its revised report on October 23, Congress refused to accept it. During the winter of 1783 the matter rested. Under the Articles of Confederation an affirmative vote of the representatives of nine states was required for the exercise of certain important powers, including military matters, and on few occasions during this winter were enough states represented for Congress to renew the debate.

In the spring of 1784 the question of a permanent peacetime army became involved in the politics of state claims to western lands. The majority of men in the remaining infantry regiment and artillery battalion were from Massachusetts and New Hampshire, and those states wanted to be rid of the financial burden of providing the extra pay that they had promised the men on enlistment. Congress refused to assume the responsibility unless the New England states would vote for a permanent military establishment. The New England representatives, led by Elbridge Gerry of Massachusetts, insisted that Congress had no authority to maintain a standing army, but at the same time they wanted the existing troops to occupy the western forts, situated in land claimed by the New England states. New York vigorously contested the New England claims to western lands, particularly in the region around Oswego and Niagara, and refused to vote for any permanent military establishment unless Congress gave it permission to garrison the western forts with its own forces.

The posts that had been the object of concern and discussion dominated the Great Lakes and the St. Lawrence River. (*Map 13*) Located on American

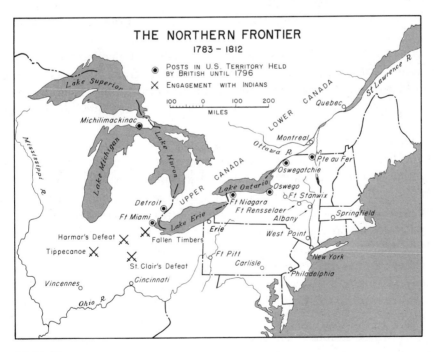

MAP 13

territory south of the boundary established by the peace treaty of 1783, the posts were in the hands of British troops when the war ended, but by the terms of the treaty they were to be turned over to the United States as speedily as possible. Congress agreed that a force should be retained to occupy the posts as soon as the British left. The problem was how and by whom the troops were to be raised. A decision was all the more urgent because the government was in the midst of negotiating a treaty with the Indians of the Northwest, and, as Washington had suggested, a sizable force "to awe the Indians" would facilitate the negotiations. But the deadlock between the New England states and New York continued until early June 1784.

Finally, on the last two days of the session, Congress rushed through a compromise. It ordered the existing infantry regiment and battalion of artillery disbanded, except for 80 artillerymen retained to guard military stores at West Point and Fort Pitt. It tied this discharge to a measure providing for the immediate recruitment of a new force of 700 men, a regiment of eight infantry and two artillery companies, which was to become the nucleus of a new Regular Army. By not making requisitions on the states for troops, but merely recommending that the states provide them from their militia, Congress got rid of most of the New England opposition on this score; by not assigning a quota for Massachusetts and New Hampshire, Congress satisfied the objections of most of the other states.

Four states were called upon to furnish troops: 260 men from Pennsylvania, 165 from Connecticut, 165 from New York, and 110 from New Jersey. Lt. Col. Josiah Harmar of Pennsylvania was appointed commanding officer. By the end of September 1784 only New Jersey and Pennsylvania had filled their quotas by enlisting volunteers from their militia.

Congress had meanwhile learned that there was little immediate prospect that the British would evacuate the frontier posts. Canadian fur traders and the settlers in Upper Canada had objected so violently to this provision of the peace treaty that the British Government secretly directed the Governor-General of Canada not to evacuate the posts without further orders. The failure of the United States to comply with a stipulation in the treaty regarding the recovery of debts owed to loyalists provided the British with an excuse to postpone the evacuation of the posts for twelve more years. So the New Jersey contingent of Colonel Harmar's force was sent to Fort Stanwix, in upstate New York, to assist in persuading the Iroquois to part with their lands, while the remainder of the force moved to Fort MacIntosh, thirty miles down the Ohio River from Fort Pitt, where similar negotiations were carried on with the Indians of the upper Ohio.

Toward a More Perfect Union

Postwar problems revealed a number of serious defects in the Articles of Confederation. The federal government lacked a separate executive branch and a judiciary, and although Congress exercised a certain amount of executive as well as legislative power, it lacked the power to tax. To some of the delegates the conflicts and dissension between the states over the western lands seemed to carry the seeds of civil war. Rioting and disturbances in Massachusetts throughout the fall and winter of 1786 strengthened the pessimism of those who feared the collapse of the new nation. A severe commercial depression following on the heels of an immediate postwar boom was causing particular distress among the back-country farmers. Angry mobs gathered in the Massachusetts hills, broke up the meetings of the courts, harried lawyers and magistrates out of the villages, and began to threaten the government arsenal in Springfield.

On October 20, 1786, Congress responded to the threat by calling on several states to raise a 1,340-man force to serve for three years. This time the New England states did not object to Congressional action, but before any of the soldiers voted by Congress could reach the scene, local militiamen repulsed an attack on the Springfield Arsenal led by Daniel Shays in late January 1787, and a few days later a large reinforcement from the eastern part of the state arrived at Springfield and put an end to the disorders. Recruiting for the force authorized by Congress continued until the following April. By then about 550 men had been enlisted and the question of expense was becoming bothersome. Congress therefore directed the states to stop recruiting and to discharge the troops already raised, except those in two artillery companies retained to guard West Point and the Springfield Arsenal. Shays' Rebellion was thus responsible for the first augmentation of the federal Army. More important, it helped persuade Americans that a stronger government was needed.

Rising concern over the ineffectiveness of the federal government, particularly in matters of finance and commercial regulation, finally led to the convening of a Constitutional Convention in the spring of 1787. To strengthen the military powers of the government was one of the principal tasks of the convention, a task no less important than establishing its financial and commercial authority. The general problem facing the convention, that of power and the control of power, came into sharp focus in the debates on military matters, since the widespread suspicion of a strong central government and the equally widespread fear of a standing army were merged in the issue of the government's military powers. Those who mistrusted a powerful government argued against a broad grant of authority not only in the fields of taxation and commercial regulation, but, and with especial force, in military matters as well. Even those, like Hamilton, who wanted to give the central government wide latitude in handling both purse and sword were also somewhat wary of standing armies. They too were concerned over the possible usurpation of political power by a military force or its use by officeholders as an instrument for perpetuating their personal power. The Hamiltonians nevertheless were willing to have the country run the risk of being less free in order to be more safe. In the final compromise the problem of the military powers of the central government was resolved through the system of checks and balances built into the new Constitution.

The Constitution clothed the central government with adequate authority to raise and maintain an army without calling upon the states. By giving Congress power to levy taxes, the Constitution provided the central government with the necessary financial means; by creating a separate executive branch, the Constitution made it possible for the daily business of the government to be conducted without constant reference to the states. The Constitution gave the power to declare war, raise armies, and provide for a navy exclusively to Congress. It also empowered Congress to call forth the militia "to execute the Laws of the Union, suppress Insurrections and repel Invasions." But authority over the militia was a shared power. Congress could provide for organizing, arming, and disciplining the militia and governing "such Part of them as may be employed in the Service of the United States," but the Constitution specifically reserved to the states the authority to appoint militia officers and to train the militia "according to the discipline prescribed by Congress."

The new Constitution introduced an important innovation by assigning all executive power to the President. The Secretary of War, therefore, became directly responsible to the President and not to Congress. The Constitution specifically provided that the President should be Commander in Chief of the Army and Navy. As such, his powers were exclusive, limited only "by their nature and by the principles of our institutions." The President had the right to assume personal command of forces in the field, but he could also delegate that right. As Commander in Chief he was responsible for the employment and disposition of the armed forces in time of peace and for the general direction of military and naval operations in war.

Washington became the first President under the new Constitution in April 1789, and on August 7 Congress created the Department of War. There was no change, however, in either the policy or the personnel of the department. General Knox, who had succeeded Washington as commander of the Army and had been handling military affairs under the old form of government, remained in charge. Since there was no navy, a separate department was unnecessary, and at first the War Department included naval affairs under its jurisdiction. Harmar, who had been given the rank of brigadier general during the Confederation period, was confirmed in his appointment, as were his officers, and the existing miniscule Army was taken over intact by the new government. In August 1789 this force amounted to about 800 officers and men. All the troops, except the two artillery companies retained after Shays' Rebellion, were stationed along the Ohio River in a series of forts built after 1785.

So small an Army required no extensive field organization to supply its needs. In keeping with the accepted military theory that the Quartermaster was a staff officer necessary only in time of war, the Confederation Congress had included the Quartermaster General and his assistants among the others discharged in 1783 and placed the military supply system under civilian control. It had made the civilian Secretary responsible for the transport, safe-keeping, and distribution of military supplies and the Board of Treasury responsible for procuring and purchasing all military stores, including food and clothing. Except during a brief period in which the Secretary of War was allowed to execute contracts for Army clothing and subsistence, the new federal government retained the Confederation system, adding in 1792 a civilian Office of the Quartermaster General to transport supplies to the frontier posts during the Indian expeditions. In 1794 Congress established the Office of the Purveyor of Public Supplies in the Treasury and the Office of Superintendent of Military Stores in the War Department to continue the same broad supply functions established in the Confederation period. This organization of military supply remained in effect with only slight modification until 1812.

The contract system used by the Purveyor of Public Supplies for the procurement of food and equipment operated much as it did in colonial times. Contracts were awarded to the lowest bidder who agreed to deliver and issue authorized subsistence at a fixed price to troops at a given post. The contractor was obliged to have on hand sufficient rations to feed the troops at all times, providing subsistence for at least six months in advance at the more distant posts. The procurement, storage, and distribution of all other supplies for the Army were centralized in Philadelphia where the Purveyor contracted for all clothing, camp utensils, military stores, medicines, and hospital stores, and the Superintendent of Military Stores collected and issued them when needed by the troops. The contract system was supposed to be more economical and efficient than direct purchase, but its weaknesses were soon apparent. The quality of the supplies and the promptness of their delivery were dictated by the contractor's profit interest.

The method of arms procurement was a variation of the contract purchase system. Convinced that the development of a domestic arms industry was essential to independence, Hamilton had urged as early as 1783 "the public manufacture of arms, powder, etc." A decade later Secretary Knox reported to Congress that although arms could be purchased more cheaply in Europe the bargain price was of little significance "compared with the solid advantages which would result from extending and perfecting the means upon which our safety may ultimately depend." Congress responded by expanding the number of U.S. arsenals and magazines for the stockpiling of weapons and by establishing national armories for the manufacture of weapons. The first national armory was established at Springfield, Massachusetts, in 1794, and a second the same year at Harpers Ferry, Virginia. Despite these developments the government still purchased most of its armament abroad, and many years would pass before domestic industry could supply the government's needs.

The Militia

Time and again Washington pointed out that the only alternative to a large standing army was an effective militia, yet his efforts and those of Knox and Hamilton to make the militia more effective by applying federal regulation failed. Congress passed the basic militia law in May 1792. It called for the enrollment of "every able-bodied white male citizen" between 18 and 45 and the organization of the militia into divisions, brigades, regiments, battalions, and companies by the individual states, each militiaman providing his own "arms, munitions, and other accouterments." The law that survived the legislative process bore little resemblance to the one proposed by Washington and Knox. It left compliance with its provisions up to the states and in the end did little more than give federal recognition to the colonial militia organization that had plagued Washington during the Revolution. Despite these limitations, the act did preserve the idea of a citizen soldiery, a concept of profound importance to the future of the country, and it also provided for the creation of special volunteer units to supplement the obligatory mass system. The volunteers, organized into companies, met regularly for military training under elected officers. With antecedents in the organized military associations of the colonial era, this volunteer force later became the National Guard.

Training and discipline were the key to an effective militia, but after the act of 1792 the militia was to be neither disciplined nor well trained. When permitted to fight in less standardized fashion—either from behind fortifications or as irregulars—militiamen could give a good account of themselves, but only highly trained troops could be expected to employ successfully the complicated, formal linear tactics of the day. Strictly interpreting the constitutional provision that reserved to the states the authority to train the militia, Congress left the extent and thoroughness of training completely to the states and merely prescribed General von Steuben's system of discipline and field exercises as the rules to be followed.

The limitations placed on the length of tours of duty and the circumstances for which it might be called into federal service further impaired the usefulness of the militia. No militiaman could be compelled to serve more than three months in any one year, nor could the President order the militia to duty outside the United States. The effect of these limitations would be readily apparent during the War of 1812.

The President first exercised his authority to employ militia for suppressing insurrection and executing the laws of Congress in 1794 when Washington sent a large force of militia under Maj. Gen. Henry Lee into western Pennsylvania during the Whiskey Rebellion. Lee encountered no resistance. As a show of force, the demonstration was impressive; as an indication of the military value of the militia in an emergency, it was inconclusive.

Military Realities in the Federalist Period

The military policies of the new nation evolved realistically in response to foreign and domestic developments. First, there was little actual military threat to the United States from a foreign nation. Britain had no desire or design to reconquer its lost colonies, although both Britain and Spain sought to curb the United States from expanding beyond the borders established by the treaty of 1783. The military alliance that bound the United States to England's arch rival, France, was a potential source of danger, but England and France were at peace until 1793. Second, the jealousy of the individual states toward one another and toward the federal government made it difficult to establish a federal Army at all and defeated efforts to institute federal regulation of the militia beyond the minimum permitted by the Constitution. Third, the federal government, plagued by financial problems, had to pare expenditures to the bone. Fourth, there was extreme reluctance on the part of Americans to serve in the Army, either as Regulars or as volunteers, for more than a brief period. At no time could the government recruit enough men to bring the Regular Army up to authorized strength. In view of these drawbacks, a larger military establishment was not feasible, even though a well-trained militia to take its place was lacking.

The Indian Expeditions

Free of the threat of foreign invasion, the young republic nevertheless faced a serious security problem in the West where the new settlers demanded protection against the Indians as well as an equitable administration of the vast new territories won in the peace of 1783. The Indian problem was an old one. Under the relentless pressure of the pioneers and because of the grants made to Continental soldiers, the frontier was rapidly receding. The Confederation Congress had tried to cope with the situation by concluding a series of treaties with the various Indian groups, but the treaties failed to keep pace with the expansion of the frontier boundaries, and the Indians, supported by British arms and the British presence in the Northwest, ferociously resisted the incursions of the settlers. In the years of the Confederation, they killed or captured over 1,500 settlers in the Kentucky Territory alone.

The Indians fought the settlers all along the frontier, but several factors militated against federal intervention in the Southwest during the first years of Washington's administration. In 1790 the United States concluded a treaty with the Creeks, the most powerful of the Southwest tribes, a treaty that the Spanish in Louisiana, eager to maintain their profitable trade with the Indians, would be likely to support. Georgia and South Carolina introduced a further argument against intervention when they objected to the presence of federal forces within their borders.

The situation was entirely different in the Northwest. There federal troops had been chiefly occupied in driving squatters out of the public domain and protecting the Indian's treaty rights, a type of duty that neither endeared them to the settlers nor trained them in the art of war. Since the enactment of the Northwest Ordinance in 1787, settlers had been pouring into the Ohio country and were demanding federal protection. Their demands carried a veiled threat: ignore their plight and they would turn to Spain and England for succor. The federal union could be destroyed in its infancy.

Tardily and somewhat inadequately, the new government groped for a response to the West's challenge. In his first annual message to Congress President Washington called for the defense of the frontier against the Indians, and Congress responded by raising the authorized strength of Regulars to

1,283. Aware that this force was inadequate to protect the entire frontier, Secretary Knox planned to call on the militia to join the Regulars in an offensive to chastise the Miami Indian group as a show of force. In June 1790 he ordered General Harmar, in consultation with Arthur St. Clair, governor of the Northwest Territory, to lead the expedition. Under an authorization given him the preceding fall, St. Clair called on Pennsylvania and Kentucky to send 1,500 militiamen to Harmar at Fort Washington (now Cincinnati). (*See Map 13.*)

The untrained and undisciplined militia was a weak reed on which to lean in a sustained campaign against the Indians, but Knox knew the militia's strengths as well as its weaknesses. Depending on the fast-striking, mounted militiamen to support the Regulars, Knox wanted Harmar to conduct a "rapid and decisive" maneuver, taking advantage of the element of surprise, to find and destroy the Indian forces and their food supplies. But the two-phased operation concocted by Harmar and St. Clair bore little resemblance to Knox's proposed tactics. Harmar planned a long march northward from Fort Washington to the Miami villages concentrated at the headwaters of the Wabash River. A second column under Maj. John Hamtramck would ascend the Wabash from Fort Vincennes, Indiana, destroying villages along the way and finally joining with Harmar's column after a 150-mile march.

The expedition failed. Hamtramck left Vincennes with 330 Regulars and Virginia militia on September 30, but after an 11-day march during which a few Indian villages were burned, the militia refused to advance farther. Harmar also set out on September 30. After struggling through the wilderness for more than two weeks with a force of 1,453 men, including 320 Regulars, he reached the neighborhood of the principal Indian village near what is now Fort Wayne, Indiana. Instead of pushing on with his entire strength, Harmar on three successive occasions sent forward unsupported detachments of about 200 to 500 militiamen plus 50 or 60 Regulars. The undisciplined militia could not be restrained from scattering in search of Indians and plunder, and, after two of the detachments suffered heavily in brushes with the Indians, Harmar took the rest of his army back to Fort Washington. His conduct was severely criticized, but a court of inquiry, noting the untrained troops with which Harmar had been provided and the lateness of the season, exonerated him.

Secretary Knox's injunctions for a "rapid and decisive" maneuver were again ignored when the government decided to send another expedition against the Northwest Indians in 1791. Congress raised the size of the invasion force, adding a second infantry regiment to the Regular Army and authorizing the President to raise a corps of 2,000 men for a term of six months, either by calling for militia or by enlisting volunteers into the service of the United States. The President commissioned Governor St. Clair a major general and placed him in command of the expedition. So slowly did recruiting and the procuring of supplies proceed that St. Clair was unable to set out before September 17, and only by calling on the neighboring states for militia was he able to bring his force up to strength. When St. Clair's force finally marched out of Fort Washington, it consisted of about 600 Regulars, almost all the actual infantry strength of the U.S. Army, in addition to about 800 enlisted "levies" and 600 militiamen.

By November 3 St. Clair had advanced about 100 miles northward from Cincinnati, and most of his force, now numbering about 1,400 effectives, encamped for the night near the headwaters of the Wabash. Neglecting the principle of security, St. Clair had not sent out scouts, and just before dawn a horde of about 1,000 Indians fell upon the unsuspecting troops. Untrained, low in morale as a result of inadequate supplies, and led by a general who was suffering from rheumatism, asthma, and "colic," the army was thrown into confusion by the sudden assault. St. Clair and less than half his force survived unscathed—637 were killed and 263 wounded.

The United States was alarmed and outraged over St. Clair's defeat. Some urged that the government abandon the Indian wars and accept the British proposal for an Indian buffer state in the Northwest, but Washington well understood the strategic implications of such a scheme and decided instead to mount a third expedition. He appointed Anthony Wayne, the dashing commander of the Pennsylvania Line during the Revolution, a major general to succeed St. Clair, and Congress doubled the authorized strength of the Army by providing for three additional regiments, two of which were to be infantry and the other a composite regiment of infantry and light dragoons. It tried to avoid the bad effects of short-term enlistment by adding the new regiments to the Regular Army as a temporary augmentation to be "discharged as soon as the United States shall be at peace with the Indian tribes." Congress also agreed to Secretary of War Knox's proposed reorganization of the Army into a "Legion," a term widely used during the eighteenth century and which had come to mean a composite organization of all combat arms under one command. Instead of regiments, the Army was composed of four "sub-legions," each commanded by a brigadier general and consisting of two infantry battalions, one battalion of riflemen, one troop of dragoons (cavalrymen trained to fight either mounted or dismounted), and one company of artillery.

Egotistical, blustery, and cordially disliked by many of his contemporaries, General Wayne nevertheless displayed little of his celebrated "madness" during the expedition. His operation was skillfully planned. Correcting previous mistakes, he insisted on rigid discipline and strict training, and conscious of the welfare of his men, he saw to it that supplies were adequate and equipment satisfactory. These military virtues finally won for the United States its elusive victory.

In the spring of 1793 General Wayne took the Legion down the river to Cincinnati where he tried to persuade the Indians to submit peacefully. When negotiations broke down, the Legion followed the route that Harmer and St. Clair had taken. Wayne was in even poorer health than St. Clair, but more determined. Like St. Clair he moved slowly and methodically, building a series of forts and blockhouses along his line of march. Despite his efforts to improve morale, he found desertion as serious a problem as had his predecessors.

Reinforced by mounted militia in July 1794, Wayne led about 3,000 men to within a few miles of Fort Miami, a post recently established by the British on the site of what is now Toledo. There, on August 20, 1794, almost within sight of the British guns, the Indians attacked. The Americans held their ground and then with a furious bayonet charge drove the enemy out of the cover of fallen trees that gave the Battle of Fallen Timbers its name. In the open prairie the Indians were at the mercy of Wayne's mounted volunteers, and in less than an hour the rout was complete.

Ignoring the protest of the British commander at Fort Miami, Wayne remained for several days, burning the Indian villages and destroying crops before leading the Legion back to Cincinnati. The western tribes, their resistance broken, finally agreed on August 3, 1795, in the Treaty of Greenville to make peace and cede their lands in Ohio to the United States. Their submission had been hastened by news that England was about to evacuate the frontier posts.

In the years following the Battle of Fallen Timbers settlers pushed rapidly into Ohio and beyond into lands still claimed by the Indians. To resist these encroachments, Tecumseh, chief of the Shawnees, and his brother, the Prophet, organized a tribal confederacy aimed at keeping the settlers out. Urged on by the settlers, Governor William Henry Harrison of the Indiana Territory decided in the summer of 1811 to strike at the Indians before they could descend on the settlements. Secretary of War William Eustis approved Harrison's scheme and placed 300 Regulars under Harrison's command in addition to his approximately 650 militia, including mounted riflemen. Moving north from Vincennes at the end of September, Harrison built a fort on the edge

BATTLE OF FALLEN TIMBERS

of the Indian country and then continued to the neighborhood of Tecumseh's principal village on Tippecanoe Creek. (*See Map 13.*) On November 6 he halted about a mile west of the village, encamping his force in the form of a trapezoid around the wagons and baggage on a piece of high-wooded ground that rose above the marshy prairies.

The Indians struck just before dawn. Harrison's situation was very similar to that of St. Clair, and for a time his force seemed about to suffer the same fate. Furious hand-to-hand combat followed the Indians' wild charge that carried them into the camp itself. Although taken by surprise, the soldiers rallied and then counterattacked. The end came when the mounted riflemen charged in on the Indians and drove them from the field. Harrison lost 39 men killed and missing and had 151 wounded, of whom 29 died. The engagement by no means solved the frontier problem in the Northwest, but this problem was soon overshadowed by the outbreak of war with England. Its most permanent legacy was a tradition that helped Harrison win the Presidency in 1841.

The Perils of Neutrality

While the United States was launching a new government and defending the frontier, France had undergone a revolution, which within a few years led to a general European war. Britain joined the coalition against France in 1793 and in the first year of the war instituted a blockade, seizing at least 300 American merchant vessels. In 1794 Jay's treaty eased the mounting crisis in Anglo-American relations. By acquiescing in the British doctrine of contraband, the United States obtained a settlement of some long-standing questions, including evacuation of the frontier posts, but only at the expense of domestic unity and peaceful relations with the French. Regarding Jay's treaty as evidence of a pro-British policy on the part of the United States, France retaliated by seizing American vessels that were trading with the British, by sending secret agents to stir up the Creek Indians along the southern frontier, and by meddling in American politics in an attempt to bring about the defeat of the "pro-British" administration. These were the new and serious problems that President Washington bequeathed to his successor, John Adams, in 1797.

Adams inherited a military establishment with an authorized strength of about 3,300 officers and men. In 1797 Congress dropped the legion type of organization that had served well in the frontier fighting, and the Army returned to a regimental type of organization with four regiments of infantry, a Corps of Artillerists and Engineers, and two companies of light dragoons more appropriate to the duties of border defense. During 1796 and early 1797 there had been some redeployment into the Southwest, so that by 1797 nine companies of infantry, about two companies of artillery, and the entire force of dragoons were stationed along the southwestern frontier. Up in the old Northwest there were five infantry companies at Detroit and smaller detachments at a dozen scattered forts elsewhere in the territory. Fort Washington, garrisoned by a full regiment, was the major installation. There were also small garrisons at the important seaports, which had been fortified after 1794 by French technicians, émigrés of the recent revolution. The rest of the Army was stationed along the Canadian border from the lakes eastward and at the older posts, like West Point, Carlisle, and Fort Pitt.

The Quasi War With France

When the French continued to attack American vessels and refused to receive the newly appointed American Minister, President Adams called Congress into special session to consider national defense. He particularly urged that immediate steps be taken to provide a navy. He also recommended that harbor defenses be improved, additional cavalry be raised, the Militia Act of 1792 be revised to provide for better organization and training, and the President be authorized to call an emergency force, although he saw no immediate need for the last. Congress approved the naval recommendations, but except for a modest appropriation for harbor defenses and an act authorizing the

President to call out 80,000 militia for a maximum term of three months, it voted down the military recommendations.

By the spring of 1798 France's actions had thoroughly aroused the country. President Adams again recommended an expanded defense program, which this time fared somewhat better in Congress. Congress passed the recommended naval increases and created a separate Navy Department. Of the three regiments the administration recommended adding to the Regular Army, Congress authorized the additional artillery but not the cavalry. With respect to the infantry regiment, the Secretary of War proposed to Congress that it might act in the double capacity of marines and infantrymen. Instead, Congress voted the U.S. Marine Corps into existence, making it part of the Army or Navy, according to whether the marines served on land or on shipboard. Congress also increased the number of companies in each of the 4 Regular infantry regiments from 8 to 10; voted a sizable sum for harbor defenses and ordnance; and authorized a Provisional Army, the emergency force that Adams had suggested the year before.

Again Congress tried to avoid the defects of short-term enlistments by setting the duration of the "existing differences between the United States and the French Republic" as the term of enlistment for the Provisional Army. Reluctant to abandon its traditional reliance on short-term militia volunteers, Congress turned down another Presidential request for an increase in the Regular Army, giving him instead the authority to accept privately armed and equipped volunteer units for short-term service. Adams never made use of this authority, but went ahead with the plans to raise the twelve infantry regiments and one cavalry regiment that made up the Provisional Army. He persuaded Washington to come out of retirement to accept command as lieutenant general, and at Washington's request appointed Alexander Hamilton senior major general. By the beginning of 1799 the officers had been appointed and in May 1799 recruiting began. By the time the Provisional Army was disbanded in June 1800, about 4,100 men had been mobilized, assembled in camps, and given from six to twelve months' training. Hamilton directed the preparation of new drill regulations to replace Steuben's, but before the task was finished the French crisis had ended and the Provisional Army was discharged.

The possibility that the United States might ally itself with Britain helped persuade the French to agree to negotiations. Furthermore, the French had been pressing Spain to return Louisiana as a step toward restoring their colonial empire in America, and for this venture peace with the United States was necessary. On September 30, 1800, a treaty was signed in which France agreed to recognize American neutrality, thus formally ending the alliance of 1778, and to refrain from seizing American vessels that were not carrying contraband. On the very next day, October 1, 1800, France and Spain signed a secret treaty turning Louisiana over to France, and a few months later England and her allies made peace with France.

Defense Under Jefferson

President Jefferson took office in 1801 committed to a policy of peace and economy. With Europe at peace and American relations with France and England better than they had been for ten years past, Congress proceeded to economize. It sold the Navy that had acquitted itself so well in the quasi war with France, retaining only the frigates and a few of the other larger ships. The Army did not feel the effect of the economy drive until March 1802. Until then the military establishment was much as Adams had left it after the Provisional Army troops had been discharged, with an authorized strength of 5,438 officers and men and an actual strength of about 4,000. In the reduction of March 1802 Congress cut back the total strength of the Army to 3,220 men, approximately what it had been in 1797 when Adams took office. It was more than 50 percent stronger in artillery, but the more expensive cavalry was eliminated.

Congress also abolished the Office of the Quartermaster General when it reduced the size of the Army and in its place instituted a system of contract agents. It divided the country into three military departments with a military agent in each who, with his assistants, was responsible for the movement of supplies and troops within his department. Since the assistant agents were also appointed by the President, the three military agents had no way to enforce accountability on their subordinates. This system soon led to large property losses.

Since the Revolution the Army had suffered from a lack of trained technicians, particularly in engineering science, and had depended largely upon foreign experts. As a remedy Washington, Knox, Hamilton, and others had recommended the establishment of a military school. During Washington's administration, Congress had added the rank of cadet in the Corps of Artillerists and Engineers with two cadets assigned to each company for instruction. But not until the Army reorganization of 1802 did Congress create a separate Corps of Engineers, consisting of 10 cadets and 7 officers, and assign it to West Point to serve as the staff of a military academy. Within a few years the U.S. Military Academy became a center of study in military science and a source of trained officers. By 1812 it listed 89 graduates, 65 of them still serving in the Army and playing an important role in operations and the construction of fortifications.

The Army and Westward Expansion

Not long after Thomas Jefferson became President, rumors reached America that France had acquired Louisiana from Spain. The news was upsetting. Many Americans, including Jefferson, had believed that when Spain lost its weak hold on the colonies the United States would automatically fall heir to them. But, with a strong power like France in possession, it was useless to wait for the colonies to fall into the lap of the United States. The presence of France in North America also raised a new security problem. Up to this time the problem of frontier defense had been chiefly one of pacifying the Indians, keeping the western territories from breaking away, and preventing American settlers from molesting the Spanish. Now, with a strong, aggressive France as backdoor neighbor, the frontier problem became tied up with the question of security against possible foreign threats. The transfer of Louisiana to France also marked the beginning of restraints on American trade down the Mississippi. In the past, Spain had permitted American settlers to send their goods down the river and to deposit them at New Orleans. Just before transferring the colony, however, it revoked the American right of deposit, an action which made it almost impossible for Americans to send goods out by this route.

These considerations persuaded Jefferson in 1803 to inquire about the possibility of purchasing New Orleans from France. When Napoleon, anticipating the renewal of the war in Europe, offered to sell the whole of Louisiana, Jefferson quickly accepted, suddenly doubling the size of the United States. The Army, after taking formal possession of Louisiana on December 20, 1803, established small garrisons at New Orleans and the other former Spanish posts on the lower Mississippi. Jefferson later appointed Brig. Gen. James Wilkinson, who had survived the various reorganizations of the Army to become senior officer, first governor of the new territory. (*Map 14*)

Before the Louisiana Purchase, Jefferson had persuaded Congress to support an exploration of the unknown territory west of the Mississippi. The acquisition of this territory now made such an exploration even more desirable. To lead the expedition, Jefferson chose Capt. Meriwether Lewis and Lt. William Clark, both of whom had served under General Wayne in the Northwest. Leaving St. Louis in the spring of 1804 with twenty-seven men, Lewis and Clark traveled up the Missouri River, crossed the Rocky Mountains, and followed the Columbia River down to the Pacific, which they reached after much

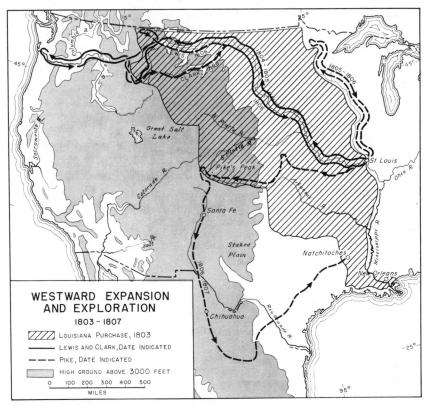

WESTWARD EXPANSION
AND EXPLORATION
1803 – 1807

////// LOUISIANA PURCHASE, 1803
——— LEWIS AND CLARK, DATE INDICATED
– – – PIKE, DATE INDICATED
       HIGH GROUND ABOVE 3000 FEET
0   100 200 300 400 500
              MILES

MAP 14

hardship in November 1805. On the return journey, the party explored the
region of central Montana and returned to St. Louis in September 1806.

While Lewis and Clark were exploring beyond the Missouri, General
Wilkinson sent out Capt. Zebulon M. Pike on a similar expedition to the head-
waters of the Mississippi. In 1807 Wilkinson organized another expedition.
This time he sent twenty men under Captain Pike westward into what is now
Colorado. After exploring the region around the peak that bears his name,
Pike encountered some Spaniards who, resentful of the incursion, escorted his
party to Santa Fe. From there the Spanish took the Americans into Mexico and
then back across Texas to Natchitoches, once more in American territory. The
Lewis and Clark expedition and those of Captain Pike contributed much to the
geographic and scientific knowledge of the country, and today remain as great
epics of the West.

To march across the continent might seem the manifest destiny of the
Republic, but it met with an understandable reaction from the Spanish. The

dispute over the boundary between Louisiana and Spain's frontier provinces and the question of the two Floridas became burning issues during Jefferson's second administration. Tension mounted in 1806 as rumors reached Washington of the dispatch of thousands of Spanish Regulars to reinforce the mounted Mexican militiamen in east Texas. Jefferson reacted to the rumors by calling up the Orleans and Mississippi Territories' militia and sending approximately 1,000 Regulars to General Wilkinson to counter the Spanish move. The rumors proved unfounded; at no time did the Spanish outnumber the American forces in the area. A series of cavalry skirmishes occurred along the Sabine River, but the opposing commanders prudently avoided war by agreeing to establish a neutral zone between the Arroyo Hondo and the Sabine River. The two armies remained along this line throughout 1806, and the neutral zone served as a *de facto* boundary until 1812.

American Reaction to the Napoleonic Wars

The second round of the great conflict between England and France began in 1803, shortly after the purchase of Louisiana. It was a much more serious affair than the earlier one. Both Britain and France adopted policies under which American merchant shipping, whether carrying contraband or not, was subject to search and seizure. The Napoleonic Wars and the consequent depredations on American commerce were less a threat to national security than a blow to national pride. Jefferson responded to the challenge by withdrawing American shipping from the seas. Madison adopted the even riskier policy of economic coercion. Jefferson's Embargo Act of 1807 prohibited trade with all foreign countries. It was replaced by the Non-Intercourse Act of 1809, which prohibited trade only with England and France. The Non-Intercourse Act was, in turn, replaced by an act in May 1810, known as Macon's Bill No. 2, which reopened trade with England and France but provided that, if either of those countries repealed its restrictive measures and the other failed to follow suit, the Non-Intercourse Act would be put into effect against the nation that continued its restrictions.

The legislation failed to keep the United States from becoming embroiled in the war and was unsuccessful in forcing England and France to respect neutral trade. Neither Jefferson nor Madison recognized that under the new scheme of economic warfare being waged by both England and France the American measures were in effect provocative acts, likely to bring the United States into the war on one side or the other. The Embargo Act and, to a lesser extent, the Non-Intercourse Act of 1809 did cripple American trade, something that neither Britain nor France had succeeded in doing. As a result, the American people, already divided by sectional jealousies and by the French crisis during Adams' administration, were so thoroughly disunited that the government could not count on the loyalty and support of a sizable part of the population.

International tension was so great in the months after the embargo went into effect that Congress, while rejecting Jefferson's proposal for recruiting a 24,000-man volunteer force, authorized the recruitment of 6,000 men as a temporary addition to the Army. In the last month of his administration President Jefferson sent more than 2,000 of these men to General Wilkinson to defend "New Orleans and its dependencies" against an expected English invasion. The invasion never materialized, but poor leadership and bureaucratic mismanagement bordering on the criminal combined with the tropical heat to accomplish what no British invasion could have done. Over 1,000 men, half of Wilkinson's army, died in Louisiana.

By January 1810 relations with Britain had so deteriorated that President Madison recommended the recruitment of a volunteer force of 20,000. Congress, apparently satisfied with the existing militia system, again refused to vote a volunteer force; not until January 1812 did it increase the Army's strength when it added thirteen additional regiments, totaling about 25,700 men, and authorized the President to call 50,000 militiamen into service.

The additional men would soon be needed. On June 18, 1812, Congress declared war against England. At the same time a Senate proposal to declare war against France failed by only two votes.

CHAPTER 6

The War of 1812

To Great Britain the War of 1812 was simply a burdensome adjunct of its greater struggle against Napoleonic France. To the Canadians it was clearly a case of naked American aggression. But to the Americans it was neither simple nor clear. The United States entered the war with confused objectives and divided loyalties and made peace without settling any of the issues that had induced the nation to go to war.

Origins of the War

The immediate origins of the war were seizure of American ships, insults and injuries to American seamen by the British Navy, and rapid expansion of the American frontier. The British outrages at sea took two distinct forms. One was the seizure and forced sale of merchant ships and their cargoes for allegedly violating the British blockade of Europe. Although France had declared a counterblockade of the British Isles and had seized American ships, England was the chief offender because its Navy had greater command of the seas. The second, more insulting, type of outrage was the capture of men from American vessels for forced service in the Royal Navy. The pretext for impressment was the search for deserters, who, the British claimed, had taken employment on American vessels.

The reaction in the United States to impressment differed from that aroused by the seizure of ships and cargoes. In the latter case the maritime interests of the eastern seaboard protested vigorously and demanded naval protection, but rather than risk having their highly profitable trade cut off by war with England they were willing to take an occasional loss of cargo. Impressment, on the other hand, presented no such financial hardship to the shipowners, whatever the consequences for the unfortunate seamen, and the maritime interests tended to minimize it.

To the country at large the seizure of American seamen was much more serious than the loss of a few hogsheads of flour or molasses. When a British naval vessel in June 1807 attacked and disabled the USS *Chesapeake* and impressed several members of the crew, a general wave of indignation rose in which even the maritime interests joined. This was an insult to the flag, and had Jefferson chosen to go to war with England he would have had considerable support. Instead he decided to clamp an embargo on American trade. In New England scores of prosperous shipowners were ruined, and a number of thriving little seaports suffered an economic depression from which few recovered. While the rest of the country remembered the *Chesapeake* affair and stored up resentment against Britain, maritime New England directed its anger at Jefferson and his party.

The seat of anti-British fever was in the Northwest and the lower Ohio Valley, where the land-hungry frontiersmen had no doubt that their troubles with the Indians were the result of British intrigue. Stories were circulated after every Indian raid of British Army muskets and equipment being found on the field. By 1812 the westerners were convinced that their problems could best be solved by forcing the British out of Canada.

While the western "war hawks" urged war in the hope of conquering Canada, the people of Georgia, Tennessee, and the Mississippi Territory entertained similar designs against Florida, a Spanish possession. The fact that Spain and England were allies against Napoleon presented the southern war hawks with an excuse for invading Florida. By this time, also, the balance of political power had shifted south and westward; ambitious party leaders had no choice but to align themselves with the war hawks, and 1812 was a Presidential election year.

President Madison's use of economic pressure to force England to repeal its blockade almost succeeded. The revival of the Non-Intercourse Act against Britain, prohibiting all trade with England and its colonies, coincided with a poor grain harvest in England and with a growing need of American provisions to supply the British troops fighting the French in Spain. As a result, on June 16, 1812, the British Foreign Minister announced that the blockade would be relaxed on American shipping. Had there been an Atlantic cable, war might have been averted. President Madison had sent a message to Congress on June 1 listing all the complaints against England and asking for a declaration of war. Dividing along sectional lines the House had voted for war on June 4, but the Senate approved only on June 18 and then by only six votes.

The Opposing Forces

At the outbreak of the war the United States had a total population of about 7,700,000 people. A series of border forts garrisoned by very small Regular Army detachments stretched along the Canadian boundary: Fort Michili-

mackinac, on the straits between Lake Michigan and Lake Huron; Fort Dearborn, on the site of what is now Chicago; Fort Detroit; and Fort Niagara, at the
mouth of the Niagara River on Lake Ontario. (*Map 15*) The actual strength
of the Regular Army in June 1812 totaled approximately 11,744 officers and
men, including an estimated 5,000 recruits enlisted for the additional force
authorized the preceding January, in contrast to an authorized strength of
35,600. The Navy consisted of 20 vessels: the 3 large 44-gun frigates, 3 smaller
frigates of the *Constellation* class rated at 38 guns, and 14 others.

Congress did not lack the will to prepare for war. In March 1812 it had
tried to place the Army's supply system on a more adequate footing by establishing a Quartermaster Department on the military staff in place of the
inefficient and costly military agent system. At the same time Congress created
the Office of the Commissary General of Purchases in the War Department,
and for the first time since the Revolution the Army's supply system was
placed under the exclusive control of the Secretary of War. In May Congress
had made provision for an Ordnance Department, responsible for the inspection and testing of all ordnance, cannon balls, shells, and shot, the construction
of gun carriages and ammunition wagons, and the preparation and inspection
of the "public powder." It enlarged the Corps of Engineers by adding a company of bombardiers, sappers, and miners, and expanded and reorganized the
Military Academy at West Point. In addition to increasing the Regular Army,
Congress had authorized the President to accept volunteer forces and to call
upon the states for militia. The difficulty was not planning for an army, but
raising one.

One of the world's major powers was ranged against the United States,
but on the basis of available resources the two belligerents were rather evenly
matched. Most of Britain's forces were tied up in the war against Napoleon,
and for the time being very little military and naval assistance could be spared
for the defense of Canada. At the outbreak of the war, there were approximately
7,000 British and Canadian Regulars in Upper and Lower Canada (now the
provinces of Ontario and Quebec). With a total white population of only about
half a million, Canada itself had only a small reservoir of militia to draw upon.
When the war began, Maj. Gen. Isaac Brock, the military commander and
civil governor of Upper Canada, had 800 militiamen available in addition to
his approximately 1,600 Regulars. In the course of the war, the two provinces
put a total of about 10,000 militia in the field, whereas in the United States
probably 450,000 of the militia saw active service, although not more than half
of them ever got near the front. The support of Indian tribes gave Canada one
source of manpower that the United States lacked. After the Battle of Tippe-

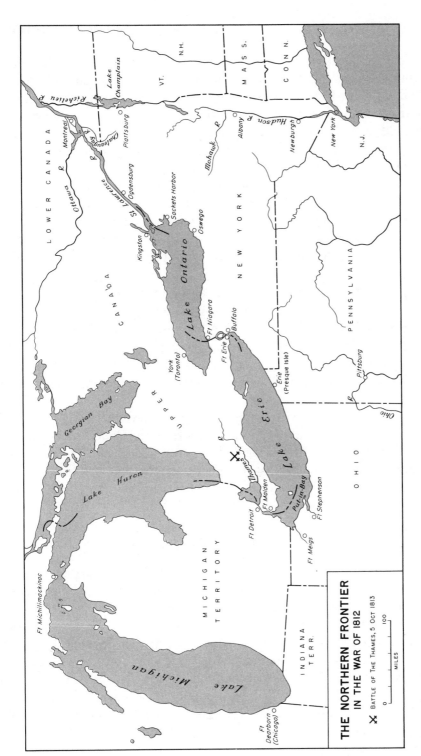

THE NORTHERN FRONTIER
IN THE WAR OF 1812

✗ BATTLE OF THE THAMES, 5 OCT 1813

MILES
0   100

MAP 15

canoe, Tecumseh had led his warriors across the border into Canada, where, along with the Canadian Indians, they joined the forces opposing the Americans. Perhaps 3,500 Indians were serving in the Canadian forces during the Thames River campaign in the fall of 1813, probably the largest number that took the field at any one time during the war.

The bulk of the British Navy was also fighting in the war against Napoleon. In September 1812, three months after the outbreak of war with the United States, Britain had no more than eleven ships of the line, thirty-four frigates, and about an equal number of smaller naval vessels in the western Atlantic. These were all that could be spared for operations in American waters, which involved the tremendous task of escorting British merchant shipping, protecting the St. Lawrence River, blockading American ports, and at the same time hunting down American frigates.

A significant weakness in the American position was the disunity of the country. In the New England states public opinion ranged from mere apathy to actively expressed opposition to the war. A good many Massachusetts and Connecticut shipowners fitted out privateers—privately owned and armed vessels that were commissioned to take enemy ships—but New England contributed little else to the prosecution of the war, and continued to sell grain and provisions to the British.

Canada was not faced with the same problem. Nevertheless, many inhabitants of Upper Canada were recent immigrants from the United States who had no great desire to take up arms against their former homeland, and there were other Canadians who thought that the superiority of the United States in men and material made any defense hopeless. That General Brock was able to overcome this spirit of defeatism is a tribute to his leadership.

The Strategic Pattern

The fundamental strategy was simple enough. The primary undertaking would be the conquest of Canada. The United States also planned an immediate naval offensive, whereby a swarm of privateers and the small Navy would be set loose on the high seas to destroy British commerce. The old invasion route into Canada by way of Lake Champlain and the Richelieu River led directly to the most populous and most important part of the enemy's territory. The capture of Montreal would cut the line of communications upon which the British defense of Upper Canada depended, and the fall of that province would then be inevitable. But this invasion route was near the center of disaffection in the United States, from which little local support could be expected. The west, where enthusiasm for the war ran high and where the Canadian forces were weak, offered a safer theater of operations though one with fewer strategic opportunities. Thus, in violation of the principles of objective and economy of force, the first assaults were delivered across the Detroit River and across the Niagara River between Lake Erie and Lake Ontario.

The war progressed through three distinct stages. In the first, lasting until the spring of 1813, England was so hard pressed in Europe that it could spare neither men nor ships in any great number for the conflict in North America. The United States was free to take the initiative, to invade Canada, and to send out cruisers and privateers against enemy shipping. During the second stage, lasting from early 1813 to the beginning of 1814, England was able to establish a tight blockade but still could not materially reinforce the troops in Canada. In this stage the American Army, having gained experience, won its first successes. The third stage, in 1814, was marked by the constant arrival in North America of British Regulars and naval reinforcements, which enabled the enemy to raid the North American coast almost at will and to take the offensive in several quarters. At the same time, in this final stage of the war, American forces fought their best fights and won their most brilliant victories.

The First Campaigns

The first blows of the war were struck in the Detroit area and at Fort Michilimackinac. President Madison gave Brig. Gen. William Hull, governor of the Michigan Territory, command of operations in that area. Hull arrived at Fort Detroit on July 5, 1812, with a force of about 1,500 Ohio militiamen and 300 Regulars, which he led across the river into Canada a week later. (*See Map 15.*) At that time the whole enemy force on the Detroit frontier amounted to about 150 British Regulars, 300 Canadian militiamen, and some 250 Indians led by Tecumseh. Most of the enemy were at Fort Malden, about twenty miles south of Detroit, on the Canadian side of the river. General Hull had been a dashing young officer in the Revolution, but by this time age and its infirmities had made him cautious and timid. Instead of moving directly against Fort Malden, Hull issued a bombastic proclamation to the people of Canada and stayed at the river landing almost opposite Detroit. He sent out several small raiding detachments along the Thames and Detroit Rivers, one of which returned after skirmishing with the British outposts near Fort Malden. In the meantime General Brock, who was both energetic and daring, sent a small party of British Regulars, Canadians, and Indians across the river from Malden to cut General Hull's communications with Ohio. By that time Hull was discouraged by the loss of Fort Michilimackinac, whose sixty defenders had quietly surrendered on July 17 to a small group of British Regulars supported by a motley force of fur traders and Indians that, at Brock's suggestion, had swiftly marched from St. Joseph Island, forty miles to the north. Hull also knew that the enemy in Fort Malden had received reinforcements (which he overestimated tenfold) and feared that Detroit would be completely cut off from its base of supplies. On August 7 he began to withdraw his force across the river into Fort Detroit. The last American had scarcely returned before the first men of Brock's force appeared and began setting up artillery opposite Detroit. By August 15 five guns were in position and opened fire on the fort, and the next morning Brock led his troops across the river. Before Brock could launch his assault, the Americans surrendered. Militiamen were released under parole; Hull and the Regulars were sent as prisoners to Montreal. Later paroled, Hull returned to face a court-martial for his conduct of the campaign, was sentenced to be shot, and was immediately pardoned.

On August 15, the day before the surrender, the small garrison at distant Fort Dearborn, acting on orders from Hull, had evacuated the post and started out for Detroit. The column was almost instantly attacked by a band of Indians who massacred the Americans before returning to destroy the fort.

With the fall of Michilimackinac, Detroit, and Dearborn, the entire territory north and west of Ohio fell under enemy control. The settlements in Indiana lay open to attack, the neighboring Indian tribes hastened to join the winning side, and the Canadians in the upper province lost some of the spirit of defeatism with which they had entered the war.

Immediately after taking Detroit, Brock transferred most of his troops to the Niagara frontier where he faced an American invasion force of 6,500 men. Maj. Gen. Stephen van Rensselaer, the senior American commander and a New York militiaman, was camped at Lewiston with a force of 900 Regulars and about 2,300 militiamen. Van Rensselaer owed his appointment not to any active military experience, for he had none, but to his family's position in New York. Inexperienced as he was in military art, van Rensselaer at least fought the enemy, which was more than could be said of the Regular Army commander in the theater, Brig. Gen. Alexander Smyth. Smyth and his 1,650 Regulars and nearly 400 militiamen were located at Buffalo. The rest of the American force, about 1,300 Regulars, was stationed at Fort Niagara.

Van Rensselaer planned to cross the narrow Niagara River and capture Queenston and its heights, a towering escarpment that ran perpendicular to the river south of the town. From this vantage point he hoped to command the area and eventually drive the British out of the Niagara peninsula. Smyth, on the other hand, wanted to attack above the falls, where the banks were low and the current less swift, and he refused to co-operate with the militia general. With a force ten times that of the British opposite him, van Rensselaer decided to attack alone. After one attempt had been called off for lack of oars for the boats, van Rensselaer finally ordered an attack for the morning of October 13. The assault force numbered 600 men, roughly half New York militiamen; but several boats drifted beyond the landing area, and the first echelon to land, numbering far less than 500, was pinned down for a time on the river bank below the heights until the men found an unguarded path, clambered to the summit, and, surprising the enemy, overwhelmed his fortified battery and drove him down into Queenston.

The Americans repelled a hastily formed counterattack later in the morning, during which General Brock was killed. This, however, was the high point of van Rensselaer's fortunes. Although 1,300 men were successfully ferried across the river under persistent British fire from a fortified battery north of town, less than half of them ever reached the American line on the heights. Most of the militiamen refused to cross the river, insisting on their legal right to remain on American soil, and General Smyth ignored van Rensselaer's request for Regulars. Meanwhile, British and Canadian reinforcements arrived in Queenston, and Maj. Gen. Roger Sheaffe, General Brock's successor, began to advance on the American position with a force of 800 troops and 300 Indian skirmishers. Van Rensselaer's men, tired and outnumbered, put up a stiff resistance on the heights but in the end were defeated—300 Americans were killed or wounded and nearly 1,000 were captured.

After the defeat at Queenston, van Rensselaer resigned and was succeeded by the unreliable Smyth, who spent his time composing windy proclamations. Disgusted at being marched down to the river on several occasions only to be marched back to camp again, the new army that had assembled after the battle of Queenston gradually melted away. The men who remained lost all sense of discipline, and finally at the end of November the volunteers were ordered home and the Regulars were sent into winter quarters. General Smyth's request for leave was hastily granted, and three months later his name was quietly dropped from the Army rolls.

Except for minor raids across the frozen St. Lawrence, there was no further fighting along the New York frontier until the following spring. During the Niagara campaign the largest force then under arms, commanded by Maj. Gen. Henry Dearborn, had been held in the neighborhood of Albany, more than 250 miles from the scene of operations. Dearborn had had a good record in the Revolutionary War and had served as Jefferson's Secretary of War. Persuaded to accept the command of the northern theater, except for Hull's forces, he was in doubt for some time about the extent of his authority over the Niagara front. When it was clarified he was reluctant to exercise it. Proposing to move his army, which included seven regiments of Regulars with artillery and dragoons, against Montreal in conjunction with a simultaneous operation across the Niagara River, Dearborn was content to wait for his subordinates to make the first move. When van Rensselaer made his attempt against Queenston, Dearborn, who was still in the vicinity of Albany, showed no sign of marching toward Canada. At the beginning of November he sent a large force north to Plattsburg and announced that he would personally lead the army into Montreal, but most of his force got no farther than the border. When his advanced guard was driven back to the village of Champlain by Canadian militiamen and Indians, and his Vermont and New York volunteers flatly refused to cross the border, Dearborn quietly turned around and marched back to Plattsburg, where he went into winter quarters.

If the land campaigns of 1812 reflected little credit on the Army, the war at sea brought lasting glory to the infant Navy. Until the end of the year the American frigates, brigs-of-war, and privateers were able to slip in and out of harbors and cruise almost at will, and in this period they won their most brilliant victories. At the same time, American privateers were picking off English merchant vessels by the hundreds. Having need of American foodstuffs, Britain was at first willing to take advantage of New England's opposition to the war by not extending the blockade to the New England coast, but by the beginning of 1814 it was effectively blockading the whole coast and had driven most American naval vessels and privateers off the high seas.

The Second Year, 1813

On land, the objects of the American plan of campaign for 1813 were the recapture of Detroit and an attack on Canada across Lake Ontario. (*See Map 15.*) For the Detroit campaign, Madison picked Brig. Gen. William H. Harrison, governor of the Indian Territory and hero of Tippecanoe. The difficulties of a winter campaign were tremendous, but the country demanded action. Harrison therefore started north toward Lake Erie at the end of October 1812 with some 6,500 men. In January 1813 a sizable detachment, about 1,000, pushed on to Frenchtown, a small Canadian outpost on the Raisin River twenty-six miles south of Detroit. There the American commander, Brig. Gen. James Winchester, positioned his men, their backs to the river with scant natural protection and their movements severely hampered by deep snow. A slightly larger force of British Regulars, militiamen, and Indians under Col. Henry Proctor soundly defeated the Americans, killing over 100 Kentucky riflemen and capturing approximately 500. The brutal massacre of wounded American prisoners by their Indian guards made "Remember the Raisin" the rallying cry of the Northwestern Army, but any plans for revenge had to be postponed, for Harrison had decided to suspend operations for the winter. He built Forts Meigs and Stephenson and posted his army near the Michigan border at the western end of Lake Erie.

The Ontario campaign was entrusted to General Dearborn, who was ordered to move his army from Plattsburg to Sackett's Harbor, where Commodore Isaac Chauncey had been assembling a fleet. Dearborn was to move across the lake to capture Kingston and destroy the British flotilla there, then proceed to York (now Toronto), the capital of Upper Canada, to capture military stores, and finally he was to co-operate with a force from Buffalo in seizing the forts on the Canadian side of the Niagara River.

The American strategy was sound. The capture of Kingston, the only tenable site for a naval station on the Canadian side of Lake Ontario, would give the United States control of the lake and, by cutting the British lines of communications, frustrate enemy plans for operations in the west. After the fall of Kingston, the operations against York and the Niagara forts would be simple mopping-up exercises. When the time came to move, however, Dearborn and Chauncey, hearing a rumor that the British forces in Kingston had been reinforced, decided to bypass that objective and attack York first. About 1,700 men were embarked and sailed up Lake Ontario without incident, arriving off York before daybreak on April 27. Dearborn, who was in poor health, turned over the command of the assault to Brig. Gen. Zebulon Pike, the explorer of the Southwest. The landing, about four miles west of the town, was virtually unopposed. The British garrison of about 600 men, occupying a fortification about halfway between the town and the landing, was overwhelmed after sharp resistance, but just as the Americans were pushing through the fort toward the town, a powder magazine exploded, killing or disabling many Americans and a number of British soldiers. Among those killed was General Pike. Remnants of the garrison fled toward Kingston, 150 miles to the east. The losses were heavy on both sides—almost 20 percent of Dearborn's forces had been killed or wounded. With General Dearborn incapacitated and General Pike dead, the troops apparently got out of hand. They looted and burned the public buildings and destroyed the provincial records. After holding the town for about a week, they recrossed the lake to Niagara to join an attack against the forts on the Canadian side of the Niagara River.

Meanwhile, Sackett's Harbor had been almost stripped of troops for the raid on York and for reinforcing the army at Fort Niagara. At Kingston, across the lake, Sir George Prevost, the Governor-General of Canada, had assembled a force of 800 British Regulars in addition to militia. Taking advantage of the absence of Chauncey's fleet, which was at the other end of the lake, Prevost launched an attack on Sackett's Harbor with his entire force of Regulars on the night of May 26. The town was defended by about 400 Regulars and approximately 750 militiamen, under the command of Brig. Gen. Jacob Brown of the New York militia. Brown posted his men in two lines in front of a fortified battery to cover a possible landing. Coming ashore under heavy fire the British nevertheless pressed rapidly forward, routed the first line, and pushed the second back into the prepared defenses. There the Americans held. The British then tried two frontal assaults, but were repulsed with heavy losses. While they were re-forming for a third attack, General Brown rallied the militia and sent them toward the rear of the enemy's right flank. This was the turning point. Having suffered serious losses and in danger of being cut off, the British hurriedly withdrew to their ships.

On the same day that Prevost sailed against Sackett's Harbor, General Dearborn at the western end of Lake Ontario was invading Canada with an army of 4,000 men. The operation began with a well-executed and stubbornly resisted amphibious assault led by Col. Winfield Scott and Commander Oliver Hazard Perry, USN, with Chauncey's fleet providing fire support. Outnumbered more than two to one, the British retreated, abandoning Fort George and Queenston to the Americans. (*Map 16*) An immediate pursuit might have sealed the victory, but Dearborn, after occupying Fort George, waited several days and then sent about 2,000 men after the enemy. The detachment advanced to within ten miles of the British and camped for the night with slight regard for security and even less for the enemy's audacity. During the night a force of about 700 British attacked the camp and thoroughly routed the Americans. Dearborn withdrew his entire army to Fort George. About two weeks later, a 500-man detachment ventured fifteen miles outside the fort and surrendered to a force of British and Indians that was half as large. After these reverses there was no further action of consequence on the Niagara front for the remainder of the year. Dearborn, again incapacitated by illness, resigned his commission in early July. Both armies were hard hit by disease, and the

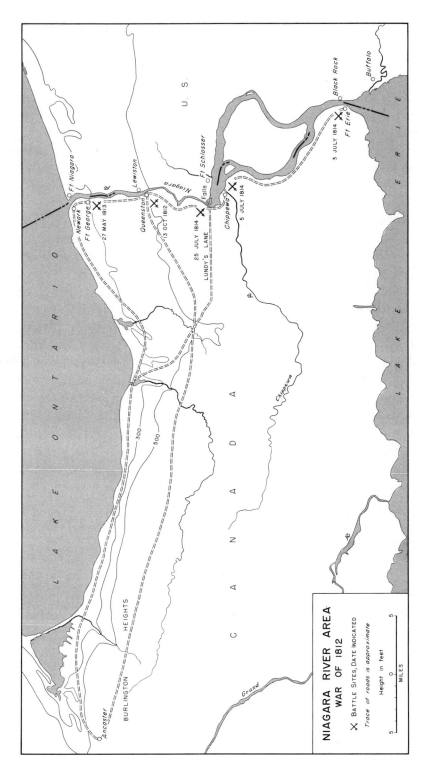

NIAGARA RIVER AREA
WAR OF 1812

X BATTLE SITES, DATE INDICATED

Trace of roads is approximate

Height in feet

MILES

MAP 16

American forces were further reduced by the renewal of the war in the west and by an attempt against Montreal.

Hull's disaster at Detroit in 1812 and Harrison's unsuccessful winter campaign had clearly shown that any offensive action in that quarter depended upon first gaining control of Lake Erie. Commander Perry had been assigned the task of building a fleet and seizing control of the lake. Throughout the spring and summer of 1813, except for the time he had joined Dearborn's force, the 27-year-old Perry had been busy at Presque Isle assembling his fleet, guns, and crews. By the beginning of August his force was superior to that of the British in every respect except long-range armament. Sailing up the lake, he anchored in Put-in-Bay, near the line still held by General Harrison in the vicinity of Forts Meigs and Stephenson, and there on September 10 Perry met the British Fleet, defeated it, and gained control of Lake Erie.

As soon as the damage to Perry's ships and the captured British vessels had been repaired, Harrison embarked his army and sailed against Fort Malden. A regiment of mounted Kentucky riflemen under Col. Richard M. Johnson moved along the shore of the lake toward Detroit. Vastly outnumbered on land and now open to attack from the water, the British abandoned both Forts Malden and Detroit and retreated eastward. Leaving a detachment to garrison the forts, Harrison set out after the enemy with the Kentucky cavalry regiments, five brigades of Kentucky volunteers, and a part of the 27th Infantry, a force of about 3,500 men. On October 5 he made contact with the British on the banks of the Thames River about eighty-five miles from Malden. (*See Map 15.*) The enemy numbered about 2,900, of whom about 900 were British Regulars and the remainder Indians under Tecumseh. Instead of attacking with infantry in the traditional line-against-line fashion, Harrison ordered a mounted attack. The maneuver succeeded completely. Unable to withstand the charging Kentuckians, the British surrendered in droves. The Indians were routed, and Tecumseh, who had brought so much trouble to the western frontier, was killed. Among those who distinguished themselves on that day was Commander Perry, who had ridden in the front rank of Johnson's charge.

As a result of the victory, which illustrated successful employment of the principles of offensive and mass, Lake Erie became an American lake. The Indian confederacy was shattered. The American position on the Detroit frontier was re-established, a portion of Canadian territory was brought under American control, and the enemy threat in that sector was eliminated. There was no further fighting here for the rest of the war.

The small remnant of the British force that had escaped capture at the Thames—no more than 250 soldiers and a few Indians—made its way overland to the head of Lake Ontario. Harrison, after discharging his Kentucky volunteers and arranging for the defenses of the Michigan Territory, sailed after it with the remainder of his army. He arrived at the Niagara frontier at an opportune time, since the American forces in that theater were being called upon to support a 2-pronged drive against Montreal.

The expedition against Montreal in the fall of 1813 was one of the worst fiascoes of the war. It involved a simultaneous drive by two forces: one, an army of about 4,000 men assembled at Plattsburg on Lake Champlain under the command of Brig. Gen. Wade Hampton and another, of about 6,000 men under the command of Maj. Gen. James Wilkinson, which was to attack down the St. Lawrence River from Sackett's Harbor. Hampton and Wilkinson were scarcely on speaking terms, and there was no one on the spot to command the two of them. Neither had sufficient strength to capture Montreal without the other's aid; each lacked confidence in the other, and both suspected that the War Department was leaving them in the lurch. At first contact with the British, about halfway down the Chateaugay River, Hampton retreated and, after falling back all the way to Plattsburg, resigned from the Army. Wilkinson, after a detachment of about 2,000 men was severely mauled in an engagement just north of Ogdensburg, also abandoned his part of the operation and followed Hampton into Plattsburg.

In the meantime, during December 1813 the British took advantage of the weakened state of American forces on the Niagara frontier to recapture Fort George and to cross the river and take Fort Niagara, which remained in British hands until the end of the war. Before evacuating Fort George the Americans had burned the town of Newark and part of Queenston. In retaliation the British, after assaulting Fort Niagara with unusual ferocity, loosed their Indian allies on the surrounding countryside and burned the town of Buffalo and the nearby village of Black Rock.

During 1813 a new theater of operations opened in the south. Andrew Jackson, an ardent expansionist and commander of the Tennessee militia, wrote the Secretary of War that he would "rejoice at the opportunity of placing the American eagle on the ramparts of Mobile, Pensacola, and Fort St. Augustine." (*Map 17*) For this purpose Tennessee had raised a force of 2,000 men to be under Jackson's command. Congress, after much debate, approved only an expedition into that part of the gulf coast in dispute between the United States and Spain, and refused to entrust the venture to the Tennesseans. Just before he went north to take part in the Montreal expedition, General Wilkinson led his Regulars into the disputed part of West Florida and, without meeting any

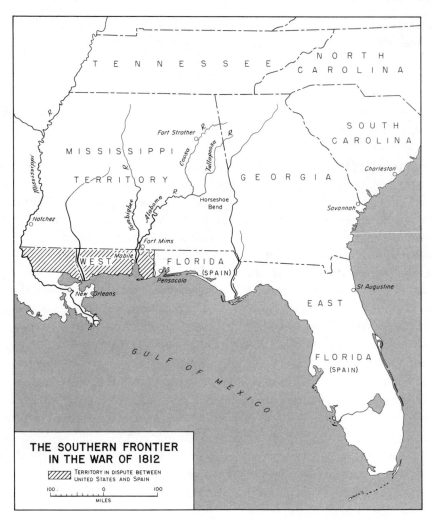

MAP 17

resistance, occupied Mobile, while the Tennessee army was left cooling its heels in Natchez.

An Indian uprising in that part of the Mississippi Territory soon to become Alabama saved General Jackson's military career. Inspired by Tecumseh's earlier successes, the Creek Indians took to the warpath in the summer of 1813 with a series of outrages culminating in the massacre of more than 500 men, women, and children at Fort Mims. Jackson, with characteristic energy, reassembled his army, which had been dismissed after Congress rejected its services for an attack on Florida, and moved into the Mississippi Territory. His own energy added to his problems, for he completely outran his primitive supply system and dangerously extended his line of communications. The hardships of the campaign and one near defeat at the hands of the Indians destroyed any enthusiasm the militia might have had for continuing in service. Jackson was compelled to entrench at Fort Strother, on the Coosa River, and remain there for several months until the arrival of a regiment of the Regular Army gave him the means to deal with the mutinous militia. At the end of March 1814 he decided that he had sufficient strength for a decisive blow against the Indians, who had gathered a force of about 900 warriors and many women and children in a fortified camp at the Horseshoe Bend of the Tallapoosa River. Jackson had about 2,000 militia and volunteers, nearly 600 Regulars, several hundred friendly Indians, and a few pieces of artillery. The attack was completely successful. A bayonet charge led by the Regulars routed the Indians, who were ruthlessly hunted down and all but a hundred or so of the warriors were killed. "I lament that two or three women and children were killed by accident," Jackson later reported. The remaining hostile tribes fled into Spanish territory. As one result of the campaign Jackson was appointed a major general in the Regular Army. The campaign against the Creeks had no other effect on the outcome of the war, but for that matter neither had any of the campaigns in the north up to this point.

Fighting also broke out during 1813 along the east coast where a British fleet blockaded the Delaware and Chesapeake Bays, bottling up the American frigates *Constellation* at Norfolk and *Adams* in the Potomac. (*Map 18*) Opposed only by small American gunboats, the British under Admiral Sir John Warren sought "to chastise the Americans into submission," and at the same time to relieve the pressure on Prevost's forces in Canada. With a flotilla, which at times numbered fifteen ships, Rear Adm. Sir George Cockburn, Warren's second-in-command, roamed the Chesapeake during the spring of 1813, burning and looting the prosperous countryside. Reinforced in June by 2,600 Regulars, Warren decided to attack Norfolk, its navy yard and the anchored *Constellation* providing the tempting targets. Norfolk's defenses rested chiefly on Craney Island, which guarded the narrow channel of the Elizabeth River. The island had a 7-gun fortification and was manned by 580 Regulars and militia in addition to 150 sailors and marines from the *Constellation*. The British planned to land an 800-man force on the mainland and, when low tide permitted, march onto the island in a flanking movement. As the tide rose, another 500 men would be rowed across the shoals for a frontal assault. On June 22 the landing party debarked four miles northwest of the island, but the flanking move was

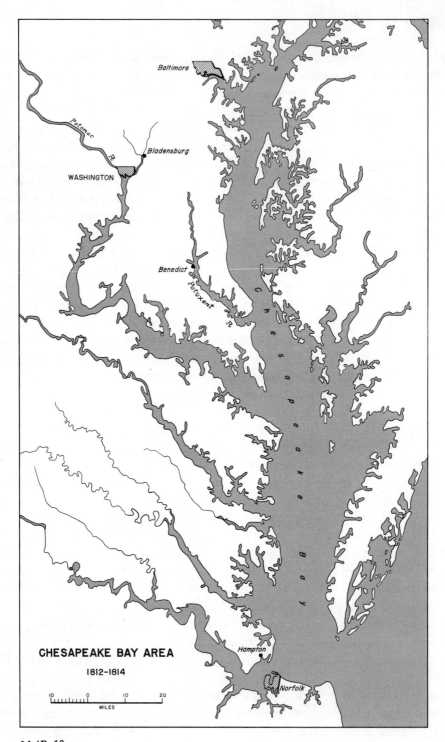

CHESAPEAKE BAY AREA

1812-1814

MILES

MAP 18

countered by the highly accurate marksmanship of the *Constellation's* gunners and was forced to pull back. The frontal assault also suffered from well-directed American fire, which sank three barges and threw the rest into confusion. After taking 81 casualties, the British sailed off in disorder. The defenders counted no casualties.

Frustrated at Norfolk, Warren crossed the Roads to Hampton where he overwhelmed the 450 militia defenders and pillaged the town. A portion of the fleet remained in the bay for the rest of the year, blockading and marauding, but the operation was not an unalloyed success. It failed to cause a diversion of American troops from the northern border and, by strengthening popular resentment (Cockburn was vilified throughout the country), helped unite Americans behind the war effort.

The conduct of the war in 1812 and 1813 revealed deficiencies in the administration of the War Department that would plague the American cause to the end. In early 1813 Madison replaced his incompetent Secretary of War William Eustis with John Armstrong, who instituted a reorganization that eventually resulted in the substitution of younger, more aggressive field commanders for the aged veterans of the Revolution. Congress then authorized an expansion of the Army staff to help the Secretary manage the war. In March it re-created the offices of Adjutant General, Inspector General, Surgeon, and Apothecary General and assigned eight topographical Engineers to the staff.

Competent leadership meant little, however, without sufficient logistical support, and logistics, more than any other factor, determined the nature of the military campaigns of the war. Lack of transportation was a major problem. The United States was fighting a war on widely separated fronts that required moving supplies through a wilderness where roads had to be built for wagons and packhorses. For this reason, ammunition and clothing supplies proved inadequate. General Harrison had to depend on homemade cartridges and clothing from Ohio townsmen for his northwestern campaign, and General Scott's Regulars would fight at Chippewa in the gray uniforms of the New York militia. Winter found the troops without blankets, inadequately housed, and without forage for their horses. Most important, the subsistence supply failed so completely that field commanders found it necessary to take local food procurement virtually into their own hands.

Transportation difficulties accounted for only part of the problem. The supply system devised in 1812 proved a resounding failure. Congressional intent notwithstanding, the Quartermaster General had never assumed accountability for the money and property administered by his subordinates or administrative control over his deputies in the south and northwest. Moreover, the functions of his office, never clearly defined, overlapped those of the Commissary General. In a vain attempt to unravel the administrative tangle, Congress created the office of Superintendent General of Military Supplies to keep account of all military stores and reformed the Quartermaster Department, giving the Quartermaster General stricter control over his deputies. In practice, however, the deputies continued to act independently in their own districts.

Both Congress and the War Department overlooked the greatest need for reform as the Army continued to rely on contractors for the collection and delivery of rations for the troops. With no centralized direction for subsistence supply, the inefficient, fraud-racked contract system proved to be one of the gravest hindrances to military operations throughout the war.

The Last Year of the War, 1814

After the setbacks at the end of 1813, a lull descended on the northern frontier. In March 1814 Wilkinson made a foray from Plattsburg with about 4,000 men and managed to penetrate about eight miles into Canada before some 200 British and Canadian troops stopped his advance. It was an even more miserable failure than his attempt of the preceding fall.

In early 1814 Congress increased the Army to 45 infantry regiments, 4 regiments of riflemen, 3 of artillery, 2 of light dragoons, and 1 of light artillery. The number of general officers was fixed at 6 major generals and 16 brigadier generals in addition to the generals created by brevet. Secretary of War Armstrong promoted Jacob Brown, who had been commissioned a brigadier general in the Regular Army after his heroic defense of Sackett's Harbor, to the rank of major general and placed him in command of the Niagara–Lake Ontario theater. He also promoted the youthful George Izard to major general and gave him command of the Lake Champlain frontier. He appointed six new brigadier generals from the ablest, but not necessarily most senior, colonels in the Regular Army, among them Winfield Scott, who had distinguished himself at the battle of Queenston Heights and who was now placed in command at Buffalo.

British control of Lake Ontario, won by dint of feverish naval construction during the previous winter, obliged the Secretary of War to recommend operations from Buffalo, but disagreement within the President's cabinet delayed adoption of a plan until June. Expecting Commodore Chauncey's naval force at Sackett's Harbor to be strong enough to challenge the British Fleet, Washington decided upon a co-ordinated attack on the Niagara peninsula. (*See Map 16.*) Secretary Armstrong instructed General Brown to cross the Niagara

River in the vicinity of Fort Erie and, after assaulting the fort, either to move against Fort George and Newark or to seize and hold a bridge over the Chippewa River, as he saw fit.

Brown accordingly crossed the Niagara River on July 3 with his force of 3,500 men, took Fort Erie, and then advanced toward the Chippewa River, sixteen miles away. There a smaller British force, including 1,500 Regulars, had gathered to oppose the Americans. General Brown posted his army in a strong position behind a creek with his right flank resting on the Niagara River and his left protected by a swamp. In front of the American position was an open plain, beyond which flowed the Chippewa River; on the other side of the river were the British.

In celebration of Independence Day, General Scott had promised his brigade a grand parade on the plain the next day. On July 5 he formed his troops, numbering about 1,300, but on moving forward discovered British Regulars who had crossed the river undetected, lined up on the opposite edge of the plain. Scott ordered his men to charge and the British advanced to meet them. The two lines approached each other, alternately stopping to fire and then moving forward, closing the gaps torn by musketry and artillery fire. They came together first at the flanks, while about sixty or eighty yards apart at the center. At this point the British line crumbled and broke. By the time a second brigade sent forward by General Brown reached the battlefield, the British had withdrawn across the Chippewa River and were retreating toward Ancaster, on Lake Ontario. Scott's casualties amounted to 48 killed and 227 wounded; British losses were 137 killed and 304 wounded.

Brown followed the retreating British as far as Queenston, where he halted to await Commodore Chauncey's fleet. After waiting two weeks for Chauncey, who failed to co-operate in the campaign, Brown withdrew to Chippewa. He proposed to strike out to Ancaster by way of a crossroad known as Lundy's Lane, from which he could reach the Burlington Heights at the head of Lake Ontario and at the rear of the British.

Meanwhile the British had drawn reinforcements from York and Kingston, and more troops were on the way from Lower Canada. Sixteen thousand British veterans, fresh from Wellington's victories over the French in Europe, had just arrived in Canada, too late to participate in the Niagara campaign but in good time to permit the redeployment of the troops that had been defending the upper St. Lawrence. By the time General Brown decided to pull back from Queenston, the British force at Ancaster amounted to about 2,200 men under General Phineas Riall; another 1,500 British troops were gathered at Fort George and Fort Niagara at the mouth of the Niagara River.

As soon as Brown began his withdrawal, Riall sent forward about 1,000 men along Lundy's Lane, the very route by which General Brown intended to advance against Burlington Heights; another force of more than 600 British moved out from Fort George and followed Brown along the Queenston road; while a third enemy force of about 400 men moved along the American side of the Niagara River from Fort Niagara. Riall's advance force reached the junction of Lundy's Lane and the Queenston road on the night of July 24, the same night that Brown reached Chippewa, about three miles distant. Concerned lest the British force on the opposite side of the Niagara cut his line of communications and entirely unaware of Riall's force at Lundy's Lane, General Brown on July 25 ordered Scott to take his brigade back along the road toward Queenston in the hope of drawing back the British force on the other side of the Niagara; but in the meantime that force had crossed the river and joined Riall's men at Lundy's Lane. Scott had not gone far when much to his surprise he discovered himself face-to-face with the enemy.

The ensuing battle, most of which took place after nightfall, was the hardest fought, most stubbornly contested engagement of the war. For two hours Scott attacked and repulsed the counterattacks of the numerically superior British force, which, moreover, had the advantage in position. Then both sides were reinforced. With Brown's whole contingent engaged the Americans now had a force equal to that of the British, about 2,900. They were able to force back the enemy from its position and capture its artillery. The battle then continued without material advantage to either side until just before midnight, when General Brown ordered the exhausted Americans to fall back to their camp across the Chippewa River. The equally exhausted enemy was unable to follow. Losses on both sides had been heavy, each side incurring about 850 casualties. On the American side, both General Brown and General Scott were severely wounded, Scott so badly that he saw no further service during the war. On the British side, General Riall and his superior, General Drummond, who had arrived with the reinforcements, were wounded, and Riall was taken prisoner.

But sides claimed Lundy's Lane as a victory, as well they might; but Brown's invasion of Canada was halted. Commodore Chauncey, who failed to prevent the British from using Lake Ontario for supply and reinforcements, contributed to the unfavorable outcome. In contrast to the splendid co-operation between Harrison and Perry on Lake Erie, relations between Brown and Chauncey were far from satisfactory. A few days after the Battle of Lundy's Lane the American army withdrew to Fort Erie and held this outpost on Canadian soil until early in November.

Reinforced after Lundy's Lane, the British laid siege to Fort Erie at the beginning of August but were forced to abandon the effort on September 21 after heavy losses. Shortly afterward General Izard arrived with reinforcements from Plattsburg and advanced as far as Chippewa, where the British were strongly entrenched. After a few minor skirmishes, he ceased operations for the winter. The works at Fort Erie were destroyed, and the army withdrew to American soil on November 5.

During the summer of 1814 the British had been able to reinforce Canada and to stage several raids on the American coast. Eastport, Maine, on Passamaquoddy Bay, and Castine, at the mouth of the Penobscot River, were occupied without resistance. This operation was something more than a raid since Eastport lay in disputed territory, and it was no secret that Britain wanted a rectification of the boundary. No such political object was attached to British forays in the region of Chesapeake Bay. (*See Map 18.*) On August 19 a force of some 4,000 British troops under Maj. Gen. Robert Ross landed on the Patuxent River and marched on Washington. At the Battle of Bladensburg, five days later, Ross easily dispersed 5,000 militia, naval gunners, and Regulars hastily gathered together to defend the Capital. The British then entered Washington, burned the Capitol, the White House, and other public buildings, and returned to their ships.

Baltimore was next on the schedule, but that city had been given time to prepare its defenses. The land approach was covered by a rather formidable line of redoubts; the harbor was guarded by Fort McHenry and blocked by a line of sunken gunboats. On September 13 a spirited engagement fought by Maryland militia, many of whom had run at Bladensburg just two weeks before, delayed the invaders and caused considerable loss, including General Ross, who was killed. When the fleet failed to reduce Fort McHenry, the assault on the city was called off.

Two days before the attack on Baltimore, the British suffered a much more serious repulse on Lake Champlain. After the departure of General Izard for the Niagara front, Brig. Gen. Alexander Macomb had remained at Plattsburg with a force of about 3,300 men. Supporting this force was a small fleet under Commodore Thomas Macdonough. Across the border in Canada was an army of British veterans of the Napoleonic Wars whom Sir George Prevost was to lead down the route taken by Burgoyne thirty-seven years before. Moving slowly up the Richelieu River toward Lake Champlain, he crossed the border and on September 6 arrived before Plattsburg with about 11,000 men. There he waited for almost a week until his naval support was ready to join the attack. With militia reinforcements, Macomb now had about 4,500 men manning a strong line of redoubts and blockhouses that faced a small river. Macdonough had anchored his vessels in Plattsburg Bay, out of range of British guns, but in a position to resist an assault on the American line. On September 11 the British flotilla appeared and Prevost ordered a joint attack. There was no numerical disparity between the naval forces, but an important one in the quality of the seamen. Macdonough's ships were manned by well-trained seamen and gunners, the British ships by hastily recruited French-Canadian militia and soldiers, with only a sprinkling of regular seamen. As the enemy vessels came into the bay the wind died, and the British were exposed to heavy raking fire from Macdonough's long guns. The British worked their way in, came to anchor, and the two fleets began slugging at each other, broadside by broadside. At the end the British commander was dead and his ships battered into submission. Prevost immediately called off the land attack and withdrew to Canada the next day.

Macdonough's victory ended the gravest threat that had arisen so far. More important it gave impetus to peace negotiations then under way. News of the two setbacks—Baltimore and Plattsburg—reached England simultaneously, aggravating the war weariness of the British and bolstering the efforts of the American peace commissioners to obtain satisfactory terms.

New Orleans: The Final Battle

The progress of the peace negotiations influenced the British to continue an operation that General Ross, before his repulse and death at Baltimore, had been instructed to carry out, a descent upon the gulf coast to capture New Orleans and possibly sever Louisiana from the United States. (*See Map 17.*) Major General Sir Edward Pakenham was sent to America to take command of the expedition. On Christmas Day, 1814, Pakenham arrived at the mouth of the Mississippi to find his troops disposed on a narrow isthmus below New Orleans between the Mississippi River and a cypress swamp. They had landed two weeks earlier at a shallow lagoon some ten miles east of New Orleans and had already fought one engagement. In this encounter, on December 23, General Jackson, who had taken command of the defenses on December 1, almost succeeded in cutting off an advance detachment of 2,000 British, but after a 3-hour fight in which casualties on both sides were heavy, he was compelled to retire behind fortifications covering New Orleans.

Opposite the British and behind a ditch stretching from the river to the swamp, Jackson had raised earthworks high enough to require scaling ladders for an assault. The defenses were manned by about 3,500 men with another 1,000 in reserve. It was a varied group, composed of the 7th and 44th Infantry Regi-

BATTLE OF NEW ORLEANS

ments, Major Beale's New Orleans Sharpshooters, LaCoste and Daquin's battalions of free Negroes, the Louisiana militia under General David Morgan, a
band of Choctaw Indians, the Baratorian pirates, and a motley battalion of fash-
ionably dressed sons and brothers of the New Orleans aristocracy. To support his
defenses, Jackson had assembled more than twenty pieces of artillery, including
a battery of nine heavy guns on the opposite bank of the Mississippi.

After losing an artillery duel to the Americans on January 1, Pakenham
decided on a frontal assault in combination with an attack against the American
troops on the west bank. The main assault was to be delivered by about 5,300
men, while about 600 men under Lt. Col. William Thornton were to cross the
river and clear the west bank. As the British columns appeared out of the early
morning mist on January 8, they were met with murderous fire, first from the
artillery, then from the muskets and rifles of Jackson's infantry. Achieving mass
through firepower, the Americans mowed the British down by the hundreds.
Pakenham and one other general were killed and a third badly wounded. More
than 2,000 of the British were casualties; the American losses were trifling.

Suddenly, the battle on the west bank became critical. Jackson did not make
adequate preparations to meet the advance there until the British began their
movement, but by then it was too late. The heavy guns of a battery posted on the
west bank were not placed to command an attack along that side of the river

and only about 800 militia, divided in two groups a mile apart, were in position
to oppose Thornton. The Americans resisted stubbornly, inflicting greater losses
than they suffered, but the British pressed on, routed them, and overran the
battery. Had the British continued their advance Jackson's position would have
been critical, but Pakenham's successor in command, appalled by the repulse of
the main assault, ordered Thornton to withdraw from the west bank and rejoin
the main force. For ten days the shattered remnant of Pakenham's army remained in camp unmolested by the Americans, then re-embarked and sailed
away.

The British appeared off Mobile on February 8, confirming Jackson's fear
that they planned an attack in that quarter. They overwhelmed Fort Bowyer, a
garrison manned by 360 Regulars at the entrance to Mobile Harbor. Before they
could attack the city itself, word arrived that a treaty had been signed at Ghent
on Christmas Eve, two weeks before the Battle of New Orleans.

The news of the peace settlement followed so closely on Jackson's triumph
in New Orleans that the war as a whole was popularly regarded in the United
States as a great victory. Yet at best it was a draw. American strategy had
centered on the conquest of Canada and the harassment of British shipping; but
the land campaign failed, and during most of the war the Navy was bottled
up behind a tight British blockade of the North American coast.

If it favored neither belligerent, the war at least taught the Americans
several lessons. Although the Americans were proud of their reputation as the
world's most expert riflemen, the rifle played only a minor role in the war.
On the other hand, the American soldier displayed unexpected superiority in
gunnery and engineering. Artillery contributed to American successes at
Chippewa, Sackett's Harbor, Norfolk, the siege of Fort Erie, and New Orleans.
The war also boosted the reputation of the Corps of Engineers, a branch which
owed its efficiency chiefly to the Military Academy. Academy graduates completed the fortifications at Fort Erie, built Fort Meigs, planned the harbor
defenses of Norfolk and New York, and directed the fortifications at Plattsburg. If larger numbers of infantrymen had been as well trained as the
artillerymen and engineers, the course of the war might have been entirely
different.

Sea power played a fundamental role in the war. In the west both opponents
were handicapped in overland communication, but the British were far more
dependent on the Great Lakes for the movement of troops and supplies for the
defense of Upper Canada. In the east, Lake Champlain was strategically important as an invasion corridor to the populous areas of both countries. Just

as Perry's victory on Lake Erie decided the outcome of the war in the far west, Macdonough's success on Lake Champlain decided the fate of the British invasion in 1814 and helped influence the peace negotiations.

The militia performed as well as the Regular Army. The defeats and humiliations of the Regular forces during the first years of the war matched those of the militia, just as in a later period the Kentucky volunteers at the Thames and the Maryland militia before Baltimore proved that the state citizen soldier could perform well. The keys to the militiaman's performance, of course, were training and leadership, the two areas over which the national government had little control. The militia, occasionally competent, was never dependable, and in the nationalistic period that followed the war when the exploits of the Regulars were justly celebrated, an ardent young Secretary of War, John Calhoun, would be able to convince Congress and the nation that the first line of defense should be a standing army.

CHAPTER 7

The Thirty Years' Peace

When an express rider galloped into Washington on the night of February 13, 1815, with the news that the War of 1812 was over, ended by the treaty signed at Ghent on Christmas Eve 1814, there began the period in American military history sometimes called "The Thirty Years' Peace." Though border warfare with the Indians flared up from time to time, no foreign enemy during these thirty years seriously menaced the peace of the United States.

Toward a Professional Army

Yet in 1815 a long period of freedom from foreign aggression could hardly have been foreseen. After Wellington's victory at Waterloo in June, there was a general expectation in Europe that America would have another war with England. This was reported to Secretary of State James Monroe by Brig. Gen. Winfield Scott, who was in Paris in the summer of 1815 observing the magnificent victory parades of Britain and its allies, collecting every current book, in French and in English, on army management and training, and studying the tactics of the Napoleonic Wars.

The Napoleonic Wars had revived the old tactical issue of column versus line. Linear tactics, well adapted to the highly trained professional armies of the eighteenth century, which aimed to win battles by maneuver, were unsuited to the huge conscript armies under Napoleon. He therefore employed the massed column as the formation for attack, using skirmishers to provide flexibility. In addition, by giving his artillery an unprecedented degree of mobility he was able to mass his firepower at critical points on the battlefield. Yet the issue of massed column versus line had not really been settled, for Napoleon had after all lost the war and the British ascribed their victories to their "thin red lines."

Those who sought to return to the "good old days" while at the same time retaining the best features of Napoleonic warfare found support in the writings of Maj. Gen. Antoine Henri Jomini, who analyzed the Napoleonic Wars in terms of basic principles and of classic, traditional warfare. His first work, *Traité des Grandes Operations Militaires,* published in 1804–05, was early brought to the United States; his greatest work, *Précis de l'Art de la Guerre,* published in 1838, had a profound effect on military thought in America. The influence of Jomini's great contemporary, Maj. Gen. Karl von Clausewitz, was not felt in the United States until long after; the latter's *Vom Krieg,* published posthumously in 1831, was not translated into English until 1873.

The Americans of 1815 were less receptive to the concept of "total war" than were the Americans of the Revolutionary period. In the War of 1812 there had been no surge of revolutionary ardor. Only a small portion of the nation had been directly involved. Neither side had attempted to destroy the other's capacity for continuing the war.

The glory of the victories on the Niagara frontier in 1814 had gone not to the citizen soldier but to the professional. The citizen soldier properly led, as at the Battle of New Orleans, had on occasion done well; but after the war many military realists questioned the ability of the Army to employ him effectively. There were several reasons. It was extremely hard to obtain from state governments accurate figures on how many militiamen were available. Moreover, the states jealously kept control of arming, disciplining, and training their militia. Though training was crucial, the War Department was limited to making recommendations and supplying training manuals. The Army could not enforce the type of rigorous training that had enabled General Scott to convert Regular soldiers—some of them as raw as militiamen—into the professionals who had excited the admiration even of the British at Chippewa and Lundy's Lane.

As soon as President Madison proclaimed the peace in February 1815, the Congress, forced to meet at Blodgett's Hotel because the Capitol lay in blackened ruins, acted promptly to create a small but efficient professional army that was thought adequate—with the addition of the militia—to guard against a repetition of the disasters of the War of 1812. Congress voted a peacetime army of 10,000 men (in addition to the Corps of Engineers), about a third of the actual wartime strength, a figure in marked contrast to the 3,220-man Regular peacetime establishment under President Jefferson. Organization and leadership were improved. The 9 wartime military districts, headed generally by superannuated holdovers from the Revolution, were converted into 2 divisions, a northern with 4 territorial departments and a southern with 5, commanded by officers who had made their reputations in the War of 1812, Maj. Gen. Jacob Brown, Division of the North, and Maj. Gen. Andrew Jackson, Division of the South.

By midsummer 1815, for the first time in nearly a year, President Madison had a full-time Secretary of War. After the forced resignation of Secretary of War John Armstrong at the end of August 1814, mainly as a result of the burning of Washington, Secretary of State James Monroe served as Secretary of War until March 1815 when illness induced him to turn over the office to Secretary of the Treasury Alexander J. Dallas as an additional duty. In the spring of 1815 President Madison appointed William H. Crawford, Minister to France, Secretary of War. By August 1815 he had returned from Paris and was able to take up his duties.

Crawford had a record of distinguished service in the U.S. Senate. He had declined the appointment as Secretary of War later offered to Armstrong, but had maintained a deep interest in the War Department, especially in the General Staff created by Congress in the spring of 1813. Because its purpose was mainly to conduct the housekeeping functions of the Army, it was not a general staff as the term was used a hundred years later, but resembled rather the modern special staff. Under it had been placed the Quartermaster's, Topographical, Adjutant General's, Inspector General's, Ordnance, Hospital, Purchasing, and Pay Departments; the Judge Advocates; the Chaplains; the Military Academy; and the commanding generals of the nine military districts and their logistical staffs. Furthermore, by stationing in Washington at the War Department certain officers of the General Staff—the Adjutant and Inspector General (a dual function performed by one officer) with two assistants, the Commissary General of Ordnance with three assistants, the Paymaster of the Army, and the Assistant Topographical Engineer—Congress had provided a management staff for the Secretary of War, who hitherto had only a few clerks to assist him.

Watching events from Paris in the fall of 1813, Crawford begged Albert Gallatin "For God's sake" to "endeavor to rid the army of old women and blockheads, at least on the general staff." The reorganization of the Army in the spring of 1815 weeded out most of the incompetents. When Crawford took office he recommended to Congress the retention of the General Staff because, as he stated in his recommendation, the history of the early campaigns in the late war had convinced him of "the necessity of giving to the military establishment, in time of peace, the organization which it must have to render it efficient in a state of war."

The only major change he recommended was the addition of the Quartermaster General to the management staff in Washington. He also recommended an increase in the Corps of Engineers. Congress put Crawford's proposals into effect by the act of April 24, 1816, and a few days later authorized the President to employ a "skilful assistant" in the Corps of Engineers, thus securing the services of a brilliant military engineer, General Simon Bernard, who had served under Napoleon. Congress also voted $838,000 for a major program of coast fortification, an effort intended to prevent a repetition of the humiliations suffered in the War of 1812.

At the same time, $115,800 was appropriated for new buildings at the U.S. Military Academy at West Point and $22,171 for the Academy's books, maps, and instruments. Under Crawford's sponsorship, facilities and staff of the Academy were expanded, the curriculum was broadened, regulations for admission were tightened, and provision was made for a Board of Visitors. In September 1816 the cadets first received gray uniforms, honoring (according to tradition) the Regulars of Chippewa and Lundy's Lane, who wore rough gray kersey because they lacked jackets of regulation blue.

Having fostered a peacetime professional army, Crawford might have used his considerable influence with Congress to strengthen it if he had been left in office longer, as he wished, but in the fall of 1816 President Madison asked him to resign and become Secretary of the Treasury in order to bring Henry Clay into the cabinet as Secretary of War. Clay and several others declined the appointment. For more than a year George Graham, the War Department's chief clerk, was Acting Secretary of War. During that period, as the threat from Europe lessened, Congress began to lose interest in the peacetime army. The actual strength had fallen to about 8,200 men at the time John C. Calhoun took the oath as Secretary of War on December 8, 1817. The new Secretary was faced with proposals to cut the Army's authorized strength, abolish the General Staff, and discontinue the Military Academy. But before Calhoun could devote his talents to staving off such proposals, he was faced with an outbreak of Indian warfare on the border between Georgia and the Spanish province of Florida.

The War Hatchet Raised in Florida

The Indians threatening the Georgia frontier were the Lower Creeks, a faction of the Creek Nation which had fled to Florida after being defeated in 1814. Called the "Red Sticks" from their red war clubs, they settled in the swamps and palmetto forests along with Seminole Indians and bands of fugitive Negro slaves and were unrestrained by weak Spanish officials, shut up in their enclaves at St. Augustine on the east coast, St. Marks in central northern Florida, and Pensacola on the west.

The Lower Creeks and Seminoles had been incited to attack American settlers in Georgia by two British adventurers from the Bahamas. One was Lt. Col. Edward Nicholls, who had employed the Indians in his abortive expedition against Mobile in the summer of 1814 and had left them well armed when he sailed away to England in 1815. Another was a trader, Alexander Arbuthnot. Both preached to the Lower Creeks the same false doctrine that the southern part of Georgia, which had been surrendered by the Creeks in the treaty of 1814, had been returned to them by the Treaty of Ghent, and that therefore Americans were settling on lands that belonged to the Indians.

By the fall of 1817 the U.S. Army was attempting to protect the settlers by reinforcing Fort Scott, a log fort built at the southwestern tip of Georgia where the Chattahoochee and Flint Rivers combine to form the Apalachicola, which, flowing through Florida to the Gulf, provided a supply route from Mobile or New Orleans to the fort. At the end of November 1817 an Army keelboat ascending the Apalachicola in advance of supply transports was attacked from the bank by a party of Indians who killed or captured thirty-four of the forty persons aboard—soldiers and wives of soldiers.

The news of the attack, reaching Washington on December 26, 1817, brought on the conflict known as the First Seminole War. Calhoun ordered Maj. Gen. Andrew Jackson to proceed immediately from Nashville to Fort Scott and take command, authorizing him, in case he thought the force on the scene insufficient—800 Regulars and about 1,000 Georgia militia—to request additional militia. Jackson, who had already reported to the War Department that he was expecting trouble in Florida, "The war hatchet having been raised," acted promptly. Calculating that the 3-month Georgia militia might have gone home before he could arrive at Fort Scott, he sent out a call for a thousand 6-month volunteers from West Tennessee. Dispatching to Fort Hawkins, in central Georgia, an officer with $2,000 to buy provisions and ordering further stores to come forward by ship from New Orleans, Jackson, escorted by two mounted companies, set off in advance of the troops.

Riding into Fort Hawkins on the evening of February 9, he was enraged to discover that the contractor who had agreed to supply him with rations had failed to do so. For more than a thousand men, he reported to Calhoun, there was not "a barrel of flour or a bushel of corn." Procuring locally some pigs, corn, and peanuts, he kept going, arriving at Fort Scott on March 9. There he learned that ships loaded with provisions from Mobile had come into the mouth of the Apalachicola. To Jackson it was all-important to protect these boats from Indians who might attack them from the riverbank. He set off next morning with his Georgia militiamen and about 400 Regulars from Fort

Scott on a protective march down the east bank of the Apalachicola. Six days later he was at the river mouth. There he halted his force and ordered Lt. James Gadsden of the Corps of Engineers to build a fort, named Fort Gadsden, for storing the supplies he was expecting from New Orleans.

His supply flotilla, delayed by a gale, did not arrive until March 25. The following day he began his campaign. His objective was a large Indian settlement on the Suwannee River, some 150 miles to the east, where a force of several thousand Indians and Negroes under a Seminole chief, Billy Bowlegs, was said to be preparing for battle. But because Jackson needed a supply base nearer than Fort Gadsden, he decided to take the Spanish fort of St. Marks on the way and arranged for his supplies to be brought by ship to the bay of St. Marks.

Stopping at the Ochlokonee River to make canoes for the crossing and farther along to clean out some Indian villages, on April 7 Jackson took St. Marks, in the process capturing Arbuthnot, whom he imprisoned. In the meantime a brigade of friendly Upper Creek Indians had ridden up, also the first detachment of the Tennessee volunteers. Because of the failure in supply, the main body of Tennesseeans did not catch up with Jackson until April 11, when he was well on the swampy trail to Bowlegs' Town.

The campaign was something of an anticlimax. From Bowlegs' Town the Indians and Negroes had fled, having been warned by Arbuthnot. The only gains were corn and cattle to feed the troops and the capture of a third adventurer from the Bahamas, Robert C. Ambrister, who had been arming and drilling Bowlegs' men. Ambrister was taken back to St. Marks and along with Arbuthnot was tried by a military court and executed. Dismissing the Georgia militia and the Indian brigade, Jackson proceeded west with his Regulars and Tennesseeans. At Fort Gadsden early in May he learned that Indians were assembling in Pensacola. He seized Pensacola, ran up the American flag, and left a garrison there as well as at St. Marks when he returned to Nashville late in May.

Jackson's highhanded actions in the First Seminole War—his invasion of Spanish territory, capture of Spanish forts, and execution of British subjects—might have had serious diplomatic repercussions if Spain or Great Britain had chosen to make an issue of them; but neither nation did. Negotiations with Spain for the purchase of Florida were already under way, and shortly after the return of the forts to Spain, Florida was ceded to the United States in February 1819 by the Adams-Onís Treaty.

For the Army, the most significant aspect of the war had been the breakdown in supply. From the time Jackson rode out of Nashville in late January 1818 until his first encounter with the Indians early in April, he had had to devote all his energies to feeding his troops. The reason had been the failure of civilian contractors. The folly of depending on civilians for so essential an item as rations had been demonstrated by the War of 1812, to Calhoun as well as to the Army. Jackson's experience in the First Seminole War underlined it. At Calhoun's suggestion the Congress in April 1818 required contractors to deliver rations in bulk at depots and provided a better system of transportation and stricter control by the Army. For the first time since the Revolutionary War, the Army had a Subsistence Department, headed by a Commissary General of Subsistence.

John C. Calhoun and the War Department

Calhoun was convinced that the American frontier ought to be protected by Regulars rather than by militia. Calling the militia into active service, he wrote Brig. Gen. Edmund P. Gaines, was "harassing to them and exhausting to the treasury. Protection is the first object, and the second is protection by the regular force." But providing a Regular force capable of protecting the frontiers north, south, and west, as well as the seacoast, was another matter. In 1820 the Congress called upon the Secretary of War to report upon a plan for the reduction of the Army to about 6,000 men. Calhoun suggested that the reduction, if it had to come, could be effected by cutting the enlisted personnel of each company to half strength. In time of war the Army could be quickly expanded to a force of approximately 19,000 officers and men. This was the start of the "expansible army" concept. Congress rejected Calhoun's plan, however, and reduced not only the company strength—in the case of the infantry companies 26 men were dropped, leaving only 42—but also the number of regiments.

The act of March 2, 1821, provided for 7 regiments of infantry and 4 regiments of artillery instead of the existing 8 regiments of infantry, a rifle regiment, a regiment of light artillery, and a corps of artillery comprising 8 battalions. The Ordnance Department was staffed by artillery officers; no ordnance officers were commissioned until 1832. The Northern and Southern Divisions were abolished and replaced by an Eastern and a Western Department, under the respective commands of Brig. Gen. Winfield Scott and General Gaines. Only one major general was provided. Because General Jackson had resigned from the Army to become Governor of Florida, the commission remained with Maj. Gen. Jacob Brown.

To provide a senior line officer in the chain of command, lack of which had been a serious deficiency in the War of 1812, Calhoun brought Brown to Washington in a position which later became known as Commanding General of the Army. Brown held it until his death in 1828, when he was succeeded by

Maj. Gen. Alexander Macomb. When Macomb died in 1841, Maj. Gen. Winfield Scott was appointed. Made brevet lieutenant general in 1847 (the first three-star general since George Washington), Scott served until his retirement in 1861.

In Calhoun's administration other important innovations in Army management were accomplished. Beginning in mid-1822 recruiting depots were opened in major cities, east and west, to enlist men for the Army at large, not for specific units. Though regimental recruiting continued, the General Recruiting Service in its first three years of operation enlisted about 68 percent more men than did the regiments. General Scott prepared a new manual of infantry tactics for Regulars and militia and, on the basis of his research in Paris in 1815, prepared the Army regulations of 1821, going minutely into every detail of the soldier's life, including the ingredients of his soup. The soldier's diet was further improved by the first commissioned Surgeon General, Joseph Lovell, who was appointed by Calhoun. Also, by requiring daily weather reports from all medical officers, in an attempt to find some correlation between weather and army diseases, Lovell provided basic data for the first study of weather in the United States and the most complete data of the sort in the world.

Under Calhoun, the work of seacoast fortification went steadily forward. By 1826 eighteen harbors and ports from the Penobscot River to the mouth of the Mississippi had been fortified with a total of thirty-one works, consisting in general of sloping earthworks covered with grass and backed by stone or brick walls. By 1843 the harbor defense program had been extended to 35 or 40 coastal areas with 69 fortifications either in place or under construction. By then greater emphasis was being placed on heavy artillery (24- and 32-pounder guns a. d 8-inch howitzers) to keep pace with increasingly heavy naval armaments.

Calhoun early turned his attention to the Military Academy, where Crawford's attempts at rehabilitation had been impeded by controversy stirred up by the arbitrary actions of the superintendent, Capt. Alden Partridge. After Partridge was removed and Bvt. Maj. Sylvanus Thayer was appointed superintendent in July 1817, the Academy became a vital force in maintaining a corps of professionally trained officers. Thayer had been sent by the War Department to Europe in 1815—one of the first of a succession of Army officers sent abroad in the early nineteenth century—to study, among other things, foreign military schools. With Calhoun's support, he organized the West Point cadets into tactical units, created the office of the commandant of cadets, improved the curriculum, and introduced new methods of instruction. For his achievements during his 16-year superintendency, Thayer became known as the father of the Academy. Military education was further advanced in 1824, when, as a result of

U.S. MILITARY ACADEMY, 1828

a proposal by Calhoun for a "school of practice" for men in service, the Artillery School at Fortress Monroe was established—the first of the Army's specialist schools, though unlike most modern schools it instructed not individuals but an entire unit, which was assigned to it for a year's tour of duty. It was closed in 1835 when all the students were sent to Florida to meet the threat of the Second Seminole War, and it was not reopened until 1858.

The first official and complete artillery system for the three categories of artillery—field, siege-and-garrison, and seacoast—was put into effect by Calhoun in 1818, following recommendations by a board of artillery and ordnance officers he had appointed to study the problem. It was based largely on the system of field carriages developed by the famous French artillerist, General Jean Baptiste de Gribeauval. During the next twenty years, growing doubts about the Gribeauval system led succeeding Boards of Ordnance to recommend a newer French system (based on that of the British) called the stock-trail because the carriage used a single trail, of a solid block of wood, rather than the old twin trail. It was simpler than the previous system and introduced interchangeability in carriages and parts. Approved by Secretary of War Joel R. Poinsett and adopted in 1839, it was substantially the artillery system used in the Mexican War. The same board that recommended it also endorsed the introduction of rockets and rocket units into the U.S. Army. The rocket contemplated was patterned after the famous Congreve used by the British in the War of 1812.

Pioneering in the West

In the three decades after 1815, the Army pushed westward ahead of the settlers, surveying, fortifying, and building roads. (*Map 19*) Stockades and forts built and garrisoned in Iowa, Nebraska, and Kansas became the footholds of settlement in the wild frontier; just outside the walls could be found gristmills, sawmills, and blacksmith shops, all of them erected by the troops. Fort Leavenworth, established in 1827 on the Missouri River, was the base for Army expeditions sent out along the Santa Fe and Oregon Trails. An important Army explorer in the 1830's was Capt. Benjamin L. E. Bonneville of the 7th Infantry who on a four years' leave of absence made valuable observations concerning the Pacific coast.

These early expeditions were made by infantrymen using steamboats, wagons, and oxcarts. The discovery that the Indians on the Great Plains were horsemen led the Army in 1832 to organize its first battalion of mounted rangers, which was expanded the following year into a regiment of dragoons—the first cavalry to appear in the Regular Army since 1815.

A western man became Secretary of War in 1831. He was Lewis Cass, former Governor of Michigan, and he was to be the first long-term Secretary since Calhoun. Like Calhoun, he had hardly assumed office when an Indian war broke out. By 1831 American emigrants pouring westward after the opening of the Erie Canal in 1824 were settling on lands in western Illinois from which the Sac and Fox Indians had been pushed out to the prairies west of the Mississippi River. A band of Sac warriors under Chief Black Hawk, called the "British Band" because they had served with the British during the War of 1812, crossed the Mississippi in the spring of 1831 and began burning settlers' houses. General Gaines, commanding the Western Department, moved in with a large body of Regulars and volunteers, and Black Hawk retired across the river. But the chief returned a year later with 500 warriors and 1,500 women and children with the intention of establishing himself on the east bank of the river.

Cass, who knew the importance of impressing the Indians with a show of force, ordered Col. Henry Atkinson, commanding at Jefferson Barracks, Missouri, to take the field with Regulars of the 6th Infantry and also ordered General Scott to bring about 1,000 infantry and artillery from the east coast. The Governor of Illinois called out a large force of militia, most of them mounted. After an inconclusive brush with the Indians, most of the Illinois volunteers returned home. On August 2, 1832, Atkinson with about 500 Regulars and as many volunteers as he had been able to collect caught up with the Indians in southern Wisconsin at the confluence of the Bad Axe River and the Mississippi

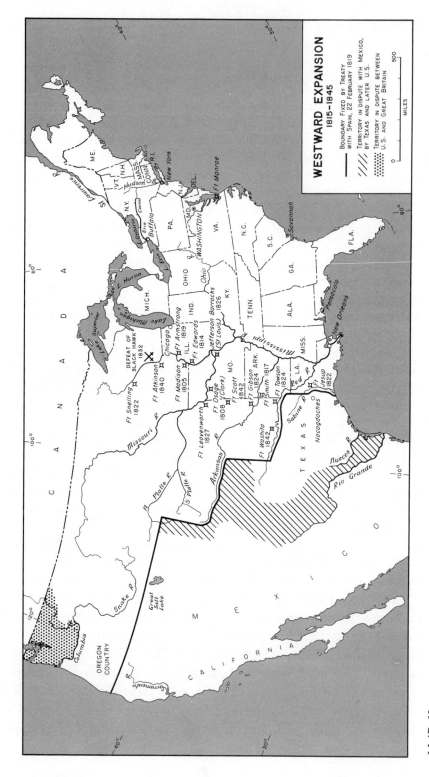

WESTWARD EXPANSION
1815-1845

— BOUNDARY FIXED BY TREATY
WITH SPAIN, 22 FEBRUARY 1819
/// TERRITORY IN DISPUTE WITH MEXICO,
BY TEXAS AND LATER U.S.
::: TERRITORY IN DISPUTE BETWEEN
U.S. AND GREAT BRITAIN

MILES
0   500

MAP 19

and defeated them decisively, with the help of an Army steamboat carrying a 6-pounder gun firing canister. Five days after the battle, General Scott arrived; but he had with him only a remnant of his forces. Asiatic cholera had broken out aboard his crowded transports on the Great Lakes, killing or disabling one third of the force; others had deserted or could not be brought forward for fear of contagion.

The Second Seminole War

Early in 1832 at the direction of Secretary Cass, the U.S. Indian commissioner in Florida negotiated a treaty with the Seminoles, ratified in 1834, by which the Indians would relinquish their lands in Florida and move to Arkansas. The time limit was eventually set at January 1, 1836. Long before the deadline, the Seminoles, led by a half-breed named Osceola, demonstrated that they would not go peaceably. Outbreaks of violence led the Army to reinforce Fort Brooke on Tampa Bay and Fort King about a hundred miles to the northeast. By December 1835, 9 companies of artillery and 2 of infantry—536 officers and men—were in Florida, under the command of Bvt. Brig. Gen. Duncan L. Clinch.

On the afternoon of December 28, 1835, Osceola with sixty warriors hidden near Fort King killed Wiley Thompson, the agent appointed to superintend the removal, as he was taking a walk outside the fort. The same day another party of warriors attacked a column of 110 Regulars marching from Fort Brooke to Fort King, led by Bvt. Maj. Francis L. Dade and moving at the pace of the oxen drawing their 6-pounder cannon. The Indians massacred all but two men, who escaped severely wounded. The Second Seminole War had begun.

Although the Dade Massacre took place west of a line dividing the Eastern and Western Departments and was therefore in General Gaines' department, President Andrew Jackson and Secretary Cass preferred to give the command to General Scott. Gaines, who was then on an inspection trip at New Orleans, was ordered to the western frontier of Louisiana to take command of all U.S. troops in the region adjoining the boundary with Texas.

General Scott left Washington on January 21, 1836. Stopping in South Carolina and Georgia to arrange for militia and supplies and to set up a depot in Savannah, he did not arrive at his headquarters in Florida near St. Augustine until February 22. Because of logistical troubles and the difficulty of moving troops over primitive, unexplored terrain to Tampa Bay, where he had planned a three-pronged offensive to bottle up the Seminoles in a swamp nearby, it was April 5 before he could begin his campaign at Tampa. By that time, the Seminoles had melted away into the Everglades. Since hot weather had set in, the militiamen, whose three months' term of service had expired, were ready to go home. As a South Carolina militia officer summed up the campaign, "Two months were consumed in preparations and effecting nothing, and the third in marching to Tampa and back again."

Though Scott's experiences in the Second Seminole War resembled in some respects those of Jackson in the First Seminole War eighteen years before, there were two important differences. First, the logistical failure was a failure in transportation, not in supply; the depots had been adequately stocked by the Commissary General of Subsistence, but wagons, roads, and Army maps were lacking. Second, General Scott had to contend with the intrusion of a subordinate commander, General Gaines, who, disregarding orders, brought a large force of Louisiana militiamen from New Orleans by ship to Tampa Bay in February. Supplying this force with rations intended for Scott's troops, Gaines fought an inconclusive battle with the Indians, which he reported as a victory—thus further impeding supply—and returned to New Orleans in March.

During May, General Scott at his headquarters near St. Augustine antagonized the Florida settlers by accusing them of cowardice and also the volunteers by officially requesting Washington that he be sent 3,000 "good troops (not volunteers)." Floridians burned him in effigy and cheered when he was transferred to Georgia at the end of May to put down an uprising of the Creek Nation, which was threatening to spill over from eastern Alabama into Georgia and Florida. There the general got into trouble with Bvt. Maj. Gen. Thomas S. Jesup, in command of operations in Alabama, who won a battle with the Indians before Scott could put his own elaborate plans into effect. In a letter to one of the President's advisers, Jesup charged Scott with unnecessary delay—"the Florida scenes enacted all over again."

The upshot of the controversy with Jesup was Scott's recall to Washington to face a court of inquiry. The court absolved him of all blame for the Florida fiasco, but he was not returned to the Seminole War. Instead, he was given diplomatic missions, for which he had demonstrated his ability during the South Carolina Nullification Crisis in 1833, when he managed to strengthen the federal forts around Charleston without provoking hostilities. He was successful in resolving several conflicts that broke out between American and Canadian settlers on the northern frontier and in persuading 15,000 Cherokee Indians in Georgia to move west peaceably.

The war in Florida continued for six years. General Jesup, commanding from late 1836 to May 1838, was not able either to persuade the Indians to leave Florida or to drive them out. His successor, Bvt. Brig. Gen. Zachary Taylor, adopted a policy of dividing the disaffected region into small districts and searching out the Indians with a pack of bloodhounds provided at one time by the state of Florida—a brief and unsuccessful experiment that aroused a furor in the United States. Taylor's search-and-destroy methods might have produced results, given time, but the War Department insisted on another attempt at negotiation and suspended hostilities. The raids were resumed. Taylor asked to be relieved and was followed by Bvt. Brig. Gen. Walker K. Armistead, who again tried negotiation and failed. In May 1841 Armistead was succeeded by Col. William J. Worth, who brought about a radical change. Hitherto the campaign in Florida had been suspended during the summer season when fever and dysentery were prevalent. Worth campaigned throughout the summer of 1841, preventing the Indians from raising and harvesting crops. By waging a ruthless war of extermination and by destroying food supplies and dwellings, he routed the Indians out of their swamps and hammocks and permitted the war to be officially ended in August 1842.

The Second Seminole War had been guerrilla warfare, of a kind the Army was not equipped to fight. The effort depleted the Regular Army so seriously that in July 1838 its authorized strength had to be increased from around 7,000 to about 12,500 men. A total of about 10,000 Regulars and perhaps 30,000 short-term volunteers had been engaged. Almost 1,600 men had lost their lives in battle or from disease and about $30 million had been spent in order that 3,800 half-starved Indians might be shipped west.

With some of this money and effort, the Army had bought experience, especially in transportation—the most pressing problem of the war. For example, the Quartermaster General had developed a light ponton wagon, lined with India rubber cloth, for crossing rivers. At General Jesup's request, the Secretary of War revived the corps of artificers that had been authorized for the War of 1812. It provided mechanics and laborers to keep wagons and boats in repair. The war taught a great deal about water transportation. Before it was over the Army was turning away from dependence on steamboats hired from private contractors to Army-owned steamboats, more reliable and cheaper in the end. The problem of navigating shallow rivers was solved by building flat-bottomed bateaux. These lessons in transportation were to be put to good use in the Mexican War.

Westward Expansion and the Texas Issue

Army pioneering expeditions from Fort Leavenworth in the 1820's and 1830's had been undertaken mainly for making treaties with the Great Plains Indians and for protecting trading caravans. Beginning in the early 1840's the prime consideration was to help the American settlers pouring westward. In

1842 2d Lt. John C. Fremont of the Corps of Topographical Engineers led an expedition to explore and map the Platte River country for the benefit of emigrants moving over the Oregon Trail; on a second expedition in 1843 he reached Sacramento, Upper California.

In 1842 Fremont reported seeing emigrant parties totaling 64 men and 16 or 17 families. Three years later, when Col. Stephen W. Kearny took five companies of the 1st Dragoons over the Oregon Trail on a march undertaken primarily for the protection of the emigrants, he saw on the trail 850 men and about 475 families in long caravans followed by thousands of cattle.

Some of the pioneers on the Oregon Trail settled in Upper California; but the main stream of American emigration into Mexican territory went to Texas. Between 1825 and 1830 approximately 15,000 emigrants with several thousand Negro slaves poured into Texas. In March of 1836 they proclaimed their independence from Mexico. The Mexicans, under General Antonio Lopez de Santa Ana, moved against the rebels and destroyed the garrison in the Alamo after a siege that lasted thirteen days. American volunteers rushed across the Sabine River to help the Texans. General Gaines, stationed on the western frontier of Louisiana to defend Louisiana and maintain American neutrality, was authorized to cross the Sabine River, generally regarded as the boundary line, but not to go beyond Nacogdoches, fifty miles west of the Sabine, which marked the extreme limit of American claims. He was at the Sabine when General Sam Houston won his victory over Santa Ana at San Jacinto on April 21, 1836. Fired by wild rumors of Mexican reinforcements, Gaines crossed the Sabine with a force of Regulars and in July occupied Nacogdoches, remaining there until recalled in December 1836.

For nearly ten years Texas existed as an independent nation, desiring annexation to the United States but frustrated because annexation had become tied up with the slavery controversy. Northerners saw annexation as an attempt by the South to extend slavery. During this decade Mexico, refusing to recognize Texan independence, made sporadic attempts to recover its lost province. Raids marked by extreme ruthlessness and ferocity by both Texans and Mexicans kept the country along the border in constant turmoil.

CHAPTER 8

The Mexican War and After

Receiving by the new telegraph the news that James K. Polk had been elected to the Presidency in November 1844, President John Tyler interpreted the verdict as a mandate from the people for the annexation of Texas, since Polk had come out strongly in favor of annexation. On March 1, 1845, Congress jointly resolved to admit Texas into the Union and the Mexican Government promptly broke off diplomatic relations. President Polk continued to hope that he could settle by negotiation Mexico's claim to Texas and acquire Upper California by purchase as well. In mid-June, nevertheless, anticipating the Fourth of July acceptance by Texas of annexation, he ordered Bvt. Brig. Gen. Zachary Taylor to move his forces from Fort Jesup on the Louisiana border to a point "on or near" the Rio Grande to repel any invasion from Mexico.

The Period of Watchful Waiting

General Taylor selected a wide sandy plain at the mouth of the Nueces River near the hamlet of Corpus Christi and beginning July 23 sent most of his 1,500-man force by steamboat from New Orleans. Only his dragoons moved overland, via San Antonio. By mid-October, as shipments of Regulars continued to come in from all over the country, his forces had swollen to nearly 4,000, including some volunteers from New Orleans. A company of Texas Rangers served as the eyes and ears of the Army. For the next six months drilling, horse-breaking, and parades, interspersed with boredom and dissipation, went on at the big camp on the Nueces. Then in February Taylor received orders from Washington to advance to the Rio Grande. Negotiations with the Mexican Government had broken down.

The march of more than a hundred miles down the coast to the Rio Grande was led by Bvt. Maj. Samuel Ringgold's battery of "flying artillery," organized in late 1838 on orders from Secretary of War Joel R. Poinsett. It was the last word in mobility, for the cannoneers rode on horseback rather than on limbers and caissons. The rear was brought up by Taylor's supply train of three hundred wagons drawn by oxen. On March 23 the columns came to a road that forked left to Point Isabel, ten miles away on the coast, where Taylor's supply ships were waiting, and led on the right to his destination on the Rio Grande, some eighteen miles southwest, opposite the Mexican town of Matamoros. Sending the bulk of his army ahead, Taylor went to Point Isabel to set up his supply base, fill his wagons, and bring forward four 18-pounder siege guns from his ships.

At the boiling brown waters of the Rio Grande opposite Matamoros he built a strong fort, which he called Fort Texas, mounting his siege guns. At the same time he sent pacific messages to the Mexican commander on the opposite bank. These were countered by threats and warnings, and on April 25, the day after the arrival at Matamoros of General Mariano Arista with two or three thousand additional troops, by open hostilities. The Mexicans crossed the river in some force and attacked a reconnoitering detachment of sixty dragoons under Capt. Seth B. Thornton. They killed eleven men and captured Thornton and the rest, many of whom were wounded.

Taylor reported to President Polk that hostilities had commenced and called on Texas and Louisiana for about 5,000 militiamen. His immediate concern was that his supply base might be captured. Leaving an infantry regiment and a small detachment of artillery at Fort Texas under Maj. Jacob Brown, he set off May 1 with the bulk of his forces for Point Isabel, where he stayed nearly a week strengthening his fortifications. After loading two hundred supply wagons and acquiring two more ox-drawn 18-pounders, he began the return march to Fort Texas with his army of about 2,300 men on the afternoon of May 7. About noon next day near a clump of tall trees at a spot called Palo Alto, he saw across the open prairie a long dark line with bayonets and lances glistening in the sun. It was the Mexican Army.

The Battles of Palo Alto and Resaca de la Palma

General Arista's forces barring the road to Fort Texas stretched out on a front a mile long and were about 4,000 strong. Taylor, who had placed part of his force in the rear to guard the supply wagons, was outnumbered at least two to one; and in terrain that favored cavalry, Arista's cavalry overwhelmingly outnumbered Taylor's dragoons. But the American artillery was superior. Also, among Taylor's junior officers were a number of West Point graduates who were to make their reputations in the Civil War, notably 2d Lt. George C. Meade and 2d Lt. Ulysses S. Grant.

On the advice of the young West Pointers on his staff, Taylor emplaced his two 18-pounder iron siege guns in the center of his line and blasted the advancing Mexicans with canister. His field artillery—bronze 6-pounder guns firing solid shot and 12-pounder howitzers firing shell—in quick-moving attacks threw back Arista's flanks. The Mexicans were using old-fashioned bronze 4-pounders and 8-pounders that fired solid shot and had such short range that their fire did little damage. During the battle Lieutenant Grant saw their cannon balls striking the ground before they reached the American troops and ricocheting so slowly that the men could dodge them.

During the afternoon a gun wad set the dry grass afire, causing the battle to be suspended for nearly an hour. After it was resumed the Mexicans fell back rapidly. By nightfall when both armies went into bivouac, Mexican casualties, caused mostly by cannon fire, numbered about 320 killed and 380 wounded. Taylor lost only 9 men killed and 47 wounded. One of the mortally wounded was his brilliant artilleryman, Major Ringgold.

At daybreak the Americans saw the Mexicans in full retreat. Taylor decided to pursue but did not begin his advance until afternoon, spending the morning erecting defenses around his wagon train, which he intended to leave behind. About two o'clock he reached Resaca de la Palma, a dry river bed about five miles from Palo Alto. There his scouts reported that the Mexicans had taken advantage of his delay to entrench themselves strongly a short distance down the road in a similar shallow ravine known as Resaca de la Guerra, whose banks formed a natural breastwork. Narrow ponds and thick chaparral protected their flanks.

Taylor sent forward his flying artillery, now commanded by Lt. Randolph Ridgely. Stopped by a Mexican battery, Ridgely sent back for help and Taylor ordered in a detachment of dragoons under Capt. Charles A. May. The dragoons overran the Mexican guns but on their return were caught in infantry crossfire from the thickets and could not prevent the enemy from recapturing the guns. The pieces were later captured by American infantrymen. Dense chaparral prevented Taylor from making full use of his artillery. The battle of Resaca de la Palma was an infantry battle of small parties and hand-to-hand fighting.

The Mexicans, still demoralized by their defeat at Palo Alto and lacking effective leadership, gave up the fight and fled toward Matamoros. Their losses at Resaca de la Palma were later officially reported as 547 and were probably much greater. The Americans lost 33 killed and 89 wounded. In the meantime Fort Texas had been attacked by the Mexicans May 3 and had withstood a two-day siege with the loss of only two men, one of them its commander for whom the fort was later renamed Fort Brown.

The panic-stricken Mexicans fleeing to Matamoros crossed the Rio Grande as best they could, some by boats, some by swimming. Many drowned, others were killed by the guns of Fort Texas. If Taylor's Regulars, flushed with victory and yelling as they pursued the enemy, had been able to catch up with Arista, they could probably have taken his demoralized army, complete with guns and ammunition. But Taylor had failed to make any provision for crossing the Rio Grande. He blamed the War Department's failure to provide him with ponton equipment (developed during the Second Seminole War), which he had requested while he was still at Corpus Christi. Since that time, however, he had done nothing to acquire bridge materials or boats, although he had been urged to do so by the West Pointers. Lieutenant Meade reported that "the old gentleman would never listen or give it a moment's attention." Not until May 18, after Taylor had brought up some boats from Point Isabel, was he able to cross into Matamoros. By that time Arista's army had melted away into the interior to rest, recoup, and fight another day.

War Is Declared

On the evening of May 9, the day of the battle of Resaca de la Palma, President Polk received a message from the War Department telling of the attack on Captain Thornton's detachment on April 25. Polk, who was already convinced by the breakdown in negotiations with Mexico that war was justified, immediately drafted a message declaring that a state of war existed between the United States and Mexico. Congress passed the declaration and Polk signed it on May 13. Congress then appropriated $10 million and substantially increased the strength of the Army. After the Second Seminole War the authorized strength had been cut from 12,500 to 8,500. This had been done by reducing the rank and file strength of the regiments, instead of eliminating units, thus firmly establishing the principle of an expansible Army. To meet the needs of the Mexican War the Congress raised the authorized enlisted strength of a company from 64 to 100 men, bringing the rank and file up to 15,540, and added a regiment of mounted riflemen and a company of sappers, miners, and pontoniers. Also, the President was authorized to call for 50,000 volunteers for a term of one year or the duration of the war.

The President went into the war with one object clearly in view—to seize all of Mexico north of the Rio Grande and the Gila River and westward to the Pacific. After discussions with General Scott, the outlines of a three-pronged thrust emerged. (*Map 20*) General Taylor was to advance westward from Matamoros to the city of Monterrey, the key to further progress in northern Mexico. A second expedition under Brig. Gen. John E. Wool was to move from San Antonio to the remote village of Chihuahua in the west, an expedition later directed southward to Saltillo near Monterrey. A third prong under Col. Stephen W. Kearny was to start at Fort Leavenworth

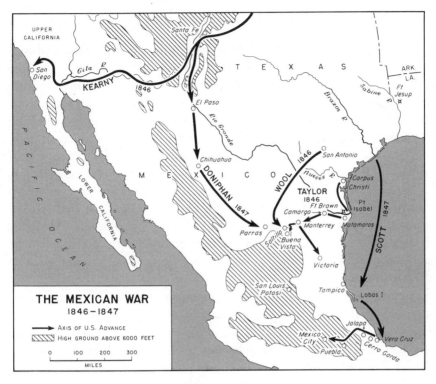

MAP 20

for Santa Fe, ultimately to continue to San Diego on the coast of California;
part of Kearny's forces under Col. Alexander W. Doniphan was later sent
south through Chihuahua to Parras.

Polk was counting on "a brisk and a short war"; not until July did he and
his Secretary of War, William L. Marcy, even begin to consider the possibility
of an advance on Mexico City by landing a force on the Gulf near Vera Cruz.
General Scott was not so optimistic. He was more aware of the problems
of supply, transportation, communications, and mobilization involved in operations against Mexico, a country with a population of seven million and an
army of about thirty thousand, many with experience gained by some twenty
years of intermittent revolution. Scott's preparations seemed too slow to Polk.
Ostensibly for that reason, but also because success in the field might make
Scott a too powerful contender for the Presidency, Polk decided not to give him
command of the forces in the field. When news came of the victories at Palo
Alto and Resaca de la Palma, Polk promoted Zachary Taylor to the brevet rank
of major general and gave him command of the army in Mexico.

The Monterrey Campaign

Taylor's plan was to move on Monterrey with about six thousand men via Camargo, a small town on the San Juan River, a tributary of the Rio Grande about 130 miles upriver. From Camargo, where he intended to set up a supply base, a road led southwest about 125 miles to Monterrey in the foothills of the Sierra Madres. His troops were to march overland to Camargo, his supplies to come by steamboat up the Rio Grande. But he could not move immediately because he lacked transportation—partly because of his failure to requisition in time and partly because of the effort required to build more wagons in the United States and to collect shallow-draft steamboats at river towns on the Mississippi and the Ohio and send them across the Gulf of Mexico. Ten steamboats were in operation at the end of July, but wagons did not begin arriving until November, after the campaign was over. To supplement his wagon train, reduced to 175, Taylor had to rely on 1,500 Mexican pack mules and a few native oxcarts.

In manpower Taylor had an embarrassment of riches. May saw the arrival of the first of the three-months militia he had requested on April 26 from the governors of Texas and Louisiana, and with them thousands of additional six-months volunteers from neighboring states recruited by Bvt. Maj. Gen. Edmund P. Gaines, commander of the Department of the West, on his own initiative—a repetition of his impulsive actions in the Second Seminole War. More than 8,000 of these short-term volunteers were sent before Gaines was censured by a court-martial for his unauthorized and illegal recruiting practices and transferred to New York to command the Department of the East. Very few of his recruits had agreed to serve for twelve months. All the rest were sent home without performing any service; in the meantime they had to be fed, sheltered, and transported. In June the volunteers authorized by Congress began pouring into Point Isabel and were quartered in a string of camps along the Rio Grande as far as Matamoros.

By August Taylor had a force of about 15,000 men at Camargo, an unhealthy town deep in mud from a recent freshet and sweltering under heat that rose as high as 112 degrees. Many of the volunteers became ill and more than half were left behind when Taylor advanced toward Monterrey at the end of August with 3,080 Regulars and 3,150 volunteers. The Regulars (with a few volunteers) were organized into the First and Second Divisions, the volunteers mainly into a Field Division, though two regiments of mounted Texans were thought of as the Texas Division. More than a fourth of the troops were mounted, among them the First Mississippi Rifle

Regiment under a West Point graduate recently elected to Congress, Col. Jefferson Davis. The mounted riflemen had percussion rifles; the infantrymen were armed with flintlock muskets. Taylor placed great reliance on the bayonet. He had a low opinion of artillery, and though warned that field pieces were not effective against the stone houses of Mexican towns, he had in addition to his four field batteries only two 24-pounder howitzers and one 10-inch mortar, the latter his only real siege piece.

By September 19 Taylor's army reached Monterrey, a city of stone in a pass of the Sierra Madres leading to the city of Saltillo. It was strongly fortified and defended by more than 7,000 Mexicans with better artillery than the Mexicans had had at Palo Alto—new British 9- and 12-pounder guns. Taylor, encamped on the outskirts of Monterrey, sent out reconnoitering parties accompanied by engineers and on September 20 began his attack. On the north the city was protected by a formidable citadel, on the south by a river; and it was ringed with forts. Taylor sent one of his Regular divisions, with four hundred Texas Rangers in advance, around to the west to cut off the road to Saltillo, and after a miserable night of drenching rain it accomplished its mission the next day, September 21, though at a cost of 394 dead or wounded, a high proportion of them officers. Taylor placed his heavy howitzers and one mortar in position to fire on the citadel and sent the remainder of his forces to close in from the eastern outskirts of the town. By the third day both attacks were driving into the city proper, the men battering down doors of the stone and adobe houses with planks, tossing lighted shells through apertures, and advancing from house to house rather than from street to street—tactics that were to be used a century later by American troops in Italian and German towns.

The climax came when the 10-inch mortar was brought up to lob shells on the great plaza into which the Mexican troops had been driven. On September 24 the Mexican commander offered to surrender on condition that his troops be allowed to withdraw unimpeded and that an eight-week armistice go into effect. Taylor agreed to the proposal. He had lost some 800 men to battle casualties and sickness, besides quantities of arms and ammunition, and he was about 125 miles from his base. Moreover, he believed that magnanimity would advance negotiations for peace which had begun when President Polk allowed General Antonio Lopez de Santa Ana to return to Mexico from exile in Havana to exert his influence in favor of a treaty.

When Polk received the news from Monterrey by courier October 11, he condemned Taylor for allowing the Mexican Army to escape and ordered the armistice terminated. Thereupon, Taylor on November 13 sent a thousand men 68 miles southwestward to occupy Saltillo, an important road center commanding the only road to Mexico City from the north that was practicable for wagons and guns. Saltillo also commanded the road west to Chihuahua and east to Victoria, capital of Tamaulipas, the province that contained Tampico, the second largest Mexican port on the Gulf. The U.S. Navy captured Tampico November 15. On the road to Chihuahua was the town of Parras, where General Wool's expedition of about 2,500 men arrived early in December after a remarkable march from San Antonio. On the way Wool had learned that the Mexican troops holding Chihuahua had abandoned it; accordingly, he joined Taylor's main army. Taylor thus acquired a valuable young engineer who had been scouting with Wool, Capt. Robert E. Lee.

Taylor was planning to establish a strong defensive line, Parras-Saltillo-Monterrey-Victoria, when he learned that most of his troops would have to be released to join General Scott's invasion of Mexico at Vera Cruz, an operation which had been decided upon in Washington in mid-November. Scott arrived in Mexico in late December. He proceeded to Camargo and detached almost all of Taylor's Regulars, about 4,000, and an equal number of volunteers, ordering them to rendezvous at Tampico and at the mouth of the Brazos River in Texas. Taylor, left with fewer than 7,000 men, all volunteers except two squadrons of dragoons and a small force of artillery, was ordered to evacuate Saltillo and go on the defensive at Monterrey.

Enraged, Taylor attributed Scott's motive to politics. Hurrying back to Monterrey from Victoria, he decided to interpret Scott's orders as "advice" rather than as an order. Instead of retiring his forces to Monterrey, he moved 4,650 of his troops (leaving garrisons at Monterrey and Saltillo) to a point about 18 miles south of Saltillo, near the hacienda of Agua Nueva. This move brought him almost 11 miles closer to San Luis Potosi, 200 miles to the south, where General Santa Ana was assembling an army of 20,000. Most of the 200 miles were desert, which Taylor considered impassable by any army; moreover, both he and Scott believed that Santa Ana would make his main effort against Scott's landing at Vera Cruz, the news of which had leaked to the newspapers. On February 8, 1847, Taylor wrote a friend, "I have no fears."

At the time he wrote, Santa Ana was already on the march northward toward Saltillo. Stung by newspaper reports that he had sold out to the Americans, Santa Ana was determined to win a quick victory and he thought he saw his opportunity when his troops brought him a copy of Scott's order depleting Taylor's forces, found on the body of a messenger they had ambushed and killed. Leading his army across barren country through heat, snow, and rain, by February 19 Santa Ana had 15,000 men at a hacienda at the edge of the desert, only 35 miles from Agua Nueva. The hardest battle of the Mexican War was about to begin.

The Battle of Buena Vista

On the morning of February 21 scouts brought the word to General Taylor that a great Mexican army was advancing, preceded by a large body of cavalry swinging east to block the road between Agua Nueva and Saltillo. That afternoon Taylor withdrew his forces up the Saltillo road about 15 miles to a better defensive position near the hacienda Buena Vista, a few miles south of Saltillo. There, about a mile south of the clay-roofed ranch buildings, mountain spurs came down to the road on the east, the longest and highest known as La Angostura; between them was a wide plateau cut by two deep ravines. West of the road was a network of gullies backed by a line of high hills. Leaving General Wool to deploy the the troops, Taylor rode off to Saltillo to look after his defenses there.

By next morning, Washington's Birthday (the password was "Honor to Washington"), the little American army of less than 5,000 troops, most of them green volunteers, was in position to meet a Mexican army more than three times its size. The American main body was east of the road near La Angostura, where artillery had been emplaced, commanding the road. West of the road, the gullies were thought to be sufficient protection.

Santa Ana arrived with his vanguard around eleven o'clock. Disliking the terrain, which by no means favored cavalry, his best arm, he sent a demand for surrender to Taylor, who had returned from Saltillo. Taylor refused. Then Santa Ana planted artillery on the road and the high ground east of it and sent a force of light infantry around the foot of the mountains south of the plateau. About three o'clock a shell from a Mexican howitzer on the road gave the signal for combat; but the rest of the day was consumed mainly in jockeying for position on the mountain spurs, a competition in which the Mexicans came off best, and the placing of American infantry and artillery well forward on the plateau. After a threatening movement on the Mexican left, Taylor sent a Kentucky regiment with two guns of Maj. Braxton Bragg's battery to the high hills west of the road, but no attack occurred there. Toward evening Taylor returned to Saltillo, accompanied by the First Mississippi Rifles and a detachment of dragoons. At nightfall his soldiers, shaken by the size and splendid appearance of the Mexican army, got what sleep they could.

The next day, February 23, the battle opened in earnest at dawn. Santa Ana sent a division up the road toward La Angostura, at the head of the defile, but it was quickly broken up by American artillery and infantrymen, and no further action occurred in that sector. The strongest assault took place on the plateau, well to the east, where Santa Ana launched two divisions, backed by a strong battery at the head of the southernmost ravine. The Americans farthest forward, part of an Indiana regiment supported by three cannons, held off the assault for half an hour; then their commander gave them an order to retreat. They broke and ran and were joined in their flight by adjoining regiments. Some of the men ran all the way back to Buena Vista, where they fired at pursuing Mexican cavalrymen from behind the hacienda walls.

About nine o'clock that morning, when the battle had become almost a rout, General Taylor arrived from Saltillo with his dragoons, Col. Jefferson Davis' Mississippi Rifles, and some men of the Indiana regiment whom he had rallied on the way. They fell upon the Mexican cavalry that had been trying to outflank the Americans north of the plateau. In the meantime Bragg's artillery had come over from the hills west of the road, and the Kentucky regiment also crossed the road to join in the fight. A deafening thunderstorm of rain and hail broke early in the afternoon, but the Americans in the north field continued to force the Mexicans back.

Just when victory for the Americans seemed in sight, Santa Ana threw an entire division of fresh troops, his reserves, against the plateau. Rising from the broad ravine where they had been hidden, the Mexicans of the left column fell upon three regiments—two Illinois and one Kentucky—and forced them back to the road with withering fire, while the right stormed the weak American center. They seemed about to turn the tide of battle when down from the north field galloped two batteries, followed by the Mississippians and Indianans led by Jefferson Davis, wounded, but still in the saddle. They fell upon the Mexicans' right and rear and forced them back into the ravine. The Mexicans' left, pursuing the Illinois and Kentucky regiments up the road, was cut to pieces by the American battery at La Angostura.

That night Santa Ana, having lost 1,500 to 2,000 men killed and wounded, retreated toward San Luis Potosi. The Americans, with 264 men killed, 450 wounded, and 26 missing, had won the battle. A great share of the credit belonged to the artillery; without it, as General Wool said in his report, the army could not have stood "for a single hour." Moving with almost the speed of cavalry, the batteries served as rallying points for the infantry. The fighting spirit of the volunteers, most of them frontiersmen, and the able and courageous leadership of the officers were beyond praise. Perhaps the greatest contribution to the victory had been Zachary Taylor himself. Stationed all day conspicuously

THE MISSISSIPPI RIFLES AT BUENA VISTA

in the center of the battle hunched on his horse "Old Whitey," with one leg hooked over the pommel of his saddle, disregarding two Mexican bullets that ripped through his coat, and occasionally rising in his stirrups to shout encouragement, he was an inspiration to his men, who swore by him. Under such a leader they felt that defeat was impossible.

Taylor knew little of the art of war. He was careless in preparing for battle and neglected intelligence; he often misunderstood the intention of the enemy and underestimated the enemy's strength. But he possessed to a superlative degree physical courage and moral courage, which according to Jomini are the most essential qualities for a general.

Buena Vista ended any further Mexican threat against the lower Rio Grande. On the Pacific coast, Colonel Kearny by December 1846 had reached San Diego after one of the most extraordinary marches in American history, across deserts and rugged mountains, to find that a naval squadron had already seized the California ports. Early in February 1847 a force of Missouri volunteers detached from Kearny's command and led by Col. Alexander W. Doniphan had set out from Santa Fe to pacify the region of the upper Rio Grande. Crossing the river at El Paso, they defeated a large force of Mexicans, mostly militia, at Chihuahua, less than a week after Taylor's victory at Buena Vista. Thus by March 1847, America's hold on Mexico's northern provinces was secure. All that remained was the capture of Mexico City.

The Landing at Vera Cruz

From a rendezvous at Lobos Island almost 50 miles south of Tampico, General Scott's force of 13,660 men, of whom 5,741 were Regulars, set sail on March 2, 1847, for the landing near Vera Cruz—the first major amphibious landing in the history of the U.S. Army. On March 5 the transports were off the coast of their target, where they met a U.S. naval squadron blockading the city. In a small boat Scott, his commanders, and a party of officers including Robert E. Lee, George G. Meade, Joseph E. Johnston, and Pierre G. T. Beauregard ran close inshore to reconnoiter and came near being hit by a shell fired from the island fortress of San Juan de Ulua opposite Vera Cruz, a shell that might have changed the course of the Mexican War and the Civil War as well.

Scott chose for the landing a beach nearly 3 miles south of the city, beyond the range of the Mexican guns. On the evening of March 9, in four hours more than 10,000 men went ashore in landing craft, consisting of 65 heavy surf boats that had been towed to the spot by steamers. The troops proceeded inland over the sand hills with little opposition from the Mexican force of 4,300 behind the city's walls. The landing of artillery, stores, and horses, the last thrown overboard and forced to swim for shore, was slowed by a norther that sprang up on March 12 and blew violently for four days, but by March 22 seven 10-inch mortars had been dragged inland and emplaced about half a mile south of Vera Cruz. That afternoon the bombardment began.

Town and fort replied, and it was soon apparent that the mortars were ineffective. Scott found himself compelled to ask for naval guns from the commander of the naval force, Commodore Matthew C. Perry. The six naval guns—three 32-pounders firing shot and three 8-inch shell guns—soon breached the walls and demoralized the defenders. On March 27, 1847, Vera Cruz capitulated.

Scott's next objective was Jalapa, a city in the highlands about 74 miles from Vera Cruz on the national highway leading to Mexico City. Because on the coast the yellow fever season was approaching, Scott was anxious to move forward to the uplands at once, but not until April 8 was he able to collect enough pack mules and wagons for the advance. The first elements, under Bvt. Maj. Gen. David E. Twiggs, set out with two batteries. One was equipped with 24-pounder guns, 8-inch howitzers, and 10-inch mortars. The other was a new type of battery equipped with mountain howitzers and rockets, officered and manned by the Ordnance Corps. The rocket section, mainly armed with the Congreve, carried for service tests a new rocket, the Hale, which depended for stability not on a stick but on vents in the rear, which also gave it a spin like that of an artillery projectile. The rockets were fired from troughs mounted on portable stands. In addition to his two batteries, General Twiggs had a squadron of dragoons, in all about 2,600 men. He advanced confidently, though warned by Scott that a substantial army commanded by Santa Ana lay somewhere ahead. On April 11, after Twiggs had gone about 30 miles, his scouts brought word that Mexican guns commanded a pass near the hamlet of Cerro Gordo.

The Battle of Cerro Gordo

Near Cerro Gordo the national highway ran through a rocky defile. On the left of the approaching Americans, Santa Ana with about 12,000 men had emplaced batteries on mountain spurs and on the right of the Americans farther down the road his guns were emplaced on a high hill, El Telegrafo. He thus had firm command of the national highway, the only means he thought Scott had of bringing up his artillery.

Fortunately for Twiggs, advancing on the morning of April 12, the Mexican gunners opened fire before he was within range and he was able to pull his forces back. Two days later Scott arrived with reinforcements, bringing his army up to 8,500. A reconnaissance by Capt. Robert E. Lee showed that the rough country to the right of El Telegrafo, which Santa Ana had considered impassable, could be traversed, enabling the Americans to cut in on the Mexican rear. The troops hewed a path through forest and brush, and when they came to ravines, lowered the heavy siege artillery by ropes to the bottom, then hoisted it up the other side. By April 17 they were able to occupy a hill to the right of El Telegrafo, where they sited the rocket battery. Early on the morning of April 18 the battle began.

Though Santa Ana, by then forewarned, had been able to plant guns to protect his flank, he could not withstand the American onslaught. The Mexicans broke and fled into the mountains. By noon Scott's army had won a smashing victory at a cost of only 417 casualties, including 64 dead. Santa Ana's losses were estimated at more than a thousand.

Scott moved next morning to Jalapa. The way seemed open to Mexico City, only 170 miles away. But now he faced a serious loss in manpower. The term of enlistment of seven of his volunteer regiments was about to expire and only a handful agreed to re-enlist. The men had to be sent home at once to minimize the danger of yellow fever when they passed through Vera Cruz. The departure of the volunteers, added to wounds and sickness among the men remaining, reduced the army to 5,820 effectives.

In May Scott pushed forward cautiously to Puebla, then the second largest city in Mexico. Its citizens were hostile to Santa Ana and had lost hope of winning the war. It capitulated without resistance on May 15 to an advance party under General Worth. Scott stayed there until the beginning of August, awaiting reinforcements from Vera Cruz, which by mid-July more than doubled his forces, and awaiting also the outcome of peace negotiations then under way. A State Department emissary, Nicholas P. Trist, had arrived on the scene and made contact with Santa Ana through a British agent in Mexico City. Trist learned that Santa Ana, elected President of Mexico for the second time, would discuss peace terms for $10,000 down and $1,000,000 to be paid when a treaty was ratified. After receiving the down payment through the intermediary, however, Santa Ana made it known that he could not prevail upon the Mexican Congress to repeal a law it had passed after the battle of Cerro Gordo making it high treason for any official to treat with the Americans. It was clear that Scott would have to move closer to the capital of Mexico before Santa Ana would seriously consider peace terms.

Contreras, Churubusco, Chapultepec

For the advance on Mexico City, Scott had about 10,000 men. He had none to spare to protect the road from Vera Cruz to Puebla; therefore his decision to move forward was daring: it meant that he had abandoned his line of communications, as he phrased it, "thrown away the scabbard." On August 7 Scott moved off with the lead division, followed at a day's march by three divisions with a three-mile-long train of white-topped supply wagons bringing up the rear. Meeting no opposition—a sign that Santa Ana had withdrawn to defend Mexico City—Scott by August 10 was at Ayolta, located on a high plateau 14 miles from the city.

The direct road ahead, entering the capital on the east, was barred by strongly fortified positions. Scott therefore decided to take the city from the west by a wide flanking movement to the south, using a narrow muddy road that passed between the southern shores of two lakes and the mountains and skirted a fifteen-mile-wide lava bed, the Pedregal, before it turned north and went over a bridge at Churubusco to the western gates of Mexico City.

The Pedregal had been considered impassable, but Captain Lee found a mule path across its southwestern tip that came out at the village of Contreras.

Scott sent a force under Bvt. Maj. Gen. Gideon J. Pillow to work on the road, supported by Twiggs's division and some light artillery. They came under heavy fire from a Mexican force under General Valencia. Pillow, manhandling his guns to a high position, attacked on August 19, but his light artillery was no match for Valencia's 68-pounder howitzer, nor his men for the reinforcements Santa Ana brought to the scene. American reinforcements made a night march in pouring rain through a gully the engineers had found through the Pedregal and fell upon the Mexicans' rear on the morning of August 20, simultaneously with an attack from the front. In seventeen minutes the battle of Contreras was won, with a loss to Scott of only 60 killed or wounded; the Mexicans lost 700 dead and 800 captured, including 4 generals.

Scott ordered an immediate pursuit, but Santa Ana was able to gather his forces for a stand at Churubusco, where he placed a strong fortification before the town at the bridge and converted a thick-walled stone church and a massive stone convent into fortresses. When the first American troops rode up around noon on August 20 they were met by heavy musket and cannon fire. The Mexicans fought as never before; not until midafternoon could Scott's troops make any progress. At last the fire of the Mexicans slackened, partly because they were running out of ammunition, and the Americans won the day, a day that Santa Ana admitted had cost him one third of his forces. About 4,000 Mexicans had been killed or wounded, not counting the many missing and captured. The battle had also been costly for Scott, who had 155 men killed and 876 wounded.

The victory at Churubusco brought an offer from Santa Ana to reopen negotiations. Scott proposed a short armistice and Santa Ana quickly agreed. For two weeks Trist and representatives of the Mexican Government discussed terms until it became clear that the Mexicans would not accept what Trist had to offer and were merely using the armistice as a breathing spell. On September 6 Scott halted the discussions and prepared to assault Mexico City.

Though refreshed by two weeks of rest, his forces now numbered only about 8,000 men. Santa Ana was reputed to have more than 15,000 and had taken advantage of the respite to strengthen the defenses of the city. And ahead on a high hill above the plain was the Castle of Chapultepec guarding the western approaches.

Scott's first objective, about half a mile west of Chapultepec, was a range of low stone buildings, containing a cannon foundry, known as El Molino del Rey. It was seized on September 8, though at heavy cost from unexpected resistance. At eight o'clock on the morning of September 13, after a barrage from the 24-pounder guns, Scott launched a three-pronged attack over the causeways leading to Chapultepec and up the rugged slopes. Against a hail of Mexican projectiles from above, his determined troops rapidly gained the summit, and though they were delayed at the moat, waiting for scaling ladders to come up, by half past nine o'clock the Americans were overrunning the castle. Scarcely pausing, they pressed on to Mexico City by the two routes available and by night-fall held two gates to the city. Exhausted and depleted by the 800 casualties suffered that day, the troops still faced house-to-house fighting; but at dawn the next day, September 14, the city surrendered.

Throughout the campaign from Vera Cruz to Mexico City General Scott had displayed not only dauntless personal courage and fine qualities of leader-ship but great skill in applying the principles of war. In preparing for battle he would order his engineers to make a thorough reconnaissance of the enemy's position and the surrounding terrain. He was thus able to execute brilliant flank-ing movements over terrain that the enemy had considered impassable, notably at Cerro Gordo and the Pedregal, the latter a fine illustration of the principle of surprise. Scott also knew when to break the rules of warfare, as he had done at Puebla when he deliberately severed his line of communications.

"He sees everything and counts the cost of every measure," said Robert E. Lee. Scott on his part ascribed his quick victory over Mexico, won without the loss of a single battle, to the West Pointers in his army, Lee, Grant, and many others. As for the troops, the trained and disciplined Regulars had come off somewhat better than the volunteers, but the army on the whole had fought well. Scott had seen to it that the men fought at the right time and place. Grant summed it up: "Credit is due to the troops engaged, it is true, but the plans and strategy were the general's."

Occupation and Negotiation in Mexico City

For two months the only responsible government in Mexico was the Ameri-can military government under Scott. The collection of revenues, suppression of disorder, administration of justice, all the details of governing the country were in the hands of the Army. When the Mexicans finally organized a government with which Commissioner Trist could negotiate a peace treaty, dispatches arrived from Washington instructing Trist to return to the United States and ordering Scott to resume the war. Knowing that the Mexicans were now sin-cerely desirous of ending the war and realizing that the government in Wash-ington was unaware of the situation, both Trist and Scott decided to continue the negotiations.

On February 2, 1848, the Treaty of Guadalupe Hidalgo was signed. It was ratified by the U.S. Senate on March 10, but powerful opposition to it developed

in Mexico. Not until May 30 were ratifications exchanged by the two govern-
ments. Preparations began immediately to evacuate American troops from
Mexico. On June 12 the occupation troops marched out of Mexico City, and on
August 1, 1848, the last American soldiers stepped aboard their transports at
Vera Cruz and quitted Mexican soil.

By the Treaty of Guadalupe Hidalgo the United States agreed to pay
Mexico $15 million and to assume the unpaid claims by Americans against
Mexico. In return Mexico recognized the Rio Grande as the boundary of Texas
and ceded New Mexico (including the present states of Arizona, New Mexico,
Utah, and Nevada, a small corner of present-day Wyoming, and the western
and southern portions of Colorado) and Upper California (the present state
of California) to the United States.

The Army on the New Frontier

The victory over Mexico, as well as the settlement of the Oregon boundary
frontier in June 1846, added to the United States a vast territory that was to
occupy the Army almost exclusively in the postwar years.

The first task was exploration, one in which the Corps of Topographical
Engineers played the leading role. Some knowledge of the new frontier had
been gained by expeditions such as those of Bonneville, Kearny, and Fremont;
more had been gained during the Mexican War by "topogs" attached to
Kearny's march to California and Wool's to Saltillo and after the war by
Maj. William H. Emory's work with the Mexican Boundary Commission, but
much still remained to be done.

The most significant and far-reaching explorations were those to locate
routes for transcontinental railroads. The first effort was directed toward the
southwest, an "ice-free, mountain-free" route. In that area the necessity for
defense against Comanches, Apaches, and Navahoes meant that most of the
Army had to be stationed between San Antonio and Fort Yuma. Forts had
to be constructed, roads built, rivers sought as avenues of supply, and Indian
trails mapped. In 1853 Congress authorized similar explorations on a northern
route to the Pacific from Chicago and a central route from St. Louis.

Railroad construction did not begin until after the Civil War. Emigrants
setting out for the West, in increasing numbers after the discovery of gold in
California in 1849, used wagon trails across plains populated by warlike Indian
tribes. The Army guarded the several transcontinental wagon routes and
managed to keep the tribes in check. During the decade of the fifties there
were no less than twenty-two distinct Indian "wars." Upon a report in 1857

Topographical Engineers Exploring the Colorado River *near Chimney Peak.*

that the Mormons in Utah were defying federal authority, two sizable expeditions were sent from Fort Leavenworth to Utah, but the "Mormon War" never became a reality.

Army expeditions, marching through primitive country where no local procurement was possible, had to carry all requirements, from horseshoe nails to artillery. Supplying the frontier posts, some as far as a thousand miles from inland waterways, entailed great effort. All goods had to be hauled in wagons or carried by pack train. The difficulty of supplying posts in the arid regions of the Southwest led in 1855 to an interesting experiment, strongly backed by Secretary of War Jefferson Davis, in the use of camels as pack animals. Seventy-five were imported from the Middle East and sent to Texas. They showed that they could carry heavy loads, walk surefootedly over ground no wagon could traverse, and subsist by grazing and on little water; but their appearance on the roads stampeded wagon and pack trains, and teamsters hated and feared them. The public and the Army turned against them and the camel experiment ended in failure.

Increasing the Peacetime Army

By the end of 1848 the Army had reverted to a peacetime strength somewhat smaller than the 10,000 authorized in 1815. It was stretched very thin by its manifold duties on the vast new frontier. On the recommendations of General

Scott and Secretary of War George W. Crawford, Congress in June 1850 approved enlarging the companies serving on the frontier to 74 privates, a considerable increase over the 50 in the dragoons, 64 in the mounted rifles, and 42 in the artillery and infantry authorized at the end of 1848. Thereafter 90 of the 158 companies were enlarged, so that by the end of 1850 the Army was authorized 12,927 officers and men.

When Jefferson Davis became Secretary of War in 1853, he strongly urged a larger Army, one that could be expanded to 27,818 men in time of war by enlarging the company to 128 men. Davis desired new mounted regiments for frontier service, because only highly mobile units could hope to handle the Indians. In March 1855 Congress added 4 new regiments to the existing 15 (2 of dragoons, 1 of mounted rifles, 4 of artillery, and 8 of infantry). They were the 1st and 2d Cavalry Regiments and the 9th and 10th Infantry Regiments. The mounted arm thus consisted of dragoons, mounted rifles, and cavalry until the Civil War, when all mounted regiments were called cavalry.

Weapons and Tactics on the Eve of the Civil War

At Davis' insistence the new infantry units were armed with percussion-cap, muzzle-loading rifle muskets instead of smoothbore muskets. Nineteenth century technological developments had made possible an accurate, dependable muzzle-loading rifle with at least as fast a rate of fire as the smoothbore musket. This was partly due to the application of the percussion-cap principle to the rifle and partly to the adoption in 1855 of the Minié ball, a lead projectile tapering forward from its hollow base. To load and fire, the soldier bit open the paper cartridge, poured the powder down the barrel, rammed in the paper to seat the charge, and then rammed the bullet home. He then put the cap in place, full-cocked the piece, aimed, and fired. Sparks from the cap fired the powder. The force of the explosion expanded the hollow base of the bullet to fit the rifling, and the bullet left the barrel spinning, and thus with considerable accuracy. Its effective range was about 400 to 600 yards as compared with 100 to 200 yards for smoothbore muskets. The rate of fire was a theoretical three rounds a minute, though this was seldom attained in practice.

In 1855 the national armories began making only rifles and started converting smoothbores into rifles, but the work took time. By the end of 1858 the Springfield and Harpers Ferry Armories had manufactured only 4,000 of the new type of rifle called the Springfield .58. It was a muzzle-loader. Breech-loading, permitting a much more rapid rate of fire, had to await the development of a tight-fitting but easy-moving bolt and a cartridge that would effectively seal the breech. Many breechloaders were on the market in the 1850's and the Army began testing all available models but did not complete its tests before 1861. Effective breech-loading rifles required metallic rather than paper cartridges to prevent escape of gases at the breech. Metallic cartridges were invented in 1856 but were not produced in large numbers until after 1861.

The introduction of rifling into field and coast artillery increased the accuracy and more than doubled the effective range; but rifled guns, which had to await the development of advanced manufacturing techniques, did not immediately supplant the smoothbores. During this period an important smoothbore piece was introduced for the light batteries, the 12-pounder bronze cannon called the "Napoleon" for Napoleon III. Capt. Robert P. Parrott's rifled cannon was developed in 1851 but did not come into use on an appreciable scale until the Civil War. The application of the Minié principle to artillery did much to further the use of rifled artillery, though grape and canister, shell (high explosive and shrapnel), and solid shot, all used in the Mexican War, were still standard.

Rockets declined in favor. The brief experience with them in the Mexican War had not been impressive. After the war, continued experimentation failed to remove faults of eccentricity in flight and instability. The rockets often exploded prematurely, so that troops were reluctant to use them; moreover, they tended to deteriorate in storage. More important than any of these considerations was the fact that the new rifled artillery was decidedly superior to rockets in range and accuracy.

Tactical doctrine did not entirely keep pace with the development of weapons. In an effort in that direction, Secretary Davis prescribed light infantry tactics for all infantry units. In general, this meant reducing the line of the infantry from three to two ranks and placing increased emphasis on skirmishers. Formations, however, were still rigid: men stood shoulder to shoulder (it was almost impossible to load a muzzle-loader lying down) and intervals between units were small. These relatively dense formations would, in the early days of the Civil War, offer inviting targets.

At the U.S. Military Academy during this period, such great names as Robert E. Lee and Dennis Mahan, author of many works on engineering and fortification, appeared on the roster of staff and faculty. The Artillery School of Practice was reopened; and, with the appearance in 1849 of Bvt. Maj. Alfred Mordecai's *Artillery for the United States Land Service,* the Army had for the first time a full, accurate description of its system of artillery. Secretary Davis sent Mordecai, along with Maj. Richard Delafield and Capt. George B. McClellan, to Europe to study all aspects of the Crimean War in particular and

European military institutions and development in general. The study of American military theory was stimulated by the publication in 1846 of Henry Wager Halleck's *Elements of Military Art and Science*. Such volumes as Scott's *Instructions for Field Artillery*, the *General Regulations for the Army of the United States, Hardee's Tactics*, and the new volume on infantry tactics sponsored by Davis were made available to Army officers and a few others, although not enough were obtained to furnish copies to the militia. A number of military schools had been founded throughout the country, with the South having a slight edge, an advantage that was to provide officers to the Confederacy when the Civil War broke out.

CHAPTER 9

The Civil War, 1861

During the administration of President James Buchanan, 1857–61, tensions over the issue of extending slavery into the western territories mounted alarmingly and the nation ran its inexorable course toward disunion. Along with slavery, the shifting social, economic, political, and constitutional problems of the fast-growing country fragmented its citizenry. After open warfare broke out in Kansas Territory among slaveholders, abolitionists, and opportunists, the battle lines of opinion hardened rapidly. President Buchanan quieted Kansas by using the Regular Army, but it was too small and too scattered to suppress the struggles that were almost certain to break out in the border states.

In 1859 John Brown, who had won notoriety in "Bleeding Kansas," seized the federal arsenal at Harpers Ferry in a mad attempt to foment a slave uprising within a slaveholding state. Again federal troops were called on to suppress the new outbreak, and pressures and emotions rose on the eve of the 1860 elections. Republican Abraham Lincoln was elected to succeed Buchanan; although he failed to win a majority of the popular vote, he received 180 of the 303 electoral votes. The inauguration that was to vest in him the powers of the Presidency would take place March 4, 1861. During this lame-duck period, Mr. Buchanan was unable to control events and the country continued to lose its cohesion.

Secession, Sumter, and Standing to Arms

Abraham Lincoln's election to the Presidency on November 6, 1860, triggered South Carolina on December 20 to enact an ordinance declaring "the union now subsisting between South Carolina and other States, under the name of the 'United States of America,' is hereby dissolved." Within six weeks, six other deep-South states seceded from the Union and seized federal property inside their borders, including military installations, save Fort Pickens outside Pensacola and Fort Sumter in Charleston Harbor. (*Map 21*) To the seven states that formed the Confederate States of America on February 18, 1861, at Montgomery, Alabama, retention of the forts by the U.S. Government was equivalent to a warlike act. To provide his fledgling government with a military force, on

March 6 the new Confederate Executive, Jefferson Davis, called for a 100,000-man volunteer force to serve for twelve months.

The creation of a rival War Department south of the 35th parallel on February 21 shattered the composition of the Regular Army and disrupted its activities, particularly in Texas, where Maj. Gen. David E. Twiggs surrendered his entire command. With an actual strength of 1,080 officers and 14,926 enlisted men on June 30, 1860, the Regular Army was based on 5-year enlistments. Recruited heavily from men of foreign birth, the United States Army consisted of 10 regiments of infantry, 4 of artillery, 2 of cavalry, 2 of dragoons, and 1 of mounted riflemen. It was not a unified striking force. The Regular Army was deployed within seven departments, six of them west of the Mississippi. Of 198 line companies, 183 were scattered in 79 isolated posts in the territories. The remaining 15 were in garrisons along the Canadian border and on the Atlantic coast.

Created by Secretary of War John C. Calhoun and expanded by Secretary of War Davis in 1853, the departments of the United States Army had become powerful institutions by the eve of the Civil War. Within each of the trans-Mississippi departments a senior colonel or general officer by brevet commanded some 2,000 officers and men. All the states east of the Mississippi constituted the Department of the East, where Bvt. Maj. Gen. John E. Wool controlled 929 Regulars. A department commander was responsible for mobilizing and training militia and volunteer forces called into federal service, and for co-ordinating his resources with any expeditionary force commander who operated inside his territory or crossed through his department. A department commander often doubled in command. He was responsible for the administration of his department as well as for conduct of operations in the field. He often had a dual staff arrangement, one departmental and another for the campaign. For strategic guidance and major decisions he looked to the President and General in Chief; for administrative support he channeled his requirements through the Secretary of War to the appropriate bureau chief. In the modern sense he had no corps of staff experts who could assist him in equating his strategic goals with his logistical needs. In many respects the departmental system was a major reason why the Union armies during the Civil War operated like a team of balky horses.

The 1,676 numbered paragraphs of the U.S. Army Regulations governed the actions of a department commander. The provisions concerning Army organization and tactics were archaic in most cases despite Davis' efforts in 1857 to update the Regulations to reflect the experience of the Mexican War. During the Civil War the Regulations would be slightly modified to incorporate the

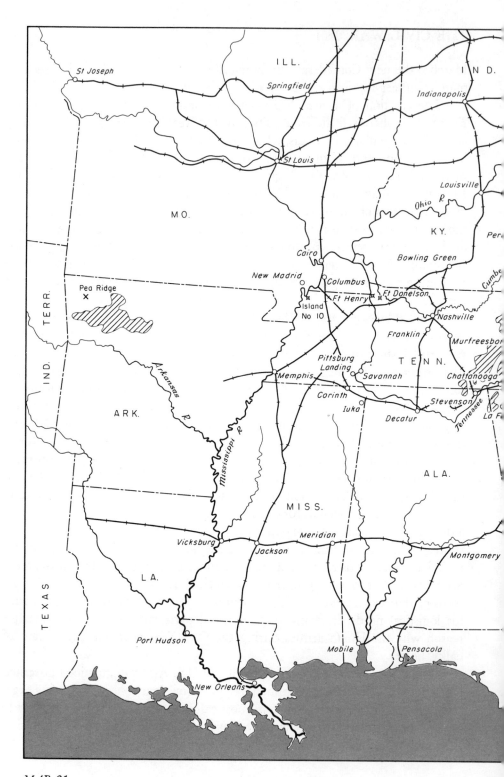

MAP 21

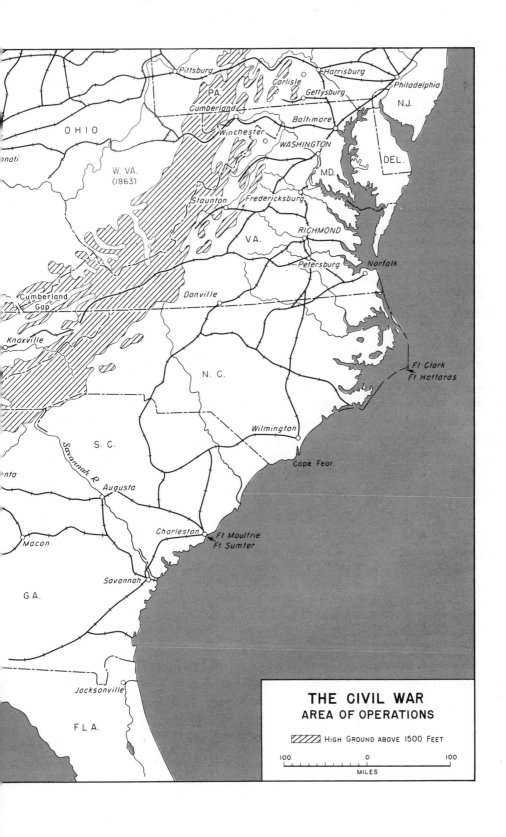

Pittsburg

Carlisle
Harrisburg

PA

Gettysburg

Philadelphia

Cumberland

N.J.

OHIO

Baltimore

Winchester

WASHINGTON

DEL.

W. VA.
(1863)

MD.

nnati

Staunton

Fredericksburg

VA.

RICHMOND

Petersburg

Norfolk

Cumberland
Gap

Danville

Ft Clark
Ft Hattaras

Knoxville

N. C.

Wilmington

S. C.

Cape Fear.

Savannah R.

Augusta

nta

Charleston

Ft Moultrie
Ft Sumter

Macon

Savannah

G A.

GA.

Jacksonville

FL A.

THE CIVIL WAR
AREA OF OPERATIONS

HIGH GROUND ABOVE 1500 FEET

100   0   100

MILES

military laws passed by two wartime Congresses. In the South these same Regulations would govern the policy and procedures of the Confederate forces.

The roster of the Regular Army was altered considerably by Davis' action in creating a Confederate Army. Of the active officer corps numbering 1,080, 286 resigned or were dismissed and entered the Confederate service. (At least 26 enlisted men are known to have violated their oaths.) West Point graduates on the active list numbered 824; of these, 184 were among the officers who offered their swords to the Confederacy. Of the approximately 900 graduates then in civil life, 114 returned to the Union Army and 99 others sought southern commissions. General in Chief Scott and Col. George H. Thomas of Virginia were southerners who fought for the Union. More serious than their numbers, however, was the high caliber of the officers who joined the Confederacy; many were regimental commanders and three had commanded at departmental level.

With military preparations under way, Davis dispatched commissioners to Washington a few days after Lincoln's inauguration on March 4, 1861, to treat for the speedy takeover of Forts Sumter and Pickens. Informally reassured that the forts would not be provisioned without proper notice, the envoys returned to Montgomery expecting an uneventful evacuation of Sumter. President Lincoln had to move cautiously, for he knew Sumter's supplies were giving out. As each March day passed, Sumter aggravated the harshness of Lincoln's dilemma. In case of war, the fort had no strategic value. If Lincoln reinforced it, Davis would have his act of provocation and Lincoln might drive eight more slaveholding states out of the Union. If Sumter was not succored, the North might cool its enthusiasm for the Union concept and become accustomed to having a confederation south of the Mason-Dixon line.

President Lincoln spent a fortnight listening to the conflicting counsel of his constitutional advisers, and made up his own mind on March 29 to resupply Fort Sumter with provisions only. No effort would be made to increase its military power. By sea he soon dispatched a token expedition and on April 8 notified South Carolina's governor of his decision. The next move was up to the local Confederate commander, Brig. Gen. Pierre G. T. Beauregard. On the 11th, Maj. Robert Anderson, Sumter's commander, politely but firmly rejected a formal surrender demand. At 4:30 the next morning Confederate batteries began a 34-hour bombardment. Anderson's 90-man garrison returned it in earnest, but Sumter's guns were no match for the concentric fire from Confederate artillery. Offered honorable terms on April 14,

Anderson surrendered the federal fort, saluted his U.S. flag with fifty guns, and, with his command, was conveyed to the fleet outside the harbor to be taken to New York City.

Unquestionably, the Confederates fired the first shot of the war, and with that rash act removed many difficulties from Lincoln's path to preserve the Union. On the 15th Lincoln personally penned a proclamation declaring the seven southern states in insurrection against the laws of the United States. To strangle the Confederacy, on the 19th Lincoln declared the entire coast from South Carolina to Texas under naval blockade. To augment the reduced Regular Army, Lincoln asked the governors of the loyal states for 75,000 militiamen to serve for three months, the maximum time permissible under existing laws. With a unanimity which astonished most people, the northern states responded with 100,000 men. Within the eight slave states still in the Union, the militia call to suppress the rebellion was angrily and promptly rejected, and the President's decision to coerce the Confederacy moved Virginia, North Carolina, Tennessee, and Arkansas to join it.

As spring changed into summer the magnitude of the job that the Union had proclaimed for itself—the conquest of an area the size of western Europe, save Scandinavia and Italy, defended by a plucky and proud people and favored by military geography—was imperfectly understood. Although Lincoln later emerged as a diligent student of warfare, he was as yet unversed in the art. His rival, Davis, from the outset knew his military men quite well and thoroughly understood the mechanics of building a fighting force. Yet, as time passed, Davis was to mismanage his government and its military affairs more and more.

Virginia's secession caused Col. Robert E. Lee, Scott's choice to be the Union's field leader, to resign his commission and offer his services to his state. The Confederates moved their capital to Richmond, Virginia, site of the largest iron works in the south and one hundred miles south of the Union capital, Washington. On May 23, Union forces crossed into northern Virginia, occupying Arlington Heights and Alexandria. With Virginia and North Carolina in rebellion, Lincoln extended the naval blockade and called for a large volunteer army backed by an increased Regular force.

Correctly anticipating that Congress in its session to open July 4 would approve his actions, Lincoln, on his own authority, established 40 regiments of U.S. Volunteers (42,034 men) to serve three years or for the duration of the war. He ordered the Regular Army increased by 1 regiment of artillery, 1 of

INSIDE FORT SUMTER *the day after its surrender.*

cavalry, and 8 of infantry (actually, 9 regiments were added), or 22,714 men, and the Navy by 18,000 sailors. The new Regular infantry regiments were each to have 3 battalions of about 800 men, in contrast to the 1-battalion structure in the existing Regular and volunteer regiments. Because the recruits preferred the larger bonuses, laxer discipline, and easy-going atmosphere of the volunteers, most of the newly constituted regiments were never able to fill their additional battalions to authorized strength.

The enthusiastic response to Lincoln's various calls had forced him to ask the governors to scale down the induction of men. The overtaxed camps could not handle the increased manpower. In raising the Army Lincoln used methods that dated back to Washington's day. The combat efficiency and state of training of the new units varied from good to very poor. Some militia regiments were well trained and equipped, others were regiments in name only. The soldiers often elected their own company officers, and the governors commissioned majors and colonels. The President appointed generals. Although many of the newly commissioned officers proved to be enthusiastic, devoted to duty, and eager to learn, incompetents were also appointed. Before the end of 1861, however, officers were being required to prove their qualifications before examining boards; those found unfit were allowed to resign.

Frequently advised by governors and congressmen, Mr. Lincoln selected generals from among leading politicians in order to give himself a broader base of political support. Some political generals, such as John A. Logan and Francis P. Blair, Jr., distinguished themselves, whereas others proved military hindrances. Lincoln gave a majority of the commissions in the first forty volunteer units to Regulars on active duty, to former West Pointers like George B. McClellan who had resigned to pursue a business career, or to those who had held volunteer commissions during the Mexican War. On the other hand, Davis never gave higher than a brigade command to a Confederate volunteer officer until he had proved himself in battle.

Both North and South failed to develop a good system of replacement of individuals in volunteer units. The Confederacy, though hamstrung by its insistence that Texans be commanded by Texans and Georgians by Georgians and by governors' demands for retaining home guards, did devise a regimental system that stood up well until the closing days of the war. Except for Wisconsin, Illinois, and Vermont, the Union armies never had an efficient volunteer replacement system. As battle losses mounted and the ranks of veteran regiments thinned, commanders were forced to send men back to their home states on recruiting duty or face the disbandment of their regiments. Northern governors with patronage in mind preferred to raise new regiments, allowing battle-tested ones to decline to company proportions.

GENERAL LEE. (*Photograph taken after his promotion to lieutenant general.*)

The enlisted Regular Army was kept intact for the duration of the war. Many critics believed that the Regulars should have been used to cadre the volunteer units. But this practice was initially impossible during the summer of 1861 for at least two reasons. Lincoln did not foresee a long war, and the majority of Regulars were needed on the frontier until trained men could replace them. In addition, Lincoln's critics overlooked the breakdown in morale that would have accompanied the breakup of old line regiments, many of which had histories and honors dating back to the War of 1812. An officer holding a Regular commission in 1861 had to resign to accept a commission in the volunteers unless the War Department specifically released him. Most Regulars were loath to resign, uncertain that they would be recalled to active duty after the war. Thus, during 1861 and part of 1862, promotion in the Regular Army was slow. All Regulars could accept commissions in the volunteers by 1862, and in many cases the year that they had spent in small unit command seasoning had its reward in advancing them to higher commands. Ulysses S. Grant and William T. Sherman, both U.S. Military Academy graduates returning from civilian life, asked specifically for volunteer regimental commands at first and soon advanced rapidly to general officer posts.

The Opponents

As North and South lined up for battle, clearly the preponderance of productive capacity, manpower, and agricultural potential lay on the side of the North. Its crops were worth more annually than those of the South, which had concentrated on growing cotton, tobacco, and rice. Between February and May 1861 the Confederate authorities missed the opportunity of shipping baled cotton to England and drawing bills against it for the purchase of arms. In seapower, railroads, material wealth, and industrial capacity to produce iron and munitions the North was vastly superior to the South. This disparity became even more pronounced as the ever-tightening blockade gradually cut off the Confederacy from foreign imports. The North had more mules and horses, a logistical advantage of great importance since supplies had to be carried to the troops from rail and river heads.

According to the census of 1860 the population of the United States numbered 31,443,321 persons. Approximately 23,000,000 of them were in the twenty-two northern states and 9,000,000 in the eleven states that later seceded. Of the latter total, 3,500,000 were slaves. The size of the opposing armies would reflect this disparity. At one time or another about 2,100,000 men would serve in the northern armies, while some 800,000 to 900,000 men would serve the South. Peak strength of the two forces would be about 1,000,000 and 600,000, respectively.

Yet not all the advantages lay with the North. The South possessed good interior lines of communications, and its 3,550-mile coast line, embracing 189 harbors and navigable river mouths, was most difficult to blockade effectively. Possessors of a rich military record in wars against the British, Spanish, Mexicans, and Indians, the southerners initially managed to form redoubtable cavalry units more easily than the North and used them with considerable skill against the invading infantry. As the war moved along, the armies on both sides demonstrated high degrees of military skill and bravery. Man for man they became almost evenly matched, and their battles were among the bloodiest in modern history.

Jefferson Davis hoped that the sympathy or even intervention of European powers might more than compensate for the Confederacy's lack of material resources. This hope, largely illusory from the start, became less and less likely of realization with the emancipation of the slaves, with every Union victory, and with the increasing effectiveness of the blockade.

Militarily, the South's greatest advantage over the North was simply the fact that if not attacked it could win by doing nothing. To restore the Union the Federal forces would have to conquer the Confederacy. Thus the arena of action lay below the strategic line of the Potomac and Ohio Rivers. Here geography divided the theater of war into three interrelated theaters of operations. The eastern theater lay between the Atlantic Ocean and the Appalachian Mountains; the western theater embraced the area from the Appalachians to the Mississippi; and the trans-Mississippi theater ran westward to the Pacific Ocean. (*Map 22*)

In the east, the strategic triangle of northern Virginia shielded invasion routes. Its apex aimed arrowlike at the Federal capital; the Potomac River and the lower Chesapeake Bay formed its right leg; its left bounded on the Blue Ridge and the adjacent Shenandoah Valley; and the base of the triangle followed the basin of the James and Appomattox Rivers, whereon stood Richmond, halfway between the bay and the valley. For three and a half years Federal commanders would be defeated on the legs and in the center of this triangle as they tried to take Richmond and defeat the Army of Northern Virginia under Lee. In three neighboring counties within this triangle more than half a million men would clash in mortal combat; more would die in these counties than in the Revolutionary War, the War of 1812, the War with Mexico, and all the Indian wars combined. To bring the Confederates out of this triangle the North would have to execute an operation aimed at breaking through the base line along the James and Appomattox Rivers.

The hammer for swinging against the anvil of Virginia came from the line of the Ohio River as Union forces moved along the invasion routes of the Green, Cumberland, Tennessee, and Mississippi Rivers. To breach the lower reaches of the Appalachians, the Federals needed the railroad centers at Nashville, Chattanooga, and Atlanta; with them they could strike northward through the Carolinas toward the line of the James. But in the spring of 1861, the anvil and hammer concept had not yet occurred to the military leaders in Washington. Only the General in Chief, Winfield Scott, had a concrete strategic proposal for waging total war. He recommended to Lincoln that time be taken to train an army of 85,000 men and that the naval blockade of the Confederacy be enforced. Then the Army was to advance down the Mississippi to divide and conquer the South. The press ridiculed the strategy, calling it the Anaconda Plan. But few leaders examined the South in terms of its military geography or concentrated on a strategy to prevail over it. Instead, most thought in terms of political boundaries and a short war that would end with the capture of Richmond.

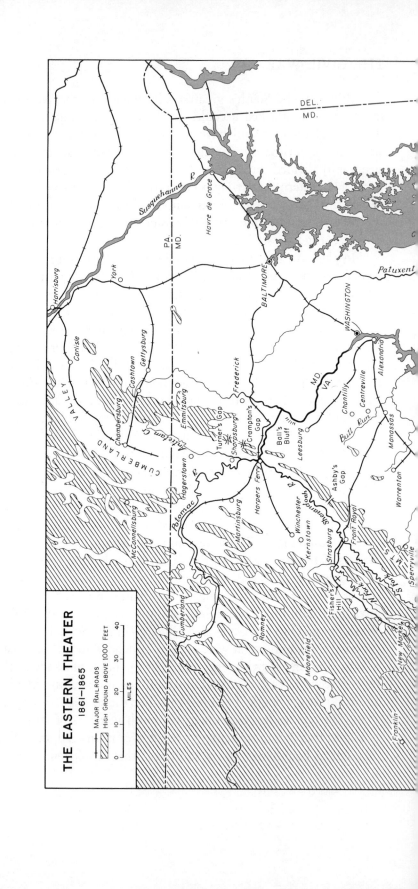

THE EASTERN THEATER
1861–1865

|‡‡‡‡| MAJOR RAILROADS
|▨▨▨| HIGH GROUND ABOVE 1000 FEET

MILES
0   10   20   30   40

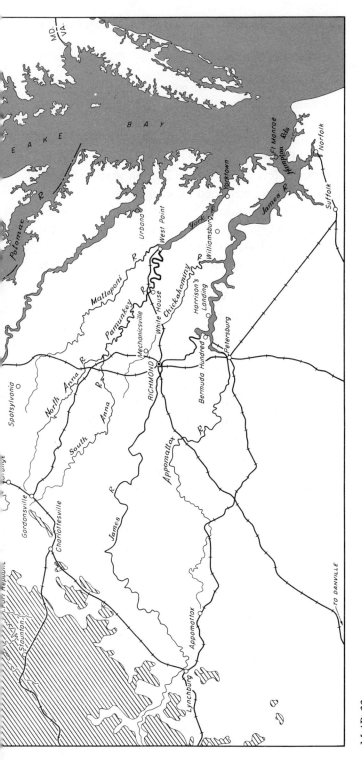

MAP 22

Manassas (Bull Run)

In the early summer of 1861 the partly trained 90-day militia, the almost untrained volunteers, and one newly organized battalion of Regulars—a total force of 50,000 Federals commanded by Brig. Gen. Irvin McDowell—defended the nation's capital. Thirty miles to the southwest, covering the rail and road hub at Manassas, Virginia, General Beauregard posted some 20,000 Confederates, to be joined by 2,000 more within a few days. To the left, on their defensive line along the Potomac, the Confederates stationed another 11,000 men under Brig. Gen. Joseph E. Johnston in the Shenandoah Valley town of Winchester. Opposing Johnston around Martinsburg, with the mission of keeping the Confederates in place, was Maj. Gen. Robert Patterson with 18,000 Federals. On the extreme right of the Confederate northern Virginia defense line was Col. Joseph B. Magruder's force, which had recently repulsed Maj. Gen. Benjamin F. Butler's Union troops at Big Bethel, Virginia, on 10 June, and forced them back into their sanctuary at Fort Monroe.

Big Bethel, the first large-scale meeting engagement of the Civil War, demonstrated that neither opponent was as yet well trained. The Confederates had started preparations earlier to protect northern Virginia and therefore might have had a slight edge on their opponents. General McDowell, only recently a major of Regulars, had less than three months to weld his three types of units—militia, volunteer, and Regular—into a single fighting force. He attempted to do too much himself, and there were few competent staff officers in the vicinity to help him. McDowell's largest tactical unit was a regiment until just before he marched out of Alexandria. Two to four brigades, plus a battery of Regular artillery—the best arm against raw infantry—formed a division. In all, thirteen brigades were organized into five divisions. McDowell parceled out his forty-nine guns among his brigade commanders, who in turn attached them to their regiments. His total force for the advance was 35,732 men, but of these one division of 5,752 men dropped off to guard roads to the rear.

McDowell's advance against Beauregard, on four parallel routes, was hastened by northern opinion, expressed in editorials and Congressional speeches, demanding immediate action. Scott warned Lincoln against undertaking the "On to Richmond" campaign until McDowell's troops had become disciplined units. But Lincoln, eager to use the 90-day militia before they departed, demanded an advance, being aware that the Confederates were also unseasoned and cherishing the belief that one defeat would force the South to quit. Scott, influenced by false intelligence that Beauregard would move immedi-

ately on Washington, acceded. Accordingly, McDowell's battle plan and preparations were expedited. The plan, accepted in late June, called for Butler and
Patterson to prevent the Confederates facing them from reinforcing Beauregard,
while McDowell advanced against Manassas to outflank the southern position.
Scott called it a good plan on paper but knew Johnston was capable of frustrating
it if given the chance. McDowell's success against the Confederate center depended upon a rapid 30-mile march, if 35,000 Federals were to keep 22,000
Confederates from being reinforced.

On July 16, 1861, the largest army ever assembled on the North American
continent up to that time advanced slowly on both sides of the Warrenton pike
toward Bull Run. McDowell's march orders were good, but the effect was
ruined by one unwise caution to the brigade commanders: "It will not be
pardonable in any commander . . . to come upon a battery or breastwork
without a knowledge of its position." The caution recalled to McDowell's subordinates the currently sensationalized bugbear of the press of being fooled by
"masked batteries," a term originating at Sumter where a certain battery was
constructed, masked by a house which was demolished just before the guns
opened fire. Accordingly, 35,000 men moved just five miles on the 17th. Next
day the Federals occupied Centreville, some four miles east of Stone Bridge,
which carried the Warrenton pike over Bull Run. (*Map 23*)

Beauregard's advanced guards made no effort to delay the Federals, but fell
back across the battle line, now extending some three miles along the west bank
of Bull Run, which meandered from Stone Bridge southeast until it joined the
Occoquan stream. The country was fairly rough, cut by streams, and thickly
wooded. It presented formidable obstacles to attacking raw troops, but a fair
shelter for equally raw troops on the defensive. On the 18th, while McDowell's
main body waited at Centreville for the trains to close up, the leading division
demonstrated against Beauregard's right around Mitchell's Ford. The Federal
infantry retired after a sharp musketry fight, and a 45-minute artillery duel ensued. It was the first exchange of four standard types of artillery ammunition
for all muzzle-loading guns, whether rifled or smoothbore. Solid shot, shell,
spherical case or shrapnel, and canister from eight Federal guns firing 415
rounds were answered by seven Confederate pieces returning 310 rounds.
Steadily withdrawing its guns, the oldest and best drilled unit of the South, the
Washington Light Artillery of New Orleans, broke off the fight against well-
trained U.S. Regular artillery. Both sides had used rifled artillery, which greatly
increased the accuracy and gave a range more than double that of the smoothbores. Yet rifled guns never supplanted the new, easily loaded Napoleons. In the
fight, defective Confederate ammunition fired from three new 3-inch iron rifles

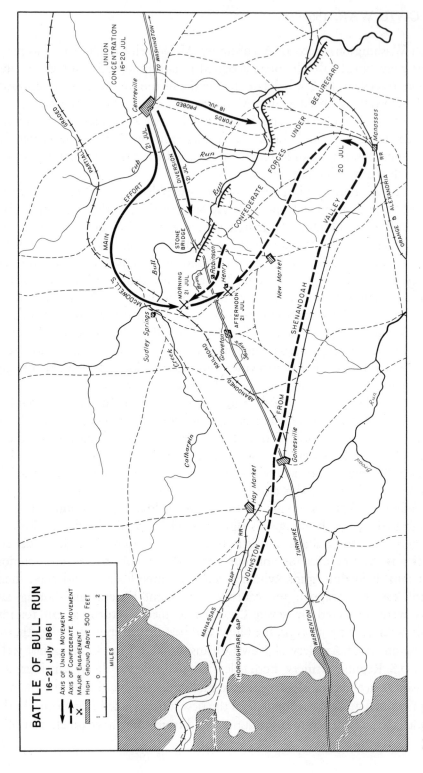

BATTLE OF BULL RUN
16-21 July 1861

AXIS OF UNION MOVEMENT
AXIS OF CONFEDERATE MOVEMENT
MAJOR ENGAGEMENT
HIGH GROUND ABOVE 500 FEET

MILES

UNION CONCENTRATION 16-20 JUL

TO WASHINGTON

Centreville

PROBED 18 JUL

FORDS

BEAUREGARD

Manassas

CONFEDERATE FORCES UNDER

DIVERSION 21 JUL

20 JUL

ORANGE & ALEXANDRIA RR

MAIN EFFORT 21 JUL

STONE BRIDGE

Bull

Run

Cub

Run

Robinson

Henry

New Market

SHENANDOAH

VALLEY

MCDOWELL'S

Sudley Springs

MORNING 21 JUL

AFTERNOON 21 JUL

Branch

Creek

Catharpin

Groveton

ABANDONED RAILROAD

Sudley

FROM

Gainesville

Run

Hay Market

JOHNSTON

MANASSAS GAP RR

THOROUGHFARE GAP

WARRENTON TURNPIKE

Broad

Run

MAP 23

would not fly point foremost but tumbled and lost range against McDowell's gunners. That the error went undetected for days reveals the haste in which Davis had procured his ordnance.

Sure that his green troops could not flank the Confederate right, McDowell tarried two more fateful days before he attacked in force. Engineers reconnoitered for an undefended ford north of Stone Bridge. Finding no vedettes at the ford near Sudley Springs, McDowell decided to envelop the Confederate left on July 21 and destroy the Manassas Gap Railroad to keep Johnston from reinforcing the outnumbered Beauregard. The idea was excellent, but the timing was slow.

While McDowell frittered away four and a half days before he was ready to envelop in force, new tools of warfare swung the advantages of mobility, surprise, and mass at critical points toward Beauregard. On July 17 spies in Washington told of McDowell's departure from Alexandria. By electric telegraph Beauregard in turn alerted Richmond. Davis, also telegraphing, ordered commanders around Richmond, at Aquia Creek, and at Winchester to concentrate their available strength at Manassas. Johnston lost no time in deceiving Patterson by using Col. J. E. B. Stuart's cavalry as a screen and adroitly maneuvering his infantry away from the valley. Johnston selected the best overland routes for his artillery and cavalry marches and arranged for railroad officials to move his four infantry brigades. Brig. Gen. Thomas Jackson's lead brigade, accompanied by Johnston himself, covered fifty-seven miles in twenty-five hours by road and rail, reaching Beauregard on the 20th.

At daylight on the 21st, McDowell unmasked the first phase of his attack plan. Three brigades of Brig. Gen. Daniel Tyler's division appeared before Stone Bridge, and a huge, 30-pounder Parrott rifle dragged into place by ten horses commenced a slow fire, directed by six cannoneers of the 2d U.S. Artillery. Five brigades in two divisions directly under McDowell's command meanwhile marched on an 8-mile circuitous route toward the undefended ford at Sudley Springs. McDowell's goal was the Confederate left rear and a chance to cut the railroad. At 9:00 a.m. a signal flag wigwag from the Henry house announced the point of the enveloping columns at Sudley's crossing, and the intelligence was immediately relayed to Beauregard and Johnston, who were three miles away on the Confederate right.

The first weight of the Federal attack fell against eleven Confederate companies and two guns. For an hour McDowell's regiments, firing one by one and moving forward cautiously in piecemeal fashion, tried to overrun Beauregard's left flank. The timid tactics gave Beauregard time to redeploy ten regiments across a 3-mile front to form a second defensive line across the north face of the hill behind the Henry house. At 10:30 a.m., as the summer sun grew hotter, a portentous dust cloud, rising ten miles northwest of Manassas, heralded the arrival of Kirby Smith's brigade, the tail of Johnston's reinforcements from the Shenandoah Valley.

For two hours the roar of the battle swelled in volume. Federal musketry crashes and the thunder from the heavier pieces indicated that McDowell was now committing whole brigades, supported by four batteries of artillery. North of the Warrenton turnpike, the Confederate infantry began to lose its brigade cohesion and fall back in disorder. As Beauregard and Johnston rode to the sound of battle, some 10,000 Federals were punishing 7,000 Confederates in the vicinity of the Henry and Robinson houses. Johnston, though senior in command, turned the battle over to Beauregard and galloped off toward Manassas to direct the arrival of reinforcements. Brig. Gen. Barnard E. Bee's brigade was pushed back from its advanced position toward the flat-crested hill behind the Henry house, where Jackson's newly arrived brigade had formed. In rallying his routed troops, Bee shouted: "Look at Jackson's Brigade; it stands like a stone wall! Rally behind the Virginians!" (Out of these words came a nickname that Jackson would carry to his grave, and after his death in 1863 the Confederate War Department officially designated his unit the Stonewall Brigade.) Screened by a wooded area, three brigades regrouped behind Jackson's lines, and the rally became a great equalizer as McDowell's strength dissipated to 9,000 men, with no immediate infantry reserves in sight.

The cloud of dust moved closer to Manassas Junction, but McDowell ignored it and allowed a lull to settle over his front for almost two hours. At 2:00 p.m., having deployed two batteries of Regular artillery directly to his front around the Henry house with insufficient infantry protection, McDowell renewed the battle. By midafternoon the dust had blended sweaty uniforms into a common hue, and more and more cases of mistaken identity were confusing both sides in the smoke of the battle. Then, as part of the confusion, came a fateful episode. To the right front of McDowell's exposed artillery, a line of advancing blue-clad infantry, the 33d Regiment, Virginia Volunteers, suddenly appeared through the smoke. The Federal artillery commander ordered canister, but the chief artillery officer on McDowell's staff overruled the order, claiming that the oncoming blue uniforms belonged to friendly infantry arriving in support. The Virginians advanced to within seventy yards of the Federal guns, leveled their muskets, and let loose. The shock of their volley cut the artillery to shreds, and for the remainder of the day nine Federal guns stood silent, unserved, and helpless between the armies.

About 4:00 p.m., Beauregard, with two additional fresh brigades, advanced his entire line. Shorn of their artillery, the faltering Federal lines soon lost cohesion and began to pull back along the routes they knew; there was more and more confusion as they retired. East of Bull Run, Federal artillery, using Napoleon smoothbores in this initial pullback from the field, proved to the unsuspecting Confederate cavalry, using classic saber-charging tactics, that a determined line of artillerymen could reduce cavalry to dead and sprawling infantry in minutes.

As in so many battles of the Civil War yet to come, there was no organized pursuit in strength to cut the enemy to ribbons while he fled from the immediate area of the battlefield. At Bull Run the Federal withdrawal turned into a panic-stricken flight about 6:30 p.m., when Cub Run bridge, about a mile west of Centreville, was blocked by overturned wagons. Sunset would fall at 7:15 p.m., and President Davis, just arrived from Richmond, had two daylight hours to arrive at a decision for pursuit. In council with Johnston and Beauregard, Davis instructed the whole Confederate right to advance against the Centreville road, but apparently his orders were never delivered or Beauregard neglected to follow them. Davis thus lost a splendid opportunity for seeing in person whether the unused infantry and artillery on the right of his line could have made a concerted effort to destroy McDowell's fleeing forces. Logistically, Federal booty taken over the next two days by the Confederates would have sustained them for days in an advance against Washington.

Strategically, Bull Run was important to the Confederates only because the center of their Virginia defenses had held. Tactically, the action highlights many of the problems and deficiencies that were typical of the first year of the war. Bull Run was a clash between large, ill-trained bodies of recruits, who were slow in joining battle; masked batteries frightened commanders; plans called for maneuvering the enemy out of position, but attacks were frontal; security principles were disregarded; tactical intelligence was nil; and reconnaissance was poorly executed. Soldiers were overloaded for battle. Neither commander was able to employ his whole force effectively. Of McDowell's 35,000 men, only 18,000 crossed Bull Run and casualties among these, including the missing, numbered about 2,708. Beauregard, with 32,000 men, ordered only 18,000 into action and lost 1,982.

Both commanders rode along the front, often interfering in small unit actions. McDowell led his enveloping column instead of directing all his forces from the rear. Wisely, Johnston left the battlefield and went to the rear to hasten up his Shenandoah Valley reserves. Regiments were committed piecemeal. Infantry failed to protect exposed artillery. Artillery was parceled out under infantry command; only on the retreat was the Union senior artillery officer on the scene allowed to manage his guns. He saved 21 guns of the 49 that McDowell had. Beauregard's orders were oral, vague, and confusing. Some were delivered, others were never followed.

The Second Uprising in 1861

The southern victory near Manassas had an immediate and a long-range effect on the efforts of both the northern and the southern states. First, it compelled northern leaders to face up to the nature and scope of the struggle and to begin the task of putting the Union on a full war footing. Second, it made them more willing to give heed to the advice of professional soldiers charged with the task of directing military operations along a vast continental land front extending from Point Lookout, Maryland, to Fort Craig in central New Mexico. Third, Confederate leaders, after their feeling of invincibility quickly wore off, called for 400,000 volunteers, sought critical military items in Europe, and turned to planning operations that might swing the remaining slaveholding states and territories into the Confederacy. Finally, the most potent immediate influence of Bull Run was upon the European powers, which eyed the Confederacy as a belligerent with much potential for political intervention and as a source of revenue. Unless the Federal Navy could make it unprofitable for private merchant ships to deliver arms to southern ports and depart with agricultural goods, speculative capital would flow increasingly into the contraband trade.

Strategically, in 1861 the U.S. Navy made the most important contribution toward an ultimate Union victory. At considerable expense and in haste to make the blockade effective, the Navy by the end of the year had assembled 200 ships of every description, armed them after a fashion, and placed them on station. With new Congressional acts regarding piracy, revenue, confiscation, and enforcement in hand, commanders of this motley fleet intercepted more and more swift blockade runners steaming out of Nassau, Bermuda, and Havana on their three-day run to Wilmington, North Carolina, Charleston, South Carolina, or Savannah, Georgia. In two round trips a blockade runner, even if lost on its third voyage, still produced a considerable profit to its owner. By the end of 1861 such profit was no longer easy, because the Navy had many new fast ships in service, specially fitted for blockade duty.

After 1861 the naval character of the war changed. There was no Civil War on the high seas except for the exciting exploits of three or four Confederate cruisers which raided commercial shipping. As the war progressed, both opponents perfected the nature and construction of ships and naval ordnance for a war that would be fought in coastal waters or inside defensible harbors. The three main weapons, the rifled naval gun, the armored ram, and the torpedo mine, were developed and used in novel ways. To offset the defensive use of these weapons by the South, the Federal Navy beginning in August 1861 landed more and more Army expeditionary forces and gradually obtained footholds in the vicinity of Mobile, Savannah, Charleston, and Wilmington. By the end of the war, joint Navy-Army expeditions would convert the sea blockade into a military occupation and would seal off all major ports in the South.

The defeat at Bull Run was followed by "a second uprising" in the North, greatly surpassing the effort after Sumter's surrender. President Lincoln and Congress set to with a will to raise and train the large Federal armies that would be required to defeat the South, to select competent Army field commanders, and to reorganize and strengthen the War Department. On July 22, 1861, Lincoln called for a 500,000-man force of 3-year volunteers and during the rest of July quickly disbanded the 90-day militiamen. The more experienced entered the newly authorized volunteer force. Meanwhile, the volunteer quota and the increase of Regulars, mobilized after Sumter, had so far progressed that camps and garrisons, established at strategic points along the 1,950-mile boundary with the border states and territories, were bustling with activity. As July ended, Congress authorized the volunteers to serve for the duration of the war and perfected their regimental organization. Four regiments were grouped into a brigade, and three brigades formed a division. The infantry corps structure would be fixed when the President directed. In effect, the Lincoln administration was building a federal force, as opposed to one based on joint state-federal control and support. State governors, given a quota according to a state's population, raised 1,000-man volunteer regiments, bought locally whatever the units needed, shipped them to federal training centers, and presented all bills to the U.S. Government. Accordingly, Congress floated a national loan of $250 million.

Pending the transformation of their volunteer forces, both opponents necessarily suspended major military operations for the remainder of 1861. President Lincoln conferred frequently with General Scott and his military advisers about steps already taken to strengthen Union forces along the continental front. Regular Army units were consolidating their position at Forts Craig and Union to protect the upper Rio Grande valley against any Confederate columns coming from Texas. To protect communication lines to the Pacific and the southwest and to guard federal supplies at Fort Leavenworth, Kansas, and St. Louis, Missouri, Union troops were deployed in eastern Kansas and across central Missouri. In August Union troops fought a drawn battle at Wilson's Creek,

UNION VOLUNTEERS IN CAMP

and Missouri became a state divided against itself. The loss of Kentucky, in Lincoln's judgment, would be "nearly the same as to lose the whole game"; so he carefully respected Kentucky's decision of May to remain neutral. After Bull Run, Illinois, Indiana, and Ohio volunteers were assembled north of the Ohio at exposed river towns to keep watch on the situation in Kentucky. In western Virginia forty counties elected to secede from Virginia and asked for federal troops to assist them in repelling any punitive expeditions emerging from the Shenandoah Valley. Between May and early July 1861, Ohio volunteers, under the command of Maj. Gen. George B. McClellan, occupied the Grafton area of western Virginia, hoping to protect the railroad that linked the Ohio Valley with Baltimore. In a series of clashes at Philippi, Beverly, and along the Cheat River, McClellan's forces checked the invading Confederates, paving the way for West Virginia's entrance into the Union.

Although the border strife intensified in the west, Scott attended to the more important front facing Virginia. The nation's capital was imperiled, the Potomac was directly under Confederate guns, and Maryland and Delaware were being used as recruiting areas for the southern cause. On July 22, Lincoln, following Scott's advice, had summoned McClellan, who was thirty-five years old at the time, to Washington, and assigned him command, under Scott, of all the troops in the Washington area. McClellan's reputation was unrivaled, and the public had acclaimed him for his victories in western Virginia. On August 21 McClellan named his force the Army of the Potomac, and commenced molding it into a formidable machine.

McClellan organized the Army of the Potomac into eleven 10,000-man divisions, each with three brigades of infantry, a cavalry regiment, and four 6-gun batteries. In general this structure was adopted by the other Union armies, and the Confederates deviated from the model only in their cavalry organization. In the Army of Northern Virginia, for example, General Lee treated his cavalry as a tactical arm, grouped first as a division, and later as a cavalry corps. Union cavalry consisted of little more than mounted infantry, carrying out a multitude of duties for the division commander, such as serving as pickets, wagon train escorts, and couriers. McClellan planned, once Lincoln activated corps, to withdraw one-half of the artillery pieces from each infantry division and center them at corps level as a reserve to be deployed under army command. He insisted that the .58-caliber single-shot, muzzle-loading Springfield rifle be the standard weapon of the infantry, and most of the Army of the Potomac possessed it when corps were organized on March 8, 1862.

McClellan completely transformed the military atmosphere around Washington before the end of 1861. But, although he was an able administrator, his critics doubted his abilities as a top field commander. And from the day he activated the Army of the Potomac, McClellan was politically active in trying to oust Scott. Finally, on November 1, the aged and harassed General in Chief, taking advantage of a new law, retired from the Army. That same day, acting on assurances that McClellan could handle two tasks concurrently, Lincoln made McClellan the General in Chief and retained him in command of the Army of the Potomac. By the 9th, basing his action on Scott's earlier groundwork, McClellan carved out five new departments in the west, all commanded by Regular Army officers. In addition, he continued the work of the new Department of New England, where General Butler was already forming volunteer regiments for scheduled seaborne operations off the Carolina capes and in the Gulf of New Mexico.

For the Union cause in Kentucky, the new General in Chief's move came none too soon. As early as September 4, a Confederate force from Tennessee had violated Kentucky's neutrality by occupying the Mississippi River town and railroad terminal of Columbus. The next day Illinois troops under Brig. Gen. Ulysses S. Grant seized Paducah and Smithland, strategic river towns in Kentucky at the confluence of the Tennessee and Cumberland Rivers with the Ohio. After Kentucky declared for the Union on September 20, both sides rapidly concentrated forces in western Kentucky. Maj. Gen. Albert S. Johnston, recently appointed to command Confederate forces in the west, fortified Bowling Green, Kentucky, and extended his defensive line to Columbus. Union troops immediately occupied Louisville and planned advances down the railroad to Nashville and eastward into the Appalachians. By November 15, the commanders of the Department of the Ohio and the Department of the Missouri, dividing their operational boundaries in Kentucky along the Cumberland River, were exchanging strategic plans with McClellan in anticipation of a grand offensive in the spring of 1862.

The outpouring of troops and their preparations for battle disrupted the leisurely pace of the War Department. In their haste to supply, equip, and deploy the second quota of volunteers, a score or more of states competed not only against one another but against the federal government as well. Profiteers demanded exorbitant prices for scarce items, which frequently turned out to be worthless. Unbridled graft and extravagance were reflected in the bills which the states presented to the War Department for payment. After Bull Run a concerted, widespread movement emerged for the dismissal of Secretary of War Simon Cameron, who had failed to manage his office efficiently. Cameron selected Edwin M. Stanton, former Attorney General in President Buchanan's cabinet, as his special counsel to handle all legal arguments justifying the War Department's purchasing policies. Knowing that the cabinet post had considerable potential, Stanton worked hard to restore the War Department's prestige. Behind the scenes Stanton aided his fellow Democrat, McClellan, in outfitting the Army of the Potomac. As the summer faded Stanton, having once scoffed at Lincoln early in the war, ingratiated himself with the President and his key cabinet members by urging his pro-Union views. In January 1862 Lincoln replaced Cameron with Stanton, who immediately set out to make his cabinet position the most powerful in Lincoln's administration.

Self-confident, arrogant, abrupt, and contemptuous of incompetent military leaders, Stanton was also fiercely energetic, incorruptible, and efficient. Respecting few men and fearing none, he did his best to eliminate favoritism and see to it that war contracts were honestly negotiated and faithfully filled. Few men liked Stanton, but almost all high officials respected him. Stanton insisted that the Army receive whatever it needed, and the best available, and no campaign by any Union army would ever fail for want of supplies.

From the day that Stanton took office, the structure of the War Department was centralized to handle the growing volume of business. Each bureau chief reported directly to Stanton, but the responsibility became so heavy that he delegated procurement and distribution matters to three assistant secretaries. Because the Quartermaster General's Department transported men and matériel, operated the depot system, constructed camps, and handled the largest number of contracts, it soon became the most important agency of the general staff. Hard-working, efficient, and loyal, Montgomery C. Meigs as Quartermaster General was an organizing genius, and was one of the few career officers to whom Stanton would listen. To complete his department, Stanton added three major bureaus during the war: the Judge Advocate General's Office in 1862; the Signal Department in 1863; and the Provost Marshal General's Bureau, established in 1863 to administer the draft (enrollment) act. In the same year the Corps of Topographical Engineers was merged with the Corps of Engineers.

Stanton faced mobilization problems and home front crises of unprecedented magnitude. Loyal states were bringing half a million men under arms. Grain, wool, leather, lumber, metals, and fuel were being turned into food, clothing, vehicles, and guns, and thousands of draft animals were being purchased and shipped from every part of the North. A well-managed federal authority was needed to assume the states' obligations, to train volunteer units in the use of their tools of war, and then to deploy them along a vast continental front. By exploiting the railroad, steamship, and telegraph, the War Department provided field commanders a novel type of mobility in their operations. Stanton's major task was to control all aspects of this outpouring of the nation's resources. If war contracts were tainted, the Union soldiers might despair. Moral as well as financial bankruptcy could easily wreck Union hopes of victory. In addition, Stanton had the job of suppressing subversion, of timing the delicate matter of putting Negroes in the Army, and of co-operating with a radical-dominated Congress, a strong-willed cabinet, and a conservative-minded Army. With a lawyer's training, Stanton, like Lincoln, knew little about military affairs, and there was little time for him to learn. Anticipating that President Lincoln would soon call for War Department plans for the spring 1862 offensives, Stanton researched every document he could find on Army administration, consulted his bureau chiefs about readiness, and prepared himself to work with the General in Chief on strategic matters.

When he took office, Stanton found that the War Department had a rival in the form of the Joint Congressional Committee on the Conduct of the War. It had its origins in an investigation of a badly executed reconnaissance at Ball's Bluff on the Potomac, October 21, 1861, in which a volunteer officer and popular former senator, Col. Edward D. Baker, was killed. By subsequently searching out graft and inefficiency, the committee did valuable service, but it also vexed the President, Stanton, and most of the generals during the war. Composed of extreme antislavery men without military knowledge and experience, the committee probed the battles, tried to force all its views regarding statecraft and strategy on the President, and put forward its own candidates for high command. Suspicious of proslavery men and men of moderate views, it considered that the only generals fit for office were those who had been abolitionists before 1861.

As the year ended both North and South were earnestly preparing for a hard war. Both opponents were raising and training huge armies totaling nearly a million men. Fort Sumter and bloody Bull Run were over and each side was gathering its resources for the even bloodier struggles to come.

CHAPTER 10

The Civil War, 1862

In 1862 the armed forces of the United States undertook the first massive campaigns to defeat the southern Confederacy. Better organization, training, and leadership would be displayed on both sides as the combat became more intense. Young American citizen soldiers would find that war was not a romantic adventure and their leaders would learn that every victory had its price.

As the winter of 1861–62 wore on, McClellan exaggerated his difficulties and the enemy's strength, and discounted the Confederacy's problems. He drilled and trained the Army of the Potomac while western forces under his general command accomplished little. Lincoln and the Union waited impatiently for a conclusive engagement. But neither the Union nor the Confederate Army showed much inclination to move, each being intent on perfecting itself before striking a heavy blow.

The President was particularly eager to support Unionist sentiment in east Tennessee by moving forces in that direction. Above all he wanted a concerted movement to crush the rebellion quickly. In an effort to push matters Lincoln issued General War Order No. 1 on January 27, 1862. This order, besides superfluously telling the armies to obey existing orders, directed that a general movement of land and sea forces against the Confederacy be launched on February 22, 1862. Lincoln's issuance of an order for an offensive several weeks in advance, without considering what the weather and the roads might be like, has been scoffed at frequently. But apparently he issued it only to get McClellan to agree to move. Even before Lincoln sent the directive his intentions were overtaken by events in the western theater.

The Twin Rivers Campaign

Students of the Civil War often concentrate their study upon the cockpit of the war in the east—Virginia. The rival capitals lay only a hundred miles apart and the country between them was fought over for four years. But it was the Union armies west of the Appalachians that struck the death knell of the Confederacy.

GENERAL GRANT. (*Photograph taken after his promotion to lieutenant general.*)

These Union forces in late 1861 were organized into two separate commands. Brig. Gen. Don Carlos Buell commanded some 45,000 men from a headquarters at Louisville, Kentucky, while Maj. Gen. Henry W. Halleck with headquarters at St. Louis, Missouri, had 91,000 under his command. These troops were generally raw, undisciplined western volunteers. Logistical matters and training facilities were undeveloped and as Halleck once wrote in disgust to his superior in Washington, "affairs here are in complete chaos."

Affairs were no better among Confederate authorities farther south. Facing Buell and Halleck were 43,000 scattered and ill-equipped Confederate troops under General Albert Sidney Johnston. Charged with defending a line which stretched for more than 500 miles from western Virginia to the border of Kansas, Johnston's forces mostly lay east of the Mississippi River. They occupied a system of forts and camps from Cumberland Gap in western Virginia through Bowling Green, Kentucky, to Columbus, Kentucky, on the Mississippi. Rivers and railroads provided Johnston with most of his interior lines of communications since most of the roads were virtually impassable in winter. To protect a lateral railroad where it crossed two rivers in Tennessee and yet respect Kentucky's neutrality, the Confederates had built Fort Henry on the Tennessee River and Fort Donelson on the Cumberland River just south of the boundary between the two states. On the other hand, hampering the Confederate build-up were southern governors whose states' rights doctrine led them to believe that defense of their respective states had higher priority than pushing forward the needed men and munitions to a Confederate commander, Johnston, at the front.

At the beginning of 1862, Halleck and Buell were supposed to be co-operating with each other but had yet to do so effectively. On his own, Buell moved in mid-January to give token response to Lincoln's desire to help the Unionists in east Tennessee. One of his subordinates succeeded in breaching the

Confederate defense line in eastern Kentucky in a local action near Mill Springs, but Buell failed to exploit the victory.

In Halleck's department, Brig. Gen. Ulysses S. Grant, at the time an inconspicuous district commander at Cairo, Illinois, had meanwhile proposed a river expedition up the Tennessee to take Fort Henry. After some hesitancy and in spite of the absence of assurance of support from Buell, Halleck approved a plan for a joint Army-Navy expedition. On January 30, 1862, he directed 15,000 men under Grant, supported by armored gunboats and river craft of the U.S. Navy under Flag Officer Andrew H. Foote, to "take and hold Fort Henry." The actions of subordinate commanders were at last prodding the Union war machine to move.

Capture of Forts Henry and Donelson

Grant landed his troops below Fort Henry and together with Foote's naval force moved against the Confederate position on February 6. At the Federals' approach the Confederate commander sent most of his men to Fort Donelson. Muddy roads delayed the Union Army's advance, but Foote's seven gunboats plunged ahead and in a short fire fight induced the defenders of Fort Henry to surrender. Indeed, the Confederates had lowered their colors before Grant's infantry could reach the action. The Tennessee River now lay open to Foote's gunboats all the way to northern Alabama.

General Grant was no rhetorician. Sparing with words, he never bombarded his troops with Napoleonic manifestos as McClellan did. After the capture of Fort Henry he simply telegraphed the somewhat surprised Halleck: "I shall take and destroy Fort Donelson on the 8th and return to Fort Henry." But inclement weather delayed the Federal movement until February 12. Then river craft carried some of the troops by water around to Fort Donelson. The rest of the troops moved overland under sunny skies and unseasonably mild temperatures. The springlike weather caused the youthful soldiers to litter the roadside with overcoats, blankets, and tents.

But winter once more descended upon Grant's forces (soon to swell to nearly 27,000 men) as they invested Fort Donelson. Johnston, sure that the fall of this fort would jeopardize his entrenched camp at Bowling Green, hurried three generals and 12,000 reinforcements to Fort Donelson and then retired toward Nashville with 14,000 men. Even without reinforcements, Fort Donelson was a strong position. The main earthwork stood 100 feet above the river and with its outlying system of rifle pits embraced an area of 100 acres. The whole Confederate position occupied less than a square mile. Grant and Foote first attempted to reduce it by naval bombardment, which had succeeded at Fort

Henry. But this time the Confederate defenders handled the gunboats so roughly that they withdrew. Grant then prepared for a long siege, although the bitter cold weather and lack of assault training among his troops caused him to have some reservations.

The Confederates, sensing they were caught in a trap, essayed a sortie on February 15, and swept one of Grant's divisions off the field. But divided Confederate command, not lack of determination or valor on the part of the fighting men, led to ultimate defeat of the attack. The three Confederate commanders could not agree upon the next move, and at a critical moment, Grant ordered counterattacks all along the line. By the end of the day Union troops had captured a portion of the Confederate outer works. Now surrounded by Union forces that outnumbered them almost two to one, the Confederate leaders decided they were in a hopeless situation. In a scene resembling *opéra bouffe*, Brig. Gen. John B. Floyd, who had been Buchanan's Secretary of War and feared execution as a traitor, passed the command to Brig. Gen. Gideon Pillow. Pillow passed the command immediately to Brig. Gen. Simon B. Buckner, who asked Grant, an old friend, for terms. Soon afterward Grant sent his famous message: "No terms except unconditional and immediate surrender can be accepted. I propose to move immediately upon your works."

Some Confederates escaped with Floyd and Pillow, and Col. Nathan Bedford Forrest led his cavalry through frozen backwaters to safety. But the bulk of the garrison "from 12,000 to 15,000 prisoners . . . also 20,000 stand of arms, 48 pieces of artillery, 17 heavy guns, from 2,000 to 4,000 horses, and large quantities of commissary stores" fell into Federal hands.

Poor leadership, violation of the principle of unity of command, and too strict adherence to position defense had cost the South the key to the gateway of the Confederacy in the west. The loss of the two forts dealt the Confederacy a blow from which it never fully recovered. Johnston had to abandon Kentucky and most of middle and west Tennessee. The vital industrial and transportation center of Nashville soon fell to Buell's advancing army. Foreign governments took special notice of the defeats. For the North the victories were its first good news of the war. They set the strategic pattern for further advance into the Confederacy. In Grant the people had a new hero and he was quickly dubbed "Unconditional Surrender" Grant.

Confederate Counterattack at Shiloh

As department commander, Halleck naturally received much credit for these victories. President Lincoln decided to unify command of all the western armies, and on March 11 Halleck received the command. Halleck, nicknamed "Old Brains," was well known as a master of the theory and literature of war. Lincoln's decision gave him jurisdiction over four armies—Buell's Army of the Ohio, Grant's Army of the Tennessee, Maj. Gen. Samuel Curtis' Army of the Southwest in Missouri and Arkansas, and Maj. Gen. John Pope's Army of the Mississippi. While Pope, in co-operation with Foote's naval forces, successfully attacked New Madrid and Island No. 10 on the Mississippi River, Halleck decided to concentrate Grant's and Buell's armies and move against Johnston at Corinth in northern Mississippi. Grant and Buell were to meet at Shiloh (Pittsburgh Landing) near Savannah on the Tennessee River. Well aware of the Federal movements, Johnston decided to attack Grant before Buell could join him. (*Map 24*) The Confederate army, 40,000 strong, marched out of Corinth on the afternoon of April 3. Muddy roads and faulty staff co-ordination made a shambles of Confederate march discipline. Mixed up commands, artillery and wagons bogged down in the mud, and green troops who insisted upon shooting their rifles at every passing rabbit threatened to abort the whole expedition. Not until late in the afternoon of April 5 did Johnston's army complete the 22-mile march to its attack point. Then the Confederate leader postponed his attack until the next morning and the delay proved costly.

Grant's forces were encamped in a rather loose battle line and apparently anticipated no attack. The position at Shiloh itself was not good, for the army was pocketed by the river at its back and a creek on each flank. Because the army was on an offensive mission, it had not entrenched. Grant has often been criticized for this omission, but entrenchment was not common at that stage of the war. The fact that the principle of security was disregarded is inescapable. Very little patrolling had been carried out, and the Federals were unaware that a Confederate army of 40,000 men was spending the night of April 5 just two miles away. The victories at Forts Henry and Donelson had apparently produced overconfidence in Grant's army, which like Johnston's, was only partly trained. Even Grant reflected this feeling, for he had established his headquarters at Savannah, nine miles downstream.

Johnston's men burst out of the woods early on April 6, so early that Union soldiers turned out into their company streets from their tents to fight. Some fled to the safety of the landing, but most of the regiments fought stubbornly and yielded ground slowly. One particular knot of Federals rallied along an old sunken road, named the Hornet's Nest by Confederates because of the stinging shot and shell they had to face there. Although this obstacle disrupted Johnston's timetable of attack, by afternoon the Confederates had attained local success elsewhere all along the line. At the same time the melee of battle badly

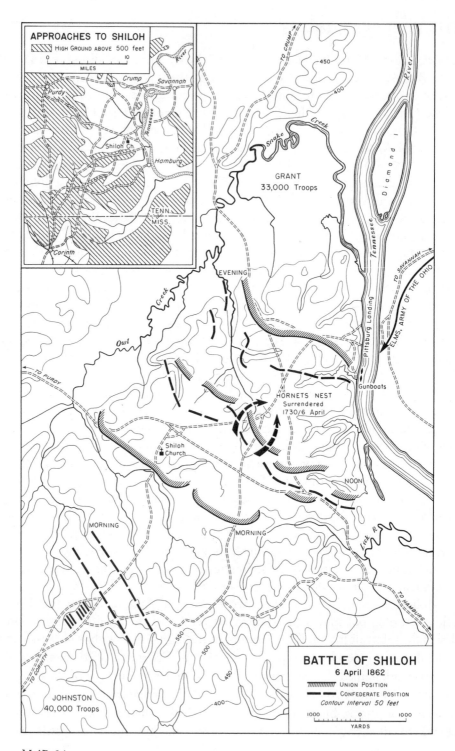

APPROACHES TO SHILOH

High Ground Above 500 feet

0   10
MILES

River
Crump
Savannah
Purdy
Tennessee
Shiloh Ch.
Hamburg
TENN.
MISS.
Corinth

TO CRUMP
450
400

Snake Creek

GRANT
33,000 Troops

Diamond I

Tennessee River

Pittsburg Landing

TO SAVANNAH

ELMS, ARMY OF THE OHIO

EVENING

Owl
Creek

TO PURDY

HORNETS NEST
Surrendered
1730/6 April

Gunboats

Shiloh
Church

NOON

MORNING

MORNING

Lick R.

TO HAMBURG

550

500

450

400

TO CORINTH

JOHNSTON
40,000 Troops

BATTLE OF SHILOH
6 April 1862

Union Position
Confederate Position
Contour Interval 50 feet

1000   0   1000
YARDS

MAP 24

disorganized the attackers. Johnston's attack formation had been awkward from the beginning. He had formed his three corps into one column with each corps deployed with divisions in line so that each corps stretched across the whole battlefront, one behind the other. Such a formation could be effectively controlled neither by army nor corps commanders.

Then, almost at the moment of victory, Johnston himself was mortally wounded while leading a local assault. General Beauregard, Johnston's successor, suspended the attack for the day and attempted to straighten out and reorganize his command. As the day ended, Grant's sixth division, which had lost its way while marching to the battlefield, reached Shiloh along with advance elements of Buell's army.

Next morning Grant counterattacked to regain the lost ground and the Confederates withdrew to Corinth. There was no pursuit. Shiloh was the bloodiest battle fought in North America up to that time. Of 63,000 Federals, 13,000 were casualties. The Confederates lost 11,000. Fortunate indeed for the Federals had been Lincoln's decision to unify the command under Halleck, for this act had guaranteed Buell's presence and prevented Johnston from defeating the Union armies separately. Grant came in for much denunciation for being surprised, but President Lincoln loyally sustained him. "I can't spare this man; he fights."

Halleck was a master of military maxims, but he had failed to concentrate all his forces immediately for a final defeat of Beauregard. As it was, Pope and Foote took Island No. 10 in April, opening the Mississippi as far as Memphis. Halleck, taking personal command of Grant's and Buell's forces, then ponderously advanced toward Corinth. Remembering Shiloh, he proceeded cautiously, and it was May 30 before he reached his objective. Beauregard had already evacuated the town. Meanwhile Capt. David G. Farragut with a naval force and Maj. Gen. Benjamin F. Butler's land units cracked the gulf coast fortifications of the Mississippi and captured New Orleans. By mid-1862, only strongholds at Vicksburg and Port Hudson on the Mississippi blocked complete Federal control of that vital river.

Perryville to Stones River

Despite these early setbacks the Confederate armies in the west were still full of fight. As Federal forces advanced deeper into the Confederacy it became increasingly difficult for them to protect the long lines of river, rail, and road supply and communications. Guerrilla and cavalry operations by colorful

Confederate "wizards of the saddle" like John Hunt Morgan, Joseph Wheeler, and Nathan Bedford Forrest followed Forrest's adage of "Get 'em skeered, and then keep the skeer on 'em." Such tactics completely disrupted the timetable of Federal offensives.

By summer and fall rejuvenated Confederate forces under General Braxton Bragg, Lt. Gen. Edmund Kirby Smith, and Maj. Gen. Earl Van Dorn were ready to seize the initiative. Never again was the South so close to victory, nor did it ever again hold the initiative in every theater of the war.

Over-all Confederate strategy called for a three-pronged advance from the Mississippi River all the way to Virginia. Twin columns under Bragg and Smith were to bear the brunt of the western offensive by advancing from Chattanooga into east Tennessee, then northward into Kentucky. They were to be supported by Van Dorn, who would move north from Mississippi with the intention of driving Grant's forces out of west Tennessee. The western columns of the Confederacy were then to unite somewhere in Kentucky.

At the same time, these movements were to be co-ordinated with the planned invasion of Maryland, east of the Appalachians, by General Robert E. Lee's Army of Northern Virginia. Much depended upon speed, good co-ordination of effort and communications, and attempts to woo Kentucky and Maryland into the arms of the Confederacy. Victory could stimulate peace advocates and the Copperheads in the North to bring peace. Furthermore there was always the possibility that a successful invasion might induce Great Britain and France to recognize the Confederacy and to intervene forcibly to break the blockade. This last hope was a feeble one. Emperor Napoleon III was primarily interested in advancing his Mexican schemes; he considered both recognition and intervention but would not move without British support. Britain, which pursued the policy of recognizing *de facto* governments, would undoubtedly have recognized the Confederacy eventually had it won the war. But the British Government only briefly flirted with the idea of recognition and throughout the war adhered to a policy of neutrality and respect for the Union blockade.

At first things went well for the Confederates in the west. Bragg caught Buell off guard and without fighting a battle forced Federal evacuation of northern Alabama and central Tennessee. But when Bragg entered Kentucky he became engaged in "government making" in an effort to set up a state regime which would bind Kentucky to the Confederacy. Also, the Confederate invasion was not achieving the expected results since few Kentuckians joined Bragg's forces and an attempt at conscription in east Tennessee failed completely.

Buell finally caught up with Bragg's advance at Perryville, Kentucky, on October 7. Finding the Confederates in some strength, Buell began concentrating his own scattered units. The next morning fighting began around Perryville over possession of drinking water. Brig. Gen. Philip H. Sheridan's division forced the Confederates away from one creek and dug in. The battle as a whole turned out to be a rather confused affair as Buell sought to concentrate units arriving from several different directions upon the battlefield itself. Early in the afternoon, Maj. Gen. Alexander M. McCook's Union corps arrived and began forming a line of battle. At that moment Maj. Gen. Leonidas Polk's Confederate corps attacked and drove McCook back about a mile, but Sheridan's troops held their ground. Finally a Union counterattack pushed the Confederates out of the town of Perryville. Buell himself remained at headquarters, only two and a half miles from the field, completely unaware of the extent of the engagement until it was nearly over. The rolling terrain had caused an "acoustic shadow" whereby the sounds of the conflict were completely inaudible to the Federal commander. While the battle ended in a tactical stalemate, Bragg suffered such severe casualties that he was forced to retreat. Coupled with Van Dorn's failure to bypass Federal defenses at Corinth, Mississippi, and carry out his part of the strategic plan, this setback forced the Confederates to abandon any idea of bringing Kentucky into the Confederacy.

By Christmas Bragg was back in middle Tennessee, battered but still anxious to recoup his losses by recapturing Nashville. Buell had been dilatory in pursuing Bragg after Perryville and had been replaced in command of the Army of the Ohio (now restyled the Army of the Cumberland) by Maj. Gen. William S. Rosecrans. In spite of urgent and even threatening letters from the War Department, the new commander would not move against Bragg until he had collected abundant supplies at Nashville. Then he would be independent of the railroad line from Nashville to Louisville, a line of communications continually cut by Confederate cavalry.

On December 26 Rosecrans finally marched south from Nashville. Poorly screened by Union cavalry, his three columns in turn knew little about Confederate concentrations near Murfreesboro, thirty miles southeast of the Tennessee capital. Here Bragg had taken a strong position astride Stones River on the direct route to Chattanooga and proposed to fight it out. Rosecrans moved into line opposite Bragg on the evening of December 30. Both army commanders proceeded to develop identical battle plans—each designed to envelop the opponent's right flank. Bragg's objective was to drive Rosecrans off his communications line with Nashville and pin him against the river. Rosecrans' plan had the same objective in reverse, that of pinning the Confederates against the stream. Victory would probably belong to the commander who struck first and hard.

Insufficient Federal security and Rosecrans' failure to insure that the pivotal units in his attack plan were also properly posted to thwart Confederate counterattacks resulted in Confederate seizure of the initiative as the battle of Stones River opened on December 31. (*Map 25*) At dawn, Maj. Gen. William J. Hardee's corps with large cavalry support began the drive on the Federal right. Undeceived by their opponent's device of extra campfires to feign a longer

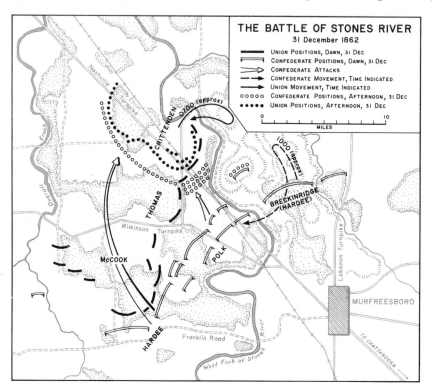

MAP 25

battle line, Confederate attacking columns simply pushed farther around the Union flank and promptly rolled the defenders back. Applying the principles of mass and surprise to achieve rapid success, Bragg's battle plan forced Rosecrans to modify his own. The Union leader pulled back his left flank division, which had jumped off to attack Maj. Gen. John C. Breckinridge's Confederate units north of Stones River. While Sheridan's division, as at Perryville, provided stubborn resistance to General Polk's corps in the center, Hardee's units continued their drive, which by noon saw the Union battle line bent back against the Nashville pike. Meanwhile the Confederate cavalry had wrought havoc among Rosecrans' rear area elements. As was typical of many Civil War battles the attacking columns of Polk and Hardee became badly intermingled. Their men began to tire, and by afternoon repeated Confederate assaults against the constricted Union line along the Nashville pike had bogged down.

That night Rosecrans held a council of war. Some of the subordinate commanders wanted to retreat. Rosecrans and two of his corps commanders, Maj. Gen. Thomas L. Crittenden and Maj. Gen. George H. Thomas, vetoed the scheme. Brigades were then returned to their proper divisions, stragglers rounded up, and various other adjustments made in the Federal position. New Year's Day, 1863, dawned quiet and little action occurred that day.

The sunrise of January 2 revealed Rosecrans still in position. Bragg directed Breckinridge to attack the Union left wing, once more thrown across Stones River on the north. But massed Union artillery shattered the assaults and counterattacking Federals drove Breckinridge's men back to their line of departure. The armies remained stationary on January 3 but Bragg finally withdrew from the battlefield that evening, permitting victory to slip from his grasp. Tactically a draw, Stones River so badly mangled the Army of the Cumberland that it would be immobilized for six months. Yet, more than most other battles of the war, Stones River was a conflict between the wills of the opposing army leaders. Rosecrans, supported by Thomas and others, would not admit himself beaten and in the end won a victory of sorts.

The great Confederate counteroffensives of 1862 had failed in the west, yet Chattanooga, the key to east Tennessee and Georgia, remained in southern hands. Farther west Federal forces had penetrated only slightly into northern Mississippi. The war was simply on dead center in the west at the end of the year.

The Army of the Potomac Moves South

As the year 1862 began in the eastern theater, plans prepared in Washington were aimed at the capture of Richmond rather than destruction of the army commanded by Joseph E. Johnston, now a full general. Precise methods for reaching the Confederate capital differed. President Lincoln favored an overland advance which would always keep an army between the Confederates and Washington. McClellan agreed at first, then changed his views in favor of a waterborne move by the Army of the Potomac to Urbana on the Rappahannock. From there he could drive to Richmond before Johnston could retire from the Manassas area to intercept him. The Washington fortifications, an elaborate system of earthen forts and battery emplacements then in advanced stages of construction, would adequately protect the capital while the field army was away. Johnston, however, rendered this plan obsolete; he withdrew from Manassas to Fredericksburg, halfway between the two capitals and astride McClellan's prospective route of advance. Early in March McClellan moved his army out to the deserted Confederate camps around Manassas to give his troops some field experience. While he was in the field President Lincoln relieved him as General in Chief, doubtless on the ground that he could not command one army in the field and at the same time supervise the operations of all the armies of the United States. Lincoln did not appoint a successor. For a time he and Stanton took over personal direction of the Army, with the advice of a newly constituted Army board consisting of the elderly Maj. Gen. Ethan A. Hitchcock and the chiefs of the War Department bureaus.

When events overtook the Urbana scheme, McClellan began to advocate a seaborne move to Fort Monroe, Virginia (at the tip of the peninsula formed by the York and James Rivers), to be followed by an overland advance up the peninsula. If the troops moved fast, he maintained, they could cover the seventy-five miles to Richmond before Johnston could concentrate his forces to stop them. This plan had promise, for it utilized Federal control of the seas and a useful base of operations at Fort Monroe and there were fewer rivers to cross than by the overland route. Successful neutralization of the *Merrimac* by the *Monitor* on March 9 had eliminated any naval threat to supply and communications lines, but the absence of good roads and the difficult terrain of the peninsula offered drawbacks to the plan. Lincoln approved it, providing McClellan would leave behind the number of men that his corps commanders considered adequate to insure the safety of Washington. McClellan gave the President his assurances, but failed to take Lincoln into his confidence by pointing out that he considered the Federal troops in the Shenandoah Valley to be covering Washington. In listing the forces he had left behind, he counted some men twice and included several units in Pennsylvania not under his command.

Embarkation began in mid-March, and by April 4 advance elements had moved out of Fort Monroe against Yorktown. The day before, however, the commander of the Washington defenses reported that he had insufficient forces to protect the city. In addition, Stonewall Jackson had become active in the Shenandoah Valley. Lincoln thereupon told Stanton to detain one of the two corps which were awaiting embarkation at Alexandria. Stanton held back McDowell's corps, numbering 30,000 men, seriously affecting McClellan's plans.

Jackson's Valley Campaign

While a small Confederate garrison at Yorktown made ready to delay McClellan, Johnston hurried his army to the peninsula. In Richmond Confederate authorities had determined on a spectacularly bold diversion. Robert E. Lee, who had rapidly moved to the rank of general, had assumed the position of military adviser to Jefferson Davis on March 13. Charged with the conduct of operations of the Confederate armies under Davis' direction, Lee saw that any threat to Washington would cause progressive weakening of McClellan's advance against Richmond. He therefore ordered Jackson to begin a rapid campaign in the Shenandoah Valley close to the northern capital. The equivalent of three Federal divisions was sent to the valley to destroy Jackson. Lincoln and Stanton, using the telegraph and what military knowledge they had acquired, devised plans to bottle Jackson up and destroy him. But Federal forces in the valley were not under a locally unified command. They moved too slowly; one force did not obey orders strictly; and directives from Washington often neglected to take time, distance, or logistics into account. Also, in Stonewall Jackson, the Union troops were contending against one of the most outstanding field commanders America has ever produced. Jackson's philosophy of war was:

Always mystify, mislead, and surprise the enemy, if possible; and when you strike and overcome him, never give up the pursuit as long as your men have strength to follow; for an army routed, if hotly pursued, becomes panic-stricken and can then be destroyed by half their number.

By mobility and maneuver, achieved by rapid marches, surprise, deception, and hard fighting, Jackson neutralized and defeated in detail Federal forces three times larger than his own. In a classic campaign between March 23 and June 9, 1862, he fought six battles: Kernstown, McDowell, Front Royal, Winchester, Cross Keys, and Port Republic. All but Kernstown were victories. His presence alone in the Shenandoah immobilized McDowell's corps by keeping these reinforcements from joining McClellan before Richmond.

The Peninsular Campaign: Fair Oaks

When McClellan reached the peninsula in early April he found a force of ten to fifteen thousand Confederates under Maj. Gen. John B. Magruder barring his path to Richmond. Magruder, a student of drama and master of deception, so dazzled him that McClellan, instead of brushing the Confederates aside, spent a month in a siege of Yorktown. But Johnston, who wanted to fight the decisive action closer to Richmond, decided to withdraw slowly up the peninsula. At Williamsburg, on May 5, McClellan's advance elements made contact with the Confederate rear guard under Maj. Gen. James Longstreet, who successfully delayed the Federal advance. McClellan then pursued in leisurely fashion. By May 25, two corps of the Army of the Potomac had turned southwest toward Richmond and crossed the sluggish Chickahominy River.

The remaining three corps were on the north side of the stream with the expectation of making contact with McDowell, who would come down from Fredericksburg. Men of the two corps south of the river could see the spires of the Confederate capital, but Johnston's army was in front of them. (*Map 26*)

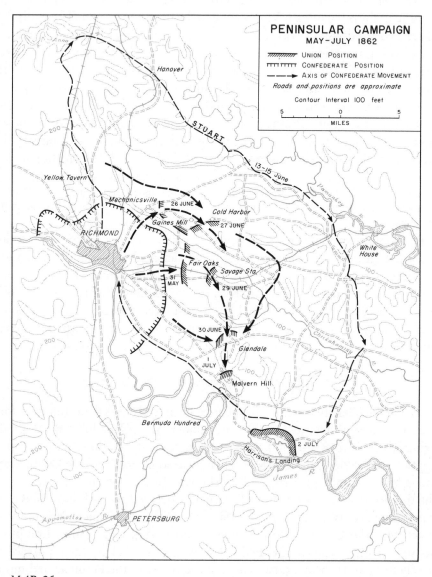

MAP 26

Drenching rains on May 30 raised the Chickahominy to flood stage and seriously divided McClellan's army. Johnston decided to grasp this chance to defeat the Federals in detail. He struck on May 31 near Fair Oaks. His plans called for his whole force to concentrate against the isolated corps south of the river, but his staff and subordinate commanders were not up to the task of executing them. Assaulting columns became confused, and attacks were delivered piecemeal. The Federals, after some initial reverses, held their ground and bloodily repulsed the Confederates.

When Johnston suffered a severe wound at Fair Oaks, President Davis replaced him with General Lee. Lee for his part had no intention of defending Richmond passively. The city's fortifications would enable him to protect Richmond with a relatively small force while he used the main body of his army offensively in an attempt to cut off and destroy the Army of the Potomac. He ordered Jackson back from the Shenandoah Valley with all possible speed.

The Seven Days' Battles

McClellan had planned to utilize his superior artillery to break through the Richmond defenses, but Lee struck the Federal Army before it could resume the advance. Lee's dispositions for the Battle of Mechanicsville on June 26 present a good illustration of the principles of mass and economy of force. On the north side of the Chickahominy, he concentrated 65,000 men to oppose Brig. Gen. Fitz-John Porter's V Corps of 30,000. Only 25,000 were left before Richmond to contain the remainder of the Union Army. When Lee attacked, the timing and co-ordination were off; Jackson of all people was slow and the V Corps defended stoutly during the day. McClellan thereupon withdrew the V Corps southeast to a stronger position at Gaines' Mill. Porter's men constructed light barricades and made ready. Lee massed 57,000 men and assaulted 34,000 Federals on June 27. The fighting was severe but numbers told, and the Federal line broke. Darkness fell before Lee could exploit his advantage, and McClellan took the opportunity to regroup Porter's men with the main army south of the Chickahominy.

At this point McClellan yielded the initiative to Lee. With his line of communications cut to White House—his supply base on the York River— and with the James River open to the U.S. Navy, the Union commander decided to shift his base to Harrison's Landing on the south side of the peninsula. His rear areas had been particularly shaky since Confederate cavalry under Brig. Gen. J. E. B. Stuart had ridden completely around the Federal Army in a daring raid in early June. The intricate retreat to the James, which involved

90,000 men, the artillery train, 3,100 wagons, and 2,500 head of cattle, began on the night of June 27 and was accomplished by using two roads. Lee tried to hinder the movement but was held off by Federal rear guards at Savage Station on June 29 and at Frayser's Farm (Glendale) on the last day of the month.

By the first day of July McClellan had concentrated the Army of the Potomac on a commanding plateau at Malvern Hill, northwest of Harrison's Landing. The location was strong, with clear fields of fire to the front and the flanks secured by streams. Massed artillery could sweep all approaches, and gunboats on the river were ready to provide fire support. The Confederates would have to attack by passing through broken and wooded terrain, traversing swampy ground, and ascending the hill. At first Lee felt McClellan's position was too strong to assault. Then, at 3:00 p.m. on July 1, when a shifting of Federal troops deceived him into thinking there was a general withdrawal, he changed his mind and attacked. Again staff work and control were poor. The assaults, which were all frontal, were delivered piecemeal by only part of the army against Union artillery, massed hub to hub, and supporting infantry. The Confederate formations were shattered because Lee failed to carry out the principle of mass. On the following day, the Army of the Potomac fell back to Harrison's Landing and dug in. After reconnoitering McClellan's position, Lee ordered his exhausted men back to the Richmond lines for rest and reorganization.

The Peninsular Campaign cost the Federal Army some 15,849 men killed, wounded, and missing. The Confederates, who had done most of the attacking, lost 20,614. Improvement in the training and discipline of the two armies since the disorganized fight at Bull Run was notable. Also significant was the fact that higher commanders had not yet thoroughly mastered their jobs. Except in McClellan's defensive action at Malvern Hill, which was largely conducted by his corps commanders, neither side had been able to bring an entire army into co-ordinated action.

Second Manassas

Failure of the Union forces to take Richmond quickly forced President Lincoln to abandon the idea of exercising command over the Union armies in person. On July 11, 1862, he selected as new General in Chief Henry W. Halleck, who had won acclaim for the victories in the west. The President did not at once appoint a successor in the west, which was to suffer from divided command for a time. Lincoln wanted Halleck to direct the various Federal armies in close concert to take advantage of the North's superior strength. If all Federal armies co-ordinated their efforts, Lincoln reasoned, they could strike where the Confederacy was weak or force it to strengthen one army at the expense of another, and eventually they could wear the Confederacy down, destroy the various armies, and win the war.

Halleck turned out to be a disappointment. He never attempted to exercise field command or assume responsibility for strategic direction of the armies. But, acting more as military adviser to the President, he performed a valuable function by serving as a channel of communication between the Chief Executive and the field commanders. He adeptly translated the President's ideas into terms the generals could comprehend, and expressed the soldier's views in language that Mr. Lincoln could understand.

Shortly before Halleck's appointment, Lincoln also decided to consolidate the various Union forces in the Shenandoah Valley and other parts of western Virginia—some 45,000 men—under the victor at Island No. 10, Maj. Gen. John Pope. Pope immediately disenchanted his new command by pointing out that in the west the Federal armies were used to seeing the backs of their enemies. Pope's so-called Army of Virginia was ordered to divert pressure from McClellan on the peninsula. But Jackson had left the valley and Federal forces were scattered. On August 3, Halleck ordered McClellan to withdraw by water from the peninsula to Aquia Creek on the Potomac and to effect a speedy junction at Fredericksburg with Pope. Meanwhile Pope began posting the Army of Virginia along the Orange and Alexandria Railroad to the west of Fredericksburg.

Lee knew that his Army of Northern Virginia was in a dangerous position between Pope and McClellan, especially if the two were to unite. On July 13, he sent Jackson, with forces eventually totaling 24,000 men, to watch Pope. After an initial sparring action at Cedar Mountain on August 9, Jackson and Pope stood watching each other for nearly a week. Lee, knowing that McClellan was leaving Harrison's Landing, had departed Richmond with the remainder of the Army of Northern Virginia and joined Jackson at Gordonsville. The combined Confederate forces outnumbered Pope's, and Lee resolved to outflank and cut off the Army of Virginia before the whole of McClellan's force could be brought to bear.

A succession of captured orders enabled both Lee and Pope to learn the intentions of the other. Pope ascertained Lee's plan to trap him against the Rappahannock and withdrew to the north bank astride the railroad. Lee, learning that two corps from the Army of the Potomac would join Pope within days, acted quickly and boldly. He sent Jackson off on a wide turning movement

TRESTLE OF THE ORANGE AND ALEXANDRIA RAILROAD *built by soldiers.*

through Thoroughfare Gap in the Bull Run Mountains around the northern flank of Pope's army and subsequently followed the same route with the divisions commanded by General Longstreet.

Pope took note of Jackson's move, but first assumed that it was pointed toward the Shenandoah Valley. Then Jackson, covering nearly sixty miles in two days, came in behind Pope at Manassas on August 26, destroyed his supply base there, and slipped away unmolested. Pope marched and countermarched his forces for two days trying to find the elusive Confederates. At the same time the Union commander failed to take Lee's other forces into account. As a result he walked into Lee's trap on the site of the old battlefield of Manassas, or Bull Run. Pope attacked Jackson, posted behind an abandoned railroad embankment, but again the attack consisted of a series of piecemeal frontal assaults which were repulsed with heavy casualties. By then Porter's V Corps from the Army of the Potomac had reached the field and was ordered to attack Jackson's right (south) flank. By this time also, Longstreet's column had burst through Thoroughfare Gap, and deploying on Jackson's right, it blocked Porter's move.

Next day, August 30, Pope renewed his attacks against Jackson, whom he thought to be retreating. Seizing the opportunity to catch the Federal columns in an exposed position, Lee sent Longstreet slashing along the Warrenton turnpike to catch Pope's flank in the air. The Federal army soon retired from the field and Pope led it back to Washington, fighting an enveloping Confederate force at Chantilly on the way.

Lee, by great daring and rapid movement, and by virtue of having the Confederate forces unified under his command, had successfully defeated one formidable Union army in the presence of another even larger one. Halleck, as General in Chief, had not taken the field to co-ordinate Pope and McClellan, and Pope lost the campaign despite the advantage of interior lines.

President Lincoln, desiring to use McClellan's admitted talents for training and reorganizing the battered eastern armies, had become convinced that bitter personal feelings between McClellan and Pope prevented them from working effectively in the same theater. On September 5, Halleck, upon the President's order, dissolved the Army of Virginia and assigned its units to the Army of the Potomac. He sent Pope to a command in Minnesota. The Union authorities expected that McClellan would be able to devote several months to training and reorganization, but Lee dashed these hopes.

Lee Invades Maryland

Up to this point the Confederates in the east had been following defensive strategy, though tactically they frequently assumed the offensive. But Davis and Lee, for a complicated set of political and military reasons, determined to take the offensive and invade the North in co-ordination with Bragg's drive into Kentucky. Militarily, in the east, an invasion of Maryland would give Lee a chance to defeat or destroy the Army of the Potomac, uncovering such cities as Washington, Baltimore, and Philadelphia, and to cut Federal communications with the states to the west.

The Army of Northern Virginia, organized into 2 infantry commands (Longstreet's consisting of 5 divisions, and Jackson's of 4 divisions) plus Stuart's 3 brigades of cavalry, and the reserve artillery, numbered 55,000 effectives. Lee did not rest after Manassas but crossed the Potomac and encamped near Frederick, Maryland, from which he sent Jackson to capture an isolated Federal garrison at Harpers Ferry. The remainder of Lee's army then crossed South Mountain and headed for Hagerstown, about twenty-five miles northwest of Frederick, with Stuart's cavalry screening the right flank. In the meantime

McClellan's rejuvenated Army of the Potomac, 90,000 men organized into 6 corps, marched northwest from Washington and reached Frederick on September 12.

At this time McClellan had a stroke of luck. Lee, in assigning missions to his command, had detached Maj. Gen. D. H. Hill's division from Jackson and attached it to Longstreet and had sent copies of his orders, which prescribed routes, objectives, and times of arrival, to Jackson, Longstreet, and Hill. But Jackson was not sure that Hill had received the order. He therefore made an additional copy of Lee's order and sent it to Hill. One of Hill's orders, wrapped around some cigars, was somehow left behind in an abandoned camp where it was picked up on September 13 by Union soldiers and rushed to McClellan. This windfall gave the Federal commander an unmatched opportunity to defeat Lee's scattered forces in detail if he pushed fast through the gaps. McClellan vacillated for sixteen hours. Lee, informed of the lost order, sent all available forces to hold the gaps, so that it was nightfall on the 14th before McClellan fought his way across South Mountain.

Lee retreated to Sharpsburg on Antietam Creek where he turned to fight. Pinned between Antietam Creek and the Potomac with no room for maneuver, and still outnumbered since Jackson's force had yet to return to the main body after capturing Harpers Ferry, Lee relied on the advantage of interior lines and the boldness and the fighting ability of his men.

McClellan delayed his attack until September 17, when he launched an un-co-ordinated series of assaults which drove back the Confederates in places but failed to break their line. Heavy fighting swelled across ripe fields and up through rocky glens that became known to history as the West Wood, the Cornfield, the East Wood, Bloody Lane, and Burnside's Bridge. One southerner remembered the attacking Union columns: "With flags flying and the long unfaltering lines rising and falling as they crossed the rolling fields, it looked as though nothing could stop them." But when the massed fire of field guns and small arms struck such human waves, a Union survivor recalled, it "was like a scythe running through our line."

McClellan, like too many leaders during the Civil War, could not bring himself to commit his reserve (the V Corps under Porter) at the strategic moment. Although adored by his men, as one of the veterans wrote after the war, he "never realized the metal that was in his grand Army of the Potomac." Jackson's last division arrived in time to head off the final assaults by Maj. Gen. Ambrose Burnside's corps, and at the end of the day Lee still held most of his line. Casualties were heavy. Of 70,000 Federal troops nearly 13,000 were killed, wounded, or missing, and the 40,000 or more Confederates engaged lost almost as many. Although Lee audaciously awaited new attacks on September 18, McClellan left him unmolested, and that night the Army of Northern Virginia withdrew across the Potomac.

Lincoln's Emancipation Proclamation

Antietam was tactically a draw, but the fact that Lee was forced to call off the invasion made it a strategic victory and gave President Lincoln an opportunity to strike at the Confederacy psychologically and economically by issuing the Emancipation Proclamation on September 22, 1862. Lincoln, while opposed to slavery and its extension to the western territories, was not an abolitionist. He had stated publicly that the war was being fought over union or secession, with the slavery question only incidental, and had earlier overruled several generals who were premature emancipators. But anticipating the total psychological warfare techniques of the twentieth century, he had for some time desired to free the slaves of the Confederate states in order to weaken their economies and to appeal to antislavery opinion in Europe. He had awaited the opportune moment that a Union victory would give him and decided that Antietam was suitable. Acting on his authority as Commander in Chief he issued the Proclamation which stated that all slaves in states or districts in rebellion against the United States on January 1, 1863, would be thenceforward and forever free. The Proclamation set no slaves free on the day it took effect. Negroes in the four slave states still in the Union were not touched, nor were the slaves in those Confederate areas that had been subjugated by Union bayonets. It had no immediate effect behind the Confederate lines, except to cause a good deal of excitement. But thereafter, as Union forces penetrated the South, the newly freed people deserted the farms and plantations and flocked to the colors.

Negroes had served in the Revolution, the War of 1812, and other early wars, but they had been barred from the Regular Army and, under the Militia Act of 1792, from the state militia. The Civil War marks their official debut in American military forces. Recruiting of Negroes began under the local auspices of Maj. Gen. David Hunter in the Department of the South as early as April 1862. There was a certain appeal to the idea that Negroes might assure their freedom by joining in the battle for it even if they served for lower pay in segregated units under white officers. On July 17, 1862, Congress authorized recruitment of Negroes while passing the antislavery Second Confiscation Act. The Emancipation Proclamation put the matter in a new light, and on May 22, 1863, the War Department established a Bureau of Colored Troops, another innovation of the Civil War since it was an example of Federal volunteer formations without official ties to specific states (others being the various U.S. sharp-shooter regiments and the invalid Veteran Reserve Corps). By the end of the war 100,000 Negroes were enrolled as U.S. Volunteers. Many other Negroes served in state units, elsewhere in the armed forces, and as laborers for the Union Army.

Fiasco at Fredericksburg

After Antietam both armies returned to face each other in Virginia, Lee situated near Culpeper and McClellan at Warrenton. But McClellan's slowness, his failure to accomplish more at Antietam, and perhaps his rather arrogant habit of offering gratuitous political advice to his superiors, coupled with the intense anti-McClellan views of the joint Congressional Committee on the Conduct of the War, convinced Lincoln that he could retain him in command no longer. On November 7 Lincoln replaced him with Burnside, who had won distinction in operations that gained control of ports on the North Carolina coast and who had led the IX Corps at Antietam. Burnside accepted the post with reluctance.

Burnside decided to march rapidly to Fredericksburg and then advance along the railroad line to Richmond before Lee could intercept him. (*Map 27*) Such a move by the army—now 120,000 strong—would cut Lee off from his main base. Burnside's advance elements reached the north bank of the Rappahannock on November 17, well ahead of Lee. But a series of minor failures delayed the completion of ponton bridges, and Lee moved his army to high ground on the south side of the river before the Federal forces could cross. Lee's situation resembled McClellan's position at Malvern Hill which had proved the folly of frontal assaults against combined artillery and infantry strongpoints. But Burnside thought the sheer weight of numbers could smash through the Confederates.

To achieve greater ease of tactical control, Burnside had created three headquarters higher than corps—the Right, Center, and Left Grand Divisions under Maj. Gens. Edwin V. Sumner, Joseph Hooker, and William B. Franklin, respectively—with two corps plus cavalry assigned to each grand division. Burnside originally planned to make the main thrust by Center and Left Grand Divisions against Jackson's positions on a long, low-wooded ridge southeast of the town. The Right Grand Division would cross three ponton bridges at Fredericksburg and attack Marye's Heights, a steep eminence about one mile from the river where Longstreet's men were posted. On the morning of December 13, he weakened the attack on the left, feeling that under cover of

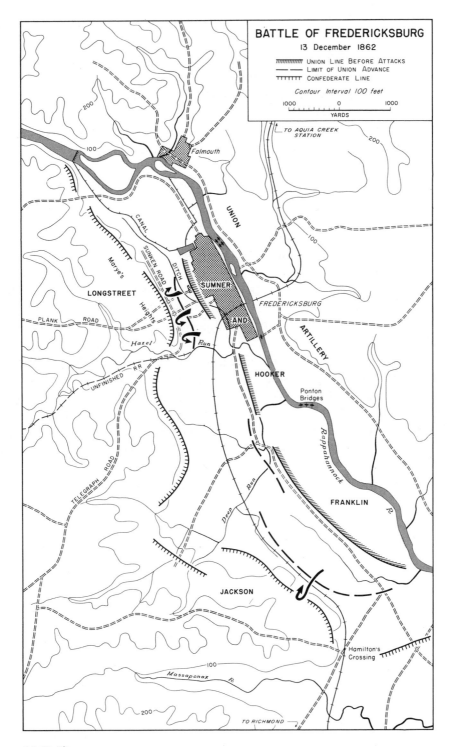

BATTLE OF FREDERICKSBURG
13 December 1862

UNION LINE BEFORE ATTACKS
LIMIT OF UNION ADVANCE
CONFEDERATE LINE

Contour Interval 100 feet

1000   0   1000
YARDS

MAP 27

147 heavy siege and field guns on the heights on the Union side of the river much could be achieved by a better-balanced attack along the whole line.

Burnside's engineers had begun laying the bridges as early as December 11. But harassment from Confederate sharpshooters complicated the operation, and it was not until the next day that all the assault units were over the river. After an artillery duel on the morning of the 13th, fog lifted to reveal dense Union columns moving forward to the attack. Part of the Left Grand Division, finding a weakness in Jackson's line, drove in to seize the ridge, but as Burnside had weakened this part of the assault the Federals were not able to hold against Confederate counterattacks. On the right, the troops had to cross a mile of open ground to reach Marye's Heights, traverse a drainage canal, and face a fusillade of fire from the infamous sunken road and stone wall behind which Longstreet had placed four ranks of riflemen. In a series of assaults the Union soldiers pushed to the stone wall but no farther. As a demonstration of valor the effort was exemplary; as a demonstration of tactical skill it was tragic. Lee, observing the shattered attackers, commented: "It is well that war is so terrible—we should grow too fond of it."

The Army of the Potomac lost 12,000 men at Fredericksburg while the Army of Northern Virginia suffered only 5,300 casualties. Burnside planned to renew the attack on the following day and Jackson, whose enthusiasm in battle sometimes approached the point of frenzy, suggested that the Confederates strip off their clothes for better identification and strike the Army of the Potomac in a night attack. But Lee knew of Burnside's plans from a captured order and vetoed the scheme. When the Federal corps commanders talked Burnside out of renewing the attack, both armies settled into winter quarters facing each other across the Rappahannock. Fredericksburg, a disastrous defeat, was otherwise noteworthy for the U.S. Army in that the telegraph first saw extensive battlefield use, linking headquarters with forward batteries during the action—a forerunner of twentieth century battlefield communications.

West of the Mississippi

If the major fighting of the Civil War occurred in the "older" populated sections of the United States, the youthful area of the American frontier across the Mississippi saw its share of action also. Missouri and Kansas, and indeed the distant New Mexico Territory (all areas involved in the root causes for the conflict), were touched by the Civil War.

The Southwest was a particularly rich plum, for as one Confederate commander observed: "The vast mineral resources of Arizona, in addition to its

affording an outlet to the Pacific, makes its acquisition a matter of some importance to our Govt." Also it was assumed that Indians and the Mormons in Utah
would readily accept allegiance to almost any government other than that in
Washington.

It was with these motives in mind that early in 1862 Confederate forces
moved up the Rio Grande valley and proceeded to establish that part of New
Mexico Territory north of the 34th parallel as the Confederate territory of
Arizona. Under Brig. Gen. Henry H. Sibley, inventor of a famous tent bearing
his name, the Confederates successfully swept all the way to Santa Fe, capital of
New Mexico, bypassing several Union garrisons on the way. But Sibley was
dangerously overextended, and Federal troops, reinforced by Colorado volunteers, surprised the advancing Confederates in Apache Canyon on March 26
and 28, as they sought to capture the largest Union garrison in the territory at
Fort Union.

One of the bypassed Federal columns under Col. Edward R. S. Canby from
Fort Craig meanwhile joined the Fort Union troops against the Confederates.
Unable to capture the Union posts, unable to resupply his forces, and learning
of yet a third Federal column converging on him from California, Sibley began
a determined retreat down the Rio Grande valley. By May he was back in Texas
and the Confederate invasion of New Mexico was ended. The fighting, on a
small scale by eastern standards, provided valuable training for Federal troops
involved later in Indian wars in this area. Indeed, while the Confederate dream
of a new territory and an outlet to the Pacific was shattered by 1862, Indian
leaders in the mountain territories saw an opportunity to reconquer lost land
while the white men were otherwise preoccupied. In 1863 and 1864 both Federal
and Confederate troops in the southwest were kept busy fighting hostile tribes.
(*Map 28*)

In Missouri and Arkansas, fighting had erupted on a large scale by the early
spring of 1862. Federal authorities had retained a precarious hold over Missouri
when Maj. Gen. Samuel R. Curtis with 11,000 men chased disorganized Confederates back into Arkansas. But under General Van Dorn and Maj. Gen. Sterling
Price, the Confederates regrouped and embarked upon a counteroffensive which
only ended at Pea Ridge on March 7 and 8. Here Van Dorn executed a double
envelopment as half his army stole behind Pea Ridge, marched around three-
fourths of Curtis' force, and struck Curtis' left rear near Elkhorn Tavern while
the other half attacked his right rear. But in so doing the Confederates uncovered
their own line of communications and Curtis' troops turned around and fought
off the attacks from the rear. After initial success, Van Dorn and Price were

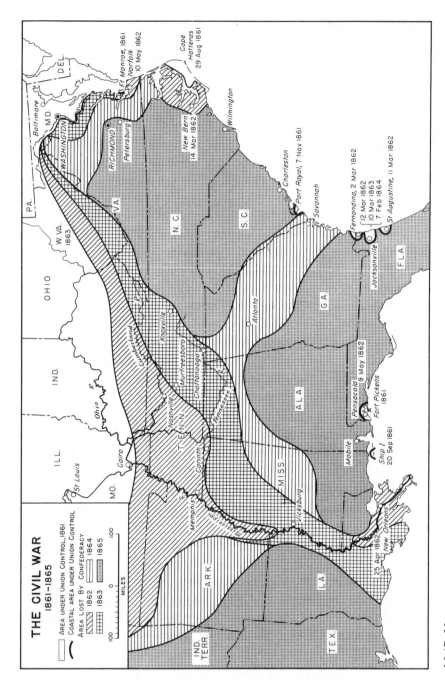

THE CIVIL WAR
1861-1865

AREA UNDER UNION CONTROL, 1861
COASTAL AREA UNDER UNION CONTROL
AREA LOST BY CONFEDERACY
1862   1864
1863   1865

MILES
100   0   100   200

MAP 28

unable to continue the contest and withdrew. For three more years guerrilla warfare would ravage Missouri but the Union grip on the state was secure.

The year 1862, which began with impressive Union victories in the west, ended in bitter frustration in the east. Ten full-scale and costly battles had been fought, but no decisive victory had yet been scored by the forces of the Union. The Federals had broken the great Confederate counteroffensives in the fall only to see their hopes fade with the advent of winter. Apparently the Union war machine had lost its earlier momentum.

CHAPTER 11

The Civil War, 1863

At the beginning of 1863 the Confederacy seemed to have a fair chance of ultimate success on the battlefield. But during this year three great campaigns would take place that would shape the outcome of the war in favor of the North. One would see the final solution to the control of the Mississippi River. A second, concurrent with the first, would break the back of any Confederate hopes for success by invasion of the North and recognition abroad. The third, slow and uncertain in its first phases, would result eventually in Union control of the strategic gateway to the South Atlantic region of the Confederacy—the last great stronghold of secession and the area in which the internecine conflict would come of age as modern total war.

Confusion Over Clearing the Mississippi

When Halleck went east in September 1862 to become General in Chief, his splendid army was divided between Grant and Buell. Grant, with over 60,000 men, remained in western Tennessee guarding communication lines. Buell's army of 56,000, after containing Bragg's invasion of Kentucky, had been taken over by Rosecrans, whose hard-won victory at Murfreesboro at the end of 1862 nevertheless immobilized the Army of the Cumberland for nearly half a year. To the west, only the posts at Vicksburg and Port Hudson prevented the Union from controlling the entire length of the Mississippi and splitting the Confederacy in two. Naval expeditions, under Capt. David G. Farragut, supported by the army, tried to seize Vicksburg in May and again in July 1862, but the Confederates easily repulsed the attempts. In the autumn Grant pressed Halleck to let him get on with the campaign down the Mississippi and finally received the response: "Fight the enemy where you please." But while Halleck and Grant were planning to move against Vicksburg by water and land, Lincoln and Stanton also outlined a similar move, but without consulting the military leaders.

The Chief Executive had long seen the importance of controlling the Mississippi, and in the fall of 1862 he and the Secretary of War prepared plans for a simultaneous advance northward from New Orleans and southward from Tennessee. Somewhat vague orders were drawn up giving command of the northbound expedition to Maj. Gen. Nathaniel Banks, who had replaced Butler as commander of the Department of the Gulf. Command of the southbound expedition was to go to Maj. Gen. John A. McClernand. Both officers were relatively untried, unstable, volunteer officers and politicians who often dabbled in intrigue in order to gain favors. Further, McClernand was to operate within Grant's department but independently of him. When Halleck found out about the Lincoln-Stanton plan, he persuaded the President to put Grant in command of the southbound expedition and to make McClernand one of his subordinates.

Grant's Campaign Against Vicksburg

Grant first tried a combined land and water expedition against Vicksburg in December 1862–January 1863. He sent Maj. Gen. William T. Sherman down river from Memphis, but the Confederates under Van Dorn and Forrest raided and cut the 200-mile-long line of communications. Sherman himself bogged down before Vicksburg, and Grant, perhaps also wishing to keep close rein on McClernand, who ranked Sherman, then determined on a river expedition which he would lead in person. Late in January Grant arrived before Vicksburg. He had upwards of 45,000 men, organized into three corps, the XIII Corps under McClernand, the XV Corps under Sherman, and Maj. Gen. James B. McPherson's XVII Corps. During the ensuing campaign Grant received two more corps as reinforcements to bring his total strength to 75,000 men.

Vicksburg had almost a perfect location for defense. (*Map 29*) At that point on the river, bluffs rose as high as 250 feet above the water and extended for about 100 miles from north to south. North of Vicksburg lay the Yazoo River and its delta, a gloomy stretch of watery, swampy bottom land extending 175 miles from north to south, 60 miles from east to west. The ground immediately south of Vicksburg was almost as swampy and impassable. The Confederates had fortified the bluffs from Haynes' Bluff on the Yazoo, some 10 miles above Vicksburg, to Grand Gulf at the mouth of the Big Black River about 40 miles below. Vicksburg could not be assaulted from the river, and sailing past it was extremely hazardous. The river formed a great U here, and Vicksburg's guns threatened any craft that tried to run by. For the Union troops to attack successfully, they would have to get to the high, dry ground east of town. This would put them in Confederate territory between two enemy forces. Lt. Gen. John C. Pemberton commanded some 30,000 men in Vicksburg, while the Confederate area commander, General Joseph E. Johnston (now recovered from his wound at Fair Oaks), concentrated the other scattered Confederate forces in Mississippi at Jackson, the state capital, 40 miles east of Vicksburg.

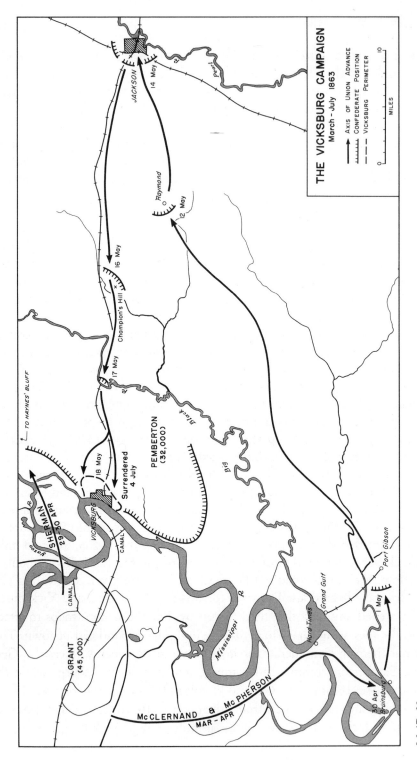

THE VICKSBURG CAMPAIGN
March – July 1863

Axis of Union Advance
Confederate Position
Vicksburg Perimeter

MILES

JACKSON

14 May

Pearl

Raymond

12 May

16 May

Champion's Hill

17 May

PEMBERTON
(32,000)

Black R.

Big

18 May

Surrendered
4 July

TO HAYNES' BLUFF

SHERMAN
29-30 APR

VICKSBURG

CANAL

CANAL

Yazoo

GRANT
(45,000)

Mississippi R.

Hard Times

Grand Gulf

Port Gibson

May

30 Apr
Bruinsburg

McCLERNAND & McPHERSON
MAR – APR

MAP 29

During late winter and early spring, with the rains falling, the streams high, and the roads at their wettest and muddiest, overland movement was impossible. Primarily to placate discontented politicians and a critical press, Grant made four attempts to reach high ground east of Vicksburg. All four were unsuccessful, foiled either by Confederate resistance or by natural obstacles. One of the more spectacular efforts was digging canals. These projects had as their objective the clearing of an approach by which troops could sail to a point near the high ground without being fired on by Vicksburg's guns, and all failed. That Grant kept on trying in the face of such discouragement is a tribute to his dogged persistence, and that Lincoln supported him is a tribute to his confidence in the general. The trouble was that Grant had been on the river for two months, and by early spring, Vicksburg was no nearer falling than when he came.

On April 4 in a letter to Halleck, Grant divulged his latest plan to capture Vicksburg. Working closely with the local naval commander, Flag Officer David D. Porter, Grant evolved a stroke of great boldness. He decided to use part of his force above Vicksburg to divert the Confederates while the main body marched southward on the west side of the Mississippi, crossed to the east bank, and with only five days' rations struck inland to live off a hostile country without a line of supply or retreat. As he told Sherman, the Union troops would carry "what rations of hard bread, coffee, and salt we can and make the country furnish the balance." Porter's gunboats and other craft, which up to now were on the river north of Vicksburg, were to run past the batteries during darkness and then ferry the troops over the river. Sherman thought the campaign too risky, but the events of the next two months were to prove him wrong.

While Sherman demonstrated near Vicksburg in March, McClernand's and McPherson's corps started their advance south. The rains let up in April, the waters receded slightly, and overland movement became somewhat easier. On the night of April 16 Porter led his river fleet past Vicksburg, whose guns, once the move was discovered, lit up the black night with an eerie bombardment. All but one transport made it safely, and starting on April 30, Porter's craft ferried the troops eastward over the river at Bruinsburg below Grand Gulf. The final march against Vicksburg was ready to begin.

At this time the Confederates had more troops in the vicinity than Grant had but never could make proper use of them. Grant's swift move had bewildered Pemberton. Then too, just before marching downstream, Grant had ordered a brigade of cavalry to come down from the Tennessee border, riding between the parallel north-south railroad lines of the Mississippi Central and Mobile and Ohio. Led by Col. Benjamin H. Grierson, this force sliced the length of the state, cutting railroads, fighting detachments of Confederate cavalry, and finally reaching Union lines at Baton Rouge, Louisiana. Most important, for the few days that counted most, it drew Pemberton's attention away from Grant and kept the Confederate general from discerning the Union's objectives.

Once more divided counsel hampered co-ordination of Confederate strategy. Johnston had been sent west by Davis to take over-all command, an imposing task, for Pemberton's army in Mississippi and Bragg's in Tennessee were widely separated. Things were further confused by Davis' directive to Pemberton to hold Vicksburg at all costs while Johnston recognized the potential trap and ordered him to move directly against Grant. In such a situation Pemberton could do little that was right. He tried to defend too wide an area; he had not concentrated but dispersed his forces at Vicksburg, the Big Black River, and along the railroad line to Jackson, where Johnston was gathering more troops.

After Grant had captured Port Gibson on May 1, and Sherman's corps had rejoined the main force, the Union commander decided that he must defeat Johnston before turning on Vicksburg. He moved northeastward and fought his way into Raymond on May 12, a move which put him squarely between Johnston and Pemberton and in a position to cut the Confederate line of communications. Next day Sherman and McPherson marched against the city of Jackson, with McClernand following in reserve, ready to hold off Pemberton. The leading corps took Jackson on May 14 and drove its garrison eastward. While Sherman occupied the state capital to fend off Johnston, the other two corps turned west against Pemberton and Vicksburg. Pemberton tried too late to catch Grant in open country. He suffered severe defeats at Champion's Hill (May 16) and Black River Bridge (May 17) and was shut up in Vicksburg. In eighteen days' Grant's army had marched 200 miles, had won four victories, and had finally secured the high ground along the Yazoo River that had been the goal of all the winter's fruitless campaigning.

Grant assaulted the Vicksburg lines on May 18 and 22, but as Sherman noted of the attacks: "The heads of columns have been swept away as chaff from the hand on a windy day." The only recourse now was a siege. Grant settled down, and removed McClernand from command after the attack of May 22 during which the corps commander sent a misleading report, then later slighted the efforts of the other corps and publicly criticized the army commander. Grant replaced him with Maj. Gen. Edward O. C. Ord, and ordered the army to implant batteries and dig trenches around the city.

The rest was now a matter of time, as Sherman easily kept Johnston away and the Federals advanced their siegeworks toward the Confederate fortifications. Food became scarce and the troops and civilians inside Vicksburg were soon reduced to eating mules and horses. Shells pounded the city, and the Federal lines were drawn so tight that one Confederate soldier admitted that "a cat could not have crept out of Vicksburg without being discovered." The front lines were so close that the Federals threw primitive hand grenades into the Confederate works. By July 1 the Union troops had completed their approaches and were ready for another assault. But Vicksburg was starving and Pemberton asked for terms. Grant offered to parole all prisoners, and the city surrendered on Independence Day. Since Grant was out of telegraphic contact with Washington, the news reached the President via naval channels on July 7, the day before General Banks' 15,000-man army, having advanced up river from New Orleans, captured Port Hudson. The whole river was now repossessed by the Union, the Confederacy sliced in two. Once more Grant had removed an entire Confederate army from the war—40,000 men—losing only one-tenth that number in the process.

Hooker Crosses the Rappahannock

Events in the western theater in the spring and early summer of 1863 were impressive. Those in the east during the same period were fewer in number but equally dramatic. After the battle of Fredericksburg, Burnside's Army of the Potomac went into winter quarters on the north bank of the Rappahannock, while the main body of Lee's Army of Northern Virginia held Fredericksburg and guarded the railway line to Richmond. During January, Burnside's subordinates intrigued against him and went out of channels to present their grievances to Congress and the President. When Burnside heard of this development, he asked that either he or most of the subordinate general officers be removed. The President accepted the first alternative, and on January 25, 1863, replaced Burnside with Maj. Gen. Joseph Hooker. The new commander had won the sobriquet of "Fighting Joe" for his intrepid reputation as a division and corps commander. He was highly favored in Washington, but in appointing him the President took the occasion to write a fatherly letter in which he warned the general against rashness and overambition, reproached him for plotting against Burnside, and concluded by asking for victories.

Under Hooker's able administration, discipline and training improved. Morale, which had fallen after Fredericksburg, rose as Hooker regularized the furlough system and improved the flow of rations and other supplies to his front-line troops. Abolishing Burnside's grand divisions Hooker returned to the orthodox corps, of which he had seven, each numbering about 15,000 men. One of Hooker's most effective innovations was the introduction of distinctive

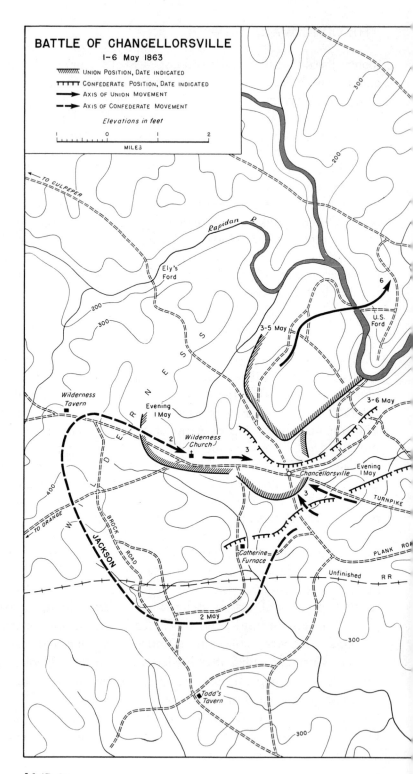

BATTLE OF CHANCELLORSVILLE
1–6 May 1863

UNION POSITION, DATE INDICATED
CONFEDERATE POSITION, DATE INDICATED
AXIS OF UNION MOVEMENT
AXIS OF CONFEDERATE MOVEMENT

Elevations in feet

0   2
MILES

TO CULPEPER

Rapidan R

Ely's
Ford

6

U.S.
Ford

3–5 May

200
300

W I L D E R N E S S

Wilderness
Tavern

Evening
I May

3–6 May

2

Wilderness
Church

3

Chancellorsville

Evening
I May

TO ORANGE

400

BROCK ROAD

JACKSON

3

TURNPIKE

Catherine
Furnace

PLANK ROAD

Unfinished   R R

2 May

300

Todd's
Tavern

300

MAP 30

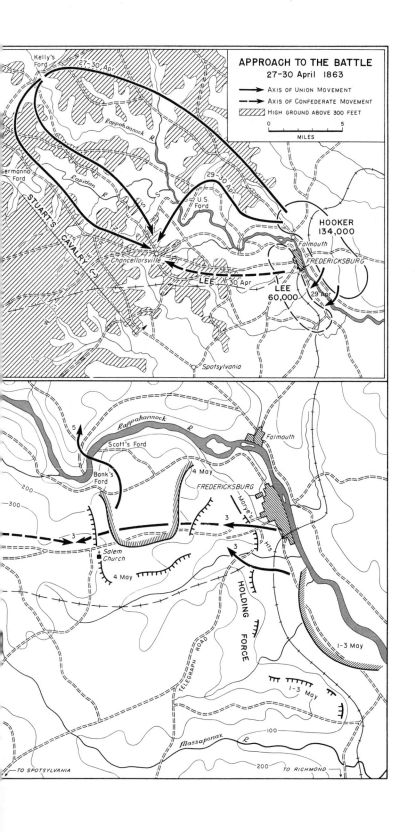

APPROACH TO THE BATTLE
27-30 April 1863

→ AXIS OF UNION MOVEMENT
⤏ AXIS OF CONFEDERATE MOVEMENT
▨ HIGH GROUND ABOVE 300 FEET

0 _____ 5
MILES

Kelly's Ford

27-30 Apr

Rappahannock R.

Germanna Ford

Rapidan R.

29-30 Apr

U.S. Ford

STUART'S CAVALRY

Chancellorsville

LEE 30 Apr

LEE 60,000

HOOKER 134,000

Falmouth

FREDERICKSBURG

29 Apr

Spotsylvania

Rappahannock R.

Scott's Ford

Falmouth

Bank's Ford

4 May

FREDERICKSBURG

200

300

3

Marye's Hts.

3

Salem Church

4 May

3

HOLDING FORCE

1-3 May

TELEGRAPH ROAD

1-3 May

100

Massaponax R.

200

TO SPOTSYLVANIA

TO RICHMOND

corps and division insignia. He also took a long step toward improving the cavalry arm of the army, which up to this time had been assigned many diverse duties and was split up into small detachments. Hooker regarded cavalry as a combat arm of full stature, and he concentrated his units into a cavalry corps of three divisions under Brig. Gen. George Stoneman. On the other hand Hooker made a costly mistake in decentralizing tactical control of his artillery to his corps commanders. As a result Union artillery would not be properly massed in the coming action at Chancellorsville.

Hooker had no intention of repeating Burnside's tragic frontal assault at Fredericksburg. With a strength approaching 134,000 men, Hooker planned a double envelopment which would place strong Union forces on each of Lee's flanks. (*Map 30*) He ordered three of his infantry corps to move secretly up the Rappahannock and ford the stream, while two more corps, having conspicuously remained opposite Fredericksburg, were to strike across the old battlefield there. Two more corps were in reserve. The cavalry corps, less one division which was to screen the move up river, was to raid far behind Lee's rear to divert him. Hooker's plan was superb; his execution faulty. The three corps moved quickly up the river and by the end of April had crossed and advanced to the principal road junction of Chancellorsville. They were now in the so-called "Wilderness," a low, flat, confusing area of scrub timber and narrow dirt roads in which movement and visibility were extremely limited. Maj. Gen. John Sedgwick crossed the Rappahannock at Fredericksburg on the 29th, and the two remaining corps moved to within supporting distance of Hooker at Chancellorsville. So far everything had gone according to plan, except that Stoneman's diversion had failed to bother Lee. One of Stuart's brigades kept Stoneman under surveillance while the main body of cavalry shadowed Hooker so effectively that the southern commander knew every move made by the Union army. By the morning of April 30, Lee was aware of what was afoot and knew that he was threatened by double envelopment. Already Hooker was sending his columns eastward toward the back door to Fredericksburg. A less bold and resolute man than Lee would have retreated southward at once, and with such ample justification that only the captious would have found fault. But the southern general, his army numbering only 60,000, used the principles of the offensive, maneuver, economy of force, and surprise to compensate for his inferior numbers. Instead of retreating, he left a part of his army to hold the heights at Fredericksburg and started west for Chancellorsville with the main body.

Chancellorsville: Lee's Finest Battle

When Lee began to move, Hooker simply lost his courage. Over protests of his corps commanders, he ordered the troops back into defensive positions around Chancellorsville. The Federals established a line in the forest, felled trees for an abatis, and constructed earth-and-log breastworks. Their position faced generally south, anchored on the Rappahannock on the east; but in the west it was weak, unsupported, and hanging in the air. Lee brought his main body up and on May 1 made contact with Hooker's strong left. That day Stuart's cavalry discovered Hooker's vulnerable right flank and promptly reported the intelligence to Lee. Conferring that night with Stonewall Jackson, Lee made another bold decision. Facing an army much greater than his own, he decided to divide his forces and further envelop the envelopers. Accordingly, Lee committed about 17,000 men against Hooker's left to hold it in place while Jackson with some 26,000 men made a wide 15-mile swing to get beyond the right flank. At first glance Lee's decision might appear a violation of the principles of mass and concentration, but while Lee's two forces were initially separated their common objective was the Army of the Potomac, and their ultimate routes converged on a common center.

Jackson's force, in a 10-mile-long column, moved out at daybreak of May 2, marching southwest first, then swinging northwest to get into position. The Federals noted that something was happening off to the south but were unable to penetrate the defensive screen; Hooker soon began to think Lee was actually retreating. In late afternoon Jackson turned onto the Orange turnpike near Wilderness Tavern. This move put him west of Hooker's right flank, and since the woods thinned out a little at this point it was possible to form a line of battle. Because time was running short and the hour of the day was late, Jackson deployed in column of divisions, with each division formed with brigades abreast, the same kind of confusing formation Johnston had used at Shiloh. Shortly after 5:00 p.m. Jackson's leading division, shrieking the "rebel yell" and driving startled rabbits and deer before it, came charging out of the woods, rolling up Maj. Gen. Oliver O. Howard's XI Corps in wild rout. The Confederates pressed forward, but fresh Union troops, disorganization of his own men, and oncoming darkness stymied the impatient Jackson. While searching for a road that would permit him to cut off Hooker from United States Ford across the Rappahannock, Jackson fell prey to a mistaken ambush by his own men. The Confederate leader was wounded and died eight days later. During the night of May 2, Stuart, Jackson's successor as corps commander, re-formed his lines. Against Stuart's right, Hooker launched local counterattacks which at first gained some success, but the next morning withdrew his whole line. Once more Hooker yielded the initiative at the moment he had a strong force between Lee's two divided and weaker forces.

Stuart renewed the attack during the morning as Hooker pulled his line back. Hooker was knocked unconscious when a shell struck the pillar of the Chancellor house against which he was leaning. Until the end of the battle he was dazed and incapable of exercising effective command, but he did not relinquish it nor would the army's medical director declare him unfit. Meanwhile Sedgwick, who shortly after Jackson's attack had received orders to proceed through Fredericksburg to Chancellorsville, had assaulted Marye's Heights. He carried it about noon on May 3, but the next day Lee once more divided his command, leaving Stuart with 25,000 to guard Hooker, and moved himself with 21,000 to thwart Sedgwick. In a sharp action at Salem Church, Lee forced the Federals off the road and northward over the Rappahannock. Lee now made ready for a full-scale assault against the Army of the Potomac huddled with its back against the river on May 6, but Hooker ordered retirement to the north bank before the attack. Confederate losses were approximately 13,000; Federal losses, 17,000. But Lee lost far more with the death of Jackson. Actually, Lee's brilliant and daring maneuvers had defeated only one man— Hooker—and in no other action of the war did moral superiority of one general over the other stand out so clearly as a decisive factor in battle. Chancellorsville exemplified Napoleon's maxim: "The General is the head, the whole of the army."

Hooker was a talented tactical commander with a good reputation. But in spite of Lincoln's injunction, "This time, put in all your men," he allowed nearly one-third of his army to stand idle during the heaviest fighting. Here again was a general who could effectively lead a body of troops under his own eyes, but could not use maps and reports to evaluate and control situations that were beyond his range of vision. Hooker, not the Army of the Potomac, lost the battle of Chancellorsville. Yet for the victors, Chancellorsville was a hollow triumph. It was dazzling, a set piece for the instruction of students of the military art ever since, but it had been inconclusive, winning glory and little more. It left government and army on both sides with precisely the problems they had faced before the campaign began.

Lee's Second Invasion of the North

By 1863 the war had entered what Sherman called its professional phase. The troops were well trained and had ample combat experience. Officers had generally mastered their jobs and were deploying their forces fairly skillfully in accordance with the day's tactical principles. Furthermore, the increased range and accuracy of weapons, together with the nature of the terrain, had induced some alterations in tactics, alterations which were embodied in a revised infantry manual published in 1863. Thus, by the third year of the war, battles had begun to take on certain definite characteristics. The battle of Gettysburg is a case in point.

Gettysburg was, first of all, an act of fate—a 3-day holocaust, largely unplanned and uncontrollable. Like the war itself, it sprang from decisions that men under pressure made in the light of imperfect knowledge. It would someday symbolize the war with all the blunders and heroism, hopes and delusions, combativeness and blinding devotion of the American man in arms of that period. With its enormous destruction, tactical maneuvers, and use of weapons, Gettysburg was one of the most dramatic and most typical of the 2,000-odd land engagements of the Civil War.

After the great victory at Chancellorsville, the Confederate cause in the eastern theater looked exceptionally bright. If 60,000 men could beat 134,000, then the Confederacy's inferiority in manpower was surely offset by superior generalship and skill at arms. Vicksburg was not yet under siege, although Grant had ferried his army over to the east bank of the Mississippi. If Davis and Lee were overly optimistic, they could hardly be blamed. Both men favored another invasion of the North for much the same political and military reasons that led to invasion in 1862. Longstreet, on the other hand, was concerned over the Federal threats in the west. He proposed going on the defensive in Virginia and advised taking advantage of the Confederacy's railroads and interior lines to send part of the Army of Northern Virginia to Tennessee to relieve pressure on Vicksburg. But he was overruled and Lee made ready to move into Pennsylvania. By this time Union strategy in the east was clearly defined: to continue operations against Confederate seaports—an attempt to seize Fort Sumter on April 7 had failed—and to destroy Lee's army. President Lincoln's orders made clear that the destruction of the Army of Northern Virginia was the major objective of the Army of the Potomac. Richmond was only incidental.

On June 30, 1863, the Army of the Potomac numbered 115,256 officers and enlisted men, with 362 guns. It consisted of 51 infantry brigades organized into 19 divisions, which in turn formed 7 infantry corps. The cavalry corps had 3 divisions. The field artillery, 67 batteries, was assigned by brigades to the corps, except for army reserve artillery. The Army of Northern Virginia, numbering 76,224 men and 272 guns in late May, comprised 3 infantry corps, each led by a lieutenant general, and Stuart's cavalry division. (The Confederacy was much more generous with rank than was the U.S. Army.) In each corps were 3 divisions, and most divisions had 4 brigades. Of the 15 field artillery battalions of 4 batteries each, 5 battalions were attached to each corps under command of the corps' artillery chiefs.

In early June Lee began moving his units away from Fredericksburg. In his advance he used the Shenandoah and Cumberland Valleys, for by holding the east-west mountain passes he could readily cover his approach route and line of communications. Hooker got wind of the move; he noted the weakening of the Fredericksburg defenses, and on June 9 his cavalry, commanded by Brig. Gen. Alfred Pleasonton, surprised Stuart at Brandy Station, Virginia. Here on an open plain was fought one of the few mounted, saber-swinging, cut-and-thrust cavalry combats of the Civil War. Up to now the Confederate cavalry had been superior, but at Brandy Station the Union horsemen "came of age," and Stuart was lucky to hold his position.

When the Federals learned that Confederate infantrymen were west of the Blue Ridge heading north, Hooker started to move to protect Washington and Baltimore and to attempt to destroy Lee. Earlier, Lincoln had vetoed Hooker's proposal to seize Richmond while Lee went north. As the Army of Northern Virginia moved through the valleys and deployed into Pennsylvania behind cavalry screens, the Army of the Potomac moved north on a broad front to the east, crossing the Potomac on June 25 and 26. Lee, forced to disperse by the lack of supplies, had extended his infantry columns from McConnellsburg and Chambersburg on the west to Carlisle in the north and York on the east.

After Brandy Station, and some sharp clashes in the mountain passes, Stuart set forth on another dramatic ride around the Union army. With only vague instructions and acting largely on his own initiative, he proved of little use to Lee. It was only on the afternoon of July 2 with his troopers so weary that they were almost falling from their saddles, that Stuart rejoined Lee in the vicinity of Gettysburg, too late to have an important influence on the battle. His absence had deprived Lee of prompt, accurate information about the Army of the Potomac. When Lee learned from Longstreet on June 28 that Hooker's men were north of the Potomac, he ordered his widespread units to concentrate at once between Gettysburg and Cashtown.

After Chancellorsville, Lincoln, though advised to drop Hooker, had kept him in command of the Army of the Potomac on the theory that he would not throw away a gun because it has misfired once. But Hooker soon became embroiled with Halleck and requested his own relief. He was replaced by a corps commander, Maj. Gen. George G. Meade, who before dawn on June 28 received word of his promotion and the accompanying problems inherent in assuming command of a great army while it was moving toward the enemy. Meade, who was to command the Army of the Potomac for the rest of the war, started north on a broad front at once but within two days decided to fight a defensive action in Maryland and issued orders to that effect. However, not all his commanders received the order, and events overruled him.

Gettysburg

Outposts of both armies clashed during the afternoon of June 30 near the quiet little Pennsylvania market town of Gettysburg. The terrain in the area included rolling hills and broad shallow valleys. Gettysburg was the junction of twelve roads that led to Harrisburg, Philadelphia, Baltimore, Washington, and the mountain passes to the west which were controlled by Lee. The rest was inevitable; the local commanders sent reports and recommendations to their superiors, who relayed them upward, so that both armies, still widely dispersed, started moving toward Gettysburg. (*Map 31*)

On July 1, Union cavalrymen fought a dismounted delaying action against advance troops of Lt. Gen. Ambrose P. Hill's corps northwest of town. By this stage of the war cavalrymen, armed with saber, pistol, and breech-loading carbine, were often deployed as mounted infantrymen, riding to battle but fighting on foot. The range and accuracy of the infantry's rifled muskets made it next to impossible for mounted men to attack foot soldiers in position. With their superior speed and mobility, cavalrymen, as witnessed in the Gettysburg campaign, were especially useful for screening, reconnaissance, and advance guard actions in which they seized and held important hills, river crossings, and road junctions pending the arrival of infantry. During the morning hours of July 1, this was the role played by Union horsemen on the ridges north and west of Gettysburg.

By noon both the I and the XI Corps of the Army of the Potomac had joined in the battle, and Lt. Gen. Richard S. Ewell's Corps of Confederates had moved to support Hill. The latter, advancing from the north, broke the lines of the XI Corps and drove the Federals back through Gettysburg. The Union infantry rallied behind artillery positioned on Cemetery and Culp's Hills south of the town. Lee, who reached the field about 2:00 p.m. ordered Ewell to take Cemetery Hill, "if possible." But Ewell failed to press his advantage, and the Confederates settled into positions extending in a great curve from northeast of Culp's Hill, westward through Gettysburg, thence south on Seminary

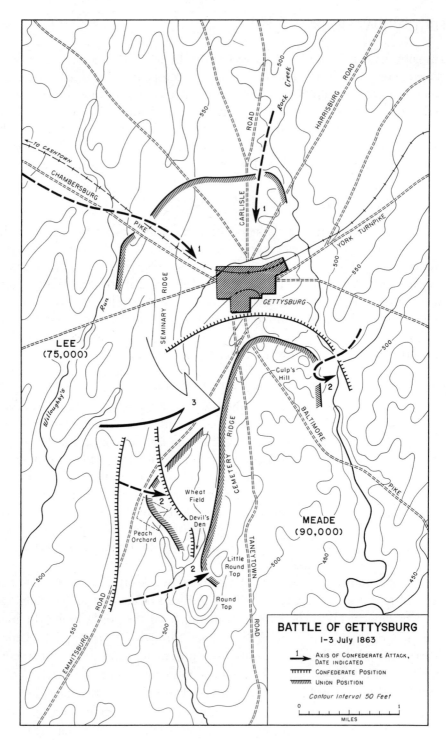

BATTLE OF GETTYSBURG
1-3 July 1863

→1 AXIS OF CONFEDERATE ATTACK, DATE INDICATED
⊥⊥⊥⊥⊥ CONFEDERATE POSITION
⫰⫰⫰⫰ UNION POSITION

Contour Interval 50 Feet

0 ———————————— 1
MILES

LEE
(75,000)

MEADE
(90,000)

TO CASHTOWN

CHAMBERSBURG PIKE

CARLISLE ROAD

HARRISBURG ROAD

Rock Creek

YORK TURNPIKE

SEMINARY RIDGE

GETTYSBURG

Willoughby's Run

Culp's Hill

CEMETERY RIDGE

BALTIMORE PIKE

Wheat Field

Devil's Den

Peach Orchard

Little Round Top

Round Top

TANEYTOWN ROAD

EMMITSBURG ROAD

MAP 31

Ridge. During the night the Federals, enjoying interior lines, moved troops onto the key points of Culp's Hill, Cemetery Hill, Cemetery Ridge, and Little Round Top.

Meade had completed his dispositions by the morning of July 2, and his line was strong except in two places. In the confusion, Little Round Top was occupied only by a signal station when the supporting cavalry was dispatched to guard the army trains and not replaced; and the commander of the III Corps, Maj. Gen. Daniel E. Sickles, on his own responsibility moved his line forward from the south end of Cemetery Ridge to higher ground near the Peach Orchard, so that his corps lay in an exposed salient. By early afternoon, seven corps were arrayed along the Union battle line.

On the Confederate side, Lee had not been able to attack early; reconnaissance took time, and Longstreet's leading division did not arrive until afternoon. Generals in the Civil War tried to combine frontal assaults with envelopments and flanking movements, but the difficulty of timing and coordinating the movements of such large bodies of men in broken terrain made intricate maneuvers difficult. The action on the second day at Gettysburg graphically illustrates the problem. Lee wanted Longstreet to outflank the Federal left, part of Hill's corps was to strike the center, while Ewell's corps was to envelop the right flank of Meade's army. The attack did not start until 3:00 p.m. when Longstreet's men, having deployed on unfamiliar ground, under a corps commander that preferred to take a defensive stance, advanced toward Little Round Top. The brigade was the basic maneuver element, and it formed for the attack with regiments in a two-rank line. Divisions usually attacked in columns of brigades, the second 150 to 300 yards behind the first, the third a similar distance behind the second. Skirmishers protected the flanks if no units were posted on either side. But such textbook models usually degenerated under actual fighting conditions, and so it was with Longstreet's attack. Divisions and brigades went in piecemeal, but with savage enthusiasm. Attacks started in close order as most men were using single-shot muzzle-loaders and had to stand shoulder to shoulder in order to get enough firepower and shock effect. But intervals between units soon increased under fire, troops often scattered for cover and concealment behind stone walls and trees, and thereafter units advanced by short rushes supported by fire from neighboring units. Thus, by late afternoon the smoke of battle was thick over the fields south of Gettysburg and the cries of the wounded mingled with the crash of musketry. The whole sector had become a chaos of tangled battle lines.

At this point Meade's chief engineer, Brig. Gen. Gouverneur Warren, discovering that no infantry held Little Round Top, persuaded the commander of the V Corps, Maj. Gen. George Sykes, to send two brigades and some artillery to the hill. They arrived just in time to hold the summit against a furious Confederate assault. When this attack bogged down, Longstreet threw a second division against Sickles' troops in the Peach Orchard and Wheatfield; this cracked the Federal line and drove as far as Cemetery Ridge before Meade's reserves halted it. Lee then ordered his troops to attack progressively from right to left and one of Hill's divisions assaulted Cemetery Ridge in piecemeal fashion, but was driven off. On the north Ewell attacked about 6:00 p.m. and captured some abandoned trenches, but Federals posted behind stone walls proved too strong. As the day ended the Federals held all their main positions. The Confederates had fought hard and with great bravery, but the progressive attack, which ignored the principle of mass, never engaged the Union front decisively at any point. The assaults were delivered against stoutly defended, prepared positions; Malvern Hill and Fredericksburg had shown this tactic to be folly, although perhaps Lee's successes against prepared positions at Chancellorsville led him to overoptimism.

Meade, after requesting the opinions of his corps commanders, decided to defend, rather than attack, on July 3. He also estimated that Lee, having attacked his right and left, would try for his center. He was right. Lee had planned to launch a full-scale, co-ordinated attack all along the line but then changed his mind in favor of a massive frontal assault by 10 brigades from 4 divisions of Longstreet's and Hill's corps against the Union center, which was held by Maj. Gen. Winfield Scott Hancock's II Corps. The assault was to be preceded by a massive artillery barrage.

The infantry's main support during the war was provided by field artillery. Rifled guns of relatively long range were available, but the soldiers preferred the 6-pounder and 12-pounder smoothbores. Rifled cannon were harder to clean; their projectiles were not as effective; their greater range could not always be effectively used because development of a good indirect fire control system would have to await the invention of the field telephone and the radio; and, finally, the rifled guns had flat trajectories, whereas the higher trajectories of the smoothbores enabled gunners to put fire on reverse slopes. Both types of cannon were among the artillery of the two armies at Gettysburg.

At 1:00 p.m. on July 3 Confederate gunners opened fire from approximately 140 pieces along Seminary Ridge in the greatest artillery bombardment witnessed on the American continent up to that time. For two hours the barrage continued, but did little more than tear up ground, destroy a few caissons, and expend ammunition. The Union artillery in the sector, numbering only 80 guns, had not been knocked out. It did stop firing in order to conserve ammunition,

PICKETT'S CHARGE

and the silence seemed to be a signal that the Confederates should begin their attack.

Under command of Maj. Gen. George E. Pickett, 15,000 men emerged from the woods on Seminary Ridge, dressed their three lines as if on parade, and began the mile-long, 20-minute march toward Cemetery Ridge. The assault force—47 regiments altogether—moved at a walk until it neared the Union lines, then broke into a run. Union artillery, especially 40 Napoleons on the south end of the ridge and some rifled guns on Little Round Top, opened fire, enfiladed the gray ranks, and forced Pickett's right over to the north. Despite heavy casualties the Confederates kept their formation until they came within rifle and canister range of the II Corps, and by then the lines and units were intermingled. The four brigades composing the left of Pickett's first line were heavily hit but actually reached and crossed the stone wall defended by Brig. Gen. John Gibbon's 2d Division of the II Corps, only to be quickly cut down or captured. Pickett's survivors withdrew to Seminary Ridge, and the fighting was over except for a suicidal mounted charge by Union cavalry, which Longstreet's right flank units easily halted. Both sides had fought hard and with great valor, for among 90,000 effective Union troops and 75,000 Confederates there were more than 51,000 casualties. The Army of the Potomac lost 3,155 killed, 14,529 wounded, and 5,365 prisoners and missing. Of the Army of Northern Virginia, 3,903 were killed, 18,735 wounded, and 5,425 missing and prisoners. If Chancellorsville was Lee's finest battle, Gettysburg was clearly his worst; yet the reverse did not unnerve him or reduce his effectiveness as a commander. The invasion had patently failed, and he retired at once toward the Potomac. As that river was flooded, it was several days before he was able to cross. Mr. Lincoln, naturally pleased over Meade's defensive victory and elated over Grant's capture of Vicksburg, thought the war could end in 1863 if Meade launched a resolute pursuit and destroyed Lee's army on the north bank of the Potomac. But Meade's own army was too mangled, and the Union commander moved cautiously, permitting Lee to return safely to Virginia on July 13.

Gettysburg was the last important action in the eastern theater in 1863. Lee and Meade maneuvered against each other in Virginia, but there was no more fighting. After Gettysburg and Vicksburg the center of strategic gravity shifted to Tennessee.

The Chickamauga Campaign

One week before the surrender of Vicksburg and the Union victory at Gettysburg, General Rosecrans moved out of Murfreesboro, Tennessee, and headed for Chattanooga, one of the most important cities in the south because of its location. (*See Map 21.*) It was a main junction on the rail line linking Richmond with Knoxville and Memphis. President Lincoln had long recognized the importance of railroads in this area. In 1862 he said, "To take and hold the railroad at or east of Cleveland [near Chattanooga], in East Tennessee, I think fully as important as the taking and holding of Richmond." Furthermore, at Chattanooga the Tennessee River cuts through the parallel ridges of the Appalachian Mountains and forms a natural gateway to either north or south. By holding the city, the Confederates could threaten Kentucky and prevent a Union penetration of the southeastern part of the Confederacy. If the Union armies pushed through Chattanooga, they would be in position to attack Atlanta, Savannah, or even the Carolinas and Richmond from the rear. As Lincoln told Rosecrans in 1863, "If we can hold Chattanooga and East Tennessee I think the rebellion must dwindle and die."

After the spring and summer campaigns in the east, the Davis government in Richmond approved a movement by Longstreet's corps of Lee's army to the west to reinforce the hard-pressed Bragg. Longstreet's move—a 900-mile trip by rail—involving some 10,000–15,000 men and six batteries of artillery, began on September 9. But a force under Burnside, now commanding the Department of the Ohio, which was not part of Rosecrans' command, had penetrated the Cumberland Gap and driven the Confederates from Knoxville; Longstreet had to go around by way of Savannah and Augusta to Atlanta, Georgia, and did not reach Bragg until September 18. The rail network was rickety, and Longstreet's soldiers quipped that such poor rolling stock had never been intended to carry such good soldiers. Movement of Longstreet's troops from Virginia was nevertheless an outstanding logistical achievement for the Confederacy.

Rosecrans had meanwhile reached the north bank of the Tennessee River near Stevenson, Alabama, on August 20. By September 4 his forces were across and on their way toward Chattanooga. After months of delay Rosecrans had accomplished the feat of completely outmaneuvering Bragg without a major battle. He planned to get in behind Bragg from the southwest and bottle him up in Chattanooga, but the Confederate general saw through the scheme and slipped away southward, carefully planting rumors that his army was demoralized and in flight. Rosecrans then resolved to pursue, a decision that would have been wise if Bragg has been retreating in disorder.

There were few passes through the mountains and no good lateral roads. Rosecrans' army was dispersed in three columns over a 40-mile front in order to make use of the various passes. Bragg concentrated his army about September 10 at Lafayette, Georgia, some twenty miles south of Chattanooga. As his force was three times as large as any one of the Union columns, Bragg hopefully anticipated that he could defeat Rosecrans in detail. But his intelligence service failed him: he thought there were two, rather than three Union columns, and prepared plans accordingly. He first planned to strike what he thought was Rosecrans' right—actually the center—then the left, but his subordinates did not support him promptly, and the attacks were made in desultory fashion. Thus, twice in three days Bragg missed a fine opportunity to inflict a serious reverse upon the Federals because of his subordinates' failure to carry out orders.

By September 12 Rosecrans was at last aware that Bragg was not retreating in disorder but was preparing to fight. The Union commander ordered an immediate concentration, but this would take several days and in the meantime his corps were vulnerable. Although Bragg was usually speedy in executing attacks, this time he delayed, awaiting the arrival of Longstreet's corps. He intended to push Rosecrans southward away from Chattanooga into a mountain cul-de-sac where the Federals could be destroyed.

By September 17 Bragg was poised just east of Chickamauga Creek. (*Map 32*) (Chickamauga, translated from Cherokee into English, means "River of Death.") When Longstreet's three leading brigades arrived on September 18, Bragg decided to cross the Chickamauga and attack. But the Federals, with two corps almost concentrated, defended the fords so stoutly that only a few units got over that day. During the night more Confederates slipped across, and by morning of the 19th about three-fourths of Bragg's men were over.

Rosecrans' third corps went into the line on the 19th, and now Bragg faced a much stronger force than he had expected. The heavily wooded battlefield had few landmarks, and some units had difficulty maintaining direction. Fighting continued throughout much of the day, but by nightfall the Federals still controlled the roads to Chattanooga. That night Lee's "Warhorse," Longstreet, arrived in person with two more brigades. He went looking for Bragg to report to him and lost his way in the woods. Encountering some soldiers, he asked them to identify their unit. When they replied with numbers—Confederate divisions were named for their commanders—he realized he was within

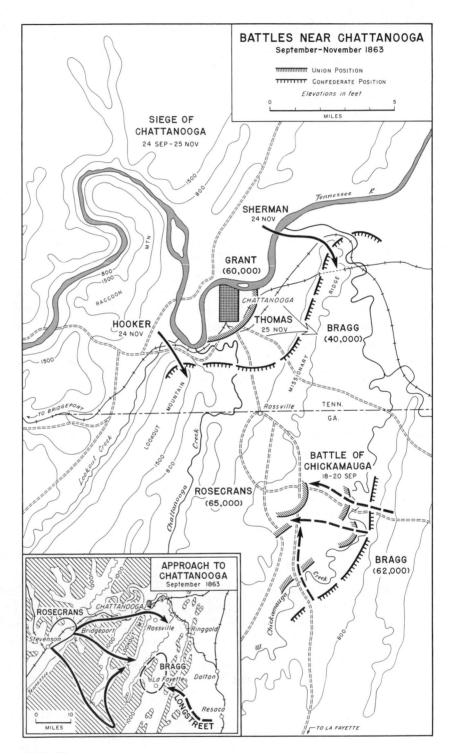

BATTLES NEAR CHATTANOOGA
September–November 1863

UNION POSITION
CONFEDERATE POSITION
Elevations in feet

0   MILES   5

SIEGE OF
CHATTANOOGA
24 SEP–25 NOV

Tennessee R.

SHERMAN
24 NOV

GRANT
(60,000)

CHATTANOOGA

HOOKER
24 NOV

THOMAS
25 NOV

BRAGG
(40,000)

RACCOON MTN

LOOKOUT MOUNTAIN

TO BRIDGEPORT

Lookout Creek

Chattanooga Creek

MISSIONARY RIDGE

Rossville   TENN.
                   GA.

BATTLE OF
CHICKAMAUGA
18–20 SEP

ROSECRANS
(65,000)

BRAGG
(62,000)

Chickamauga Creek

W.

TO LA FAYETTE

APPROACH TO
CHATTANOOGA
September 1863

ROSECRANS   CHATTANOOGA

Stevenson   Bridgeport   Rossville   Ringgold

LOOKOUT MT

Tennessee

BRAGG
La Fayette   Dalton

LONGSTREET

Resaca

0   10   MILES

MAP 32

Union lines, hastily rode off in the darkness, and eventually found Bragg. During the night Rosecrans regrouped and dug in.

Bragg decided to renew the attack the next day and to attack progressively from his right to left (sometimes known in military parlance as "oblique order"). He reorganized the Army of Tennessee into two wings under Polk and Longstreet with little regard for its existing corps organization. The attack began about 9:00 a.m. and hit Thomas' corps first. The Union line held until Rosecrans received an erroneous report that one of his units was not supported, and ordered another unit to move in and help. In the ensuing confusion, orders designated a unit which was already in line of battle. When this force obediently abandoned its position, Longstreet, just beginning his attack, saw the hole and drove into it at once. Thomas' right flank was bent back and most of the Union right wing simply melted from the field and streamed in rout back toward Chattanooga. Rosecrans, considering himself defeated, retired to Chattanooga to organize it for defense. Thomas, with about two-thirds of the disorganized army, stood fast and checked vicious attacks by Longstreet and Polk until nightfall. This resolute stand and the valorous performance of the U.S. 19th Infantry won for Thomas and that unit the title "Rock of Chickamauga." A Confederate remembered that afternoon how "the dead were piled upon each other in ricks, like cord wood, to make passage for advancing columns. The sluggish Chickamauga ran red with human blood."

Bragg concluded that no decisive results could be attained that day. Polk, Longstreet, and Forrest pleaded with him to push the routed Federals and recapture Chattanooga. But 18,000 casualties (the Federals had lost only 1,500 less) so unnerved Bragg that he permitted Thomas to withdraw unmolested from the field to a blocking position extending from Missionary Ridge west to Lookout Mountain. Next day Thomas retired into Chattanooga. Polk wrote to President Davis of Bragg's "criminal negligence," and Forrest a week later insubordinately told the army commander, "You have played the part of a damned scoundrel, and are a coward and if you were any part of a man I would slap your jaws." Yet nothing could erase completely the fact that the Confederates had won a great victory and had Rosecrans' army bottled up in a trap.

Grant at Chattanooga

Rosecrans' army, having started out offensively, was now shut up in Chattanooga, as Bragg took up positions on Lookout Mountain and Missionary Ridge. The Union commander accepted investment and thus surrendered his freedom of action. Burnside, at Knoxville, was too far away to render immediate aid. There were no strong Confederate units north of Chattanooga, but Rose-crans' line of communications was cut away. The Nashville and Chattanooga Railroad, instead of running directly into the city, reached the river at Stevenson, crossed at Bridgeport southwest of Chattanooga, and ran through Confederate territory into town. River steamers could get to within only eight miles of Chattanooga; beyond, the Tennessee River was swift and narrow. Supplies therefore came over the mountains in wagons, but starting September 30 Confederate cavalry under Maj. Gen. Joseph Wheeler, one of Bragg's cavalry corps commanders, raided as far north as Murfreesboro. Though heavily and effectively opposed in his effort to tear up the railroad, he managed to destroy many precious Union supply wagons. With the mountain roads breaking down under the heavy traffic in wet weather, rations within Chattanooga ran short. Men went hungry, and horses and mules began to die of starvation. Rosecrans prepared to reopen his line of communications by means of an overland route to the west. But this route was dominated by Confederate troops on Raccoon and Lookout Mountains. Additional troops to clear these strongpoints were required if the Army of the Cumberland was to survive.

Washington finally awoke to the fact that an entire Union army was trapped in Chattanooga and in danger of capture. In a midnight council meeting on September 23, the President met with Secretary Stanton, General Halleck, and others to determine what could be done. As General Meade was not then active in the east, they decided to detach two corps, or about 20,000 men, from the Army of the Potomac and send them by rail to Tennessee under the command of General Hooker, who had been without active command since his relief in June. The forces selected included 10 artillery batteries with over 3,000 mules and horses. The 1,157–mile journey involved four changes of trains, owing to differing gauges and lack of track connections, and eclipsed all other such troop movements by rail up to that time. The troops began to entrain at Manassas Junction and Bealton Station, Virginia, on September 25 and five days later the first trains arrived at Bridgeport, Alabama. Not all of the troops made such good time—for the majority of the infantry the trip consumed about nine days. And movement of the artillery, horses, mules, baggage, and impedimenta was somewhat slower. Combined with a waterborne movement of 17,000 men under Sherman from Mississippi, the reinforcement of the besieged Rosecrans was a triumph of skill and planning.

Chickamauga had caused Stanton and his associates to lose confidence in Rosecrans. For some time Lincoln had been dubious about Rosecrans, who, he said, acted "like a duck hit on the head" after Chickamauga, but he did not immediately choose a successor. Finally, about mid-October, he decided to

UNION TRANSPORTS ON THE TENNESSEE RIVER

unify command in the west and to vest it in General Grant, who still commanded the Army of the Tennessee. In October Stanton met Grant in Louisville and gave him orders which allowed him some discretion in selecting subordinates. Grant was appointed commander of the Military Division of the Mississippi, which embraced the Departments and Armies of the Ohio, the Cumberland, and the Tennessee, and included the vast area from the Alleghenies to the Mississippi River north of Banks' Department of the Gulf. Thomas replaced Rosecrans, and Sherman was appointed to command Grant's old army.

Now that Hooker had arrived, the line of communications, or the "cracker line" to the troops, could be reopened. Rosecrans had actually shaped the plan, and all that was needed was combat troops to execute it. On October 26 Hooker crossed the Tennessee at Bridgeport and attacked eastward. Within two days he had taken the spurs of the mountains, other Union troops had captured two important river crossings, and the supply line was open once more. Men, equipment, and food moved via riverboat and wagon road, bypassing Confederate strongpoints, to reinforce the besieged Army of the Cumberland.

In early November Bragg weakened his besieging army by sending Longstreet's force against Burnside at Knoxville. This move reduced Confederate strength to about 40,000 at about the same time that Sherman arrived with two army corps from Memphis. The troops immediately at hand under Grant—Thomas' Army of the Cumberland, two corps of Sherman's Army of the Tennessee, and two corps under Hooker from the Army of the Potomac—now numbered about 60,000. Grant characteristically decided to resume the offensive with his entire force.

The Confederates had held their dominant position for so long that they seemed to look on all of the Federals in Chattanooga as their ultimate prisoners. One day Grant went out to inspect the Union lines and he reached a point where Union and Confederate picket posts were not far apart. Not only did his own troops turn out the guard, but a smart set of Confederates came swarming out, formed a neat military rank, snapped to attention, and presented arms. Grant returned the salute and rode away. But plans were already afoot to divest the Confederates of some of their cockiness.

Grant planned to hit the ends of the Confederates' line at once. Hooker would strike at Lookout Mountain, and Sherman moving his army upstream, across the river from Chattanooga, and crossing over by pontons, would hit the upper end of Missionary Ridge. While they were breaking the Confederate flanks, Thomas' men could make limited attacks on the center, and the Army of the Cumberland's soldiers, already nursing a bruised ego for the rout at Chickamauga, realized that in the eyes of the commanding general they were second-class troops.

Hooker took Lookout Mountain on November 24. On the same day Sherman crossed the Tennessee at the mouth of Chickamauga Creek and gained positions on the north end of Missionary Ridge. The next day his attacks bogged down as he attempted to drive southward along the Ridge. To help Sherman, Grant directed the Army of the Cumberland to take the rifle pits at the foot of the west slope of Missionary Ridge. These rifle pits were the first of three lines of Confederate trenches. Thomas' troops rushed forward, seized the pits, and then, having a score to settle with the Confederates positioned above them, took control of this phase of the battle. Coming under fire from the pits above and in front of them, the Federals simply kept on going. When Grant observed this movement he muttered that someone was going to sweat for it if the charge ended in disaster. But Thomas' troops drove all the way to the top, and in the afternoon Hooker swept the southern end of the ridge. The Federals then had the unusual experience of seeing a Confederate army disintegrate into precipitate retreat and beckoned to their Northern comrades: "My God! Come and see them run!" Grant pursued Bragg the next day, but one Confederate division skillfully halted the pursuit while Bragg retired into Georgia to regroup.

The battles around Chattanooga ended in one of the most complete Union victories of the war. Bragg's army was defeated, men and matériel captured, and the Confederates driven south. The mountainous defense line which the Confederates had hoped to hold had been pierced; the rail center of Chattanooga was permanently in Union hands; and the rich, food-producing eastern Tennessee section was lost to the Confederacy. Relief had come at last for the Union sympathizers in eastern Tennessee. With Chattanooga secured as a base, the way was open for an invasion of the lower South.

CHAPTER 12

The Civil War, 1864–1865

From Bull Run to Chattanooga, the Union armies had fought their battles without benefit of either a grand strategy or a supreme field commander. During the final year of the war the people of the North grew restless, and as the election of 1864 approached, many of them advocated a policy of making peace with the Confederacy. President Lincoln never wavered. Committed to the policy of destroying the armed power of the Confederacy, he sought a general who could pull all the threads of an emerging strategy together, and then concentrate the Union armies and their supporting naval power against the secessionists. After Vicksburg in July 1863, Lincoln leaned more and more toward Grant as the man whose strategic thinking and resolution would lead the Union armies to final victory.

It is the strategic moves of the armies during the last year of the war, rather than the tactical details, that are most instructive.

Strategy of Annihilation and Unity of Command

Acting largely as his own General in Chief after McClellan's removal in early 1862, Mr. Lincoln had watched the Confederates fight from one ephemeral victory to another inside their cockpit of northern Virginia. In the western theater, Union armies, often operating independently of one another, had scored great victories at key terrain points. But their hold on the communications base at Nashville was always in jeopardy as long as the elusive armies of the Confederacy could escape to fight another day at another key point. The twin, un-co-ordinated victories at Gettysburg and Vicksburg, 900 airline miles apart, only pointed up the North's need for an over-all strategic plan and a general who could carry it out.

Having cleared the Mississippi River, Grant wrote to Halleck and the President about the opportunities now open to his army. Grant first called for the consolidation of the autonomous western departments and the co-ordination of their individual armies. After this great step, he proposed to isolate the area west of the line Chattanooga-Atlanta-Montgomery-Mobile. Within this region, Grant urged a "massive rear attack" that would take Union armies in the Gulf Department under Maj. Gen. Nathaniel P. Banks and Grant's Army of the Tennessee to Mobile and up the Alabama River to Montgomery. The U.S. Navy would play a major role in this attack. Simultaneously, Rosecrans was to advance overland through Chattanooga to Atlanta. All military resources within this isolated area would be destroyed.

Lincoln vetoed Grant's plan in part by deferring the Mobile-Montgomery phase. The President favored a demonstration by Banks up the Red River to Shreveport in order to show the American flag to Napoleon III's interlopers in Mexico, and Banks' Department of the Gulf was left out of the consolidation of the other western commands under Grant in October 1863.

After his own victory at Chattanooga in November, Grant wasted few hours in writing the President what he thought the next strategic moves should be. As a possible winter attack, Grant revived the touchy Mobile campaign while the Chattanooga victors were gathering strength for a spring offensive to Atlanta. Grant reasoned that Lee would vacate Virginia and shift strength toward Atlanta. For the Mobile-Montgomery plan, Grant asked for Banks' resources in the Gulf Department. Lincoln again balked because the Texas seacoast would be abandoned. Grant's rebuttal explained that Napoleon III would really be impressed with a large Army-Navy operation against Mobile Bay. The Red River campaign, Grant believed, would not deter Napoleon III. The President told Grant again that he had to heed the demands of Union diplomacy, but at the same time he encouraged Grant to enlarge his strategic proposals to include estimates for a grand Federal offensive for the coming spring of 1864.

Grant's plan of January 1864 projected a four-pronged continental attack. In concert, the four armies were to move on Atlanta, on Mobile—after Banks took Shreveport—on Lee's communications by a campaign across the middle of North Carolina on the axis New Bern–Neuse River–Goldsboro–Raleigh–Greensboro, and on Lee's Army of Northern Virginia in the hope of defeating it in an open battle. Lincoln opposed the North Carolina phase, fearing that Grant's diversion of 60,000 effective bayonets from formations covering Washington was too dangerous. Lincoln knew that Lee's eyes were always fixed on the vast amount of supplies in the depots around the Washington area.

Though Lincoln scuttled some of Grant's professional schemes, he never lost his esteem for Grant's enthusiasm and intelligence. In February 1864 Congress revived Scott's old rank of lieutenant general, to which Grant was promoted on March 9. Lincoln relieved Halleck as General in Chief, ordered Grant to Washington to assume Halleck's post, and during March the President, the new General in Chief, and the Secretary of War ironed out top-level command arrangements which had plagued every President since the

War of 1812. Lincoln and Stanton relinquished powerful command, staff, and communications tools to Grant. Stanton, greatly impressed with Grant's public acclaim, cautioned his General Staff Bureau chiefs to heed Grant's needs and timetables.

In twentieth century terms, Grant was a theater commander. As General in Chief, he reported directly to the President and Secretary of War, keeping them informed about the broad aspects of his strategic plans and telling them in advance of his armies' needs. Grant removed himself from the politics of Washington and established his headquarters in northern Virginia. Though he planned to go quickly to troubled spots, Grant elected to accompany Meade's Army of the Potomac in order to assess Lee's moves and their effects on the other columns of the Union Army. By rail or steamboat, Grant was never far from Lincoln, and in turn the President visited Grant frequently. To tie his far-flung commands together, Grant employed a vast telegraph system.

In a continental theater of war larger than Napoleon's at its zenith, Grant's job, administratively, eventually embraced four military divisions, totaling seventeen subcommands, wherein 500,000 combat soldiers would be employed. At Washington, Halleck operated a war room for Grant and eased his heavy burden of studying the several Army commanders' detailed field directives by preparing brief digests, thus saving the General in Chief many hours of reading detailed reports. Bearing the then nebulous title of "Chief of Staff, U.S. Army," Halleck had a major job in keeping Grant informed about supply levels at base depots and advance dumps in Nashville, St. Louis, City Point, Washington, Philadelphia, Louisville, and New York City. Under Stanton, Quartermaster General Montgomery C. Meigs, the most informed logistician and supply manager of his day, dispatched men and munitions to Grant's subcommands according to a strategic timetable. As the spring offensive progressed, Stanton, Halleck, and Meigs gave Grant a rear-area team that grasped the delicate balance between theater objectives and the logistical support required to achieve them.

Grant spent the month of April on the Rapidan front developing his final strategic plan for ending the war. In essence, he recapped all of his views on the advantages to be gained from his victories in the western theater. He added some thoughts about moving several Federal armies, aided by naval power when necessary, toward a common center in a vast, concentrated effort. He planned to stop the Confederates from using their interior lines. He intended to maneuver Lee away from the Rapidan Wilderness and defeat the Army of Northern Virginia in open terrain by a decisive battle. Another Union force collected from the Atlantic seaport towns of the deep South was to cut the James-Appomattox River line to sever Lee's rail and road links with the other parts of the Confederacy. Simultaneously, Sherman's group of armies would execute a wide wheeling movement through the South to complete the envelopment of the whole country east of the Mississippi. Banks was still scheduled to make the attack through Mobile. As Lincoln described the plan, "Those not skinning can hold a leg."

By mid-April 1864 Grant had issued specific orders to each commander of the four Federal armies that were to execute the grand strategy. In round numbers the Union armies were sending 300,000 combat troops against 150,000 Confederates defending the invasion paths. Meade's Army of the Potomac and Burnside's independent IX Corps, a combined force of 120,000 men, constituted the major attack column under Grant's over-all direction. The enemy had 63,000 troops facing Grant along the Rapidan. Two subsidiary thrusts were to support Meade's efforts. Commanding a force of 33,000 men, Butler with his Army of the James was to skirt the south bank of the James, menace Richmond, take it if possible, and destroy the railroads below Petersburg. Acting as a right guard in the Shenandoah Valley, Maj. Gen. Franz Sigel's 23,000 Federals were to advance on Lee's rail hub at Lynchburg, Virginia. With the northern Virginia triangle under attack, in the continental center of the line Sherman's 100,000 men were to march on Atlanta, annihilating Joseph E. Johnston's 65,000 soldiers, and devastating the resources of central Georgia. On the continental right of the line, Banks was to disengage as soon as possible along the Red River and with Rear Adm. David C. Farragut's blockading squadron in the Gulf of Mexico make a limited amphibious landing against Mobile. The day for advance would be announced early in May.

In rising from regimental command to General in Chief, Grant had learned much from experience, and if he sometimes made mistakes he rarely repeated them. Not a profound student of the literature of warfare, he had become, by the eve of his grand campaign, one of those rare leaders who combine the talents of the strategist, tactician, and logistician and who marry those talents to the principle of the offensive. His operations, especially the "rear mass attack," were models of the execution of the principles of war. He was calm in crisis; reversals and disappointments did not unhinge his cool judgment. He mastered the dry-as-dust details of a logistical system and used common sense in deciding when to use the horse-drawn wagon, the railroad, or the steamboat in his strategic moves. Above all, Grant understood and applied the principle of modern war that the destruction of the enemy's economic resources is as necessary as the annihilation of the enemy's armies.

Lee Cornered at Richmond

On the morning of May 4, 1864, Meade and Sherman moved out to execute Grant's grand strategy. The combat strength of the Army of the Potomac, slimmed down from seven unwieldy corps, consisted of three infantry corps of 25,000 rifles each and a cavalry corps. Commanding the 12,000-man cavalry corps was Maj. Gen. Philip H. Sheridan, an energetic leader brought east by Grant on Halleck's recommendation. Meade again dispersed his cavalry, using troopers as messengers, pickets, and train guards, but young Sheridan, after considerable argument, eventually succeeded in concentrating all of his sabers as a separate combat arm. Grant reorganized Burnside's IX Corps of 20,000 infantrymen, held it as a strategic reserve for a time, and then assigned the IX Corps to Meade's army. Lee's army, now 70,000 strong, was also organized into a cavalry and three infantry corps.

Grant and Lee were at the height of their careers and this was their first contest of wills. Having the initiative, Grant crossed the Rapidan and decided to go by Lee's right, rather than his left. (*Map 33*) First, Grant wanted to rid himself of the need to use an insecure railroad with limited capacity back to Alexandria, Virginia. Second, he wanted to end the Army of the Potomac's dependence on a train of 4,000 wagons; the Army's mobility was hobbled by having to care for 60,000 animals. Finally, Grant wanted to use the advantages of Virginia's tidewater rivers and base his depots on the Chesapeake Bay. He was willing to accept the risk inherent in moving obliquely across Lee's front in northern Virginia.

With little room for maneuver, Grant was forced to advance through the Wilderness, where Hooker had come to grief the year before. As the army column halted near Chancellorsville to allow the wagon trains to pass the Rapidan, on May 5 Lee struck at Meade's right flank. Grant and Meade swung their corps into line and hit hard. The fighting in the battle of the Wilderness, consisting of assault, defense, and counterattack, was close and desperate in tangled woods and thickets. Artillery could not be brought to bear. The dry woods caught fire and some of the wounded died miserably in the flame and smoke. On May 6 Lee attacked again. Longstreet's I Corps, arriving late in battle but as always in perfect march order, drove the Federals back. Longstreet himself received a severe neck wound, inflicted in error by his own men, that took him out of action until October 1864. Lee, at a decisive moment in the battle, his fighting blood aroused to a white heat, attempted to lead an assault in person; but men of the Texas brigade with whom Lee was riding persuaded

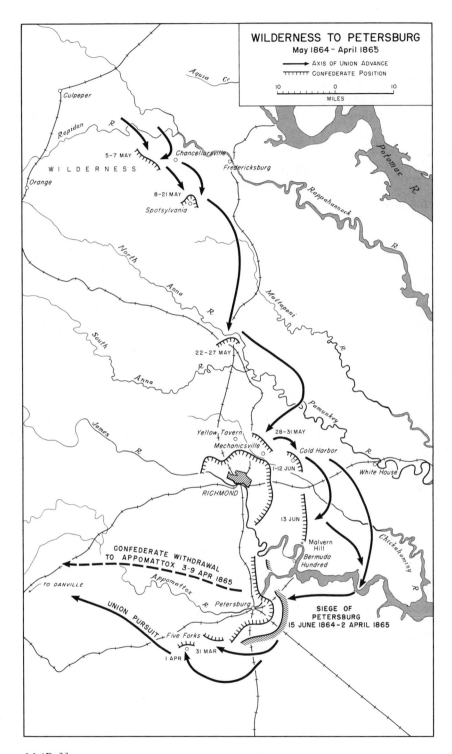

MAP 33

the southern leader to go to the rear and direct the battle as their Army commander. On May 7 neither side renewed the battle.

Now came the critical test of Grant's execution of strategy. He had been worsted, though not really beaten, by Lee, a greater antagonist than Bragg, Joseph E. Johnston, and Pemberton. After an encounter with Lee, each of the former Army of the Potomac commanders, McClellan, Burnside, and Hooker, had retired north of the Rappahannock River and postponed any further clashes with that great tactician. But Grant was of a different breed. He calmly ordered his lead corps to move south toward Spotsylvania as rapidly as possible to get around Lee's flank and interpose the Army of the Potomac between Lee and Richmond.

Lee detected Grant's march and, using roads generally parallel to Grant's, also raced toward the key road junction at Spotsylvania. J.E.B. Stuart's cavalry harassed and slowed Grant; Lee arrived first and quickly built strong earth-and-log trenches over commanding ground which covered the roads leading to Richmond. In this crossroads race, Sheridan's cavalry would have been useful, but Meade had dissipated the cavalry corps' strength by deploying two divisions of horse to guard his already well-protected trains. Sheridan and Meade argued once again over the use of cavalry, and the General in Chief backed Sheridan, allowing him now to concentrate his cavalry arm. Grant gave Sheridan a free hand in order to stop Stuart's raids. Leading his corps southward in a long ride toward Richmond, its objective a decisive charge against Stuart, Sheridan did the job. He fought a running series of engagements that culminated in a victory at Yellow Tavern, in which the gallant Stuart was mortally wounded. The South was already short of horses and mules, and Sheridan's 16-day raid ended forever the offensive power of Lee's mounted arm.

For four days beginning May 9 Meade struck repeatedly at Lee's roadblock at Spotsylvania but was beaten back. Twice the Federals broke through the trenches and divided Lee's army, but in each case the attackers became disorganized. Supporting infantry did not or could not close in, and Confederate counterattacks were delivered with such ferocity that the breakthroughs could be neither exploited nor held. On the morning of the 11th, Grant wrote Halleck: "I propose to fight it out on this line if it takes all summer." On May 20, having decided the entrenchments were too strong to capture, Grant sideslipped south again, still trying to envelop Lee's right flank.

With smaller numbers, Lee skillfully avoided Grant's trap and refused to leave entrenched positions and be destroyed in open battle. Lee retired to the North Anna River and dug in. Grant then continued to move south, to his left, in a daring and difficult tactical maneuver. Butler had meanwhile advanced

up the peninsula toward Richmond, but
Beauregard outmaneuvered him in May
and bottled up Butler's men at Bermuda
Hundred between the James and Appomattox Rivers. Eventually Butler and
Banks, who did not take Mobile, were
removed from command for their failure to carry out their assignments in the
grand strategy.

Lee easily made his way into the
Richmond defenses with his right flank
on the Chickahominy and his center
at Cold Harbor, the site of the Gaines'
Mill action in 1862. The front extended
for eight miles. On June 3 Grant assaulted Lee's center at Cold Harbor.
Though bravely executed, the attack was
badly planned. The Confederates re-

GUNS AND AMMUNITION *stored at City Point.*

pulsed it with gory efficiency, and Grant later regretted that he had ever
made the attempt. Cold Harbor climaxed a month of heavy fighting in which
Grant's forces had casualties totaling about 55,000 as against about 32,000 for
those of Lee. After Cold Harbor, Grant executed a brilliant maneuver in the
face of the enemy. All Union corps were on the north bank of the deep, wide
James by June 14 and crossed over a 2,100-foot ponton bridge, the longest up to
that time in modern history. Having established a new and modern base depot
at City Point, complete with a railroad line to the front, Grant on June 18, 1864,
undertook siege operations at Petersburg below Richmond, an effort which
continued into the next year.

After forty-four days of continuous fighting, Lee was fixed finally in
position warfare, a war of trenches and sieges, conducted ironically enough
by two masters of mobile warfare. Mortars were used extensively, and heavy
siege guns were brought up on railway cars. Grant still sought to get around
Lee's right and hold against Lee's left to prevent him from shortening his line
and achieving a higher degree of concentration. When Lee moved his lines to
counter Grant, the two commanders were, in effect, maneuvering their
fortifications.

Now that Lee was firmly entrenched in front of Grant, and could spare
some men, he decided to ease the pressure with one of his perennial raids up
the Shenandoah Valley toward Washington. Confederate Maj. Gen. Jubal A.

Early's corps in early July advanced against Maj. Gen. David Hunter, who had replaced Sigel. Hunter, upon receiving confused orders from Halleck, retired up the valley. When he reached the Potomac, he turned west into the safety of the Appalachians and uncovered Washington. Early saw his chance and drove through Maryland. Delayed by a Union force on July 9 near Frederick, he reached the northern outskirts of Washington on July 11 and skirmished briskly in the vicinity of Fort Stevens. Abraham Lincoln and Quartermaster General Meigs were interested spectators. At City Point, Grant had received the news of Early's raid calmly. Using his interior waterway, he embarked the men of his VI Corps for the capital, where they landed on the 11th. When Early realized he was engaging troops from the Army of the Potomac, he managed to escape the next day.

Grant decided that Early had eluded the Union's superior forces because they had not been under a single commander. He abolished four separate departments and formed them into one, embracing Washington, western Maryland, and the Shenandoah Valley. In August, Sheridan was put in command with orders to follow Early to the death. Sheridan spent the remainder of the year in the valley, employing and co-ordinating his infantry, cavalry, and artillery in a manner that has won the admiration of military students ever since. He met and defeated Early at Winchester and Fisher's Hill in September and shattered him at Cedar Creek in October. To stop further raids and prevent Lee from feeding his army on the crops of that fertile region, Sheridan devastated the Shenandoah Valley.

Sherman's Great Wheel to the East

On March 17, 1864, Grant had met with Sherman at Nashville and told him his role in the grand strategy. Sherman, like Grant, held two commands. As Division of the Mississippi commander, he was responsible for the operation and defense of a vast logistical system that reached from a communications zone at St. Louis, Louisville, and Cincinnati to center on a large base depot at Nashville. Strategically, Nashville on the Cumberland River rivaled Washington, D.C., in importance. A 90-mile military railroad, built and operated by Union troops, gave Nashville access to steamboats plying the Tennessee River. Connected with Louisville by rail, Nashville became one vast storehouse and corral. If the city was destroyed, the Federal forces would have to fall back to the Ohio River line. Wearing his other hat, Sherman was a field commander, with three armies under his direction.

With the promise of the return of his two crack divisions from the Red River expedition by May 1864 and with a splendid administrative system working behind him, Sherman was ready to leave Chattanooga in the direction of Atlanta. (*Map 34*) His mission was to destroy Johnston's armies and capture Atlanta, which after Richmond was the most important industrial center in the Confederacy. With 254 guns, Sherman matched his three small armies, and a separate cavalry command—a total force of more than 100,000 men—against Joseph E. Johnston's Army of Tennessee and the Army of Mississippi including Wheeler's cavalry, consisting of 65,000 men.

Sherman moved out on May 4, 1864, the same day the Army of the Potomac crossed the Rapidan. Johnston, realizing how seriously he was outnumbered, decided to go on the defensive, preserve his forces intact, hold Atlanta, and delay Sherman as long as possible. There was always the hope that the North would grow weary of the costly struggle and that some advocate of peaceful settlement might defeat Abraham Lincoln in the election of 1864. From May 4 through mid-July, the two forces maneuvered against each other. There were daily fights but few large-scale actions. As Sherman pushed south, Johnston would take up a strong position and force Sherman to halt, deploy, and reconnoiter. Sherman would then outflank Johnston, who in turn would retire to a new line and start the process all over again. On June 27 Sherman, unable to maneuver because the roads were muddy and seriously concerned by the unrest in his armies brought about by constant and apparently fruitless marching, decided to assault Johnston at Kennesaw Mountain. This attack against prepared positions, like the costly failure at Cold Harbor, was beaten back. Sherman returned to maneuver and forced Johnston back to positions in front of Atlanta.

Johnston had done his part well. He had accomplished his missions and had so slowed Sherman that Sherman covered only 100 miles in 74 days. Johnston, his forces intact, was holding strong positions in front of Atlanta, his main base; but by this time Jefferson Davis had grown impatient with Johnston and his tactics of cautious delay. In July he replaced him with Lt. Gen. John B. Hood, a much more impetuous commander.

On July 20, while Sherman was executing a wide turning movement around the northeast side of Atlanta, Hood left his fortifications and attacked at Peach Tree Creek. When Sherman beat him off, Hood pulled back into the city. While Sherman made ready to invest, Hood attacked again and failed again. Sherman then tried cavalry raids to cut the railroads, just as Johnston had during the advance from Chattanooga, but Sherman's raids had as little success as Johnston's. Sherman then began extending fortifications on August 31. Hood, who had dissipated his striking power in his assaults, gave up and retired to

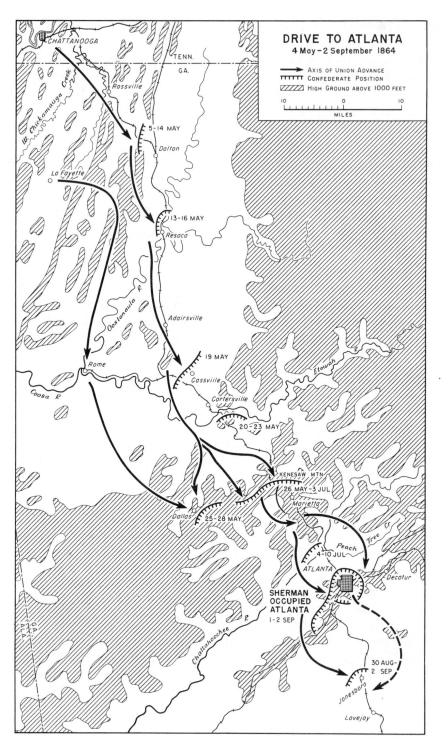

DRIVE TO ATLANTA
4 May – 2 September 1864

→ AXIS OF UNION ADVANCE
⊥⊥⊥⊥ CONFEDERATE POSITION
///// HIGH GROUND ABOVE 1000 FEET

10   0   10
MILES

CHATTANOOGA

TENN.
GA.

Rossville

W. Chickamauga Creek

5-14 MAY
Dalton

La Fayette

13-16 MAY
Resaca

Oostanaula R.

Adairsville

Etowah R.

Rome

Coosa R.

19 MAY
Cassville

Cartersville

20-23 MAY

KENESAW MTN.
26 MAY-3 JUL
Marietta

Dallas 25-28 MAY

Peach Tree Cr.

4-10 JUL
ATLANTA
Decatur

SHERMAN
OCCUPIED
ATLANTA
1-2 SEP

Chattahoochee R.

GA.
ALA.

30 AUG-
2 SEP
Jonesboro

Lovejoy

MAP 34

northwest Alabama, and Sherman marched into Atlanta on the first two days of September. Sherman hoped that Mobile had fallen, and a shorter line for his supplies by way of Montgomery, Alabama, or still better by the lower Chattahoochee to Columbus, Georgia, was open. Admiral Farragut had entered Mobile Bay on August 5, 1864, but had no troops to take Mobile itself.

The fall of Atlanta gave President Lincoln's campaign for re-election in 1864 a tremendous boost. In addition, the psychological lift given the Union by Admiral Farragut's personal heroism in the battle of Mobile Bay greatly added to Lincoln's prestige.

Atlanta was only a halfway point in Sherman's vast wheel from the western theater toward the rear of Lee's Army of Northern Virginia. Abandoning the idea of catching up with Hood, Sherman by telegraph outlined his next strategic move to Lincoln and Grant in early September 1864. Sherman's two proposals proved him an able strategist as well as a consummately bold and aggressive commander. To defend Nashville, he suggested that he send two corps, 30,000 men, back to Thomas, where that commander would raise and train more men and be in position to hold Tennessee if Hood came north. To carry the offensive against the economic heart of the Confederacy, Sherman recommended that he himself take four corps—62,000 men—cut his own communications, live off the country, and march to the seacoast through Georgia, devastating and laying waste all farms, railways, and storehouses in his path. Whether he arrived at Pensacola, Charleston, or Savannah, Sherman reasoned he could hold a port, make contact with the U.S. Navy, and be refitted by Stanton and Meigs. Meigs promised to do the logistical job, and Lincoln and Grant, though their reaction to the plan was less than enthusiastic, accepted it in a show of confidence in Sherman.

Before marching out of Atlanta, Sherman's engineers put selected buildings to the torch and destroyed all railroads in the vicinity. On November 12, moving away from the Nashville depots toward Savannah, the Division of the Mississippi troops broke telegraphic contact with Grant. They had twenty days' emergency rations in their wagons, but planned to replenish them by living off the country. Operating on a 60-mile-wide front, unimpeded by any Confederate force, Sherman's army systematically burned and destroyed what it did not need. The march became something of a rowdy excursion. Sherman's campaign, like Sheridan's in the Shenandoah, anticipated the economic warfare and strategic aerial bombardments of the twentieth century. Yet the victims of his methods could hardly be blamed if they regarded Sherman's strategy as an excuse for simple thievery.

On December 10 Sherman, having broken the classic pattern by moving away from his logistical base, arrived in front of Savannah. Confederate forces evacuated the seaport on December 21 and Sherman offered it to the nation as a Christmas present. Awaiting him offshore was Meigs' floating seatrain, which enabled him to execute the last phase of Grant's strategy, a thrust north toward the line of the James River.

Thomas Protects the Nashville Base

Sherman, as the western theater commander, did not learn of Nashville's fate until he reached Savannah. He had planned Nashville's defense well enough by sending his IV and XXII Corps under Maj. Gen. John M. Schofield to screen Hood's northward move from Florence, Alabama. Schofield was to allow Thomas some time to assemble 50,000 men and strengthen Nashville. The aggressive Hood with his 30,000 men had lost a golden opportunity to trap Schofield at Spring Hill, Tennessee, on November 29, 1864. Unopposed, the Union troops made a night march across Hood's front to escape capture. Bitterly disappointed, Hood overtook Schofield the next day at Franklin.

Grant's continental timetable could have at this point been upset by Hood. Booty at Nashville might carry Hood to the Ohio or allow him to concentrate with Lee before Richmond. But Franklin turned into one of the Confederacy's most tragic battles. It commenced about 3:30 p.m. on November 30 and ended at dusk as Hood threw 18,000 of his veterans against a solidly entrenched force of Federals. Like Pickett's charge at Gettysburg, Hood's frontal assault gained nothing. He lost over 6,000 men, including 13 general officers. At nightfall Schofield brought his troops in behind Thomas' defenses at Nashville.

Hood was in a precarious position. He had been far weaker than Thomas to begin with; the battle of Franklin had further depleted his army; and, even worse, his men had lost confidence in their commander. The Federals in Nashville were securely emplaced in a city which they had been occupying for three years. Hood could do little more than encamp on high ground a few miles south of Nashville and wait. He could not storm the city; his force was too small to lay siege; to sidestep and go north was an open invitation to Thomas to attack his flank and rear; and to retreat meant disintegration of his army. He could only watch Thomas' moves.

Thomas, the Rock of Chickamauga, belonged to the last bootlace school of soldiering. In comparison with Grant and Sherman, he was slow; but he was also thorough. He had gathered and trained men and horses and was prepared to attack Hood on December 10, but an ice storm the day before made movement impossible. Grant and his superiors in Washington fretted at the delay, and the General in Chief actually started west to remove Thomas. But on December 15 Thomas struck like a sledgehammer in an attack that militarily students have regarded as virtually faultless.

Thomas' tactical plan was a masterly, co-ordinated attack. His heavily weighted main effort drove against Hood's left flank while a secondary attack aimed simultaneously at Hood's right. Thomas provided an adequate reserve and used cavalry to screen his flank and extend the envelopment of the enemy left. Hood, on the other hand, was overextended and his thin line was concave to the enemy, denying him the advantage of interior lines. Hood's reserve was inadequate, and his cavalry was absent on a minor mission.

The two-day battle proceeded according to Thomas' plan as the Federals fixed Hood's right while slashing savagely around the Confederate left flank. They broke Hood's first line on December 15, forcing the southerners to retire to a new line two miles to the rear. The Federals repeated their maneuver on the 16th, and by nightfall the three-sided battle had disintegrated into a rout of Hood's army. Broken and defeated, it streamed southward, protected from hotly pursuing Union cavalry only by the intrepid rear-guard action of Forrest's horsemen. The shattered Army of the Tennessee reached Tupelo, Mississippi, on January 10, 1865. It no longer existed as an effective fighting force; Hood was relieved of command and his scattered units were assigned to other areas of combat. The decisive battle of Nashville had eliminated one of the two great armies of the Confederacy from a shrinking chessboard.

Lee's Last 100 Days

President Lincoln was delighted with Savannah as a Christmas present, and in his congratulatory letter to Sherman and Grant the Commander in Chief said that he would leave the final phases of the war to his two leading professional soldiers. Accordingly, from City Point, Grant directed Sherman, on December 27, 1864, to march overland toward Richmond. At 3:00 p.m. on December 31, Sherman agreed to execute this last phase of Grant's continental sweep. In the final 100 days of the war, the two generals would clearly demonstrate the art of making principles of warfare come alive and prove that each principle was something more than a platitude. Each commander had a common objective: Grant and Meade would continue to hammer Lee. Sherman was to execute a devastating invasion northward through the Carolinas toward a juncture with Meade's Army of the Potomac, then on the line of the James River. Their strategy was simple. It called for the massing of strength and exemplified an economy of force. It would place Lee in an unmaneuverable position, cutting him off from all other Confederate commanders. Surprise would be achieved by reuniting all of Sherman's original corps when Schofield, moving from central Tennessee by rail, river, and ocean transport, arrived at the Carolina capes. Solidly based on a centralized logistical system with protected Atlantic sea trains at their side, Grant and Sherman were ready to end Lee's stay in Richmond.

Robert E. Lee, the master tactician, divining his end, wrote to Davis that the Confederates would have to concentrate their forces for a last-ditch stand. In February 1865 the Confederate Congress conferred supreme command of all Confederate armies on Lee, but it was an empty honor. Lee could no longer control events. Sherman moved through Columbia, South Carolina, in February, took Wilmington, North Carolina, the Confederacy's last port, then pushed on. Johnston, newly reappointed to a command, had the mission of stopping Sherman's forces, but could not. At Richmond and Petersburg toward the end of March, Grant renewed his efforts along a thirty-eight-mile front to get at Lee's right (west) flank. By now Sheridan's cavalry and the VI Corps had returned from the Shenandoah Valley, and the total force immediately under Grant numbered 101,000 infantry, 14,700 cavalry, and 9,000 artillery. Lee had 46,000 infantry, 6,000 cavalry, and 5,000 artillery.

On March 29 Grant began his move to the left. Sheridan and the cavalry pushed out ahead by way of Dinwiddie Court House in order to strike at Burke's Station, the intersection of the Southside and Danville Railroads, while Grant's main body moved to envelop Lee's right. But Lee, alerted to the threat, moved west. General A.P. Hill, who never stood on the defense if there was a chance to attack, took his corps out of its trenches and assaulted the Union left in the swampy forests around White Oak Road. He pushed General Warren's V Corps back at first, but Warren counterattacked and by March 31 had driven Hill back to his trenches. Next day Sheridan advanced to Five Forks, a road junction southwest of Petersburg, and there encountered a strong Confederate force under General Pickett—cavalry plus two infantry divisions—which Lee had dispatched to forestall Sheridan. Pickett attacked and drove Sheridan back to Dinwiddie Court House, but there Sheridan dug in and halted him. Pickett then entrenched at Five Forks instead of pulling back to make contact with Hill, whose failure to destroy Warren had left a gap between him and Pickett, with Warren's corps in between. Sheridan, still formally the commander of the Army of the Shenandoah, had authority from Grant to take control of any nearby infantry corps of the Army of the Potomac. He wanted Warren to fall upon Pickett's exposed rear and destroy him, but Warren moved too slowly, and Pickett consolidated his position. Next day Sheridan attacked again but failed to destroy Pickett because Warren had moved his corps too slowly and put most of it in the wrong place. Sheridan, another devotee of the offensive principle who would not tolerate failure to engage the enemy, summarily relieved Warren of command.

Grant renewed his attack against Lee's right on April 2. The assault broke the Confederate line and forced it back northward. The Federals took the line of the Southside Railroad, and the Confederates withdrew toward Petersburg. Lee then pulled Longstreet's corps away from the shambles of Richmond to hold the line, and in this day's action Hill was killed. With his forces stretched thin, Lee had to abandon Richmond and the Petersburg fortifications. He struck out and raced west toward the Danville Railroad, hoping to get to Lynchburg or Danville, break loose, and eventually join forces with Johnston. But Grant had him in the open at last. He pursued relentlessly and speedily, with troops behind (east of) Lee and south of him on his left flank, while Sheridan dashed ahead with the cavalry to head Lee off. A running fight ensued from April 2 through 6. Ewell's corps was surrounded and captured at Sayler's Creek. Lee's rations ran out; his men began deserting and straggling. Finally, Sheridan galloped his men to Appomattox Court House, squarely athwart Lee's line of retreat.

Lee resolved that he could accomplish nothing more by fighting. He met Grant at the McLean House in Appomattox on April 9, 1865. The handsome, well-tailored Lee, the very epitome of southern chivalry, asked Grant for terms. Reserving all political questions for his own decision, Lincoln had authorized Grant to treat only on purely military matters. Grant, though less impressive in his bearing than Lee, was equally chivalrous. He accepted Lee's surrender, allowed 28,356 paroled Confederates to keep their horses and mules, furnished rations to the Army of Northern Virginia, and forbade the soldiers of the Army of the Potomac to cheer or fire salutes in celebration of victory over their old antagonists. Johnston surrendered to Sherman on April 26, twelve days after the assassination of the President. The last major trans-Mississippi force gave up the struggle on May 26, and the grim fighting was over.

Attrition in manpower had forced both South and North to turn from volunteers to conscription in order to keep their armies up to effective strength. The Confederate government had enacted a draft law as early as April 1862. Late in that year Union governors were no longer able to raise enough troops for the Federal armies and on March 3, 1863, Congress passed the Enrollment Act, an outright assertion of national conscription by the central government. This law made able-bodied males between 20 and 45 years of age liable for national

TRENCHES BEFORE PETERSBURG

military service. The Enrollment Act was not popular, as bloody draft riots in New York demonstrated after Gettysburg. Both the Confederate and the U.S. laws were undemocratic in that they did not apply equally to all individuals. They provided for exemptions that allowed many to escape military service entirely. Comparatively few men were ever drafted into the Federal service, but by stimulating men to volunteer the Enrollment Act had its desired effect.

The principal importance of the Enrollment Act of 1863, however, does not lie in the effect it had on manpower procurement for the Civil War. This measure established firmly the principle that every citizen is obligated to defend the nation and that the Federal government can impose that obligation directly on the citizen without mediation of the states. In addition, the act recognized that the previous system of total reliance on militia and volunteers would not suffice in a modern, total war.

Dimensions of the War

Viewing the war in its broadest context, a historian could fairly conclude that a determined general of the North had bested a legendary general of the South, probably the most brilliant tactician on either side, because the Union could bring to bear a decisive superiority in economic resources and manpower.

Lee's mastery of the art of warfare staved off defeat for four long years, but the outcome was never really in doubt. Grant—and Lincoln—held too many high cards. And during the last year of the war, the relations between the Union's Commander in Chief and his General in Chief set an unexcelled example of civil-military co-ordination.

In this costly war, the Union Army lost 138,154 men killed in battle. This figure seems large, but it is scarcely half the number—221,374—who died of other causes, principally disease, bringing the total Union dead to 359,528. Men wounded in action numbered 280,040. Figures for the Confederacy are incomplete, but at least 94,000 were killed in battle, 70,000 died of other causes, and some 30,000 died in northern prisons.

With the advent of conscription, mass armies, and long casualty lists, the individual soldier seemed destined to lose his identity and dignity. These were the days before regulation serial numbers and dog tags (although some soldiers made individual tags from coins or scraps of paper). But by the third year of the war various innovations had been introduced to enhance the soldier's lot. Union forces were wearing corps badges which heightened unit identification, *esprit de corps*, and pride in organization. The year 1863 saw the first award of the highest United States decoration, the Medal of Honor. Congress had authorized it on July 12, 1862, and the first medals were given by Secretary Stanton in 1863 to Pvt. Jacob Parrott and five other soldiers. They had demonstrated extraordinary valor in a daring raid behind the Confederate lines near Chattanooga. The Medal of Honor remains the highest honor the United States can bestow upon any individual in the armed services.

Throughout the western world, the nineteenth century, with its many humanitarian movements, evidenced a general improvement in the treatment of the individual soldier, and the U.S. soldier was no exception. The more severe forms of corporal punishment were abolished in the U.S. Army in 1861. Although Civil War medical science was primitive in comparison with that of the mid-twentieth century, an effort was made to extend medical services in the Army beyond the mere treatment of battle wounds. As an auxiliary to the regular medical service, the volunteer U.S. Sanitary Commission fitted out hospital ships and hospital units, provided male and, for the first time in the U.S. Army, female nurses, and furnished clothing and fancier foods than the regular rations. Similiarly, the U.S. Christian Commission augmented the efforts of the regimental chaplains and even provided, besides songbooks and Bibles, some coffee bars and reading rooms.

The Civil War forced changes in the traditional policies governing the burial of soldiers. On July 17, 1862, Congress authorized the President to establish national cemeteries "for the soldiers who shall die in the service of the country." While little was done during the war to implement this Congressional action, several battlefield cemeteries—Antietam, Gettysburg, Chattanooga, Stones River, and Knoxville—were set up, ". . . as a final resting place for those who here gave their lives . . ." in lieu of some nameless corner of a forgotten field.

As the largest and longest conflict of the nineteenth century in the western world, save for the Napoleonic struggle, the American Civil War has been argued and analyzed for the more than a hundred years since the fighting stopped. It continues to excite the imagination because it was full of paradox. Old-fashioned, in that infantry attacked in the open in dense formations, it also foreshadowed modern total war. Though not all the ingredients were new, railroads, telegraph communications, steamships, balloons, armor plate, rifled weapons, wire entanglements, the submarine, large-scale photography, and torpedoes—all products of the burgeoning industrial revolution—gave new and awesome dimensions to armed conflict.

CHAPTER 13

Darkness and Light
The Interwar Years, 1865–1898

With the end of the Civil War, the great volunteer army enlisted for that struggle was quickly demobilized and the U.S. Army became once again a Regular organization. During the ensuing period the Army faced a variety of problems, some old and some new. These included, besides demobilization, occupation duty in the South, a French threat in Mexico, domestic disturbances, Indian troubles, and, within the Army itself, the old awkward relationship between the line and the staff departments. Despite a relative isolation from civilian society during the period 1865–98, the Army developed professionally, experimented with new equipment of various kinds, and took halting steps toward utilizing the period's new technology in weapons. In a period of professional introspection, the Army still contributed to the nation's civil progress.

Demobilization, Reorganization, and the French Threat in Mexico

The military might of the Union was put on display late in May 1865, when Meade's and Sherman's armies participated in a grand review in Washington, Sherman's army alone taking six and one-half hours to pass the reviewing stand on Pennsylvania Avenue. It was a spectacle well calculated to impress on Confederate and foreign leaders alike that only a strong government could field such a powerful force. But even as these troops were preparing for their victory march, the War Department sent Sheridan to command an aggregate force of about 80,000 men in the territory west of the Mississippi and south of the Arkansas, of which he put about 52,000 in Texas. There Sheridan's men put muscle behind previous diplomatic protests against the presence of French troops in Mexico. The French had entered that country several years earlier ostensibly to collect debts, but since 1864 had maintained their puppet Maximilian on a Mexican throne in the face of opposition from

Mexican patriot forces under Benito Juárez. While the Civil War lasted, the United States had been unable to do more than protest this situation, for even a too vigorous diplomacy might have pushed France into an alliance with the South. Now stronger measures seemed necessary.

The military might in being in May 1865 was ephemeral, for the volunteers wanted to go home and Congress wanted to decrease the size of the Army. Because of the needs of occupation in the South and the French threat in Mexico, demobilization was spread over a period of eighteen months instead of the three in which it could have been accomplished. Nevertheless, it was rapid. On May 1, 1865, there were 1,034,064 volunteers in the Army, but by November 15, 800,963 of them had been paid, mustered out, and transported to their home states by the Quartermaster Corps. A year later there were only 11,043 volunteers left in the service, most of whom were United States Colored Troops. These were almost all mustered out by late October 1867.

General Grant, the General in Chief, wanted to increase the Regular Army, kept small during the Civil War, to 80,000 men, but neither Secretary Stanton nor Congress would agree. Congress, on July 28, 1866, voted an establishment of 54,302 officers and enlisted men. Actual strength reached about 57,000 on September 30, 1867, a peak for the whole period down to 1898. In 1869 Congress cut the number of infantry regiments to 25 and the authorized strength to 45,000; in 1876 the regimental tables of organization were reduced so as to limit the total authorized force to 27,442, an authorization that remained virtually stationary until the Spanish-American War. A significant effect of the Civil War on the new organization of the Army was a provision in the 1866 act for four Negro infantry regiments, which were reduced to two in 1869, and two Negro cavalry regiments, though most of their officers would be white. In 1877, Henry O. Flipper of Thomasville, Georgia, became the first Negro graduate of West Point and was assigned to one of these regiments, the 10th Cavalry.

Demobilization was not so rapid that Napoleon III was unaware of the strength of U.S. forces in being. In the spring of 1867 he finally withdrew his troops from Mexico and left Maximilian to die before a *juarista* firing squad. While there were other factors that help explain the French emperor's action, and historians are not agreed on his motives, he could not have ignored the determination to enforce the Monroe Doctrine embodied in Sheridan's show of force, especially since Maj. Gen. John M. Schofield was then on a special mission in France to make this point clear.

Reconstruction

The Civil War settled once and for all the questions of slavery and of state sovereignty, but the problems of reconstruction remained after Appomattox and with them the Army's involvement in southern affairs. The nation had to be put back together, and the peace had to be won or the sacrifices of a terrible war would have been in vain. The Army had a principal role in reconstruction from the very beginning. As the Union armies advanced in the South, civil government collapsed, except in Sherman's military district, and the Army found itself acting in place of the civil government by extending the function of its provost marshals from policing troops to policing and, in effect, governing the occupied areas. The duties of these provost marshals ranged from establishing garbage regulations to trying to determine the loyalty of southern citizens. Near the end of the war, Congress created the Bureau of Refugees, Freedmen, and Abandoned Lands—the Freedmen's Bureau—and put it under the Army. Its primary purpose was to protect and help the former slaves. In late 1865 most of the governmental functions of the provost marshals were transferred to this bureau, which was headed by Maj. Gen. Oliver O. Howard, a professional officer with antislavery convictions of long standing. As early as 1862, President Lincoln appointed military governors, who were civilians functioning with military support, in Tennessee, Louisiana, and North Carolina.

After Lincoln's death, President Andrew Johnson went ahead with his own reconstruction plans. He declared the Civil War formally at an end in April 1866, liberally pardoned most former Confederates upon their taking a loyalty oath, and then permitted them to re-establish civil government. The leniency of this program, some historians now maintain, led the Army, under Grant, with Stanton in the War Department, to look to Congress rather than to the President, the Commander in Chief, for aid in protecting the Union forces in the South from harassment. Congress, at the same time, was in fundamental disagreement with the President's course. It therefore asserted its supremacy in a series of legislative acts, undoing all that President Johnson had done and placing the South under military control.

The Congress set forth its basic plan in the Command of the Army Act (actually a part of the Army Appropriations Act of 1867) and the Tenure of Office and the First Reconstruction Acts of March 1867. The first of these provided that all Presidential orders to the Army should be issued through the General in Chief, whose headquarters would be in Washington, and who could be removed only with Senate approval. Similarly, the Tenure of Office Act denied the President authority to remove Cabinet officers without approval of the Senate. The first of these acts sought to make Grant rather than the President supreme over the Army, while the Tenure of Office Act sought to keep Stanton in the War Department and the next year provided the principal basis for the impeachment of President Johnson when he suspended the Secretary from office without the Senate's consent.

The First Reconstruction Act divided the South into five military districts. The commanders of these districts were major generals who reported directly to Washington. This was an interesting command relationship, for it was customary to divide the country into geographical commands called divisions, whose subordinate parts were called departments. In March 1867, however, there were only two divisions, the Missouri and the Pacific, with the rest of the country divided into the five military districts of the South and into departments which, like the five districts, reported directly to Washington. As time went by, the Army created additional geographical divisions, and in 1870 a Division of the South comprising three territorial departments administered military affairs in what had been the five reconstruction districts. There is a difference of opinion as to how much the First Reconstruction Act removed control of the reconstruction forces from President Johnson, although Grant advised Sheridan, one of the district commanders, that these commanders, rather than the Executive in Washington, were the sole interpreters of the act. In July 1867, Congress incorporated this interpretation in the Third Reconstruction Act, which declared that "no district commander . . . shall be bound in his action by any opinion of any civil officer of the United States." As a consequence of the First and Third Reconstruction Acts, some historians regard the reconstruction forces as virtually a separate army under Congressional control, thus distinguishing them from the forces in the territorial divisions and departments which remained clearly under the President.

Under the Reconstruction Acts the district commanders had to cope with such matters as horse stealing, moonshining, rioting, civil court proceedings, regulating commercial law, public education, fraud, removing public officials, registering voters, holding elections, and the approving of new state constitutions by registered voters. This occupation duty absorbed somewhat more than one-third of the Army's strength in 1867. As the southern states were restored to the Union under the reconstruction governments, military rule came to an end and civil authorities assumed full control of state offices. This process was largely completed in 1870.

With the ending of Congressional reconstruction, the Army's direct supervision of civil affairs in the South came to an end and the number of troops on occupation duty, which already had fallen off markedly, was reduced still further. Now its mission was to preserve the new state governments by continuing its protection of the Negroes and their white allies upon whom the governments rested, policing elections, helping to apprehend criminals, and keeping the peace in conflicts between rival state officials. The Ku Klux Klan, a postwar organization that had a considerable membership by 1870–71, became an object of special concern to the Army, as it did to the Congress, because of the Klan's terroristic efforts to deliver the South from Negro-Radical Republican control. Consequently, one of the most important Army functions in this period was support of federal marshals in an effort to suppress the Klan. This became an Army responsibility despite the restoration of state militia forces under the reconstruction governments as a means of relieving some of the burden on the Regular troops, which were spread thin. Since many of these new militia forces consisted of Negroes, they were not very effective against white terrorists, who directed some of their acts against the militiamen themselves. These militia forces mainly performed general police duty and watched over elections and voting. Eventually, because of the opposition of white southerners to Negroes in uniform, the Negro militia forces were disbanded.

In April 1877, as a result of the compromise by which Rutherford B. Hayes became President after the disputed election of 1876, the last of the troops on reconstruction duty in the South were transferred to other duty and the federal military occupation of the South came to an end. The Army's role in the South in the years 1865–77 was without precedent in the United States.

Domestic Disturbances

Aside from the Indian wars and Sheridan's show of force on the Mexican border, the Army engaged in no conventional military operations of any consequence until the Spanish-American War, that is, for a period of over thirty years. There were, however, a number of domestic disturbances in which armed forces were used, not only in the South during the reconstruction period but elsewhere as well. Indeed, by 1878, when Congress forbade the use of federal troops without authorization by either "the Constitution or . . . Congress," there had been literally hundreds of instances of their use by federal marshals in strikes, enforcement of local laws, collection of revenues, and arrests of offenders.

In the summer of 1877 the Hayes administration used troops in the wave of railway strikes that marked the country's first great national labor dispute. These strikes spread to a dozen or more states and led to a number of requests for federal help. Thereupon, the Hayes administration pursued a policy of moving troops only to protect federal property or upon the request of a governor or federal judge. The Army stripped every post in Maj. Gen. Winfield Scott Hancock's Military Division of the Atlantic of its available men and also obtained troops from other posts. Additionally, President Hayes used some marines. The President had his own source of information during the strikes in Signal Corps observer-sergeants at weather stations, who reported to Washington at intervals concerning conditions as they saw them in their localities.

Under the circumstances of their use, federal troops came into only limited contact with mobs during the 1877 strikes. They nevertheless contributed greatly to the restoration of order, as Hancock reported, "by their presence alone." The positive results were not due to the size of the forces, for with only about 24,000 troops in the entire Army in 1877 only a small detachment could be used at any one place. But these Regular troops were well disciplined and, taking their cue from the President himself, they acted with considerable restraint in putting down the strikes, neither losing a single soldier nor causing the death of any civilian.

Although the Army became involved in other strike duty in the succeeding years of the century, the best-known instance was in the Pullman, or railway, strike of 1894 which, though centered in Chicago, also affected other parts of the country. President Grover Cleveland's order hastily putting troops in Chicago against the wishes of Governor John Peter Altgeld provided that they should execute the orders and processes of federal courts, prevent obstructions to the movement of the mails, and generally enforce U.S. laws. In fact, they put down the strike. Other governors also protested the use of federal troops in their states. Maj. Gen. Nelson A. Miles, who commanded the 2,000 federal troops in Chicago (and who had advised against using them in the strike), did not use his men effectively at first because he broke them up in small detachments in support of policemen and marshals at scattered points. New orders, however, required him to concentrate his forces and authorized him to fire upon rioters after a proper warning. A small company of Regular troops under his command did fire upon a mob in Hammond, Indiana, on July 7, 1894, when about to be overwhelmed by many times their own number. At least one rioter was killed and more than a dozen rioters were wounded in this action.

The violence was actually much less in 1894 than in 1877, but with only about 28,000 officers and enlisted men in the Army, Schofield, the Commanding General, reported that while his troops performed their duty "promptly and effectively," the situation taxed them "nearly to the limit." He might have added that, at least in California, both sailors and marines were used. The

United States Supreme Court unanimously sustained President Cleveland's actions in Chicago during the 1894 strike, with the result that a legal precedent was set for using federal troops within a state without its consent.

The National Guard Movement

Despite the use of Regular troops in notable instances, the organized militia under state control saw more strike duty than the Regulars in the years after the Civil War. The volunteer militia organizations that had existed since the colonial period became, in effect, the only real militia in existence in those years. The events of the seventies in particular led many persons to fear another insurrection, and as a result legislation was introduced to improve and to provide better arms for the organized militia. In 1879, in support of this effort, the National Guard Association came into being in St. Louis, and between 1881 and 1892 every state revised its military code to provide for an organized militia, which most states, following the lead of New York, called the National Guard. As such, it was by 1898 the principal reserve standing behind the Regular Army.

There was a certain martial enthusiasm in the seventies and eighties, despite the general antimilitarism of the period, that swelled the ranks of the Guard. Also, the Guard attracted some persons because it was a fraternal group that appealed to the manly virtues of physical fitness, duty, and discipline; and it attracted many because it was a kind of social club whose members enjoyed a local prestige. Although organized by states, the Guard had roots in the new nationalism of the period, as may be seen in its very name. Despite this new interest in the Guard, and although the War Department supported the Guard's proposal for a new militia act, apathy, states' rights, and antimilitarism prevented Congress from enacting the desired legislation. Through the efforts of the National Guard Association, the Guard nevertheless succeeded in securing an act in 1887 that doubled the $200,000 annual federal grant for firearms that the militia had enjoyed since 1808.

Isolation and Professional Development

The industrial unrest of the seventies and later was a manifestation of the growing industrialization and urbanization of the nation in the last decades of the nineteenth century, but while labor organizations grew as never before they were of relatively little influence until much later. Meanwhile, perhaps partly as a reaction to the terrible experiences of the Civil War, the ideals and philosophy of what Samuel P. Huntington calls "business pacifism" became dominant. Among other things, business pacifism rejected things military as outmoded in an industrial world designed to produce and sell goods, and it made an impression upon both intellectuals and the popular mind. It manifested itself as either indifference or outright hostility to the Regular Army, affected military appropriations, and philosophically separated the Army from the people. In the late sixties and in the seventies, as Army appropriations fell off (and in 1877 were not even made until November) the Army became isolated from the society at large. It became isolated not only socially, but physically as well, for much of the Army was on lonely duty in the West. Those years, according to William Addleman Ganoe, were "The Army's Dark Ages." They caused the Army and the Navy as well to look inward and to develop a truly military viewpoint that differed fundamentally from business pacifism and civilian liberal thought in general.

Paradoxically, in Huntington's words, the post-Civil War years were actually "the most fertile, creative, and formative in the history of the American armed forces." It took such a period of peace to develop the professionalism that would find employment in the world wars of the next century. In the Army, this professionalism took shape largely under the impetus of two men, General William T. Sherman and Col. Emory Upton, who were helped by other reformers of lesser rank. Their contemporary, Rear Adm. Stephen B. Luce, was similarly the architect of a new professionalism in the Navy.

Sherman's fame, of course, rests upon his record in the Civil War, but he was also the Commanding General of the Army for almost fifteen years from 1869, when he succeeded Grant, to 1883, when Sheridan succeeded him—a record second only to that of Winfield Scott. Unlike Grant and two of the other five Commanding Generals before him, Sherman remained out of politics and thus began the tradition of political neutrality, which would be adhered to long after his time, although not religiously. In this and other ways he oriented the thought of the professional soldier. As Commanding General he became the architect for a system of postgraduate schools beyond the Military Academy through which an officer could learn the skills of his own branch of the service and finally the principles of higher command.

Emory Upton, a protégé of Sherman, was the most influential of the younger officers who worked to reform the Army. He was graduated from West Point in 1861 and was brevetted a major general during the Civil War. After the war he prepared a new system of infantry tactics; served as commandant of cadets at the Military Academy, 1870–75; went on a mission to study the armies of Asia and Europe, which left him especially impressed by the German military system; and then became superintendent of theoretical instruction in the Artillery School at Fort Monroe. His best known writings, *The Armies of Asia and Europe* (1878) and *The Military Policy of the United States* (1904), argued for numerous reforms. The second of these two books was unfinished at the time of his death by suicide in 1881, but was put in order by an associate and, circulating in the Army, became influential long before its publication. It presented a case for a strong Regular military force based upon U.S. experience and subsequently provided the Regular Army with intellectual ammunition for shooting down the arguments of militia advocates, for whom John A. Logan provided a text in his posthumously published *Volunteer Soldier of America* (1887). In Upton's view, a wartime army should consist entirely of Regular formations, which meant that all volunteers should serve under Regular officers. Upton borrowed this plan for an expansible Regular Army from John C. Calhoun. Without giving due weight to the strength of tradition, he wanted the United States to abandon its traditional dual military system and replace it with a thoroughgoing professional army on the German model.

The Military Academy at West Point was at the base of the pyramidal structure of the Army educational system. Unfortunately, much of the vitality went out of the instruction at West Point after 1871 with the departure of Dennis Hart Mahan, the intellectual godfather of the postwar reformers. Although the War Department removed West Point from control of the Corps of Engineers in 1866, the Academy continued to provide a heavily mathematical training and to turn out military technicists but at the same time lost its former eminence as an engineering school. As time went by, the technical content of the curriculum in both the Military Academy and the Naval Academy was reduced, but by 1900 the effort to combine basic military and liberal arts subjects set both institutions off from other collegiate institutions and from the mainstream of education in the United States.

The period of reduced emphasis on technicism at the Military Academy saw the rise of the special postgraduate technical schools that Sherman favored. When the Engineers lost their responsibility for West Point in 1866, a group of engineer officers founded the Essayons Club, which became the Engineer School of Application in 1885. In 1868 Grant revived Calhoun's Artillery School at Fort Monroe, which had been closed since 1860. Also in 1868, a signal school of instruction opened at Fort Greble and, in 1869, moved to Fort Whipple (later Fort Myer), where it continued until 1885. In 1881, Sherman founded the School of Application for Infantry and Cavalry at Fort Leavenworth. Although at its beginning this school was little different from any of the other branch schools, it eventually fulfilled Sherman's hopes and evolved, with much of the credit due Col. Arthur L. Wagner, into the General Service and Staff College.

The Medical Department under the Surgeon General, George Miller Sternberg, founded the Army Medical School in 1893.

Included in the act of 1866 that fixed the organization of the postwar Army was a provision authorizing the President to detail as many as twenty officers to teach military science in schools of higher learning. This supplemented the part of the Morrill Act of 1862 that had provided for military instruction in land-grant colleges. By 1893 the number of instructors had increased to one hundred. In this program can be seen the beginnings of the Reserve Officers' Training Corps, although it would not be organized as such for many years.

Another significant aspect of the developing military professionalism of the years following the Civil War was the founding of professional associations and journals. Notable among them were the United States Naval Institute, founded in 1873, whose *Proceedings* would become well known; the Military Service Institution of the United States, whose *Journal* would become a casualty of World War I; the United States Cavalry Association, which published the *Cavalry Journal;* and the Association of Military Surgeons, which published *The Military Surgeon.* In 1892 the Artillery School at Fort Monroe founded *The Journal of the United States Artillery;* and in 1893 a group of officers at Fort Leavenworth founded the Infantry Society, which became the United States Infantry Association the following year and later published the *Infantry Journal.* Earlier, in 1879, *United Service* began publication as a journal of naval and military affairs. Still earlier, in 1863, the *Army and Navy Journal,* as it came to be called, began a long run. It was not a professional journal like the others mentioned, but along with its social and other items about service personnel it carried articles, correspondence, and news of interest to military people that helped bind its readers together in a common professional fraternity.

Before the Civil War the Army had no professional personnel system in the modern sense. Traditionally, most officers came into the service from the Military Academy at the lowest rank and received promotions on the basis of seniority. The war, however, made at least the need for a retirement system evident, and in 1861 Congress provided for compulsory retirement for incapacity. In 1862 and 1870 it provided that after thirty years' service an officer might retire either voluntarily or compulsorily at the President's discretion. Finally, in 1882, legislation made retirement compulsory at age sixty-four, which prompted the retirement of Sherman, Meigs, and Surgeon General Joseph K. Barnes. Beginning in 1890, promotions for all officers below the rank of major were by examination, thus insuring a minimum level of professional competence. In the mid-nineties, the Army instituted systematic character and efficiency reports for all officers.

Line and Staff

There was no end, during the years between the Civil War and the turn of the century, to the old controversy between the line of the Army and the staff departments. The controversy had its roots in a legally divided responsibility and received nourishment from a conception of war as a science and as the natural purpose of the military. Although Congress made Grant a full general in 1866, and although Sherman and Sheridan both held that rank after him, neither these officers (except only Grant during postwar reconstruction) nor their successors were able to avoid the basic organizational frustrations of the office of Commanding General. The problem was inevitable because, as Army regulations put it as late as 1895, the military establishment in the territorial commands was under the Commanding General for matters of discipline and military control, while the Army's fiscal affairs were conducted by the Secretary of War through the staff departments. At the same time, no statutory definition of the functions of the Commanding General existed except to a limited extent late in the century in the matter of research and development. In practice this situation also diluted the Commanding General's control of the territorial departments, since obviously the distribution and diversion of logistical support for these departments by the staff heads and the Secretary of War would affect troop operations.

Basic to the controversy was an assertion of the primacy of the line over the staff departments, for which there was a theoretical foundation in the developing conception of war as a science and the practice of that science as the sole purpose of military forces. Since the Army existed only to fight, it followed that its organization, training, and every activity should be directed to the single end of efficiency in combat. Therefore, the staff departments, which represented technicism, existed only to serve the purposes of the line, which represented professionalism. From that proposition it followed that the line, in the person of the Commanding General, should control the staff. It also followed that the Army should not become involved, as it did, in such activities as the advancement of science or exploration.

"The regular Army now is a very curious compound," Sherman observed in 1874 in hearings on a bill to reduce the Army. As the Commanding General, he had "no authority, control or influence over anything but the cavalry, artillery, and infantry, and such staff officers as are assigned by their respective chiefs, approved by the Secretary of War, and attached to these various bodies for actual service." To him the three services that he named were "the Army of the United States," while the rest simply went "to make up the military peace establishment." If the Army had to be pruned, he advised pruning the branches of this peace establishment, not the active regiments. To a question about who commanded the engineer battalion, he replied that "God only knows, for I do not." In his opinion the Ordnance Department was "the softest place in the Army." Sons and nephews wanted to go into it, he declared, "especially young men with influential congressional friends." As for the 450 men of the "signal detachment," Sherman regarded them as "no more soldiers than the men at the Smithsonian Institution. They are making scientific observations of the weather, of great interest to navigators and the country at large. But what does a soldier care about the weather? Whether good or bad, he must take it as it comes."

Sherman's view was that of the Army command and of the line, but it did not prevail. In 1894, the situation in which heads of the staff departments spent their entire careers with their specialty and became technical rather than military experts was modified by the requirement that thereafter appointments to the staff departments should be from the line of the Army. This left the basic command problem still unresolved.

Technical Development

The record of the Army's technical development in the years down to the end of the century was not one of marked and continuous progress in every field, for it was hampered by military conservatism, insufficient funds, and the nation's slowness in adapting inventive genius to the art of war. Yet there was considerable progress. In transportation, with the extension of the trans-Mississippi railroads, it became possible to move whole wagon trains by lashing the wagons to flatcars and transporting the mules in closed cars. In ordnance there was progress, however slow, and there were notable beginnings, some of them of vast potential, in signal communications.

The Army was about as slow in adopting new weapons as it was in solving the problem of command that had plagued it for so long. Although Henry and Spencer breech-loading repeating rifles using rim-fire cartridges were used during the Civil War, the typical Civil War infantry shoulder arm was a muzzle-loading rifle musket. In the years immediately following the war, the Ordnance Department, faced with a shortage of funds, converted thousands of the Civil War muzzle-loaders to breechloaders. Desiring a better weapon, however, the Army convened a board in 1872 to examine and test existing weapons. After the board had examined over a hundred weapons the Army adopted the single-shot Model 1873 Springfield breechloader. This fired a center-fire, .45-caliber cartridge, the caliber that the Ordnance Department selected as most desirable for all rifles, carbines, and pistols. The 1889 model of this gun, which embodied its final modifications, was the last of the Army's single-shot, large-caliber, black-powder rifles and the principal shoulder arm of the National Guard as late as 1898.

The Springfield remained in service even after the adoption of newer weapons and despite the trend toward smokeless powder and repeating arms abroad. U.S. manufacturers were slow to develop the new powder, which had several clear advantages. It burned progressively, gradually increasing the velocity of the bullet as it traveled through the barrel. In addition, its increasing pressures permitted a refinement in the rifling that gave a greater spin to the bullet and produced a higher velocity and a flatter trajectory.

When smokeless powder became available in the United States, a board in 1890 recommended adoption of the Danish .30-caliber, bolt-action Krag-Jörgensen rifle, which fired smokeless cartridges and had a box magazine holding five cartridges. The Army adopted the Krag, as it came to be known, in 1892, but Congress delayed production at the Springfield Armory for two years until tests of fourteen American models failed to turn up a superior weapon. By 1897 the Krag had been issued throughout the Regular Army. When its manufacture was discontinued in 1904, the original 1892 model had been twice modified, in 1896 and 1898.

Of the several types of the early machine gun available during the Civil War, the most successful was the Gatling gun, which the Army did not adopt until 1866, when the war was over. Even the advocates of this gun failed to recognize its usefulness as an infantry weapon, but instead looked upon it as either auxiliary to artillery or as a useful weapon for defending bridges.

In artillery as in shoulder arms American technical genius lagged behind that of Europe, where breech-loading artillery using smokeless powder became common in the late nineteenth century. Other European improvements were explosive shells and recoil-absorbing devices, which permitted refiring without reaiming after every shot and opened the way to sophisticated sighting mechanisms and to indirect fire. Also, the year before the Spanish-American War the French invented their famous 75-mm. gun. The U.S. Army nevertheless adopted some good rifled breechloaders, the 3.2-inch rifle being the standard light field piece. These new guns replaced the old smoothbores and steel replaced iron in their construction, but they still used black powder. The Army also had begun to experiment with steel carriages, pneumatic or hydraulic brakes, and mechanisms for elevating, traversing, and sighting artillery pieces.

The progress that had been made in artillery and armor plate was at least partly the result of the work of several boards. The first of these was the joint Army-Navy Gun Foundry Board, provided by the Naval Appropriations Act of 1883. Its purpose was to consider the problem of how American industry could produce both armor plate and armor-piercing guns, upon which a modern navy depended, that would be comparable to the products of European industry. After touring European armament factories, the board recommended that the government award generous contracts to U.S. companies to stimulate their development of steels and forgings, and that the government itself assemble the new materials into weapons at both the Naval Gun Factory and Army arsenals.

The new interest in the Navy in those years resulted in a need to examine coastal fortifications, which would have to be improved if new ships were not to be tied down to defense of the principal harbors. As a consequence the Endicott Board was set up in 1885 to plan for restoration of the coastal fortifications. Neither the world situation nor the existing naval technology justified the estimated cost of implementing the board's recommendations, but in 1888 Congress voted an initial appropriation and established a permanent body, the Board of Ordnance and Fortification, to supervise programs concerned with preparing coastal fortifications. This board was significant as the first War Department-wide agency for supporting research and development and as an attempt to place the important staff departments partly under the control of the Commanding General. Moreover, its failure served to point up the defects in the War Department's organization. The board remained in existence until 1920, but in 1890 and 1891 engineer expenditures and in 1892 ordnance expenditures were removed from the board's supervision. The actual work on the fortifications that followed was never completed, but during the nineties the Army abandoned the old forts around the principal harbors in favor of earthworks, armor-plated concrete pits, and great 10-inch and 12-inch disappearing rifles.

During the years after the Civil War there were several significant, some even germinal, developments in signal communications under the Signal Corps, or the Signal Service as it was known for many years. In 1867 the War Department restored electric field telegraphy to the Signal Corps, which had lost responsibility for it about three years earlier; and the corps quickly developed a new flying or field telegraph train, using batteries, sounders, and insulated wire. Then after constructing a telegraph line along the east coast in 1873 as an aid to the Life-Saving Service, the Signal Corps built long telegraph lines in both the Southwest and Northwest to provide communication between isolated military posts. These also provided facilities for transmitting weather reports. By 1881 these lines extended for slightly more than 5,000 miles.

In the late seventies, within a year or two of Alexander Graham Bell's patenting of the telephone, the Army was using it experimentally at Fort Whipple and between that post and Signal Corps offices in Washington. By 1889 a field-telephone kit, combining the Bell telephone, a Morse key, and a battery, had been developed but was believed to be too expensive for manufacture and issue at that time. About three years later, of ninety-nine garrisoned posts, fifty-nine had telephone equipment, some belonging to the Signal Corps and some rented from the Bell Telephone Company. At about the same time that the Army began using the telephone, it also became interested in the heliograph and found it to be particularly useful in the Southwest. There were also experiments as early as 1878 with homing pigeons.

Perhaps most significant of all the Signal Corps experimentation and developments of the period was the reintroduction of balloons into the Army in the early nineties for the first time since the Civil War. In 1893 the Signal Corps exhibited a military balloon at the World's Columbian Exposition in Chicago, and in 1896 it organized a model balloon train at Fort Logan, Colorado. Here were the beginnings that would lead without interruption to the development of Army aviation.

The backwardness of the United States in military technology in the nineties, despite some important developments, would be misleading unless one looked beyond the specific military facts to examine the nation's industrial base. The United States was already an industrial giant. In 1890, only twenty-nine years after the beginning of the Civil War, the United States pulled ahead of Great Britain in the production of both pig iron and steel and thus became the world's leading producer. Moreover, in the decade of the nineties, the United States also surpassed Great Britain in coal production. In total manufactures, the nation's share jumped from less than 20 percent of the world volume in 1880 to more than 35 percent in 1913. With such an industrial base and potential, the Army of the nineties had no real need for concern.

Civil Accomplishment

The U.S. Army performed a variety of highly useful civil functions in the interwar years, despite the new professionalism that decried such activities as contrary to the natural purpose of an army. Upon the purchase of Alaska from Russia in 1867 the Army occupied the new territory and, through the Depart-

MEMBERS OF THE GREELY EXPEDITION. *Lieutenant Greely is fourth from the left, front row.*

ment of Alaska, served as a temporary caretaker until Congress could provide civil government. Over a period of ten years the Army established posts, maintained law and order, and regulated the affairs of the territory. With the withdrawal of Army troops from Alaska in June 1877, military control over the territory ceased. For the next twenty years the Army's principal role in Alaska was in support of various explorations conducted by Army personnel, which had begun at least as early as 1869 when Capt. Charles P. Raymond of the Army Engineers explored the Yukon. Thereafter there were other explorations in the Yukon, the region of the Copper and Tanana Rivers, and to Point Barrow by, variously, 1st Lt. Frederick Schwatka of the 3d Cavalry, 2d Lt. William R. Abercrombie of the 2d Infantry, 2d Lt. Henry T. Allen of the 2d Cavalry, and 1st Lt. Patrick Henry Ray of the Signal Corps.

Ray's expedition to Point Barrow, 1881–83, was successful in carrying out various meteorological and other observations. It returned safely, but the companion Lady Franklin Bay expedition to Ellesmere Island, 1881–84, under 1st Lt. Adolphus Washington Greely of the Signal Corps, was not nearly so fortunate. Although the Greely expedition reached a point farther north than any prior expedition and carried out its scientific observations, all but seven members of the party died before rescue (and one person died afterward) through failure of prearranged plans for receiving supplies. The Greely expedition grew out of the plans of Signal Corps 1st Lt. Henry W. Howgate for an Arctic colony at Lady Franklin Bay. The Ray expedition stemmed from the proposals of the International Polar Conference, which met in Hamburg in 1879, for a chain of stations about the North Pole to make meteorological studies.

After the Civil War, the rivers and harbors work of the Corps of Engineers increased considerably, contributing substantially to development of the nation's water resources. Other notable contributions of the Engineers were their construction of public buildings, including supervision of the final work on the Washington Monument and on the State, War, and Navy Building, together with Brig. Gen. Thomas Lincoln Casey's planning and supervision from 1888 to 1895 of the construction of what is now the main building of the Library of Congress. Beginning in 1878, the Engineers provided an officer to serve by Presidential appointment as one of the three governing commissioners of the District of Columbia.

EARLY SIGNAL CORPS WEATHER OFFICE, *Washington, D.C.*

Of the four great surveys undertaken in the United States prior to establishment of the Geological Survey in the Interior Department in 1879, the Corps of Engineers had responsibility for two. They were the King Survey, 1867–72, which made a geological exploration of the 40th parallel; and the Wheeler Survey, 1871–79, as the geographical survey west of the 100th meridian was called. The latter was more of a military survey in the tradition of the old Corps of Topographical Engineers than was the former, which was essentially a civilian undertaking. Both of these surveys nevertheless collected specimens of great use to scientists in the fields of botany, zoology, paleontology, and related disciplines.

Although the Navy was largely responsible for interoceanic canal surveys in the post-Civil War years, the first United States Isthmian Canal Commission, appointed by President Grant in 1872, had Brig. Gen. Andrew A. Humphreys, Chief of Engineers, as one of its three members. In 1874 Maj. Walter McFarland,

Corps of Engineers, went out, with naval assistance, to examine the Nicaragua and Atrato-Napipi canal routes; and in 1897 Col. Peter C. Hains of the Engineers was one of the members appointed by President William McKinley to the Nicaragua Canal Commission.

In the years from 1870 to 1891 the War Department organized and operated under the Signal Corps the nation's first modern weather service using both leased telegraph lines and, after they were built, the Army's own military lines for reporting simultaneous observations to Washington. Under Brig. Gen. Albert J. Myer, the Chief Signal Officer, the service gained international renown, but partly because of the hostility of the War Department and the Army to the essentially civil character of the weather service and to its cost, Congress in 1890 directed transfer of the service to the Department of Agriculture, where it became the Weather Bureau in 1891. This loss of the weather service marked a general decline in the role of the military services in the cause of science. Although the Signal Corps retained responsibility for military meteorology, the Army had little need of it until World War I.

Of all the Army's civil contributions, those of its Medical Department, with immeasurable implications for the entire society, may well have been the most important. Indeed, medical research in the Army, in which a few outstanding men were predominant, did not reflect the decline in research that affected the other military branches of the period. One of the most notable of the Army's medical contributions was the Army Medical Library, or the Surgeon General's Library, which, though founded in 1836, did not come into its own until after 1868, when Assistant Surgeon John Shaw Billings began to make it into one of the world's great medical libraries. Similarly, in the same period, Billings developed the Army Medical Museum, which had been founded during the Civil War, into what would become in fact a national institute of pathology.

George Sternberg, who became the Surgeon General in 1893, was the leading pioneer in bacteriology in the United States and a worthy contemporary of Louis Pasteur and Robert Koch. Sternberg's official duties provided some opportunity for his studies, although he performed most of his research independently, some of it in the Johns Hopkins Hospital in Baltimore under the auspices of the American Public Health Association. He was appreciated by all except the more conservative of his colleagues who resisted the germ theory to about the same degree as physicians in private practice.

The more than three decades from the end of the Civil War to the Spanish-American War took the Army through a period of isolation and penury in which it engaged in no large war but in which it had opportunity for introspection. It took advantage of this opportunity and in professional ways that would mean much to its future success moved from darkness and near despair into the light of a new military day. Yet as the century drew to a close, the Army had yet another war to fight before it would see accomplished at least some of the reforms toward which the new military professionalism looked. Meanwhile, it became caught up in numerous Indian campaigns, or Indian wars, as they are now called.

CHAPTER 14

Winning the West: The Army in the Indian Wars, 1865–1890

Perhaps because of a tendency to view the record of a military establishment in terms of conflict, the U.S. Army's operational experience in the quarter century following the Civil War has come to be known as the Indian wars. Previous struggles with the Indian, dating back to colonial times, had been limited as to scope and opponent and took place in a period when the Indian could withdraw or be pushed into vast reaches of uninhabited and as yet unwanted territory to westward. By 1865 this safety valve was fast disappearing; routes of travel and pockets of settlement had multiplied across the western two-thirds of the nation, and as the Civil War closed, white Americans in greater numbers and with greater energy than before resumed the quest for land, gold, commerce, and adventure that had been largely interrupted by the war. The showdown between the older Americans and the new—between two ways of life that were basically incompatible—was at hand. The besieged red man, with white civilization pressing in and a main source of livelihood—the buffalo—threatened with extinction, was faced with a fundamental choice: surrender or fight. Many chose to fight, and over the course of some twenty-five years the struggle ranged over the plains, mountains, and deserts of the American West, a guerrilla war characterized by skirmishes, pursuits, massacres, raids, expeditions, battles, and campaigns, of varying size and intensity. Given its central role in dealing with the Indian, the Army made a major contribution to continental consolidation.

The Setting and the Challenge

After Appomattox the Army had to muster out over a million volunteers and reconstitute a Regular establishment that had languished during the Civil War when bounties and short enlistments made service in the volunteers more profitable. There were operational commitments to sustain during and after the transition, some an outgrowth of the war just ended, others the product of internal and external situations that could not be ignored. Whereas the prewar Army of the 1850's was essentially a frontier Army, the postwar Army became something more. To defense of the frontier were added military occupation of the southern states, neutralization of the Mexican border during Napoleon's colonial enterprise under Maximilian, elimination of a Fenian (Irish Brotherhood) threat to Canada in the Northeast, and dispersion of white marauders in the border states. But these and other later involvements were passing concerns. The conflict with the red man was the overriding consideration in the next twenty-five years until Indian power was broken.

Unfortunately, the military assets released from other tasks were lost through reductions in force instead of being diverted to frontier defense. For even though the country during the Indian campaigns could not be said to be at peace, neither Congress nor the war-weary citizens in the populous Atlantic states were prepared to consider it in a state of war. And in any case, there was strong sentiment against a large standing army as well as a widely held belief that the Indian problem could be settled by other than military means.

As the postwar Army took shape, its strength began a decade of decline, dropping from an 1867 level of about 57,000 to half that in the year that General Custer was killed, then leveling off at an average of about 26,000 for the remaining years up to the War with Spain. Effective strength always lay somewhere below authorized strength, seriously impaired, for example, by high rates of sickness and desertion.

Because the Army's military responsibilities were of continental proportions, involving sweeping distances, limited resources, and far-flung operations, an administrative structure was required for command and control. The Army was, therefore, organized on a territorial basis, with geographical segments variously designated as divisions, departments, and districts. There were frequent modifications of organization, rearrangements of boundaries, and transfers of troops and posts to meet changing conditions. (*Map 35*)

Development of a basic defense system in the trans-Mississippi West had followed the course of empire; territorial acquisition and exploration succeeded by emigration and settlement brought the whites increasingly into collision with the Indians and progressively raised the need for military posts along the transcontinental trails and in settled areas.

The annexation of Texas in 1845, the settlement of the Oregon boundary dispute in 1846, and the successful conclusion of the Mexican War with the cession to the United States in 1848 of vast areas of land, all drew the outlines of the major task facing the Army in the West in the middle of the nineteenth century. During the period between the Mexican and Civil Wars the Army

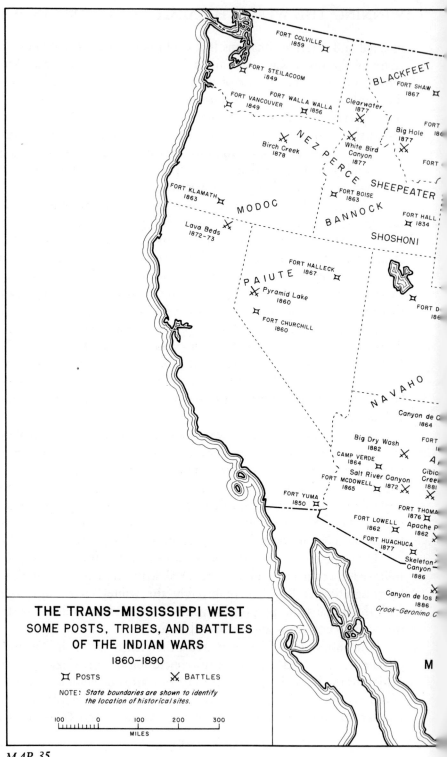

FORT COLVILLE
1859

BLACKFEET

FORT STEILACOOM
1849

FORT SHAW
1867

FORT WALLA WALLA

FORT VANCOUVER   Clearwater   FORT
1849   1856   1877   FORT   186

NEZ PERCE   Big Hole
1877

Birch Creek   White Bird   FORT
1878   Canyon
1877

SHEEPEATER

FORT KLAMATH   FORT BOISE
1863   1863

MODOC   BANNOCK   FORT HALL
1834

Lava Beds   SHOSHONI
1872-73

FORT HALLECK
1867

PAIUTE   Pyramid Lake   FORT D
1860   186

FORT CHURCHILL
1860

NAVAHO

Canyon de C
1864

Big Dry Wash   FORT
1882

CAMP VERDE   A
1864
Salt River Canyon   Cibic
FORT MCDOWELL   1872   Cree
1865   1881

FORT YUMA   FORT THOMA
1850   1876

FORT LOWELL   Apache P
1862   1862

FORT HUACHUCA
1877

Skeleton
Canyon
1886

Canyon de los
1886
Crook-Geronimo C

M

THE TRANS-MISSISSIPPI WEST
SOME POSTS, TRIBES, AND BATTLES
OF THE INDIAN WARS
1860-1890

⊐ POSTS   ✕ BATTLES

NOTE: *State boundaries are shown to identify
the location of historical sites.*

100   0   100   200   300
MILES

MAP 35

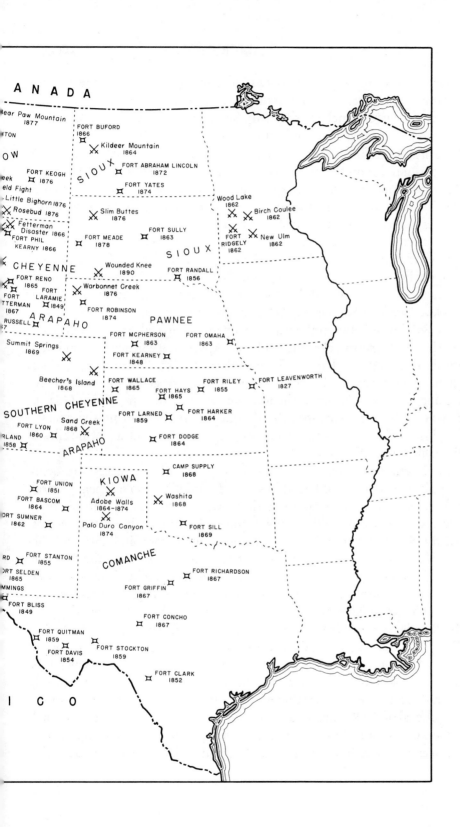

CANADA

Bear Paw Mountain
1877
TON

OW

eek
eld Fight
Little Bighorn 1876
Rosebud 1876
Fetterman
Disaster 1866
FORT PHIL
KEARNY 1866

CHEYENNE
FORT RENO
1865   FORT
FORT   LARAMIE
TTERMAN   1849
1867
RUSSELL
7

ARAPAHO

Summit Springs
1869

Beecher's Island
1868

SOUTHERN CHEYENNE
FORT LYON   Sand Creek
1860   1868
RLAND
1858

ARAPAHO

FORT UNION
1851
FORT BASCOM
1864
RT SUMNER
1862

FORT STANTON
RD   1855
RT SELDEN
1865
MMINGS

FORT BLISS
1849

FORT QUITMAN
1859
FORT DAVIS
1854

FORT BUFORD
1866
Kildeer Mountain
1864
FORT ABRAHAM LINCOLN
1872
FORT YATES
1874

SIOUX

FORT KEOGH
1876

Slim Buttes
1876
FORT SULLY
FORT MEADE   1863
1878
SIOUX

Wounded Knee   FORT RANDALL
1890   1856
Warbonnet Creek
1876
FORT ROBINSON
1874

PAWNEE
FORT MCPHERSON   FORT OMAHA
1863   1863
FORT KEARNEY
1848

FORT WALLACE   FORT RILEY   FORT LEAVENWORTH
1865   1855   1827
FORT HAYS
1865
FORT LARNED   FORT HARKER
1859   1864
FORT DODGE
1864

CAMP SUPPLY
1868
KIOWA
Washita
Adobe Walls   1868
1864-1874
Palo Duro Canyon   FORT SILL
1874   1869

COMANCHE
FORT RICHARDSON
1867
FORT GRIFFIN
1867

FORT CONCHO
1867

FORT STOCKTON
1859

FORT CLARK
1852

Wood Lake
1862
Birch Coulee
1862
FORT
RIDGELY   New Ulm
1862   1862

I C O

established a reasonably comprehensive system of forts to protect the arteries of white travel and areas of white settlement across the frontier. At the same time, operations were launched against Indian tribes that represented actual or potential threats to movement and settlement.

Militarily successful in some cases, these operations nevertheless hardened Indian opposition, prompted wider red provocation, and led to the delineation of an Indian barrier to westward expansion extending down the Great Plains from the Canadian to the Mexican border. Brig. Gen. William S. Harney, for example, responded to the massacre of Lt. John L. Grattan's detachment by Sioux with a punishing attack on elements of that tribe on the Blue Water in Nebraska in 1855. Farther south Col. Edwin V. Sumner hit the Cheyennes on the Solomon Fork in Kansas in 1857, and Bvt. Maj. Earl Van Dorn fought the Comanches in two successful battles, at Rush Spring in future Oklahoma and Crooked Creek in Kansas, in 1858 and 1859, respectively.

In the Southwest between the wars, Army units pursued Apaches and Utes in New Mexico Territory, clashing with the Apaches at Cieneguilla and Rio Caliente in 1854 and the Utes at Poncha Pass in 1855. There were various expeditions against various branches of the elusive Apaches involving hard campaigning but few conclusive engagements such as the one at Rio Gila in 1857. It was in this region in 1861 that Lt. George N. Bascom moved against Chief Cochise, precipitating events that opened a quarter century of hostilities with the Chiricahua Apaches.

In the Northwest, where numerous small tribes existed, there were occasional hostilities between the late 1840's and the middle 1860's. Their general character was similar to operations elsewhere: white intrusion, Indian reaction, and white counteraction with superior force. The more important events involved the Rogue River Indians in Oregon between 1851 and 1856 and the Yakima, Walla Walla, Cayuse, and other tribes on both sides of the Cascade Mountains in Washington in the last half of the 1850's. The Army, often at odds with civil authority and public opinion in the area, found it necessary on occasion to protect Indians from whites as well as the other way around.

The Regular Army's frontier mission was interrupted by the onset of the Civil War, and the task of dealing with the Indians was transferred to the volunteers. Although the red man demonstrated an awareness of what was going on and took some satisfaction from the fact that white men were fighting each other, there is little evidence that he took advantage of the transition period between removal of the Regulars and deployment of the volunteers. The so-called Great Sioux Uprising in Minnesota in 1862 that produced active campaigning in the Upper Missouri River region in 1863 and 1864 was spontaneous, and other clashes around the West were the result, not of the withdrawal of the Regular Army from the West, but of the play of more fundamental and established forces. In any case, by 1865 Army strength in the frontier departments was about double what it had been at the time of Fort Sumter. The volunteers were generally able to keep pace with a continuing and gradually enlarging westward movement by developing further the system of forts begun by their predecessors.

Thus the regional defense systems established in the West in the 1850's and 60's provided a framework for the deployment of the Army as it turned from the Civil War to frontier responsibilities. In the late summer of 1866 the general command and administrative structure for frontier defense comprised the Division of the Missouri, containing the Departments of Arkansas, Missouri, Dakota, and the Platte; the Division of the Pacific, consisting of the Departments of California and the Columbia; and the independent Department of the Gulf, whose area included Texas.

The Army's challenge in the West was one of environment as well as adversary, and in the summer of 1866 General Grant sent a number of senior officer inspectors across the country to observe and report on conditions. The theater of war was uninhabited or only sparsely settled, and its great distances and extreme variations of climate and geography accentuated manpower limitations, logistical and communications problems, and the difficulties of movement. The extension of the rail system only gradually eased the situation. Above all, the mounted tribes of the Plains were a different breed from the Indians the Army had dealt with previously in the forested areas of the East. Despite the fact that the Army had fought Indians in the West in the period after the Mexican War, much of the direct experience of its officers and men had been lost during the Civil War years. Until frontier proficiency could be re-established, the Army would depend upon the somewhat intangible body of knowledge that marks any institution, fortified by the seasoning of the Civil War.

Of the officers who moved to the forefront of the Army in the Indian wars, few had frontier and Indian experience. At the top levels at the outset, Grant as a captain had had only a taste of the loneliness of the frontier outpost. Western duty was unknown to Sherman, and, while Sheridan had served about five years in the Northwest as a junior officer, neither Nelson A. Miles nor Oliver Otis Howard knew frontier service of any kind. Wesley Merritt, George Armstrong Custer, and Ranald S. Mackenzie all graduated from West Point into the Civil War, and John Gibbon had only minor involvement in the Seminole War and some garrison duty in the West. Alfred Sully, also a veteran of the Seminole War and an active campaigner against the Sioux during Civil

War years, fell into obscurity, while Philip St. George Cooke was overtaken by age and Edward R. S. Canby's experience was lost prematurely through his death at Indian hands. George Crook almost alone among the Army leaders at the upper levels of the Indian wars had pre-Civil War frontier experience, dating from 1852, that he could bring back to the West in 1866.

Thus to a large degree the officers of the Indian wars were products of the Civil War. Many brought outstanding records to the frontier, but this was a new conflict against an unorthodox enemy. Those who approached their new opponent with respect and learned his ways became the best Indian fighters and in some cases the most helpful in promoting a solution to the Indian problem. Some who had little respect for the "savages" and placed too much store in Civil War methods and achievements paid the penalty on the battlefield. Capt. William J. Fetterman was one of the first to fall as the final chapter of the Indian wars opened in 1866.

The Bozeman Trail

While the Civil War was still in progress, gold was discovered in Montana and fortune seekers flocked to the area. Lines of communications to the fields around Virginia City lay along circuitous routes and pressure mounted for more direct access. The Army explored the possibilities and adopted a route, pioneered by John Bozeman, extending from Fort Laramie on the North Platte River and Oregon Trail, northwestward along the eastern base and around the northern shoulder of the Big Horn Mountains. Unfortunately, the trail cut through hunting grounds reserved to the Sioux, Northern Cheyennes, and Arapahoes by treaty in 1865.

The Indians resisted white incursions and Maj. Gen. Patrick E. Connor's Powder River Expedition failed to stop their depredations. In 1866 the government, under public pressure and officially attracted to the gold resources as a means of relieving the financial strains of the Civil War, opened new negotiations, but with indifferent results. A few friendly chiefs signed a new agreement at Fort Laramie, but others led by Red Cloud of the Sioux stalked out defiantly when Col. Henry B. Carrington marched in with a battalion of the 18th Infantry, on his way to establish posts along the Bozeman Trail even before agreement with the Indians had been reached.

Although motivated by a sense of justice, treaty-making with the Indians more often than not constituted an exercise in futility for both parties. On the Indian side the tribes were loosely knit societies of individualists living a nomadic existence under leaders whose control and influence fluctuated with the fortunes of war. A treaty was no more binding than the degree of power, authority, and allegiance a leader might muster at any given time, Washington's understanding to the contrary. On the white side, although the authority of negotiating officials was unquestioned, the power to enforce treaty provisions on highly independent westering whites was another thing, and as breach after breach provoked the red man to action the Army was invariably called in to protect the offending citizens and punish the Indians.

Colonel Carrington's battalion of about 700 men departed Fort Laramie in June 1866 for the Big Horn country. Despite Red Cloud's threat to oppose the move, several families, including the commanding officer's, accompanied the force. At Fort Reno on Powder River, some miles beyond the end of the telegraph, Carrington with a Regular company relieved two companies of the 5th U.S. Volunteers, former Confederate prisoners who became so-called galvanized Yankees when they agreed to frontier Indian service in exchange for their freedom. Farther northwestward, 225 miles from Fort Laramie, he selected a site on the Piney tributary of Powder River to construct his headquarters post—Fort Phil Kearny. Five companies remained there while the remaining two were sent another 90 miles out to establish Fort C. F. Smith at the northern edge of the Big Horns.

Fort Phil Kearny became the focus of enemy attention and during its brief existence remained virtually in a state of siege. On December 21, 1866, the Indians attacked a wood train six miles from the fort. Captain Fetterman, who had been brevetted lieutenant colonel in Civil War actions and now boasted that with eighty men he could ride through the whole Sioux Nation, asked to lead a relief column. Indian decoys demonstrated invitingly before the rescue party, withdrawing gradually over Lodge Trail Ridge northwest of the post. Fetterman fell for the ruse and, against Carrington's orders, with eighty men at his back crossed the ridge. In a carefully executed ambush the Indians wiped out the entire force, including two civilians who had gone along to try out their new Henry repeating rifles, weapons far superior to the Springfield muzzle-loaders carried by the infantrymen and the Spencer carbines carried by the cavalrymen in the detail.

The Army was more successful in two other notable actions on the Bozeman Trail. In August 1867 the Indians launched separate but apparently co-ordinated attacks against a haying detail near Fort Smith and a wood detail outside Fort Kearny. In the Hayfield Fight 19 soldiers and 6 civilians, under Lt. Sigismund Sternberg, equipped with converted breech-loading Springfields and several repeating rifles, held off vastly superior odds with a loss of only 3 killed and 3 wounded. In the Wagon Box Fight, Capt. James Powell, with 31 men similarly armed and stationed behind wagon boxes removed from their running gear, held off an investing force of several thousand Sioux and Cheyennes for a good four hours, withstanding mounted and dismounted attacks by several hundred warriors at various times with only 3 killed and 2 wounded.

It is risky to deal in statistics concerning Indian participation and casualties in western campaigns. Accounts vary widely, are founded on shaky evidence, and require some balancing and juggling merely to reach a general order of magnitude, much less an accurate assessment of the facts in a given situation. There is no doubt that the Sioux and Cheyennes suffered serious casualties in the Hayfield and Wagon Box fights. For the Army, however, these were defensive engagements and it lacked sufficient force in the Upper Plains to undertake offensive operations. At the same time there was sentiment in the East to treat with rather than chastise the Indians. The government withdrew the garrisons and abandoned the Montana road in July 1868.

The Southern Plains

The Army during the Indian wars was habitually unable to balance resources with requirements, both because of limited manpower and because of the continental size of the theater of operations. As Lt. Gen. William T. Sherman, commanding the Division of the Missouri, put it, "Were I or the department commanders to send guards to every point where they are clamored for, we would need alone on the plains a hundred thousand men, mostly of cavalry. Each spot of every road, and each little settlement along five thousand miles of frontier, wants its regiment of cavalry or infantry to protect it against the combined power of all the Indians, because of the bare possibility of their being attacked by the combined force of all the Indians."

It was the good fortune of both the Army and the citizen in the West that the Indians rarely acted in concert within or between tribes, although had they done so the Army might have been able regularly to employ large units instead of dispersing troops in small detachments all over the frontier, and might also have had better luck in forcing the elusive opponent to stand and fight. But troops and units were at a premium, so much so in 1868 that Maj. Gen. Philip H. Sheridan decided to try an unusual expedient to carry out his responsibilities in the Department of the Missouri.

Sheridan directed Maj. George A. Forsyth to "employ fifty first-class hardy frontiersmen, to be used as scouts against the hostile Indians, to be commanded by yourself." Recruited at Forts Harker and Hays in Kansas, the command took the field in late August in a region frequented by Comanches, Kiowas,

Southern Cheyennes, and Arapahoes, augmented by some Sioux roaming south of the Platte. The tribes were restive. The Kansas Pacific Railroad was advancing through their country, frightening the buffalo—their source of food, clothing, and shelter—and attracting white settlement. The Cheyennes were still smoldering over the massacre of some 200 of Black Kettle's band, including women and children, by Col. John M. Chivington and his Colorado volunteers on Sand Creek in 1864, and had demonstrated their mistrust of the whites when Maj. Gen. Winfield Scott Hancock penetrated their area with a large and presumably peaceful expedition in 1867.

Forsyth and the Indians collided on the Arickaree Fork of the Republican River at dawn on November 17, 1868, when a combined war party of about 600 Cheyennes, Sioux, and Arapahoes attacked him in a defensive position on a small island in the river bed. The Indians pressed the fight for three days, wounding Forsyth and upwards of 20 of his scouts and killing his second in command, Lt. Frederick H. Beecher, and his surgeon and 3 scouts. Among Indian casualties in this Battle of Beecher Island was the influential Cheyenne leader Roman Nose. The first rescue force on the scene was Capt. Louis H. Carpenter's company of Negro troopers of the 10th Cavalry Regiment.

By the late 1860's the government's policy of removing Indians from desirable areas (graphically represented by the transfer of the Five Civilized Tribes from the Southeast to Oklahoma—the Cherokees called it the "Trail of Tears") had run its course and was succeeded by one of concentrating them on reservations. The practice of locating tribes in other than native or salubrious surroundings and of joining uncongenial bands led to more than one Indian war. Some bands found it convenient to accept reservation status and government rations during the winter months, returning to the warpath and hunting trail in the milder seasons. Many bands of many tribes refused to accept the treaties offered by a peace commission and resisted the government's attempt to confine them to specific geographical limits; it fell to the Army to force compliance. In his area, General Sheridan now planned to hit the Indians in their permanent winter camps.

While a winter campaign presented serious logistical problems, it offered opportunities for decisive results. If the Indians' shelter, food, and livestock could be destroyed or captured, not only the warriors but their women and children were at the mercy of the Army and the elements, and there was little left but surrender. Here was the technique of total war, a practice that raised certain moral questions for many officers and men that were never satisfactorily resolved.

Sheridan devised a plan whereby three columns would converge on the wintering grounds of the Indians just east of the Texas Panhandle, one from Fort Lyon in Colorado, one from Fort Bascom in New Mexico, and one from Camp Supply in Oklahoma. The 7th Cavalry Regiment under Lt. Col. George Armstrong Custer fought the major engagement of the campaign. Custer found the Indians on the Washita River and struck Black Kettle's Cheyenne village with eleven companies from four directions at dawn on November 29, 1868, as the regimental band played "Garry Owen." A fierce fight developed which the Indians continued from surrounding terrain. By mid-morning Custer learned that this was only one of many villages of Cheyennes, Arapahoes, Kiowas, and Comanches extending for miles along the Washita. Facing such odds, Custer hastened to destroy the village and its supplies and horses, used an offensive maneuver to deceive the enemy, and under cover of darkness withdrew from the field, taking 53 women and children as prisoners. The 7th lost 21 officers and men killed and 13 wounded in the Battle of the Washita; the Indians perhaps 50 killed and as many wounded.

The Kiowas and Comanches did not lightly relinquish their hunting grounds and forsake their way of life. Some lived restlessly on a reservation in Indian Territory around Fort Sill, others held out. Sherman, now Commanding General of the U.S. Army, Sheridan, commanding the Division of the Missouri, and their field commanders were forced into active compaigning before these tribes were subdued. In 1871 reservation Kiowas raided into Texas, killing some teamsters of a government wagon train. General Sherman, visiting at Fort Sill, had the responsible leaders—Satanta, Satank, and Big Tree—arrested in a dramatic confrontation on the post between armed Indians and soldiers in which only Sherman's coolness prevented an explosion. Satank was later killed attempting escape, while Satanta and Big Tree were tried and imprisoned for two years. Again in custody in 1876, Satanta took his own life.

There were other incidents on the Southern Plains before the Indians there were subjugated. An Army campaign in 1874, involving about 3,000 troops under Col. Nelson A. Miles' over-all command, was launched in five columns from bases in Texas, New Mexico, and Indian Territory against the Texas Panhandle refuge of the Plains tribes. On September 24 Col. Ranald S. Mackenzie and the 4th Cavalry found the winter camp of the Comanches, Kiowas, Cheyennes, and Arapahoes in a last stronghold, the deep Palo Duro Canyon on the Staked Plains. Mackenzie's surprise attack separated the Indians from their horses and belongings, and these were destroyed. With winter coming on the Indians had little alternative to the reservation.

The Northwest

Not all the Indian wars were fought with Plains tribes. The Army engaged in wars with several Pacific slope tribes in the 1870's, and the operations were widely scattered over the mountainous northwestern quarter of the trans-Mississippi West.

The Modoc War of 1872–73 began when the Modocs, who had been placed on a reservation in southern Oregon with the more numerous and traditionally unfriendly Klamaths, returned without permission to their home in the Lost River country on the California border. When the Army attempted in November of 1872 to take them back to the reservation, fighting broke out and the Indians retreated into a natural fortress—the Lava Beds at the southern end of Tule Lake. Over the course of six month there were four engagements in which Regular and volunteer troops with superior strength and weapons incurred heavier losses than their opponents. Extended efforts by a peace commission made little headway and ended in tragedy when two of the members, Brig. Gen. Edward R. S. Canby and Reverend Eleaser Thomas, both unarmed, were shot while in conference with the Indians. The Modocs finally surrendered and four of their leaders, including Canby's murderer, Captain Jack, were hanged.

The practice of uprooting the Indians from their homeland was also the cause of the Nez Perce War in 1877. The Nez Perces had been friendly to the whites from the days of their contact with Lewis and Clark. Although they ceded some of their lands to the whites, they refused to give up the Wallowa Valley in northeastern Oregon. White encroachment increased, stiffening the lines of political pressure back to Washington and leading inevitably to decisions favorable to white settlement and removal of the Nez Perces to the Lapwai Reservation across the Snake River in Idaho. Some elements of the tribe complied, but Chief Joseph and his people did not and the Army was ordered to move them. An inevitable course of events and irresponsible actions by both reds and whites made hostilities unavoidable.

In a remarkable campaign that demonstrated the unique capabilities of guerrilla forces and the difficulties that formal military units have in dealing with them, the Nez Perces led the Army on a 1,300-mile chase over the Continental Divide, punctuated by a number of sharp engagements. The Indians used the terrain to great advantage, fighting when circumstances favored them, sideslipping around opposing forces or breaking contact when the situation dictated it. They lived off the land, while the Army was tied to supply trains that were vulnerable to Indian attack. But their freedom of

SURRENDER OF CHIEF JOSEPH

movement was hindered by their women and children, while Army superiority in strength and weapons gradually began to tell. Indian rifles were no match for howitzers and Gatling guns, and Indian mobility could not outstrip the Army's use of the telegraph to alert additional forces along the Nez Perce line of flight. The battles of White Bird Canyon, Clearwater, Big Hole, Canyon Creek, and Bear Paw Mountain involved hundreds of troops and numerous units under Howard, Gibbon, Samuel D. Sturgis, and Miles. There were heavy casualties on both sides before Chief Joseph, in a poignant speech, surrendered. "Hear me, my Chiefs," were his closing words to Generals Howard and Miles, "my heart is sick and sad. From where the sun now stands I will fight no more forever."

In 1878 and 1879 Army forces took the field against various bands of Indians in mountain areas of the Northwest. Operations against the Bannocks, Sheepeaters, and Utes were relatively minor. The Bannock War was caused by white intrusion on the Camas Prairie in Idaho, where camas roots were a prime source of food for the Indians. The Sheepeater War, also centered in Idaho, broke out when the Indians were charged wtih several murders they probably did not commit. The Ute War in northwestern Colorado grew out of the misguided methods and impractical idealism of Indian Agent Nathan C.

Meeker. All of these clashes represented a last convulsion against fate for the tribes involved, while for the Army they meant hard campaigning and casualties.

The Southwest

The Apaches were among the Army's toughest opponents in the Indian wars. The zone of operations embraced the territories of Arizona and New Mexico, western Texas, and Mexico's northern provinces, and, despite the fact that hostile Apaches were relatively few in number and the theater was essentially a secondary one, they tied down sizable forces over a long period of time.

Post-Civil War Apache troubles extended from the late 1860's, when the Army campaigned against Cochise, on through the seventies and eighties, when Victorio and Geronimo came to the fore. On the Army side the important factor was the assignment of Bvt. Maj. Gen. George Crook to the Southwest, where he served two tours between 1871 and 1886. Crook was an able administrator as well as an outstanding soldier, and proved to be a relentless opponent of the Indian on the battlefield and a steadfast friend off it. As commander of the Department of Arizona he organized at key locations a number of mobile striking forces under experienced frontier officers and launched them in a concerted campaign supported by mule pack trains. Acting under an 1866 Congressional act, which authorized the Army to enlist up to a thousand Indian scouts (they came from traditionally friendly tribes like the Crow and Pawnee or from friendly elements of warring tribes), Crook also employed Apache scouts. Converging columns and persistent pursuit brought results, and he left Arizona in relative quiet when he went to the Department of the Platte in 1875.

But the quiet in the Southwest did not last long. Largely at the instigation of politicians, merchants, contractors, and other self-serving whites, several bands of mutually uncongenial Apaches were transferred from desirable areas to the unhealthy San Carlos Reservation in the Arizona lowlands. As a result, much of what Crook had accomplished was undone as disgruntled Apaches again turned to raiding and killing. In the summer of 1881, for example, an Apache medicine man stirred the Indians to heights of religious fervor that led to a sharp clash on Cibicu Creek with troops commanded by Col. Eugene A. Carr, one of the Army's most experienced Indian fighters. The action was highlighted by perhaps the most notable instance of disaffection when the Indian scouts with the command turned on the Regulars.

GERONIMO (*left center*) AT THE CONFERENCE WITH GENERAL CROOK
(*second from right, seated*), *1886*.

Throughout the Indian wars there was constant friction between the
War and the Interior Departments over the conduct of Indian affairs. A
committee of the Continental Congress had first exercised this responsibility.
In 1789 it was transferred to the Secretary of War, and in 1824 a Bureau of
Indian Affairs was created in the War Department. When the Department
of the Interior was established in 1849, the Indian bureau was transferred
to that agency. Thus administration of Indian affairs was handled by one
department while enforcement lay with another. As General Crook put it
to a Congressional committee in 1879: "As it is now you have a divided responsibility. It is like having two captains on the same ship."

Crook returned to Arizona in 1882 to restore confidence among the Apaches
in white administration, move them along the paths of civilization, and spar
constantly with the Indian bureau. On the military side, he took the field against
dwindling numbers of hostiles, co-operating with Mexican officials and authorized to cross the international boundary in pursuit of the renegades. Crook met
with Geronimo in the Sierra Madre Mountains in March of 1886 and negotiated
a surrender that brought in all but Geronimo and a few followers who backed
out at the last moment. When Washington failed to back the field commander
in the conditions on which he had negotiated the surrender, Crook asked to
be relieved. Nelson A. Miles replaced him, and Lt. Charles B. Gatewood entered

Geronimo's mountain fastness to arrange a surrender and bring the Apache campaigns to a close.

The Northern Plains

All of the elements of the clash of red and white civilizations were present in the events leading to final subjugation of the Indians. The mounted tribes of the Great Plains were astride the main corridors of westward expansion, and this was the area of decision. The treaty of 1868 had set aside the Great Sioux Reservation in South Dakota and the Army had abandoned the Bozeman Trail, leaving the Powder River region as unceded Indian country. The Sioux and their allies were thus north of the main transcontinental artery along the Platte. Although the arrangement worked for several years, it was doomed by the irresistible march of civilization. The Sioux rejected white overtures for a right-of-way for the Northern Pacific Railroad, and when surveyors went ahead anyway they ran into Indian resistance, which led to the dispatch in 1873 of a large military expedition under Col. David S. Stanley up the Yellowstone Valley. The next year General Sheridan sent Custer and the 7th Cavalry on a reconnaissance through the Black Hills, within the Sioux Reservation. When geologists with the expedition found gold, the word spread rapidly and prospectors filtered into the area despite the Army's best efforts to keep them out. Another treaty was broken and, band by band, angry reservation Indians slipped away to join nontreaty recalcitrants in the unceded Powder River region of Wyoming and Montana.

In December 1875 the Indian bureau notified the Sioux and Cheyennes that they had to return to the reservation by the end of the following month. Since the Indians were in winter quarters in remote areas and would have had little chance against the elements, they did not obey. As the deadline passed, the Commissioner of Indian Affairs appealed to the Army to force compliance. Sheridan, mindful of his success with converging columns against the Southern Plains tribes, determined upon a similar campaign in the north.

Columns were organized to move on the Powder River area from three directions. Brig. Gen. Alfred H. Terry marched westward from Fort Abraham Lincoln in Dakota Territory, his principal element the 7th Cavalry under Custer. Col. John Gibbon moved eastward from Fort Ellis in western Montana with a mixed force of infantry and cavalry, while Brig. Gen. George Crook moved northward from Fort Fetterman on the North Platte in Wyoming with a force heavily weighted in cavalry. In March 1876 a part of Crook's force under Col. Joseph J. Reynolds had entered the valley of the Powder and surprised a

Cheyenne-Sioux camp, but Reynolds had failed to press an initial advantage and had withdrawn without punishing the Indians. In June, with the major campaign under way, Crook made the first contact. The Sioux and Cheyennes learned of his approach along Rosebud Creek, and some 1,500 warriors moved to meet him. Crook had fifteen companies of cavalry and five of infantry, about 1,000 men, plus another 300 friendly Indians and civilians. The two forces met on roughly equal terms on the 17th in heavy fighting. Tactically, neither side carried the field conclusively enough to claim a victory. Strategically, Crook's withdrawal to a supply base to southward gave the Battle of the Rosebud the complexion of a defeat for the Army, especially in view of developments on the Little Bighorn River about fifty miles to northwestward, which his continued advance might have influenced decisively.

While Crook was moving northward to his collision on the Rosebud, Terry and Gibbon, marching from east and west, had joined forces on the Yellowstone River at its confluence with the Powder, where a supply base serviced by river steamer was established. Terry sent out the 7th Cavalry to scout for Indian sign, and Maj. Marcus A. Reno with six companies (the cavalry "company" was not called a "troop" until 1883) reconnoitered up the Powder, across the Tongue River, and into the valley of the Rosebud. Here on June 17 Reno found a fresh trail leading west out of the valley and across the Wolf Mountains in the direction of the Little Bighorn. He was unaware, and was thus unable to inform his superiors, that Crook was also in the Rosebud valley and had been engaged and blocked by a large force of Indians not far upstream on this very same day.

Terry held a council of war aboard the steamer *Far West* to outline his plan. Custer's 7th Cavalry would move south up the Rosebud, cross the Wolf Mountains, and enter the Little Bighorn valley from the south. Gibbon, joined by Terry, would ascend the Bighorn River and its tributary, the Little Bighorn, from the north, trapping the Indians between the two forces.

As it happened, Custer moved at least a day early for the co-operative action envisioned in Terry's plan. On June 25, 1876, the 7th crossed the Wolf Mountains and moved into the valley of the Little Bighorn. Custer was confident of his capability to handle whatever he ran up against, convinced that the Indians would follow their usual practice of scattering before a show of force, and completely unaware that he was descending upon one of the largest concentrations of Indians ever assembled on the Plains—perhaps as many as 12,000 to 15,000 Sioux and Northern Cheyennes, with between 3,000 and 4,000 warriors under such leaders as Crazy Horse, Sitting Bull, Gall, Crow King, Lame Deer, Hump, and Two Moon.

Around noon of this Sunday in June, Custer sent Capt. Frederick W. Benteen with three companies to scout to the left of the command, not an unusual move for a force still attempting to fix the location of an elusive enemy and expecting him to slip away on contact. About 2:30 p.m., still two miles short of the river, when the upper end of an Indian village came into view, Custer advanced three more companies under Major Reno with instructions to cross the river and charge the Indian camp. With five companies Custer moved off to the right, still screened by a fold of ground from observing the extent of his opposition, perhaps with the thought of hitting the Indians from the flank—of letting Reno hold the enemy by the nose while he, Custer, kicked him in the seat of the pants. As he progressed, Custer rushed Sgt. Daniel Kanipe to the rear to hurry the pack train and its one-company escort forward, and shortly afterward dispatched Trumpeter John Martin with a last message to Benteen informing him that a "big village" lay ahead and to "be quick— bring packs."

The main phase of the Battle of the Little Bighorn lasted about two hours. Reno, charging down the river with three companies and some Arickara scouts, ran into hordes of Indians, not retreating, but advancing, perhaps mindful of their creditable performance against Crook the week before, and certainly motivated by a desire to protect their women and children and cover a withdrawal of the villages. Far outnumbered, suffering heavy casualties, and in danger of being overrun, Reno withdrew to the bluffs across the river and dug in.

Custer and his five companies—about 230 strong—moved briskly along the bluffs above the river until, some four miles away, beyond supporting distance and out of sight of the rest of the command, they were brought to bay and overwhelmed by an Indian force that outnumbered them by perhaps 20 to 1. When the last man had fallen and the dead had been plundered, the Indians turned their attention to Reno once again.

While the Indians had been chiefly absorbed on the Custer section of the field, Benteen's battalion and the pack train and its escorting company had moved up and gone into a defensive perimeter with Reno's force. An attempt to move in force in Custer's direction, despite a complete lack of knowledge of his location and situation, failed; the Reno defensive position was reoccupied and remained under attack until dark of the 25th and on through daylight hours of the 26th. The siege was finally lifted with the arrival of the Terry-Gibbon column on June 27th.

The Custer disaster shocked the nation and was the climax of the Indian wars. The Army poured troops into the Upper Plains and the Indians scattered, some, like Sitting Bull's band, to Canada. But gradually, under Army pressure or seeing the futility of further resistance, the Indians surrendered and returned to the reservation.

The last gasp of the Indian wars occurred in 1890 and grew out of the fervor of the Ghost Dance religion. The Sioux were particularly susceptible to the emotional excitement and the call of the old way of life represented in these ceremonies, and their wild involvement frightened the agent on the Sioux Reservation into calling for military protection. The 7th Cavalry, now commanded by Col. James W. Forsyth, moved to Wounded Knee Creek on the Pine Ridge Agency where, on December 29, 1890, the regiment attempted to disarm Big Foot's band. An Indian's rifle was discharged into the air as two soldiers disarmed him, precipitating a battle in which more than 150 Indians, including women and children, were killed and a third as many wounded, while 25 soldiers were killed and another 37 wounded.

The Battle of Wounded Knee was the last Indian engagement to fall in the category of warfare; later incidents were more in the realm of civil disturbance. The nineteenth century was drawing to a close and the frontier was rapidly disappearing. Territories were being replaced by states, and people, settlements, government, and law were spreading across the land. The buffalo were gone and the Indians were confined to reservations and dependent upon the government for subsistence. An expanded rail system was available to move troops quickly to trouble spots, and the Army could now concentrate its forces at the larger and more permanent posts and relinquish numerous smaller installations that had outgrown their usefulness. By 1895 the Army was deployed more or less equally around the country on the basis of regional rather than operational considerations.

In the quarter century of the Indian wars the Army met the Indian in over a thousand actions, large and small, all across the American West. It fought these wars with peacetime strength and on a peacetime budget, while at the same time it helped shape Indian policy, contributed to the red man's acculturation, and was centrally involved in numerous other activities that were part and parcel of westward expansion and of the nation's attainment of its "manifest destiny." Operations against the Indians seasoned the Army and forged a core of experienced leaders who would serve the republic well as it moved onto the world scene at the turn of the century.

CHAPTER 15

Emergence to World Power
1898–1902

In the latter part of the nineteenth century the United States, hitherto largely provincial in thought and policies, began to emerge as a new world power. Beginning in the late 1880's more and more Americans displayed a willingness to support involvement of the nation in frankly imperialistic ventures, justifying this break with traditional policy on strategic, economic, religious, and emotional grounds. Much of the energy that had been channeled earlier into internal development of the country, and especially into westward expansion along the frontier (which, according to the Census Bureau, ceased to exist as of 1890), was now diverted to enterprises beyond the continental limits of the United States. It was only a matter of time before both the Army and the Navy were to be called upon to support and protect the new American interests overseas.

A New Manifest Destiny

This new manifest destiny first took the form of vigorous efforts to expand long-established American trade and naval interests overseas, especially in the Pacific and Caribbean. Thus, in the Pacific the United States took steps to acquire control of coaling and maintenance stations for a growing steam-propelled fleet. In 1878 the United States obtained the right to develop a coaling station in Samoa and in 1889, to make this concession more secure, recognized independence of the islands in a tripartite pact with Great Britain and Germany. In 1893, when a new native government in Hawaii threatened to withdraw concessions, including a site for a naval station at Pearl Harbor, American residents tried unsuccessfully to secure annexation of the islands by the United States. Development of a more favorable climate of opinion in the United States in the closing years of the century opened the way for annexation of Hawaii in 1898 and Eastern Samoa (Tutuila) in 1899.

In the same period, the Navy endeavored with little success to secure coaling stations in the Caribbean, and Americans watched with interest abortive efforts of private firms to build an isthmian canal in Panama. American businessmen promoted establishment of better trade relations with Latin American countries, laying the groundwork for the future Pan American Union. And recurrent diplomatic crises, such as that with Chile in 1891–92, arising from a mob attack on American sailors in Valparaiso, and with Great Britain over the Venezuelan–British Guiana boundary in 1895, drew further attention to the southern continent.

Trouble in Cuba

While economic and strategic motives contributed significantly to the new manifest destiny, it was traditional American humanitarian concern for the oppressed peoples of Cuba that ultimately proved most important in launching the United States on an imperialistic course at the turn of the century. Cuba's geographic proximity to the United States and strategic location had long attracted the interest of American expansionists. Yet they were a small minority, and only when the Cubans rebelled against the repressive colonial policies of Spain did the attention of most Americans turn to the Caribbean island. This was true in 1868, when Cubans revolted against the Spanish regime in a rebellion destined to last for a decade, and again in 1895, when they rose up once more against continuing repression by the mother country. Many Americans soon favored some kind of intervention, but President Grover Cleveland was determined that the United States should adhere to a policy of strict neutrality. Events in Cuba, however, soon were to make this position increasingly difficult to maintain.

When after almost a year of costly fighting the Spanish had failed to suppress the rebellion, they turned to harsher measures. To carry these out the Madrid Government appointed a new Captain-General for Cuba, Valeriano Weyler, an officer with a reputation as an able soldier. Weyler arrived in Havana in early February 1896 with additional troops and immediately instituted new tactics designed to isolate the insurrectionist forces—entrenchments, barbed-wire fences, and, at narrow parts of the island, lines of blockhouses. Simultaneously, he inaugurated a policy of *reconcentrado,* herding women, children, and old people from the countryside into detention camps and garrisoned towns, where thousands died from disease and starvation. Weyler's methods gave newspapers in the United States, especially those practicing a newly fashionable yellow journalism, opportunity for renewed attacks on Spanish policies in Cuba. They portrayed the Spanish general as an inhuman "butcher" inflicting his cruel tactics on high-minded patriots struggling bravely for freedom from the oppression of an out-dated Old World authoritarianism.

In early 1896 both houses of Congress adopted by overwhelming majorities concurrent resolutions proposing that the United States grant belligerent status to the insurgents and employ its good offices to gain Spain's recognition of Cuban independence. Politicians, both in and out of Congress, saw in the Cuban situation an opportunity to gain popular support in the upcoming election of 1896. And a few expansion-minded American leaders perceived the insurrection as a chance to acquire naval bases in the Caribbean and open the way further for the country to play a more prominent role in world affairs. But neither Cleveland, nor his successor as President in 1897, William McKinley, wanted a war with Spain.

The Republican party platform of 1896, however, committed McKinley to a policy of using the nation's "influences and good offices to restore peace and give independence . . ." to Cuba. Consistent with this pledge, the newly elected President, in the face of a crescendo of demands for immediate American intervention, worked courageously and patiently, seeking to find a diplomatic solution that would satisfy the Cuban insurrectionists yet avoid a conflict between the United States and Spain.

In early February 1898, after serious rioting in Havana, the jingoistic New York *Journal* published a private letter written by Enrique Dupuy de Lôme, the Spanish Minister in Washington, to a Spanish editor then traveling in the United States. This communication, which a Cuban official in the Havana Post Office had stolen and passed on to the newspaper, expressed de Lôme's adverse personal reaction to McKinley's message to Congress in December 1897. The President was, he thought, "weak and a bidder for admiration of the crowd . . . a would-be politician who tries to leave a door open behind himself while keeping on good terms with the jingoes in his party." For the majority of Americans this unprecedented insult to a President was only further confirmation of the arrogance and insolence with which they felt Spain regularly conducted its Cuban policies. Even de Lôme's prompt resignation did little to calm the storm of indignation that swept the country. Nevertheless when Spain, at American insistence, somewhat reluctantly offered an apology, McKinley was inclined to accept it. Privately he was horrified at the possibility that what he viewed as a strictly personal matter might lead to war.

Despite this development McKinley still might have achieved a diplomatic solution had the American battleship *Maine* not been sunk on February 15, 1898, in Havana harbor as a result of a mysterious explosion, with a loss of 260 lives. The vessel was in the port ostensibly on a courtesy call—but actually to provide closer protection for American citizens in Cuba—dispatched there rather reluctantly by McKinley upon the advice of the American consul in Havana.

A naval investigating commission appointed by the President announced on March 25 that the *Maine* had gone down as a result of an external explosion, which to most Americans indicated Spanish treachery. But McKinley, in reporting to Congress on the commission's verdict, once again counseled "deliberate consideration" and, on March 27, sent to Madrid a new plan for peaceful settlement of the Cuban problem. The Spanish reply on March 31 agreed to end the *reconcentrado* policy and arbitrate the *Maine* disaster, but procrastinated on granting the insurrectionists an immediate armistice and refused to accept mediation by McKinley or to promise eventual independence for Cuba.

In spite of this discouraging response from Spain, the President continued to move slowly, leaving the door open for last-minute negotiations. Twice he postponed his war message to Congress before finally delivering it on April 11. Eight days later Congress passed a joint resolution proclaiming Cuba independent and authorizing the President to take necessary measures to expel the Spanish from the island. It included a significant amendment by Senator Teller of Colorado forbidding annexation of Cuba. With this authorization McKinley immediately ordered a blockade of Cuba, and an American naval squadron promptly took up a position off Havana. On April 25 Congress declared a state of war had existed since April 21. So began the conflict with Spain which McKinley and Cleveland had tried so hard to avoid—a war for which, despite the months of negotiation preceding its outbreak, the country was militarily most ill prepared.

Mobilizing for War

The extent of unpreparedness for overseas combat varied considerably in the two military services. In the decade preceding the war, the Navy, thanks to the efforts of career officers such as Rear Adm. Stephen B. Luce and Capt. Alfred T. Mahan, and to Benjamin Tracy, Secretary of the Navy in Harrison's administration, and also to the willingness of Congress, in a period of expanding overseas interests and relative prosperity, to appropriate the necessary funds, had carried out an extensive construction and modernization program. During the same period, the Naval War College at Newport, Rhode Island (established in 1885 through the efforts of Admiral Luce), had provided the Navy with a strong corps of professional officers trained in the higher levels of warfare and strategy, including the far-ranging doctrines of Mahan.

The Army was not so fortunate. With an average size in the quarter of a century preceding 1898 of only about 26,000 officers and men, most of whom were scattered widely across the country in company- and battalion-size organizations, the Army never had an opportunity for training and experience in the operation of units larger than a regiment. And while the individual soldier was well trained, the Army lacked a mobilization plan, a well-knit higher staff, and experience in carrying on joint operations with the Navy. The National Guard, with somewhat more than 100,000 members, was composed mostly of infantry units. Still lacking a consistent program of supervision by the Regular forces, most Guard units were poorly trained and disciplined, understrength, and inadequately equipped. Thus, typically, although most Regulars by 1898 were armed with Krag-Jörgensen rifles firing smokeless powder cartridges, most Guardsmen were still equipped with Springfield rifles which could fire only black powder ammunition.

Despite obvious deficiencies, the Guard might have supplied many of the units used in the conflict had it not been for other factors that made it difficult to employ Guardsmen on short notice in overseas theaters of war. Under existing law, there was some question as to whether it was legal for Guard units to serve abroad. Furthermore, Guard organization varied greatly from state to state, and most Guardsmen objected to any move that would place them under control of the Regular Army for the sake of achieving greater uniformity in organization. The War Department proposed to form a new federal volunteer force with officers appointed by the President. But again the Guard opposed this, and Congress in the mobilization act of April 22, 1898, settled for a make-shift arrangement providing for a wartime force composed of both Regular and volunteer units organized into brigades, divisions, and army corps. Some Guard units did, in effect, serve under an arrangement whereby if enough members of a state unit volunteered for service, they were kept together to form a comparable federal volunteer unit.

Although the act of April 22 provided for 125,000 volunteers, popular demand soon led Congress to increase this number by 75,000 and authorize additional special volunteer forces, including 10,000 enlisted men "possessing immunity from diseases incident to tropical climates"—the so-called Immunes. Simultaneously it also authorized more than doubling the size of the Regular Army to nearly 65,000. By war's end in August 1898, the Regular forces numbered 59,000 and the volunteers, 216,000, a total of 275,000.

Mobilizing, equipping, and supplying these wartime forces placed a severe burden upon the War Department. With neither a military planning staff nor the funds necessary to plan for war in peacetime, the department inevitably was ill prepared for any kind of major mobilization or military operation.

Further complicating matters was a basic disagreement within the department concerning the strategy to be followed and the way mobilization should be carried out.

To the extent the United States had a strategy for conduct of the war against Spain in the Caribbean, it consisted of maintaining a naval blockade of Cuba while native insurgent forces carried on a harassing campaign against Spanish troops on the island. Supporters of this policy—Captain Mahan was among its more articulate advocates—believed that it would lead eventually to surrender of the Spanish forces and the freeing of Cuba. No direct clash between American and Spanish troops was visualized; American land forces would simply occupy Cuba as soon as the Spanish departed.

More or less in conformity with this strategy, Maj. Gen. Nelson Miles, Commanding General of the Army, proposed to assemble, train, and equip a small force of about 80,000, using the Regular Army as a nucleus. There would be ample time for mobilizing this force, since Miles deemed it unwise to land any troops in Cuba before the end of the unhealthy rainy season in October. The first step was to concentrate the entire Regular Army at Chickamauga Park, Georgia, where it could receive much-needed instruction in combined arms operations.

So deliberate and cautious a plan, however, was, by mid-April 1898, not in harmony with the increasing public demand for immediate action against the Spanish. With an ear to this demand, Secretary of War Russell M. Alger, who had been a general officer in the Civil War and subsequently had pursued a political career for thirty years, ignored the advice of General Miles. He ordered the Regular infantry regiments to go to New Orleans, Tampa, and Mobile, where presumably they would be ready for an immediate descent on Cuba. (*Map 36*) (Later some infantry troops did go to Chickamauga Park, where they trained with the Regular cavalry and artillery concentrated there.)

The decision to mobilize large volunteer forces compounded the problems of equipping, training, and supplying the wartime Army. In the spring and summer of 1898, thousands of enthusiastic volunteers, a few with some militia training but most only raw recruits, poured into newly established camps in the South—located there so as to be near Cuba and, at the same time, help the soldiers to become accustomed to semitropical climatic conditions. But a taste of military life in the training camps soon curbed the enthusiasm of most volunteers, for there they found chronic shortages of the most essential equipment—even of such basic items as underwear, socks, and shoes—a steady diet of badly prepared food, unbelievably poor sanitary conditions, inadequate

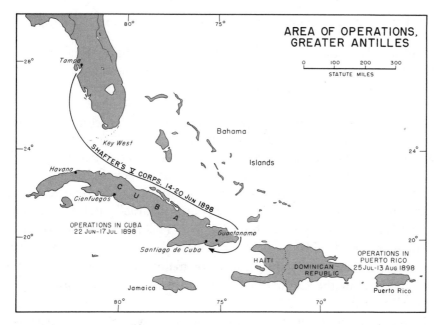

MAP 36

medical facilities, and a lack of up-to-date weapons. Red tape and poor management in the War Department's supply bureaus (the Ordnance Department possibly excepted) continued to delay correction of some of the worst deficiencies and combined with the shortage of capable volunteer officers to limit the effectiveness and quality of training received in the camps.

A similar general inefficiency characterized the War Department's conduct of actual operations against Spain. Since Congress had provided no machinery in the department for peacetime co-ordination of foreign policy with the country's military posture, the nation went to war without any kind of over-all plan of operations or even adequate intelligence about the enemy or the Cuban insurgents. Suddenly confronted in April 1898 with the necessity for launching overseas amphibious attacks on hostile shores—under the best circumstances always a difficult type of operation, requiring careful planning and close interservice co-operation—the War Department bureaus and the Army high command found themselves almost totally unprepared. Given time, they might have devised at least adequate operational plans; but public opinion, political pressures, and the trend of events demanded the launching of an immediate expedition against the Spanish in Cuba.

Victory at Sea: Naval Operations in the Caribbean and Pacific

Fortunately, it turned out that the really decisive fighting of the war fell to the much better prepared Navy, although last-minute alterations in its strategic plan for dealing with the Spanish Fleet seriously threatened to reduce its effectiveness. Shortly after the war began, rumors circulated that an enemy fleet under Admiral Pascual Cervera y Topete was approaching the Atlantic coast of the United States. An alarmed public demanded that measures be taken to defend the Atlantic seaboard. In deference to this demand, the Navy Department in late April 1898 withheld some of its best fighting ships from Rear Adm. William T. Sampson's North Atlantic Squadron, sent to blockade Cuba. These ships, formed into a "flying squadron" under Commodore Winfield S. Schley, set up a watch for Cervera. This move was in conflict with the provisions in the Navy's strategical plan for a war with Spain. Based upon Mahan's doctrines, the plan called for maintaining Sampson's squadron at full strength in the Caribbean, ready to intercept any Spanish fleet sent out to relieve Cuba.

In the western Pacific, meantime, the Navy was able to adhere to its strategical plan—the latest version of which had been completed in June 1897. Worked out after 1895 by officers at the Naval War College in collaboration with the Office of Naval Intelligence, this plan, known to President McKinley and the high officials in the Navy Department, provided for an attack on the Philippines, leading to destruction of Spanish warships there, capture of Manila, and blockade of the principal Philippine ports. The basic objectives of the plan were to weaken Spain by cutting off revenues from the Philippines and to place the United States in the position of having something to offer the Spanish as an inducement to make peace after Cuba had been freed.

Active Navy preparation for war began in January 1898, and in late February Theodore Roosevelt, as Acting Secretary of the Navy (Secretary John D. Long was ailing), cabled orders to American naval commanders, instructing them to get their squadrons in readiness to carry out existing war plans against Spain. Commodore George Dewey of the Asiatic Squadron received instructions to assemble his ships at Hong Kong, where they could take on coal and supplies preparatory to an attack on the Philippines.

Thus, on April 24, when McKinley finally ordered the Asiatic Squadron to execute the war plan against the Philippines Dewey was ready. He sailed into Manila Bay on the night of April 30 and next morning located the Spanish warships at Cavite. In a few hours and without loss of a single

American life, he sank or disabled the entire Spanish Fleet. In the days immediately following, he also silenced the land batteries defending Manila harbor, but the city itself continued to resist. (*See Map 44.*)

Since Dewey's 1,700 men were barely sufficient to maintain his own naval squadron, he requested dispatch of land forces from the United States to take Manila. In the two months before their arrival, he blockaded the port and gave assistance to Emilio Aguinaldo, Filipino insurgent leader, who, with Dewey's aid, had returned to the Philippines from exile in Hong Kong. Aguinaldo undertook guerrilla operations to keep the Spanish land forces in the vicinity of Manila. Dewey had to deal as well with the ticklish problem of British, French, and German naval contingents in Manila Bay, which arrived ostensibly to protect their nationals from the insurgents, but actually also to help uphold any claims their governments might advance to Filipino territory should the United States fail to take control over the islands. Most troublesome was the German squadron under Rear Adm. Otto von Diederichs, but Dewey's patience and firmness prevented a serious incident, and Berlin withdrew its fleet when it became apparent that the United States was not going to abandon the Philippines.

Operations in the Caribbean

As in the Pacific so also in the Caribbean the course of naval developments would determine when and where the Army undertook operations against Spanish land forces. During the early part of May 1898, the whereabouts of the Spanish Fleet under Admiral Cervera remained a mystery. Lacking this information, the Army could not fix precisely the point where it would launch an attack. Nevertheless, the War Department pushed preparations at Tampa, Florida, for an expedition under General Miles to be put ashore somewhere near Havana. But persistent rumors of the approach of the Spanish Fleet to Cuban waters delayed this expedition while the Navy searched further for Cervera. News at last reached Washington near the end of May that the Spanish admiral had skillfully evaded the American naval blockade and, on the 19th of the month, had slipped into the bay at Santiago de Cuba. (*See Map 36.*)

The Navy, at first not at all certain that it was actually Cervera's fleet in Santiago, sent Admiral Sampson to inspect the harbor. As soon as the American naval commander had ascertained that the four cruisers and several smaller war vessels were indeed Spanish, he bombarded the forts at the entrance to Santiago Bay. Unable to silence them, Sampson decided against trying to run the heavily mined harbor entrance. Instead, he sent Lt. (jg) Richmond P. Hobson to bottle up the enemy fleet by sinking the collier *Merrimac* athwart the channel. When this bold project failed, Sampson requested land forces to seize the Spanish batteries, at the same time dispatching marines ashore to secure a site for a naval base east of Santiago. In the first land skirmish of the Cuban campaign, the marines quickly overcame enemy resistance and established the base at Guantánamo Bay.

Upon receipt of Sampson's request for land forces, the War Department, already under strong public pressure to get the Army into action, ordered Maj. Gen. William R. Shafter to embark with the V Corps from Tampa as soon as possible to conduct operations against Santiago in co-operation with the Navy. This corps was the only one of the eight that the War Department had organized for the war that was anywhere near ready to fight. Composed chiefly of Regular Army units, it had been assembling at Tampa for weeks when the order came on May 31 for its embarkation; it would require another two weeks to get the corps and its equipment on board and ready to sail for Cuba.

The slow pace of preparation and loading of the expedition was attributable to many factors. There was no over-all plan and no special staff to direct it. Although selected because of its port facilities and proximity to Cuba, Tampa, from the logistical point of view, proved to be a poor choice for marshaling a major military expedition. With only one pier for loading ships and a single-track railroad connecting with mainline routes from the north, the resulting backup of freight cars for miles delayed shipment of much needed supplies and equipment. Incoming soldiers waited interminably in uncomfortable railroad cars. When freight cars finally did reach the port area, there were no wagons to unload them and no bills of lading to indicate what was in them. When it came to loading the ships, of which there were not enough to carry the entire corps, supplies and equipment were put on board with little regard for unloading priorities in the combat zone should there be enemy resistance during the landings.

In spite of the confusion and inefficiency at Tampa, by June 14 nearly 17,000 men were ready to sail. On board were 18 Regular and 2 volunteer infantry regiments; 10 Regular and 2 volunteer cavalry squadrons, serving dismounted; 1 mounted cavalry squadron; 6 artillery batteries; and a machine gun (Gatling gun) company. The expedition comprised a major part of the Regular forces, including all of the Regular Negro combat regiments. Moving out from Tampa on the morning of the 14th, the V Corps joined its naval convoy next day off the Florida Keys and by June 20 had reached the vicinity of Santiago.

TRANSPORTS AT TAMPA

While the troops on board endured tropical heat, unsanitary conditions, and cold rations—the canned beef was especially unpalatable—Shafter and Sampson conferred on how to proceed against the Spanish in Santiago. Sampson wanted the Army to storm the fort on the east side of the bay entrance, driving the Spanish from their guns. Then his fleet could clear away the mines and enter Santiago Bay to fight Cervera's squadron. Lacking heavy artillery, Shafter was not sure his troops could take the fort, which crowned a steep hill. He decided instead to follow the suggestion of General Calixto Garcia, the local insurgent leader, and land his forces at Daiquirí, east of Santiago Bay. (*Map 37*)

On June 22, after heavy shelling of the landing areas, the V Corps began disembarking amid circumstances almost as confused and hectic as those at Tampa. Captains of many of the chartered merchant ships resisted bringing their vessels close inshore. Their reluctance slowed the landing of troops and equipment, already handicapped by a shortage of lighters (the Navy could not spare the additional ones needed). Horses, simply dropped overboard to get ashore on their own, swam out to sea in some instances and were lost. An alert enemy defense might well have taken advantage of the chaotic conditions

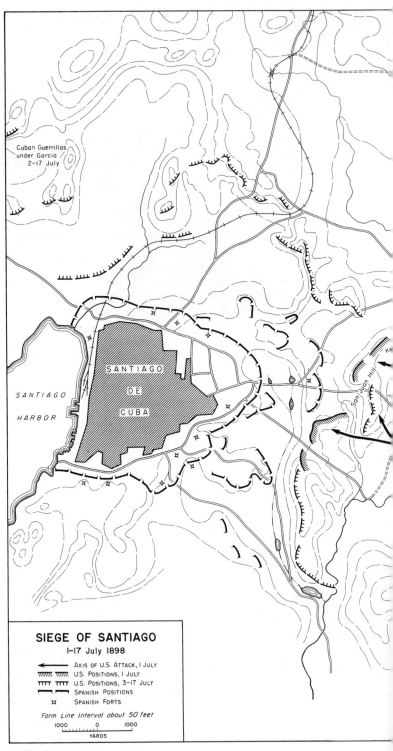

Cuban Guerrillas
under Garcia
2-17 July

SANTIAGO

SANTIAGO
D E
CUBA

HARBOR

San Juan Hill

SIEGE OF SANTIAGO
1-17 July 1898

Axis of U.S. Attack, 1 July
U.S. Positions, 1 July
U.S. Positions, 3-17 July
Spanish Positions
¤ Spanish Forts

Form Line Interval about 50 feet

1000   0   1000
YARDS

MAP 37

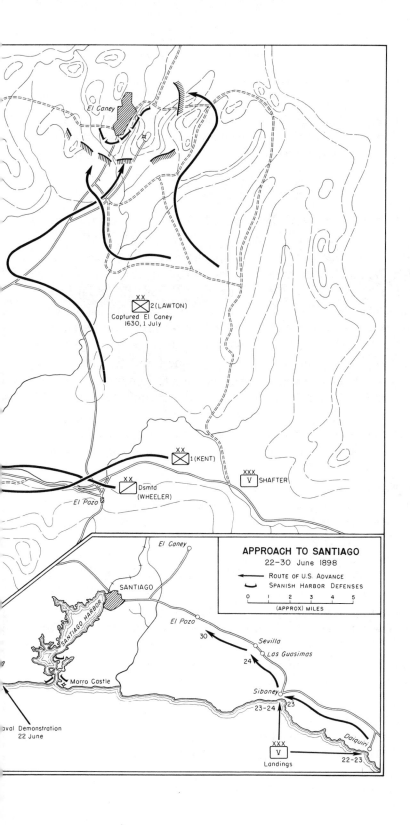

El Caney

$\boxed{\times\times}$ 2 (LAWTON)
Captured El Caney
1630, 1 July

$\boxed{\times\times}$ 1 (KENT)

$\boxed{\times\times\times}$ SHAFTER
V

$\boxed{\times\times}$ Dsmtd
(WHEELER)

El Pozo

El Caney

SANTIAGO

APPROACH TO SANTIAGO
22–30 June 1898

↞ ROUTE OF U.S. ADVANCE
⌢ SPANISH HARBOR DEFENSES

0 1 2 3 4 5
(APPROX) MILES

SANTIAGO HARBOR

El Pozo

30

Sevilla
Las Guasimas

24

Morro Castle

Sibaney

23–24   23

aval Demonstration
22 June

$\boxed{\times\times\times}$
V
Landings

Daiquiri

22–23

to oppose the landings effectively. But the Spanish, though they had more than 200,000 troops in Cuba—some 36,000 of them in Santiago Province—did nothing to prevent Shafter's men from getting ashore. Some 6,000 landed on June 22 and most of the remaining 11,000 on the two days following. In addition, some 4,000 to 5,000 insurgents under General Garcia supplemented the American force.

The Battle of Santiago

Once ashore, elements of the V Corps moved westward toward the heights of San Juan, a series of ridge lines immediately east of Santiago, where well-entrenched enemy troops guarded the land approaches to the city. On June 23, Brig. Gen. Henry W. Lawton, commanding the vanguard, advanced along the coast from Daiquirí to occupy Siboney, which then became the main base of operations. The next day, Brig. Gen. Joseph Wheeler, the Confederate Army veteran, pushed inland along the road to Santiago with dismounted cavalry to seize Las Guásimas, after a brief skirmish with rear guard elements of a retiring Spanish force. This move brought American units within five miles of the San Juan Heights, where they paused for a few days while General Shafter assembled the rest of his divisions and brought up supplies. Even in this short time, Shafter could observe the debilitating effects of tropical climate and disease on his men. He was aware, too, that the hurricane season was approaching. Consequently, he decided in favor of an immediate attack on the defenses of Santiago.

Shafter's plan was simple: a frontal attack on the San Juan Heights. For this purpose, he deployed Brig. Gen. Jacob F. Kent's infantry division on the left and Wheeler's dismounted cavalry on the right, the entire force with supporting elements comprising some 8,000 troops. But before he made the main advance on the heights Lawton's infantry division with a supporting battery of artillery—more than 6,500 men—was to move some two miles north to seize the fortified village of El Caney, cutting off Santiago's water supply and, if necessary, intercepting rumored Spanish reinforcements. This action completed—Shafter thought it would take about two hours—Lawton was to turn southwestward and form on the right flank of Wheeler's division for participation in the main assault. A brigade which had just landed at Siboney was to advance meanwhile along the coast in a feint to deceive the enemy.

The attack, which moved out at dawn on July 1, soon became badly disorganized because of poor co-ordination, difficult terrain, and tropical heat. The corpulent Shafter, virtually prostrated by the heat, had to leave the direction of the battle to others. At a stream crossing on the crowded main trail to

San Juan Heights enemy gunners scored heavily when a towed Signal Corps balloon pinpointed the front of the advancing line of troops. And Lawton's division, delayed in its seizure of El Caney by a stubborn enemy defense, misplaced artillery, and the necessity of withdrawing a volunteer unit armed only with telltale black powder, did not rejoin the main force until after the assault had ended. Despite these unexpected setbacks, Kent's and Wheeler's divisions at midday launched a strong frontal attack on the Spanish forward defensive positions. Cavalry units of Wheeler's division, including the 9th Cavalry and part of the 10th, both Negro regiments, and the volunteer Rough Riders, who were commanded by Lt. Col. Theodore Roosevelt, seized Kettle Hill, separate from the central heights. Then Kent's infantry regiments, sup-

THE SIGNAL CORPS BALLOON *at Santiago.*

ported by the unorthodox employment of Gatling guns in the attack, stormed up San Juan Hill in the main ridge line, driving the Spanish from blockhouse and trench defenses and compelling them to retire to a strongly fortified inner line. Thus the day ended with the Americans having achieved most of their initial objectives. But the cost was high—nearly 1,700 casualties sustained since the start of operations against Santiago.

Concerned with the increasing sickness that was further thinning the ranks of the V Corps and faced by a well-organized Spanish second line of defense, General Shafter cabled Secretary Alger on July 3 that he was considering withdrawing about five miles to higher ground between the San Juan River and Siboney. The shift would place his troops in a position where they would be less exposed to enemy fire and easier to supply. Alger replied that "the effect upon the country would be much better" if Shafter continued to hold his advanced position.

The V Corps commander then again sought to get the Navy to enter Santiago Bay and attack the city. But neither the Navy Department nor President McKinley was willing to sanction this move. Just when the whole matter threatened to become an embarrassing public debate between the two services, the Spanish themselves resolved the issue.

Deteriorating conditions within Santiago—lack of food and ammunition were seriously affecting the health and morale of the defending forces—convinced the defenders that the city must soon fall. While Cervera considered flight from the port hopeless, he had no recourse but to attempt it. Officials in both Havana and Madrid had ordered him, for reasons of honor, to escape when Santiago appeared about to surrender. Finally, on the morning of July 3, while Sampson and Shafter conferred ashore, Cervera made his dash for the open sea, hoping to reach the port of Cienfuegos on the south coast of Cuba. As soon as the Spanish Fleet appeared, Sampson's squadron, temporarily under command of Commodore Schley, gave chase and in less than two hours destroyed Cervera's fleet; four cruisers were crippled and run ashore and one destroyer was beached and another sunk.

A few days later, General Shafter persuaded the Spanish leaders in Santiago that they had no choice except to surrender. On July 16 they signed the unconditional terms demanded by the McKinley administration, which provided for surrender of 11,500 troops in the city and some 12,000 others in the vicinity of Santiago. The formal surrender ceremony took place on the following day.

During preparations for the Santiago campaign, General Miles personally had been overseeing organization of a second expedition to seize Puerto Rico. On July 21 he sailed from Guantánamo with more than 3,000 troops. His original strategy was to land first at Cape Fajardo in the northeast part of the island, where he could establish a base of operations for a subsequent advance westward to the capital, San Juan. For reasons not entirely clear, but probably because of a desire not to have to co-operate with the Navy in the attack on San Juan, Miles, while still at sea, changed his plans and on July 25 landed forces first at Guánica on the southeastern coast. Meeting virtually no opposition, the Americans shortly occupied the port of Ponce. In early August, after arrival of more than 10,000 additional troops from ports in the United States, General Miles, using Ponce as a base of operations, launched a four-column drive toward San Juan. There was little bloodshed—casualties for the campaign totaled fewer than fifty—and, in fact, most Puerto Ricans welcomed the American troops. The campaign ended on August 13 when word reached the island that Spain had signed a peace protocol the previous day.

Back in Cuba, meanwhile, conditions for the Army were much less pleasant. Spread of malaria, typhoid, and yellow fever among Shafter's troops at Santiago threatened to have far deadlier consequences than had the actual fighting. Concern over this problem led to the drafting of a joint letter by a number of Shafter's senior officers, proposing immediate evacuation of the Army from Cuba. Addressed to the commanding general, this round robin letter unfortunately came to the attention of the press before it reached Shafter. Hence, Washington officials read it in the newspapers before learning of its content from the general himself. Naturally the whole episode, coming at the time when peace negotiations were beginning, caused a sensation. Although acutely embarrassing for the Army and General Shafter, the incident did have the salutary effect of hastening measures to evacuate thousands of troops to Montauk Point, Long Island, where the Army Medical Department already had taken steps to establish an isolated detention camp. Here those who had contracted tropical infections received the necessary treatment. And out of the Army's nearly disastrous experience with the debilitating effects of disease and climate in Cuba came the impetus for the Medical Corps' notable project to determine the causes of yellow fever, inaugurating a long-term program of research and study into what henceforth would be a permanent concern of the Army—the maintenance of the health and effectiveness of American troops in a tropical environment.

The Fall of Manila

In another tropical setting halfway around the world from Cuba the final military episode of the war took place. During May and June 1898 Admiral Dewey, while awaiting the arrival in the Philippines of land forces from the United States, kept in contact with the insurgent leader, General Aguinaldo. The Filipino forces occupied lines on the land side of Manila, preventing the Spanish garrison from moving beyond the immediate outskirts of the city.

Although the Americans and the Philippine insurgents shared a common interest in bringing about the defeat of the Spanish, relations between them tended to deteriorate during the period of waiting. The most important reason was a fundamental difference in objectives. The goal of the insurgents, who controlled most areas outside the towns and cities on Luzon and the other important islands, was immediate independence for the Philippines. But after some hesitation the McKinley administration and more and more Americans were coming around to the view that the United States ought to retain the islands. Once Aguinaldo became aware of this he endeavored to counteract it by taking steps to establish a revolutionary government with himself as president. On August 6 he appealed to foreign governments to recognize the independence of the Philippines. Hence by late summer there was serious doubt as to just what might be expected from the increasingly hostile insurgent forces.

In the interim, the long-awaited ground forces needed to complete the campaign in the Philippines began arriving in the Manila area. By the end of July 1898, some 13,000 volunteer and 2,000 Regular troops, constituting the VIII Corps under Maj. Gen. Wesley Merritt, had reached the islands. These troops had embarked from west coast ports (chiefly San Francisco) with a minimum of the confusion and difficulty that had characterized the launching of the Cuban expedition. In spite of the long voyage across the Pacific, they were in good condition and ready to start operations against the Spanish as soon as enough troops could be moved into the vicinity of Manila.

By early August General Merritt had 11,000 troops of the VIII Corps in lines immediately to the rear of those occupied by the insurgents, ready to attack the city. Inside the Philippine capital and in fortified lines just beyond the city walls were about 10,000 to 15,000 Spanish troops. Although their leaders were fully aware of the relative hopelessness of the situation, efforts of Dewey and Merritt to secure a peaceful surrender failed because the Spanish Government in Madrid insisted that the garrison should make at least a token show of resistance.

On the morning of August 13 the VIII Corps launched an assault on Manila. As the tide receded, American units moved quickly to the beaches on the south side of the city and then, supported by concentrated fire from Dewey's ships, advanced through the insurgent lines. By prior arrangement, somewhat reluctantly agreed to by Aguinaldo, the insurgents were to retire as the Americans moved toward the Spanish entrenchments. But in carrying out this difficult maneuver, Americans and insurgents unintentionally became intermixed and some troops—presumably for the most part insurgents—began firing on the Spanish lines. Momentarily, this flare-up threatened to thwart the enemy's plan to offer only token resistance, but quick action by American officers brought the firing under control and the garrison surrendered. Operations at Manila cost the Americans a total of 17 killed and 105 wounded.

Formal surrender ceremonies came the following day—actually two days after the government in Madrid had signed a peace protocol ending hostilities. News of the protocol had not yet reached Manila because the cable Dewey cut when he first entered Manila Bay still had not been repaired.

After negotiations in Paris in the fall of 1898, the United States and Spain signed a treaty on December 10 ending the war. By its terms Spain gave up sovereignty over Cuba, which became an independent state, ceded Puerto Rico and Guam to the United States, and accepted $20 million in payment for the Philippines. Thus fatefully did Americans commit the nation to a new role as a colonial power in the Far East, with momentous future consequences that few at the turn of the century could anticipate.

The Philippine Insurrection, 1899–1902

Signing of the Treaty of Paris brought only a brief pause in military operations for the Army in the Philippines. With defeat and departure of the Spanish, the Americans inherited the complex problems of governing a populous Far Eastern archipelago about which they still knew relatively little. Even with full co-operation of all the heterogeneous peoples of differing cultures living in the islands, the task would have been formidable. Leaders of the native nationalist movement were no more ready to accept American rule peacefully than Spanish.

In the period following the fall of Manila while peace negotiations were in progress an uneasy truce existed between the insurgents and the American occupation forces. Under leadership of Aguinaldo, the insurgents established a provisional republic with a capital at Malolos, northeast of Manila, and organized a congress which began preparing a constitution. After the United States in January 1899 officially proclaimed possession of the Philippines and its intention to extend political control over all the islands, the insurgent congress ratified the constitution, formally establishing a Filipino republic, and prepared to resist the Americans.

The circumstances surrounding the start of fighting on the night of February 4, 1899, are vague. An insurgent patrol apparently deliberately challenged without provocation an American guard post near Manila. Since the incident occurred on the eve of ratification of the Treaty of Paris by the United States Senate, it is conceivable that the insurgents may have wished by this surprise move to inflict an embarrassing setback on the Americans before reinforcements could arrive in the Philippines, hoping thus to influence the vote on the treaty. Or it may simply have been a spontaneous outburst, stemming from Aguinaldo's known inability to exercise very tight discipline over his loosely organized army. Whatever the reason, the VIII Corps reacted promptly and decisively. Against an estimated 40,000 insurgents in the Manila area, Maj. Gen. Elwell S. Otis, who had replaced General Merritt, could commit only about 12,000 of his 21,000 troops, since the remainder were volunteers scheduled to go home for early demobilization. Nevertheless, in extensive operations around the Philippine capital in the several days immediately following the attack on the 4th, the VIII Corps drove back the insurgents at all points, inflicting some 3,000 casualties, and then, late in the month, thwarted what appeared to be the beginning of a widespread uprising in the city, potentially fraught with the most serious consequences.

Although the insurgents suffered a severe setback in these first major engagements of the Philippine Insurrection, they continued more or less organized resistance on a smaller scale for more than two years, with spasmodic outbursts in the Visayas, the islands immediately south of Luzon. The Americans also met resistance from the predominantly Moslem Moro peoples residing in Mindanao and the Sulu Archipelago in the southern Philippines, areas where even the Spanish during their long period of rule had never exercised effective control.

When news of the insurrection reached Washington it quickly dispelled any doubts the McKinley administration might have had concerning the need for more troops in the Philippines to establish effective American control. The War Department responded promptly, arranging to raise ten additional federal volunteer regiments and, at the same time, ordering immediate dispatch of much needed Regular units to the islands. By late summer of 1899, more than 35,000 additional troops had joined the VIII Corps and more were on the way. Before it ended more than 100,000 American soldiers took part in some phase of the Philippine Insurrection.

Short of firearms and ammunition, the insurgents depended primarily upon unconventional tactics. Avoiding open confrontation with the better armed and organized Americans whenever possible, they relied upon surprise attacks and ambush, where bolo knives and other more primitive weapons could be employed with the most devastating effect. Resort to guerrilla operations enabled the insurgents to exploit their superior knowledge of the jungle and the mountainous country in which much of the fighting took place. To cope with these tactics, the Army found itself drawing upon its long experience in fighting the western Indians. Hampered logistically by the lack of roads and by rough terrain in the interior, the Americans had to depend primarily upon small arms fire and the bayonet in repelling hit-and-run insurgent attacks. Keeping the poorly organized and poorly co-ordinated insurgent bands under constant pursuit and pressure, VIII Corps troops gradually extended their control over most of Luzon and the other important islands.

Beginning in April 1899, the Army carried out a series of carefully co-ordinated offensives, aimed at securing control of the important population centers and lines of communications as a first step in establishing stable government and restoring normal economic activities. Immediately after the outbreak of insurgent hostilities in February, American columns had pushed north, south, and east from Manila, capturing the rebel capital at Malolos, and securing the Pasig River, which cut the main line of communications between insurgent forces in north and south Luzon. Now in April, General Otis sent General Lawton, veteran of the Santiago campaign, south toward Santa Cruz in the Laguna de Bay area and Maj. Gen. Arthur MacArthur north up the central plain from Malolos toward San Fernando. By mid-May, the success of these drives had seriously undermined insurgent ability to continue organized resistance and forced Aguinaldo to flee to the mountains in northern Luzon. Advent of the rainy season and shortage of manpower halted further operations until fall.

In the autumn of 1899, General Otis launched a three-pronged drive in north central Luzon against Aguinaldo's remaining forces. Moving up on the right, Lawton recaptured San Isidro and approached San Fabian on Lingayen Gulf; MacArthur, in the center, seized Tarlac and reached Dagupan; Brig. Gen. Loyd Wheaton, on the left, went by ship from Manila to San Fabian, moving inland to defeat the insurgents at San Jacinto, and then linked up with MacArthur at Dagupan. Aguinaldo again managed to escape, but eventually was captured in March 1901 through a ruse skillfully carried out by a small party of Filipino scouts and American soldiers led by Brig. Gen. Frederick Funston.

Operations in the winter of 1899–1900 cleared insurrectionist remnants from the Manila region and permanently secured important lines of communications in central Luzon. By March 1900 the Army also controlled southern Luzon and the Visayas. In May, Otis, believing the insurrection virtually over, requested his own relief and General MacArthur replaced him. Events proved Otis mistaken, for the Army had to continue in the field for many more months, dealing with sporadic but persistent resistance in numerous small engagements. The guerrilla warfare was bitter and costly, resulting in more casualties for the Army than in the entire preceding fifteen months of extensive military operations. In early 1902, unrest among the Moros in Mindanao and the Sulu Archipelago intensified, and was by no means really settled when President Theodore Roosevelt announced on July 4 the formal end of the Philippine Insurrection.

The Boxer Uprising

Acquisition of the Philippines tended to stimulate further a growing interest in China among Americans for both commercial and humanitarian reasons. One important argument advanced for retaining the Philippines was that they would serve as a convenient way station in carrying on trade and protecting American interests in the Manchu empire. The dominant problem in China at the end of the nineteenth century was its threatened partition by the Great Powers. Both the Americans and the British opposed this, and in

September 1899 the United States announced it had secured agreement from the interested powers for maintenance of an Open Door policy in their relations with China.

The already extensive exploitation of their country by foreign states, however, had aroused widespread resentment among younger Chinese. They formed the nucleus of a secret group called Boxers by Westerners which, with tacit support of the Dowager Empress, undertook a campaign against foreign influences and foreigners. By early 1900 this movement had brought much of China to the verge of revolution. Boxers in the northern provinces attacked and killed hundreds of Chinese Christians and foreigners, mostly missionaries. The wave of violence was climaxed by murder of the German Minister on June 20. In fear for their lives in what appeared to be the beginning of a general uprising, most remaining foreigners as well as many Chinese converts fled to the foreign legations area in Peking, defended by a composite force of some 600 soldiers and civilians. Soon they were besieged there by a much larger force of Boxers assisted by Chinese imperial troops.

Although the McKinley administration disliked the idea of becoming involved in an election year in an international incident with overtones of entangling foreign alliances, it agreed to join with the other powers in taking such steps as seemed necessary to rescue their beleaguered nationals. In establishing the limits of American diplomatic co-operation with the intervening powers, Secretary of State John Hay admonished the United States Minister that ". . . we have no policy in China except to protect with energy American interests and especially American citizens. . . . There must be no alliances." And on July 3 Hay circulated a second Open Door note among the interested powers, stating that it was the policy of the United States "to seek a solution which may bring about permanent safety and peace to China, preserve Chinese territorial and administrative entity, protect all rights guaranteed to friendly powers by treaty and international law, and safeguard for the world the principle of equal and impartial trade with all parts of the Chinese Empire."

Already in June the Navy's China squadron, under Rear Adm. Louis Kempff, had joined with other foreign naval units in bombardment of the Taku forts guarding Tientsin, the port city nearest to Peking, and had supplied a contingent for an international landing force composed of marines and other available troops. Formed into a rescue column, including more than a hundred Americans, this force had encountered overwhelming opposition and failed to break through to Peking. The powers then had taken immediate steps to organize a large relief expedition to drive through to the Chinese capital.

Because of the Philippine Insurrection the United States had sizable Army units available fairly near China. It could therefore contribute one of the larger contingents to the international relief force. Although General MacArthur, commanding in the Philippines, was somewhat reluctant to weaken his already overextended forces, he agreed to dispatch to China immediately the 9th Infantry and later the 14th Infantry and some artillery units. Other units, including the 6th Cavalry, came directly from the United States. Using Manila as a base and Nagasaki, Japan, as an advance port, the United States eventually assembled some 2,500 soldiers and marines in China under command of Maj. Gen. Adna R. Chaffee. On July 13, elements of this force, officially designated the China Relief Expedition, participated with troops from several other nations in the attack on Tientsin, which surrendered on the same day.

By early August, an allied force of some 19,000, including British, French, Japanese, Russian, German, Austrian, Italian, and American troops, was ready to move out of Tientsin toward Peking, some seventy miles distant. Fighting a number of sharp skirmishes en route, this force reached the Manchu capital on August 12 and prepared immediately to assault the gates leading into the Outer City. Lacking effective central direction, the relief expedition's attack was poorly executed. The Russian contingent prematurely forced an entrance into the Outer City on August 13, only to be thrown into confusion and require rescue by other allied troops. The next day, in a more carefully co-ordinated assault, elements of the U.S. 14th Infantry scaled the so-called Tartar Wall and provided cover for the British as they entered the Outer City in force, relieving the legations compound. Then on August 15, Capt. Henry J. Reilly's Light Battery F of the U.S. 5th Artillery shattered the gates leading into the Inner City with several well-placed salvos, opening the way for the allied troops to occupy the center of Peking. Although American troops had suffered comparatively light losses—slightly more than 200 killed and wounded—they did not take part in subsequent military operations, which consisted primarily of suppressing scattered Boxer elements and rescuing foreigners in the provinces. The McKinley administration, anxious to avoid further involvement in China, wanted to get Army units back to the Philippines before winter.

In a few months all resistance had ended and the Dowager Empress sued for peace, offering to pay an indemnity and reaffirm previously existing commercial concessions. During prolonged negotiations an international army of occupation to which the United States contributed a small contingent of Regulars remained in north China. It was withdrawn in September 1901 under terms of the Boxer Protocol. This agreement also provided that the powers maintain a fortified legation in Peking, garrison the Tientsin-Peking railway—an American contingent served as a part of this force until 1938—and receive reparations of $333 million. Of this amount the United States claimed only $25 million. In a few years it became apparent that even this sum was more than was needed to indemnify claims of American nationals and in 1907, and again in 1924, the United States returned portions totaling nearly $17 million to China, which placed the money in a trust fund for education of Chinese youths in both countries.

Participation of the United States in the Boxer Uprising at the beginning of the twentieth century marked the first time since the American Revolution that the country had joined with other powers in an allied military operation. The intervention in China represented one more instance of the gradual change taking place at the turn of the century in the traditional policies and attitudes of the United States in world affairs as a result of the triumph of imperialism. As they entered the new century most Americans still believed that despite the acquisition of overseas colonies the nation could continue to adhere to the historic principles of isolationism. Developments in the early years of the twentieth century would demonstrate, however, that the nation had to make changes and adjustments in many long-established institutions and policies—including those relating to military defense of the country—to meet the requirements of its new status as a world power.

CHAPTER 16

Transition and Change, 1902–1917

For the United States the opening years of the twentieth century were a time of transition and change. At home they marked the beginning of a peaceful revolution—often designated the "Progressive Era"—when political leaders such as Theodore Roosevelt undertook to solve the economic and social problems arising out of the rapid growth of large-scale industry in the late nineteenth century. Increasing public awareness of these problems as a result of the writings of the "Muckrakers" and social reformers provided popular support for efforts to solve them by legislative and administrative measures. In foreign affairs it was a period when the country had to begin adjusting its institutions and policies to the requirements of its new status as a world power. In spite of a tendency after the end of the War with Spain to follow traditional patterns and go back to essentially isolationist policies, the nation's new responsibility for overseas possessions, its expanding commercial interests abroad, and the continued unrest in the Caribbean made a reversion to insularity increasingly unfeasible.

The changing conditions at home and abroad inevitably affected the nation's military establishment. During the decade and a half between the War with Spain and American involvement in World War I, both the Army and the Navy would undergo important reforms in organization and direction. Although the United States did not become a participant in any major conflict during these years, both services were frequently called upon to assist with administration of the newly acquired overseas possessions. Both aided with protection of investments abroad threatened by native insurrections, revolutions, and other internal disturbances. And both contributed in other ways to upholding the vital interests of the nation in an era of greatly increased competition for commercial advantage and colonial empire.

Modernizing the Armed Forces

The intensification of international rivalries led most of the Great Powers to seek additional protection and advantage in diplomatic alliances and alignments. By the early years of the twentieth century the increasingly complex network of agreements had resulted in a new and precarious balance of power in world affairs. This balance was constantly in danger of being upset, particularly because of an unprecedented arms race, characterized by rapid enlargement of armies and navies and development of far more deadly weapons and tactics. While the United States remained aloof from "entangling alliances," it nevertheless continued to modernize and strengthen its own armed forces, giving primary attention to the Navy—the first line of defense.

The Navy's highly successful performance in the Spanish-American War increased the willingness of Congress and the American public to support its program of expansion and modernization. For at least a decade after the war Theodore Roosevelt, Senator Henry Cabot Lodge of Massachusetts, and other leaders who favored a "Big Navy" policy with the goal of an American fleet second only to that of Great Britain experienced little difficulty in securing the necessary legislation and obtaining the funds required for the Navy's expansion program.

For the Navy another most important result of the War with Spain was the decision to retain possessions in the Caribbean and the western Pacific. In the Caribbean the Navy acquired more bases for its operations such as that at Guantánamo Bay in Cuba. The value of these bases soon became apparent as the United States found itself intervening more frequently in the countries of that region to protect its expanding investments and trade. In the long run, however, acquisition of the Philippines and Guam was even more significant, for it committed the United States to defense of territory thousands of miles distant from the home base. American naval strength in the Pacific had to be increased immediately to insure maintenance of a secure line of communications for the land forces that had to be kept in the Philippines. One way to accomplish this increase, with an eye to economy of force, was to build a canal across the Isthmus of Panama, so that Navy ships could move more rapidly from the Atlantic to the Pacific as circumstances demanded. Another was to acquire more bases in the Pacific west of Hawaii, which was annexed in 1898. Japan's spectacular naval victories in the war with Russia and Roosevelt's dispatch of an American fleet on a round-the-world cruise lasting from December 1907 to February 1909 drew public attention to the problem. But most Americans failed to perceive the growing threat of Japan to United States possessions in the western Pacific, and the line of communications to the Philippines remained incomplete and highly vulnerable.

The Navy fared much better in its program to expand the fleet and incorporate the latest technological developments in ship design and weapons. The modernization program that had begun in the 1880's and had much to do with the Navy's effectiveness in the Spanish-American War continued in the early 1900's. Construction of new ships, stimulated by the war and Roosevelt's active support, continued at a rapid rate after 1898 until Taft's administration, and at a somewhat slower pace thereafter. By 1917 the United States had a Navy unmatched by any of the Great Powers except Great Britain and Germany.

The Army, aware of the serious deficiencies revealed in the War with Spain and of the rapid technological changes taking place in the methods of warfare, also undertook to modernize its weapons and equipment. Development of high-velocity, low-trajectory, clip-loading rifles capable of delivering a high rate of sustained fire had already made obsolete the Krag-Jörgensen rifle, adopted by the Army in 1892. In 1903 the Regular Army began equipping its units with the improved bolt-action, magazine-type Springfield rifle, which incorporated the latest changes in weapons technology. The campaigns of 1898 also had shown that the standard rod bayonet was too flimsy; starting in 1905, the Army replaced it by a one pound knife bayonet with a 16-inch blade. In 1906 addition of a greater propellant charge in ammunition for the Springfield provided even higher muzzle velocity and deeper penetration of the bullet. Combat at close quarters against the fierce charges of the Moros in the Philippines demonstrated the need for a hand arm less cumbersome and having greater impact than the .38-caliber revolver. The Army found the answer in the recently developed .45-caliber Colt automatic pistol, adopted in 1911.

Far more significant in revolutionizing the nature of twentieth century warfare than these improved hand weapons was the rapid-firing machine gun. The manually operated machine gun—the Gatling gun—which the Army had adopted in 1866, was employed successfully in the Indian wars and the Spanish-American War. American inventors, including Hiram Maxim, John Browning, and Isaac N. Lewis, the last an officer in the Army's coast artillery, took a leading part in developing automatic machine guns in the years between the Civil War and World War I. Weapons based upon their designs were adopted by many of the armies of the world. But not until fighting began in World War I was it generally realized what an important role the machine gun was to have in modern tactics. Thus in the years between 1898 and 1916, Congress appropriated only an average of $150,000 annually for procurement of machine guns, barely enough to provide four weapons for each Regular regiment and a few for the National Guard. Finally in 1916 Congress voted $12 million for machine gun procurement, but the War Department held up its expenditure until 1917 while a board tried to decide which type of weapon was best suited to the needs of the Army.

Development of American artillery and artillery ammunition continued to lag behind that of western European armies. The Army did adopt in 1902 a new basic field weapon, the 3-inch gun with an advanced recoil mechanism. Also, to replace the black powder that had been the subject of such widespread criticism in the War with Spain, both the Army and the Navy took steps to increase the domestic output of smokeless powder. By 1903 production was sufficient to supply most American artillery.

Experience gained in the Spanish-American War also brought some significant changes in the Army's coastal defense program. The hurriedly improvised measures taken during the war to protect Atlantic ports from possible attack by the Spanish Fleet emphasized the need for modern seacoast defenses. Under the strategical concepts in vogue, construction and manning of these defenses were primarily an Army responsibility since in wartime the naval fleet had to be kept intact, ready to seek out and destroy the enemy's fleet. On the basis of recommendations by the Endicott Board, the Army already had begun an ambitious coastal defense construction program in the early 1890's, and in 1905 a new board headed by Secretary of War William Howard Taft made important revisions in this program with the goal of incorporating the latest techniques and devices. Added to the coastal defense arsenal were fixed, floating, and mobile torpedoes and submarine mines. At the same time, the Army's Ordnance Department tested 16-inch rifles for installation in the coastal defense fortifications, in keeping with the trend toward larger and larger guns to meet the challenge of naval weapons of ever-increasing size.

Of the many new inventions that came into widespread use in the early twentieth century in response to the productive capacity of the new industrial age, none was to have greater influence on military strategy, tactics, and organization than the internal combustion engine. It made possible the motor vehicle, which, like the railroad in the previous century, brought a revolution in military transportation, and the airplane and tank, both of which would figure importantly in World War I.

Reorganization of the Army: Establishment of the General Staff

After the Spanish-American War the Army also underwent important organizational and administrative changes aimed in part at overcoming some of the more glaring defects revealed during the war. Although the nation had won the war with comparative ease, many Americans realized that the victory was attributable more to the incompetence of the enemy than to any special qualities displayed by the Army. In fact, as a postwar investigating commission appointed by President McKinley and headed by Maj. Gen. Granville M. Dodge brought out, there was serious need for reform in the administration and direction of the Army's high command and for elimination of widespread inefficiency in the operations of the War Department.

No one appreciated the need for reform more than Elihu Root, a New York lawyer appointed Secretary of War in 1899 by McKinley. The President had selected Root primarily because he seemed well qualified to solve the legal problems that would arise in the Army's administration of recently acquired overseas possessions. But Root quickly realized that if the Army was to be capable of carrying out its new responsibilities as an important part of the defense establishment of a world power, it had to undergo fundamental changes in organization, administration, and training. Root, as a former corporation lawyer, tended to see the Army's problems as similar to those faced by business executives. "The men who have combined various corporations . . . in what we call trusts," he told Congress, "have reduced the cost of production and have increased their efficiency by doing the very same thing we propose you shall do now, and it does seem a pity that the Government of the United States should be the only great industrial establishment that cannot profit by the lessons which the world of industry and of commerce has learned to such good effect."

Beginning in 1899, Root outlined in a series of masterful reports his proposals for fundamental reform of Army institutions and concepts to achieve that "efficiency" of organization and function required of armies in the modern world. He based his proposals partly upon recommendations made by his military advisers (among the most trusted were Maj. Gen. Henry C. Corbin, The Adjutant General, and Lt. Col. William H. Carter) and partly upon the views expressed by officers who had studied and written about the problem in the post-Civil War years. Root arranged for publication of Col. Emory Upton's *The Military Policy of the United States* (1904), an unfinished manuscript which advocated a strong, expansible Regular Army as the keystone of an effective military establishment. Concluding that after all the true object of any army must be "to provide for war," Root took prompt steps to reshape the American Army into an instrument of national power capable of coping with the requirements of modern warfare. This objective could be attained, he hoped, by integrating the bureaus of the War Department, the scattered elements of the Regular Army, and the militia and volunteers.

Root perceived as the chief weakness in the organization of the Army the long-standing division of authority, dating back to the early nineteenth century, between the Commanding General of the Army and the Secretary of War. The

Commanding General exercised discipline and control over the troops in the field while the Secretary, through the military bureau chiefs, had responsibility for administration and fiscal matters. Root proposed to eliminate this division of authority between the Secretary of War and the Commanding General and to reduce the independence of the bureau chiefs. The solution, he suggested, was to replace the Commanding General of the Army with a Chief of Staff, who would be the responsible adviser and executive agent of the President through the Secretary of War. Under Root's proposal, formulation of broad American policies would continue under civilian control.

A lack of any long-range planning by the Army had been another obvious deficiency in the War with Spain, and Root proposed to overcome this by the creation of a new General Staff, a group of selected officers who would be free to devote full time to preparation of military plans. Planning in past national emergencies, he pointed out, nearly always had been inadequate because it had to be done hastily by officers already overburdened with other duties. Pending Congressional action on his proposals, Root in 1901 appointed an *ad hoc* War College Board to act as an embryonic General Staff. In early 1903, in spite of some die-hard opposition, Congress adopted the Secretary of War's recommendations for both a General Staff and a Chief of Staff, but rejected his request that certain of the bureaus be consolidated.

By this legislation Congress provided the essential framework for more efficient administration of the Army. Yet legislation could not change overnight the long-held traditions, habits, and views of most Army officers, or of some Congressmen and the American public. Secretary Root realized that effective operation of the new system would require an extended program of re-education. This need for re-education was one important reason for the establishment of the Army War College in November 1903. Its students, already experienced officers, would receive education in problems of the War Department and of high command in the field. As it turned out they actually devoted much of their time to war planning, becoming in effect the part of the General Staff which performed this function.

In the first years after its establishment the General Staff achieved relatively little in the way of genuine staff planning and policy making. While staff personnel did carry out such appropriate tasks as issuing in 1905 the first Field Service Regulations for government and organization of troops in the field, drawing up the plan for an expeditionary force sent to Cuba in 1906, and supervising the Army's expanding school system, far too much of their time was devoted to day-to-day routine administrative matters.

The General Staff did make some progress in overcoming its early weaknesses. Through experience, officers assigned to the staff gradually gained awareness of its real purpose and powers. In 1910 when Maj. Gen. Leonard Wood became Chief of Staff he reorganized the General Staff, eliminating many of its time-consuming procedures and directing more of its energies to planning. With the backing of Secretary of War Henry L. Stimson (1911–13), Wood dealt a decisive blow to that element in the Army itself that opposed the General Staff. In a notable controversy, he and Stimson forced the retirement in 1912 of the leader of this opposition, Maj. Gen. Fred C. Ainsworth, The Adjutant General.

The temporary closing of most Army schools during the Spanish-American War and the need to co-ordinate the Army's educational system with the Root proposals for creating a War College and General Staff had provided an opportunity for a general reorganization of the whole system, with the over-all objective of raising the standards of professional training of officers. In 1901 the War Department directed that the schools of instruction for officers thereafter should be the Military Academy at West Point; a school at each post of elementary instruction in theory and practice; the five service schools—the Artillery School, Engineer School of Application, School of Submarine Defense (mines and torpedoes), School of Application for Cavalry and Field Artillery, and Army Medical School; a General Staff and Service College at Leavenworth; and a War College. The purpose of the school at Leavenworth henceforth was to train officers in the employment of combined arms and prepare them for staff and command positions in large units. To meet the requirements for specialized training as a result of new developments in weapons and equipment, the Army expanded its service school system, adding the Signal School in 1905, the Field Artillery School in 1911, and the School of Musketry in 1913.

Creation of the General Staff unquestionably was the most important organizational reform in the Army during this period, but there were also a number of other changes in the branches and special staff designed to keep the Army abreast of new ideas and requirements. The Medical Department, for example, established Medical, Hospital, Army Nurse, Dental, and Medical Reserve Corps. In 1907 Congress approved of division of the artillery into the Coast Artillery Corps and the Field Artillery, and in 1912 it enacted legislation consolidating the Subsistence and Pay Departments with the Quartermaster to create the Quartermaster Corps, a reform earlier recommended by Secretary Root. The act of 1912 also established an enlisted Quartermaster service corps, marking the beginning of the practice of using service troops instead of civilians and combat soldier details.

In the new field of military aviation, the Army failed to keep pace with early twentieth century developments. Contributing to this delay were the reluctance of Congress to appropriate funds and resistance within the military bureaucracy to diversion of already limited resources to a method of warfare as yet unproved. The Army did not entirely neglect the new field—it had used balloons for observation in both the Civil and Spanish-American Wars and, beginning in 1898, the War Department subsidized for several years Samuel P. Langley's experiments with power-propelled, heavier-than-air flying machines. In 1908, after some hesitation, the War Department made funds available to the Aeronautical Division of the Signal Corps (established a year earlier) for the purchase and testing of Wilbur and Orville Wright's airplane. Although the Army accepted this airplane in 1909, another two years passed before Congress appropriated a relatively modest sum—$125,000—for aeronautical purposes. Between 1908 and 1913, it is estimated that the United States spent only $430,000 on military and naval aviation, whereas in the same period France and Germany each expended $22 million, Russia, $12 million, and Belgium, $2 million. Not until 1914 did Congress authorize establishment of a full-fledged Aviation Section in the Signal Corps. The few military airplanes available for service on the Mexican border in 1916 soon broke down, and the United States entered World War I far behind the other belligerents in aviation equipment, organization, and doctrine.

Reorganization of the Army: The Regular Army and the Militia

In the years after the Spanish-American War nearly a third of the Regular Army troops, on the average, served overseas. Most were in the Philippines suppressing the insurrection and when that conflict officially ended in mid-1902, stamping out scattered resistance and organizing and training a native force known as the Philippine Scouts. Other Regulars were garrisoned in Alaska, Hawaii, China, and elsewhere. To carry out its responsibilities abroad and to maintain an adequate defense at home, the Regular Army from 1902 to 1911 had an average of about 75,000 officers and men, far below the 100,000 that Congress had authorized in 1902 to fill thirty infantry and fifteen cavalry regiments, supported by a corps of artillery. To make up for this deficiency in size of the Regular forces and at the same time to remedy some of the defects revealed in the mobilization for the War with Spain, the planners in the War Department recommended a reorganization of the volunteer forces.

Secretary Root took the lead in presenting to Congress in 1901 a program for reform of the National Guard. In response to his recommendations, Congress in 1903 passed the Dick bill, which thoroughly revised the obsolete Militia Act of 1792. It separated the militia into two classes—the Organized Militia, to be known as the National Guard, and the Reserve Militia—and provided that, over a five-year period, the Guard's organization and equipment be patterned after that of the Regular Army. To help accomplish these changes in the Guard, the Dick bill made available federal funds; prescribed drill at least twice a month, supplemented with short annual training periods; permitted detailing of Regular officers to Guard units; and directed holding of joint maneuvers each year. Failure of the new measure, however, to modify significantly the long-standing provisions that severely restricted federal power to call up Guard units and control Guard personnel limited its effectiveness. Subsequent legislation in 1908 and 1914 reduced these restrictions to some extent, giving the President the right to prescribe the length of federal service and, with the advice and consent of the Senate, to appoint all officers of the Guard while the Guard was in federal service.

Although the largest permanent unit of the Regular Army in peacetime continued to be the regiment, experience in the Spanish-American War, observation of new developments abroad, and lessons learned in annual maneuvers all testified to the need for larger, more self-sufficient units, composed of the combined arms. Beginning in 1905, the *Field Service Regulations* laid down a blueprint for the organization of divisions in wartime, and in 1910 the General Staff drew up a plan for three permanent infantry divisions to be composed of designated Regular Army and National Guard regiments. Because of trouble along the Mexican border in the spring of 1911, the plan was not carried out. Instead, the Army organized a provisional maneuver division, ordering its component units, consisting of three brigades comprised of nearly 13,000 officers and men, to concentrate at San Antonio, Texas. The division's presence there, it was hoped, would end the border disturbances.

The effort proved only how unready the Army was to mobilize quickly for any kind of national emergency. Assembly of the division required several months. The War Department had to collect Regular Army troops from widely scattered points in the continental United States and denude every post, depot, and arsenal to scrape up the necessary equipment. Even so, when the maneuver division finally completed its concentration in August 1911, it was far from fully operational, since none of its regiments were up to strength or adequately armed and equipped. Fortunately, the efficiency of the division was not put to any battle test, and within a short time it was broken up and its component units were returned to their home stations. Because those members of Congress who had Army installations in their own districts insisted on retaining them, the War Department was prevented from relocating units so that there would be a greater concentration of troops in a few places. The only immediate result of the Army's attempt to gain experience in the handling of large units was an effort to organize on paper the scattered posts of the Army so that their garrisons, which averaged 700 troops each, could join one of three divisions. But these abortive attempts to mobilize larger units were not entirely without value. In 1913 when the Army again had to strengthen the forces along the Mexican border, a division assembled in Texas in less than a week, ready for movement to any point where it might be needed.

Caribbean Problems and Projects

The close of the War with Spain brought no satisfactory solution for the Cuban problem. As a result of years of misrule and fighting, conditions on the island when the war ended were deplorable. Under provisions of the Teller amendment, the United States was pledged to turn over the rule of Cuba to its people. American forces, however, stayed on to assist the Cubans in achieving at least a modicum of economic and political stability. The first step was to set up a provisional government, headed in the beginning by Maj. Gen. John R. Brooke and later by General Wood. This government promptly undertook a program of rehabilitation and reform. An outstanding achievement was eliminating yellow fever, which had decimated Army troops during the war. Researches and experiments carried out by the Army Medical Department culminated in the discovery that the dread disease is transmitted by a specific type of mosquito.

When order had been restored in Cuba, a constituent assembly met. Under the chairmanship of General Wood, it drew up an organic law for the island patterned after the American Constitution. At the insistence of the United States, this law included several clauses known as the Platt amendment, which also appeared in the subsequent treaty concluded in 1903 by the two countries. The amendment limited the amount of debt Cuba could contract, granted the United States naval bases at Guantánamo and Bahia Honda, and gave the United States the right to intervene to preserve "Cuban independence" and maintain a government "adequate to the protection of life, property and individual liberty." In 1902, after a general election and the inauguration of the republic's first president, the Americans ended their occupation. But events soon demonstrated that the period of tutelage in self-government had been too short. In late 1906, when the Cuban Government proved unable to cope with a new rebellion, the United States intervened to maintain law and order. On the advice of Secretary of War Taft, President Roosevelt dispatched more than 5,000 troops to Havana, the so-called Army of Cuban Pacification, which remained in Cuba until early 1909. Again in 1912 and 1917, the United States found it necessary to intervene, but each time withdrew its occupying forces as soon as order was restored. Not until 1934 did the United States, consistent with its new Good Neighbor Policy, give up the right of intervention embodied in the Platt amendment.

Emergence of the United States as a world power with a primary concern for developments in the Caribbean Sea increased the long-time American interest in an isthmian canal. Discovery of gold in California in 1848 and the rapid growth of the west coast states had underlined the importance of developing a shorter sea route from Atlantic ports to the Pacific. The strategic need for a canal was dramatized for the American people during the Spanish-American War by the sixty-six-day voyage of the battleship *Oregon* from Puget Sound around Cape Horn to Santiago, where it joined the American Fleet barely in time to participate in the destruction of Cervera's ships.

A few months after the end of the War with Spain, McKinley told Congress that a canal under American control was "now more than ever indispensable." By the Hay-Pauncefote Treaty of 1901, the United States secured abrogation of the terms of the Clayton-Bulwer Treaty of 1850 that required the United States to share equally with Great Britain in construction and operation of any future isthmian canal. Finally, in 1903, the long-standing question of where the canal should be built—Nicaragua or Panama—was resolved in favor of Panama. An uprising in Panama against the government of Colombia provided President Roosevelt with an opportunity to send American naval units to support the rebels, assuring establishment of an independent republic. The new republic readily agreed to permit the United States to acquire control of a ten-mile strip across the isthmus, to purchase the property formerly belonging to the French syndicate that had attempted to construct a canal in the 1880's, and to build, maintain, and operate an interoceanic canal. Congress promptly appropriated the necessary funds for work to begin and the Isthmian Canal Commission set about investigating the problem of who should construct the canal.

When the commission advised the President that overseeing the construction of so vast a project was beyond the capabilities of any private concern, Roosevelt decided to turn the job over to the Army. He reorganized the commission, assigning to it new members—the majority were Army officers—and in 1907 appointed Col. George W. Goethals as its chairman and chief engineer. In this capacity, Goethals, a graduate of the Military Academy who had served in the Corps of Engineers since 1882, had virtually sole responsibility for administration of the canal project. Displaying great organizational ability, he overcame many serious difficulties, including problems of engineering, employee grievances, housing, and sanitation, to complete the canal by 1914. Goethals owed a part of his success to the support he received from the Army's Medical Department. Under the leadership of Col. William C. Gorgas, who earlier had played an important role in administering the sanitation program in Cuba, the Army carried through measures to control malaria and virtually wipe out yellow fever, ultimately converting the Canal Zone into a healthy and attractive place to live and work.

The completed Panama Canal stood as a magnificent engineering achievement and an outstanding example of the Army's fulfillment of a peacetime mission; but its opening and operation under American administration were also highly significant from the point of view of military strategy. For the Navy, the Canal achieved economy of force by eliminating the necessity for maintaining large fleets in both the Atlantic and Pacific. For the Army, it created a new strategic point in the continental defense system that had to be strongly protected by the most modern fortifications manned by a large and well-trained garrison.

The Army on the Mexican Border

Early in the twentieth century, the Army found itself frequently involved in hemispheric problems, not only with the countries of the Caribbean region, but also with the United States' southern neighbor, Mexico. That nation, after a long era of relative political stability, entered a period of revolutionary turmoil. Beginning in 1911, internal conflicts in the northern part of the country led to recurrent incidents along the Mexican border, posing a serious threat to peace. President William Howard Taft first ordered strengthening of the border patrols and then, in the summer of 1911, concentration of the maneuver division at San Antonio. After a period of quiet, General Victoriano Huerta in 1913 deposed and replaced President Francisco Madero. The assassination of Madero shortly thereafter led to full-scale civil war between Huerta's forces and those of General Venustiano Carranza, leader of the so-called Constitutionalists, and Emiliano Zapata, chief of the radicals. Woodrow Wilson, who had succeeded Taft as President, disapproved of the manner in which Huerta had come to power. In a significant shift from traditional American policy, the President decided not to recognize Huerta on the grounds that his assumption of power did not meet the test of "constitutional legitimacy." At the same time, Wilson imposed an arms embargo on both sides in the civil war. But in early 1914, when Huerta's forces halted the Constitutionalists, Wilson endeavored to help Carranza by lifting the embargo.

Resentment over Wilson's action contributed to the arrest in February of American sailors by followers of Huerta in the port of Tampico. Although they were soon released with an expression of regret from Huerta, Rear Adm. Henry T. Mayo, commanding the American Fleet in the area, demanded a public apology. Huerta refused. Feeling that intervention was unavoidable and seeing an opportunity to deprive Huerta of important ports, President Wilson supported Admiral Mayo and proposed to occupy Tampico, seize Veracruz, and blockade both ports. When a German steamer carrying a cargo of ammunition arrived unexpectedly at Veracruz in late April, the United States put ashore a contingent of marines and sailors to occupy the port and prevent unloading of the ship. Naval gunfire checked a Mexican counterattack and by the end of the month an American force of nearly 8,000—about half marines and half Army troops—under command of Maj. Gen. Frederick Funston occupied the city. For a time war with Mexico seemed inevitable, but both Wilson and Huerta accepted mediation and the Mexican leader agreed to resign. Carranza had barely had time to assume office when his erstwhile ally, Francisco "Pancho" Villa, rebelled and proceeded to gain control over most of northern Mexico.

Despite the precariousness of Carranza's hold on Mexico, President Wilson decided to recognize his government. It was now the turn of Villa to show resentment. He instigated a series of border incidents which culminated in a surprise attack by 500 to 1,000 of his men against Columbus, New Mexico, on March 9, 1916. Villa's troops killed a substantial number of American soldiers and civilians and destroyed considerable property before units of the 13th Cavalry drove them off. The following day, President Wilson ordered Brig. Gen. John J. Pershing into Mexico to assist the Mexican Government in capturing Villa.

On March 15 the advance elements of this punitive expedition entered Mexico in "hot pursuit." For the next several months, Pershing's troops chased Villa through unfriendly territory for hundreds of miles, never quite catching up with him but managing to disperse most of his followers. Although Carranza's troops also failed to capture Villa, Carranza soon showed that he had no desire to have the United States do the job for him. He protested the continued presence of American troops in Mexico and insisted upon their withdrawal. Carranza's unfriendly attitude, plus orders from the War Department forbidding attacks on Mexicans who were not followers of Villa, made it difficult for Pershing to deal effectively with other hostile Mexicans who blocked his path

GENERAL PERSHING AND HIS TROOPS *during the pursuit of Villa.*

without running the risk of precipitating war. Some clashes with Mexican Government troops actually occurred. The most important took place in June at Carrizal where scores were killed or wounded. This action once again created a critical situation and led President Wilson to call 75,000 National Guardsmen into federal service to help police the border.

Aware that the majority of Americans favored a peaceful solution, Wilson persuaded Carranza to resume diplomatic negotiations. The two leaders agreed in late July to submit the disputes arising out of the punitive expedition to a joint commission for settlement. Some time later the commission ruled that the American unit commander in the Carrizal affair was at fault. Although the commission broke up in January 1917 without reaching agreement on a plan for evacuating Pershing's troops, relations between the United States and Germany had reached so critical a stage that Wilson had no alternative but to order withdrawal of the punitive expedition.

Pershing failed to capture Villa, but the activities of the American troops in Mexico and along the border were not entirely wasted effort. Dispersal of Villa's band put an end to serious border incidents. More important, from a military point of view, was the intensive training in the field received by both Regular Army and National Guard troops who served on the border and in Mexico. Too, the partial mobilization drew further attention to the still unsolved problem of developing a satisfactory system for maintaining in peacetime the nucleus of those trained forces that would be required to supplement the Regular Army in national emergencies. Fortunately, many defects in the military establishment, especially in the National Guard, came to light in time to be corrected before the Army plunged into the war already under way in Europe.

CHAPTER 17

World War I: The First Three Years

As the armed camp that Europe had become by the summer of 1914 approached the point of explosion, the United States was markedly unprepared for any role that a European holocaust might create for the New World. Nor was there any widespread agitation to alter that situation, for despite the nation's increased involvement in world affairs, most Americans looked to the tactic of the ostrich to keep them out of the trouble. Americans, President Woodrow Wilson would admonish once war came, should remain "impartial in thought as well as in action."

Although the Navy, the nation's first line of defense, was the world's third largest, the Army was woefully inadequate for coping with anything much more complex than domestic disturbances or border defense. In striking contrast to 1.5 million trained men available in France and more than 2 million in Germany, the U.S. Army was short even the 100,000-man strength that Congress had authorized in 1902. Within the Army high command the contest of authority between the General Staff and the powerful bureau chiefs still went on, for all Elihu Root's reforms, and argument persisted over Emory Upton's rejection of the militia system in favor of the concept of an expansible army.

How War Came in Europe

The event that set off war in Europe came in late June at Sarajevo where a fanatical Serbian nationalist assassinated the heir to the Austro-Hungarian throne. In other times and under different conditions, this act might not have been enough to catapult the world into the most widespread and costly conflict man had yet known, one that eventually would put under arms sixty-five million men from thirty countries representing every continent, and one that would involve sea battles around the globe and major land campaigns not only in Europe but in parts of Africa and Asia Minor.

Yet as matters stood that summer of 1914, Europe was a tinderbox awaiting a spark. The situation was, in the words of President Wilson's personal adviser, Col. Edward M. House, "militarism run stark mad."

European nationalism had much to do with it. In Germany, a newly united nation forged from a loose-knit confederation of quarreling states no longer had the strong guiding hand of its able creator, Chancellor Otto von Bismarck, but instead had the chauvinistic direction of Wilhelm II, the kaiser. In Italy, also only recently united, vacillation and indecision reigned. In Russia, center of bellicose pan-Slavism, an autocratic czar already was feeling the pressure of people's revolt. In the Balkans, various minorities, particularly the Serbs, were challenging the patchwork amalgamation that was the Austro-Hungarian empire.

At the same time the industrial revolution, with its attendant commercial expansion, had prompted Germany to seek entry into the colonial system that long had been the province of France and Britain. As the Germans built the navy that was essential to their ambition, Britain's age-old supremacy of the seas was challenged. Germany's rise also threatened France on the ground, already tangibly demonstrated in the war of 1870–71, which produced in the French a lasting bitterness and such a burning desire to regain the lost provinces of Alsace and Lorraine that many saw a war of irredentism as inevitable.

The Germans continued to expand their military machine in keeping with their ever-growing aspirations, and as the French followed suit, an arms race of frightening proportions ensued. Meanwhile, the nations banded together in alliances designed to offset one another. There was at first the Triple Alliance composed of Germany, Austria, and Italy. On the other side, the Entente Cordiale between Britain and France gradually merged with the Dual Alliance of France and Russia to become the Triple Entente. With the defection of Italy, Germany and Austria became the Central Powers, which Bulgaria and Turkey eventually joined. The Triple Entente became, with the addition of Italy, the nucleus of the Allied Powers.

Despite some halfhearted efforts to localize the dispute over the assassinated prince, the fact that Russia backed Serbia and the kaiser promised Austria full support meant that the only real question was the date when the war was to begin. The answer to that came on July 28 when Austria declared war on Serbia. In view of the entangling alliances and the bulging arsenals, entry of all the major powers into the conflict was all but preordained.

The Early Campaigns

The bellicosity of Germany toward both Russia and France dictated for the Germans a two-front war. To meet this contingency, the German General Staff had laid its plans to defeat France swiftly before the Russians with their ponderous masses could fully mobilize, then to shift forces rapidly to the east and destroy the Russians at will.

The maneuver designed to defeat the French was the handiwork of Germany's gifted former Chief of Staff, Count Alfred von Schlieffen, who lent his name to the plan. Deducing that the French would attack in Alsace and Lorraine, Schlieffen proposed to trap them in a massive single envelopment, a great scythelike movement through the Low Countries and into northern France, thence west and south of Paris. Schlieffen was prepared to give ground on his left wing in Alsace-Lorraine to insure keeping the French armies occupied until a powerful right wing—the tip of the scythe—could complete the envelopment. So basic to the plan was the power of the right wing that the old man reputedly stressed it in his dying words. (*Map 38*)

Schlieffen's successor, Helmuth von Moltke, failed to heed this proviso. Moltke eliminated the invasion of the Netherlands, thus confining the German right wing to a narrow fortified corridor on either side of the Belgian city of Liège. Wary of the theory of giving ground in Alsace-Lorraine, he shifted troops from the right to strengthen the defense on the left. Similarly worried about the strength of the German forces assigned to contain the Russians, Moltke withdrew four and a half corps from the right wing to move to the east.

These vagaries almost did in the Schlieffen plan, yet such surprise did the maneuver achieve that by late August French and British were in full retreat, the threat to Paris so real that the French Government abandoned the city. At that point Moltke again wavered, for word came that the Russians had mobilized far faster than expected and had begun to attack. Under pressure from the kaiser, Moltke again violated Schlieffen's dictum, pulling out two more corps from his right wing. In an effort to compensate for this diminution by reducing the depth of the envelopment, he ordered the tip of the scythe to pass east rather than west of Paris.

The two corps that Moltke withdrew had no effect in the east, since they arrived only after the Germans already had repelled the Russians in the battles of Tannenberg and the Masurian Lakes. Had Moltke retained them, they might not have been enough to carry the Schlieffen plan through to victory; but since their departure was what had prompted Moltke to alter the scope of the envelopment, their presence would have sharply changed the nature of what followed, the "Miracle of the Marne."

Paris spared, the French Commander in Chief, General Joseph Joffre, rallied the retreating French and British armies along the Marne east of the city, while in Paris the city's commander assembled the garrison—some of them transported in sputtering Parisian taxis—and hurled them against the German flank. That

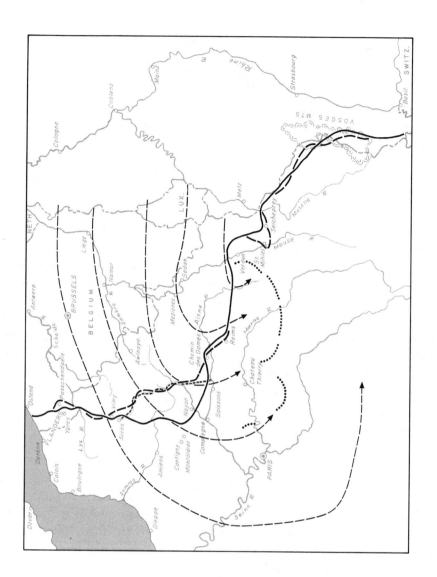

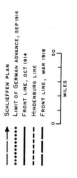

WESTERN FRONT

Sep 1914 – Mar 1918

→ SCHLIEFFEN PLAN
●●●●● LIMIT OF GERMAN ADVANCE, SEP 1914
——— FRONT LINE, OCT 1914
– – – HINDENBURG LINE
||||| FRONT LINE, MAR 1918

0   50

MILES

MAP 38

action afforded time for main British and French forces to turn, halt the Germans at the Marne River east of Paris, and drive them back to the Aisne River, forty miles to the north.

As stalemate developed along the Aisne, each side tried to envelop the northern flank of the other in successive battles that by October had extended the opposing lines all the way to the Belgian coast. The year would end with the Germans in control of most of Belgium and of the rich mining and industrial provinces of northern France, while the Allies, to their good fortune, managed to hold on to most of the Channel ports, which were vital if the British were to supply their troops on the Continent and if the Germans were to be denied critical bases for operations against the Royal Navy.

Hurting from unexpectedly brutal losses and stunned at the indecision of the first four months of warfare, Allied and German armies alike went to ground. The landscape from Switzerland to the sea soon was scarred with opposing systems of zigzag, timber-revetted trenches, fronted by tangles of barbed wire sometimes more than 150 feet deep and featured here and there by covered dugouts providing shelter for troops and horses and by observation posts in log bunkers or concrete turrets. Out beyond the trenches and the barbed wire was a muddy desert called no man's land where artillery fire had eliminated habitation and vegetation alike, where men in nighttime listening posts strained to hear what the enemy was about, and where rival patrols clashed.

It would eventually be apparent to both sides that they had miscalculated, that the newly developed machine gun and improved indirect fire artillery had bolstered not the offense but the defense, and that which had been presaged—but ignored—in the U.S. Civil War and in the Russo-Japanese War had come to be. The spade had become the *sine qua non* of the battlefield, lessening the applicability of such principles of war as maneuver, economy of force, surprise, and making critical the principle of mass. Masses of men—nearly 2 million Germans, 3 million Allied troops; masses of artillery—barrages lasted days and even weeks before an offensive; and masses of casualties—British and French in 1915 lost 1.5 million men killed, wounded, and missing. Yet through it all the opposing lines stood much as they had at the start. For more than two years they would vary less than ten miles in either direction.

To meet the high cost of the long, deadly struggle, the opposing powers turned more than ever before in history to the concept of the nation in arms. Even Britain, for so many years operating on the theory of a powerful navy and only a small though highly professional army, resorted to conscription and sent massive new armies to the Continent. To appease the appetite of the vast armies for munitions, equipment, and supplies, the nations harnessed their mines, factories, and railroads to war production, levied high income taxes, froze wages and prices, rationed food and other commodities.

On the battlefield, commanders persisted in a vain hope that somehow the stalemate might be ended and breakthrough and exploitation achieved. Although the Germans spent much of their effort in 1915 in a futile campaign for quick victory against the Russians, it was they who first came close to a breakthrough on the Western Front. They did so in April with a greenish mist of chlorine gas released from thousands of canisters against a French colonial division on the British sector of the front. The colonials broke, but the Germans were unprepared to exploit the advantage. The first use of poison gas thus was a strategic blunder wasting total surprise for nothing more than local gains.

The British similarly blundered the next year when they also introduced a new weapon prematurely. This was the tank, an ungainly, ponderous offspring of a marriage of armor with the caterpillar tractor; it owed its name to British attempts to deceive the Germans that the vehicle was a water storage device. In the first commitment in September 1916, 34 tanks helped British infantry advance a painful mile and a half. There would be other attacks in later months involving tanks in strengths close to 500, but the critical element of surprise already had passed. Tanks later would prove sufficient to achieve the penetration everybody sought, but they were too slow and too subject to mechanical failure to fill the old role of horse cavalry as the tool of exploitation.

For all the lack of decision, both poison gas and the tank soon were established weapons, although the Germans were slow to accept the tank. Another weapon, meanwhile, found full acceptance on both sides: the airplane, frail forerunner of modern tactical and strategic bombers. Used at first primarily for reconnaissance, then as a counterreconnaissance weapon to fight the enemy's planes, and finally as an offensive weapon to attack ground troops, before the war ended aircraft engaged in strategic missions against railroads, factories, and cities, presaging the mass destruction that was to follow in another great war.

A fourth new weapon was the submarine, which the Germans employed with a ruthless skill that would bring them close to victory but would in the end provoke the instrument of their downfall. When the Germans first opened submarine warfare early in 1915, only 27 U-boats, as the submarines were called, were ready for action. Even this number quickly achieved impressive results, soon sinking more than 150,000 tons of Allied shipping each month. U-boat crews could not always correctly identify vessels which they attacked, and many neutral ships were sunk. The first American vessel to be involved was the merchant ship *Gulflight*, struck by a torpedo on the first day of May, but the event with sharpest impact on public opinion followed a week later when a submarine off the coast of Ireland sank the British liner *Lusitania*, with the loss of 1,198 lives, including 128 Americans.

The Impact of the War on the United States

The sinking of the *Lusitania* shocked an American public that, while unable to follow the President's dictum on impartiality of thought, had nevertheless displayed up to this point little desire to become directly involved in Europe's bloodbath. Although most Americans had from the first resented the submarine campaign, Britain too was violating the freedom of the seas with a blockade not only of Germany but of neutral European nations as well. This had raised the question of whether the acts of both sides were not equally reprehensible; but the heavy loss of life in the sinking of the *Lusitania* invoked fresh ire against the Germans. Membership in patriotic organizations flourished, and voices advocating preparedness found new listeners.

Among the voices were those of Elihu Root, ex-President Theodore Roosevelt, and former Secretary of War Henry L. Stimson. Another was that of General Wood, whose term as the Army's Chief of Staff had expired just over a year after President Wilson and his peace-oriented administration had come to office. Following a practice he had introduced while Chief of Staff of conducting summer camps where college students paying their own way could receive military training, Wood lent his support to a similar four-week camp for business and professional men at Plattsburg Barracks, New York. Known as the "Plattsburg idea," its success justified opening other camps, assuring a relatively small but influential cadre possessing basic military skills and imbued with enthusiasm for preparedness.

Yet these were voices of a heavily industrialized and articulate east. Few like them were to be heard from the rural south, the west, or a strongly isolationist midwest, where heavy settlements of German-Americans (called by some, derisively, "hyphenated Americans") detected in the talk of preparedness a heavy leaning toward the nation's historic Anglo-Saxon ties. There was in the country, too, a strong tide of outright pacifism, which possessed an eloquent spokesman in Wilson's Secretary of State, William Jennings Bryan.

How deep were Bryan's convictions became apparent in the government's reaction to the sinking of the *Lusitania*. Although Bryan agreed with the President's first diplomatic protest over the sinking, he dissented when the President, dissatisfied with the German reply and determined to insist on the right of neutrals to engage in commerce on the high seas, insisted on a second and stronger note. The Secretary resigned.

Although sinkings by submarine continued through the summer of 1915, Wilson's persistent protest at last produced an apparent diplomatic victory when in September the Germans promised that passenger liners would be sunk only after warning and with proper safeguards for passengers' lives. Decelerating their campaign, the Germans actually acted less in response to American protests than to a realization that they lacked enough submarines to achieve victory by that means.

American commerce with Europe meanwhile continued, particularly in munitions, but because of the British blockade almost all was with the Allied nations. The British intercepted ships carrying foodstuffs to Germany and held them until their cargoes rotted. Just after mid-1915 they put even cotton on a long list of contraband and blacklisted any U.S. firm suspected of trading with the Central Powers. These were deliberate and painful affronts, but so profitable was the munitions trade that only the southern states, hurt by the loss of markets for cotton, raised loud protest. In October 1915 President Wilson repealed a ban earlier imposed on loans to belligerents, thereby further stimulating trade with the Allies.

While Americans as a whole remained opposed to entering the war, their sympathy for the Allied cause grew. A combination of Allied propaganda and German ineptitude was largely responsible. The propagandists were careful to insure that nobody forgot the German violation of Belgian neutrality, the ordeal of "Little Belgium." Stories of babies mutilated and women violated by German soldiers were rampant. The French executed nine women as spies during the war, but it was the death of a British nurse, Edith Cavell, at the hands of the Germans that the world heard about and remembered. Clumsy German efforts at propaganda in the United States backfired when two military attachés were discovered financing espionage and sabotage. The Germans did their cause no further good when one of their submarines in October 1916 surfaced in Newport Harbor, sent an officer ashore to deliver a letter for the German ambassador, then submerged and sank nine Allied ships close off the New England coast.

Continuing to champion neutrality and seeking—however unsuccessfully— to persuade the belligerents to establish international rules of submarine warfare, President Wilson was personally becoming more aware of the necessity for military preparedness. Near the end of a nationwide speaking tour in February 1916, he not only called for creation of "the greatest navy in the world" but also urged widespread military training for civilians, lest some day the nation be faced with "putting raw levies of inexperienced men onto the modern field of battle." Still upholding the cause of freedom of the seas, he refused to go along with congressmen who sought to forbid Americans to travel on armed merchant ships.

Wilson nevertheless continued to demonstrate a fervent hope for neutrality. A submarine attack in March on the French steamer *Sussex* with Americans aboard convinced the President's adviser, Colonel House, and his new Secretary of State, Robert Lansing, that the nation should sever diplomatic relations with Germany, a course that a fiery speech of self-justification by the German chancellor in the Reichstag and a cynical reply to an American note of protest did nothing to discourage. Wilson instead went only so far as to dispatch what amounted to an ultimatum, demanding that the Germans cease the submarine war against passenger and merchant vessels or face severance of relations with the United States.

While questioning the American failure to deal as sternly with the British blockade and rejecting the charge of unrestricted submarine warfare, Germany again agreed to conform to American demands for prior warning and for protecting the lives of passengers. Wilson, in turn, saw that unless something could be done about the British blockade the German vow probably would be short-lived. When a protest to the British availed nothing, the President offered the services of the United States to negotiate a peace. That brought little positive response from either side.

The National Defense Act of 1916

Some of the President's growing sympathy for the cause of preparedness could be traced to increasing concern on the part of members of his administration, most notably the Secretary of War, Lindley M. Garrison. As an annex to the Secretary's annual report in September 1915, Garrison had submitted a study prepared by the General Staff entitled, "A Proper Military Policy for the United States." Like proposals for reform advanced earlier by Stimson and Wood, the new study turned away from the Uptonian idea of an expansible Regular Army, which Root had favored, to the more traditional American concept of a citizen army as the keystone of an adequate defense force. Garrison proposed more than doubling the Regular Army, increasing federal support for the National Guard, and creating a new 400,000-man volunteer force to be called the Continental Army, a trained reserve under federal control as opposed to the state control of the Guard.

Although Wilson refused to accept more than a small increase in the Regular Army, he approved the concept of a Continental Army. Garrison's proposal drew support, too, in the Senate, but not enough to overcome adamant opposition in the House of Representatives from strong supporters of the National Guard. Influential congressmen countered with a bill requiring increased federal responsibility for the Guard, acceptance of federal standards, and agreement by the Guard to respond to a Presidential call to service. Under pressure from these congressmen, Wilson switched his support to the Congressional plan. This, among other issues, prompted Garrison to resign.

There the matter might have bogged down had not Pancho Villa shot up Columbus, New Mexico. Facing pressing requirements for the National Guard on the Mexican border, the two halls of Congress at last compromised, incorporating the concept of the citizen army as the foundation of the American military establishment but not in the form of a Continental Army. They sought instead to make the National Guard the nucleus of the citizen force.

Passed in May and signed into law the next month, the bill was known as the National Defense Act of 1916. It provided for an army in no way comparable to those of the European combatants and produced cries of outrage from those still subscribing to the Uptonian doctrine. It also contained a severe restriction inserted by opponents of a strong General Staff, sharply limiting the number of officers who could be detailed to serve on the staff at the same time in or near Washington. The bill represented nevertheless the most comprehensive military legislation yet enacted by the U.S. Congress.

The National Defense Act of 1916 authorized an increase in the peacetime strength of the Regular Army over a period of five years to 175,000 men and a wartime strength of close to 300,000. Bolstered by federal funds and federal-stipulated organization and standards of training, the National Guard was to be increased more than fourfold to a strength of over 400,000 and obligated to respond to the call of the President. The act also established both an Officers' and an Enlisted Reserve Corps and a Volunteer Army to be raised only in time of war. Additional officers were to be trained in colleges and universities under a Reserve Officers' Training Corps program.

Going beyond the heretofore recognized province of military legislation, the National Defense Act of 1916 also granted power to the President to place orders for defense materials and to force industry to comply. The act further directed the Secretary of War to conduct a survey of all arms and munitions industries. A few months later the Congress demonstrated even greater interest in the industrial aspects of defense by creating a civilian Council of National Defense made up of leaders of industry and labor, supported by an advisory

commission composed of the secretaries of the principal government departments, and charged with the mission of studying economic mobilization. The
administration furthered the preparedness program by creating a U.S. Shipping
Board to regulate sea transport while developing a naval auxiliary fleet and a
merchant marine.

The War in 1916

As Wilson, through the fall of 1916, waged a campaign for re-election on a
peace platform, the war on the Western Front remained a stalemate despite two
of history's greatest and bloodiest battles. In a switch of main effort from Eastern
to Western Front, Moltke's successor as Chief of the General Staff, Erich von
Falkenhayn, chose the fortress town of Verdun, which he deemed of immense
moral and psychological significance to France, for massive attack in a campaign designed to bleed France white. There followed the Battle of the Somme
in which the British with French support attacked in quest of breakthrough
and victory. Neither achieved much more than to run up the casualty total:
460,000 French at Verdun, 300,000 German; 614,000 Allied troops on the
Somme, 650,000 German.

The appalling carnage of these battles brought the relief of Falkenhayn,
replaced by the heroes of the Eastern Front, Paul von Hindenburg as Chief of
the General Staff, and Erich Ludendorff as First Quartermaster General, his
deputy, although it was Ludendorff rather than the aging Hindenburg who
dominated in this command arrangement. It also wrote the end to the field
career of the French Commander in Chief, Field Marshal Joffre. In England, a
government fell.

On the Eastern Front, the Russians had rallied after giving up Poland to
the Germans and struck back with a major offensive against the Austrians that
carried almost to the passes leading through the Carpathian Mountains. It was
the greatest Russian victory of the war, but it cost a million men and left the
poorly armed, poorly equipped Russian soldier ready to embrace revolution.

That year, too, Italians and Austrians ground each other down along the
Isonzo in northeastern Italy, while an adventure in peripheral warfare, launched
the preceding year at the instigation of Winston Churchill, First Lord of the
Admiralty, ended indecisively in evacuation of the Gallipoli peninsula. Indecisive
too was the war's greatest sea battle, when a cornered German surface fleet
ventured out of the Baltic to meet the British Fleet in the Battle of Jutland, then
withdrew to the corner for the rest of the war, but only after inflicting more losses
than it received.

During the last three months of 1916, the German submarine campaign again mounted in intensity. Each month the British lost 176,000 tons of shipping. Counting Allied and neutral shipping, the losses averaged 192,000 tons a month, a shocking increase over the previous year that reflected a continuing growth of the U-boat fleet.

An End to Neutrality

As a new year of war opened, German leaders decided that they had lost so many men at Verdun and on the Somme that they would have to assume the defensive on the Western Front; their only hope of quick victory lay with the submarines, of which they now had close to 200. By operating an unrestricted campaign against all shipping, whatever the nationality, in waters off the British Isles and France, the Germans believed they could defeat the Allies within six months. While they recognized the strong risk of bringing the United States into the war by this tactic, they believed they could starve the Allies into submission before the Americans could raise, train, and deploy an Army.

The German ambassador in Washington continued to encourage Wilson to pursue his campaign for peace even as the Germans made their U-boats ready. On January 31, 1917, Germany informed the U.S. Government and other neutrals that beginning the next day U-boats would sink all vessels, neutral and Allied alike, without warning.

While the world waited to learn the American reaction, President Wilson searched for some alternative to war. Three days later, still groping desperately for a path to peace, he went before the Congress, not to ask a declaration of war, but to announce a break in diplomatic relations. This step, Wilson hoped, would be enough to turn the Germans from their new course.

Wilson could not know it at the time but an intelligence intercept already had placed in British hands a German telegram that, when released, would remove any doubt as to German intentions toward the United States. This message was sent in January from the German Foreign Secretary, Arthur Zimmermann, to the German ambassador to Mexico, proposing that in the event of war with the United States, Germany and Mexico conclude an alliance, with the adherence of Japan. In exchange for Mexico's taking up arms against the United States, Germany would provide generous financial assistance. Victory achieved, Mexico was to regain her lost territory of Texas, New Mexico, and Arizona.

Cognizant of the impact the message was bound to have on the United States, the British were nevertheless slow to release it; they had to devise a method to assure the Americans of its authenticity while concealing from the Germans that they had broken the German diplomatic code. On February 23, just over a month after intercepting the telegram, the British turned over a copy to the American ambassador in London.

When President Wilson received the news, he was angered but still unprepared to accept it as cause for war. In releasing the message to the press, he had in mind not inciting the nation to war but instead moving Congress to pass a bill authorizing the arming of American merchant ships, most of which were standing idle in American ports because of the submarine menace. As with the break in diplomatic relations, this, the President hoped, would so impress the Germans that they would abandon their unrestricted submarine campaign.

Although Congress and most of the nation were shocked by revelation of the Zimmermann message, their hopes for neutrality shattered, pacifists and pro-Germans countered with a roar of disbelief that the message was authentic. Zimmermann himself silenced them when in Berlin he admitted having sent the telegram.

In the next few weeks, four more American ships fell victim to German U-boats. Fifteen Americans died. At last convinced that the step was inevitable, the President went before Congress late on April 2 to ask for a declaration of war. Four days later, on April 6, 1917, the United States declared war on Germany.

A Year of Crisis in Europe

The United States entered the war even as Allied fortunes were approaching their nadir.

In Russia in March a spontaneous revolution had erupted, prompting the czar to abdicate and initiating a struggle for power between moderate Socialists and hard-core revolutionaries, the Bolsheviks. The moderates won, formed a provisional government, and vowed to continue the war, a development that made going to war more palatable to many Americans, since the overthrow of the old dynastic-imperial system gave logic to a Wilsonian phrase that this was a war "to make the world safe for democracy."

The reign of the moderates was destined to be brief, partly because the Germans contrived to foment trouble by permitting an exiled revolutionary leader, Nikolai Lenin, to pass from Switzerland through Germany in a special train to Russia. There Lenin joined with other leaders, including Leon Trotsky, in an open campaign to upset the moderate government. As forces of the

Central Powers launched a counteroffensive in July close behind a short-lived Russian offensive, Russian units, riven by revolutionary cells, collapsed, with soldiers deserting by the tens of thousands. The way was prepared for the Bolsheviks to seize power in the October Revolution. The new government under Lenin and Trotsky sued for peace.

On the Western Front the year's operations began with great expectations on the Allied side as a new French commander, General Robert Nivelle, prepared a grandiose, end-the-war offensive. With support from a converging British attack from the north, Nivelle planned to send four French armies to cut in behind a great bulge in the line between Soissons and Arras. Unfortunately, Nivelle was too open with his preparations. The Germans moved first, pulling back from the bulge to a previously prepared position which the Allies would name the Hindenburg Line. In the process they laid waste to the land behind them, and in occupying a shorter line gained 13 divisions for their reserve. In exchange for the usual minor gains, the British incurred 84,000 casualties, the French 187,000.

The worst was still to come. Mutiny broke out in one French regiment and spread swiftly through 54 divisions. The government relieved Nivelle, putting in his place to restore the Army's morale and discipline Henri Philippe Pétain, who had emerged as the hero of the earlier battle for Verdun.

With the French temporarily *hors de combat,* the British took up the struggle with a giant offensive in Flanders. First came a limited objective attack to straighten a minor bulge in the line known as the Messines Ridge. Working like moles, the British dug five miles of underground tunnels, laid a million pounds of explosives, then literally blew up the Messines Ridge. With some 20,000 Germans killed or wounded in one blow, the British took the ridge; but when they launched their main offensive a few miles to the north, breakthrough was as elusive as ever. In a battle that persisted into late fall—Passchendaele, they called it, after a ridge that was the first objective—British casualties totaled 245,000, German half that number.

More disastrous still were the results of an Austrian offensive launched with German assistance in Italy in the fall. In what became known as the Battle of Caporetto, the Italians in one blow lost 305,000 men; 275,000 of them surrendered as the Army fell back a hundred miles in panic. British and French divisions had to be rushed to Italy to keep the Italians in the war.

A combination of all these crises prompted the Allied governments to strive seriously for the first time to create some form of unified command. Yet for all the peril, no government was yet prepared to yield its troops to foreign command. The Allies created a Supreme War Council with both political and military representation from all the Allied nations, a step toward an over-all command, but only a step.

Despite the seriousness of the crises on land, the most portentous of all as the United States entered the war was the crisis at sea. In February 1917 alone, German U-boats had sunk 781,000 tons of Allied and neutral shipping, and the British were predicting a loss in April of almost 900,000 tons. At this rate, the British reckoned, the Germans soon would force them out of the war; by October 1917, the end would be in sight.

The United States Prepares for War

Although far from ready for war, the U.S. Navy fortunately was in a position to take immediate steps to aid the Allies. An emissary from Washington, Rear Adm. William S. Sims, helped to convince the British Admiralty to employ a new tactic to counter the rampaging submarines, a system of convoys whereby destroyers and other warships escorted groups of merchant vessels across the Atlantic. By early May, 6 U.S. destroyers had begun to participate in this system, and before the summer was out the number would grow to 37, while 5 U.S. battleships were operating in European waters.

The convoy system did not defeat the submarine, but it was effective enough to break the crisis. During the last half of 1917 total ship sinkings declined steadily; in December less than 400,000 tons of shipping was lost. In the meantime, the United States had joined Britain in a massive shipbuilding program.

The U.S. Army was in no position to make its weight felt immediately. Counting that part of the National Guard federalized for duty on the Mexican border, the Army numbered only 210,000 men with an additional 97,000 Guardsmen still in state service. Not a single unit of divisional size existed and so hobbled by the restriction written into the National Defense Act was the General Staff that only 19 officers were on duty in the headquarters in Washington. Although the experience in Mexico had given the little Army some seasoning, the main result of that involvement had been to point up shortages in equipment and other deficiencies. Except for 890,000 Springfield rifles, the Army's arsenal was nearly bare.

Given the state of the Army and the fact that the United States went to war over the limited issue of unrestricted submarine warfare, the nation conceivably might have confined its contribution to the war at sea, but such a concept received neither general nor official support. Starting with the President's war message to Congress, the intent was to send ground troops to Europe and to do all possible to defeat the German empire and end the war.

Congress, the President, the government moved swiftly in that direction. The House of Representatives authorized a $7 billion bond issue; to build up and manage the merchant marine, the President created the Emergency Fleet Corporation; the Treasury Department opened a drive to float a $2 billion Liberty Loan. The Army General Staff, meanwhile, quickly decided that to bolster Allied morale a division should be shipped as promptly as possible to France as tangible evidence that the United States intended to fight.

Forming a division required collecting as a nucleus four infantry regiments from the Mexican border, building them up to strength with men from other regiments and with recruits, and calling Reserve officers to fill out the staffs. By mid-June the 1st Infantry Division had begun to embark amid dockside confusion not unlike that in the Spanish-American War. Not only did the men lack many of their weapons but a large number had never even heard of some of them. Yet the pertinent fact was that a division was on the way to provide a much-needed boost for the war-weary Allied nations. On the Fourth of July, a battalion of the 16th Infantry marched through Paris to French cheers of near delirium, but it would be months before the 1st Division would be sufficiently trained to participate in the war even on a quiet sector of the front.

To command the American Expeditionary Forces, President Wilson chose the man with command experience in Mexico, John J. Pershing, even though Pershing was junior to five other major generals in the Army. Within three weeks of the appointment, Pershing was on his way to France to survey the situation and furnish the War Department with an estimate of the forces that would have to be provided. He was present for the 16th Infantry's parade on the Fourth of July and participated in a ceremony at the tomb of General Lafayette, where a Quartermaster colonel—not Pershing, as many would long believe—uttered the words, "Lafayette, we are here."

As Pershing was preparing to sail for Europe, Congress in mid-May passed a Selective Service Act based on a plan developed by the War Department after careful study of conscription in the Civil War. It was a model act, one that eliminated such inequities as substitutes, purchased exemptions, and bounties, and assured that conscripts would serve for the duration of the emergency. To spare the Army any opprobrium connected with administering the draft, this was made the responsibility of local civilian boards. Although these local boards were empowered to grant selective exemptions based on essential occupations and family obligations, all males between the ages of 21 and 30 had to register. These ages later were extended from 18 to 45.

The Selective Service Act also established the broad outlines of the Army's structure. There were to be three increments: (1) the Regular Army, to be raised immediately to the full wartime strength of 286,000 authorized in the National Defense Act of 1916; (2) the National Guard, also to be expanded immediately to the authorized strength of approximately 450,000; and (3) a National Army (the National Defense Act had called it a Volunteer Army), to be created in two increments of 500,000 men each at such time as the President should determine.

Much of the identity of these three segments eventually would be lost as recruits and draftees alike were absorbed in all units, so that in mid-1918 the War Department would change the designation of all land forces to one "United States Army." The original segment to which regiments, brigades, and divisions belonged nevertheless continued to be apparent from numerical designations. For the Regular Army, for example, divisions were numbered up to 25, while numbers 26 through 75 were reserved for the National Guard and higher numbers for divisions of the National Army.

Just how large an army the United States was to raise depended in large measure on the situation in Europe and on General Pershing's recommendations from his vantage point there. Soon after Pershing's arrival in France, he called for approximately a million men to be sent to France before the end of 1918. This was the smallest number, Pershing noted, that would afford an independent fighting force, a full field army of 20 divisions and necessary supporting troops. This number, Pershing warned, probably would constitute only a start.

The War Department in turn translated Pershing's recommendation into a plan to send instead by the end of 1918 30 divisions with supporting services, a total of 1,372,000 men; but so disastrous were the developments in Europe in succeeding months—the Nivelle offensive, Passchendaele, Caporetto, the Russian Revolution—that Pershing felt impelled to revise his estimate. In June 1918, he would ask for 3,000,000 men with 66 divisions to be in France by May 1919. This figure he quickly raised to an estimate of 80 divisions by April 1919, followed shortly by a request for 100 divisions by July of the same year.

Although the War Department questioned whether 100 divisions could be sent to France by the summer of 1919 and even whether that many would be necessary to win the war, detailed study produced a promise to raise 98 divisions and to have 80 of them in France by the summer of 1919. This meant, in turn, an increase in the original program of 30 divisions by the end of 1918, raising the goal to 52 divisions.

Part of the War Department's concern was based on the size of the U.S. division—28,000 men—almost double that of Allied and German divisions, which meant in numbers of men that 100 U.S. divisions were the equivalent of almost 200 Allied divisions. This size was a result of one of Pershing's early recommendations, which, along with advice of military missions sent from France and Britain, prompted radical changes in organization of the U.S. infantry division.

The need, as Pershing saw it, was for a division large enough to provide immense striking and staying power, one larger in size than most army corps of the Civil War. As determined by the War Department, the division was to be organized in 2 infantry brigades of 2 regiments each, a field artillery brigade with 1 heavy and 2 light regiments, a regiment of combat engineers, 3 machine gun battalions, plus signal, medical, and other supporting troops.

As the war proceeded, the Army actually would reach a peak strength of 3,685,458. This included 62 divisions, 43 of which were sent overseas. On this basis, when the war came to an end, the Army was running close to the projected goal of 52 divisions to be in France by the end of 1918.

How fast the Army could expand at the start depended in large measure on the availability of housing and of arms, equipment, and supplies. New Regular regiments and small units were organized immediately, using existing housing facilities, while the new National Guard formations were called in two increments and housed in tent camps, mainly in warmer southern states. Although over nine million men registered for the draft in June, the first would be called to fill the divisions of the National Army only in September after a priority building program could provide the first of the vast new cantonments that would be required. A special Cantonment Division of the Quartermaster Corps worked with a civilian Committee on Emergency Construction to provide these facilities.

In the matter of arms, munitions, and equipment, the demands were so urgent and so tremendous, not only for the Army but also for the Navy and the Allies, that as the authors of the National Defense Act of 1916 had anticipated, and as the European powers early had discovered, industry too had to be mobilized. For this task, the Council of National Defense as created by the National Defense Act provided a central planning office and control. The council early established a Munitions Standards Board, composed of industrialists to determine standards for munitions manufacturers, which grew by stages into a War Industries Board with broad powers to co-ordinate all purchasing

GRAND REVIEW, CAMP DEVENS, MASSACHUSETTS

by agencies of the Army and Navy, to establish production priorities, to create new plans and convert existing plants to priority uses, and to co-ordinate the activities of various civilian war agencies.

Despite these efforts, the demand for arms was so immense and immediate and the time required for contracts to be let and industry to retool so lengthy that the Army for a long time would have to train with obsolete and even wooden guns and in the end would have to depend heavily on Allied manufacture. The one weapon providing no particular problem was the rifle. To add to already existing stocks, the Army's own arsenals increased production of Springfields, while plants that had been filling Allied orders modified the British Lee-Enfield rifle to take U.S. ammunition for use by U.S. troops. All American units reaching France during the first year had to be equipped with Allied machine guns and automatic rifles, but new and excellent Browning machine guns and automatic rifles began coming off U.S. production lines in volume by mid-1918. Of some 2,250 artillery pieces used by American forces in France, only a hundred were of U.S. manufacture. Similarly an embryonic U.S. Tank Corps used French tanks, and in some instances British and French tank battalions supported U.S. troops. The Air Section that expanded rapidly to 11,425 flying officers, of whom 5,000 reached France, also had to depend primarily on planes provided by the Allies. The United States did produce a good 12-cylinder Liberty airplane engine, and a few U.S. planes saw service in latter weeks of the war.

The record of U.S. industry was somewhat better in terms of the soldier's personal needs, including his food. The Army worked closely with a War Food Administration to avoid the food scandals of earlier wars. Inductions had to be slowed briefly until sufficient uniforms could be accumulated, and shortages in some items persisted, but as a result less of industry's failures than of a cumbersome Quartermaster contracting system, which was eventually corrected. The Army in any case made extensive purchases abroad but mainly in bulky items to relieve the burden on transatlantic shipping—horses, coal, lumber for overseas camps, and a few textile items like blankets.

Providing officers for the new divisions was another factor affecting the speed of the Army's expansion, for at the start the Army had only 9,000 officers against an immediate requirement of 200,000. Although the General Staff at first contemplated scattering the officers and noncommissioned officers of the Regular Army to form cadres for the National Army, in keeping with Uptonian doctrine, it early became apparent that the small number of Regulars would be submerged and lost in the sea of conscripts. This was one of the factors influencing the General Staff's decision to form a division of Regulars for early shipment to France.

Eschewing the obvious though questionable expedient of appointing officers directly from civilian life, the Army provided direct commissions only for specialists like doctors and those uniquely qualified by civilian experience for the technical services. As a start, the Army conducted sixteen Officers' Training Camps for civilians and reservists on the order of the old "Plattsburg idea"; but in the main the Army drew its officers from the ranks of qualified enlisted men in the Regular Army, from the Reserve Officers' Training Corps and a Student Army Training Corps in colleges and universities, and in the largest numbers of all from Officers' Training Camps in division cantonments and later eight consolidated Officers' Training Schools. Officer candidates were admitted to these schools only after careful screening and then were given three months of intensive training. The 60 percent who made the grade were commissioned in the new National Army. Called in some circles "90-day wonders," these officers nevertheless provided the Army with a leadership far surpassing that of the average new officer in any previous war.

How much training time the soldier needed before going overseas was long a matter of conjecture, but the War Department finally settled on four months' training in the United States. This was so rudimentary, particularly since the units with which the individual soldier went to war were similarly

1ST LT. EDWARD V. RICKENBACKER, FIRST AMERICAN ACE, *with his Spad plane, France, 1918.*

inexperienced, that General Pershing set up a thorough training course for all divisions once they arrived in France. Conducted with British and French assistance, Pershing's program was so lengthy as to provoke impatience on the part of the Allies and criticism on the part of many American officers.

Getting the troops to their training centers, then to ports of embarkation, and finally across the Atlantic was such a mammoth undertaking and had to be executed on such an emergency basis that confusion and mismanagement could hardly have been unexpected. To co-ordinate rail transportation, the government established a Railway War Board, which later became the Railroad Administration, but so congested did the railroads become that the government eventually seized and ran them through the Railroad Administration. The Shipping Board that had been created close on adoption of the National Defense Act of 1916 had had more time for preparation, but shipping nevertheless remained a critical item and ports often were glutted with supplies. The government cut imports drastically to conserve shipping, established a mass construction program of standardized cargo vessels, and seized interned German vessels and a few others of foreign registry; but British vessels still had to handle much of the traffic.

Changes in the Army High Command

As expansion and overseas deployment proceeded, the unprecedented and in some cases overwhelming demands of the situation had an inevitable impact on many of the Army's historic institutions. The most marked and at the same time of the most import for the future was on the organization of the General Staff and the authority of the Chief of Staff.

The office of the Chief of Staff had yet to find an assertive incumbent until early in March 1918, when the War Department brought back from France Pershing's artillery commander, Maj. Gen. Peyton C. March. In recalling March, the Secretary of War, Newton D. Baker, had reorganization of the General Staff specifically in mind, for a recent Senate investigation of quartermaster, supply, and transportation problems had focused attention on deficiencies that the early months of expansion had revealed.

In the Overman Act, passed by the Congress in May 1918, which granted the President broad authority to reorganize executive agencies during the war emergency, March obtained the tool needed to establish at long last General Staff authority over the heretofore powerful bureau chiefs. Given the additional authority of the rank of full general, March decreed that these chiefs were subordinate to the General Staff and were to report to the Secretary of War only through the Chief of Staff.

Drastically reorganizing the General Staff, March created four main divisions: Operations; Military Intelligence; Purchase, Storage, and Traffic; and War Plans. The titles fairly well explained the functions, except that Operations and War Plans shared the functions of the former War College Division and that Purchase, Storage, and Traffic provided the Army for the first time a central control over logistics. Under this reorganization, the total military and civilian strength of the General Staff increased to just over a thousand.

Lest there remain any room for misinterpreting the role of the Chief of Staff, March, with Secretary Baker's support, issued general orders spelling out the authority in specific terms. The order read, in part:

The Chief of Staff by law (Act of May 12, 1917) takes rank and precedence over all officers of the Army, and by virtue of that position and by authority of and in the name of the Secretary of War he issues such orders as will insure that the policies of the War Department are harmoniously executed by the several corps, bureaus, and other agencies of the Military Establishment and that the Army program is carried out speedily and efficiently.

That, in theory, completed at last the reform of the General Staff that Elihu Root had started, but in practice, an obstacle remained in the person of the field commander in France, General Pershing, who had been promoted to four-star rank ahead of March. Pershing had gone to France with an almost total authority to do the job as he saw it, and, despite technical subordination to March, Pershing resisted any effort by the Chief of Staff to assert authority over his command. The Secretary of War on a number of occasions had to act as arbiter between the two and, in matters related to the American Expeditionary Forces, usually acceded to Pershing's will rather than March's.

The final evolvement of the Chief of Staff as the incontestably supreme military chief of the Army would have to await Pershing's return and his assumption of the job himself, yet Peyton C. March stood, along with Root, as a primary architect of the position.

CHAPTER 18

World War I: The U.S. Army Overseas

Included in the orders General Pershing received from the Secretary of War before he left for France was a stipulation "to cooperate with the forces of the other countries . . . but in so doing the underlying idea must be kept in view that the forces of the United States are a separate and distinct component of the combined forces, the identity of which must be preserved." This was a requirement that influenced many of Pershing's early decisions in regard to the American Expeditionary Forces and was to be for long months a recurring source of contention between Pershing and Allied commanders who were nearing the end of their manpower resources.

Training and Organizing U.S. Troops

For assembling American troops, Pershing chose the region southeast of Paris. Since the British were committed to that part of the front north of Paris and since the French had achieved their greatest concentration in protection of the capital, they had tied up the Channel ports and the railroads north and northeast of Paris. By locating southeast of the city, U.S. forces would be close to the Lorraine portion of the front, a likely spot for committing an independent American force. The French had few troops there and important objectives lay within reasonable striking distance—coal and iron mines and railroads vital to the Germans. This part of the front could be served by the ports of southern and southwestern France and by rail lines less committed to French and British requirements. Pershing set up his headquarters near the source of the Marne in Chaumont.

To Pershing, the training not only of the hastily assembled 1st Division but also of the others that followed before the end of 1917 (the 2d—half Regular Army, half Marine; 26th—New England National Guard; and 42d—called the "Rainbow Division" because it was a composite of Guardsmen from many states) was seriously inadequate. Many of the men in these divisions were recruits, replacements for those pulled out to help train newly forming units.

Pershing devised an intensive training schedule for the 1st Division and planned to follow a similar program for the other three with the idea of withholding all four from active sectors until all were ready, whereupon, late in 1918, they might be committed as the nucleus of an independent American force. Reinforced by other units arriving in 1918, Pershing in 1919 could open an offensive aimed at victory.

For training in trench warfare, Pershing gratefully accepted the help of experienced Allied officers. He also followed the Allied system of setting up special training centers and schools to teach subjects such as gas warfare, demolitions, and the use of the hand grenade and the mortar. Yet in the belief that the French and British had become too imbued with trench warfare to the exclusion of the open maneuvers that eventually would be necessary to achieve victory, he insisted on additional training in offensive tactics, including detailed work in rifle marksmanship and use of the bayonet.

Not until late October 1917 did Pershing submit the 1st Division to trial experience in the line. One battalion at a time from each regiment spent ten days with a French division. The first U.S. Army casualties of the war resulted from this deployment when early in November the Germans staged a trench raid against the same battalion that had paraded in Paris. With a loss of 3 of their own men, the Germans killed 3 Americans and captured 11.

The cycle in the trenches completed, Pershing submitted the 1st Division to further training to correct the deficiencies observed at the front. Only in mid-January of 1918, six months after its arrival in France, was the division ready in Pershing's view to move as a unit into a quiet sector of the trenches.

General Pershing had in the meantime been setting up the staff and logistical organization for managing the growing American force. Reflecting a strong similarity to the French system, his General Staff ultimately included a chief of staff, a deputy chief, and five assistant chiefs supervising five sections: G–1 (Personnel), G–2 (Intelligence), G–3 (Operations), G–4 (Supply), and G–5 (Training). Staffs for divisions and later for corps and armies followed a similar organization, while to fill the new staff positions Pershing set up a General Staff College with a 3-month course.

To provide logistical support, Pershing created a Line of Communications under a single commander responsible directly to him. It was organized into base sections, each with one or more ports, an intermediate section for storage and classification of supplies, and an advanced section for distribution to the zone of operations. After American units entered combat, depots in the advanced section made up supplies for each division in trains which moved to division railheads, whence the divisions moved the supplies to the front in wagons and trucks. The designation Line of Communications was later changed to Services of Supply under command of Pershing's original chief of staff, Maj. Gen. James G. Harbord.

Pressure From French and British

Carrying out the comprehensive training program required all the determination at Pershing's disposal, for once the first exultation accompanying the arrival of American troops in France had predictably passed, practical French and British commanders saw that it would be a long time before independent American units could assume any appreciable portion of the combat burden. They began to insist almost immediately that American soldiers be fed into Allied divisions as replacements.

The Allies felt their request was logical. They had the experienced commanders and units, the necessary artillery, aviation, and tank support, but they lacked men. The American situation was the reverse. Their way, they argued, the power of the American soldier could be quickly brought to bear and hasten the victory. Yet this was reckoning without a sense of national pride that existed among both the soldiers themselves and the American people.

Pershing refused.

Although the Allied governments tried to bypass Pershing by going directly to Washington, they found the Secretary of War and the President firmly behind their field commander. When General Tasker H. Bliss, who had served briefly as the U.S. Army Chief of Staff, was sent as the American representative to the Supreme War Council, Allied governments tried this channel to break Pershing's adamant resolve; but although Bliss was inclined to be more conciliatory than Pershing, he yielded nothing on the principle of a separate American force.

The issue arose again early in 1918 when the British offered to provide the shipping to transport 150 battalions of infantry, which would be used to fill out British divisions that because of the manpower shortage had been reduced from 12 battalions of infantry to 9. After four or five months, according to the British plan, Pershing might withdraw the battalions to form them into American divisions.

This too Pershing refused, but well aware that a lack of ships was slowing the American build-up, he suggested that the British transport divisions instead. Because the same shipping that could move 150 infantry battalions could accommodate only about 3 divisions, which would mean only 36 infantry battalions, the British declined, but eventually they agreed to transport 6 divisions without equipment on the condition that Pershing outfit and train them in the British zone. Ten divisions would eventually arrive under this program.

The matter of a separate American force stood for the moment with Pershing still in unqualified control, yet in view of Allied persistence and of pending developments at the front the question was bound to arise again and again.

The German Offensive, March 1918

As the year 1918 opened, two more U.S. divisions were destined for early arrival in France, but if Pershing kept to his training schedule the American presence was a long way from assertion on the battlefield. The original excitement among the French and British over America's entry into the war had given way to renewed pessimism, for the Allied position appeared less favorable than at any time since the opening battle of the Marne. To the weary French and British, President Wilson's January proclamation of a 14-point peace proposal, however statesmanlike, appeared too idealistic.

So perturbed by the shocking losses of Passchendaele was the British Prime Minister, Lloyd George, that he withheld replacements to assure that his field commander, Sir Douglas Haig, would have to remain on the defensive. Nor could a French Army not yet fully recovered from the mutinies be expected to swing to the attack. The Allies appeared to have no alternative for 1918 but to hold on grimly until enough American troops arrived to assure the numerical superiority essential to victory.

Aside from the calamities of the Nivelle offensive, Passchendaele, and Caporetto, the Allies faced the prospect of sharply increased German numbers made available by the Russian defection. The number of German divisions shifted from east to west would have been even greater had the new Bolshevik government not reneged on its decision to get out of the war and had the Germans not blundered in response. The Bolsheviks had come to Brest-Litovsk in December 1917 to talk only of a peace that would restore Russia's prewar boundaries and impose no indemnities, a concept that strained German credulity. What came of the first encounter at Brest-Litovsk was neither peace nor war but a bizarre new confrontation between Germany and Russia that still tied down eighty German divisions.

Russia, said the Bolsheviks, would not make peace; neither would its forces continue the war even if the Germans still fought. In response, the German armies in the east began in February 1918 to march deeper into Russia. They marched on even after the Bolsheviks at last agreed to real peace, only to become involved eventually in guerrilla warfare against their rear. Throughout the spring and summer of 1918 a million Germans that might have been decisive on the Western Front remained embroiled in Russia.

Within Germany, by the start of 1918, the duo of Hindenburg and Ludendorff had gradually accumulated almost dictatorial powers, with Ludendorff dominating more than ever. They decided that they had to strike early in 1918 in a final grand effort to achieve victory in the west before American manpower could be brought to bear. Germany, possibly more than France and Britain, was hurting gravely from the long war: on the home front, starvation was becoming a stark reality, and the previous summer there had been Marxist-inspired mutinies in the German Navy. The replacements going to German divisions were old men and boys.

By recalling divisions from Italy and some from the east, Ludendorff managed to assemble over 3,500,000 men on the Western Front, including 192 divisions. He planned to attack in early spring with 62 divisions along the Somme against the British, whose armies had little space for recoil before they would find themselves with their backs on the Channel. Having split the British and French, he then would turn to defeat the French. (*Map 39*)

For success Ludendorff counted on numerical superiority (4 to 1), surprise, and the first mass application of new tactics developed originally in the east by Lt. Gen. Oscar von Hutier. The so-called "Hutier tactics" involved a relatively short (several hours) but intensive artillery preparation, heavy on gas and smoke, followed by a rolling barrage creeping ahead of the infantry at a predetermined rate. Organized in small battle groups built around a light machine gun, the infantry infiltrated to cut off strongpoints rather than assault them, leaving that task to others who came behind. The enemy's forward positions ruptured, the infantry advanced swiftly to overrun the enemy artillery and break into the clear. In both these phases, light artillery was attached to assault battalions, a tactical use of horse-drawn field pieces heretofore considered suicidal in trench warfare.

The new tactics put a premium on courage, stamina, initiative, and co-ordination, qualities which, for lack of time, the Germans could instill in only about two dozen specially selected divisions. These were pulled from the line, filled out with men from other divisions, and put through an intensive training program.

Despite elaborate efforts to achieve surprise, a new confidence radiating from Berlin and intelligence gathered from prisoners at the front made it clear to the Allies that the Germans were readying a major offensive. The British even determined the general strength, place, and finally the date of the attack, and they had a strong indication of the tactics the Germans would employ. But Haig, short of reserves, could do little in advance to prepare to counter the blow,

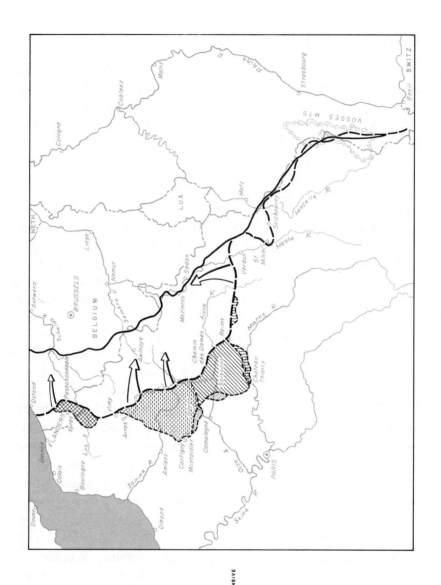

WESTERN FRONT
20 Mar – 11 Nov 1918

FRONT LINE, 20 MAR
GERMAN AMIENS OFFENSIVE
GERMAN LYS OFFENSIVE
GERMAN AISNE OFFENSIVE
GERMAN NOYON – MONTDIDIER OFFENSIVE
ALLIED OFFENSIVE, SEP – NOV
FRONT LINE, 11 NOV

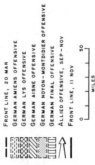

0   50
MILES

MAP 39

while the French High Command refused to believe that if Ludendorff intended a decisive offensive he would strike the British rather than the French.

The big blow came on March 21 in a fog with the main effort against the British right wing. When night fell, the Germans had achieved a penetration along a 50-mile front and were pointing toward Amiens, a communications hub on the Somme that in German hands would effectively split the French and British armies. The only question remaining was, did Ludendorff have the means to exploit his success.

If Ludendorff's success or failure depended on early commitment of Allied reserves, he had little cause for concern. Despite a mutual pledge by Haig and Pétain to go to each other's aid in event of crisis, so imbued was Pétain with the belief that the Germans were bound to strike a harder blow against the French that he was slow to send help. Although he gradually dispatched six divisions to the south flank of the penetration, these acted less to stem the German tide than to screen against any German turn toward Paris.

Ludendorff nevertheless was running into trouble. To broaden the penetration at the northern shoulder, he threw in 20 more divisions; but these were untrained in the Hutier tactics and failed to pierce a solid British defense. The long-fought-over terrain along the Somme slowed the advance of the main effort, and a hastily created British defensive force composed mainly of rear-echelon service troops occupied old trenches east of Amiens to halt the advance on that critical city. The German divisions in the lead were becoming exhausted, and supplies failed to get forward.

By the end of March, Ludendorff's offensive had bogged down. He had achieved a brilliant tactical victory—an advance of forty miles in eight days, 70,000 prisoners, 200,000 other Allied casualties; but strategically the result was empty. He had failed either to destroy the British armies or to separate them from the French, and he had taken as many casualties as he had inflicted, most of them in the highly trained shock divisions, losses he could not replace.

Unity of Command

A combination of the crisis and of Pétain's dilatory response to Haig's pleas for help also harmed German chances of ultimate victory. Although Haig himself had vitiated an earlier attempt to create a 30-division reserve for the Supreme War Council by pleading inability to spare his quota, he was so shaken by the crisis on the Somme that he volunteered to subordinate British troops around Amiens to a Frenchman, General (later Marshal of France) Ferdinand Foch. As an instructor in prewar years at the École de Guerre, Foch had established a reputation as a military theorist and earlier in the war had successfully co-ordinated British, French, and Belgian operations in Flanders. Out of this agreement to subordinate all troops around the Amiens salient to Foch grew a broader understanding to subordinate, first, all British and French troops on the Western Front, then, later, all Allied forces.

The Allies at last had a unified command, even though they qualified it with weakening provisos: one that Foch had only "strategic direction" while "tactical control" remained with national commanders, another that each national commander could appeal a decision of the supreme commander to his home government. These qualifications, in theory, sharply diminished Foch's authority; but through military acumen, determination, and force of personality, Foch would make the arrangement work.

The Lys Offensive, April 1918

Ludendorff, meanwhile, clung to a belief that with another blow he could shatter the British armies. This time he chose a point a few miles north of the Amiens salient along the Lys River in Flanders, close by the scene of the bloody British offensive known as Passchendaele. Now he had 35 divisions.

Following an intensive bombardment, mainly with gas shells, eight German divisions attacked early on April 9 along the south bank of the Lys and quickly took advantage of the collapse of a Portuguese division to plunge five miles past the last of the trenches into open country. The next day other divisions attacking along the north bank of the Lys also achieved a penetration.

By the fourth day of the attack, the British were in serious danger. Putting the new unified command to a test, Field Marshal Haig called on Foch for help, but having long observed the tenacity of the British soldier on defense, Foch was convinced Haig could hold without involving reserves that could be better saved for a counteroffensive once the Germans had exhausted their resources. Although Haig fumed, Foch would agree to send only a few divisions.

Haig at that point issued what became known as his "backs to the wall" order: "There is no other course open to us but to fight it out. . . . With our backs to the wall and believing in the justice of our cause, each one of us must fight on to the end."

As the British soldier responded nobly, hungry German troops often slowed their attack to forage for food. In the end, Ludendorff had no choice but to call off the offensive. As April drew to a close, he held another vulnerable salient that included the Passchendaele Ridge but little else of tactical importance, this at a cost to the British of 305,000 casualties of all types but to the Germans even more, 350,000.

The first major action involving an American division had developed in the meantime far from the flaming Somme and Lys on a quiet sector in Lorraine, not far from the town of St. Mihiel. Here the 26th Division on April 20 came under a heavy bombardment, followed by a German attack in regimental strength aimed at seizing the village of Seicheprey. Boxing in the defenders with artillery barrages, the Germans took the village, only to lose it in the afternoon to a U.S. counterattack. The Germans held on to a nearby wood through the day, but American riflemen, cut off and scattered early in the fighting, regrouped to regain their positions the next day. The Germans left behind 160 dead, but they took 136 prisoners and inflicted 634 casualties.

During these weeks, General Pershing came under renewed pressure from the British and French to make up losses in Allied divisions with individual American replacements. While Pershing at the height of the crisis on the Somme had offered to place U.S. troops at Foch's disposal, he had been thinking only of the existing crisis while remaining faithful in the long run to the concept of an autonomous American army. Long and sometimes tempestuous were the arguments, voluminous the cables between Allied capitals, but in the end Pershing would go only so far as to agree that infantry and engineers of the divisions being transported in British shipping might be brought to France ahead of their artillery. Allied commanders, including Foch, finally endorsed the principle of forming as soon as possible an independent American force.

The Aisne Offensive, May 1918

As these arguments proceeded, the front was for a few weeks relatively quiet. It was a quiet before a storm, for Ludendorff was determined to persist in his struggle in Flanders to pin the British armies against the Channel.

To draw off Allied reserves from Flanders, Ludendorff decided on a diversionary attack against the Chemin des Dames, an elongated, commanding ridgeline northeast of Paris covering Soissons. Although this was the sector where Pétain had feared attack in March, with no attack forthcoming he had progressively thinned the defense. So imbued with the natural strength of the position was the local commander that he had neglected to erect a defense in depth, concentrating his men instead on the forward slope of the Chemin des Dames. In the face of heavy bombardment combined with the Hutier tactics, he was inviting disaster.

It was not long in coming. Although forewarned by an American intelligence analysis that an attack was in the offing, the French refused to heed the signs until the day before the attack was to begin. All the French troops could do in the time remaining was to stand warily at their posts while Foch belatedly began moving reserves.

With 17 divisions forward and 13 in follow-up reserve, the Germans attacked early on May 27 behind a barrage by close to 5,000 guns. German infantry plunged quickly over and beyond the Chemin des Dames, jumping the Aisne and Vesle Rivers, and gaining up to 20 miles in the first 24 hours.

Although this was to have been but a diversionary attack, Ludendorff was too elated by the breakthrough, too tempted by the open road to Paris to bring it to a halt. Three days later, on the last day of May, his troops would reach the Marne at Château-Thierry, less than fifty miles from the French capital, almost as close as Moltke had come in 1914.

Under pressure of this new crisis, General Pershing again went to Foch, this time to offer 5 American divisions to be used along the Marne as Foch deemed necessary. By the night of May 31, the machine gun battalion of the 3d Division, moved up swiftly in trucks, was in position to help French troops hold the bridge site over the Marne at Château-Thierry, and the rest of the division was on the way to help hold the river line. The next day the 2d Division (which included a Marine brigade) took up defensive positions north of the Marne and west of Château-Thierry astride the main highway to Paris.

Despair gripped not only the French stragglers falling back from the front but also the Allied High Command. What they could not know was that again Ludendorff was overextended, that he could strike in earnest for Paris only after broadening the wings of his narrow salient and bringing up supplies and reserves.

For two days Ludendorff's advance troops beat vainly against a hastily dug American line. At last they desisted, but the infantrymen and marines of the 2d Division would give them no rest. Beginning on June 6, the 2d Division attacked in costly but intrepid strikes against Belleau Wood and the villages of Bouresches and Vaux. Although this fighting would continue for three weeks, it was apparent from the first that the sudden, dramatic introduction of a new force had brought Ludendorff's thrust to a halt. For the Americans it was a costly debut—9,777 casualties, including 1,811 dead—but the moral effect on both sides was great.

The moral effect was all the more pronounced because of another action that antedated the 2d Division's achievement, the first offensive by an American division in the war. It began as a preliminary to a planned French counterattack against the Amiens salient, a counterattack that because of Ludendorff's break-through to the Marne failed to come off. It was an attack by the 1st Division against the village of Cantigny on commanding ground near the tip of the salient.

Supported by American and French artillery and by French tanks, one regiment took the village in a swift maneuver early on May 28, then held on grimly as counterattack followed counterattack into the next day. The Americans lost 1,607 men, including 199 killed, but in the process they achieved a victory presaging greater events to follow.

The German Offensive, June 1918

Conscious of this new force entering the battle, conscious too of the necessity to maintain the initiative if ever the British armies were to be broken, Ludendorff wanted to pull back from the highly vulnerable Marne salient, but the effect on German morale would have been too adverse. Denied use of these troops for renewing the offensive against the British in Flanders, he decided on still another diversionary attack. By taking ground that might serve as a buffer for a railroad passing through Soissons, Ludendorff would improve supply into the Marne salient and at the same time pose a new threat to Paris that would, he hoped, pull Allied reserves from Flanders.

Ludendorff on June 9 sent one army westward from Soissons, another southward from the south flank of the Amiens salient between the towns of Noyon and Montdidier. As the two thrusts joined, they would merge the Amiens and Marne salients into one big, less vulnerable bulge in the line and release divisions to move to Flanders.

Yet this time there was no surprise and this time the French were ready with a defense in depth. They held the Germans to a tortuous advance of nine miles, then stopped them with counterattacks. By the fifth day, the attack had run its course.

A Growing American Force

As a temporary lull settled over the front, General Pershing on July 4 announced that a million Americans had arrived in France. Nine divisions had had some combat experience, mainly in quiet sectors; 2 others were completing their training; and 8 more had recently arrived. The total was 19, each one double the size of an Allied or German division.

In June Pershing had created three corps headquarters. The I Corps under Maj. Gen. Hunter Liggett first took responsibility for a sector near Château-

Thierry, while the II Corps under Maj. Gen. George W. Read controlled the 27th and 30th Divisions that were destined to fight through the rest of the war with the British. The III Corps under Maj. Gen. Robert L. Bullard had yet to enter the line.

With 250,000 U.S. troops arriving every month, the effect of the American presence on Allied troops and the French population was stimulating, electric. Winston Churchill saw it this way:

> The impression made upon the hard-pressed French by this seemingly inexhaustible flood of gleaming youth in its first maturity of health and vigour was prodigious. None were under twenty, and few over thirty. As crammed in their lorries they clattered along the roads, singing the songs of a new world at the tops of their voices, burning to reach the bloody field, the French Headquarters were thrilled with the impulse of new life. . . . Half trained, half organized, with only their courage, their numbers and their magnificent youth behind their weapons, they were to buy their experience at a bitter price. But this they were quite ready to do.

For all the influx of new strength, no one yet saw any quick ending of the war, any indication that the Germans might have only one more offensive left in them.

The Last German Offensive, July 1918

The meager gains of Ludendorff's diversionary attack in June having failed either to secure the railroad at Soissons or to draw Allied reserves from Flanders, Ludendorff planned yet another diversionary attack before returning to the offensive in Flanders. A month in preparation, the new offensive began on July 15, one army driving southeast from the Marne salient, another attacking south from positions east of the city of Reims, a total of 52 divisions. Meeting on the Marine, the two armies were to cut a sizable segment from the Allied line and in the process solve the supply problem in the Marne salient by taking the railroads at Reims.

Ludendorff called this the *Friedensturm*—Peace Offensive. That was a mistake, for should failure occur in an offensive associated with such a grandiose aim, the German soldier would be in no condition to recover from the despair that was bound to follow. The slackening of discipline among troops too long denied all but the barest necessities had first emerged in the Lys offensive, but it had become even more apparent during the drive to the Marne as many men deserted the battle to loot wine cellars in the champagne country around Soissons. Weak from malnutrition, the soldiers were peculiarly susceptible to an influenza epidemic that swept the trenches in June and was to keep recurring into November. On the eve of each new offensive, hundreds were deserting to the enemy.

A wave of desertions combined with information gleaned from aerial photographs, observation posts, and patrols told the French what was coming, when, and where. East of Reims, the French commander, whose troops included the 42d U.S. Division, elected to pull the bulk of his men from the forward trenches, leaving only outposts in what was known as a "sacrifice line." While the vacated positions absorbed the German artillery bombardment, the French laid down a counterbarrage. As German troops battered by shellfire neared the "sacrifice line," French and American troops fell back to an intermediate position. After repeating the delaying tactics, French and Americans again withdrew, this time to a main line of resistance. At this third line they held. By noon of the first day the issue was no longer in doubt.

Anxious to deny any German foothold across the Marne, the French opposite the other prong of the German attack had opted against these tactics. Here German gains were greater—up to four miles beyond the Marne at some points—and a French division, occupying a re-entrant formed by a bend in the river, folded, leaving four attached American companies of the 28th Division in a desperate plight. Most of these men were killed or captured. Yet the 3d Division on the French left held, its 38th Infantry, beset on three sides, executing such a steadfast defense that the regiment earned a nickname, "Rock of the Marne."

By noon of the second day, Ludendorff recognized that this prong of his attack also had been blunted. He called off the offensive.

Allied Counteroffensive

Even as the Germans were preparing what turned out to be their last offensive, General Foch had been assembling Allied divisions to launch a counteroffensive directed at first toward a limited objective—cutting the highway leading from Soissons to Château-Thierry, the main supply route of German troops in the Marne salient—but with the certainty that, if successful, the attack would be extended to erase the entire salient. In the forefront of the attack were two U.S. divisions—the 1st and 2d—operating under a French corps command.

A heavy rain fell as the troops moved to their jump-off positions the night of July 17, providential, as it turned out, since it helped conceal Allied preparations. After only a short but intensive artillery preparation early on the 18th, Allied infantry moved to the attack from near Soissons in the north to Château-Thierry in the south. In the corps with U.S. divisions, 350 French tanks early

MEN OF THE 26TH DIVISION NEAR CHÂTEAU-THIERRY, *July 1918.*

took the lead. When night fell, the two armies had advanced in some places up to five miles.

Although these two U.S. divisions were soon relieved by French and British units, the drive continued and expanded to the east, bringing in the 3d, 4th, 26th, and 28th Divisions and eventually the 32d, 42d, and 77th Divisions, and headquarters of the I and III Corps. The Germans began abandoning their Marne salient, though deliberately and in good order, retiring to successive defensive positions all the way to the Vesle River with the Chemin des Dames at their backs.

A Separate American Army

As the Allied drive came to a halt at the end of the first week of August, new hope of victory stirred in the ranks. The drive had carried no more than 20 miles, but the results were infinitely more important than the amount of territory regained. The counteroffensive had eliminated the threat to Paris, spoiled Ludendorff's cherished ambition of striking a deathblow in Flanders, and so dimmed German chances of victory that even Ludendorff could no longer hope for more than a stalemate. Furthermore, the initiative had passed to the Allies, whose fresh force had proven beyond doubt (though at a cost of 50,000 casualties) its ability on the offensive. In the bid to win before the Americans could intervene in force, Ludendorff had failed.

As this counteroffensive (sometimes called, in conjunction with the last German offensive, the Second Battle of the Marne) neared an end, General Pershing pressed his case for an independent American army and a separate

AMERICAN MILITARY POLICE PATROLLING A ROAD *near Château-Thierry.*

sector of the front. Foch was sympathetic, for a separate American force fitted in with plans he was formulating to eliminate three other German-held salients on the front. British and French together were to reduce the Amiens salient, then the British would erase the Lys salient while the Americans eliminated another salient in Lorraine that had stood for four years and took its name from a town at the tip, St. Mihiel.

With Pershing himself as commander, headquarters of the First Army officially opened on August 10. The new command encompassed the I and III Corps and 19 U.S. divisions.

As demonstrated earlier in making American units available to Allied armies, Pershing for all his adamant resolve to create an independent American force never objected to allowing some U.S. divisions to fight under Allied command; he objected instead to the use of American troops as individual replacements or in small increments to fill out depleted Allied units. Even as he formed the First Army he left the II Corps and its two divisions with the British, while he allowed several other divisions to serve under French command.

The one division whose employment violated Pershing's principle was the 93d, which had only infantry regiments without trains or artillery. This was a Negro division, one of only two organized and sent to France during the war, although thousands of other Negroes served overseas in the Services of Supply. The 93d's regiments were assigned to the French, reorganized according to French tables, and used as integral parts of French divisions. The other Negro division, the 92d, served in the First Army.

The Somme Offensive

As Pershing was forming the First Army, French and British armies under Haig launched converging attacks from the northwest and southwest against the Amiens salient. They achieved as much surprise as had the Germans against the Chemin des Dames. Using 300 tanks in the lead, ten British divisions, including Australians and Canadians, scored a swift breakthrough, brushing aside German units in rout, gaining seven miles in the first few hours, and making of August 8, in Ludendorff's words, a "black day" for the German Army.

Yet the slow, ponderous tanks could not long sustain such a pace, and horse cavalry was of no use when the enemy stiffened. Coming against a strong German stand in old trenches dating from 1915, Haig paused, shifted the emphasis of his attack farther north, then in a methodical campaign gradually pushed the Germans back. By the end of August the Germans were retiring into the positions whence they had begun their big March offensive, the Hindenburg Line. The Amiens salient, like that on the Marne, was a thing of the past. Meanwhile, other British units helped by the U.S. II Corps with the 27th and 30th Divisions had almost finished erasing the Lys salient.

On the German side, the events of 8 August had cast a pall over the High Command. "We have nearly reached the limit of our power to resist," said Hindenburg. "The war must be ended." When Ludendorff agreed, Wilhelm II instructed his Foreign Secretary to find a way out of the war, but the underlying idea was to retain as much as possible of the territory that the German armies had conquered. Under such a condition, there was little real hope for peace.

The St. Mihiel Offensive

As the British drive progressed, General Pershing and his staff shifted divisions to Lorraine. Their goal was to push beyond the St. Mihiel salient to seize Metz or at least to cut the highway running from Metz all the way to Antwerp, the enemy's main line of lateral communications. When Foch saw the plan, he was so enthusiastic that he increased the French participation from 4 to 10 divisions.

Foch's endorsement of the American plan preceded the British success in pushing the Germans into the Hindenburg Line. Planning an early attack along the Somme to break that line, Marshal Haig suggested to Foch that instead of attacking toward Metz the Americans should be employed from

FRENCH TANKS RETURNING FROM THE FRONT

positions west of Verdun to attack northward toward Mézières along the French-Belgian frontier northeast of Reims. Such an attack would serve not only to cut the enemy's railroad but also to converge with the British attack.

Seeing in Haig's proposal a possibility of victory before the year was out, Foch endorsed the idea. Presenting it to General Pershing, he directed that once the St. Mihiel salient was eliminated the American objective should be changed from Metz to Mézières. In the drive on Mézières, Foch was to employ two armies, one wholly American under Pershing, the other Franco-American under French command.

Foch's proposal for a Franco-American army under French command appeared to Pershing as a threat to the long-sought independent American force which he had so recently achieved. He insisted that, while the American army "will fight wherever you may decide, it will not fight except as an independent American army." Foch declined to press the issue.

Reducing the scope of the attack on the St. Mihiel salient to nine U.S. and five French divisions, Pershing and his staff began to prepare two offensives to be mounted within 23 days in areas 40 miles apart. That was something no single army had yet attempted on the Western Front.

The Germans, fortunately, were to make the task easier. Conscious of the vulnerability of the St. Mihiel salient and of a major Allied offensive in the making, they began to pull out of the salient two days before Pershing planned to attack.

Under Pershing's plan, a French corps was to press the tip of the salient while the V Corps under Maj. Gen. George H. Cameron, in its first combat action, hit the west flank. Meanwhile General Liggett's I Corps and the IV Corps under Maj. Gen. Joseph T. Dickman, also new in the line, was to attack the south flank, the two American thrusts to meet in the center of the salient at the town of Vigneulles. French and British provided the bulk of the artillery support—3,000 guns—while the only tanks available were 267 light French Renaults. Although the French furnished many of the tank crews, others were Americans of the 304th Tank Brigade, commanded by Lt. Col. George S. Patton, Jr. An Allied air force controlled by an exponent of air power, Col. William Mitchell, consisted of almost 1,500 planes (600 piloted by Americans), the largest concentration of aircraft yet assembled.

Following a four-hour artillery bombardment, the tank-infantry advance began before daylight on September 12. Most of the tanks fell victim early to mechanical failure or mud, but they were hardly needed. Resistance was from the first surprisingly moderate, particularly on the southern flank where the Germans had already thinned their forward troops as a step in the general withdrawal. By nightfall of the first day a gap of only ten miles separated the two converging American forces.

When Pershing learned that roads leading out of the salient were filled with withdrawing Germans, he urged continued attack through the night to block all escape routes. A regiment of the 26th Division pushed swiftly from the west to enter Vigneulles two hours after midnight, there to be joined soon after drawn by a regiment of the 1st Division.

This first victory of the war by an American army netted 15,000 prisoners at a cost of only 7,000 casualties. It was so easy that some have referred to it as the action in which the Americans relieved the Germans, but the observation fails to take into account that the Germans had begun to pull back because they dreaded what was coming.

The Meuse-Argonne Offensive

Even as Pershing had been preparing and launching this first big American attack, Foch's original plan had been growing by bounds. No longer was the offensive to be confined to a British strike along the Somme and an American drive on Mézières. The new plan also included a Belgian-British-French attack along the Lys and French attacks in between British and Americans. It was to be a grand assault all along the front—said Foch: "Tout le monde à la bataille!". The aim was to cut the enemy's rail line at Mézières and Aulnoye, the latter in front of the British, and thereby force the Germans to retire inside their frontier before winter set in. For the offensive Foch had 220 divisions—160 in line, 60 in reserve. They included 42 of the big American divisions, although some of these had only recently arrived and Pershing would be forced to cannibalize others to obtain replacements. Ten American divisions would still serve with British and French armies.

Assisted by the French Fourth Army on the left, the American attack was to begin first, on September 26. It posed a tremendous logistical effort involving rapid transfer of some 800,000 men, 200,000 French moving out of the new American sector west of Verdun, and 600,000 Americans moving in. That it was completed in secrecy and in time for the jump-off was attributable in large measure to the planning of a young officer on Pershing's staff, Col. George C. Marshall. Again the British and French furnished most of the artillery and tanks (190 French lights) and some of the 800 aircraft supporting the attack.

The terrain over which the advance was to pass was studded with natural and man-made obstacles. From high ground east of the Meuse River, which formed the right boundary for the attack, and from densely wooded high ground of the Argonne Forest in the left of the attack zone, German eyes could look down on much of the battlefield; and in the center, between the forest and the river, the Germans held a hogback ridge replete with fortified spurs and stone-walled villages. The Germans had established three lines with trenches, barbed wire, deep dugouts, and concrete fighting posts, while a fourth was under construction farther back. Particularly formidable were strongpoints at Montfaucon, Cunel, and Barricourt.

In a sector approximately twenty miles wide, Pershing massed three corps, each to employ two divisions forward, one in reserve. With a superiority in men of 8 to 1, he hoped to make the ten miles through the first three German positions in one sustained drive.

The infantry began to advance before daylight after a 3-hour artillery bombardment. Achieving surprise, they caught the Germans with only four divisions in the line. General Bullard's III Corps on the right pushed five miles through both the first and second German positions, but General Cameron's V Corps in the center ground to a halt before the bristling defenses of Montfaucon, and General Liggett's I Corps on the left could advance little more than a mile through the thick, almost trackless Argonne Forest.

During the next few days, the troops plodded slowly forward, at last carrying Montfaucon and putting the V Corps through the second German line, but progress amid the trees and dank ravines of the Argonne Forest still was slow. Flanking fire from east of the Meuse and from uncleared portions of the Argonne harried units on the right and in the center. Most of the supporting tanks succumbed to the usual troubles of mud and mechanical failure. Congestion and muddy roads hampered resupply. Most serious of all was the inexperience of the troops, for having used his experienced divisions in the St. Mihiel salient Pershing had had to withhold them from the first assault. Units got lost, message traffic broke down, some commanders failed.

Any hope that an advance by the French Fourth Army on the left might unhinge the Germans in front of the U.S. troops went for naught, for the French were making no more rapid gains. As September came to an end, Pershing had no choice but to pause to reorganize.

Elsewhere on the Western Front, progress was, with one exception, not much more encouraging. The Belgian-French-British effort on the Lys bogged down in rain and mud, as had every offensive in that region, while the French in the center of the Allied line were not to begin their attack until British and Americans on their flanks had driven deep enough to threaten the Germans opposite them with entrapment. Only the British along the Somme provided any indication of decisive success, scoring a deep penetration of the Hindenburg Line with the help of the 27th and 30th Divisions of the U.S. II Corps. The penetration was soon expanded to create a gap all the way through the fortifications, but the effort left British troops temporarily spent.

Despite the disappointing progress of the grand offensive from an Allied viewpoint, it was enough to start a collapse within the German High Command. On September 28, Ludendorff mused at such length on the miseries besetting him that he worked himself into a rage, foamed at the mouth, and fell to the floor. That evening he called on Hindenburg. The situation, the two agreed, was infinitely worse than in August when they had first urged the kaiser to seek peace, advice that had produced no results. They had no alternative now but to agree to surrender all conquered territory in the west and try to negotiate a peace on the basis of President Wilson's Fourteen Points.

On October 4 the German chancellor cabled Wilson asking for an armistice. Without informing the Allied governments, Wilson answered with a request for clarification. The German chancellor replied on October 12 that the Germans agreed to all Fourteen Points; but by this time word of the peace feeler had reached the French and British, who for their part were in no mood to accept Wilson's unilateral actions. Furthermore, Ludendorff himself had recovered from his convulsive fit, had seen that the Allied offensive had imposed no rout, and had come to believe the Germans could get terms that would allow them to withdraw behind their own frontier, reorganize their armies, and resist any peace proposals they deemed unacceptable.

Yet events were taking place that were destined to tie Ludendorff's hands and harden Wilson's resolve. Not the least of these were continued fierce German resistance and the revelation, in those areas where the Germans were forced to retire, of wanton destruction and a barbaric disregard for human life more flagrant than those excesses of 1917 when they had left behind a wasteland in retiring into the Hindenburg Line.

On the Meuse-Argonne front, Pershing's First Army renewed its offensive on October 4 after inserting experienced divisions into the line, but during the brief pause in operations Ludendorff had brought in reinforcements. The fight to clear the rest of the Argonne Forest and pierce the third German line progressed no more swiftly than before.

In the Argonne a "lost battalion" of the 77th Division was surrounded for five days before other troops could break through to free 194 survivors out of an original 600. In the Argonne, too, an American patrol took about 75 Germans by surprise and was herding them toward the rear when German machine gunners opened fire, killing and wounding 9 out of 17 in the patrol. When a German lieutenant led a charge aimed at the survivors, Pfc. Alvin C. York, a Tennessee sharpshooter, cut down 15 Germans one by one until at last surviving members of this group too surrendered. When a count could be taken, it revealed that York had captured 132 of the enemy.

To dispense with the troublesome German flanking fire from heights on the other side of the Meuse, General Pershing broadened his attack to include the east bank. To control that phase, Pershing created the Second Army under General Bullard. Relinquishing command of the First Army to General Liggett, Pershing himself moved up to the level of army group.

Despite the added strength on the east bank, the fight continued slow and costly, for Ludendorff looked on the offensive as such a threat to the vital railroad through Mézières that he eventually committed 27 of his reserve divisions to this sector. Some help developed on the left when on October 5 the U.S. 2d Division, attacking with the French, captured high ground known as Blanc Mont, prompting a slow German withdrawal before the Fourth Army back to the Aisne River. On the 10th, the I Corps finally cleared the last of the Argonne Forest, but bitter fighting continued through the rest of the month for the fortified hills between the forest and the Meuse. Not until the last day of October was the third German position broken all along the line.

The British in the meantime had renewed their offensive, driving forward inexorably as the Germans fell back grudgingly from one prepared position to another. It was in this section that much of the evidence of German destruction and barbarity was found.

At the same time, continuing activities of the U-boats also helped to crystallize Allied resolve. On the 10th, a submarine torpedoed a passenger steamer off the coast of Ireland with a loss of 300 lives. A few days later another U-boat sank an Irish mail boat taking the lives of 520 passengers, mostly women and children.

Affected by the public outcry over these incidents, President Wilson made clear in his reply to the second German note that the Allied military leaders would set the terms of the armistice, that there was no other way to deal with a government that persisted in illegal and inhumane acts. The note concluded that if the United States had to deal "with the military masters and the monarchial autocrats of Germany now, or if it is likely to have to deal with them later in regard to the international obligations of the German Empire, it must demand, not peace negotiations but surrender."

Confidence restored, Ludendorff called on his government to reject the terms; but the government was by this time listening to the voices of a disillusioned people, the noise of riots in the streets, and to the threat of Marxist revolution. On October 27 the kaiser dismissed Ludendorff, who repaired in disguise to Sweden, and events strode swiftly toward a climax. The German naval commander tried to take the High Seas Fleet to sea in a last bid for glory, but the crews mutinied and brought the ships back into port with revolutionary flags flying. Revolutionary councils formed among the soldiers in the trenches. Bulgaria in late September had already dropped out of the war; Turkey followed on October 30; Austria-Hungary on November 3. On November 6 Ludendorff's successor, General Wilhelm Groener, urged the government to conclude an armistice within three days or face chaos.

All along the front, meanwhile, the Allied armies had renewed their offensives in what became a general advance. In the far north two U.S. divisions—the 37th and 91st—fought with the Belgian-French-British force under the Belgian king. Haig's British troops entered their objective of Aulnoye on November 5, while the French armies maintained steady pressure against the German center.

Beginning on the first of November, the U.S. First Army renewed the attack with the V Corps in the center driving six miles the first day to take heights just south of the fourth German line near Barricourt. This feat assured success of the whole operation, for it prompted German withdrawal behind the Meuse. On November 5 the III Corps forced a crossing of the Meuse, and three days later American troops held high ground overlooking the city of Sedan, a few miles east of Mézières, and brought the lateral railroad under artillery fire. There the advance stopped as Marshal Foch shifted the American boundary eastward to allow the French the honor of retaking Sedan, scene of a disastrous French defeat in 1870.

The Meuse-Argonne was the greatest battle yet fought by the U.S. Army. Almost 1,250,000 American troops had participated during the course of the offensive. Casualties were high—120,000 of all types—but the results impressive. Until the last, this battle had worried German commanders most; unlike other sectors of the front, here they had little space short of a vital objective that they could afford to trade for time.

The German Surrender

Under pressure of continuing Allied attack and of public agitation at home, the Germans early on November 8 sent delegates to a railroad siding in the Compiègne Forest west of Soissons to discuss armistice terms. The next day the kaiser abdicated, fleeing to the Netherlands in exile, and the Germans proclaimed a republic.

Under terms of the armistice, the Germans were to withdraw from all occupied territory, including Alsace and Lorraine; retire all armies to the east bank of the Rhine; provide the Allies with bridgeheads beyond the Rhine; and relinquish specific amounts of military equipment that would preclude their continuing the war.

The fighting ended at the eleventh hour of the eleventh day of the eleventh month, 1918.

Men died right up to the last, but finally, after more than four grim years, it was over. Of the men of all nations in uniform, more than 8,500,000 died, and total casualties exceeded 37,500,000, a price that would forever invite criticism of the way commanders on both sides fought the war. American casualties alone totaled 320,710.

So ended the first adventure of the United States in departing from its traditional policy of noninvolvement in European affairs. That the nation could make such a decisive contribution in so short a time hardly could have been conceived in advance.

That there would be mistakes, blunders, shortcomings under such a rapid expansion and commitment was perhaps inevitable. Until mid-1918, for example, when separate replacement training camps were at last established, units both in the United States and overseas had to be broken up to provide replacements. This practice was damaging to morale and damaging too in that it sent many poorly trained men into the lines. So close did the American supply system in France come to breaking down that in the summer of 1918, under threat of intervention from Washington, Pershing had to exert special efforts to rescue it. Pershing himself was overburdened with command responsibilities—theater, line of communications, and tactical. The dependence on the Allies for air, artillery, and tank support, however inevitable in such a rapid deployment, did nothing for efficiency on the battlefield. On the home front some Americans vented their hostility on other Americans for no more valid reason than their ancestry.

Yet countless other things were done effectively. The nation handled conscription with minimum friction and without disruption of the economy. The Army expanded with almost incredible speed while still maintaining efficiency. The Navy performed invaluable service in defeating the submarine and, with British help, in getting the Army safely overseas. Although the war ended before American industry could demonstrate its full wartime potential, the record, with some exceptions, was impressive nevertheless.

Most important of all, the nation and its Army had provided a force that reached embattled Europe in time to rejuvenate flagging Allied fortunes and provide sufficient advantage to assure victory for the Allied side.

CHAPTER 19

Between World Wars

Soon after the armistice of November 1918 the War Department urged the Congress to authorize the establishment of a permanent Regular Army of nearly 600,000 and a three-month universal training system that would permit a quick expansion of this force to meet the requirements of a new major war. The Congress and American public opinion rejected these proposals. It was hard to believe that the defeat of Germany and the exhaustion of the other European powers did not guarantee that there would be no major war on land for years to come. Although the possibility of war with Japan was recognized, American leaders assumed that such a war, if it came, would be primarily naval in character. Indeed, the fundamental factor in the military policy of the United States during the next two decades was reliance on the United States Navy as the first line of national defense.

Another basic factor that determined the character of the Army between world wars was the decision of the United States not to join the League of Nations and therefore to reject participation in an active and co-operative world security system to maintain peace. The American people soon showed themselves unwilling to support an Army in being any larger than required to defend the continental United States and its overseas territories and possessions, to keep alive a knowledge of the military arts, and to train inexpensive and voluntary civilian components. Since the Army had huge stocks of matériel left over from its belated production for World War I, the principal concern of the War Department until the 1930's was manpower to fulfill these peacetime missions.

Demobilization

Planning for demobilization had begun less than a month before the armistice, since few in the United States had expected the war to end so quickly. When the fighting in Europe stopped, almost all officers and men in the Army became eligible for discharge. The War Department had to decide how to muster out these men as rapidly and equitably as possible without unduly disrupting the national economy, while at the same time maintaining an effective force for occupation and other postwar duties. It decided in favor of the traditional method of demobilization by units as the one best calculated to achieve these ends. Units in the United States were moved to thirty demobilization centers located throughout the country, so that men after processing could be discharged near their homes. Units overseas were brought back just as rapidly as shipping space could be found for them, processed through debarkation centers operated by the Transportation Service, and then sent to the demobilization centers for discharge. In practice the unit system was supplemented by a great many individual discharges and by the release of certain occupational groups, notably railroad workers and anthracite coal miners.

In the first full month of demobilization the Army released about 650,000 officers and men, and within nine months it demobilized nearly 3,250,000 without seriously disturbing the American economy. A demobilization of war industry and disposal of surplus matériel paralleled the release of men, but the War Department kept a large reserve of weapons for peacetime or new emergency use. Despite the lack of much advance planning demobilization worked reasonably well. The Army was concerned at the outset because it had no authority to enlist men to replace those discharged. A law of February 28, 1919, permitted enlistments in the Regular Army for either one or three years; and by the end of the year the active Army, reduced to a strength of about 19,000 officers and 205,000 enlisted men, was again a Regular volunteer force.

Immediate Duties

At home during 1919 and 1920 Army forces continued the guard on the border of Mexico required by revolutionary disturbances in that country. Because of the lack of National Guard forces (not yet reorganized) the active Army until the summer of 1921 also had to supply troops on numerous occasions to help suppress domestic disorders, chiefly arising out of labor disputes and race conflicts in a restless postwar America.

Abroad, a newly activated United States Third Army moved into Germany on December 1, 1918, to occupy a segment of territory between Luxembourg and the Rhine River around Coblenz. As many as nine divisions participated in the German occupation during the spring of 1919. Similarly, an Army regiment sent to Italy before the end of hostilities participated for four months in the occupation of Austria. In Germany, American troops had no unusual difficulties with the populace, and soon after the peace conference ended in May 1919 the occupation forces were rapidly reduced. They numbered about 15,000 at the beginning of 1920. After rejecting the Treaty of Versailles the United States remained technically at war with Germany until the summer of 1921, when a separate peace was signed. Thereafter, the occupying force was gradually withdrawn, and the last thousand troops left for home on January 24, 1923.

Revolutionary turmoil in Soviet Russia induced President Wilson in August 1918 to direct Army participation in expeditions of United States and Allied forces that penetrated the Murmansk-Archangel region of European Russia and into Siberia via Vladivostock. The north Russian force, containing about 5,000 American troops under British command, suffered heavy casualties while guarding war supplies and communication lines before being withdrawn in June 1919. The Siberian force of about 10,000 under Maj. Gen. William S. Graves had many trying experiences in attempting to rescue Czech troops and in curbing Japanese expansionist tendencies between August 1918 and April 1920. Together these two forces incurred about as many combat casualties as the Army expeditionary force of similar size had sustained in Cuba in 1898. After the withdrawals from Germany and Russia, the only Army forces stationed on foreign soil until 1941 were the garrison of about 1,000 maintained at Tientsin, China, from 1912 until 1938, and a force of similar strength dispatched from the Philippines to Shanghai for five months' duty in 1932. The Marine Corps rather than the Army provided the other small foreign garrisons and expeditionary forces required after World War I, particularly in the Caribbean area.

Reorganization Under the National Defense Act of 1920

After many months of careful consideration, Congress passed a sweeping amendment of the National Defense Act of 1916. The new National Defense Act of June 4, 1920, which governed the organization and regulation of the Army until 1950, has been widely acknowledged to be one of the most constructive pieces of military legislation ever adopted in the United States. It rejected the theory of an expansible Regular Army urged by Army leaders since the days of John C. Calhoun. Instead, it established the Army of the United States as an organization of three components, the professional Regular Army, the civilian National Guard, and the civilian Organized Reserves (Officers' and Enlisted Reserve Corps). Each component was to be so regulated in peacetime that it could contribute its appropriate share of troops in a war emergency. In effect the act acknowledged the actual practice of the United States throughout its history of maintaining a standing peacetime force too small to be expanded to meet the needs of a great war, and therefore necessarily of depending on a new Army of civilian soldiers for large mobilizations. In contrast to earlier practice, the training of civilian components now became a major peacetime task of the Regular Army, and principally for this reason the Army was authorized a maximum officer strength of 17,726—more than three times the actual officer strength of the Regular Army before World War I. At least half of the new permanent officers were to be chosen from among non-Regulars who had served during the war. The act also provided that officer promotions, except for doctors and chaplains, were henceforth to be made from a single list, a step that equalized opportunity for advancement throughout most of the Army. The Regular Army was authorized a maximum enlisted strength of 280,000, but the actual enlisted as well as officer strength would depend on the amount of money voted in annual appropriations.

The new defense act also authorized the Army to continue all of its arm and service branches established before 1917, and to add three new branches, the Air Service, the Chemical Warfare Service, and a Finance Department, the first two reflecting new combat techniques demonstrated in the late war. The Tank Corps of World War I, representing another new technique, was absorbed by the Infantry. The act specifically charged the War Department with mobilization planning and preparation for the event of war. It assigned the military aspects of this responsibility to the Chief of Staff and the General Staff and the planning and supervision of industrial procurement to the Assistant Secretary of War.

World War I experience both in Washington and in France had greatly strengthened the position and authority of the General Staff. When General Pershing became Chief of Staff in 1921 he reorganized the War Department General Staff on the model of his wartime General Headquarters staff in France, to include five divisions: G–1 dealing with personnel, G–2 with intelligence, G–3 with training and operations, G–4 with supply, and a new War Plans Division that dealt with strategic planning and related preparations for the event of war. It was the War Plans Division that helped to draft "color" plans for the event of war with individual nations (as ORANGE, for war with Japan), and it was also planned that the staff of the War Plans Division would provide the nucleus for any new wartime General Headquarters established to direct operations. The General Staff divisions assisted the Chief of Staff in his supervision of the military branches of the War Department and of the field forces. The principal organizational change thereafter in the 1920's came in 1926 with the establishment of the Air Corps as an equal combat arm and with provision for its enlargement and modernization.

The field forces in the continental United States were put under the command and administration of nine corps areas approximately equal in population, and those overseas in Panama, Hawaii, and the Philippines under departments with similar authority. The division rather than the regiment became the basic Army unit, especially in mobilization planning, and each corps area was allocated 6 infantry divisions—1 Regular Army, 2 National Guard, and 3 Reserve. In addition, a cavalry division patrolled the Mexican border, and in Pacific outposts Army mobile units were organized as separate Hawaiian and Philippine Divisions. The defense act had contemplated a higher organization of divisions into corps and armies, but no such tactical organizations existed in fact for many years.

Education for and within the Army between world wars received far greater attention than ever before. This situation reflected the emphasis in the National Defense Act on preparedness in peacetime as well as the increasing complexity of modern war. The United States Military Academy and the Reserve Officers' Training Corps program furnished most of the basic schooling for new officers. Thirty-one special service schools provided branch training. These branch schools trained officers and enlisted men of the civilian components besides those of the Regular Army, and furnished training through extension courses as well as on location. Three general service schools provided the capstone of the Army educational system. The oldest, located at Fort Leavenworth, Kansas, and known after 1928 as the Command and General Staff School, provided officers with the requisite training for divisional command and General Staff positions. In Washington the Army War College and, after 1924, the Army Industrial College trained senior officers of demonstrated ability for the most responsible command and staff positions. In establishing the Industrial College the Army recognized the high importance of logistical training for the conduct of modern warfare.

Regular Army Strength and Support

When the National Defense Act was adopted in June 1920, the Regular Army numbered about 200,000—about two-thirds the maximum strength authorized in the act. In January 1921 Congress directed a reduction in enlisted strength to 175,000, and in June 1921 to 150,000, as soon as possible. A year later Congress limited the active Army to 12,000 commissioned officers and 125,000 enlisted men, not including the 7,000 or so in the Philippine Scouts, and Regular Army strength was stabilized at about this level until 1936. Appropriations for the military expenses of the War Department also became stabilized during this same period, amounting to about $300 million a year. This was about half of what a full implementation of the National Defense Act had been estimated to cost. The United States during these years spent rather less on its

Army than on its Navy, in line with the national policy of depending on the Navy as the first line of defense. War Department officials, especially in the early 1920's, repeatedly expressed alarm over the failure of Congress to appropriate enough money to carry out the terms of the National Defense Act. They believed that it was essential for minimum defense needs to have a Regular Army with an enlisted strength of 150,000 or (after the Air Corps Act of 1926) of 165,000. As Chief of Staff Douglas MacArthur pointed out in 1933, the United States ranked seventeenth among the nations in active Army strength; but foreign observers rated its newly equipped Army Air Corps second or third in actual power.

In equipment the Air Corps offered a marked contrast to the rest of the Army. For almost two decades ground units had to get along as best they could with weapons left over from World War I. The Army was well aware that these old weapons were becoming increasingly obsolete, and that new ones were needed. For example, General MacArthur in 1933 described the Army's tanks (except for a dozen experimental models) as completely useless for employment against any modern unit on the battlefield. Although handicapped by very small appropriations for research and development, Army arsenals and laboratories worked continuously during the 1920's and 1930's to devise new items of equipment and to improve old ones. Service boards, links between branch schools and headquarters, tested pilot models and determined the doctrine for their employment so that it could be incorporated in training manuals. But not much new equipment was forthcoming for ground units in the field until Army appropriations began to rise in 1936.

For a number of years only about one-fourth of the officers and one-half of the enlisted men of the Regular Army were available for assignment to tactical units in the continental United States. Many units existed only on paper; almost all had only skeletonized strength. Instead of nine infantry divisions, there were actually three. In May 1927 one of these divisions, a cavalry brigade, and 200 planes participated in a combined arms maneuver in Texas, but for the most part Regular units had to train as battalions or companies. The continued dispersion of skeletonized divisions, brigades, and regiments among a large number of posts, many of them relics of the Indian wars, was a serious hindrance to the training of Regulars, although helpful in training the civilian components. Efforts to abandon small posts continued to meet with stubborn opposition from local interests and their elected representatives in Congress. In the infantry, for example, in 1932 the 24 regiments available in the United States for field service were spread among 45 posts, with a battalion or less at 34. Most of the organic transportation of these units was of World War I vintage, and the Army did not have the money to concentrate them for training by other means. Nor were there large posts in which they could be housed. The best training of larger units occurred overseas in the fairly sizable garrisons maintained by the Army in Hawaii, the Philippines, and Panama. In the early 1930's the great depression had the immediate effect of cuts in appropriations and pay that further reduced the readiness of Army units for military service.

Civilian Components

One of the major purposes of the National Defense Act had been to promote the integration of the Regular Army and the civilian components by establishing uniformity in training and professional standards. While in practice this purpose fell considerably short of full realization, nevertheless the new Army system saw an unprecedented amount of civilian military training. This training brought the Regular out of his traditional isolation from the civilian community, and it acquainted large numbers of civilians with the problems and views of the professional soldier. All together, the civilian components and the groups in training that contributed to their ranks had an average strength of about 400,000 between the wars. The end result of the civilian training program was to be an orderly and effective mobilization of National Guard and Reserve elements into the active Army in 1940 and 1941.

The absorption of the National Guard into the Army during World War I had left the states without any Guard units after the armistice. The act of 1920 contemplated a National Guard of 436,000, but its actual peacetime strength became stabilized at about 180,000. This force relieved the Regular Army of any duty in curbing domestic disturbances within the states from 1921 until 1941, and stood ready for immediate induction into the active Army whenever necessary. The War Department, in addition to supplying Regular officers for instruction and large quantities of surplus World War I matériel for equipment, applied about one-tenth of its military budget to the support of the Guard in the years between wars. Guardsmen engaged in 48 armory drills and 15 days of field training each year. Though not comparable to active Army units in readiness for war, the increasingly federalized Guard was better trained in 1939 than it had been when mobilized for Mexican border duty in 1916. Numerically, the National Guard was the largest component of the Army of the United States between 1922 and 1939.

In addition to the Guard, the civilian community had of course a very large number of trained officers and enlisted men after World War I, which assured the nation of a natural reservoir of manpower for the Army for

a decade or more after the war. Only a very few of these men joined the
Enlisted Reserve Corps, but large numbers of officers maintained their
commissions in the Officers' Reserve Corps through five-year periods during
which they received further training through school and extension courses
and in brief tours of active duty. The composition of the Officers' Reserve
Corps, which numbered about 100,000 between the wars, gradually changed as its
ranks were refilled by men newly commissioned after training in the Reserve
Officers' Training Corps (ROTC) or the Citizens' Military Training Camp
(CMTC) programs.

The ROTC program began long before the passage of the National Defense
Act, in military colleges of which the first was Norwich University, established
in 1819, in state land-grant schools set up under the Morrill Act of 1862, and
in a number of private colleges and universities. For several decades before
World War I the Army detailed annually up to 100 Regular officers as instructors,
and supplied equipment, for college military training; but until the defense
acts of 1916 and 1920 the program was only loosely associated with the Army's
own needs. The new dependence on the civilian components for Army
expansion, and the establishment of the Officers' Reserve Corps as a vehicle
to retain college men in the Army of the United States after graduation, gave
impetus to a greatly enlarged and better regulated ROTC program after 1920.
By 1928 there were ROTC units in 325 schools, about 225 of them being senior
units enrolling 85,000 students in colleges and universities. Regular Army
officers detailed as professors of military science instructed these units, and
about 6,000 men graduating from them were commissioned each year in the
Officers' Reserve Corps. This inexpensive program paid rich dividends when
the nation again mobilized to meet the threat of war in 1940 and 1941.

The Army's CMTC program, a very modest alternative to the system
of universal military training proposed in 1919, provided about 30,000 young
volunteers with four weeks of military training in summer camps each year.
Those who completed four years of CMTC training became eligible for Reserve
commissions, the CMTC thus providing another (though much smaller) source
for the rolls of the Officers' Reserve Corps and the National Guard.

Domestic Employment

The most notable domestic use of Regular troops in twenty years of peace
happened in the nation's capital in the summer of 1932. Some thousands of
"Bonus Marchers" remained in Washington after the adjournment of Congress
dashed their hopes for immediate payment of a bonus for military service in

World War I. On July 28, when marshals and police tried to evict one group encamped near the Capitol, a riot with some bloodshed occurred. Thereupon President Herbert C. Hoover called upon the Army to intervene. A force of about 600—cavalrymen and infantrymen with a few tanks—advanced to the scene under the leadership of Chief of Staff MacArthur in person, two other generals, and, among junior officers, two whose names would in due course become much more familiar, Majors Dwight D. Eisenhower and George S. Patton, Jr. The troops cleaned up the situation near the Capitol without firing a shot, and then proceeded with equal efficiency to clear out all of the marchers from the District of Columbia. From a military point of view the Army had performed an unpleasant task in exemplary fashion, and with only a few minor injuries to participants; but the use of military force against civilians, most of them veterans, tarnished the Army's public image and helped to defeat the administration in the forthcoming election.

Aside from the bonus incident, the most conspicuous employment of the Army within the United States during these years of peace was in a variety of nonmilitary tasks that only the Army had the resources and the organization to tackle quickly. In floods and blizzards and hurricanes it was the Army that was first on the spot with cots, blankets, and food. In another direction, Army Engineers expanded their work on rivers and harbors for the improvement of navigation and flood control. For four months in 1934 the Air Corps, on orders from President Franklin D. Roosevelt, took over the carrying of air mail for the Post Office Department with somewhat tragic consequences, since the corps was wholly unprepared for such an undertaking.

The most important and immediately disruptive nonmilitary duty began in 1933, after Congress passed an act that put large numbers of jobless young men into reforestation and other reclamation work. President Roosevelt directed the Army to mobilize these men and thereafter to run their camps without in any way making the Civilian Conservation Corps (CCC) program a military project in disguise. Within seven weeks the Army mobilized 310,000 men into 1,315 camps, a mobilization more rapid and orderly than any in the Army's history. For more than a year the War Department had to keep about 3,000 Regular officers and many noncommissioned officers assigned to this task, and in order to do so the Army had to strip tactical units of their leadership. Unit training was brought to a standstill, and the readiness of units for immediate military employment was almost destroyed. In the second half of 1934 the War Department called a large number of Reserve officers to active duty to replace the Regulars, and, by August 1935, 9,300 Reserve officers (not counted in active Army strength) were serving with the CCC. A good many of them continued in this service until 1941, but the Army never wanted to insert military training into the program, in part because the CCC camps were so small and so isolated. Despite its initial and serious interference with normal Army operations, in the long run the CCC program had a beneficial effect on military preparedness. It furnished many thousands of Reserve officers with valuable training, and it gave nonmilitary but disciplined training to many hundreds of thousands of young men who were to become soldiers and sailors in World War II.

National and Military Policy

For fifteen years, from 1921 to 1936, the American people, their representatives in Congress, and their Presidents thought that the United States could and should avoid future wars with other major powers, except possibly Japan. They believed the nation could achieve this goal by maintaining a minimum of defensive military strength, avoiding entangling commitments with Old World nations, and yet using American good offices to promote international peace and the limitation of armaments. The United States took the initiative in 1921 in calling a conference in Washington to consider the limitation of armaments. The resulting naval treaty of 1922 temporarily checked a race for naval supremacy. It froze capital ship strengths of the United States, Great Britain, and Japan in a 5–5–3 ratio for a number of years. This ratio and restrictions on new naval base construction assured that neither the United States nor Japan could operate offensively in the Pacific as long as treaty provisions were respected. In effect these provisions also meant that it would be impossible for the United States to defend the Philippines against a Japanese attack. On the other hand, a general agreement among the western nations and Japan to maintain the *status quo* in the Pacific and in China offered fair assurance against a Japanese war of aggression, but only as long as the western powers did not themselves become embroiled in the European-Atlantic area.

In 1928 the United States and France joined in drafting the Pact of Paris, which renounced war as an instrument of national policy. Thereafter, the United States announced to the world that, if other powers did likewise, it would limit its armed forces to those necessary to maintain internal order and defend national territory against aggression and invasion. In 1931 the chief of the Army's War Plans Division advised the Chief of Staff that the defense of frontiers was precisely the cardinal task for which the Army had been organized, equipped, and trained. There was no real conflict between national policy and the Army's conception of its mission during the 1920's and early 1930's. But in the Army's opinion the government and the American public, in their antipathy to war, failed to support even minimum needs for national defense.

Across the oceans, the clouds of war began to form again in 1931 when the Japanese seized Manchuria and then defied the diplomatic efforts of the League of Nations and the United States to pry them loose. In 1933 Japan quit the League and a year later announced that it would no longer be bound by the naval limitation treaties after they expired in 1936. In Europe, Adolf Hitler came to power in Germany in 1933, and by 1936 Nazi Germany had denounced the Treaty of Versailles, embarked on rearmament, and occupied the demilitarized Rhineland. Hitler's partner in dictatorship, Italy's Benito Mussolini, began his career of aggression by attacking Ethiopia in 1935. A revolution in Spain in 1936 not only produced a third dictatorship but also an extended war that became a proving ground for World War II. The neutrality acts passed by the Congress between 1935 and 1937 were a direct response to these European developments, and the United States tried to mend its international position in other ways by opening diplomatic relations with Soviet Russia in 1933, by promising eventual independence to the Philippines in 1934, and by liquidating its protectorates in the Caribbean area and pursuing the policy of the Good Neighbor toward Latin America generally.

No quick changes in American military policy followed. But beginning in 1935 the armed forces received substantially larger appropriations that permitted them to improve their readiness for action. Army improvements during the next three years reflected not only the increasingly critical international situation but also the careful planning of the War Department during General Douglas MacArthur's tour as Chief of Staff from 1930 to 1935. His recommendations led to a reorganization of the combat forces and a modest increase in their size, and were accompanied by more realistic planning for using the manpower and industrial might of the United States for war, if that should become necessary.

The Army Strengthened

The central objective of the Chief of Staff's recommendations had been to establish a small hard-hitting force ready for emergency use. In line with this objective the Army wanted to mechanize and motorize its Regular combat units as soon as it could, and to fill their ranks so that they could be trained effectively. The Army also needed new organizations to control training of the larger ground and air units and teams of combined arms in peacetime and to command them if war came. For these purposes the War Department between 1932 and 1935 created four army headquarters and a General Headquarters Air Force in the continental United States under command of the Chief of Staff. Under these headquarters, beginning in the summer of 1935, Regular and National Guard divisions and other units trained together each year in summer maneuvers and other exercises, including joint exercises with the Navy. In the same year Congress authorized the Regular Army to increase its enlisted strength to the long-sought goal of 165,000. This increase was accompanied during the following years by substantially greater expenditures for equipment and housing, so that by 1938 the Regular Army was considerably stronger and far readier for action than it had been in the early 1930's. But in the meantime the strength and power of foreign armies had been increasing even more rapidly.

In the slow rebuilding of the 1930's, the Army concentrated on equipping and training its combat units for mobile warfare rather than for the static warfare that had characterized operations on the Western Front in World War I. Through research it managed to acquire some new weapons that promised increased firepower and mobility as soon as equipment could be produced in quantity. In 1936 the Army adopted the Garand semiautomatic rifle to replace the 1903 Springfield, and during the 1930's it perfected the mobile 105-mm. howitzer that became the principal divisional artillery piece of World War II and developed light and medium tanks that were much faster than the lumbering models of World War I. In units, horse power gave way to motor power as rapidly as new vehicles could be acquired. To increase the maneuverability of its principal ground unit, the division, the Army decided after field tests to triangularize the infantry division by reducing the number of its infantry regiments from four to three, and to make it more mobile by using motor transportation only. The planned wartime strength of the new division was to be little more than half the size of its World War I counterpart.

Modern war is so complex and modern armies are so demanding in equipment that industrial mobilization for war must precede the large-scale employment of manpower by at least two years if a war is to be fought effectively. The Army's Industrial Mobilization Plan of 1930 established the basic principles for harnessing the nation's economic strength to war needs, and revisions of this plan to 1939 improved the pattern. Manpower planning culminated in the Protective Mobilization Plan of 1937. Under this plan the first step was to be the induction of the National Guard, to provide with the Regular Army an Initial Protective Force of about 400,000. The Navy and this defensive force would then protect the nation while the Army engaged in an orderly expansion to planned strengths of one, two, and four million, as necessary. Along with manpower planning there evolved for the first time prior to actual war a definite training plan, which included the location, size, and scheduling for replacement training centers, unit training centers, and schools, detailed unit and individual training programs, and the production of a variety of training manuals. While these plans were to help guide the mobilization that began in the summer of 1940, they had their faults. As it turned out the planners set their sights too low. They assumed a maximum mobilization of World War I dimension, whereas World War II was to call forth more than twice as many men and proportionately an even greater industrial effort for the Army. The plans also assumed until 1939 that mobilization for war would come more or less suddenly, instead of relatively slowly during many months of nominal peace.

The Beginnings of World War II

The German annexation of Austria in March 1938 followed by the Czech crisis in September of the same year awakened the United States and the other democratic nations to the imminence of another great world conflict. The new conflict had already begun in the Far East when Japan had invaded China in 1937. After Germany seized Czechoslovakia in March 1939, war in Europe became inevitable, since Hitler had no intention of stopping with that move and Great Britain and France for their part decided that they must fight rather than yield anything more to Hitler. In August Germany made a deal with the Soviet Union, which provided for a partition of Poland and a Soviet free hand in Finland and the northern Baltic states. Then on September 1, 1939, Germany invaded Poland. When France and Great Britain responded by declaring war on Germany, they embarked on a course that could not lead to victory without aid from the United States. Yet an overwhelming majority of the American people wanted to stay out of the new war if they could, and this sentiment necessarily governed the initial responses of the United States Government and of its armed forces to the perilous international situation.

President Roosevelt and his advisers, being fully aware of the danger, had launched the nation on a limited preparedness campaign at the beginning of 1939. By then the technological improvement of the airplane had introduced a new factor into the military calculations of the United States. The moment was approaching when it would be feasible for a hostile Old World power to establish air bases in the Western Hemisphere from which the Panama Canal—then the key to American naval defense—or the continental United States itself might be attacked. Such a development would destroy the oceanic security that the American nation had so long enjoyed. The primary emphasis in 1939 was therefore on increasing the striking power of the Army Air Corps. At the same time Army and Navy officers collaborated in drafting the RAINBOW plans that superseded existing color plans and thereafter helped to guide the development and conduct of the American armed forces toward the war. A month after the European war began the President, in formally approving the RAINBOW 1 plan, changed the avowed national military policy from one of guarding the United States and its possessions only to one of hemisphere defense, and the policy of hemisphere defense was to be the focus of Army plans and actions until the end of 1940.

Immediately after the European war started the President proclaimed a limited national emergency and authorized increases in Regular Army and National Guard enlisted strengths to 227,000 and 235,000, respectively. He also proclaimed American neutrality in the war, but at his urging Congress presently gave indirect support to the western democracies by ending the prohibition on munitions sales to nations at war embodied in the Neutrality Act of 1937. British and French orders for munitions in turn helped to prepare American industry for the large-scale war production that was to come. When the quick destruction of Poland was followed by a lull in the war, the tempo of America's own defense preparations slackened. The Army concentrated on making its Regular force ready for emergency action by providing it with full and modern equipment as quickly as possible, and in April 1940 by engaging 70,000 troops in the first genuine corps and army training maneuvers in American military history. How adequate the Army was depended on the survival of France and Great Britain. The successful German seizure of Denmark and Norway in April 1940 followed by the quick defeat of the Low Countries and France and the grave threat to Great Britain forced the United States in June to adopt a new and greatly enlarged program for defense, for it then looked as if the nation might eventually have to face the aggressors of the Old World almost alone.

The Prewar Mobilization

Under the leadership of Chief of Staff General George C. Marshall and, after July, of Secretary of War Henry L. Stimson, the Army embarked in the summer of 1940 on a large expansion designed to protect the United States and the rest of the Western Hemisphere against any hostile forces that might be unleashed from the Old World. Army expansion was matched by a naval program designed to give the United States a two-ocean Navy strong enough to deal simultaneously with the Japanese in the Pacific and the naval strength that Germany and its new war partner, Italy, might acquire in the Atlantic if they defeated Great Britain. Both expansion programs had the overwhelming support of the American people, who though still strongly opposed to entering the war were now convinced that the danger to the United States was very real. Congressional appropriations between May and October 1940 reflected this conviction. The Army received more than $8 billion for its needs during the succeeding year—a sum greater than

GENERAL MARSHALL

what had been granted for the support of its military activities during the preceding twenty years. The munitions program approved for the Army on June 30, 1940, called for procurement by October 1941 of all items needed to equip and maintain a 1,200,000-man force, including a greatly enlarged and modernized Army Air Corps, and by September the War Department was planning to create an Army of a million and a half as soon as possible.

To fill the ranks of this new Army, Congress on August 27 approved induction of the National Guard into federal service and the calling up of the Organized Reserves. Then it approved the first peacetime draft of untrained civilian manpower in the nation's history, in the Selective Service and Training Act of September 14, 1940. Units of the National Guard, and selectees and the Reserve officers to train them, entered service as rapidly as the Army could construct camps to house them. During the last six months of 1940 the active Army more than doubled in strength, and by mid-1941 it achieved its planned strength of one and a half million officers and men.

A new organization, General Headquarters, took charge of training the Army in July 1940. In the same month the Army established a separate Armored Force, and subsequently Antiaircraft and Tank Destroyer Commands, which, with the Infantry, Field Artillery, Coast Artillery, and Cavalry, broadened the front of ground combat arms to seven. The existing branch schools and a new Armored Force School concentrated during 1940 and 1941 on improving the fitness of National Guard and Reserve officers for active duty, and in early 1941 the War Department established officer candidate schools to train men selected from the ranks for junior leadership positions. In October 1940 the four armies assumed command of ground units in the continental United States, and thereafter trained them under the supervision of General Headquarters. The corps area commands became administrative and service organizations. Major overseas garrisons were strengthened, and the Army established new commands to supervise the garrisoning of Puerto Rico and Alaska where there had been almost no Regular Army troops for many years. In June 1941 the War Department established the Army Air Forces to train and administer air units in the United States. In July it began the transformation of General Headquarters into an operational post for General Marshall as Commanding General of the Field Forces. By the autumn of 1941 the Army had 27 infantry, 5 armored, and 2 cavalry divisions, 35 air groups, and a host of supporting units in training in the continental United States. But most of these units were still unready for action, in part because the United States had shared so much of its old and new military equipment with the nations that were actively fighting the Axis triumvirate of Germany, Italy, and Japan.

Toward War

On the eve of France's defeat in June 1940 President Roosevelt had directed the transfer or diversion of large stocks of Army World War I weapons, and of ammunition and aircraft, to both France and Great Britain, and after France fell these munitions helped to replace Britain's losses in the evacuation of its expeditionary force from Dunkerque. More aid to Britain was forthcoming in September when the United States agreed to exchange fifty over-age destroyers for offshore Atlantic bases, and the President announced that henceforth production of heavy bombers would be shared equally with the British. An open collaboration with Canada from August 1940 onward led to a strong support of the Canadian war effort, Canada having followed Great Britain into war in September 1939. The foreign aid program culminated in the Lend-Lease Act of March 1941, which swept away the pretense of American neutrality by openly avowing the intention of the United States to become an "arsenal of democracy" against aggression. Prewar foreign aid was nonetheless a measure of self defense; its fundamental purpose was to help contain the military might of the Axis powers until the United States could complete its own protective mobilization.

Thus by early 1941 the focus of American policy had shifted from hemisphere defense to a limited participation in the war. Indeed by then it appeared to Army and Navy leaders and to President Roosevelt that the United States might be drawn into full participation in the not too distant future. Assuming the probability of simultaneous operations in the Pacific and Atlantic, they agreed that Germany was the greater menace and that if the United States did enter the war it ought to concentrate on the defeat of Germany first. This principle was accepted in staff conversations between American and British military representatives in Washington ending on March 29, 1941.

After these conversations the Army and Navy adjusted the most comprehensive of the prewar planning concepts, RAINBOW 5, to accord with American military preparations and actions during the remaining months of 1941 before the Japanese attack. During these months the trend was steadily toward American participation in the war against Germany. In April the President authorized an active naval patrol of the western half of the Atlantic Ocean. In May the United States decided to accept responsibility for the development and operation of military air routes across the North Atlantic via Greenland and across the South Atlantic via Brazil. During May it also appeared to the President and his military advisers that a German drive through Spain and Portugal to northwestern Africa and its adjacent islands might be imminent. This prospect together with German naval activity in the North Atlantic led the President to proclaim an unlimited national emergency, and to direct the Army and Navy to prepare an expeditionary force to be sent to the Azores as a step toward blocking a German advance toward the South Atlantic. Then, in early June, the President learned that Hitler was preparing to attack the Soviet Union, a move that would divert German military power away from the Atlantic, at least for the time being.

The Germans invaded the Soviet Union on June 22, and three days later Army troops landed in Greenland to protect it against German attack and to build air bases for the air ferry route across the North Atlantic. Earlier in June the President had also decided that Americans should relieve British troops guarding Iceland, and the initial contingent of American forces reached there in early July, to be followed by a sizable Army expeditionary force in September. In August the President and British Prime Minister Winston Churchill met in Newfoundland and drafted the Atlantic Charter, which defined the general terms of a just peace for the world. By October the United States Navy was fully engaged in convoy-escort duties in the western reaches of the North Atlantic, and Navy ships, with some assistance from Army aircraft, were joining with British and Canadian forces in warring against German submarines. In November Congress voted to repeal prohibitions against the arming of American merchant vessels and their entry into combat zones, and the stage was set, as Prime Minister Churchill noted on November 9, for "constant fighting in the Atlantic between German and American ships."

Apparently all of the overt American moves in 1941 toward involvement in the war against Germany had solid backing in American public opinion, with only an increasingly small though vociferous minority criticizing the President for the nation's departures from neutrality. But the American people were still not prepared for an open declaration of war.

As the United States moved toward war in the Atlantic area, American policy toward Japan also stiffened. Although the United States wanted to avoid a two-front war, it was not ready to do so by surrendering vital areas or interests to the Japanese as the price of peace. When in late July 1941 the Japanese moved large forces into what became South Vietnam, the United States responded by freezing Japanese assets and cutting off oil shipments to Japan. At the same time the War Department recalled General MacArthur to active duty to command both United States and Philippine Army forces in the Far East and it also decided to send Army reinforcements to the Philippines, including heavy bombers intended to dissuade the Japanese from making any more southward moves. For their part the Japanese, while continuing to negotiate with the United States, tentatively decided in September to embark on a war of conquest in Southeast Asia and the Indies as soon as possible, and to try to immobilize American naval opposition by an opening air strike against the great American naval base of Pearl Harbor in Hawaii. When intensive last-minute negotiations in November failed to produce any accommodation, the Japanese made their decision for war irrevocable.

The Japanese attack of December 7, 1941 on Pearl Harbor and the Philippines at once ended the division of American opinion toward participation in the war, and America went to war with a unanimity of popular support that was unprecedented in the military history of the United States. This was also the first time in its history that the United States had entered a war with a large Army in being and an industrial system partially retooled for war. The Army numbered 1,643,477, and it was ready to defend the Western Hemisphere against invasion. But it was not ready to take part in large-scale operations across the oceans. Many months would pass before the United States could launch even limited offensives.

CHAPTER 20

World War II: The Defensive Phase

About one o'clock in Washington on the afternoon of December 7, 1941, the first news of the Japanese attack on Pearl Harbor, Hawaii, reached the War Department. The news came as a shock, even as the attack itself had come. It caught by surprise not only the American people at large, who learned of the attack a short while later, but also their leaders, including the very officers who had earlier been so much concerned over the possibility of just such an attack. One explanation is that these officers and their political superiors were momentarily expecting the Japanese to use all their forces against weakly held British and Dutch positions in the Far East (and probably, but not certainly, against the Philippines). But without warning in the early morning of December 7, powerful carrier-borne air forces had smashed the U.S. Pacific Fleet at anchor in Pearl Harbor. The same day (December 8 in the Philippines), about noon, Formosa-based bombers caught the bulk of the U.S. Far East Air Force lined up on Clark and Iba fields not far from Manila in central Luzon and virtually destroyed it. For the second time within a quarter-century, Americans found themselves fully involved in a war they had not sought—this time in the first truly global conflict.

The Outbreak of War: Action and Reaction

The attack on Pearl Harbor was one of the most brilliant tactical feats of the war. From 6 carriers which had advanced undetected to a position 200 miles north of Oahu, some 350 aircraft came in through the morning mist, achieving complete tactical surprise. They bombed and strafed the neatly aligned Army planes on Hickam and Wheeler Fields, as well as Navy and Marine Corps aircraft, and they carefully singled out as targets major units of the Navy's battle force at anchor in the harbor. Fortunately, the fleet's 3 carriers were away at the time, and the attackers failed to hit the oil tanks and naval repair shops on shore. But the blow was devastating enough. About 170 aircraft were destroyed and 102 damaged, all 8 battleships were sunk or badly damaged, besides many other vessels, and total casualties came to about 3,400, including 2,402 service men and civilians killed. Japanese losses were about 49 aircraft and 5 midget submarines. In an astonishing achievement, the enemy managed to apply in one shattering operation a combination of the principles of surprise, objective, mass, security, and maneuver. In its larger strategic context, the Pearl Harbor attack also exemplifies the principles of the offensive and economy of force. The joint Congressional committee investigating the attack called it the "greatest military and naval disaster in our Nation's history."

These two attacks—on Pearl Harbor and on the Philippines—effectively crippled American striking power in the Pacific. The Philippines and other American possessions in the western Pacific were isolated, their loss a foregone conclusion. The Hawaiian Islands and Alaska lay open to invasion; the Panama Canal and the cities, factories, and shipyards of the west coast were vulnerable to raids from the sea and air. Months would pass before the United States could regain a capacity for even the most limited kind of offensive action against its oriental enemy. As Japanese forces moved swiftly southward against the Philippines, Malaya, and the Netherlands Indies, Japan's Axis partners, Germany and Italy, promptly declared war on the United States, thus ending the uncertainty as to whether the United States would become a full-fledged belligerent in the European war. For the first time in its history, the United States was embarked upon an all-out, two-front war.

Meanwhile Britain was battling to maintain its hold on the eastern Mediterranean region which lay athwart the historic lifeline to possessions and Commonwealth associates in the Far East. Late in 1940 small British forces based in Egypt gained important successes against Italian armies in Libya, and the Greeks in the winter of 1940–41 resoundingly defeated an invading Italian army and chased it back into Albania. But German armies quickly came to the aid of their Italian ally. In April 1941 the famous panzer divisions, supported by overwhelming air power, swept through the Balkans, crushing the Yugoslav and Greek armies, and a British expeditionary force hastily dispatched to aid the latter. The following month German airborne forces descended on the island of Crete and swamped British and Greek defenders in a spectacular, though costly, attack. In Libya a powerful German-Italian army under General Erwin Rommel drove the British back across the Egyptian border, isolating a large garrison in Tobruk and threatening the Nile Delta. Against these disasters Britain could count only the final expulsion of the Italians from the Red Sea area and of the Vichy French from Syria, the suppression of pro-German uprisings in Iraq, and the achievement of a precarious naval ascendancy in the eastern and western portions of the Mediterranean. During the remainder of

1941 the British gradually built up strength in eastern Libya, and late in the year they succeeded in relieving Tobruk and pushing Rommel back to his original starting point at El Agheila.

Since mid-1940 the military fortunes of the anti-Axis powers had declined as the European war expanded. Germany had crushed all its continental European opponents in the west, and then attempted to destroy Britain's air forces as a prelude to an invasion across the English Channel. In the air battles over Britain in August and September 1940 the Royal Air Force won a brilliant victory. But during the following winter and spring the waning threat of invasion had been replaced by the equally deadly and more persistent menace of economic strangulation. German aircraft pulverized Britain's ports and inland cities, while U-boats, surface raiders, and mines decimated shipping. By 1941 the imports on which the United Kingdom depended for existence had dwindled to less than two-thirds of their prewar volume, and the British people faced the prospect of ultimate starvation.

In June 1941, however, the storm center of the war had moved elsewhere. Only slightly delayed by the conquest of the Balkans, Hitler on June 22, 1941, hurled German might against the Soviet Union, the only remaining power on the European continent capable of challenging his dominance. By early December, when the onset of winter and stiffening Soviet resistance finally brought the advance to a halt, the German armies had driven to the suburbs of Moscow, inflicted huge losses on the Red Army, and occupied a vast expanse of European Russia embracing its most densely populated and industrialized regions. This, as it turned out, was the high tide of German success in World War II; Hitler, like Napoleon, was to meet disaster on the wind-swept plains of Russia. But in December 1941 few were willing to predict this outcome. British and United States leaders assembling in Washington at the end of that month to make plans for dealing with the crisis had to reckon with the probability that in the year to come, unless the Western Allies could somehow force Germany to divert substantial forces from the eastern front, the German steamroller would complete the destruction of the Soviet armies. Hitler would then be able, with the resources and enslaved peoples of all Europe at his feet, to throw his full power against the West.

American military leaders had already given thought to this grim prospect, and to the implications it held for America's role in the war. In the Victory Program, drawn up by the Army and Navy at the President's behest during the summer of 1941, the leaders of the two services had set forth in some detail the strategy and the means they considered necessary to win ultimate victory if, as they expected, Soviet Russia succumbed to the Axis onslaught. The strategy was the one laid down in the RAINBOW 5 war plan—wear Germany down by bombing, blockade, subversion, and limited offensives, while mobilizing the strength needed to invade the European continent and to defeat Germany on its own ground. Japan meanwhile would be contained by air and sea power, local defense forces, China's inexhaustible manpower, and the Soviet Union's Siberian divisions. With Germany out of the running, Japan's defeat or collapse would soon follow. As for the means, the United States would have to provide them in large part, for the British were already weary and their resources limited. The United States would serve not merely, to use the President's catchy phrase, as the "arsenal of democracy," supplying weapons to arm its allies, but also as the main source of the armies without which wars, above all this war, could not be won. Army leaders envisaged the eventual mobilization of 215 divisions, 61 of them armored, and 239 combat air groups, requiring a grand total, with supporting forces, of 8.8 million men. Five million of these would be hurled against the European Axis. It was emphasized that victory over the Axis Powers would require a maximum military effort and full mobilization of America's immense industrial resources.

Yet the Victory Program was merely an expression of professional military views, not a statement of national military policy. That policy, on the eve of Pearl Harbor, was still ostensibly hemisphere defense. The pace of rearmament and mobilization, in the summer and fall of 1941, was actually slowing down. Signs pointed to a policy of making the American contribution to the defeat of the Axis, as columnist Walter Lippmann put it, one "basically of Navy, Air, and manufacturing," something a great deal less than the all-out effort envisaged in the Victory Program. Public and Congressional sentiment, moreover, still clung to the hope that an immediate showdown with the Axis Powers could be avoided and that the country would not be forced into full belligerent participation in the war, as evidenced by a near defeat of the bill to extend Selective Service, continuation of a prohibition against sending selectees outside the Western Hemisphere, and apathetic public response to submarine attacks on American destroyers in September and October.

The Japanese attack on Pearl Harbor and the Philippines changed the picture. A wave of patriotic indignation over Japanese duplicity and brutality swept the country. Isolationism virtually evaporated as a public issue, and all parties closed ranks in support of the war effort. Indeed, in retrospect, despite the immediate tactical success the Japanese achieved at Pearl Harbor, that attack proved to be a great blunder for them, politically and strategically. The President, early in January, dramatized the magnitude of the effort now demanded by proclaiming a new set of production goals—60,000 airplanes in

1942 and 125,000 in 1943; 45,000 tanks in 1942 and 75,000 in 1943; 20,000 anti-aircraft guns in 1942 and 35,000 in 1943; half a million machine guns in 1942 and as many more in 1943; and 8 million deadweight tons of merchant shipping in 1942 and 10 million in 1943. Vanished were the two illusions that America could serve only as an arsenal of democracy, contributing weapons without the men to wield them, or, conversely, that the nation could rely solely on its own fighting forces, leaving other anti-Axis nations to shift for themselves. "We must not only provide munitions for our own fighting forces," Roosevelt advised Secretary of War Henry L. Stimson, "but vast quantities to be used against the enemy in every appropriate theater of war." A new Victory Program boosted the Army's ultimate mobilization goal to 10 million men, and the War Department planned to have 71 divisions and 115 combat air groups organized by the end of 1942, with a total of 3.6 million men under arms. As an Army planner had predicted back in the spring of 1941, the United States now seemed destined to become "the final reserve of the democracies both in manpower and munitions."

Late in December 1941 President Roosevelt and Prime Minister Churchill met with their advisers in Washington (the ARCADIA Conference) to establish the bases of coalition strategy and concert immediate measures to meet the military crisis. They faced an agonizing dilemma. Prompt steps had to be taken to stem the spreading tide of Japanese conquest. On the other hand, it seemed likely that the coming year might see the collapse of Soviet resistance and of the British position in the Middle East. In this difficult situation the Allied leaders made a far-reaching decision that shaped the whole course of the war. Reaffirming the principle laid down in Anglo-American staff conversations in Washington ten months earlier, they agreed that the first and main effort must go into defeating Germany, the more formidable enemy. Japan's turn would come later. Defeating Germany would involve a prolonged process of "closing and tightening the ring" about Fortress Europe. Operations in 1942 would have to be defensive and preparatory, though limited offensives might be undertaken if the opportunity offered. Not until 1943 at the earliest could the Allies contemplate a return to the European continent "across the Mediterranean, from Turkey into the Balkans, or by landings in Western Europe."

Another important action taken at the ARCADIA Conference was the establishment of the Combined Chiefs of Staff (CCS). This was a committee consisting of the professional military chiefs of both countries, responsible to the President and Prime Minister for planning and directing the grand strategy of the coalition. Its American members were the Army Chief of Staff, General Marshall; the Chief of Naval Operations, Admiral Harold R. Stark (replaced early in 1942 by Admiral Ernest J. King); and the Chief (later Commanding General) of the Army Air Forces, Lt. Gen. Henry H. Arnold. In July 1942 a fourth member was added, the President's personal Chief of Staff, Admiral William D. Leahy. Since the CCS normally sat in Washington, the British Chiefs of Staff, making up its British component, attended in person only at important conferences with the heads of state. In the intervals they were represented in Washington by the four senior members of the permanent British Joint Staff Mission, headed until late in 1944 by Field Marshal Sir John Dill, the former Chief of the British Imperial General Staff. Under the CCS a system of primarily military subordinate committees grew up, specifically designated to handle such matters as strategic and logistical planning, transportation, and communications.

By February 1942 the Joint Chiefs of Staff (JCS), consisting of the U.S. members of the CCS, had emerged as the highest authority in the U.S. military hierarchy (though never formally chartered as such), and responsible directly to the President. Like the CCS, the JCS in time developed a machinery of planning and working committees, the most important of which were the Joint Staff Planners, the Joint Strategic Survey Committee, and the Joint Logistics Committee. No executive machinery was created at either the CCS or JCS level. The CCS ordinarily named either the British Chiefs or the U.S. Joint Chiefs to act as its executive agent, and these, in turn, employed the established machinery of the service departments.

In the spring of 1942 Britain and the United States agreed on a worldwide division of strategic responsibility. The U.S. Joint Chiefs of Staff were to be primarily responsible for the war in the Pacific, and the British Chiefs for the Middle East-Indian Ocean region, while the European-Mediterranean-Atlantic area would be a combined responsibility of both staffs. China was designated a separate theater commanded by its chief of state, Chiang Kai-shek, though within the United States' sphere of responsibility. In the Pacific, the Joint Chiefs established two main theaters, the Southwest Pacific Area (SWPA) and the Pacific Ocean Areas (POA), the former under General MacArthur, the latter under Admiral Chester W. Nimitz. POA was further subdivided into North, Central, and South Pacific areas, the first two directly controlled by Nimitz, the third by his deputy, Admiral William F. Halsey, Jr. (*See Map 41.*) Later in 1942, the U.S. air and service troops operating in China, India, and northern Burma were organized as U.S. Army Forces, China-Burma-India, under Lt. Gen. Joseph W. Stilwell. On various other far-flung lines of communications U.S. Army forces, mostly air and service troops during 1942, were organized under similar theater commands. In June Maj. Gen. Dwight D. Eisenhower arrived in England to take command of the newly established European Theater of Operations, and after the landings in North Africa late in the year a new U.S. theater was organized in that region.

The British and the Americans had decided at the ARCADIA Conference that Allied forces in each overseas theater would operate, as far as possible, under a single commander, and this principle was subsequently applied in most theaters. Within theaters subordinate unified commands were created, in some cases for Allied ground, naval, or air forces, and most frequently for task forces formed to carry out a specific operation or campaign. The authority of Allied theater commanders over national forces was always restricted with respect to areas and missions, and, as a last resort, senior national commanders in each theater could appeal to their own governments against specific orders or policies of the theater commander. In practice, this right of appeal was rarely invoked.

In essence, unified command at the Allied level gave the commander control of certain specific forces for operational purposes, rather than jurisdiction over a given geographical area. Administration of national forces and the allocation of resources were usually handled through separate national channels. In certain cases, inter-Allied boards or committees, responsible to the Allied theater commander, controlled the common use of critical resources (such as petroleum products) or facilities (such as railways and shipping) within a theater. Administration of U.S. forces overseas also generally followed separate Army and Navy channels, except in the Pacific where, from 1943 on, supply, transportation, and certain other services were jointly administered to a limited degree.

Even before Pearl Harbor, Army leaders had realized that the peacetime organization of the War Department General Staff, dating back to 1921, was an inadequate instrument for directing a major war effort. Originally a small co-ordinating and planning body, the General Staff, and especially its War Plans and Supply Divisions, rapidly expanded during the emergency period into a large operating organization, increasingly immersed in the details of supervision to the detriment of its planning and policy-making functions. The Chief of Staff, to whom some sixty-one officers and agencies had direct access, carried an especially heavy burden.

Three additional features of the organization demanded remedy. One was the continued subordination of the Army Air Forces to General Staff supervision, which conflicted with the Air Forces' drive for autonomy. Another was the anomalous position of General Headquarters (GHQ), whose role as command post for the field forces and responsibilities in the fields of training and logistics clashed with the authority of the General Staff at many points. Finally, the division of supply responsibilities between the Supply Division (G-4) and the Office of the Under Secretary of War—with requirements and distribution assigned to the former and procurement to the latter—was breaking down under the pressure of mobilization.

Spurred by the Pearl Harbor disaster, which seemed to accentuate the need for better staff co-ordination in Washington, General Marshall on March 9, 1942, put into effect a sweeping reorganization of the War Department. Under the new plan, which underwent little change during the war years, the General Staff, except for the War Plans and Intelligence Divisions, was drastically whittled down and limited in function to broad planning and policy guidance. An expanded War Plans Division, soon renamed Operations Division (OPD), became General Marshall's command post and, in effect, a superior general staff for the direction of overseas operations. The Army Air Forces, though in some respects on a lower level of administrative authority than before, had virtually complete control of the development of its special weapon—the airplane. Administering its own personnel and training, it organized and supported the combat air forces to be employed in theaters of operations and came also to exercise considerable influence over both strategic and operational planning.

In the reorganization of March 9 two new commands were created, the Army Ground Forces (AGF) and the Services of Supply, later renamed the Army Service Forces (ASF). The former, headed by Lt. Gen. Lesley J. McNair, took over the training mission of GHQ, now abolished, and absorbed the ground combat arms. To the ASF, commanded by Lt. Gen. Brehon B. Somervell, were subordinated the supply (renamed technical) and administrative services, the nine corps areas, and most of the Army posts and installations throughout the United States, including the ports of embarkation through which troops and supplies flowed to the forces overseas. In supply matters, Somervell now reported to two masters, the Chief of Staff for requirements and distribution and the Under Secretary of War, Mr. Robert P. Patterson, for procurement. His subordination to the latter was, in reality, only nominal since most of Patterson's organization was transferred bodily to Somervell's headquarters. Except for equipment peculiar to the Army Air Forces, the ASF thus became the Army's central agency for supply in the United States. It drew up the Army's "shopping list" of requirements, the Army Supply Program; through the seven technical services (Quartermaster, Ordnance, Signal, Chemical, Engineer, Medical, and Transportation) it procured most of the Army's supplies and equipment; it distributed these materials to the Army at home and abroad, as well as to

Allies under lend-lease; it operated the Army's fleet of transports; and it trained specialists and service units to perform various specialized jobs. General Somervell himself became General Marshall's principal logistical adviser.

All this looked to the future. In the first few weeks after Pearl Harbor, while the Navy was salvaging what it could from the wreckage at Pearl Harbor and striving to combat German submarines in the western Atlantic, the War Department made desperate efforts to bolster the defenses of Hawaii, the Philippines, the Panama Canal, Alaska, and the U.S. west coast. By the end of December, the danger of an attack on the Hawaii-Alaska-Panama triangle seemed to have waned, and the emphasis shifted to measures to stave off further disasters in the Far East. The British and Americans decided at ARCADIA that the Allies would attempt to hold the Japanese north and east of the line of the Malay Peninsula and the Netherlands Indies and to re-establish communications with the Philippines to the north. To co-ordinate operations in this vast theater, the Allied leaders created the ABDA (American-British-Dutch-Australian) Command, including the Netherlands Indies, Malaya, Burma, and the Philippines. British Lt. Gen. Sir Archibald P. Wavell was placed in over-all command. Through India from the west and Australia from the east, the Allies hoped in a short time to build up a shield of air power stout enough to blunt the Japanese threat.

For a time it seemed as though nothing could stop the Japanese juggernaut. In less than three weeks after Pearl Harbor, the isolated American outposts of Wake and Guam fell to the invaders, the British garrison of Hong Kong was overwhelmed, and powerful land, sea, and air forces were converging on Malaya and the Netherlands Indies. Picked, jungle-trained troops drove down the Malay Peninsula toward the great fortress of Singapore, infiltrating and out-flanking successsive British positions. Two of the most formidable warships in the British Navy, the battleship *Prince of Wales* and the battle cruiser *Repulse,* were sunk by Japanese torpedo planes off the east coast of Malaya, a loss that destroyed the Allies' last hope of effectively opposing Japan's naval power in the Far East. Attacked from the land side, Singapore and its British force of over 80,000 troops surrendered on February 15, 1942. Meanwhile the Japanese had invaded the Netherlands Indies from the north, west, and east. In a series of actions during January and February, the weak Dutch and Australian naval forces, joined by the U.S. Asiatic Fleet withdrawing from the Philippines, were destroyed piecemeal, only four American destroyers escaping south to Australia. On March 9 the last Allied ground and air forces in the Netherlands Indies, almost 100,000 men (mostly Indonesian troops) surrendered to the invaders. In Burma, the day before, the British had been forced under heavy bombing to evacuate Rangoon and retreat northward. Before the end of April the Japanese had completed the ocupation of Burma, driving the British westward into India and the bulk of U.S. Lt. Gen. Joseph W. Stilwell's Chinese forces back into China; General Stilwell and the remnants of other Chinese units retreated to India. In the process the Japanese had won possession of a huge section of the Burma Road, the only viable route between China and India. Henceforth and until late in the war communication between China and its allies was to be limited to an air ferry from India over the "hump" of the Himalayan Mountains. During the late spring strong Japanese naval forces reached the coastal cities of India and even attacked Britain's naval base on Ceylon.

By May 1942 the Japanese had thus gained control of Burma, Malaya, Thailand, French Indochina, and the Malay Archipelago, while farther to the east they had won strong lodgments on the islands of New Guinea and New Britain and in the Solomons, flanking the approaches to Australia and New Zealand from the United States. This immense empire had been won at remarkably little cost through an effective combination of superior air and sea power and only a handful of well-trained ground divisions. The Japanese had seized and held the initiative while keeping their opponents off balance. They had concentrated their strength for the capture of key objectives such as airfields and road junctions and for the destruction of major enemy forces while diverting only minimum forces on secondary missions, thus giving an impression of overwhelming numerical strength. They had frequently gained the advantage of surprise and had baffled their enemies by their speed and skill in maneuver. The whole whirlwind campaign, in short, had provided Japan's enemies with a capsule course of instruction in the principles of war.

Fall of the Philippines

Only in the Philippines, almost on Japan's southern doorstep, was the timetable of conquest delayed. When the Japanese struck, the defending forces in the islands numbered more than 130,000, including the Philippine Army which, though mobilized to a strength of ten divisions, was ill trained and ill equipped. Of the U.S. Army contingent of 31,000, more than a third consisted of the Philippine Scouts, most of whom were part of the Regular Army Philippine Division, the core of the mobile defense forces. The Far East Air Force, before the Japanese attack, had a total of 277 aircraft of all types, mostly obsolescent but including 35 new heavy bombers. Admiral Thomas C. Hart's Asiatic Fleet, based on the Philippines, consisted of 3 cruisers, 13 old destroyers,

6 gunboats, 6 motor torpedo boats, 32 patrol bombers, and 29 submarines. A regiment of marines, withdrawn from Shanghai, also joined the defending forces late in November 1941. Before the end of December, however, American air and naval power in the Philippines had virtually ceased to exist. The handful of bombers surviving the early attacks had been evacuated to Australia, and the bulk of the Asiatic Fleet, its base facilities in ruins, had withdrawn southward to help in the defense of the Netherlands Indies.

The main Japanese invasion of the Philippines, following preliminary landings, began on December 22, 1941. While numerically inferior to the defenders, the invading force of two divisions with supporting units was well trained and equipped and enjoyed complete mastery of the air and on the sea. The attack centered on Luzon, the northernmost and largest island of the archipelago, where all but a small fraction of the defending forces were concentrated. The main landings were made on the beaches of Lingayen Gulf, in the northwest, and Lamon Bay in the southeast. General MacArthur's plan was to meet and destroy the invaders on the beaches, but his troops were unable to prevent the enemy from gaining secure lodgments. On December 23 MacArthur ordered a general withdrawal into the mountainous Bataan Peninsula, across Manila Bay from the capital city. Manila itself was occupied by the Japanese without resistance. The retreat into Bataan was a complex operation, involving converging movements over difficult terrain into a cramped assembly area from which only two roads led into the peninsula itself. Under constant enemy attack, the maneuver was executed with consummate skill and at considerable cost to the attackers. Yet American and Filipino losses were heavy, and the unavoidable abandonment of large stocks of supplies foredoomed the defenders of Bataan to ultimate defeat in the siege that followed. An ominous portent was the cutting of food rations by half on the last day of the retreat.

By January 7, 1942, General MacArthur's forces held well-prepared positions across the upper part of the Bataan Peninsula. Their presence there, and on Corregidor and its satellite island fortresses guarding the entrance to Manila Bay, denied the enemy the use of the bay throughout the siege. In the first major enemy offensive, launched early in January, the "battling bastards of Bataan" at first gave ground but thereafter handled the Japanese so roughly that attacks ceased altogether from mid-February until April, while the enemy reorganized and heavily reinforced. The defenders were, however, too weak to seize the initiative themselves.

General MacArthur, meanwhile, was ordered by the President to leave his post and go to Australia in order to take command of Allied operations against the Japanese in the Southwest Pacific. In mid-March he and a small party made

GENERAL WAINWRIGHT BROADCASTING TO AMERICAN FORCES

their way through the Japanese lines by motor torpedo boat to Mindanao, and from there were flown to Australia. Command of the forces in the Philippines devolved upon Lt. Gen. Jonathan M. Wainwright.

By April the troops on Bataan were subsisting on about fifteen ounces of food daily, less than a quarter of the peacetime ration. Their diet, consisting mostly of rice supplemented by carabao, mule, monkey, or lizard meat, was gravely deficient in vitamins and provided less than 1,000 calories a day, barely enough to sustain life. Weakened by hunger and poor diet, thousands succumbed to malaria, dengue, scurvy, beriberi, and amoebic dysentery, made impossible to control by the shortage of medical supplies, especially quinine. Desperate efforts were made to send food, medicine, ammunition, and other supplies through the Japanese blockade to the beleaguered forces. But during the early weeks, before the enemy cordon had tightened, it proved impossible, despite promises of lavish pay and bonuses, to muster the necessary ships and crews. Even so, sizable stocks were accumulated in the southern islands, but only about 1,000 tons of rations ever reached Manila Bay. Shipments in converted destroyers from the United States were too late and too few, and only insignificant quantities could be brought in by submarine and aircraft.

At the beginning of April the Japanese, behind a pulverizing artillery barrage, attacked again. The American lines crumpled, and in a few days the defending forces virtually disintegrated. On April 9 Maj. Gen. Edward P. King, Jr., commanding the forces on Bataan, surrendered. For almost another month the garrison on Corregidor and the other islands, swelled by refugees from Bataan, held out under air bombardment and almost continuous plunging fire from heavy artillery massed on adjacent shores and heights—one of the most intense artillery bombardments, for so small a target, of the entire war. On the night of May 5, after a final terrific 5-day barrage, Japanese assault troops won a foothold on Corregidor, and the following night, when it became apparent that further resistance was useless, General Wainwright surrendered unconditionally. Under his orders, which the Japanese forced him to broadcast, other American commanders in the Philippines capitulated one by one. By early June, except for scattered guerrilla detachments in the hills, all organized resistance in the islands had ceased.

Deploying American Military Strength

After more than a year and a half of rearming, the United States in December 1941 was still in no position to carry the war to its enemies. On December 7 the Army numbered some 1,644,000 men (including about 120,000 officers), organized into 4 armies, 37 divisions (30 infantry, 5 armored, 2 cavalry), and over 40 combat air groups. Three of the divisions were overseas (2 in Hawaii, 1 in the Philippines), with other garrison forces totaling less than 200,000. By spreading equipment and ammunition thin, the War Department might have put a substantial force into the field to repel an attack on the continental United States; 17 of the divisions at home were rated as technically ready for combat. But these divisions lacked the supporting units and the training necessary to weld them into corps and armies. More serious still, they were inadequately equipped with many weapons that recent operations in Europe had shown to be indispensable—for example, tank and antitank guns, antiaircraft artillery, radios, and radar—and some of these shortages were aggravated by lack of auxiliary equipment like fire control mechanisms.

Above all, ammunition of all kinds was so scarce that the War Department was unwilling to commit more than one division and a single antiaircraft regiment for service in any theater where combat operations seemed imminent. Only one division-size task force, in fact, was sent to the far Pacific before April 1942. Against air attacks, too, the country's defenses were meager. Along the Pacific coast the Army had only 45 modern fighter planes ready to fly, and only twelve

3-inch antiaircraft guns to defend the whole Los Angeles area. On the east coast there were only 54 Army fighter planes ready for action. While the coastal air forces, primarily training commands, could be reinforced by aircraft from the interior of the country, the total number of modern fighter aircraft available was less than 1,000. Fortunately, there was no real threat of an invasion in force, and the rapidly expanding output of munitions from American factories promised to remedy one of these weaknesses within a few months. Furthermore, temporary diversions of lend-lease equipment, especially aircraft, helped to bolster the overall defense posture within the first few weeks after Pearl Harbor. The Army hoped by April to have as many as thirteen divisions equipped and supplied with ammunition for combat.

To deploy these forces overseas was another matter. Although the U.S. merchant marine ranked second only to Great Britain's and the country possessed an immense shipbuilding capacity, the process of chartering, assembling, and preparing shipping for the movement of troops and military cargo took time. Time was also needed to schedule and organize convoys, and, owing to the desperate shortage of escort vessels, troop movements had to be widely spaced. Convoying and evasive routing, in themselves, greatly reduced the effective capacity of shipping. Moreover, vast distances separated U.S. ports from the areas threatened by Japan, and to these areas went the bulk of the forces deployed overseas during the months immediately following Pearl Harbor. Through March 1942, as a result, the outflow of troops to overseas bases averaged only about 50,000 per month, as compared with upwards of 250,000 during 1944, when shipping was fully mobilized and plentiful and the sea lanes were secure.

There seemed a real danger early in 1942, however, that German U-boats might succeed in reducing transatlantic deployment to a trickle—not so much by attacking troop transports, most of which could outrun their attackers, as by sinking the slow cargo ships on which the forces overseas depended for support. Soon after Germany's declaration of war, the U-boats struck at the virtually unprotected shipping lanes in the western Atlantic, and subsequently extended their attacks to the Gulf of Mexico and Caribbean areas and the mouth of the St. Lawrence. During the spring of 1942 tankers and freighters were torpedoed in plain view of vacationers on east coast beaches, and coastal cities dimmed or extinguished their lights in order that ships might not provide silhouetted targets for the U-boats. The Navy lacked the means to cope with the peril. In late December 1941 it had only twenty assorted surface vessels and about a hundred aircraft to protect the whole North Atlantic coastal frontier. During the winter and spring these were supplemented by another hundred

Army planes of longer range, several armed British trawlers, and as many improvised craft as could be pressed into service.

But the toll of ship sinkings increased. In March 788,000 deadweight tons of Allied and neutral dry cargo shipping were lost, in June 936,000 tons. Tanker losses reached an all-time peak of 375,000 tons in March, leading to complete suspension of coastal tanker movements and to gasoline rationing in the seaboard states. During the first six months of 1942 losses of Allied shipping were almost as heavy as during the whole of 1941 and exceeded new construction by almost 2.8 million deadweight tons. Although the United States was able by May to balance its own current losses by building new ships, Britain and other Allied countries continued until the following August to lose more than they could build, and another year passed before new construction offset cumulative losses.

Slowly and with many setbacks a system of countermeasures was developed. Convoying of coastal shipping, with ships sailing only by day, began in the spring of 1942. North-South traffic between U.S. and Caribbean and South American ports was also convoyed, on schedules interlocked with those of the transatlantic convoys. The latter, during 1942, were protected in the western half of the Atlantic by the U.S. and Canadian Navies, in the eastern half by the British. Troops were transported across the Atlantic either without escort in large, speedy liners like the *Queen Elizabeth* and the *Queen Mary*—which between them carried almost a quarter of all U.S. troops sent to Europe—or in heavily escorted convoys. Throughout the war, not a single loaded troop transport was sunk on the United Kingdom run. The slow merchant ships were convoyed in large groups according to speed.

But with responsibility for U.S. antisubmarine operations divided between the Navy and Army Air Forces, effective co-operation was hampered by sharp disagreement over organization and methods, and available resources throughout 1942 were inadequate. The U-boats, meanwhile, were operating with deadly effect and in growing numbers. Late in the year they began to hunt in packs, resupplied at sea by large cargo submarines ("milch cows"). The Allied convoys to Murmansk and other northern Soviet ports suffered especially heavy losses on their long passage around the top of the Scandinavian peninsula. In November shipping losses from all causes soared above 1.1 million deadweight tons— the peak, as it turned out, for the entire war, but few at the time dared so to predict.

In the Pacific, fortunately, the principal barriers to deployment of U.S. forces were distance and lack of prepared bases, not enemy submarines. Japan's fleet of undersea craft made little effort to prey on the Allied sea lanes and probably, over the vast reaches of the Pacific, could not have inflicted serious damage in any case. The chief goal of American deployment to the Pacific during most of 1942, following the initial reinforcement of Hawaii and the Panama Canal, was to build up a base in Australia and secure the chain of islands leading to it. Australia was a vast, thinly populated, and, except in its southeastern portion, largely undeveloped island continent, 7,000 miles and almost a month's sail from the U.S. west coast. It had provided a haven for some 4,000 American troops who, on December 7, had been at sea, bound for the Philippines, and in January a task force of division size (POPPY Force) was hastily assembled and dispatched to New Caledonia to guard its eastern approaches. During the first few weeks the main effort of the small American forces went into sending relief supplies to the Philippines and aircraft and troops to Java to stem the Japanese invasion. Beginning in March, as the futility of these efforts became evident, and coincident with the arrival of General MacArthur to assume command of all Allied forces in the Southwest Pacific, the construction of base facilities and the build-up of balanced air and ground forces got under way in earnest.

This build-up had as its first object the defense of Australia itself, for at the end of January the Japanese had occupied Rabaul on New Britain Island, thus posing an immediate threat to Port Moresby, the weakly held Australian base in southeastern New Guinea. In February President Roosevelt pledged American help in countering this threat, and in March and April two infantry divisions (the 41st and 32d) left the United States for the Southwest Pacific. At the same time, construction of air and refueling bases was being rushed to completion in the South Pacific islands that formed steppingstones along the ocean routes to Australia and New Zealand. After the western anchor of this chain, New Caledonia, was secured by the POPPY Force, Army and Marine garrisons and reinforcements were sent to various other islands along the line, culminating with the arrival of the 37th Division in the Fiji Islands in June.

These moves came none too soon for, during the spring, the Japanese, after occupying Rabaul, pushed into the southern Solomons, within easy striking distance of the American bases on Espíritu Santo and New Caledonia. They also occupied the northeastern coast of New Guinea, just across the narrow Papuan peninsula from Port Moresby, which the Americans and Australians were developing into a major advanced base in preparation for an eventual offensive northward. The stage was thus set for a major test of strength in the Pacific—American forces spread thinly along an immense arc from Hawaii to Australia, with outposts far to the north in Alaska; the Japanese securely in possession of the vast areas north and west of the arc and, with the advantage of interior lines, prepared to strike in force at any point. The first test came in May, when the Japanese made an attempt from the sea to take Port Moresby. This was successfully countered in the great carrier battle of the Coral Sea. Thereupon the Japanese struck eastward, hoping to destroy the U.S. Pacific Fleet and to seize Midway—a bid for naval supremacy in the Pacific. A diversionary attack on Dutch Harbor, the most forward U.S. base in Alaska, caused considerable damage, and the Japanese were able to occupy the islands of Kiska and Attu in the foggy Aleutian chain. But the main Japanese forces, far to the south, were crushingly defeated, with especially heavy losses in carriers and aircraft. The Battle of Midway in June 1942 was one of the truly decisive engagements of the war. By seriously weakening Japan's mobile striking forces, Midway left the Japanese virtually helpless to prevent the consolidation of American positions and the eventual development of overwhelming military supremacy throughout the Pacific. Only two months later, in fact, American forces took the first step on the long "road back" by landing on Guadalcanal in the southern Solomons.

Although the RAINBOW 5 plan was put into effect immediately after Pearl Harbor, the desperate situation in the Pacific and Far East and the shortage of shipping and escorts ruled out most of the scheduled Atlantic, Caribbean, and South American deployments. In January reinforcements were sent to Iceland and a token force to Northern Ireland, and by June two full divisions (the 34th Infantry and the 1st Armored) had reached Ireland, while the remainder of the 5th Infantry had arrived in Iceland, completing the relief of the U.S. Marine brigade and most of the British garrison. No more divisions sailed eastward until August. Meanwhile, garrisons in the Atlantic and Caribbean were being built up to war strength. But plans to occupy the Azores, Canaries, and Cape Verdes, and to capture Dakar on the west African coast went by the board, primarily for lack of shipping. Also abandoned after lengthy discussion was a project (GYMNAST) proposed by Prime Minister Churchill at the ARCADIA Conference for an Anglo-American occupation of French North Africa.

Thus, despite the reaffirmation of the "Germany first" strategy at ARCADIA, the great bulk of American forces sent overseas during the first half of 1942 went to the theaters of war against Japan. Of the eight Army divisions that left the country before August, five went to the Pacific. Including two more already in Hawaii, and a Marine division at sea, bound for New Zealand (eventually for the landings on Guadalcanal in August), eight divisions were deployed against Japan in July 1942. Of the approximately 520,000 Army troops in overseas bases, 60 percent were in the Pacific (including Alaska) and the newly established China-Burma-India theater; the remainder were almost all in Caribbean and western Atlantic garrisons. Of 2,200 Army aircraft overseas, about 1,300 were in the Pacific (including Alaska) and Far East, 900 in the western Atlantic and Latin America. Not until August did the U.S. Army Air Forces in the British Isles attain sufficient strength to fly a single independent bombing mission over northern France.

Planning for a Cross-Channel Invasion

The Army's leaders and planners, schooled in a tradition that emphasized the principles of mass and offensive, had been fretting over the scale of deployment to the Pacific since early in the year. Late in January Brig. Gen. Dwight D. Eisenhower, then a War Department staff officer whom General Marshall had assigned to handle the crisis in the Pacific, noted, "We've got to go to Europe and fight—and we've got to quit wasting resources all over the world." In the joint committees Army planners urged that as soon as the situation could be stabilized in the Southwest Pacific, U.S. forces should begin to concentrate in the British Isles for an offensive against Germany. Secretary Stimson and others were pressing the same views on the President. In the middle of March the Joint Chiefs of Staff approved this course of action, and in April, at the President's order, General Marshall and Harry Hopkins, the President's personal representative, went to London to seek British approval.

Logistical considerations heavily favored both the general strategy of concentration against Germany and the specific plan of invading northwestern Europe from a base in the British Isles. Because the target area was close to the main sources of British and American power, two to three times as many forces could be hurled against northwestern Europe, with a given amount of shipping, as could be supported in operations against Japan. Britain itself was a highly industrialized country, fully mobilized after two and a half years of war, and well shielded by air and naval power—a ready-made base for a land invasion and air attacks on Germany's vitals. While invasion forces were assembling, moreover, they would serve to garrison the British Isles. Finally, an attack across the English Channel would use the only short water crossing to the Continent from a base already available and would thrust directly at the heart of Fortress Europe by the main historic invasion routes.

Even so, the plan was a desperate gamble. If northwestern Europe offered the Allies a position of strength, the Germans, too, would be strong there, close to their own heartland, served by the superb rail and road net of western and central Europe, shielded by submarines based along the entire length of Europe's Atlantic front. The limited range of fighter aircraft based in southern England narrowly restricted the choice of landing areas. Much hinged on the USSR, where for the present the bulk of Germany's land forces were pinned down. If the Soviet Union collapsed, an invasion from the west would be a suicidal venture. The invasion must therefore be launched before the Soviet armies were crushed and, moreover, in sufficient strength to draw substantial German forces away from the Eastern Front in order to avert that very catastrophe.

On the face of it, these two requirements seemed to cancel each other. For Allied planners had little hope that the Russians could stand up under another summer's onslaught, and it was obvious, in view of the scarcity of shipping, that any attack the Western Allies could mount by the coming summer or early fall would be hardly more than a pinprick. The best solution General Marshall's planners could offer to this dilemma was to set the invasion for the spring of 1943 (Roundup), in the hope that until then, through air bombardment of Germany and a continued flow of matériel to the Soviet Union, the Allies could help the Soviet armies to stave off defeat. If these measures should fail, and Soviet resistance seemed about to collapse, then, with whatever forces were on hand, the Allies would have to invade the Continent in 1942 (Sledgehammer)— and no later than September, before bad weather closed down over the Channel. The same course would be followed in the unlikely event that Germany itself showed signs of serious weakness in 1942.

In London, Mr. Hopkins and General Marshall found the British delighted that the United States was ready to commit itself to a major offensive against Germany in 1943. The British readily agreed that preparations should begin immediately for an invasion the following spring, and they undertook to provide more than half the shipping needed to move about a million American troops and immense quantities of matériel to the United Kingdom. They warned, however, that their first concern at present was to maintain their position in the Middle East, where, late in January, Rommel's revitalized Africa Korps had inflicted a serious reverse on the Eighth Army. Both sides were now feverishly building up for a new offensive. The British also expressed deep misgivings over the proposed emergency cross-Channel operation in the fall. Nevertheless, the British approved the American plan, essentially the War Department's plan, "in principle"—a phrase that was to give much trouble in the coalition war. The immediate relief felt by General Marshall's staff in Washington was reflected by General Eisenhower, then Chief, Operations Division, War Department General Staff, who noted: ". . . at long last, and after months of struggle . . . we are all definitely committed to one concept of fighting! If we can agree on major purposes and objectives, our efforts will begin to fall in line and we won't just be thrashing around in the dark."

But on the American side, too, there were strong reservations. Admiral King did not contest in principle the "Germany first" strategy. But he was determined not to allow preparations for the cross-Channel invasion to jeopardize "vital needs" in the Pacific, by which, as he candidly stated early in May, he meant the ability of U.S. forces "to hold what we have against any attack that the Japanese are capable of launching." Only the President's peremptory order on May 6 that the invasion build-up in Britain must not be slowed down (it had, indeed, scarcely begun) prevented a large-scale diversion of forces and shipping to the Pacific to counter the Japanese offensive that culminated in the great naval battles of the Coral Sea and Midway. The President himself made it clear, on the other hand, that aid to the Soviet Union would have to continue on a mounting scale, whatever the cost to Bolero (the American build-up in the United Kingdom) in matériel and shipping. And even Army leaders were unwilling to assign shipping for the movement until the scheduled build-up of garrisons in the Western Hemisphere and various other overseas stations had been completed, which, it was estimated, would not be until August at the earliest. Until then British shipping would have to carry the main burden.

Not until June 1942, therefore, did the first shipload of American troops under the new plan set sail for England in the great British luxury liner, *Queen Elizabeth*. Almost simultaneously a new crisis erupted in the Middle East. At the end of May, after a four-month lull, Rommel seized the initiative and swept around the southern flank of the British Eighth Army, which held strong positions in eastern Libya from El Gazala on the coast south to Bir Hacheim. After two weeks of hard fighting, in which the British seemed to be holding their own, Rommel succeeded in taking Bir Hacheim, the southern anchor of the British line. During the next few days British armor, committed piecemeal in an effort to cover a withdrawal to the northeast, was virtually wiped out by skillfully concealed German 88-mm. guns. The Eighth Army once again retreated across the Egyptian frontier, and on June 21 Tobruk, which the British had expected, as in 1941, to hold out behind Axis lines, was captured with its garrison and large stores of trucks, gasoline, and other supplies.

News of this disaster reached Prime Minister Churchill in Washington, where he had gone early in the month to tell the President that the British were unwilling to go through with an emergency cross-Channel landing late in 1942. General Marshall immediately offered to send an armored division to help the hard-pressed British in Egypt, but it was decided, for the present, to limit American aid to emergency shipments of tanks, artillery, and the ground components of three combat air groups. This move required the diversion for many weeks of a substantial amount of U.K. shipping from the North Atlantic on the long voyage around the Cape of Good Hope. But the heaviest impact on the invasion build-up in the United Kingdom resulted from the diversion of British shipping to the Middle East and the retention there of shipping the British had earmarked for the build-up. For the time being, British participation in the BOLERO program virtually ceased.

By the end of August, with only seven months to go before the invasion was to be launched, only about 170,000 American troops were in or on their way to the British Isles, and the shipment of equipment and supplies, particularly for the development of cantonments, airfields, and base facilities, was hopelessly behind schedule. There seemed little likelihood that enough shipping would be available to complete the movement across the Atlantic of a million troops, with the ten to fifteen million tons of cargo that must accompany them, by April 1943 as scheduled. And even if the shipping could have been found, Britain's ports and inland transportation system would have been swamped before the influx reached its peak. Thus, by the late summer of 1942, a spring 1943 ROUNDUP appeared to be a logistical impossibility.

Torch Replaces Sledgehammer-Roundup

By this time, in fact, American military leaders had become discouraged about a cross-Channel invasion in spring of 1943, though not primarily because of the lag in the build-up program. In June the British had decided that SLEDGE-HAMMER, for which they had never had any enthusiasm, could not be undertaken except in a situation which offered good prospects of success—that is, if the Germans should seem about to collapse. At the moment, with the German summer offensive just starting to roll toward the Caucasus and the lower Don, such a situation did not appear to be an imminent possibility. The British decision was influenced in part by the alarming lag in deliveries of American landing craft, of which less than two-thirds of the promised quota for the operation was expected to materialize. The British also argued that the confusion and losses attendant upon executing SLEDGEHAMMER—and the cost of supporting the beachhead once it was established—were likely to disrupt preparations for the main invasion the following spring. Since SLEDGEHAMMER, if carried out, would have to be, in the main, a British undertaking, the British veto was decisive. The operation was canceled.

As a substitute, the British proposed a less risky venture—landings in French North Africa—which they were confident could be accomplished in stride, without harm to ROUNDUP. To Stimson, Marshall, King, and Arnold this proposal was anathema. Failure would be a costly, perhaps fatal rebuff to Allied prestige.

Success might be even more dangerous, the Americans feared, for it might lead the Allies step by step into a protracted series of operations around the southern periphery of Europe, operations that could not be decisive and would only postpone the final test of strength with Germany. At the very least, an invasion of North Africa would, the Americans were convinced, rule out a spring 1943 invasion of the Continent. The Army planners preferred the safer alternative of simply reinforcing the British in Egypt.

The British proposal was, nevertheless, politically shrewd, for it was no secret that President Roosevelt had long ago expressed a predilection for this very undertaking. He was determined, besides, that American ground forces go into action somewhere in the European area before the end of 1942. Already half persuaded, he hardly needed Churchill's enthusiastic rhetoric to win him over to the new project. When General Marshall and his colleagues in the Joints Chiefs of Staff suggested, as an alternative, that the United States should immediately go on the defensive in Europe and turn all-out against Japan, Roosevelt brusquely rejected the idea.

In mid-July, Hopkins, Marshall, and King went to London under orders from the President to reach agreement with the British on some operation in 1942. After a vain effort to persuade the British to reconsider an invasion of the Continent in 1942, the Americans reluctantly agreed on July 24 to the North Africa operation, now christened TORCH, to be launched before the end of October. The President, overruling Marshall's suggestion that final decision be postponed until mid-September in order to permit a reappraisal of the Soviet situation, cabled Hopkins that he was "delighted" and that the orders were now "full speed ahead." Into the final agreement, however, Marshall and King wrote their own conviction that the decision on TORCH "in all probability" rulled out invasion of the Continent in 1943 and meant, further, that the Allies had accepted "a defensive, encircling line of action" in the European-Mediterranean war.

End of the Defensive Stage

With the decision for TORCH, the first stage in the search for a strategic plan against Germany came to an end. In retrospect, 1941–42 had been a period of defensive strategy, and a strategy of scarcity. The British and American approaches to war had had their first conflict, and the British had won the first round. That British notions of strategy had tended to prevail was not surprising. British forces had been mobilized earlier and were in the theaters in far greater numbers than American forces. The United States was still mobilizing its manpower and resources. It had taken the better part of the year after Pearl

Harbor for U.S. forces to have an appreciable effect in the theaters. Strategic planning in 1942 had been largely opportunistic, hand to mouth, and limited by critical shortages in shipping and munitions. Troops had been parceled out piecemeal to meet immediate threats and crises. Despite the "Germany first" decision, the total U.S. Army forces deployed in the war against Japan by the end of the year actually exceeded the total U.S. Army forces deployed in the war against Germany. The one scheme to put Allied planning on an orderly, long-range basis and to achieve the concepts of mass and concentration in which General Marshall and his staff had put their faith had failed. By the close of the critical first year after Pearl Harbor, an effective formula for halting the dissipation of forces and matériel in what it regarded as secondary ventures still eluded the Army high command.

CHAPTER 21

Grand Strategy and the Washington High Command

In 1943 the debate within the Grand Alliance over strategy against the Axis Powers entered a new stage. The midwar period—roughly to the establishment of a foothold in Normandy in the summer of 1944—was the period of increasing plenty. The power to call the turn on strategy and to choose the time and place to do battle passed to the Allies. U.S. troops and supplies flowed out in ever-increasing numbers and quantity, and the full impact of American mobilization and production was felt not only in the theaters but also in Allied councils. But the transition to the strategic initiative introduced many new and complex problems for the high command in Washington. Active and passive fronts were now established all over the world. The TORCH decision had thrown all Allied planning into a state of uncertainty. For General Marshall and the Army planners in the Washington command post the basic strategic question was how to limit operations in subsidiary theaters and carry the war decisively to the Axis Powers. They had to start over and seek new and firmer long-range bases upon which to plan for victory in the multifront coalition war.

Strategic Planning for Offensive Warfare: Midwar

The decision for TORCH opened a great debate on European strategy between the Americans and the British that endured down to the summer of 1944. The issues that emerged were disputed in and out of the big international conferences of midwar from Casablanca in January 1943 to Second Quebec in September 1944. In that debate Churchill eloquently urged ever onward in the Mediterranean—Sicily, landing in Italy, Rome, the Pisa-Rimini line; then "north and northeast." President Roosevelt, himself fascinated by the possibilities in the Mediterranean, to a considerable extent seconded these moves, despite the reluctance of the American Chiefs. Pleading his case skillfully, the British leader stressed the need to continue the momentum, the immediate advantages, the "great prizes" to be picked up in the Mediterranean, the need to continue the softening-up process, while the Allies awaited a favorable opportunity to invade the Continent across the English Channel. The fact that sizable Allied forces were present in the Mediterranean and that there was an immediate chance to weaken the enemy in that area were telling arguments.

At the same time the Americans—with General Marshall as the foremost military spokesman—gradually made progress toward limiting the Mediterranean advance, toward directing it to the west rather than to the east, toward linking it directly with a definite major cross-Channel operation, and thereby winning their way back to the idea of waging a war of mass and concentration on the Continent. Part of their task was to secure agreement with President Roosevelt, part with the British, and eventually the Russians. The series of decisions reached at the 1943 conferences—Casablanca in January, Washington (TRIDENT) in May, First Quebec (QUADRANT) in August, and Cairo-Tehran (SEXTANT-EUREKA) in November and December—reflect the compromises of the Americans and the British between opportunism and long-range commitments, between a war of attrition and a war of mass and concentration.

Each of these conferences marked a milestone in coalition strategy and in the maturation of American strategic planning. At Casablanca General Marshall made a last vigorous but vain stand for a cross-Channel operation in 1943. The conferees did approve a round-the-clock combined bomber offensive against Germany that both the Americans and the British viewed as a prerequisite to a future cross-Channel operation. But no real long-range plan for the defeat of the Axis Powers emerged. Casablanca merely recognized that the Anglo-Americans would retain the initiative in the Mediterranean, and defined the short-range objective in terms of a prospective operation against Sicily.

Unlike the small, disunited American delegation, the well-prepared British operated as a cohesive team and presented a united front. President Roosevelt, still attracted to the Mediterranean, had not yet made the notion of a big cross-Channel attack his own. A striking illustration of the want of understanding between the White House and the military staffs came in connection with the unconditional surrender formula to which he and Churchill publicly committed themselves at Casablanca. The President had simply informed the JCS of his intention to support that concept as the basic Allied aim in the war at a meeting at the White House shortly before the conference. But no study of the meaning of this formula for the conduct of the war was made by either the Army or the Joint Staff before or during the conference—nor did the President encourage his military advisers to do so.

To the American military staff it appeared at the time that the long experience of the British in international negotiations had carried the day. Keenly disappointed, Brig. Gen. Albert C. Wedemeyer, General Marshall's principal adviser at Casablanca, wrote: ". . . we lost our shirts and . . . are now committed to a subterranean umbilicus operation in midsummer. . . . we came, we listened, and we were conquered."

General Wedemeyer admired the way the British had presented their case: "They swarmed down upon us like locusts with a plentiful supply of planners and various other assistants with prepared plans. . . . As an American I wish that we might be more glib and better organized to cope with these super negotiators. From a worm's eye viewpoint it was apparent that we were confronted by generations and generations of experience in committee work and in rationalizing points of view. They had us on the defensive practically all the time."

The American military staff took the lessons of Casablanca to heart. If they did not become more glib, they at least organized themselves better. To meet the British on more equal terms, they overhauled their joint planning system and resolved to reach closer understandings with the President in advance of future meetings. As a by-product of the debate and negotiation over grand strategy in midwar, the planning techniques and methods of the Americans became more nearly like those of their British ally, even if their strategic ideas still differed. They became more skilled in the art of military diplomacy, of quid pro quo, or what might be termed the "tactics" of strategic planning. At the same time their strategic thinking became more sophisticated. The Casablanca Conference represented the last fling for the "either-or" school of thought in the American military staff. Henceforth, they began to think not in terms of this *or* that operation, but in terms of this *and* that—or what one planner fittingly called "permutations and combinations." The outstanding strategic questions for them were no longer to be phrased in terms of either a Mediterranean or a cross-Channel operation, but in terms of defining the precise relations between them—and the Combined Bomber Offensive.

In the debate, the American Joint Chiefs of Staff countered British demands for more emphasis upon the Mediterranean, particularly the eastern Mediterranean, by supporting further development of Pacific offensives. Holding open the "Pacific alternative" carried with it the threat of non cross-Channel operation at all—which the British did not wish. The war in the Pacific thereby offered the United States staff a significant lever for keeping the Mediterranean issue under control. At the same time General Marshall recognized that the Mediterranean offensive could not be stopped completely with North Africa or Sicily and that definite advantages would accrue from knocking out Italy, opening up the Mediterranean further for Allied shipping, and widening the air offensive against Germany.

Beginning with the compromise agreements at TRIDENT in the spring of 1943, the American representatives could point to definite steps toward fixing European strategy in terms of a major cross-Channel undertaking for 1944. At that conference they assented to a plan for eliminating Italy from the war, which the British urged as the "great prize" after Sicily. But the forces, the Americans insisted, were to be limited so far as possible to those already in the Mediterranean. At the same time, they won British agreement to the transfer of 4 American and 3 British divisions from the Mediterranean to the United Kingdom. Both sides agreed to continue the Combined Bomber Offensive from the United Kingdom in four phases to be completed by April 1944 and leading up to an invasion across the Channel. Most encouraging was the President's unequivocal announcement in favor of a cross-Channel undertaking for the spring of 1944. The British agreed that planning should start for mounting such an operation with target date, May 1944, on the basis of 29 divisions built up in the United Kingdom (Operation ROUNDHAMMER, later called OVERLORD). The bare outlines of a new pattern of European strategy began to take shape.

That pattern took clearer shape at QUADRANT. There the American Chiefs urged a firm commitment to OVERLORD, the plan developed by a British-American planning staff in London. The British agreed but refused to give it the "overriding priority" over all operations in the Mediterranean area that the Americans desired. Plans were to proceed for eliminating Italy from the war, establishing bases as far north as Rome, seizing Sardinia and Corsica, and landing in southern France. Forces for these operations would be limited to those allotted at TRIDENT. With a definite limitation on the Mediterranean offensive, authorization for a definite allocation of forces for the approved cross-Channel operation, and for an extended Combined Bomber Offensive in support of it, the strategic pattern against Germany was taking on more final form.

After QUADRANT came new danger signals for the Washington high command. The British were making overtures for active operations in the Aegean, which the Americans interpreted, wrongly or rightly, as a prelude to a move on the Balkans and a consequent threat to the cross-Channel strategy. At the Moscow Conference in October 1943 came other warning signs from another and more unexpected source. At that meeting of the foreign ministers, a prelude to the full-dress conference at Tehran to follow, the representatives of the Anglo-American staffs met for the first time with the Russian staff. In a surprise

TEHRAN CONFERENCE

maneuver, the Russians, who from the beginning had been pleading for the second front in Europe, intimated that they might be willing to accept an active campaign in Italy as the second front.

With these portents in mind, the uneasy American Joint Chiefs of Staff accompanied the President on board the USS *Iowa* en route to the Cairo Conference in November 1943. During the rehearsals on that voyage for the meetings ahead the President afforded his military advisers a rare glimpse into his reflections on the political problems that were bound up with the war and its outcome. His concern lest the United States be drawn into a permanent or lengthy occupation of Europe came out sharply in the discussion with the JCS on the zones of occupation in postwar Germany. As he told the JCS, "We should not get roped into accepting any European sphere of influence." Nor did he wish the United States to become involved in a prolonged task of reconstituting France, Italy, and the Balkans. "France," he declared, "is a British baby." Significantly, the President added, "There would definitely be a race for Berlin. We may have to put the United States Divisions into Berlin as soon as possible." With a pencil he quickly sketched on a simple map of Europe the zonal boundaries he envisaged, putting Berlin and Leipzig in a big American zone in northern Germany—one of the most unusual records of the entire war and later brought back to Washington by Army officers in the American delegation.

Tehran proved to be the decisive conference in European strategy. There, for the first time in the war, President Roosevelt, Prime Minister Churchill, and their staffs met with Marshal Stalin, the Soviet leader, and his staff. Churchill made eloquent appeals for operations in Italy, the Aegean, and the east Mediterranean, even at the expense of a delay in OVERLORD. For reasons of its own, the USSR put its weight behind the American concept of strategy. Confident of its capabilities, demonstrated in its great comeback since the critical days of Stalingrad, the Soviet Union asserted its full power as an equal member of the Allied coalition. Stalin came out vigorously in favor of OVERLORD and limiting further operations in the Mediterranean to one directly assisting OVERLORD, an invasion of southern France. In turn, the Russians promised to launch an all-out offensive on their front to accompany the Allied moves. Stalin's strong stand put the capstone on Western strategy against Germany. The Anglo-American Chiefs agreed to launch OVERLORD during May 1944 in conjunction with a southern France operation, and to consider these the supreme operations for that year.

The final blueprint for Allied victory in Europe had taken shape. Germany was to be crushed between the jaws of a gigantic vise applied from the west and the east. How much reliance President Roosevelt had come to place in General Marshall was reflected in his decision not to release Marshall for the command of the cross-Channel attack. As he told General Marshall, "I . . . could not sleep at night with you out of the country." President Roosevelt gave the nod to General Eisenhower, who had built a solid reputation as the successful leader of coalition forces in the Mediterranean. Preparations for the big cross-Channel attack began in earnest.

The last lingering issue in the long drawn-out debate was not settled until the summer of 1944. In the months following Tehran, the southern France operation came perilously close to being abandoned in favor of the British desire for further exploitation in Italy and possibly even across the Julian Alps into the Hungarian plain. Complicating the picture was a shortage of landing craft to carry off both OVERLORD and the southern France attack simultaneously. But General Marshall and the Washington military authorities, backed by President Roosevelt, remained adamant on the southern attack. The British and the Americans did not reach final agreement on a southern France operation until August—two months after the OVERLORD landings—just a few days before the operation was actually launched, when Churchill reluctantly yielded. This concluding phase of the debate represented the last gasp of the peripheral strategy with a new and sharper political twist. Churchill was now warily watching the changing European scene with one eye on the retreating Germans, and the other on the advancing Russians.

A number of misconceptions grew up in the postwar period about this Anglo-American debate over strategy. What was at stake in the midwar debate was not whether there should be a cross-Channel operation. Rather the question was: Should that operation be a full-bodied drive with a definite target date that the Americans desired, or a final blow to an enemy critically weakened in a war of opportunity that the British desired? It is a mistake to assume that the British did not from the first want a cross-Channel operation. The difference lay essentially in the precise timing of that attack and in the extent and direction of preparatory operations. Once agreed on the major blow, the British stoutly held out for a strong initial assault that would insure success in the operation. It is also a mistake to assume that the Americans remained opposed to all Mediterranean operations. Indeed, much of their effort in 1943-44 was spent in reconciling those operations with a prospective cross-Channel operation.

What about the question of a Balkan alternative that has aroused so much controversy? Would it not have been wiser to have invaded the continent through the Balkans and thereby forestall Soviet domination? The fact must be emphasized that this is a postwar debate. The Balkan invasion was never proposed by any responsible leader in Allied strategy councils as an alternative to OVERLORD; nor did any Allied debate or combined planning take place in those terms. After the war Churchill steadfastly denied that he wanted a Balkan invasion. The British contended that the Americans had been frightened by the specter rather than by the substance of their proposals. And indeed the American staff had been frightened by the implications of Churchillian proposals for raids, assistance to native populations, throwing in a few armored divisions, and the like—for the eastern Mediterranean and Balkan regions. For the American staff Mediterranean operations had offered a striking demonstration of how great the costs of a war of attrition could be. The so-called "soft underbelly" of Italy, to which the Prime Minister had glowingly referred, turned out to be a hard-shelled back demanding more and more increments of American and Allied men and means. The mere thought of being sucked step by step, by design or by circumstance, into a similar undertaking in the Balkans, an area of poor terrain and communications—even if it were an unrealistic fear on the part of the American staff—was enough to send shivers up the spines of American planners. Certainly, neither the President nor the American staff wanted to get involved in the thorny politics of the Balkan area, and both were determined to stay out. The Balkan question was never argued out in frank military or political terms by the Allies during World War II.

Frustrated by the loss of what he regarded as glittering opportunities in the Mediterranean, Churchill struck out after the war at the American wartime "logical, large-scale mass-production thinking." But as Gordon Harrison, the author of *Cross-Channel Attack,* put it: "To accuse Americans of mass-production thinking is only to accuse them of having a mass-production economy and of recognizing the military advantage of such an economy. The Americans were power-minded." From the beginning they thought in terms of taking on the main German armies and beating them. Back of the American staff's fear of a policy of attritional and peripheral warfare against Germany in midwar lay their continued anxiety over its ultimate costs in men, resources, and time. This anxiety was increased by their concern with getting on with the war against Japan. Basic in their thinking was a growing realization of the ultimate limits of American manpower and a growing anxiety about the effects of a long-continued period of maximum mobilization on the home front. All of these factors combined to confirm their faith in the doctrine of military concentration.

As it turned out, the final strategy against Germany was a compromise of American and British views—of British peripheral strategy and the American principle of concentration. To the extent that the cross-Channel operation was delayed a year later than the Americans wished in order to take advantage of Mediterranean opportunities and to continue the softening up process, the British prevailed. Perhaps still haunted by the ghosts of Passchendaele and Dunkerque, the British were particularly sensitive to the requisite conditions for OVERLORD—for example, how many enemy troops could be expected to oppose it. But, as the Americans had hoped from the beginning, the cross-Channel attack turned out to be a conclusive operation with a fixed target date; it was given the highest priority and the maximum force to drive directly at the heart of German power.

Thus, by the summer of 1944 the final blueprinting of the Allied strategy for defeating Germany was completed. Despite the compromises with opportunism, American staff notions of fighting a concentrated, decisive war had been clearly written into the final pattern. Those notions had been reinforced by the addition, from Casablanca onward, of the unconditional surrender aim. The peripheral trend had been brought under control, and General Marshall had managed to conserve American military power for the big cross-Channel blow. The Americans had learned to deal with the British on more nearly equal terms. The military chiefs had drawn closer to the President and the U.S. side was able to present a united front vis-à-vis the British.

During the Anglo-American debate of midwar, significant changes had taken place in the alignment of power within the Grand Alliance. These shifts had implications as important for war strategy as for future relations among the wartime partners. By the close of 1943 the mighty American industrial and military machine was in high gear. The growing flow of American military strength and supplies to the European theater assured the acceptance of the American strategic concept. The Soviet Union, steadily gathering strength and confidence in 1943, made its weight felt at a critical point in the strategic debate. Britain had virtually completed its mobilization by the end of 1943, and stresses and strains had begun to appear in its economy. Compared to the Soviet Union and the United States, Britain was becoming relatively weaker. In midwar the Americans drew up with and threatened to pass the British in deployed strength in the European theater. Within the coalition Britain's military power and notions of fighting the war were being overtaken. Tehran, which fixed the final European strategy, marked a subtle but important change in the foundations of the Alliance. For the strategists of the Pentagon and of the Kremlin the doctrine of concentration had provided a common bond.

Completing the Strategic Patterns

From the standpoint of the Washington high command, the main story of military strategy in World War II, except for the important and still unanswered question of how to defeat Japan, came to an end in the summer of 1944. The last stage—culminating in the surrender of Germany and of Japan—was the period of the payoff, of the unfolding of strategy in the field. In this final phase, the problems of winning the war began to run up against the problems of winning the peace.

Once the Allied forces became firmly lodged on the European continent and took up the pursuit of the German forces, the war became for General Marshall and his staff essentially a matter of tactics and logistics—the Supreme Allied Commander, General Eisenhower, assuming the responsibility for making decisions as military circumstances in the field dictated. But to Churchill, disturbed by the swift Soviet advance into Poland and the Balkans, the war seemed more than ever a contest for great political stakes. In the last year of the European conflict therefore, the two approaches often became a question of military tactics versus political considerations.

By the summer of 1944 the shape of things to come was already apparent. Once on the Continent, General Eisenhower was given more and more responsibility for political decisions, or fell heir to them by default. Lacking political guidance and direction from Washington, the commander in the field made decisions on the basis of military considerations. He fell back on the U.S. staff notions of defeating the enemy and ending the war quickly and decisively with the fewest casualties. This trend became even more marked in 1945 in the commander's decision to stop at the Elbe and not attempt to take Berlin or Prague ahead of the Russians.

As usual, General Marshall and the U.S. staff backed the decisions of the commander in the field. Typical of Marshall's approach were two statements he made in April 1945—one in response to a British proposal to capture Berlin, the other concerning the liberation of Prague. With reference to Berlin, Marshall joined with his colleagues in the JCS in emphasizing to the British Chiefs of Staff "that the destruction of the German armed forces is more important than any political or psychological advantages which might be derived from possible capture of the German capital ahead of the Russians. . . . Only Eisenhower is in a position to make a decision concerning his battle and the best way to exploit successes to the full." With respect to Prague, Marshall wrote to Eisenhower "Personally and aside from all logistic, tactical or strategic implications, I would be loath to hazard American lives for purely political purposes." Such views of the Army Chief of Staff took on added significance, for during Roosevelt's final and his successor's early days in office the burden of dealing with important issues fell heavily on the senior military advisers in the Washington high command. Marshall's stand on these issues was entirely consistent with earlier Army strategic planning. Whatever the ultimate political outcome, from the standpoint of a decisive military conclusion of the war against Germany it made little difference whether the forces of the United States or those of the Soviet Union took Berlin and Prague. At the same time, in purely military dealings with the Russians in the closing months of the European conflict, and as Soviet and American troops drew closer, the American staff began to stiffen its stand and a firmer note crept into its negotiations for co-ordination of Allied efforts. Early in 1945 Marshall advised Eisenhower to forget diplomatic niceties in dealing with the Russians and urged him to adopt a direct approach "in simple Main Street Abilene style."

Churchill's inability to reverse the course of the last year of the war underscored the changed relationships between U.S. and British national military weight and the shifting bases of the Grand Alliance. With British manpower already mobilized to the hilt, after the middle of 1944 British production became increasingly unbalanced, and the British fought the remainder of the war with a contracting economy. The Americans did not hit the peak of their military manpower mobilization until May 1945—the month Germany surrendered. Reaching their war production peak at the end of 1943, they were able to sustain it at high levels to the end of the war. The greater capacity of the American economy and population to support a sustained, large-scale Allied offensive effort showed up clearly in the last year of the European war. Once entrenched on the Continent, American divisions began to outnumber the British more and more. Through the huge stockpiles of American production already built up and through his control of the growing U.S. military manpower on the Continent, General Eisenhower was able to put the imprint of U.S. staff thinking on how to win the war. Whatever his political predilections, Churchill had to yield. As the war against Germany lengthened beyond the hoped-for end in 1944, British influence in high Allied councils went into further decline. The last year of the war saw the United States and the Soviet Union emerging as the two strongest military powers in Europe, the one as intent on leaving Europe soon as the other was on pushing its strategic frontiers westward. On the Western side the struggle was to be concluded the way the American military chiefs had wished to wage it from the beginning—as a conventional war of concentration.

Meanwhile, as the war with Germany was drawing to a close, the strategy for defeating Japan had gradually been taking shape. Despite the Germany-first principle, the so-called secondary war simply would not stand still. From the beginning, in the defensive as well as in the offensive stage, the Pacific exerted a strong pull on American forces and resources. Nor would American public opinion tolerate a strictly defensive, limited war against Japan until Germany was beaten. Though final plans had to await the defeat of Germany, the pace of advance in the Pacific became so fast that it almost caught up with the European conflict. In the Pacific, as in the Mediterranean, American strategists learned that forces in being had a way of creating their own strategy.

While European war strategy was fashioned on the international level, the war against Japan from the beginning was almost exclusively an American affair, and its strategy essentially an interservice concern. The American plans and decisions in the Pacific war were presented to the international conferences, where they usually received Allied approval with little debate. Disputes and arguments were on the service level for the most part, with General Marshall and Admiral King working out compromises between themselves. In the process General Marshall often acted as mediator between the Navy and General MacArthur.

MEDIUM TANKS ON AN AMERICAN ASSEMBLY LINE

The traditional naval concern with the Pacific and the necessarily heavy reliance in the theater upon shipping, especially assault shipping, put the main burden of developing offensive strategy upon the Navy. But Navy plans for a central Pacific offensive had to be reconciled with General MacArthur's concept of approaching Japan via the New Guinea–Philippines axis. Thus a twofold approach—"a one-two punch"—replaced the original single axis strategy. This double axis advance produced a strategy of opportunity similar to that urged by the British for the war in Europe and took the Allies to the threshold of Japan by the time the European war ended. The critical question of whether Japan could be defeated by bombardment and blockade alone, or whether an invasion would be necessary, was long debated. In Washington during the late spring of 1945 the Army's argument that plans and preparations should be made for an invasion was accepted as the safe course to follow.

The rapid pace of the Pacific advance outran the American plans for the China-Burma-India Theater, and that theater declined in strategic importance in the war against Japan. Disillusioned by the inability of China to play an active role in the final defeat of Japan, American military leaders sought to substitute the USSR. To save American lives in a Pacific OVERLORD, those leaders in general became eager to have the USSR enter the war against Japan and pin down Japanese forces on the Asiatic mainland. Before final plans for a Pacific OVERLORD could be put into effect, however, the Japanese surrendered. The dramatic dropping of atomic bombs on August 6 and 9 on Hiroshima and Nagasaki, respectively, came as a complete surprise to the American public and to the Army strategic planners, with the exception of a handful of top officers in the Washington command post who were in on the secret. In a sense the supersession of strategic plans by a revolutionary development of weapons was a fitting climax to a war that had throughout shown a strong tendency to go its own way.

The last year of the war witnessed, along with the finishing touches on grand strategy, the change-over from the predominantly military to the politico-military phase. As victory loomed, stresses and strains within the coalition became more apparent. With the Second Quebec Conference in September 1944 agreement among the Allies on military plans and war strategy became less urgent than need to arrive at acceptable politico-military terms on which the winning powers could continue to collaborate. That need became even more marked at Yalta in February 1945 and at the Potsdam Conference in July 1945. To handle these new challenges after building up a staff mechanism geared to the predominantly military business of fighting a global and coalition war necessitated considerable adjustment of Army staff processes and planning. In midwar Army planning had been geared to achieve the decisive blow on the Continent that had been a cardinal element in the planners' strategic faith. Scarcely were the Western Allies ensconced on the Continent, however, when the challenges of victory and peace were upon the Army planners. They entered the last year of the war with the coalition disintegrating, the President failing in health, and a well-organized politico-military machine lacking. Besides the frictions generating on the foreign fronts, the Army still had to cope with the immense problem of what to do with the beaten foe—with terms of surrender, occupation, and postwar bases. The military fell heir—by default—to problems no longer easily divided into military and political.

Expansion and Distribution of the Wartime Army

To the Washington high command strategic plans were one vital ingredient in the formula for victory. Manpower was another. Indeed, at stake in the midwar debate was the fresh and flexible military power of the United States. That power was also General Marshall's trump card in negotiations with the coalition partners. To put a brake on diversionary deployments to secondary theaters and ventures and to conserve American military manpower for the big cross-Channel blow became the major preoccupation of the Chief of Staff and his advisers in midwar. Behind their concern for effective presentation of the American strategic case at the midwar international conferences lay the growing uneasiness of General Marshall and his staff over the American manpower problem. To continue what appeared to them to be essentially a policy of drift in Allied strategy raised grave issues about mobilizing and deploying U.S. forces. To support a war of attrition and peripheral action, in place of concentrated effort, raised serious problems about the size and kind of Army the United States should and could maintain.

To establish a proper manpower balance for the United States in wartime was as difficult as it was important. In light of the 15 to 16 million men estimated to be physically fit for active military service, on the surface it seemed hard to understand why there should be any U.S. manpower problem at all. The problem as well as the answer stemmed basically from the fact that the Allies had from the beginning accepted the proposition that the single greatest tangible asset the United States brought to the coalition in World War II was the productive capacity of its industry. From the very beginning, U.S. manpower calculations had to be closely correlated with the needs of war industry.

The Army had therefore to compete for manpower not only with the needs of the other services but also with the claims of industry. By 1943 the "arsenal of democracy" was just beginning to hit its full productive stride. To cut too deeply into the industrial manpower of the country in order to furnish men for the Army and Navy might interfere seriously with arming U.S. and Allied troops. Furthermore, the United States was fighting a global conflict. To service its lines of communications extending around the world required large numbers of men, and great numbers of troops were constantly in transit to and from the theaters. To carry the fight across the oceans demanded a powerful Navy and a large merchant fleet, which also had to be given a high priority for manpower. Each industry as well as each theater commander was continually calling for more men. The problem for the Army was not only how much it should receive for its share of the manpower pool but also how it should divide that share most effectively to meet the diverse demands made upon it.

By 1943 the realization among the Army staff was growing that the U.S. manpower barrel did have a bottom. Even before the end of 1942 it was becoming visible. Also evident was the fact that, while the United States would remain the major "arsenal of democracy," it could no longer be regarded as a limitless source of munitions. The pool of unemployed that had cushioned the shock of mobilization for three years had been almost exhausted. Industrial expansion had slowed down, labor had become tight in many areas, and in November 1942 the President had placed a ceiling of 8.2 million officers and men upon the Army's expansion during 1943, intimating at the same time that this limit would probably hold for the duration of the war. General Marshall and his colleagues in the JCS were still determined that the United States make a major contribution in fighting forces to the defeat of the Axis Powers. But postponement of the invasion of northwestern Europe, together with the indicated limitations on American manpower and resources, made it necessary to reconsider the nature of that contribution. To match strategy, manpower, and production for the offensive phase of the war became a basic task of the Washington high command in the remainder of the war.

Supply programs for 1943 reflected prospective changes in the American role in the war. Cuts fell most heavily on the ground munitions program, which was reduced by more than one-fifth, and on lend-lease to nations other than the Soviet Union. Some reductions were also made in naval ship construction, but the program for building escort vessels was left intact and the merchant ship-building program was actually enlarged. The emphasis was on producing first of all the tools needed to defeat the U-boats and secure the sea lanes for the deployment of American forces overseas, and at the same time to insure that ample shipping would be available for this purpose. Soviet armies had to be assured a continuous flow of munitions to enable them to stave off the Germans. Meanwhile, airpower had to be built up and brought to bear as rapidly as possible, while the slower mobilization and deployment of ground forces was under way—heavy bombers to batter the German homeland, carrier-borne aircraft to restore mobility and striking power to the forces in the Pacific. The ground army, finally, had to be shaped to operate, at least during the coming year and a half, in relatively small packages at the end of long lines of communications in a great variety of terrain. Its units had to be compact, versatile, and easily transportable, but also mobile and able to hit hard. Every ton of shipping, as General McNair declared, had to deliver the maximum of fighting power.

The changing requirements and circumstances of coalition warfare in the offensive phase greatly affected plans and programs for expanding the U.S. Army—in total growth and internal distribution of strength as well as in overseas deployment. Manpower squeezes, together with strategic, logistical, and operational considerations, helped to change the shape as well as the size of the Army. By the end of 1942 the U.S. Army had grown to a strength of 5.4 million officers and men. Although this was still well under the ceiling of 8.2 million set by the President in November, the mobilization of ground combat elements was already nearing completion. Seventy-three divisions were then in being, and no more than 100 were expected to be activated. In June 1943 the goal was reduced to 90 divisions, with an overall strength ceiling of 7.7 million—far under the heavily mechanized force of 215 divisions which the framers of the Victory

Program in 1941 had considered none too large to take on the German Army
Actually the U.S. Army in 1945 reached a peak strength of 8.3 million and 89
divisions. The last division was activated in August 1943.

The strength of ground combat units in the Army increased hardly at all
after 1942, even though 16 divisions and some 350 separate artillery and engineer
battalions were added after that date. These additional units had to be formed by
means of redistribution and economies within existing personnel allotments in
the same categories. Since the Army as a whole increased by almost 3 million
men after 1942, its ground combat elements, even including replacements,
declined from over half of the Army's total strength at the beginning of 1942 to
about a third in the spring of 1945. It was no mean achievement merely to
maintain the Army's combat units at full strength during the heavy fighting of
1944 and 1945. Neither the Germans nor the Japanese were able to do as much.

Mindful of the untrained divisions sent overseas in World War I, General
Marshall from the first set as his goal thorough and realistic training of large
units in the United States, culminating in large-scale maneuvers by corps and
armies. Since all divisions had been activated by August 1943 and the mass
deployment of the Army overseas did not begin until late in that year, most
divisions were thoroughly trained. The major threat to an orderly training program came in 1944 when many trained divisions had to be skeletonized in order
to meet the demand for trained replacements. Equipment shortages were a
serious obstacle to effective training in early 1943, as in 1942, as was also the
shortage of trained commissioned and noncommissioned officers to provide
cadres.

In 1943 the Army's ground combat forces continued to undergo the drastic
reorganization and streamlining begun in 1942. Troop basis cuts reduced the
planned number of armored divisions from 20 to 16, eliminated all motorized
divisions, and cut back tank destroyer and antiaircraft units. The armored corps
disappeared. Armored and infantry divisions were reduced in personnel and
equipment. Tanks taken from armored divisions were organized into separate
tank battalions, to be attached to divisions as needed, and motor transport was
pooled under corps or army headquarters for greater flexibility.

The division remained the basic fighting team of arms and services combined
in proportions designed for continuous offensive action under normal battle
conditions. Its triangular organization was retained. The infantry division contained 3 regiments, and included, besides 4 artillery battalions (3 armed with
105-mm. howitzers, 1 with 155-mm. howitzers), a reconnaisance troop (scout
cars and light tanks), and engineer, ordnance, signal, quartermaster, medical,
and military police units. Each regiment could readily be teamed with an

artillery battalion. Reinforced with other elements of the division, or with elements assigned by corps or army headquarters, it formed the regimental combat team. The total strength of the infantry division was reduced from its prewar strength of 15,245 to 14,253.

The armored division, as organized in 1942, had consisted of 2 tank regiments and 1 armored infantry regiment, plus 3 battalions of armored artillery and an armored reconnaissance battalion. This arrangement was calculated to produce 2 combat commands, with varying proportions of tanks and infantry in division reserve. The armored division also included supporting elements corresponding to those in the infantry divisions but motorized to increase mobility. In the armored division as reorganized in 1943, battalions replaced regiments. The new model contained 3 medium tank battalions, 3 armored infantry battalions, and 3 armored artillery battalions. These, with supporting elements, could be combined readily into 3 combat commands (A, B, and Reserve). The total strength of the armored division was reduced from 14,620 to 10,937. Two armored divisions remained "heavy" divisions, with the old organization, until the end of the war.

The only other special type of division of real importance retained in 1943 was the airborne division. Including parachute and gliderborne regiments, it was designed as a miniature infantry division, with lighter, more easily transportable artillery and the minimum of vehicles and service elements needed to keep it fighting after an airdrop until it could be reinforced. Its strength was only 8,500 until early 1945 when it was raised to 12,979. By the beginning of 1945 other experimental and special-type divisions—mountain, motorized, light, jungle, and cavalry—had either disappeared or largely lost their special characteristics.

Underlying all this change were the basic aims of making ground forces mobile, flexible, and easily transportable, by increasing the proportion of standardized and interchangeable units in less rigid tactical combinations. Nor did this streamlining involve any sacrifice of effective power. Army leaders were convinced, and experience on the whole proved, that these units could not only move faster and farther, but could also strike even harder than the units they replaced.

Premobilization planning had contemplated that Negro Americans would be included in the ranks of a wartime Army proportionately to their number in the whole population and proportionately, also, in each of the arms and services. Neither goal was achieved, but the number of Negro troops in the Army reached a peak strength of over 700,000 and more than 500,000 of them served overseas. Contemporary attitudes and practices in American society kept

Negroes in segregated units throughout the war, although the Army gradually eliminated many of the obvious types of discrimination that almost inevitably flowed from their segregation. The bulk of Negro soldiers overseas were in supply and construction units; but many others who served in the two Negro divisions, in separate combat support battalions, and in a fighter group, directly engaged the enemy on the ground and in the air.

In 1944 the manpower shortage became nation-wide. The Army, under the double pressure of accelerated deployment schedules and heavy demands for infantry replacements for battle casualties in the two-front full-scale war, was driven to stringent measures. The Army Specialized Training Program, which had absorbed 150,000 soldiers in college study, was dissolved, and the aviation cadet training program was drastically curtailed. To release soldiers for battle, the Army drew heavily on limited service personnel and women for noncombat duties. The induction of female volunteers had begun in mid-1942 and in the following year, for the first time in the Army's history, women had been given a full legal military status as the Women's Army Corps (WAC). Growing in strength, the WAC reached a peak of 100,000 by the spring of 1945.

As the Army moved overseas, many posts were consolidated or closed, releasing large numbers of overhead personnel. Margins of overstrength and basic privates in tactical units were eliminated or reduced. Coast artillery units were converted to heavy artillery, hundreds of antiaircraft units were dissolved, and nondivisional infantry regiments became a source of infantry replacements. To meet the threat of the German counteroffensive in the Ardennes in December 1944, the handful of divisions remaining in the United States, most of them earmarked for the Pacific, were rushed to Europe, and the United States was left without a strategic reserve. In May 1945 the overall ground army numbered 68 infantry, 16 armored, and 5 airborne divisions.

The extent to which the Army depended on its air arm to confer striking power and mobility is suggested by the enormous growth of the Army Air Forces—from about 400,000 men at the beginning of 1942 to a peak of over 2.4 million early in 1944. At the end of the war in Europe it had 243 organized groups in being, and a numerical strength of 2.3 million men. More than 1.5 million of the worldwide AAF strength in March 1945 consisted of service troops, troops in training, and overhead.

After 1942 the growth of the ground army also was very largely in services and administrative elements. By March 1945 these comprised 2.1 million (not counting hospital patients and casuals en route) of the ground army's 5.9 million personnel. This growth reflected both the global character of the war, with its long lines of communications, and the immense numbers of noncombatant specialists needed to operate and service the equipment of a modern mechanized army. They were a manifestation, too, of the American people's insistence on providing the American citizen soldier with something like his accustomed standard of living. Less tangible and more difficult to control was the demand for large administrative and co-ordinating staffs, a demand that was self-generating since administrators themselves had to be administered and co-ordinators co-ordinated. One of the most conspicuous phenomena of global war was the big headquarters. In the European theater in 1944 "over-head" personnel, largely in higher headquarters, numbered some 114,000 men. On the eve of V–E Day, with overseas deployment for the two-front war complete, almost 1.3 million of the 2.8 million men who remained in the United States were in War Department, AGF, ASF, and AAF overhead agencies to operate the Zone of Interior establishment.

The demand for noncombatant personnel was swelled by the assignment to the Army of various administrative tasks. One was the administration of military lend-lease. Another was the development of the atomic bomb, the supersecret, $2 billion Manhattan Project assigned to the Corps of Engineers. Two of the Army's overseas commands—the China-Burma-India Theater and the Persian Gulf Command—had missions that were largely logistical in character. From the first the Pacific theaters generated the heaviest demands for service troops, to build, operate, and service the manifold facilities needed by a modern army in regions where these were virtually nonexistent. To a lesser degree these needs were also present in the Mediterranean, and operations against the Germans everywhere involved the task of repairing the ruin wrought by the enemy. Big construction projects like the Alcan Highway (from western Canada to Alaska) and the Ledo Road in Burma added to the burden. To carry out the Army's vast procurement program—to compute requirements, negotiate contracts, and expedite production—called for a multitude of highly trained administrators, mostly civilian businessmen whom the Army put into uniform.

Thus, for every three fighting men in the ground army, there were two technicians and administrators somewhere behind, engaged in functions other than killing the enemy. Behind the fighting front, too, stretched the "pipeline," filled with what General McNair once called "the invisible horde of people going here and there but seemingly never arriving." In March 1945 casuals en route or in process of assignment numbered 300,000. Far more numerous were the replacements, who at this time totaled 800,000 in the ground army; AAF replacements numbered 300,000. Almost no provision had been made for replacements in the early troop basis. The necessity of providing spaces for them, as well as for larger numbers of service and AAF troops, in the Army's total allotment of manpower went far to account for the difference between the 215 divisions in the original Victory Program and the 89 actually organized.

Replacements kept the effective strength of the Army from declining. The number of soldiers in hospitals in World War II seldom fell below 200,000, and at the beginning of 1945 reached a peak of almost 500,000. Throughout the war, the Army suffered a total of 936,000 battle casualties, including 235,000 dead; to the latter must be added 83,400 nonbattle deaths. The Army's dead represented about 3 percent of the 10,420,000 men who served in its ranks during World War II.

Despite the acknowledged primacy of the European war, only gradually did the flow of American troops overseas take the direction desired by the Army planners. Not until OVERLORD was given top priority at the Tehran Conference at the end of 1943 could the double war finally begin to assume the focus and flow into the channels planned by the War Department in the early stages of the coalition war. During 1943 the Army sent overseas close to 1.5 million men, including 13 divisions. Over two-thirds of these totals, including more than 1 million troops and 9 divisions, were deployed against Germany. In these terms the balance was finally being redressed in favor of the war against Germany. The cumulative totals at the end of 1943 showed 1.4 million men, including 17 divisions, deployed against Germany, as opposed to 913,000 troops, including 13 divisions, lined up against Japan—a sharp contrast to the picture at the end of 1942, when in manpower and number of divisions the war against Japan had maintained an edge over the war in Europe.

On the other hand, the failure of the Allies to agree on a specific plan for the cross-Channel attack until Tehran permitted deployment in the war against Japan to develop at a much quicker pace than the planners had expected. It was not until October 1943 that the divisions in Europe exceeded those in the Pacific. And when the effort expended by the Navy and Marine Corps, especially in the Pacific, is added to Army deployment overseas, a different picture emerges. Actually, after two years of war, the balance of U.S. forces—and resources—between the European and Japanese arenas was fairly even. Indeed, of the total of 3.7 million men—Army, Navy, and Marines—overseas during 1943, slightly more than half were arrayed against Japan. By the close of that year the growing costs of fighting a multifront war on an opportunistic basis and the difficulty of keeping a secondary war secondary in the absence of a firm long-range plan for the primary war had been driven home to the Army planners.

By the end of the midwar period—in September 1944—General Marshall and his staff could survey the state of Army deployment with considerable

satisfaction. Channeling U.S. military power to the United Kingdom for a
concentrated attack against Germany had been a long struggle. More divisions
were sent overseas in the first nine months of 1944—the bulk of them going
to the European theater—than had been shipped overseas during the previous
two years. To support OVERLORD and its follow-up operations, the Army funneled
forces into the European theater and later into continental Europe in ever-
increasing numbers during the first three quarters of 1944. Slightly over 2
million men, including 34 divisions and 103 air groups, were in the European
theater at the end of September 1944—over 45 percent of the total number of
troops overseas in all Theaters. By then, the overall breakdown of Army troops
overseas gave the war against Germany a 2 to 1 advantage over the Japanese
conflict, and this was matched by the Army divisional distribution. Forty
divisions were located in Europe and the Mediterranean, with 4 more en route,
against 21 in the Pacific. In the air, the preponderance lay even more heavily
in favor of Europe. With the bulk of the Army's combat strength overseas
deployed against the Reich, and with most of the divisions that were in the
United States slated to go to the European theater, General Marshall and his
planners could consider their original concept well on the way to accomplish-
ment. Although there were still over 3.5 million men left in the continental
United States at the end of September, there were only 24 combat divisions
remaining. The Army planners had hoped to maintain some of the divisions
as a strategic reserve to cope with emergencies.

When the crisis caused by the Ardennes breakthrough of December 1944
denuded the United States of all the remaining divisions, the possibility of having
raised too few divisions caused War Department leaders from Stimson on down
some anxious moments. Fortunately this was the last unpleasant surprise; another
such crisis would have found the divisional cupboard bare. Indeed, the decision
for 90 divisions—the Army's "cutting edge"—was one of the greatest gambles
taken by the Washington high command in World War II.

Thus, in the long run, Marshall and his staff were not only able to reverse
the trend toward the Pacific that had lasted well into 1943 but had gone to the
other extreme during 1944. Because of unexpected developments in the European
war, not one division was sent to the Pacific after August 1944, and planning
deployment totals for the Pacific for 1944 were never attained. European deployment, on the other hand, mounted steadily and substantially exceeded the
planners' estimates. At the end of April 1945, when the Army reached its peak
strength of 5.4 million overseas, over 3 million were in the European theater
and 1.2 million in the Pacific. Regardless of the type of war fought in World

War II—concentration and invasion in Europe, or blockade, bombardment, and island hopping in the Pacific—each required a tremendous outlay of American military strength and resources.

Balancing Means and Ends

Throughout the conflict the matching of means with ends, of logistics with strategy, continued to be a complex process, for World War II was the greatest coalition effort and the first really global war in which the United States had been involved. The wherewithal had to be produced and delivered to a multitude of allies and so far-flung fronts over long sea lines of communications and all somehow harnessed to some kind of strategic design to defeat the enemies. As the war progressed, the Army strategic planners learned to appreciate more and more the limits of logistics in the multifront war. From the standpoint of the Americans, the basic strategic decisions they supported from the beginning— the Germany-first decision and the primacy of the cross-Channel attack—were in large measure justified by logistics. Each would capitalize on the advantages of concentrating forces and material resources on a single major line of communications and link the major arsenal represented by the United States with the strategically located logistical base offered by Great Britain. The realities of logistics had in part defeated their original BOLERO strategy, and forces and resources in being in other theaters had generated their own offensive strategy.

In the midwar era, while Allied plans remained unsettled, the competing claims of the Pacific and Mediterranean for a strategy of opportunism, the continuing needs of other far-flung fronts, added to the accumulated "fixed charges"—for example, aid to China, Britain, and the Soviet Union, and the rearming of the French—took a heavy toll of American resources. The full-blown war economy was matched by the full-blown war on the global scale. In and out of the international conferences of midwar in the era of relative plenty, the adjustment of means and ends went on and logistics remained a limiting, if not always the final determining, factor in the strategic debate. The scope, timing, landing places, and even the choice of specific operations were to a large extent influenced by the availability of the wherewithal, by the quantities that could be produced and delivered to the fighting fronts.

To logisticians in World War II, the balance among supplies and equipment, trained troops, and the shipping to transport them—the only means then feasible for mass movement overseas—was of continuing concern. In planning for that balance the factor of lead time was particularly important. For example, for the invasion of Normandy in June 1944 planning for the production of material had to start two years in advance, the buildup in England at least a year in advance, and the actual planning of detailed logistical support six months before the landings. Usually the shorter the lead time for logistical preparations, the narrower the range of strategic choices tended to be.

To the end the Army was, of course, one cog in the mighty American war machine, and it had to compete for resources with its sister services and with allies. The home front, too, had to be supported. While the war cut deeply into the life of the American people, it was fought with a "guns and butter" policy without any real sacrifice in the American standard of living. The Army was not anxious to cut into that standard of living. Nor did it have final say over the allocation and employment of key resources. To balance the allocation of forces, supplies, and shipping among the many fronts and nations, within the framework of the close partnership with the British, required a degree of central logistical control and direction at both combined and national level unknown in earlier wars. A complex network of Anglo-American and national civilian and military agencies for logistical planning emerged. In the melding of resources and plans that went on in and out of the international conferences, planners took their cue from the basic decisions of the CCS—in this sense, the top logistical as well as strategic planning organization.

An imposing structure of federal agencies and committees grew up in Washington to control the nation's economic mobilization. Its keystone was the influential War Production Board (WPB) that controlled the allocation and use of raw materials, machine tools, and facilities, with powers similar to those of the War Industries Board in World War I. In the military sphere the War Department, like the Navy Department, had a large degree of autonomy in controlling requirements planning, production, and distribution of material for its forces. The actual procurement—that is, purchasing and contracting of munitions and other war materials—was carried out directly by the Army's technical services and the Navy's bureaus. Within the Joint Chiefs of Staff organization many logistical problems at issue between the services were settled by negotiation. The War Shipping Administration (WSA) operated and allocated the critical United States merchant shipping. Close co-operation between WSA and the British Ministry of War Transport resulted in the pooling of the two merchant fleets, comprising the bulk of the world's mercantile tonnage. Other civilian agencies dealt with such critical commodities as food, petroleum products, and rubber. In the spring of 1943 most of the mobilization agencies were subordinated to a new co-ordinating unit, the Office of War Mobilization headed by former Justice James F. Byrnes.

Theoretically U.S. munitions production along with that of the British empire was placed in a "common pool" and distributed according to strategic need. Allocations were made by two Munitions Assignments Boards, each representing both countries and responsible to the CCS. One board, sitting in Washington, allocated U.S. production, while a second in London allocated British production. Using the principles of lend-lease and reciprocal aid, these two boards made allocations to other Western Allied countries as well as to the United States and Britain. Supplies for the Soviet Union were governed by separate diplomatic protocols, and the boards seldom attempted to alter their provisions in making assignments. The common pool theory, however, proved somewhat too idealistic for complete application. It really applied from the start almost entirely to American production, for the British had little surplus to distribute. Their contributions to the American effort, though substantial, normally took the form of services and soft goods rather than military hardware. In these circumstances, the Americans almost inevitably came to question the application of the common pool theory and to make assignments on the premise that each partner had first call on its own resources. British participation in the allocation of American production became only nominal in the later war years.

However imperfect the application of the common pool concept, lend-lease, with its counterpart, reciprocal aid, proved an admirable instrument of coalition warfare. Lend-lease did what President Roosevelt had initially intended it should. It removed the dollar sign from Allied supply transactions and gave the Allies an unprecedented flexibility in distributing materials without generating complicated financial transactions or postwar problems such as the war debts of World War I had created. Under the Lend-Lease Act of March 1941, the War Department turned over to Allied countries approximately $25 billion worth of war materials. About 58 percent went to Britain, 23 percent to Russia, 8 percent to France, 7 percent to China, and the remainder to other countries. Included in these supplies were some 37,000 light and medium tanks, nearly 800,000 trucks, and 3,400 locomotives. The Army Service Forces was the Army's operating agency for administering this program, and from 1942 on military lend-lease requirements were included with U.S. Army requirements in the Army supply program. This American largess was distributed almost exclusively under the principle of achieving complete military victory in the war, not of contributing to the postwar political purposes of any ally.

Even with American production in high gear during 1943-45, critical shortages or bottlenecks developed to hamper operations at various stages. In early 1943, as in 1942, the most stringent limiting factor was ocean shipping to transport troops and supplies overseas. Indeed, in the spring of 1943, when

LST Discharging Cargo Over a Ponton Causeway, *Gela, Sicily.*

President Roosevelt decided to divert scarce shipping to support the faltering British economy, he had to overrule the JCS, deeply concerned over American military requirements—one of the few occasions in the war he did so. After mid-1943, amid the changing requirements of the war in full bloom, the logistical bottlenecks tended to be specialized rather than general. From late 1943 until June 1944 the most serious critical shortage became the supply of assault shipping to land troops and supplies in amphibious operations. In the case of landing craft, the shortage was most severe in one specific category, the Landing Ship Tank (LST). In April 1944 Winston Churchill became exasperated enough to wonder whether history would ever understand why "the plans of two great empires like Britain and the United States should be so much hamstrung and limited" by an "absurd shortage of the L.S.T.'s." In the last stage, after troops were ashore and fighting on the European continent, the principal bottleneck shifted to port and inland clearance capacity in both that area and in the Pacific.

The basic problem of allocating resources between the war against Germany and the war against Japan remained almost to the end. Although the basic decision of "Germany first" held throughout the conflict, one of the most persistent questions concerned the proportion in which available resources should be divided between the two wars. This question reflected some divergence of political, military, geographical, and psychological factors in the Anglo-

American strategy of the war. For Britain, the war against Japan tended to be a side show, and its leaders tended to emphasize the effort in Europe and the Mediterranean at the expense of the Pacific. The United States more than met its commitments in Europe but insisted from the beginning on a margin of safety in the war against Japan, for which it early had been given major responsibility. Furthermore, the pull to the Pacific in midwar that the U.S. Navy and General MacArthur, both now on the offensive, particularly welcomed became for the Washington high command a lever against overcommitment in the Mediterranean. At the midwar conferences the Anglo-American debate focused on the division of resources among the theaters where the two nations combined their efforts—the Mediterranean, northwest Europe, and Southeast Asia. For the Pacific, American military leaders simply presented their decisions, logistical as well as strategic, to the conferences for the stamp of approval. In effect, American military leaders in midwar went far toward asserting unilateral control over the division of American resources between the two wars.

In the final analysis, the multifront nature of the war developed as a product of changing circumstances rather than of a predetermined grand design. Coalition strategy evolved as a result of a complex, continuing process—a constant struggle to adjust ends and means, to reconcile diverse pressures, pulls, and shifting conditions in the global war, and to effect compromises among nations with diverse national interests. That strategy, frequently dictated by necessity, often emerged from events rather than determined them.

The Washington high command was to end the war as it began it—without a fully developed theory on how to match strategic plans, manpower, and resources for a coalition, global war. But throughout its search for the formula for victory it had consistently pursued its goal of winning the war decisively, of complete military victory, without concern for postwar political aims. Whatever general political objectives the President had, he was committed to no strategic doctrine except complete victory. The political and military spheres of American national policy continued their customary separate ways.

Institutionally, World War II became for American strategists and logisticians an organization war, a war of big planning staffs in the capitals and the theater headquarters. Strategy and logistics became big business—established industries in the huge American wartime military establishment. World War II contributed significantly to the education of American Army planners in these arts. General Marshall, for example, once succinctly observed that his military experience in World War I had been based on roads, rivers, and railroads; in World War II he had to learn all over again and to acquire "an education based on oceans."

Throughout Americans evinced their national habit in war—a penchant for quick, direct, and total solutions. The strategic principles they stressed were entirely in harmony with their own traditions and capacities. They proved particularly adept in adapting their mass-production economy to war purposes and in applying power on a massive scale. How far they had come in the quarter century since World War I was evidenced by a comparison of their strategic experience in the two coalition world wars of the twentieth century. In World War I the United States, a junior partner, conformed to the strategy set by the Allies; in World War II the United States came to hold its own in allied war councils and played an influential role in molding Allied strategy, virtually dictating the strategy of the Pacfic war. In meeting the problems of global coalition warfare, in the greatest conflict in which the United States had been involved, American strategists and logisticians came of age.

The multifront war of mass, technology, and mobility that taxed the strategists and logisticians in Washington also challenged the overseas commands and the tacticians in the field. As the war had progressed, the role of the theater commands in strategy, logistics, and tactics had become increasingly significant. It is appropriate, therefore, at this point to turn from Washington high command to the Army overseas and to trace the actual course of operations in the double war.

CHAPTER 22

World War II: The War Against Germany and Italy

With the invasion of North Africa (Operation TORCH), the U.S. Army in late 1942 began a ground offensive against the European Axis that was to be sustained almost without pause until Italy collapsed and Germany was finally defeated. More than a million Americans were to fight in lands bordering the Mediterranean Sea and close to four million on the European continent, exclusive of Italy, in the largest commitment to battle ever made by the U.S. Army. Alongside these Americans were to march British, Canadian, French, and other Allied troops in history's greatest demonstration of coalition warfare, while on another front massed Soviet armies were to contribute enormously to the victory.

The North African Campaign, November 1942–May 1943

Although the decision to launch Operation TORCH had been made largely because the Allies could not mount a more direct attack against the European Axis early in the war, there were specific and attractive objectives—to gain French-controlled Morocco, Algeria, and Tunisia as a base for enlisting the French empire in the war, to assist the British in the Libyan Desert in destroying Axis forces in North Africa, to open the Mediterranean to Allied shipping, and to provide a steppingstone for subsequent operations.

The Germans and their Italian allies controlled a narrow but strategic strip of the North African littoral between Tunisia and Egypt with impassable desert bounding the strip on the south. (*Map 40*) Numbering some 100,000 men under a battle-tested German leader, Field Marshal Rommel, the German-Italian army in Libya posed a constant threat to Egypt and the Near East as well as to French North Africa and, since the Axis also controlled the northern shores of the Mediterranean, served to deny the Mediterranean to Allied shipping. Only a few convoys seeking to supply British forces on the island of Malta ever ventured into the Mediterranean, and these took heavy losses.

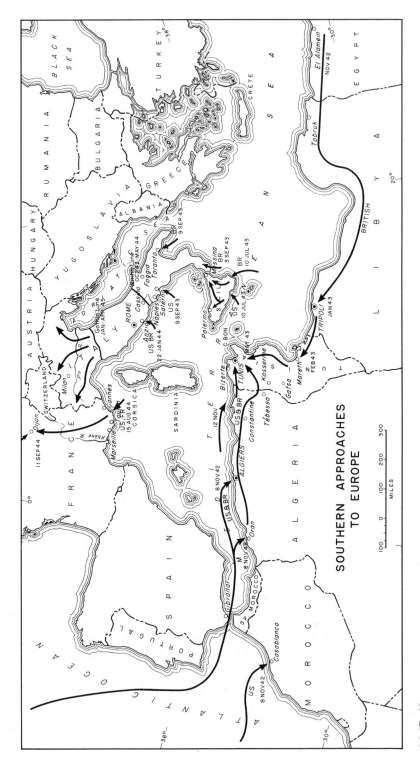

SOUTHERN APPROACHES
TO EUROPE

MAP 40

Moving against French Africa posed for the Allies special problems rooted in the nature of the armistice that had followed French defeat in 1940. Under terms of that armistice, the Germans had left the French empire nominally intact, along with much of the southern half of Metropolitan France, yet in return the French Government was pledged to drop out of the war. Although an underground resistance movement had already begun in France and an Allied-equipped force called the Free French was assembling in the British Isles, that part of the regular French Army and Navy left intact by the armistice was sworn to the service of the Vichy government. This pledge had led already to the anomaly of Frenchman fighting Frenchman and of the British incurring French enmity by destroying part of the fleet of their former ally.

If bloodshed was to be averted in the Allied invasion, French sympathies had to be enlisted in advance, but to reveal the plan was to risk French rejection of it and German occupation of French Africa. Although clandestine negotiations were conducted with a few trusted French leaders, these produced no guarantee that French forces would not resist.

Partly because of this intricate situation, the Allies designated an American, General Eisenhower, to command the invasion in order to capitalize on absence of rancor between French and Americans by giving the invasion an American rather than a British complexion. American troops were to make up the bulk of the assault force, and the Royal Navy was to keep its contribution as inconspicuous as possible.

The operation was to begin in western Egypt, where the British Commander in Chief, Middle East, General Sir Harold R. L. G. Alexander, was to attack with the veteran British Eighth Army under Lt. Gen. Bernard L. Montgomery against Field Marshal Rommel's German-Italian army. Coming ashore in French Africa, General Eisenhower's combined U.S.-British force was to launch a converging attack against Rommel's rear.

In selecting beaches for the invasion, U.S. planners insisted upon a landing on the Atlantic coast of Morocco lest the Germans seal the Strait of Gibraltar and cut off support to forces put ashore on the Mediterranean coast. Because both troops and shipping were limited, a landing on the Atlantic coast restricted the number and size of landings possible inside the Mediterranean. Although a landing as far east as Tunisia was desirable because of vast overland distances (from the Atlantic coast to Tunis is more than a thousand miles), proximity of Axis aircraft on Sicily and Sardinia made that too perilous.

Making the decision on the side of security, the Allies planned simultaneous landings at three points—in Morocco near the Atlantic port of Casablanca and in Algeria near the ports of Oran and Algiers. Once the success of these landings was assured, a convoy was to put ashore small contingents of British troops to seize ports in eastern Algeria while a ground column headed for Tunisia in a race to get there before the Germans could move in.

Given the assignment to invade North Africa only at the end of July 1942, the U.S. Army faced enormous difficulties in meeting a target date in November of the same year. Troops had had little training in amphibious warfare, landing craft were few and obsolete, and much equipment was inferior to that of the Axis forces. So few U.S. troops were available in England that troops for the landing near Casablanca had to be shipped direct from the United States, one of history's longest sea voyages preceding an amphibious assault.

After soundly defeating an Axis attack, Montgomery's Eighth Army on October 23 auspiciously opened an offensive at El 'Alamein, there to score a victory that was to be a turning point in British fortunes. A little over two weeks later, before daylight on November 8, the U.S. Navy put U.S. Army forces ashore near Casablanca, while the Royal Navy landed other U.S. troops and contingents of British troops near Oran and Algiers. The entire invasion force consisted of over 400 warships, 1,000 planes, and some 107,000 men, including a battalion of paratroopers jumping in the U.S. Army's first airborne attack.

Although the invasion achieved strategic surprise, the French in every case but one fought back at the beaches. Dissidence among various French factions limited the effectiveness of some of the opposition, but any resistance at all raised the specter of delay that might enable the Germans to beat the Allies into Tunisia. Three days passed before the French agreed to cease fire and take up arms on the Allied side.

French support at last assured, the Royal Navy put British troops ashore close to the Tunisian border while an Allied column began the long overland trek. The British troops were too few to do more than secure two small Algerian ports, the ground column too late. Over the narrow body of water between Sicily and North Africa the Germans poured planes, men, and tanks. Except for barren mountains in the interior, Tunisia was for the moment out of Allied reach.

The Tunisia Campaign

Recoiling from the defeat at El 'Alamein, Rommel's German-Italian army in January 1943 occupied old French fortifications near the southern border of Tunisia, the Mareth Line, there to face Montgomery's Eighth Army, while more than 100,000 enemy troops under General Juergen von Arnim faced westward against General Eisenhower's Allied force. Although the Italian high command in Italy exercised loose control, the Axis nations failed to establish a unified command over these two forces.

The Allied plan to defeat Rommel by converging attacks having been foiled, General Eisenhower had no choice but to dig in to defend in the Tunisian mountains until he could accumulate enough strength to attack in conjunction with a renewed strike by Montgomery against the Mareth Line. Before this could be accomplished, Rommel on February 14 sent strong armored forces through the passes in central Tunisia against the U.S. II Corps, commanded by Maj. Gen. Lloyd R. Fredendall. Rommel planned to push through the Kasserine Pass, then turn northwestward by way of an Allied supply base at Tébessa to reach the coast and trap the Allied units.

In a series of sharp armored actions, Rommel quickly penetrated thinly held American positions and broke through the Kasserine Pass. Although success appeared within his grasp, lack of unified command interfered. Planning an attack of his own, General von Arnim refused to release an armored division needed to continue Rommel's thrust. Concerned that Rommel lacked the strength for a deep envelopment by way of Tébessa, the Italian high command directed a turn northward, a much shallower envelopment.

The turn played into Allied hands, for the British already had established a blocking position astride the only road leading northward. At the height of a clash between Rommel's tanks and the British, four battalions of American artillery arrived after a forced march from Oran. On February 22 these guns and a small band of British tanks brought the Germans to a halt. Warned by intelligence reports that the British Eighth Army was about to attack the Mareth Line, Rommel hurriedly pulled back to his starting point.

The Axis offensive defeated, the U.S. II Corps, commanded now by Maj. Gen. George S. Patton, Jr., launched a diversionary attack on March 17 toward the rear of the Mareth Line, while Montgomery's Eighth Army a few days later struck the line in force. By the end of the first week of April, the two forces had joined.

With all their forces now linked under the tactical command of General Alexander, the Allies opened a broad offensive that within a month captured the ports of Bizerte and Tunis and compressed all Axis troops into a small bridgehead covering the Cape Bon peninsula at the northeastern tip of Tunisia. The last of some 275,000 Germans and Italians surrendered on May 10.

Although the original Allied strategy had been upset by the delay imposed by French resistance and the swift German build-up in Tunisia, Allied troops achieved victory in six months, which in view of their limited numbers and long lines of communications, was impressive. A few days later the first unopposed British convoy since 1940 reached beleaguered Malta.

American troops in their first test against German arms had made many mistakes. Training, equipment, and leadership had failed in many instances to meet the requirements of the battlefield, but the lessons were clear and pointed to nothing that time might not correct. More imporant was the experience gained, both in battle and in logistical support. Important too was the fact that the Allied campaign had brought a French army back into the war. Most important of all, the Allies at last had gained the initiative.

The Sicily Campaign, July–August 1943

Where the Allies were to go after North Africa had already been decided in January 1943 at the Casablanca Conference. As with the decision to invade North Africa, the next step—invading Sicily (Operation Husky)—followed from recognition that the Allies still were unready for a direct thrust across the English Channel. Utilizing troops already available in North Africa, they could make the Mediterranean safer for Allied shipping by occupying Sicily, perhaps going on after that to invade Italy and knock the junior Axis partner out of the war.

As planning proceeded for the new operation, General Eisenhower (promoted now to four-star rank) remained as supreme commander, while General Alexander, heading the 15th Army Group, served as ground commander. Alexander controlled Montgomery's Eighth Army and a newly created Seventh U.S. Army under Patton (now a lieutenant general).

How to invade the Vermont-size, three-cornered island posed a special problem. The goal was Messina, the gateway to the narrow body of water between Sicily and Italy, the enemy's escape route to the Italian mainland. Yet the Strait of Messina was so narrow and well fortified that Allied commanders believed the only solution was to land elsewhere and march on Messina by way of shallow coastal shelves on either side of towering Mount Etna.

Applying the principle of mass, Alexander directed that all landings be made in the southeastern corner of the island, British on the east coast, Americans on the southwest. Behind British beaches a brigade of glider troops was to capture a critical bridge, while a regiment of U.S. paratroopers took high ground behind American beaches. After seizing minor ports and close-in airfields, Patton's Seventh Army was to block to the northwest against Axis reserves while Montgomery mounted a main effort up the east coast.

Because Sicily was an obvious objective after North Africa, complete strategic surprise was hardly possible, but bad weather helped the Allies achieve tactical surprise. As a huge armada bearing some 160,000 men steamed across the Mediterranean, a mistral—a form of unpredictable gale common to the Mediterranean—sprang up, so churning the sea that General Eisenhower was for a time tempted to order delay. While the heavy surf swamped some landing craft and made all landings difficult, it put the beach defenders off their guard. Before daylight on July 10, both British and Americans were ashore in sizable numbers.

As presaged in North Africa, poor performance by Italian units left to German reserves the task of repelling the invasion. Although preattack bombardment by Allied planes and confusion caused by a scattered jump of U.S. paratroopers delayed German reaction, a panzer division mounted a sharp counterattack against American beaches before the first day was out. It came dangerously close to pushing some American units into the sea before naval gunfire and a few U.S. tanks and artillery pieces that had got ashore drove off the German tanks.

To speed reinforcement, the Allies on two successive nights flew in American and British paratroopers. In both instances, antiaircraft gunners on ships standing offshore and others on land mistook the planes for enemy aircraft and opened fire. Losses were so severe that for a time some Allied commanders questioned the wisdom of employing this new method of warfare.

The Germans meanwhile formed a solid block in front of the British along the east coast, prompting General Patton to urge expanding the role of his Seventh Army. First cutting the island in two with a drive by the II Corps, commanded now by Maj. Gen. Omar N. Bradley, Patton sent a provisional corps pushing rapidly through faltering Italian opposition to the port of Palermo and the northwestern tip of the island. This accomplished within fourteen days after coming ashore, Patton turned to aid the British by attacking toward Messina along a narrow northern coastal shelf.

As both Allied armies in early August readied a final assault to gain Messina, the Germans began to withdraw to the mainland. Despite Allied command of sea and air, they managed to evacuate all their forces, some 40,000 troops. When on August 17, thirty days after the invasion, U.S. patrols pushed into Messina, the Germans had incurred some 10,000 casualties, the Italians probably as many as 100,000, mostly prisoners of war. Allied losses were 22,000.

The American force that fought in Sicily was far more sophisticated than that which had gone into battle in North Africa. New landing craft, some capable of bearing tanks, had made getting ashore much quicker and surer, and new amphibious trucks called DUKW's eased the problem of supply over the beaches. Gone was the Grant tank with its side-mounted gun, lacking wide traverse; in its place was the Sherman with 360-degree power-operated traverse for a turret-mounted 75-mm. piece. Commanders were alert to avoid a mistake often made in North Africa of parceling out divisions in small increments, and the men were sure of their weapons and their own ability. Some problems of co-ordination with tactical air remained, but these soon would be worked out.

The Surrender of Italy

Even as the Allies had been preparing to invade Sicily, the Italian people and their government had become increasingly disenchanted with the war. Under the impact of the loss of North Africa, the invasion of Sicily, and a first bombing of Rome, the Italian king forced Mussolini to resign as head of the government.

Anxious to find a way out of the war, a new Italian government made contact with the Allies through diplomatic channels, leading to direct talks with General Eisenhower's representatives. The Italians, it soon developed, were in a quandary—they wanted to pull out of the war, yet they were virtual prisoners of German forces in Italy that Hitler, sensing Italian defection, strongly reinforced. Although plans were drawn for airborne landings to secure Rome coincident with announcement of Italian surrender, these were canceled in the face of Italian vacillation and inability to guarantee strong assistance in fighting the Germans. The Italian government nevertheless agreed to surrender, a fact General Eisenhower announced on the eve of the principal Allied landing on the mainland.

The Italian Campaign, September 1943–May 1945

Since the Allied governments had decided to pursue after Sicily whatever course offered the best chance of knocking Italy from the war, invading the mainland logically followed. This plan also presented an opportunity to tie down German forces and prevent their employment either on the Russian front or against the eventual Allied attack across the English Channel. Occupying Italy also would provide airfields close to Germany and the Balkans.

How far up the peninsula of Italy the Allies were to land depended almost entirely on the range of fighter aircraft based on Sicily, for all Allied aircraft carriers were committed to the war in the Pacific. Another consideration was a desire to control the Strait of Messina to shorten sea supply lines.

On September 3 a British force under Montgomery crossed the Strait of Messina and landed on the toe of the Italian boot against surprisingly moderate opposition. Following Eisenhower's announcement of Italian surrender, a British fleet steamed brazenly into the harbor of Taranto in the arch of the Italian boot to put a British division ashore on the docks, while the Fifth U.S. Army under Lt. Gen. Mark W. Clark staged an assault landing on beaches near Salerno, twenty-five miles southeast of Naples.

Reacting in strength against the Salerno invasion, the Germans two days after the landing mounted a vigorous counterattack that threatened to split the beachhead and force abandonment of part of it. For four days, the issue was in doubt. Quick reinforcement of the ground troops (including a regiment of paratroopers jumping into the beachhead), gallant fighting, liberal air support, and unstinting naval gunfire at last repulsed the German attack. On September 15 the Germans began to withdraw, and the next day patrols of the British Eighth Army arrived from the south to link the two Allied forces. Two weeks later American troops took Naples, thereby gaining an excellent port, while the British seized valuable airfields around Foggia on the other side of the peninsula.

Although the Germans seriously considered abandoning southern Italy to pull back to a line in the Northern Apennines, the local commander, Field Marshal Albert Kesselring, insisted that he could hold for a considerable time on successive lines south of Rome. This proved to be an accurate assessment. The Allied advance was destined to proceed slowly, partly because of the difficulty of offensive warfare in rugged mountainous terrain and partly because the Allies limited their commitment to the campaign, not only in troops but also in shipping and the landing craft that were necessary if the enemy's strong defensive positions were to be broken by other than frontal attack.

Because the build-up for a cross-Channel attack—the main effort against Germany—was beginning in earnest, the Allies could spare few additional troops or shipping to pursue the war in Italy. Through the fall and winter of 1943-44, the armies would have to do the job in Italy with what was at hand, a total of eighteen Allied divisions.

A renewed offensive in October 1943 broke a strong German delaying position at the Volturno River, twenty miles north of Naples, and carried as far as a so-called Winter Line, an imposing position anchored on towering peaks around the town of Cassino. Casting about for a way to break this line, General Eisenhower obtained permission to retain temporarily from the build-up in Britain enough shipping and landing craft to make an amphibious end run. General Clark was to use a corps of his Fifth U.S. Army to land on beaches near Anzio, some thirty miles south of Rome and sixty miles behind the Winter

Line. By threatening or cutting German lines of communications to the Winter Line, the troops at Anzio were to facilitate Allied advance through the line and up the valley of the Liri River, the most obvious route to Rome.

Provided support by a French corps equipped with American arms, General Clark pulled out the U.S. VI Corps under Maj. Gen. John P. Lucas to make the envelopment. While the VI Corps—which included a British division—sailed toward Anzio, the Fifth Army launched a massive attack aimed at gaining access to the Liri valley. Although the VI Corps landed unopposed at Anzio on January 22, 1944, the attack on the Winter Line gained little.

Rushing reserves to Anzio, Field Marshal Kesselring quickly erected a firm perimeter about the Allied beachhead and successfully resisted every attempt at breakout. On February 16 Kesselring launched a determined attack to eliminate the beachhead that only a magnificent defense by U.S. and British infantry supported by artillery, tanks, planes, and naval gunfire at last thwarted.

Through the rest of the winter and early spring, the Fifth and Eighth Armies regrouped and built their combined strength to twenty-five divisions, mainly with the addition of French and British Commonwealth troops. General Eisenhower, meanwhile, had relinquished command in the Mediterranean early in January to go to Britain in preparation for the coming invasion of France. He was succeeded by a Britisher, Field Marshal Sir Henry M. Wilson.

On May 11 the Fifth and Eighth Armies launched a new carefully synchronized attack to break the Winter Line. Passing through almost trackless mountains, French troops under General Clark's command scored a penetration that unhinged the German position. As the Germans began to fall back toward Rome, the VI Corps attacked from the Anzio beachhead but failed to make sufficient progress to cut the enemy's routes of withdrawal. On June 4, 1944, U.S. troops entered Rome.

With D-day in Normandy only two days off, the focus of the Allied war against Germany shifted to France, and with the shift came a gradual diminution of Allied strength in Italy. Allied forces nevertheless continued to pursue the principle of the offensive. Reaching a new German position in the Northern Apennines, the Gothic Line, they started in August a three-month campaign that achieved penetrations, but they were unable to break out of the mountains. This period also saw a change in command as General Clark became commander of the Allied army group and Lt. Gen. Lucian K. Truscott assumed command of the Fifth Army.

In the spring of 1945 the Fifth and Eighth Armies penetrated a final German defensive line to enter the fertile plains of the Po River valley. On May 2, the Germans in Italy surrendered, the first formal capitulation of the war.

A German Trench on the Gothic Line, *overlooking a circling road.*

Less generally acclaimed than other phases of World War II, the campaign in Italy nevertheless had a vital part in the overall conduct of the war. At the crucial time of the Normandy landings, Allied troops in Italy were tying down twenty-six German divisions that well might have upset the balance in France. As a result of this campaign, the Allies obtained airfields useful for strategic bombardment of Germany and the Balkans, and conquest of the peninsula further guaranteed the safety of Allied shipping in the Mediterranean.

Cross-Channel Attack

Even as the Allied ground campaign was proceeding on the shores of the Mediterranean, three other campaigns were under way from the British Isles— the campaign of the U.S. Navy and the Royal Navy to defeat the German submarine, a U.S.-British strategic bombing offensive against Germany, and a third, intricately tied in with the other two, a logistical marathon to assemble the men and tools necessary for a direct assault against the foe.

Most critical of all was the antisubmarine campaign, for without success in that, the two others could progress only feebly at best. The turning point in that campaign came in April 1943, when the full effect of all the various

devices used against the U-boat began to be apparent. Despite German introduction of an acoustical torpedo that homed on the noise of an escort's propellers,
and later of the *schnorkel*, a steel tube extending above water by means of which
the U-boat could charge its batteries without surfacing, Allied shipping losses
continued to decline. In the last two years of the war the submarines would
sink only one-seventh of the shipping they did in the earlier years.

In the second campaign, the combined bomber offensive that U.S. and
British chiefs at Casablanca had directed, the demands of the war in the
Pacific and the Mediterranean slowed American participation. Not until the
summer of 1943 were sufficient U.S. bombers available in Britain to make a
substantial contribution, and not until February 1944 were U.S. airmen at
last able to match the big thousand-plane raids of the British.

While the Royal Air Force struck by night, bombers of the U.S. Army
Air Forces hit by day, both directing much of their attention to the German
aircraft industry in an effort to cripple the German air arm before the invasion.
Although the raids imposed delays on German production, the most telling
effect was the loss of German fighter aircraft and trained pilots rising to oppose
the Allied bombers. As time for the invasion approached, the German air arm
had ceased to represent a real threat to Allied ground operations, and Allied
bombers could shift their attention to transportation facilities in France in
an effort to restrict the enemy's ability to move reserves against the invasion.

The logistical build-up in the British Isles, meanwhile, had been progressing
at an ever-increasing pace, easily the most tremendous single logistical undertaking of all time. The program entailed transporting some 1,600,000 men
across the submarine-infested Atlantic before D-day and providing for their
shelter, hospitalization, supply, training, and general welfare. Mountains of
weapons and equipment, ranging from locomotives and big bombers to dental
fillings, also had to be shipped.

Planning for the invasion had begun long before as the British, standing
alone, looked to the day when they might return to the Continent. Detailed
planning began in 1943 when the Combined Chiefs of Staff appointed a
Britisher, Lt. Gen. Frederick E. Morgan, as chief of staff to a supreme commander yet to be named. Under Morgan's direction, British and American
officers drew up plans for several contingencies, one of which, Operation
OVERLORD, anticipated a large-scale assault against a still powerful German
Army. This plan served as the basis for a final plan developed early in 1944 after
General Eisenhower, designated as the supreme commander, arrived in Britain
and established his command, Supreme Headquarters, Allied Expeditionary
Force, or SHAEF.

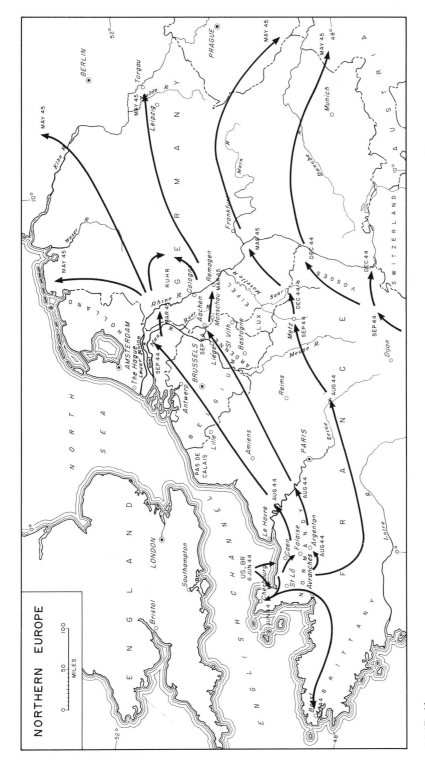

NORTHERN EUROPE

0   50   100
MILES

MAP 41

GENERAL EISENHOWER TALKING TO PARATROOPERS *before their drop behind the Normandy beaches.*

The over-all ground commander for the invasion was the former head of the British Eighth Army, General Montgomery, who also commanded the 21 Army Group, the controlling headquarters for the two Allied armies scheduled to make the invasion. The British Second Army under Lt. Gen. Sir Miles C. Dempsey was to assault on the left; the First U.S. Army under Bradley (promoted now to lieutenant general) on the right.

A requirement that the invasion beaches had to be within easy range of fighter aircraft based in Britain and close to at least one major port sharply limited the choice. The state of German defenses imposed further limitations, leaving only one logical site, the base of the Cotentin peninsula in Normandy, southeast of Cherbourg. (*Map 41*) To facilitate supply until Cherbourg or some other port could be opened, two artificial harbors were to be towed from Britain and emplaced off the invasion beaches.

Despite a weather forecast of high winds and a rough sea, General Eisenhower made a fateful decision to go ahead with the invasion on June 6. During the night over 5,000 ships moved to assigned positions, and at two o'clock, the

U.S. Troops Moving Ashore at Omaha Beach on D-Day

morning of the 6th, the operation for which the world had long and anxiously waited opened. One British and two U.S. airborne divisions (the 82d and 101st) dropped behind the beaches to secure routes of egress for the seaborne forces. Following preliminary aerial and naval bombardment, the first waves of infantry and tanks began to touch down at 6:30, just after sunrise. A heavy surf made the landings difficult but, as in Sicily, put the defenders off their guard.

The assault went well on British beaches, where one Canadian and two British divisions landed, and also at Utah, westernmost of the U.S. beaches, where the 4th Division came ashore. The story was different at Omaha Beach; there an elite German division occupying high bluffs laced with pillboxes put the landings in jeopardy. Allied intelligence had detected the presence of the enemy division too late to alter the landing plan. Only through improvisation and personal courage were the men of two regiments of the 1st Division and one of the 29th at last able to work their way up the bluffs and move slowly inland. Some 50,000 U.S. troops nevertheless made their way ashore on the two beaches before the day was out. American casualties were approximately 6,500, British and Canadian, 4,000—in both cases lighter than expected.

The German command was slow to react to the invasion, having been misled not only by the weather but also by an Allied deception plan which continued to lead the Germans to believe that this was only a diversionary assault, that the main landings were to come later on the Pas de Calais. Only in one instance, against the British who were solidly ashore, did the Germans mount a sizable counterattack on D-day.

Build-up and Breakout

While Allied aircraft and French resistance fighters impeded the movement of German reserves, the Allies quickly built up their strength and linked the beachheads. U.S. troops then moved against Cherbourg, taking the port, after bitter fighting, three weeks following the invasion. Other Allied forces had in the meantime been deepening the beachhead between Caen and the road center of St. Lô, so that by the end of June the most forward positions were twenty miles from the sea, and the Germans still had been able to mount no major counterattack.

Commanded by Field Marshal Gerd von Rundstedt, the Germans nevertheless defended tenaciously in terrain ideally suited to the defense. This was hedgerow country, where through the centuries French farmers had erected high banks of earth around every small field to fence livestock and protect crops from coastal winds. These banks were thick with the roots of shrubs and trees, and in many places sunken roads screened by a canopy of tree branches ran between two hedgerows. Tunneling into the hedgerows and using the sunken roads for lines of communication, the Germans turned each field into a small fortress.

For all the slow advance and lack of ports (a gale on June 19 demolished one of the artificial harbors and damaged the other), the Allied build-up was swift. By the end of June close to a million men had come ashore, along with some 586,000 tons of supplies and 177,000 vehicles. General Bradley's First Army included four corps with 2 armored and 11 infantry divisions. British strength was about the same.

Seeking to end the battle of the hedgerows, the British attempted to break into more open country near Caen, only to be thwarted by concentrations of German armor. General Bradley then tried a breakout on the right near St. Lô. Behind an intensive aerial bombardment that utilized both tactical aircraft and heavy bombers, the First Army attacked on July 25. By the second day American troops had opened a big breach in German positions, whereupon armored divisions drove rapidly southward twenty-five miles to Avranches at the base of the Cotentin peninsula. While the First Army turned southeastward, the

Third U.S. Army under General Patton entered the line to swing through Avranches into Brittany in quest of ports.

The arrival of the Third Army signaled a major change in command. General Bradley moved up to command the 12th Army Group, composed of the First and Third Armies, while his former deputy, Lt. Gen. Courtney H. Hodges, assumed command of the First Army. Montgomery's 21 Army Group consisted of the British Second Army and a newcomer to the front, the First Canadian Army under Lt. Gen. Henry D. G. Crerar. General Montgomery continued to function as overall ground commander, an arrangement that was to prevail for another five weeks until General Eisenhower moved his head-quarters to the Continent and assumed direct command of the armies in the field.

In terms of the preinvasion plan, General Eisenhower intended establishing a solid lodgment area in France extending as far east as the Seine River to provide room for air and supply bases. Having built up strength in this area, he planned then to advance into Germany on a broad front. Under Montgomery's 21 Army Group, he would concentrate his greatest resources north of the Ardennes region of Belgium along the most direct route to the Ruhr industrial region, Germany's largest complex of mines and industry. Bradley's 12th Army Group, meanwhile, was to make a subsidiary thrust south of the Ardennes to seize the Saar industrial region along the Franco-German frontier. A third force invading southern France in August was to provide protection on Bradley's right.

The First Army's breakout from the hedgerows changed that plan, for it opened the German armies in France to crushing defeat. When the Germans counterattacked toward Avranches to try to cut off leading columns of the First and Third Armies, other men of the First Army held firm, setting up an opportunity for exploiting the principle of maneuver to the fullest. While the First Canadian Army attacked toward Falaise, General Bradley directed mobile columns of both the First and Third Armies on a wide encircling maneuver in the direction of Argentan, not far from Falaise. This caught the enemy's counterattacking force in a giant pocket. Although a 15-mile gap between Falaise and Argentan was closed only after many of the Germans escaped, more than 60,000 were killed or captured in the pocket. Great masses of German guns, tanks, and equipment fell into Allied hands.

While the First Army finished the business at Argentan, Patton's Third Army dashed off again toward the Seine River, with two objects: eliminating the Seine as a likely new line of German defense and making a second, wider envelopment to trap those German troops that had escaped from the first pocket. Both Patton accomplished. In the two pockets the enemy lost large segments of two field armies.

Invasion of Southern France

Even as General Eisenhower's armies were scoring a great victory in Normandy, the Allies on August 15 staged another invasion, this one in southern France (Operation DRAGOON) to provide a supplementary line of communications through the French Mediterranean ports and to prevent the Germans in the south from moving against the main Allied armies in the north. Lack of landing craft had precluded launching this invasion at the same time as OVERLORD.

Under control of the Seventh U.S. Army, commanded now by Lt. Gen. Alexander M. Patch, three U.S. divisions, plus an airborne task force and French commandos, began landing just after dawn. Defending Germans were spread too thin to provide much more than token resistance, and by the end of the first day the Seventh Army had 86,000 men and 12,000 vehicles ashore. The next day French troops staged a second landing and moved swiftly to seize the ports of Toulon and Marseille.

Faced with entrapment by the spectacular Allied advances in the north, the Germans in southern France began on August 17 to withdraw. U.S. and French columns followed closely and on September 11 established contact with Patton's Third Army. Under the 6th Army Group, commanded by Lt. Gen. Jacob L. Devers, the Seventh Army and French forces organized as the 1st French Army passed to General Eisenhower's command.

Pursuit to the Frontier

As Allied columns were breaking loose all over France, men and women of the French resistance movement began to battle the Germans in the streets of the capital. Although General Eisenhower had intended to bypass Paris, hoping to avoid heavy fighting in the city and to postpone the necessity of feeding the civilian population, he felt impelled to send help lest the uprising be defeated. On August 25 a column including U.S. and French troops entered the city.

With surviving German forces falling back in defeat toward the German frontier, General Eisenhower abandoned the original plan of holding at the Seine while he opened the Brittany ports and established a sound logistical base. Determined to take advantage of the enemy's defeat, he reinforced Montgomery's 21 Army Group by sending the First U.S. Army close alongside the British, thus providing enough strength in the northern thrust to assure quick capture of ports along the English Channel, particularly the great Belgian port of Antwerp. Because the front was fast moving away from Brittany, the Channel ports were essential.

Ports posed a special problem, for with the stormy weather of fall and winter approaching, the Allies could not much longer depend upon supply over the invasion beaches, and Cherbourg had only a limited capacity. Even though Brittany now was far behind the advancing front, General Eisenhower still felt a need for the port of Brest. He put those troops of the Third Army that had driven into the peninsula under a new headquarters, the Ninth U.S. Army commanded by Lt. Gen. William H. Simpson, and set them to the task. When Brest fell two weeks later, the port was a shambles. The port problem nevertheless appeared to be solved when on September 4 British troops took Antwerp, its wharves and docks intact; but the success proved to be illusory. Antwerp is on an estuary sixty miles from the sea, and German troops clung to the banks, denying access to Allied shipping.

The port situation was symptomatic of multitudinous problems that had begun to beset the entire Allied logistical apparatus (organized much like Pershing's Services of Supply, but called the Communications Zone). The armies were going so far and so fast that the supply services were unable to keep pace. Although enough supplies were available in Normandy, the problem was to get them to forward positions that sometimes were more than 500 miles beyond the depots. Despite extraordinary measures such as establishing a one-way truck route called the Red Ball Express, supplies of such essential commodities as gasoline and ammunition began to run short. This was the penalty the Allied armies would have to pay for the decision to make no pause at the Seine.

The logistical crisis sparked a difference over strategy between General Eisenhower and General Montgomery. In view of the logistical difficulties, Montgomery insisted that General Patton's Third Army should halt in order that all transportation resources might be concentrated behind his troops and the First Army. This allocation, he believed, would enable him to make a quick strike deep into Germany and impel German surrender.

Acting on the advice of logistical experts on his staff, General Eisenhower refused. Such a drive could succeed, his staff advised, only if all Allied armies had closed up to the Rhine River and if Antwerp were open to Allied shipping. The only choice, General Eisenhower believed, was to keep pushing all along the line while supplies held out, ideally to go so far as to gain bridgeheads over the Rhine.

There were obstacles other than supply standing in the way of that goal. Some were natural, like the Moselle and Meuse Rivers, the Vosges Mountains in Alsace, the wooded hills of the Ardennes, and a dense Huertgen Forest facing the First Army near Aachen. Others were man made, old French forts around Metz and the French Maginot Line in northeastern France, as well as dense fortifications all along the German border—the Siegfried Line, or, as the Germans called it, the West Wall. By mid-September the First Army had penetrated the West Wall at several points but lacked the means to exploit the breaks.

Although General Eisenhower assigned first priority to clearing the seaward approaches to Antwerp, he sanctioned a Montgomery proposal to use Allied airborne troops in a last bold stroke to capitalize on German disorganization before logistics should force a halt. While the British Second Army launched an attack called Operation GARDEN, airborne troops of a recently organized First Allied Airborne Army (Lt. Gen. Lewis H. Brereton) were to land in Operation MARKET astride three major water obstacles in the Netherlands—the Maas, Waal, and Lower Rhine Rivers. Crossing these rivers on bridges to be secured by the airborne troops, the Second Army was to drive all the way to the IJssel Meer (Zuider Zee), cutting off Germans farther west and putting the British in a position to outflank the West Wall and drive into Germany along a relatively open north German plain.

Employing one British and two U.S. airborne divisions, the airborne attack began on September 17. On the first day alone approximately 20,000 paratroopers and glider troops landed in the largest airborne attack of the war. Although the drops were spectacularly successful and achieved complete surprise, the chance presence of two panzer divisions near the drop zones enabled the Germans to react swiftly. Resistance to the ground attack also was greater than expected, delaying quick link-up with the airheads. The combined operation gained a salient some fifty miles deep into German-held territory but fell short of the ambitious objectives, including a bridgehead across the Lower Rhine.

At this point, Montgomery (promoted now to field marshal) concentrated on opening Antwerp to Allied shipping, but so determined was German resistance and so difficult the conditions of mud and flood in the low-lying countryside that it was well into November before the job was finished. The first Allied ship dropped anchor in Antwerp only on November 28.

As a result of a cutback in offensive operations and extraordinary efforts of the supply services, the logistical situation had been gradually improving. In early November resources were sufficient to enable the U.S. armies to launch a big offensive aimed at reaching the Rhine; but, despite the largest air attack in direct support of ground troops to be made during the war (Operation QUEEN), it turned out to be a slow, arduous fight through the natural and artificial obstacles along the frontier. Heavy rain and severe cold added to the difficulties. By mid-December the First and Ninth Armies had reached the Roer River east of Aachen, twenty-three miles inside Germany, and the Third Army had come up to the West Wall along the Saar River northeast of Metz, but only the Seventh Army and the 1st French Army in Alsace had touched any part of the Rhine.

Having taken advantage of the pause imposed by Allied logistical problems to create new divisions and rush replacements to the front, the Germans in the west had made a remarkable recovery from the debacle in France. Just how remarkable was soon to be forcefully demonstrated in what had heretofore been a quiet sector held by the First Army's right wing.

The Ardennes Counteroffensive

As early as the preceding August, Adolf Hitler had been contemplating a counteroffensive to regain the initiative in the west and compel the Allies to settle for a negotiated peace. Over the protests of his generals, who thought the plan too ambitious, he ordered an attack by twenty-five divisions, carefully conserved and secretly assembled, to hit thinly manned U.S. positions in the Ardennes region of Belgium and Luxembourg, cross the Meuse River, and push on northwestward to Antwerp. In taking Antwerp, Hitler expected to cut off the British 21 Army Group and the First and Ninth U.S. Armies.

Under cover of inclement winter weather, Hitler concentrated his forces in the forests of the Eifel region, opposite the Ardennes. Before daylight on December 16, the Germans attacked along a 60-mile front, taking the VIII Corps and the south wing of the V Corps by surprise. In most places, German gains were rapid, for the American divisions were either inexperienced or seriously depleted from earlier fighting, and all were stretched thin.

The Germans nevertheless encountered difficulties from the first. Cut off and surrounded, small U.S. units continued to fight. At the northern shoulder of the penetration, divisions of the V Corps refused to budge from the vicinity of Monschau, thereby denying critical roads to the enemy and limiting the width of the penetration. At St. Vith American troops held out for six days to block a vital road center. To Bastogne to the southwest, where an armored detachment served as a blocking force, General Eisenhower rushed an airborne division which never relinquished that communications center even though

FIRST ARMY MEN SETTING UP A 57–MM. ANTITANK GUN

surrounded. Here Brig. Gen. Anthony C. McAuliffe delivered a terse one-word reply to a German demand for surrender: "Nuts!"

Denied important roads and hampered by air attacks as the weather cleared, the Germans fell a few miles short of even their first objective, the Meuse River. The result after more than a month of hard fighting that cost the Americans 75,000 casualties and the Germans close to 100,000 was nothing but a big bulge in the lines, from which the battle drew its popular name.

Faced with a shortage of infantry replacements during the enemy's counter-offensive General Eisenhower offered Negro soldiers in service units an oppor-tunity to volunteer for duty with the infantry. More than 4,500 responded, many taking reductions in grade in order to meet specified requirements. The 6th Army Group formed these men into provisional companies, while the 12th Army Group employed them as an additional platoon in existing rifle companies. The excellent record established by these volunteers, particularly those serving as platoons, presaged major postwar changes in the traditional approach to employing Negro troops.

Although the counteroffensive had given the Allied command some anxious moments, the gallant stands by isolated units had provided time for the First and Ninth Armies to shift troops against the northern flank of the penetration and for the Third Army to hit the penetration from the south and drive through to beleaguered Bastogne. A rapid shift and change in direction of attack by the Third Army was one of the more noteworthy instances during the war of successful employment of the principle of maneuver.

By the end of January 1945, U.S. units had retaken all lost ground and had thwarted a lesser German attack against the 6th Army Group in Alsace. The Germans having expended irreplaceable reserves, the end of the war in Europe was in sight.

The Russian Campaigns

Much of the hope for an early end to the war rested with tremendous successes of the Soviet armies in the east. Having stopped the invading Germans at the gates of Moscow in late 1941 and at Stalingrad in late 1942, the Russians had made great offensive strides westward in both 1943 and 1944. Only a few days after D-day in Normandy the Red Army had launched a massive offensive which by mid-September had reached East Prussia and the gates of the Polish capital of Warsaw. In January 1945, as U.S. troops eliminated the bulge in the Ardennes, the Red Army started a new drive that was to carry to the Oder River, only forty miles from Berlin.

Far greater masses of troops were employed in the east than in the west over vast distances and a much wider front. The Germans had to maintain more than two million combat troops on the Eastern Front as compared with less than a million on the Western Front. Yet the Soviet contribution was less disproportionate than would appear at first glance, for the war in the east was a one-front ground war, whereas the Allies in the west were fighting on two ground fronts and conducting major campaigns in the air and at sea, as well as making a large commitment in the war against Japan. At the same time, the United States was contributing enormously to the war in Russia through lend-lease—almost $11 billion in materials, including over 400,000 jeeps and trucks, 12,000 armored vehicles (including 7,000 tanks, enough to equip some 20-odd U.S. armored divisions), 14,000 aircraft, and 1.75 million tons of food.

The Final Offensive

Soon after the opening of the Soviet January offensive, the Western Allies began a new drive to reach and cross the Rhine, the last barrier to the industrial heart of Germany. Exhausted by the overambitious effort in the Ardennes and forced to shift divisions to oppose the Russians, the Germans had little chance of holding west of the Rhine. Although Field Marshal von Rundstedt wanted to conserve his remaining strength for a defense of the river, Hitler would authorize no withdrawal. Making a strong stand at the Roer River and at places where the West Wall remained intact, the Germans imposed some delay but paid dearly in the process, losing 250,000 troops that could have been used to better advantage on the Rhine.

Falling back behind the river, the Germans had made careful plans to destroy all bridges, but something went amiss at the Ludendorff railroad bridge in the First Army's sector at Remagen. On March 7 a task force of the 9th Armored Division found the bridge damaged but passable. Displaying initiative and courage, a company of infantry dashed across. Higher commanders acted promptly to reinforce the foothold.

To the south, a division of the Third Army on March 22 made a surprise crossing of the Rhine in assault boats. Beginning late the next day the 21 Army Group and the Ninth U.S. Army staged a full-dress crossing of the lower reaches of the river, complete with an airborne attack rivaling in its dimensions Operation MARKET. The Third Army then made two more assault crossings, and during the last few days of March both the Seventh Army and the 1st French Army of the 6th Army Group crossed farther upstream. Having expended most of their resources west of the river, the Germans were powerless to defeat any Allied crossing attempt.

As the month of April opened, Allied armies fanned out from the Rhine all along the line with massive columns of armor and motorized infantry. Encircling the Ruhr, the First and Ninth Armies took 325,000 prisoners, totally destroying an entire German army group. Although the Germans managed to rally determined resistance at isolated points, a cohesive defensive line ceased to exist.

Since the Russians were within forty miles of Berlin and apparently would reach the German capital first, General Eisenhower put the main weight of the continuing drive behind U.S. armies moving through central Germany to eliminate a remaining pocket of German industry and to link with the Russians. The 21 Army Group meanwhile sealed off the Netherlands and headed toward the base of the Jutland peninsula, while the 6th Army Group turned southeastward to obviate any effort by the Nazis to make a last-ditch stand in the Alps of southern Germany and Austria.

By mid-April Allied armies in the north and center were building up along the Elbe and Mulde Rivers, an agreed line of contact with the Red Army approaching from the east. First contact came on April 25 near the town of Torgau, followed by wholesale German surrenders all along the front and in Italy.

With Berlin in Soviet hands, Hitler a suicide, and almost every corner of Germany overrun, emissaries of the German Government surrendered on May 7 at General Eisenhower's headquarters in Reims, France. The next day, May 8, was V–E Day, the official date of the end of the war in Europe.

The Situation on V–E Day

As V–E Day came, Allied forces in Western Europe consisted of 4½ million men, including 9 armies (5 of them American—one of which, the Fifteenth, saw action only at the last), 23 corps, 91 divisions (61 of them American), 6 tactical air commands (4 American), and 2 strategic air forces (1 American). The Allies had 28,000 combat aircraft, of which 14,845 were American, and they had brought into Western Europe more than 970,000 vehicles and 18 million tons of supplies. At the same time they were achieving final victory in Italy with 18 divisions (7 of them American).

The German armed forces and the nation were prostrate, beaten to a degree never before seen in modern times. Hardly any organized units of the German Army remained except in Norway, Czechslovakia, and the Balkans, and these would soon capitulate. What remained of the air arm was too demoralized even for a final suicidal effort, and the residue of the German Navy lay helpless in captured northern ports. Through five years of war, the German armed forces had lost over 3 million men killed, 263,000 of them in the west, since D-day. The United States lost 135,576 dead in Western Europe, while Britain, Canada, France, and other Allies incurred after D-day approximately 60,000 military deaths.

Unlike in World War I, when the United States had come late on the scene and provided only those forces to swing the balance of power to the Allied side, the American contribution to the reconquest of Western Europe had been predominant, not just in manpower but as a true arsenal of democracy. American factories produced for the British almost three times more lend-lease materials than for the Russians, including 185,000 vehicles, 12,000 tanks, and enough planes to equip four tactical air forces, and for the French, all weapons and equipment for 8 divisions and 1 tactical air force, plus partial equipment for 3 more divisions.

Although strategic air power had failed to prove the decisive instrument many had expected, it was a major factor in the Allied victory, as was the role of Allied navies, for without control of the sea lanes, there could have been no build-up in Britain and no amphibious assaults. It was nonetheless true that the application of the power of ground armies finally broke the German ability and will to resist.

While the Germans had developed a flying bomb and later a supersonic missile, the weapons with which both sides fought the war were in the main much improved versions of those that had been present in World War I—the motor vehicle, the airplane, the machine gun, indirect fire artillery, the tank. The difference lay in such accouterments as excellent radio communications and in a new sophistication, particularly in terms of mobility, that provided the means for rapid exploitation that both sides in World War I had lacked.

From North Africa to the Elbe, U.S. Army generalship proved remarkably effective. Such field commanders as Bradley, Devers, Clark, Hodges, Patton, Simpson, Patch, and numerous corps and division commanders would stand beside the best that had ever served the nation. Having helped develop Army doctrine during the years between the two great wars, these same men put the theories to battlefield test with enormous success. Some indication of the magnitude of the responsibilities they carried is apparent from the fact that late in the war General Bradley as commander of the 12th Army Group had under his command four field armies, 12 corps, and 48 divisions, more than 1,300,000 men, the largest exclusively American field command in U.S. history.

These commanders throughout displayed a steady devotion to the principles of war. Despite sometimes seemingly insurmountable obstacles of weather, terrain, and enemy concentration, they were consistently able to achieve the mass, mobility, and firepower to avoid a stalemate, maintaining the principles of the objective and the offensive and exploiting the principle of maneuver to the fullest. On many occasions they achieved surprise, most notably in the amphibious assaults and at the Rhine. They were themselves taken by surprise twice, in central Tunisia and in the Ardennes, yet in both cases they recovered quickly. Economy of force was particularly evident in Italy, and simplicity was nowhere better demonstrated than in the Normandy landings, despite a complexity inherent in the size and diversity of the invasion forces. From the first, unity of command was present in every campaign, not just at the tactical level but also in the combined staff system that afforded the U.S. and Britain a unity of command and purpose never approached on the Axis side.

CHAPTER 23

World War II: The War Against Japan

In World War II, for the first time, the United States had to fight a war on two fronts. Though the central strategic principle governing allocation of resources to the two fronts provided for concentrating first on the defeat of the European Axis, on the American side this principle was liberally interpreted, permitting conduct of an offensive war against Japan as well as against Germany in the years 1943–45. The U.S. Fleet, expanding after its initial setback at Pearl Harbor much as the Army had, provided the main sinews for an offensive strategy in the Pacific, although the Army devoted at least one-third of its resources to the Pacific war, even at the height of war in Europe. In sum, the United States proved capable, once its resources were fully mobilized, of successfully waging offensives on two fronts simultaneously—a development the Japanese had not anticipated when they launched their attack on Pearl Harbor.

Japan's Strategy

Japan entered World War II with limited aims and with the intention of fighting a limited war. Its principal objectives were to secure the resources of Southeast Asia and much of China and to establish a "Greater East Asia Co-Prosperity Sphere" under Japanese hegemony. In 1895 and in 1905 Japan had gained important objectives without completely defeating China or Russia and in 1941 Japan sought to achieve its hegemony over East Asia in similar fashion. The operational strategy the Japanese adopted to start war, however, doomed their hopes of limiting the conflict. Japan believed it necessary to destroy or neutralize American striking power in the Pacific—the U.S. Pacific Fleet at Pearl Harbor and the U.S. Far East Air Force in the Philippines—before moving southward and eastward to occupy Malaya, the Netherlands Indies, the Philippines, Wake Island, Guam, the Gilbert Islands, Thailand, and Burma. Once in control of these areas, the Japanese intended to establish a defensive perimeter stretching from the Kurile Islands south through Wake, the Marianas, the Carolines, and the Marshalls and Gilberts to Rabaul on New Britain. From

MAP 42

THE PACIFIC AREAS

1 AUGUST 1942

0   500   1000
STATUTE MILES ON THE EQUATOR

Rabaul the perimeter would extend westward to northwestern New Guinea and would encompass the Indies, Malaya, Thailand, and Burma. Japan thought that the Allies would wear themselves out in fruitless frontal assaults against the perimeter and would ultimately settle for a negotiated peace that would leave it in possession of most of its conquests. (*Map 42*)

The Japanese were remarkably successful in the execution of their offensive plan and by early 1942 had reached their intended perimeter. But they miscalculated the effect of their surprise attack at Pearl Harbor which unified a divided people and aroused the United States to wage a total, not a limited, war. As a result Japan lost, in the long run, any chance of conducting the war on its own terms. The Allies, responding to their defeats, sought no negotiated peace, but immediately began to seek means to strike back. In February and March 1942 small carrier task forces of the Pacific Fleet hit the Marshalls, Wake, and Marcus, and bombers from Australia began to harass the Japanese base at Rabaul. In April Army bombers, flying off a naval carrier, delivered a hit-and-run raid on Tokyo. Meanwhile, the United States began to develop and fortify a line of communications across the southern Pacific to Australia and to strengthen the defenses of the "down-under" continent itself. These new bases, along with Alaska, Hawaii, and India, also strengthened during the period, could become the launching points for counteroffensives. And once the Allies became strong enough to threaten the Japanese defensive perimeter from several directions the Japanese would lose the advantage of interior lines, and with it the strategic initiative, for Japan did not have and could not produce the means to defend and hold at all points.

Perceiving their danger, the Japanese in a second phase offensive tried to sever the Allied lines of communications to Australia and to expand their perimeter in the Pacific. In the spring of 1942 they pushed southeast from Rabaul to Guadalcanal and Tulagi in the Solomons, and seized Attu and Kiska in the Aleutians. But they failed in their main effort to take Midway Island, northwest of Hawaii, and in the naval battles of the Coral Sea and Midway in May and June they lost the bulk of their best naval pilots and planes. Midway was the turning point, for it redressed the naval balance in the Pacific and gave the Allies the strategic initiative. The Japanese, with the mobility of their carrier striking forces curtailed, abandoned plans to cut the Allied South Pacific life line and turned instead to strengthening their defensive perimeter, planning to wage a protracted war of attrition in the hope of securing a negotiated peace.

Guadalcanal and Papua: The First Offensives

After Midway the U.S. Joint Chiefs, responsible for direction of the war in the Pacific, almost naturally turned to the elimination of the threat to their line of communications in the south as the objective of their first offensive. In so doing, they gave to American strategy in the Pacific a twist unanticipated in prewar planning, which had always presupposed that the main offensive in any war against Japan would be made directly across the Central Pacific from Hawaii toward the Philippines. The Joint Chiefs on July 2 directed Allied forces in the South and Southwest Pacific Areas to begin a series of operations aimed at the ultimate reduction of the Japanese stronghold at Rabaul on New Britain Island, thus establishing Allied control of the Bismarck Archipelago.

The campaign would consist of three stages or tasks. In Task One, forces of the South Pacific Area (under Vice Adm. Robert L. Ghormley until November 1942 and thereafter under Admiral William F. Halsey) would seize base sites in the southern Solomons. In Task Two, South Pacific forces would advance up the ladder of the Solomons while Southwest Pacific forces (under General MacArthur) would move up the north coast of New Guinea as far as Lae and Salamaua. In Task Three, the forces of the two theaters would converge on Rabaul and clear the rest of the Bismarck Archipelago. Task One was to be conducted under the general supervision of Admiral Chester W. Nimitz, whose vast Pacific Ocean Areas command included the North, Central, and South Pacific Areas as subtheaters. Tasks Two and Three would be executed under the strategic direction of General MacArthur. The Joint Chiefs of Staff, reserving to themselves final control of the assignment of tasks, allocation of resources, and timing of operations, would provide, in effect, unified command over Nimitz and MacArthur.

The offensive began on August 7, 1942, when the 1st Marine Division landed on Guadalcanal and nearby islands in the southern Solomons. The Japanese, taking full advantage of interior lines from their bases at Rabaul and Truk, reacted vigorously. Six times from August to the end of November they challenged American naval superiority in the South Pacific in a series of sharp surface engagements. Air battles were almost daily occurrences for a month or more after the landings, and the Japanese sent in strong ground reinforcements, gambling and ultimately losing substantial air and naval resources in the effort to hold Guadalcanal. The Americans had to reinforce heavily, deploying naval power, planes, soldiers, and marines in the battle at the expense of other theaters. Before the island was secured in November, another Marine

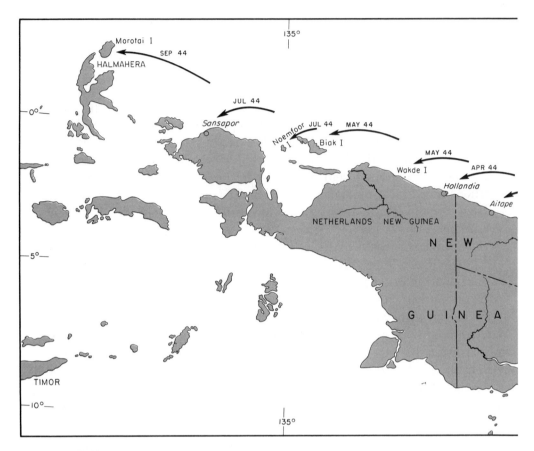

MAP 43

division (the 2d), two Army divisions (25th and Americal), and one separate regiment, to mention only the major ground combat elements, had been thrown into the battle. The last act came in February 1943, when the 43d Division moved into the Russell Islands, thirty-five miles northwest of Guadalcanal. On Guadalcanal and in the Russells, American forces then began to construct major air and logistical bases for further advances.

A Japanese overland drive toward Port Moresby in New Guinea had meanwhile forced General MacArthur to begin an offensive of his own—the Papua Campaign. (*Map 43*) During the late summer the Japanese had pushed across the towering Owen Stanley Mountains toward Port Moresby from the Buna-Gona area on New Guinea's northeastern coast, and by mid-September were only twenty miles from their objective. Australian ground forces drove the

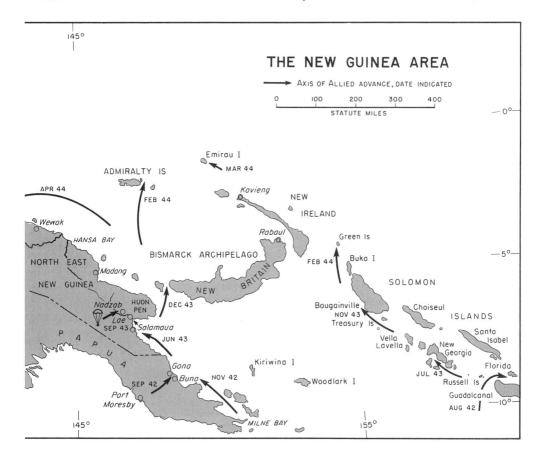

Japanese back to the north coast, where they strongly entrenched themselves around Buna and Gona. It took 2 Australian divisions, 1 U.S. Army division (32d), and another U.S. Army regiment almost four months of bitter fighting to dislodge the Japanese. Casualties were high, but as at Guadalcanal the Allied forces learned much about jungle fighting, the importance of air power, and the need for thorough logistical preparation. They also discovered that the Japanese soldier, though a skillful, stubborn, and fanatic foe, could be defeated. The myth of Japanese invincibility was forever laid to rest in the jungles of Guadalcanal and Papua.

After Papua and Guadalcanal the tempo of operations in the South and Southwest Pacific Areas slowed while General MacArthur and Admiral Halsey gathered resources and prepared bases for the next phase. The Japanese, in turn, undertook to reinforce their main bases in New Guinea and the northern Solomons. In March 1943 they attempted to send a large convoy to Lae in New Guinea but, in the Battle of the Bismarck Sea, lost some 3,500 troops and much valuable shipping, principally to Army land-based aircraft. During the following months Rabaul-based planes, reinforced by carrier planes flown in from the Carolines, sought unsuccessfully to knock out American air power in the southern Solomons.

Search for a Strategy

Meanwhile, in the spring and summer of 1943, a strategy for the defeat of Japan began to take shape within Allied councils. The major Allied objective was control of the South China Sea and a foothold on the coast of China, so as to sever Japanese lines of communications southward and to establish bases from which Japan could first be subjected to intensive aerial bombardment and naval blockade and then, if necessary, invaded. The first plans for attaining this objective envisioned Allied drives from several different directions—by American forces across the Pacific along two lines, from the South and Southwest toward the Philippines and from Hawaii across the Central Pacific; and by British and Chinese forces along two other lines, the first a land line through Burma and China and the second a sea line from India via the Netherlands Indies, Singapore, and the Strait of Malacca into the South China Sea. Within the framework of this tentative long-range plan, the U.S. Joint Chiefs fitted their existing plans for completion of the campaign against Rabaul, and a subsequent advance to the Philippines, and developed a plan for the second drive across the Central Pacific. They also, in 1942 and 1943, pressed the Chinese and British to get a drive under way in Burma to reopen the supply line to China in phase with their Pacific advances, offering extensive air and logistical support.

The North Pacific line running from Alaska through the Kuriles to the northernmost Japanese island of Hokkaido also beckoned in early 1943 as a possible additional avenue of approach to Japan. The Joint Chiefs decided, however, that although the Japanese perimeter should be pushed back in this area, the foggy, cold North Pacific with its rock-bound and craggy islands was not a profitable area in which to undertake a major offensive. In May 1943 the U.S. 7th Division went ashore on Attu and, after three weeks of costly fighting through icy muck and over wind-swept ridges in a cold, almost constant fog, destroyed the Japanese garrison. In August a combined American-Canadian expedition landed on Kiska, some distance away, only to find that the Japanese had evacuated the island three weeks earlier. With the Japanese perimeter pushed back to the Kuriles the Allied advance stopped, and further operations were limited to nuisance air raids against these Japanese-held islands. Ground forces used in the attacks on Attu and Kiska were redeployed to the Central Pacific, and some of the defensive forces deployed in Alaska were also freed for employment elsewhere.

Prospects of an advance through China to the coast faded rapidly in 1943. At the Casablanca Conference in January the Combined Chiefs agreed on an ambitious operation, called ANAKIM, to be launched in the fall of 1943 to retake Burma and reopen the supply line to China. ANAKIM was to include a British amphibious assault on Rangoon and an offensive into central Burma, plus an American-sponsored Chinese offensive in the north involving convergence of forces operating from China and India. ANAKIM proved too ambitious; even limited offensives in Southeast Asia were postponed time and again for lack of adequate resources. By late 1943 the Americans had concluded that their Pacific forces would reach the China coast before either British or Chinese forces could come in through the back door. At the SEXTANT Conference late in 1943 the Combined Chiefs agreed that the main effort against Japan should be concentrated in the Pacific along two lines of advance, with operations in the North Pacific, China, and Southeast Asia to be assigned subsidiary roles.

In this strategy the two lines of advance in the Pacific—the one across the Central Pacific via the Gilberts, Marshalls, Marianas, Carolines, and Palaus toward the Philippines or Formosa (Taiwan) and the other in the Southwest Pacific via the north coast of New Guinea to the Vogelkop and thence to the southern Philippines—were viewed as mutually supporting. (*Map 44*) Although the Joint Chiefs several times indicated a measure of preference for the Central Pacific as the area of main effort, they never established any real priority between the two lines, seeking instead to retain a flexibility that would permit striking blows along either line as opportunity offered. The Central Pacific route promised to force a naval showdown with the Japanese and, once the Marianas were secured, to provide bases from which the U.S. Army Air Forces' new B-29 bombers could strike the Japanese home islands. The Southwest Pacific route was shorter, if existing bases were taken into consideration, and offered more opportunity to employ land-based air power to full advantage. The target area for both drives, in the strategy approved at SEXTANT, was to be the Luzon-Formosa-China coast area. Within this area the natural goal of the Southwest Pacific drive was the Philippines, but that of the Central Pacific drive could be either the Philippines or Formosa. As the drives along the two lines got under way in earnest in 1944, the choice between the two became the central strategic issue.

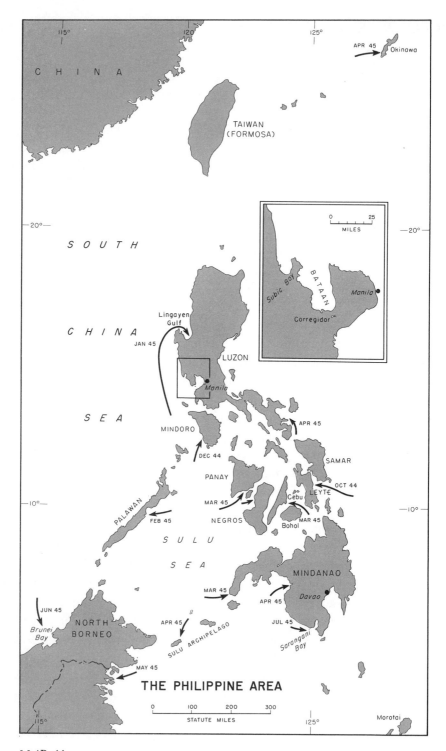

THE PHILIPPINE AREA

MAP 44

Cartwheel: The Encirclement of Rabaul

In June 1943 MacArthur and Halsey resumed their offensive to reduce the Japanese stronghold at Rabaul—a prerequisite to further advances along the Southwest Pacific axis toward the Philippines. The plan for the campaign provided for a carefully phased series of operations in each theater, each designed to secure a strategic position where air cover could be provided for further advances. The first of the series started in late June when MacArthur landed American troops on the Woodlark and Kiriwina Islands off eastern New Guinea and at Nassau Bay on the New Guinea coast, and Halsey's forces made their first landings on the New Georgia group in the Central Solomons. From these beginnings the operations proceeded up the ladder of the Solomons, along the coast of New Guinea, and across the straits to New Britain Island generally as scheduled, despite strong Japanese reaction.

In the Solomons by early August Army forces under Halsey had secured New Georgia with its important Munda airfield, but the campaign was not completed until October when U.S. and New Zealand troops occupied Vella Lavella, between New Georgia and Bougainville. At the end of October, New Zealanders and U.S. marines landed on Treasury and Choiseul Islands to secure bases for the assault on Bougainville; that assault got under way on November 1 when marines landed, followed soon after by the Army's 37th Division. In each phase of the Solomons campaign, the Japanese sought unsuccessfully to contest Allied air and naval supremacy, to land reinforcements, and to launch strong counterattacks against Allied beachheads, losing in the effort both planes and combat ships they could ill afford to spare. Air and naval losses suffered in the Solomons crippled the Japanese Fleet for months to come and helped to pave the way for the successful Central Pacific drive that got under way in November. With the repulse of the Japanese counterattack on Bougainville, by the end of November security of the American beachhead on that island was assured, permitting the development of a major American air base. With the taking of Bougainville, the main part of the South Pacific Area's task in Operation CARTWHEEL was completed.

MacArthur's forces meanwhile continued their offensives, with Australian troops carrying most of the burden in New Guinea. In early September the U.S. Army's 503d Parachute Regiment, in the first airborne operation of the Pacific war, seized an airfield at Nadzab, inland from Lae and Salamaua. Australian troops cleared Lae and Salamaua by mid-September and, flown into Nadzab, moved on to the Huon peninsula. Elements of the U.S. 32d Division landed at the western end of the peninsula in January 1944 in an attempt to trap a large Japanese force, but by the time Australian and American units had sealed the western exits to the peninsula most of the Japanese had escaped northwest to Hansa Bay and Wewak.

In the meantime, MacArthur and Halsey had assembled the forces to launch a final offensive toward Rabaul, but the Joint Chiefs decided that the actual seizure of that objective would be too costly in terms of men, equipment, and time. They preferred to encircle Rabaul, neutralize it by air bombardment, and push on to seize an offensive base farther west, in the Admiralty Islands. A new series of operations toward these ends started in MacArthur's theater on December 15, 1943, when U.S. Army units landed on the south coast of western New Britain, and on the 26th, the 1st Marine Division landed on the north coast. In mid-February 1944 New Zealand troops of the South Pacific Area secured an air base site on Green Island, north of Rabaul, and on the last day of the month MacArthur began landing the 1st Cavalry Division (an infantry unit retaining its former designation) on the Admiralties, closing the western and northwestern approaches to Rabaul. Marines under Halsey seized a final air base site on Emirau, north of Rabaul, on March 20, while Marine and Army units under MacArthur secured additional positions in western and central New Britain from March to May 1944. The major Japanese base at Rabaul, with its 100,000-man garrison, was as effectively out of the war as if it had been destroyed. In the process of encircling Rabaul, the Allies had also left to wither on the vine another important Japanese base at Kavieng on New Ireland, north of Rabaul.

In the last phase of the campaign against Rabaul, a pattern developed that came to characterize much of the war in the Pacific. The Allies would mount no frontal attacks against strongly entrenched Japanese forces if they could avoid it; they would not advance island by island across a vast ocean studded with myriad atolls and island groups. Rather, they would advance in great bounds, limited only by the range of land-based air cover or the availability of carrier-based air support. The Allies would deceive and surprise the Japanese; they would bypass major strongpoints and leave them reduced to strategic and tactical impotence.

The Central Pacific Drive Begins

The necessity for relying primarily on support of land-based aircraft curtailed the length of the jumps in the South and Southwest Pacific in 1943. The Navy's limited supply of aircraft carriers could not be employed to best advantage in the narrow waters around New Guinea and the Solomons. By mid-1943, however, new larger and faster carriers of the *Essex* class (27,000 tons) and lighter carriers of the *Independence* class (11,000 tons) were joining the Pacific

Fleet. Around these new carriers Admiral Nimitz built naval task forces tailored in each case to the particular operation at hand. The task forces consisted of a mix of carriers, destroyers, cruisers, battleships, submarines, minesweepers, and support craft. In the broad expanses of the Central Pacific, these air carrier task forces could provide both air and naval support for far longer leaps forward, while the entire Pacific Fleet stood ready to confront the main Japanese Fleet at any time it chose to give battle.

The Central Pacific drive got under way on November 20, 1943, when Nimitz sent Army and Marine forces to the Gilbert Islands to seize bases from which to support subsequent jumps into the Marshalls. Troops and supplies for the Gilberts loaded at Hawaii on newly developed assault shipping and sailed more than 2,000 miles to be set ashore by specially designed landing craft and amphibian vehicles. Makin, the Army objective, fell to the 27th Division after four days of hard fighting. Tarawa, where the 2d Marine Division went ashore, proved a bloody affair that provided a stiff test for American amphibious doctrine, techniques, and equipment. Naval gunfire vessels and carrier-based aircraft provided support during and after the assault.

The advance to the Gilberts disclosed that U.S. forces had not entirely mastered certain aspects of amphibious warfare, especially naval gunfire support, co-ordination of air support, and ship-to-shore communications. But valuable lessons were learned that, added to the earlier experiences of the South and Southwest Pacific Areas, established a pattern of island warfare which represented one of the major tactical developments of the war. First, air and naval forces isolated an objective and softened its defenses; simultaneously, joint forces would attack or feint toward other islands to deceive the Japanese. The approach of convoys carrying the ground assault forces to the main objective signaled the opening of final, intensive air and naval bombardment of the landing beaches. Whenever practicable, small forces occupied neighboring islands as sites for land-based artillery. Under cover of all these supporting fires, the landing forces moved from ship to shore in echelons, or waves, rocket-firing landing craft in the lead and amphibian tanks and tractors following to carry the assault troops directly onto the beaches and inland. Finally came landing craft with more infantry and with tanks, artillery, and supporting troops. Supplies followed rapidly as the assault forces secured and expanded the beachhead. Amphibious techniques were refined and modified to some extent after the Gilberts, but the lessons learned there made it unnecessary to effect any radical changes in amphibious doctrine throughout the rest of the war.

The Japanese did not react strongly to the loss of the Gilberts, and at the end of January 1944 Nimitz' Army and Marine forces moved into the eastern and central Marshalls to seize Majuro and Kwajalein. The strength employed in this operation proved so preponderant and Japanese defenses so weak that Nimitz was able to accelerate his next advance by two and a half months, and on February 17 landed Marine and Army units on Eniwetok Atoll in the western Marshalls. Concurrently, he conducted a long-awaited carrier strike against Truk in the central Carolines, considered Japan's key bastion in the Central Pacific. The raid revealed that the Japanese had virtually abandoned Truk as a naval base, and the capture of the atoll, set for June, no longer appeared necessary. Nimitz then drew up plans to invade the Marianas in mid-June and move on to the western Carolines and Palaus in mid-September, again accelerating the pace of the advance.

Acceleration of the Pacific Drive

General MacArthur had also pushed forward the Southwest Pacific Area's timetable. Having landed in the Admiralties a month ahead of his original schedule, he proposed to cancel operations against Hansa Bay and Wewak on the northeast coast of New Guinea in favor of a jump to Hollandia and Aitape, on the north-central coast, in April, two months earlier than previously planned. He would then continue northwestward along the coast in a campaign entailing the steady extension of land-based air cover by the seizure of successive air base sites until he reached the Vogelkop, at the eastern end of New Guinea, and then proceed to Mindanao, southernmost of the Philippine Islands.

The Joint Chiefs, quickly seizing the fruits of their strategy of opportunism, on March 12, 1944, rearranged the schedule of major Pacific operations. They provided for the assault by MacArthur's forces on Hollandia and Aitape in April with the support of a carrier task force from the Pacific Fleet, to be followed by Nimitz's move into the Marianas in June and into the Palaus in September. While Nimitz was employing the major units of the Pacific Fleet in these ventures, MacArthur was to continue his advance along the New Guinea coast with the forces at his disposal. In November, he was again to have the support of main units of the Pacific Fleet in an assault on Mindanao. Refusing yet to make a positive choice of what was to follow, the Joint Chiefs directed MacArthur to plan for the invasion of Luzon and Nimitz to plan for the invasion of Formosa early in 1945.

The March 12 directive served as a blueprint for an accelerated drive in the Pacific in the spring and summer of 1944. On April 22 Army forces under MacArthur landed at Hollandia and Aitape. At neither place was the issue ever in doubt, although during July the Japanese who had been bypassed at Wewak launched an abortive counterattack against Aitape. Protected by land-based aircraft from Hollandia, MacArthur's Army units next jumped 125 miles northwest on May 17 to seize another air base site at Wakde Island, landing first on the New Guinea mainland opposite the chief objective. A ground campaign of about a month and a half ensued against a Japanese division on the mainland, but, without waiting for the outcome of the fight, other Army troops carried the advance northwestward on May 27 another 180 miles to Biak Island.

As this point the wisdom of conducting twin drives across the Pacific emerged. The Japanese Navy was preparing for a showdown battle it expected to develop off the Marianas in June. MacArthur's move to Biak put land-based planes in position to keep under surveillance and to harry the Japanese Fleet, which was assembling in Philippine waters before moving into the Central Pacific. Reckoning an American-controlled Biak an unacceptable threat to their flank, the Japanese risked major elements of their fleet to send strong reinforcements to Biak in an attempt to drive MacArthur's forces off the island. They also deployed to bases within range of Biak about half their land-based air strength from the Marianas, Carolines, and Palaus—planes upon which their fleet depended for support during the forthcoming battle off the Marianas.

After two partially successful attempts to reinforce Biak, the Japanese assembled for a third try enough naval strength to overwhelm local American naval units; but just as the formidable force was moving toward Biak the Japanese learned the U.S. Pacific Fleet was off the Marianas. They hastily assembled their naval forces and sailed northwestward for the engagement known as the Battle of the Philippine Sea. Having lost their chance to surprise the U.S. Navy, handicapped by belated deployment, and deprived of anticipated land-based air support, the Japanese suffered another shattering naval defeat. This defeat, which assured the success of the invasions of both Biak and the Marianas, illustrates well the interdependence of operations in the two Pacific areas. It also again demonstrated that the U.S. Pacific Fleet's carrier task forces were the decisive element in the Pacific war.

Army and Marine divisions under Nimitz landed on Saipan in the Marianas on June 15, 1944, to begin a bloody three-week battle for control of the island. Next, on July 21, Army and Marine units invaded Guam, 100 miles south of Saipan, and three days later marines moved on to Tinian Island. An important turning point of the Pacific war, the American seizure of the Marianas brought the Japanese home islands within reach of the U.S. Army Air Forces' B–29 bombers, which in late November began to fly missions against the Japanese homeland.

At Biak Japanese resistance delayed capture of the best airfield sites until late June. On July 2, MacArthur's Army forces moved on to Noemfoor Island, ninety miles to the west, in a combined parachute-amphibious operation designed to broaden the base of the Southwest Pacific's air deployment. On July 30 the 6th Division continued on to the northwestern tip of New Guinea to secure another air base, and on September 15 MacArthur landed the reinforced 31st Division on Morotai Island, between New Guinea and Mindanao in the Philippines. On the same day Nimitz sent the 1st Marine Division ashore on Peleliu in the southern Palaus, and on the 17th the 81st Division from Nimitz' command landed on Angaur, just south of Peleliu. A regimental combat team of the 81st Division secured Ulithi Atoll, midway between Peleliu and the Marianas, without opposition on September 23.

With these landings the approach to the Philippines was virtually completed. The occupation of Morotai proved easy, and the island provided airfields for the support of advances into the Philippines and Indies. The Pacific Fleet employed Ulithi as a forward anchorage. Hard fighting dragged on in the Palaus through November, but as the result of another acceleration in the pace of Pacific operations these islands never played the role originally planned for them.

In twin drives, illustrative of the principles of maneuver, objective, economy of force, surprise, and mass, the Allied forces of the Pacific had arrived in mid-September 1944 at the threshold of their strategic objective, the Luzon-Formosa-China coast triangle. In seven months MacArthur's forces had moved forward nearly 1,500 miles from the Admiralties to Morotai; in ten months Nimitz' forces had advanced over 4,500 miles from Hawaii to the Palaus. The time had now arrived when a final choice had to be made of the main objective in the target area.

The Decision To Invade Luzon

During the summer of 1944, as the battles raged along both lines of advance, the strategic debate over the choice of Luzon versus Formosa also waxed hot. General MacArthur argued fervently that the proper course was to move through the Philippines to Luzon, cutting the Japanese lines of communications southward, establishing a base for bombardment and invasion of Japan, and fulfilling a solemn national obligation to liberate the Philippine people. Admiral Ernest J. King, Chief of Naval Operations, just as adamantly insisted that the war could be shortened by directing the Pacific advance from the Marianas and Palaus toward Formosa, the China coast, and Japan proper, seizing only the essential positions in the southern and central Philippines necessary to render air support for these advances. The arguments for Formosa were cogent enough. Its strategic position made it a better island steppingstone to the China coast or the Japanese home islands, a position from which Japanese communications to the south could be cut more effectively than from Luzon, and a closer-in position from which to conduct strategic bombardment. But it also could prove to be a more difficult position to take, and Nimitz did not have in his theater sufficient Army supporting and service troops, without reinforcement, to sustain a land campaign on the island. It might be difficult, too, to mount an invasion of Formosa as long as the Japanese could, from strong positions on Luzon, interfere with the Allied line of communications. Another consideration involved the real value of a foothold on the China coast. By the early fall of 1944, air base sites in east China from which the Allies had hoped to support Pacific operations and bomb Japan appeared irretrievably lost, and the Marianas already provided bases for the B–29's almost as close to Tokyo as Formosa. The need to seize and develop a port on the China coast thus lost much of its urgency, and the argument that Formosa was the best steppingstone to China became less compelling. Then, too, a successful invasion of either Luzon or Formosa required some concentration of forces from the two theaters. It was far easier to shift highly mobile naval resources in Nimitz' theater to the Philippines than it was to redeploy Army troops from the Southwest Pacific to support Nimitz' invasion of Formosa and the jump to the China coast with which he hoped to follow it.

At the time of the Morotai and Palaus landings, MacArthur's plans for invasion of the Philippines called for a preliminary assault in southern Mindanao on November 15, 1944, to secure air bases for the support of a larger attack at Leyte, in the east-central Philippines, on December 20. He would follow this with a large-scale assault on Lingayen Gulf in February 1945. Nimitz meanwhile planned to mount an invasion of Yap in the Carolines in October 1944 and then would prepare to launch his attack on Formosa as soon afterward as the elements of the Pacific Fleet required for operations in the southern and central Philippines could be returned. Obviously, there had to be a choice between Luzon and Formosa, for the Pacific Fleet would be required to support either operation.

The course of events went far to dictate the final choice. In mid-September Admiral Halsey's carrier task forces providing strategic support for the Morotai and Palaus operations struck the central and southern Philippines. Halsey found Japanese air strength unexpectedly weak and uncovered few signs of significant ground or naval activity. On the basis of Halsey's reports, MacArthur and Nimitz proposed to the Joint Chiefs a move directly to Leyte in October, bypassing Mindanao. Nimitz agreed to divert to the Leyte invasion the 3-division corps then mounting out of Hawaii for the assault against Yap. The Joint Chiefs quickly approved the new plan, and the decision to invade Leyte two months ahead of schedule gave MacArthur's arguments to move onto Luzon almost irresistible force. MacArthur now reported that he could undertake the invasion of Luzon in December 1944, whereas all the planners' estimates indicated that resources for an invasion of Formosa—particularly service troops and shipping—could not be readied before February 1945 at the earliest. Nimitz proposed to shift the Central Pacific attack northward against Iwo Jima in the Bonins in January 1945 and then against Okinawa and other islands in the Ryukyus early in March. On October 3, Admiral King bowing to the inevitable, accepted the new plans and the Joint Chiefs issued directives to MacArthur for the invasion of Luzon on December 20 and to Nimitz for the invasion of Iwo Jima and Okinawa early in 1945.

Pacific strategy had been cast into almost its final mold. In the end, the China coast objective disappeared entirely from planning boards. Final plans for the defeat of Japan envisaged gradual tightening of the ring by blockade and bombardment from the Marianas, Philippines, and Ryukyus with an invasion of the home islands to be mounted from these bases.

The Philippines Campaign

The main assault at Leyte took place on October 20, 1944, as four Army divisions landed abreast in the largest amphibious operation yet conducted in the Pacific. Vice Adm. Thomas C. Kinkaid, MacArthur's naval commander, controlled the amphibious phases, including naval gunfire support and close air support by planes based on escort carriers. Ground forces were under Lt. Gen. Walter Krueger, commanding the U.S. Sixth Army; land-based air forces of the Southwest Pacific Area in general support were commanded by Lt. Gen. George C. Kenney. MacArthur himself exercised unified command over the air, ground, and naval commanders. The fast carrier task forces of the Pacific Fleet, providing strategic support, operated under the control of Admiral Halsey, who reported to Nimitz, not MacArthur. There was no provision for unified naval command, and Halsey's orders were such that he could make his principal mission the destruction of the Japanese Fleet rather than the support of MacArthur's entry into the Philippines.

The Japanese had originally planned to make their stand in the Philippines on Luzon, but the invasion of Leyte moved them to reconsider, since they now decided that the entire Philippine Archipelago would be strategically lost if the

UNLOADING SUPPLIES ON A LEYTE BEACH

U.S. Army secured a foothold in the central islands. They therefore began sending ground reinforcements to Leyte; increased their land-based air strength in the Philippines in the hope of destroying Allied shipping in Leyte Gulf and maintaining local air superiority; and dispatched their remaining naval strength to Leyte Gulf to destroy Kinkaid's invasion fleet and to block Allied access to the Philippines. The ensuing air-naval Battle of Leyte Gulf was the most critical moment of the campaign, and proved one of the most decisive actions of the Pacific war.

Admiral Halsey, without consulting MacArthur or Kinkaid, pulled the bulk of his carrier forces northward to intercept part of the Japanese Fleet, leaving Leyte Gulf open to other Japanese Fleet units. Gallant, desperate action by Kinkaid's old battleships and escort carrier planes turned back the Japanese in the gulf, assuring the safety of the landing forces. It had been a close thing, clearly demonstrating the dangers of divided command. In the end, however, the combined operations of Kinkaid's and Halsey's forces virtually eliminated the Japanese Navy as a factor in the Pacific war.

With the Leyte beaches secure, U.S. Army units proceeded to destroy the Japanese ground forces. Miserable weather bogged down the pace of operations, made supply difficult, delayed airfield construction, curtailed air support, and permitted the Japanese to continue to ship reinforcements to the island. The reinforcement program came to a sudden halt early in December when the 77th Division executed an amphibious envelopment on Leyte's west coast,

GENERAL MACARTHUR AND MEMBERS OF HIS STAFF *wading ashore at Leyte.*

and by late December the Sixth Army had secured the most important sections of the island, those required for air and logistical bases. Japanese troops in the mountains of northwestern Leyte continued organized resistance well into the spring of 1945, occupying the energies of large portions of Lt. Gen. Robert L. Eichelberger's newly formed Eighth Army.

While the fight on Leyte continued, MacArthur's forces moved on to Luzon only slightly behind schedule. The first step of the Luzon Campaign was the seizure of an air base in southwestern Mindoro, 150 miles south of Manila, on December 15, 1944, two Army regiments accomplishing the task with ease. The invasion of Luzon itself started on January 9, 1945, when four Army divisions landed along the shores of Lingayen Gulf. Command arrangements were similar to those at Leyte, and again fast carrier task forces under Halsey operated in general support and not under MacArthur's control. Within three days five Army divisions, a separate regimental combat team, two artillery groups, an armored group, and supporting service units were ashore and had begun a drive down the Central Plains of Luzon toward Manila. The Japanese were incapable of naval intervention at Lingayen Gulf, and their most significant reaction was to throw a number of kamikaze (suicide plane) attacks against Kinkaid's naval forces for four days.

General Tomoyuki Yamashita, commanding Japanese forces in the Philippines, did not intend to defend the Central Plains—Manila Bay region, the strategic prize of Luzon. Knowing he would receive no reinforcements and believing the issue in the Philippines had been decided at Leyte, he sought only to pin down major elements of MacArthur's forces in the hope of delaying Allied progress toward Japan. For this purpose he moved the bulk of his troops into mountain strongholds, where they could conduct a protracted, bloody defensive campaign. But Japanese naval forces on Luzon, only nominally under Yamashita, decided to ignore this concept in favor of defending Manila and Manila Bay. Thus, when U.S. Army units reached Manila on February 3, it took them a month of bitter building-to-building fighting to root out the Japanese. Meanwhile, operations to clear Manila Bay had begun with a minor amphibious landing at the southern tip of Bataan on February 15. The next day a combined parachute-amphibious assault, involving two Army regiments, initiated a battle to clear Corregidor Island. Other forces cleared additional islands in Manila Bay and secured the south shore. By mid-March the bay was open for Allied shipping, but an immense salvage and repair job was necessary before the Allies could fully exploit Manila's excellent port facilities.

The reinforced 38th Division had landed meanwhile near Subic Bay and had cut across the base of Bataan peninsula to prevent the Japanese from holing up on Bataan as had MacArthur's forces three years earlier. The 11th Airborne Division undertook both amphibious and parachute landings in southern Luzon to start clearing that region, and the 158th Regimental Combat Team made an amphibious assault in southeastern Luzon to secure the Bicol peninsula. Turning against the Japanese mountain strongholds, MacArthur continued to pour reinforcements onto Luzon, and the land campaign there ultimately evolved into the largest of the Pacific war. MacArthur committed to Luzon ten divisions, two regiments of another division, and three separate regimental combat teams. Guerrillas also played a large role. One guerrilla unit came to substitute for a regularly constituted division, and other guerrilla forces of battalion and regimental size supplemented the efforts of the Army units. Moreover, the loyal and willing Filipino population immeasurably eased the problems of supply, construction, and civil administration.

Except for a strong pocket in the mountains of north central Luzon, organized Japanese resistance ended by late June 1945. The rugged terrain in the north, along with rainy weather, prevented Krueger's Sixth Army from applying its full strength to the reduction of this pocket. Eichelberger's Eighth Army took over responsibility for operations on Luzon at the end of June and continued the pressure against Yamashita's force in the last-stand area, but they held out there until the end of the war.

While Sixth Army was destroying Japanese forces on Luzon, Eighth Army ultimately employed five divisions, portions of a sixth division, a separate

U.S. PARATROOPERS DROPPING ON CORREGIDOR

regimental combat team, and strong guerrilla units in its campaign to re-conquer the southern Philippines. This effort began when a regimental combat team of the 41st Division landed on Palawan Island on February 28, 1945. Here engineers built an air base from which to help cut Japan's line of communications to the south and to support later advances in the southern Philippines and the Indies. On March 10, another regimental combat team of the 41st, later reinforced, landed near Zamboanga in southwestern Mindanao, and soon thereafter Army units began moving southwest toward Borneo along the Sulu Archipelago. In rapid succession Eighth Army units then landed on Panay, Cebu, northwestern Negros, Bohol, central Mindanao, southeastern Negros, northern Mindanao, and finally at Sarangani Bay in southern Mindanao, once intended as the first point of re-entry into the Philippines. At some locales bitter fighting raged for a time, but the issue was never in doubt and organized Japanese resistance in the southern Philippines had largely collapsed by the end of May. Mopping up continued to the end of the war, with reorganized and re-equipped guerrilla forces bearing much of the burden.

The last offensives in the Southwest Pacific Area started on May 1 when an Australian brigade went ashore on Tarakan Island, Borneo. Carried to the beaches by landing craft manned by U.S. Army engineers, the Australians had air support from fields on Morotai and in the southern Philippines. On June 10 an Australian division landed at Brunei Bay, Borneo, and another Australian division went ashore at Balikpapan on July 1 in what proved to be the final amphibious assault of the war.

Iwo Jima and Okinawa

Since slow-base development at Leyte had forced MacArthur to delay the Luzon invasion from December to January, Nimitz in turn had to postpone his target dates for the Iwo Jima and Okinawa operations, primarily because the bulk of the naval resources in the Pacific—fast carrier task forces, escort carrier groups, assault shipping, naval gunfire support vessels, and amphibious assault craft—had to be shifted between the two theaters for major operations. The alteration of schedules again illustrated the interdependence of the Southwest and Central Pacific Areas.

The Iwo Jima assault finally took place on February 19, 1945, with the 4th and 5th Marine Divisions, supported by minor Army elements, making the landings. The 3d Marine Division reinforced the assault, and an Army regiment ultimately took over as island garrison. The marines had to overcome fanatic resistance from firmly entrenched Japanese, who held what was probably the strongest defensive system American forces encountered during the Pacific war, and it took a month of bloody fighting to secure the island. In early March a few crippled B–29's made emergency landings on Iwo; by the end of the month an airfield was fully operational for fighter planes. Later, engineers constructed a heavy bomber field and another fighter base on the island.

The invasion of the Ryukyus began on March 26 when the 77th Division landed on the Kerama Islands, fifteen miles west of Okinawa, to secure a forward naval base, a task traditionally assigned to marines. On April 1 the 7th and 96th Divisions and the 2d and 6th Marine Divisions executed the assault on the main objective, Okinawa. Two more Army divisions and a Marine infantry regiment later reinforced it. Another amphibious assault took place on April 16, when the 77th Division seized Ie Shima, four miles west of Okinawa, and the final landing in the Ryukyus came on June 26, when a small force of marines went ashore on Kume Island, fifty miles west of Okinawa. Ground forces at Okinawa were first under the U.S. Tenth Army, Lt. Gen. Simon B. Buckner commanding. When General Buckner was killed on June 18, Marine Lt. Gen. Roy S. Geiger took over until General Joseph W. Stilwell assumed command on the 23d.

The Japanese made no attempt to defend the Okinawa beaches, but instead fell back to prepared cave and tunnel defenses on inland hills. Bitterly defending every inch of ground, the Japanese continued organized resistance until late June. Meanwhile, Japanese suicide planes had inflicted extensive damage on Nimitz' naval forces, sinking about 25 ships and damaging nearly 165 more in an unsuccessful attempt to drive Allied naval power from the western Pacific. Skillful small unit tactics, combined with great concentrations of naval, air, and artillery bombardment, turned the tide of the ground battle on Okinawa itself. Especially noteworthy was the close support that naval gunfire vessels provided the ground forces and the close air support furnished by Army, Navy, and Marine aircraft.

Capture of Okinawa and other positions in the Ryukyus gave the Allies both air and naval bases within easy striking distance of Japan. By early May fighter planes from Okinawa had begun flights over Japan, and as rapidly as fields became available bombers, including units from the Southwest Pacific Area, came forward to mount attacks in preparation for the invasion of the home islands. The forward anchorages in the Ryukyus permitted the Pacific Fleet to keep in almost continuous action against Japanese targets. The Ryukyus campaign had brought Allied forces in the Pacific to Japan's doorstep.

The American Effort in China, Burma, and India

While American forces in the Pacific, under the unified direction of the U.S. Joint Chiefs of Staff, made spectacular advances, the Allied effort in Southeast Asia bogged down in a mire of conflicting national purposes. The hopes Americans held, in the early stages of the war, that Chinese manpower and bases would play a vitally important role in the defeat of Japan were doomed to disappointment. Americans sought to achieve great aims on the Asiatic mainland at small cost, looking to the British in India and the Chinese, with their vast reservoirs of manpower, to carry the main burden of ground conflict. Neither proved capable of exerting the effort the Americans expected of them.

Early in 1942 the United States had sent General Stilwell to the Far East to command American forces in China, Burma, and India and to serve as Chief of Staff and principal adviser to Chiang Kai-shek, the leader of Nationalist China and Allied commander of the China theater. Stilwell's stated mission was "to assist in improving the efficiency of the Chinese Army." The Japanese conquest of Burma, cutting the last overland supply route to China, frustrated Stilwell's designs, for it left a long and difficult airlift from Assam to Kunming over the high peaks of the Himalayas as the only remaining avenue for the flow of supplies. The Americans assumed responsibility for the airlift, but its development was slow, hampered by a scarcity of transport planes, airfields, and trained pilots. Not until late in 1943 did it reach a monthly capacity of 10,000 tons, and in the intervening months few supplies flowed into China. The economy of the country continually tottered on the brink of collapse, and the Chinese Army, although it was a massive force on paper, remained ill organized, ill equipped, poorly led, and generally incapable of offensive action.

Stilwell thought that the only solution was to retake Burma and reopen the land supply line to China, and this became the position of the U.S. Joint Chiefs of Staff. To achieve the goal Stilwell undertook the training and equipping of a Chinese force in India that eventually consisted of three divisions, and sought to concentrate a much larger force in Yunnan Province in China and to give it offensive capability. With these two Chinese forces he hoped to form a junction in north Burma, thus re-establishing land communications between China and India. Stilwell's scheme became part of the larger plan, ANAKIM, that had been approved by the Combined Chiefs of Staff at the Casablanca Conference. Neither the British nor the Chinese, however, had any real enthusiasm for ANAKIM, and in retrospect it seems clear that its execution in 1943 was beyond the capabilities of forces in the theater. Moreover, Chiang was quite dilatory in concentrating a force in Yunnan; Maj. Gen. Claire L. Chennault, commanding the small American air force in China, urged that the Hump air line should be used to support an air effort in China, rather than to supply Chinese ground forces. Chennault promised amazing results at small cost, and his proposals attracted President Roosevelt as well as the British and the Chinese. As an upshot, at the TRIDENT Conference in May 1943, the amphibious operation against Rangoon was canceled and a new plan for operations emerged that stressed Chennault's air operations and provided for a lesser ground offensive in central and northern Burma. Under this concept a new road would be built from Ledo in Assam Province, India, to join with the trace of the old Burma Road inside China. The Americans assumed responsibility for building the Ledo Road in the rear of Chinese forces advancing from India into Burma.

Logistical difficulties in India, however, again delayed the opening of any land offensive and kept the airlift well below target figures. Until the supply line north from Calcutta to the British and Chinese fronts could be improved— and this job took well over a year—both air and ground operations against the Japanese in Burma were handicapped. In October 1943 Chinese troops under Stilwell did start to clear northern Burma, and in the spring of 1944 a U.S. Army unit of regimental size, Merrill's Marauders, spearheaded new offensives to secure the trace for the overland road. But Myitkyina, the key point in the Japanese defenses in north Burma, did not fall until August 2 and by that time the effort in Burma had been relegated to a subsidiary role.

After the Sextant Conference in late 1943, in fact, the American staff no longer regarded it as probable that the overland route to China could be opened in time to permit Chinese forces to drive to the coast by the time American forces advancing across the Pacific reached there. While the Americans insisted on continuing the effort to open the Ledo Road, they now gave first priority to an air effort in China in support of the Pacific campaigns. The Army Air Forces, in May 1944, started to deploy the first of its B–29 groups to airfields in East China to commence bombing of strategic targets in Korea, Manchuria, and Japan. At the same time, Chennault's Fourteenth Air Force was directed to stockpile supplies for missions in support of Pacific forces as they neared the China coast. Again these projects proved to be more than could be supported over the Hump air line, particularly since transports had also to be used to supply the ground effort of both British and Chinese forces. Then the Japanese reacted strongly to the increased air effort and launched a ground offensive that overran most of the existing fields and proposed air base sites in east China. Both air and ground resources inside China had to be diverted to oppose the Japanese advance. The B–29's were removed to India in January 1945, and two months later were sent to Saipan where the major strategic bombing offensive against Japan was by that time being mounted. In sum, the air effort in China without the protection of an efficient Chinese Army fulfilled few of the goals proclaimed for it.

To meet the crisis in east China, President Roosevelt urged Chiang to place his U.S. supported armies under the command of General Stilwell; Chiang eventually refused and asked for Stilwell's recall, a request the President honored. In September 1944, Maj. Gen. Albert C. Wedemeyer replaced Stilwell as Chief of Staff to Chiang and commander of American forces in the China Theater; a separate theater in India and Burma was created with Lt. Gen. Dan I. Sultan as its commanding general. The command issue was dropped and the American strategy in China became simply one of trying to realize at least something from previous investments without additional commitments.

Ironically enough, it was in this phase, after the Pacific advances had outrun those in Southeast Asia, that objects of the 1942 strategy were realized, in large part because the Japanese, hard-pressed everywhere, were no longer able to support their forces in Burma and China adequately. British and Chinese forces advanced rapidly into Burma in the fall of 1944, and, on January 27, 1945, the junction between Chinese forces advancing from India and Yunnan finally took place, securing the trace of the Ledo Road. To the south, the British completed the conquest of central Burma and entered Rangoon from the north early in May. The land route to China was thus finally secured on all sides, but the Americans had already decided that they would develop the Ledo Road only as a one-way highway, though they did expand the airlift to the point where, in July 1945, it carried 74,000 tons into China.

With increased American supply support, Wedemeyer was able to make more progress in equipping and training the Chinese Army. Under his tutelage the Chinese were able to halt the Japanese advance at Chihchiang in April 1945, and, as the Japanese began to withdraw in order to prepare a citadel defense of their home islands, Wedemeyer and the Chinese laid plans to seize a port on the Chinese coast. The war came to an end, however, before this operation even started and before the training and equipping of a Chinese Army was any-where near completion. Chiang's forces commenced the reoccupation of their homeland still, for the most part, ill equipped, ill organized, and poorly led.

The Japanese Surrender

During the summer of 1945, Allied forces in the Pacific had stepped up the pace of their air and naval attacks against Japan. In June and July carrier-based planes of the U.S. Pacific Fleet and U.S. Army Air Forces planes from the Marianas, Iwo Jima, and Okinawa struck the Japanese home islands contin-uously. During July Pacific Fleet surface units bombarded Japan's east coast, and in the same month a British carrier task force joined in the attack. Planes from the Philippines hit Japanese shipping in the South China Sea and extended their strikes as far as Formosa and targets along the South China coast. American submarines redoubled their efforts to sweep Japanese shipping from the sea and sever the shipping lanes from Japan to the Indies and Southeast Asia. Throughout the war, in fact, submarines had preyed on Japanese merchant and combat vessels, playing a major role in isolating Japan from its conquests and thereby drastically reducing Japan's ability to wage war.

After Germany's surrender in May the United States embarked upon a huge logistical effort to redeploy more than a million troops from Europe, the United States, and other inactive theaters to the Pacific. The aim was to complete the redeployment in time to launch an invasion of Japan on November 1, and the task had to be undertaken in the face of competing shipping demands for demobilization of long-service troops, British redeployment, and civil relief in Europe. By the time the war ended, some 150,000 men had moved directly from Europe to the Pacific, but a larger transfer from the United States across the Pacific had scarcely begun. In the Pacific, MacArthur and Nimitz had been sparing no effort to expand ports and ready bases to receive the expected influx and to mount invasion forces. The two commanders were also completing plans

ATOMIC CLOUD OVER NAGASAKI

for the invasion of Japan. In the last stage of the war, as all forces converged on Japan, the area unified commands were replaced by an arrangement that made MacArthur commander of all Army forces in the Pacific and Nimitz commander of all Navy forces.

By midsummer of 1945 most responsible leaders in Japan realized that the end was near. In June, those favoring peace had come out in the open, and Japan had already dispatched peace feelers through the Soviet Union, a country it feared might also be about to enter the war despite the existence of a non-aggression treaty between the two nations. As early as the Tehran Conference in late 1943 Stalin had promised to enter the war against Japan, and it was agreed at Yalta in February 1945 that the USSR would do so three months after the defeat of Germany. At the Potsdam Conference in July 1945 the Soviet Union reaffirmed its agreement to declare war on Japan. At this conference the United States and Britain, with China joining in, issued the famed Potsdam Declaration calling upon Japan to surrender promptly, and about the same time President Truman decided to employ the newly tested atomic bomb against Japan in the event of continued Japanese resistance.

Despite the changing climate of opinion in Japan, the Japanese did not immediately accept the terms of the Potsdam Declaration. Accordingly, on August 6 a lone American B–29 from the Marianas dropped an atomic bomb on Hiroshima; on the 9th the Soviet Union came into the war and attacked Japanese forces in Manchuria; and on the same day another B–29 dropped a second atomic bomb on Nagasaki. The next day Japan sued for peace, and, with the signing of surrender terms aboard the USS *Missouri* in Tokyo Bay on September 2, the bitter global war came to an end.

Retrospect

In winning the Pacific war the Allies had found it unnecessary to press home their attacks and destroy the Japanese military forces except for the

Japanese Fleet. By the end of the war Japan's Navy had virtually ceased to exist; Japanese industry had been so hammered by air bombardment that Japan's ability to wage war was seriously reduced; and U.S. submarine and air actions had cut off sources of raw material. At the time of the surrender Japan still had 2,000,000 men under arms in the homeland and was capable of conducting a tenacious ground defense; about 3,000 Japanese aircraft were also operational. Nevertheless, the Japanese could hardly have continued the war for more than a few months. On the other hand, the fact that an invasion was not necessary certainly spared many American lives.

The great arbiter of the Pacific war had been American industrial power, which produced a mighty war machine. Out of this production had come the Pacific Fleet, a potent force that could overcome the vast reaches of the Pacific upon which the Japanese had depended so heavily as a defensive advantage. The decisive combat element of the fleet was the fast carrier task force, which carried the war deep into Japanese territory and supported advances far beyond the range of land-based aircraft. Land-based air power also played a decisive part. When carriers were not available to support offensives, it was land-based aviation that measured the distance of each forward move. Land-based aviation proved important as well in providing close support for ground operations, while aerial supply operations and troop movements contributed greatly to the success of the Allied campaigns.

Both naval and air forces were dependent upon shore bases, and the war in the Pacific demonstrated that even in a predominantly naval-air theater, ground combat forces are an essential part of the offensive team. The Japanese had also been dependent upon far-flung bases, so that much of the Allied effort during the war had gone into the seizure or neutralization of Japan's bases. Thus, the Pacific war was in large measure a war for bases. On the other hand, the U.S. Pacific Fleet, in one of the greatest logistical developments of the war, went far in the direction of carrying its bases with it by organizing fleet trains of support vessels that were capable of maintaining the fleet at sea over extended periods.

Another important facet of the Pacific war was the development and employment of amphibious assault techniques, repeatedly demonstrating the need for unified command. Air, ground, and naval teamwork, supremely important in the struggle against Japan, occasionally broke down, but the success of the Allied campaigns illustrates that all three elements achieved it to a large degree. Strategic air bombardment in the Pacific, designed to cripple Japan's industrial capacity, did not get under way until well along in 1945. The damage inflicted on Japanese cities was enormous, but the effect, as in the case of the bomber offensive against Germany, remains unsettled, though the bombardment finally brought home to the Japanese people that the war was lost. The submarine played a vital role in reducing Japan's capabilities by taking a huge toll of Japanese shipping and by helping to cut Japan off from the resources of Southeast Asia.

In the final analysis Japan lost because the country did not have the means to fight a total war against the combination of industrial, air, naval, and human resources represented by the United States and its Allies. Admiral Isoroku Yamamoto, commander of the Japanese Fleet at the outbreak of the war, put his finger on the fatal weakness of the Japanese concept of the war, when he stated: "It is not enough that we should take Guam and the Philippines, or even Hawaii and San Francisco. We should have to march into Washington and sign the treaty in the White House." This the Japanese could never do, and because they could not they had to lose the war.

CHAPTER 24

Peace Becomes Cold War, 1945–1950

The United States did not return to its prewar isolationism after World War II. The balance of power in Europe and Asia and the safety of ocean distances east and west that made isolation possible had vanished, the balance upset by the war, the protection of oceans eliminated by advances in air transportation and weaponry. There was now little inclination to dispute the essential rightness of the position espoused by Woodrow Wilson after World War I that the nations of the world were interdependent, the peace indivisible. "We are participants," Wilson had said, "whether we would or not, in the life of the world. We are partners with the rest. What affects mankind is inevitably our affair as well as the affair of the nations of Europe and of Asia." Indeed, in the years immediately following World War II, full participation in world events became a governing dynamic of American life.

In the immediate wake of the war the hopes of the American Government and people rested in the United Nations Organization formed at San Francisco in 1945 to provide a world program of collective security. The fifty countries signing the U.N. Charter agreed to employ ". . . effective collective measures for the prevention and removal of threats to the peace and for the suppression of acts of aggression . . .," including the use of armed force if peaceful measures failed. A U.N. Security Council received authority to determine when the peace was threatened and what counteraction was to be taken and to call on member states to furnish military formations when armed force was deemed necessary. Founder members of the United Nations included the United States, Union of Soviet Socialist Republics, United Kingdom, China, and France; each of them received permanent representation on the Security Council and the power of veto over any council action. Since the United Nations' effectiveness depended largely upon the full cooperation of these five countries, the primary objective of American foreign policy as the postwar era opened was to continue and strengthen the solidarity those nations had displayed during the war.

A clear responsibility of U.S. membership in the United Nations was to maintain sufficient military power to permit an effective contribution to any U.N. force that might be necessary. Other than this, it was difficult, in the immediate aftermath of war, to foresee national security requirements in the changed world and, consequently, to know the proper shape of a military establishment to meet them. The immediate task was to demobilize the great war machine assembled during the war and, at the same time, maintain occupation troops in conquered and liberated territories. Beyond this lay the problems of deciding the size and composition of the postwar armed forces and of establishing the machinery through which national security policy would be determined and the military establishment governed.

Demobilization

The Army and Navy had worked separately during the war to determine what their postwar strengths should be and had produced plans for an orderly demobilization. The Navy developed a program for 600,000 men, 370 combat and 5,000 other ships, and 8,000 aircraft. The Army Air Forces was equally specific, setting its sights on becoming a separate service with 400,000 members, 70 air wings, and a complete organization of supporting units. The Army initially established as an over-all postwar goal a Regular and Reserve structure capable of mobilizing four million men within a year of any future outbreak of war; later it set the strength of the active ground and air forces at one and a half million. Demobilization plans called for the release of troops on an individual basis, each man receiving point credit for length of service, combat participation and awards, time spent overseas, and parenthood. The shipping available to bring overseas troops home and the capacity to process discharges were considered in setting the number of points determining eligibility for release, with the whole scheme aimed at producing a systematic transition to a peacetime military structure.

Pressure for faster demobilization from an articulate public, the Congress, and the troops themselves upset the plans for an orderly demobilization. The Army, which felt the greatest pressure, responded by easing the eligibility requirement and releasing half its eight million troops by the end of 1945. Early in 1946, when the Army cut down the return of troops from abroad in order to meet its overseas responsibilities, a crescendo of protest greeted the move, including troop demonstrations in the Philippines, China, England, France, Germany, Hawaii, and even California. The public cry diminished only after the Army more than halved its remaining strength during the first six months of 1946.

President Truman, determined to balance the national budget, meanwhile developed and through fiscal year 1950 employed a "remainder method" of calculating military budgets, subtracting all other expenditures from revenues before recommending a military appropriation. The dollar ceiling applied for fiscal year 1947 dictated a new maximum Army strength of just over one million. To reach it, the Army issued no more draft calls and released all postwar draftees along with the remaining troops eligible for demobilization. By June 30, 1947, the Army was a volunteer body of 684,000 ground troops and 306,000 airmen. (The Navy was meanwhile reduced to a strength of 484,000, the Marine Corps to 92,000.) It was still a large peacetime Army, but shortages of capable maintenance troops resulted in a widespread deterioration of equipment, and remaining Army units, understrength and infused with briefly trained replacements, were only shadows of the efficient organizations they had been at the end of the war.

Unification

While demobilization proceeded, civil and military officials alike wrestled with the task of reorganizing the national security system to cope with a changed world. The basic need, long recognized and proved anew by World War II, was unified control at the national level and at major military command levels. During the war this control had been accomplished through temporary arrangements. After the war, some permanent merger of ground, air, and naval forces under the authority of a single civilian member of the President's cabinet and the establishment of a statutory body where all plans and policies bearing on national security could be integrated seemed necessary. After long arguments over the degree of central authority to be imposed on the armed forces and over roles and missions to be assigned each service, the National Security Act of 1947 was passed as a first effort to achieve these ends.

The principal creations of the act were a National Security Council and a National Military Establishment. The latter, though not an executive department of the Federal government, was headed by a civilian Secretary of Defense with cabinet rank. The Air Force became a separate service equal with the Army and Navy; and all three were designated as executive departments and headed by civilian secretaries who, though they lacked cabinet rank, had direct access to the President.

Members of the National Security Council included the Secretary of State, Secretary of Defense, the three service secretaries, and heads of other governmental agencies as appointed by the President. One of the appointees was the Chairman of the National Security Resources Board, an agency also established by the act to handle the problems of industrial, manpower, and raw material mobilization in support of an over-all national strategy. In theory, the National

Security Council was to develop co-ordinated diplomatic, military, and industrial plans; recommend integrated national security policies to the President; and guide the execution of those policies approved. In practice, because the responsibility was inherently so complicated, the council would produce something less than precise policy determinations.

The national military establishment included the Departments of the Army, Navy, and Air Force and the Office of the Secretary of Defense. The Secretary of Defense exercised general direction over the three departments. The Joint Chiefs of Staff, composed of the military chiefs of the three services, became a statutory body seated in the Office of the Secretary of Defense and functioned as the principal military advisers to the President, the National Security Council, and the Secretary of Defense. They were also responsible for formulating joint military plans, establishing unified commands in various areas of the world, and giving strategic directon to those commands. Under this dispensation, unified commands were established by mid-1950 in the Far East, the Pacific, Alaska, the Caribbean, and Europe. Within each, at least theoretically, Army, Navy, and Air Force troops were under commanders of their respective services and under the overall supervision of a commander in chief designated from one of the services by the Joint Chiefs. But it would take some time for the principle of unity of command to be completely applied in all areas.

Under the Security Act, each military service retained much of its former autonomy since it was administered within a separate department. Interservice accord on roles and missions negotiated in 1948 by James V. Forrestal, the first Secretary of Defense, tended to harden the separation. The Army received primary responsibility for conducting operations on land, for supplying anti-aircraft units to defend the United States against air attack, and for providing occupation and security garrisons overseas. The Navy, besides remaining responsible for surface and submarine operations, retained control of its sea-based aviation and of the Marine Corps with its organic aviation. The new Air Force received jurisdiction over strategic air warfare, air transport, and combat air support of the Army.

The signal weakness of the act, however, was not that it left the armed forces more federated than unified, but that the Secretary of Defense, empowered to exercise only general supervision, could do little more than encourage cooperation among the departments. Furthermore, the direct access to the President given the three service secretaries tended to confuse the lines of authority. These faults prompted an amendment to the act in 1949 by which the National Military Establishment was converted into an executive department and renamed the Department of Defense. The Departments of the Army, Navy, and Air Force were reduced from executive departments to military departments within the Department of Defense; a chairman without vote was added to the Joint Chiefs; and the Secretary of Defense received the appropriate responsibility and authority to make him truly the central figure in co-ordinating the activities of the three services. In extension of civilian control, the three service secretaries retained authority to administer affairs within their respective departments; and the departments remained the principal operating agencies for administering, training, and supporting their respective forces.

Unification also touched the military school system, although each service continued to conduct courses to meet its own specialized needs. Three schools were opened to educate senior officers of all the services and selected civilians: an Armed Forces Staff College to train selected officers in planning and executing joint military operations, an Industrial College of the Armed forces to instruct senior officers in the many aspects of mobilizing the nation's resources for war, and a National War College to develop selected officers and civilians for duties connected with the execution of national policy.

A new Uniform Code of Military Justice applying to all the armed forces was enacted by Congress in May 1950. This code, besides prescribing uniformity, reduced the severities of military discipline in the interest of improving the lot of the individual serviceman. In another troop matter, part of a larger effort in the area of civil rights, President Truman directed the armed forces to eliminate all segregation of troops by race. The Navy and the Air Force abolished their all-Negro units by June 1950, whereas the Army, with more Negro members than its sister services, would take some four years longer to desegregate.

Occupation

Throughout demobilization about half the Army's diminishing strength remained overseas, the bulk involved in the occupation of Germany and Japan. Another large force was in liberated Korea, along with a Soviet force, both armies having sent units to accept the surrender of Japanese troops stationed there and to occupy the country.

Under a common occupation policy developed principally in conferences at Yalta and Potsdam in 1945, the Allied Powers assumed joint sovereign authority over Germany. American, British, Soviet, and French forces occupied separate zones, and national matters came before an Allied Control Council composed of the commanders of the four occupation armies. Berlin, itself lying deep in the Soviet zone in eastern Germany, was similarly divided and governed.

In the American zone, Army occupation troops proceeded rapidly with disarmament, demilitarization, and the eradication of Nazi influence from German life. American officials meanwhile participated as members of an International Military Tribunal which tried 22 major leaders of the Nazi party, sentencing 12 to death, imprisoning 7, and acquitting 3. An Office of Military Government supervised German civil affairs within the American zone, working increasingly through German local, state, and zonal agencies which military government officials staffed with men who were politically reliable. A special U.S. Constabulary, organized by the Army as demobilization cut away the strength of units in Germany, operated as a mobile police force.

Each of the other occupying powers organized its zone along similar lines. But the Allied Control Council, which could act only by unanimous agreement, failed to achieve unanimity on such nationwide matters as central economic administrative agencies, political parties, labor organizations, foreign and internal trade, currency, and land reform. USSR demands and dissents were chiefly responsible for the failures. Each zone inevitably became a self-contained administrative and economic unit, and some two years after the German surrender very little progress had been made toward the reconstruction of German national life. The eventual result, first taking shape in September 1949, was a divided Germany: the Federal Republic of Germany in the area of the American, British, and French zones; a Communist government in the Soviet zone in the east.

The occupation of Japan proceeded along different lines as a result of President Truman's insistence that the whole of Japan come under American control. Largely because the war in the Pacific had been primarily an American war, the President secured Allied approval of General of the Army Douglas MacArthur as Supreme Commander, Allied Powers, for the occupation of Japan. A Far East Advisory Commission representing the eleven nations that had fought against Japan was seated in Washington; and a branch of that body, with representatives from the United States, Great Britain, China, and the USSR, was located in Tokyo. These provided forums for Allied viewpoints on occupation policies, but the real power rested in General MacArthur.

Unlike Germany, Japan retained its government, which, under the supervision of General MacArthur's occupation troops, disarmed the nation rapidly and without incident. An International Military Tribunal similar to the one that functioned in Germany tried twenty-five high military and political officials, sentencing seven to death. MacArthur meanwhile encouraged reforms to alter the old order of government in which the emperor claimed power by divine right and exercised rule through an oligarchy of military, bureaucratic, and economic cliques. By mid-1947, the free election of a new Diet and a thorough revision of the nation's constitution began the transformation of Japan into a constitutional democracy with the emperor's role limited to that of a constitutional monarch. The way was thus open for the ultimate restoration of Japan's sovereignty.

West of the Japanese islands, on the peninsula of Korea jutting out from the central Asian mainland, the course of occupation resembled that in Germany. USSR forces, following their brief campaign against the Japanese in Manchuria, had moved into Korea from the north in August 1945. U.S. Army forces, departing their last battleground on Okinawa, entered from the south a month later. The 38th parallel of north latitude crossing the peninsula at its waist was set as the boundary between forces as the two nations released Korea from forty years of Japanese rule, the Americans accepting the Japanese surrender south of the line, the Soviets above it.

According to wartime agreements, Korea was to receive full independence following a period of Allied military occupation during which native leadership was to be regenerated and the country's economy rehabilitated. Very quickly the 38th parallel represented a complication in restoring Korea's sovereignty. For while the parallel had been designated only as a boundary between forces, the Soviets considered it a permanent delineation between occupation zones. This interpretation, as in Germany, ruptured the administrative and economic unity of the country.

Hope of removing this obstacle rose when the United States presented the problem during a meeting of foreign ministers at Moscow in December 1945. The ministers agreed that a joint U.S.-USSR commission would develop a provisional Korean government and that a four-power trusteeship composed of the United States, the Soviet Union, the United Kingdom, and China would guide the provisional government for a maximum of five years. But in the meetings of the commission, the Soviet members revealed a willingness to reunite Korea only if the provisional government was Communist-dominated. Persistent Soviet demands to this end were matched by equally persistent American refusals. The resulting impasse finally prompted the United States to lay the whole Korean question before the General Assembly of the United Nations in September 1947.

The Rise of a New Opponent

Soviet intransigence, as demonstrated in Germany, in Korea, and in other areas, dashed American hopes for Great Power unity. The USSR, Winston Churchill warned in a speech at Fulton, Missouri, early in 1946, was lowering an "iron curtain" across the European continent. It successfully, and quickly, drew eastern Germany, Poland, Hungary, Rumania, Bulgaria, Yugoslavia, and Albania behind that curtain. In Greece, where political and economic disorder led to civil war, the rebels received support from Albania, Bulgaria, and Yugoslavia. In the Near East, the Soviets kept a grip on Iran by holding troops placed there during the war beyond the time specified in the wartime arrangement. They also tried to intimidate Turkey into giving them special privileges in connection with the strategic Dardanelles. In Asia, besides insisting on full control in northern Korea, the USSR, it appeared, had turned Manchuria over to the Chinese Communists under Mao Tse-tung and was encouraging Mao in his renewed effort to wrest power from Chiang Kai-shek and the Kuomintang government.

Whatever the impulse behind the Soviet drive, whether it was a search for national security or a desire to promote Communist world revolution in keeping with Marxist doctrine, the USSR strategy appeared to be one of expansion. The United States could see no inherent limits to the outward push. Each Communist gain, it seemed, would serve as a springboard from which to try another; and a large part of the world, still suffering from the ravages of war, offered tempting opportunities for further Soviet expansion. The American response was a policy of containment, of blocking any extension of Communist influence. But, viewing the European continent as the main area of Soviet expansion, the United States at first limited its containment policy to western Europe and the Mediterranean area and attempted other solutions to the problem in Asia.

China, in any case, presented a dilemma. On the one hand, it was doubtful that Chiang Kai-shek could defeat the Communists with aid short of direct American participation in the civil war. Such participation was considered unacceptable. On the other hand, an attempt, through the efforts of General of the Army George C. Marshall following his Army retirement, to negotiate an end to the war on terms that would place the Kuomintang in full authority proved futile. The United States, consequently, adopted the attitude of "letting the dust settle." Part of the basis for this attitude was a prevalent American view that the Chinese Communist revolt was more Chinese than Communist, that its motivation was nationalistic, not imperialistic. Hence, though the dust appeared to be settling in favor of the Chinese Communists by the end of 1948, there was some hope that American-Chinese friendship could be restored whenever and however the conflict ended.

Next door in Korea, the division between north and south had become a reality by the end of 1948. After the Korean problem was referred to the United Nations, that body sent a commission to supervise free elections throughout the peninsula. But USSR authorities, declaring the U.N. project illegal, refused the commission entry above the 38th parallel. The U.N. then sponsored an elected government in the southern half of the peninsula, which in August 1948 became the Republic of Korea (South Korea). The Soviets countered during the following month by establishing a Communist government, the Democratic People's Republic of Korea (North Korea), above the parallel. Three months later, they announced the withdrawal of their occupation forces. The United States followed suit, withdrawing its troops by mid-1949 except for an advisory group left behind to help train the South Korean armed forces.

In the main arena in western Europe and in the Mediterranean area, blunt diplomatic exchanges finally produced a withdrawal of Soviet forces from Iran. But it was around American economic strength that the United States constructed a basic containment strategy, a resort based on judgment that the American monopoly on atomic weapons would cause the USSR to forgo direct military aggression in favor of exploiting civil strife in those countries prostrated by the war. The American strategy hence was to provide economic assistance to friends and former enemies alike to alleviate the conditions of distress conducive to Communist expansion.

To ease the situations in Turkey and Greece, President Truman in 1947 obtained $400 million from Congress with which to assist those two countries. "I believe," the President declared, "that it must be the policy of the United States to support free peoples who are resisting attempted subjugation by armed minorities or by outside pressures   .   .   .   that we must assist free peoples to work out their own destinies in their own way   .   .   .   that our help should be primarily through economic and financial aid which is essential to economic stability and orderly political processes." This philosophy, to become well known as the Truman Doctrine, was limited in application at the time, but it was destined to have wide significance for it, in effect, placed the United States in the position of opposing Communist expansion in any part of the world.

A broader program of economic aid followed. General Marshall, who became Secretary of State in January 1947, proposed that economic recovery in Europe be pursued as a single task, not nation by nation, and that the resources of European countries be combined with American aid within a single program. This "Marshall Plan" drew an immediate response wherein sixteen nations (who also considered the needs and resources of western Germany) devised a four-year European Recovery Program incorporating their resources and requiring some $16 billion from the United States. The Congress balked when President Truman first asked for approval of the program but appropriated funds for the first year in April 1948, after the USSR had engineered a *coup d'etat* that placed a Communist government in power in Czechoslovakia. The USSR, though invited in a last effort to promote Great Power unity, had refused to participate in the program and discouraged the initial interest displayed by some countries within its sphere of influence. In further counteraction, the Soviet Union in October 1947 had organized the Cominform, a committee for co-ordinating Communist parties in Europe whose aim was to fight the Marshall Plan as "an instrument of American imperialism."

Meanwhile, to protect the Western Hemisphere against Communist intrusion, the United States in September 1947 helped devise the Inter-American Treaty of Reciprocal Assistance (Rio Treaty), the first regional arrangement for collective defense under provisions of the U.N. Charter. Eventually signed by all twenty-one American republics, the treaty served notice that armed aggression against one signatory would be considered an attack upon all. Responses, by independent choice of each signatory, could range from severance of diplomatic relations through economic sanctions to military counteraction.

In March 1948, a second regional arrangement, the Brussels Treaty, drew five nations of western Europe—Great Britain, France, Belgium, the Netherlands, and Luxembourg—into a long-term economic and military alliance. The signatories received encouragement from President Truman, who declared before the Congress his confidence ". . . that the determination of the free countries of Europe to protect themselves will be matched by an equal determination on our part to help them. . . ." Senator Arthur H. Vandenberg of Michigan followed with a resolution, passed in the Senate in June 1948, authorizing the commitment of American military strength to regional alliances such as the Brussels Treaty.

Out of all of this grew the real basis of postwar international relations: West versus East, anti-Communists against Communists, those nations aligned with the United States confronting those assembled under the leadership of the Soviet Union, a cold war between power blocs. Leadership of the western bloc fell to the United States, since the fortunes of war had left it the only western power with sufficient resources to take the lead in containing Soviet expansion.

The Trends of Military Policy

Although pursued as a program of economic assistance, the American policy of containment nonetheless needed military underwriting. Containment, first of all, was a defensive measure. The USSR, moreover, had not completely demobilized. On the contrary, it was maintaining over four million men under arms, keeping armament industries in high gear, and rearming some of its satellites. Hence, containment needed the support of a military policy of deterrence, of a military strategy and organizational structure possessing sufficient strength and balance to discourage any Soviet or Soviet-supported military aggression.

Postwar military policy, however, did not develop as a full response to the needs of containment. For one reason, mobilization in the event of war, not the maintenance of ready forces to prevent war, was the traditional and current trend of American peacetime military thinking. A principal feature of mobilization planning was an effort to install universal military training. This effort was a particular response to technological advances which had eliminated the grace of time and distance formerly permitting the nation to mobilize its untrained citizenry after a threat of war became real, and which therefore posed a need for a huge reservoir of trained men. Late in 1945, President Truman asked the Congress for legislation requiring male citizens to undergo a year of military training (not *service*) upon reaching the age of eighteen or after completing high school. Universal military training quickly became the subject of wide debate. Objections ranged from mild criticism that it was ". . . a system in which the American mind finds no pleasure" to its denunciation as a "Nazi program." Regardless of the President's urgings, studies that produced further justification, and various attempts to make the program more palatable, the Congress over the five years following the President's first proposal refused to act on the controversial issue.

Without universal military training, the provision of trained strength with which to reinforce a nucleus of Regular forces at mobilization depended almost entirely upon the older system of using civilian components. This Reserve strength, like that of the Regular forces, was affected by limited funds. Enrollment in the National Guard and Reserves of all three services at mid-1950 totaled over two and a half million. But, owing in large part to restricted budgets, members in active training numbered less than one million. The bulk of this active strength rested in the Army's National Guard and Organized Reserve Corps. The National Guard, with 325,000 members, included twenty-seven understrength divisions. The active strength of the Organized Reserve Corps, some 186,000, was vested mainly in a multitude of small combat support and service units, these, too, generally understrength. A final source of trained strength was the Reserve Officers' Training Corps program, in which at midterm in fiscal year 1950 about 219,000 high school and college students were enrolled.

Also inhibiting a response to the military needs of containment was the influence of World War II, above all, the advent of the atomic bomb. The tendency was to consider the American nuclear monopoly as the primary deterrent to direct Soviet military action and to think only in terms of total war. Obversely, the possibility of lesser conflicts in which the bomb would be neither politically nor militarily relevant was almost completely disregarded.

Budgetary limitations to a great extent governed the size of the armed forces. From the figure reached at the end of demobilization, the total strength of active forces gradually decreased under the limited appropriations. The Army, Navy, and Marine Corps suffered losses in strength, whereas the Air Force actually grew somewhat larger. About a third of the Air Force constituted the Strategic Air Command, whose heavy bombers armed with atomic bombs represented the main deterrent to Soviet military aggression. Louis A. Johnson, who became Secretary of Defense in March 1949, gave full support to a defense based primarily on strategic air power, largely because of his dedication to economy. Intent on ridding the Department of Defense of what he considered "costly war-born spending habits," Secretary Johnson reduced defense expenditures below even the restrictive ceilings in President Truman's recommendations. As a result, by mid-1950 the Air Force, with 411,000 members, was barely able to maintain forty-eight air wings. The Navy, with a strength of 377,000, had 670 ships in its active fleet and 4,300 operational aircraft. In the Marine Corps, which had 75,000 men, the battle units amounted to skeletons of two divisions and two air wings. The Army, down to 591,000 members, had its combat strength vested in ten divisions and five regimental combat teams. The constabulary in Germany was equal to another division.

As evident in the strength reductions, mobilization strategy, and heavy reliance on the atomic bomb and strategic air power, the idea of deterring aggression through balanced ready forces had little place in the development of postwar military policy. The budgetary limitations made clear that military policy, caught as it often is between conflicting domestic pressures and foreign challenges, had responded more to domestic interests; and the roles played by traditional thinking and the influence of World War II invite the observation that, while foreign policy was being adjusted to a new opponent and a new kind of conflict, military policy was being developed mainly with earlier enemies and an all-out war in mind.

The Army of 1950

As the Army underwent its postwar reduction, from 8 million men and 89 divisions in 1945 to 591,000 men and 10 divisions in 1950, it also underwent numerous structural changes. At the department level, changes were made in

1946 to restore the General Staff to its prewar position. The principal adjustment toward this end was the elimination of the very powerful Operations Division (OPD), where control of wartime operations had been centralized. The prewar structure of the General Staff was restored with five coequal divisions under new names: Personnel and Administration; Intelligence; Organization and Training; Service, Supply and Procurement; and Plans and Operations. Also in 1946, Headquarters, Army Service Forces, was abolished, and the administrative and technical services serving under that headquarters during the war regained their prewar status as departmental agencies. In 1948, Army Ground Forces was redesignated Army Field Forces.

These and other organizational changes instituted or planned over the first five postwar years became a matter of statute with passage of an Army Reorganization Act in 1950. The act confirmed the power of the Secretary of the Army to administer departmental affairs. Under him, the Army Chief of Staff was responsible for the Army's readiness and operational plans, and for carrying out, worldwide, the approved plans and policies of the department. He had the assistance of general and special staffs whose size and composition could be adjusted as requirements changed. Below the Chief of Staff, the Chief of Army Field Forces was directly responsible for developing tactical doctrine, for controlling the Army school system, and for supervising the field training of Army units. Most of the training and schools were conducted within six Continental Army Areas into which the United States was divided.

Under the new act, the Secretary of the Army received authority to determine the number and strength of the Army's combat arms and services. Three combat arms—infantry, armor, and artillery—received statutory recognition. The last represented a merger of the old field artillery, coast artillery, and anti-aircraft artillery. Armor was made a continuation of another older arm, now eliminated, the cavalry. The services numbered fourteen and included The Adjutant General's Corps, Army Medical Service, Chaplains Corps, Chemical Corps, Corps of Engineers, Finance Corps, Inspector General's Corps, Judge Advocate General's Corps, Military Police Corps, Ordnance Corps, Quartermaster Corps, Signal Corps, Transportation Corps, and Women's Army Corps. Army Aviation, designated neither arm nor service, existed as a quasi arm equipped with small fixed-wing craft and helicopters.

The better Army troops at mid-1950 were among a large but diminishing group of World War II veterans. The need to obtain replacements quickly during demobilization, the distractions and relaxed atmosphere of occupation duty, and a postwar training program less demanding than that of the war years impeded the combat readiness of newer Army members. The new Uniform Code of Military Justice, because it softened military discipline, was considered in some quarters as likely to blunt the Army's combat ability even more.

Half the Army's major combat units were deployed overseas. Of the ten divisions, four infantry divisions were part of the Far East Command on occupation duty in Japan. Another infantry division was with the European Command in Germany. The remaining five were in the United States, constituting a General Reserve to meet emergency assignments. These included two airborne infantry divisions, two infantry divisions, and an armored division. All ten had undergone organizational changes, most of them prompted by the war experience. Under new tables of organization and equipment, the firepower and mobility of a division received a boost through the addition of a tank battalion and an antiaircraft battalion and through a rise in the number of pieces in each artillery battery from four to six. At regimental level, the cannon and antitank companies of World War II days were dropped; the new tables added a tank company, 4.2-inch mortar company, and 57-mm. and 75-mm. recoilless rifles. The postwar economies, however, had forced the Army to skeletonize its combat units. Nine of the 10 divisions were far understrength, infantry regiments had only 2 of the normal 3 battalions, most artillery battalions had only 2 of the normal 3 firing batteries, and organic armor was generally lacking. No unit had its wartime complement of weapons, and those weapons on hand as well as other equipment were largely worn leftovers from World War II. None of the combat units, as a result, came anywhere near possessing the punch conceived under the new organizational design.

The Cold War Intensifies

The deterioration in military readiness through mid-1950 proceeded in the face of a worsening trend in international events, especially from mid-1948 forward. In Germany, in further protest against western attempts to establish a national government, and in particular against efforts to institute currency reforms in Berlin, the USSR in June 1948 moved to force the Americans, British, and French out of the capital by blockading the road and rail lines through the Soviet occupation zone over which troops and supplies from the west reached the Allied sectors of the city. General Lucius D. Clay, the American military governor, countered by devising an airlift in which U.S. Army and U.S. Air Force troops, with some help from the British, loaded and flew in food, fuel, and other necessities to keep the Allied sectors of Berlin supplied. The success of the airlift and a telling counterblockade in which shipments of goods formerly reaching the Soviet sector from western Germany were shut off finally moved the Soviets to lift the blockade in May 1949.

Meanwhile, in April 1949, the United States joined the North Atlantic Treaty Organization (NATO), a military alliance growing out of the Brussels Treaty. NATO joined the United States with Canada and ten western European nations under terms by which ". . . an armed attack against one or more of them . . . shall be considered an attack against them all," a provision specifically aimed at discouraging a Soviet march in Europe. The signatories agreed to earmark forces for service under NATO direction. In the United States, the budgetary restrictions, mobilization strategy, and continuing emphasis on air power and the bomb handicapped military commitment to the alliance. An effort at the time by some officials to increase the nation's conventional forces against the possibility of a conflict in which atomic retaliation would be an excessive answer was defeated by the basic budget ceiling and Secretary of Defense Johnson's ardent economy drive. Through NATO membership, nevertheless, the United States certified that it would fight if necessary to protect common Allied interests in Europe and thus enlarged the policy of containment beyond the economic realm.

Concurrently with negotiations leading to the NATO alliance, the National Security Council reconsidered the whole course of postwar military aid. Under different programs, some of them continuations of World War II aid, the United States was by 1949 providing military equipment and training assistance to Greece, Turkey, Iran, China, Korea, the Philippines, and the Latin American republics. The National Security Council recommended and President Truman proposed to the Congress that all existing programs, including those conceived for NATO members, be combined into one. The result was the Mutual Defense Assistance Program of October 1949. The Department of the Army, made executive agency for the program, sent each recipient country a military assistance advisory group. Composed of Army, Navy, and Air Force sections, each advisory group assisted its host government in determining the amount and type of aid needed and helped train the armed forces of each country in the use and tactical employment of matériel received from the United States.

A new and surprising turn came in the late summer of 1949 when, from two to three years ahead of western bloc estimates, an explosion over Siberia announced Soviet possession of an atomic weapon. On the heels of the USSR's achievement, the civil war in China ended in favor of the Chinese Communists. Chiang Kai-shek was forced to withdraw to the island of Taiwan (Formosa) in December 1949. Two months later, Communist China and the USSR negotiated a treaty of mutual assistance, an ominous event for the rest of Asia.

The loss of the nuclear monopoly prompted a broad review of the entire political and strategic position of the United States, a task carried out at top staff levels in the National Security Council, Department of State, and Department of Defense. A special National Security Council committee at the same time considered the specific problem posed by the Soviet achievement. Out of the committee effort came a decision to intensify research already begun on the development of a hydrogen bomb to assure the United States the lead in the field of nuclear weapons. Out of the broader review, completed in April 1950, came recommendations for a large expansion of American military, diplomatic, and economic efforts to meet the changed world situation. The planning staffs in the Department of Defense began at once to translate the military recommendations into force levels and budgets. There remained the question of whether the plans when completed would persuade President Truman to lift the ceiling on military appropriations, but as a result of events in Asia this question was never put to the test.

After the Communist victory in China, the United States applied its policy of containment in Asia. In January 1950, Dean G. Acheson, who a year earlier had become Secretary of State, publicly defined the U.S. "defense line" in Asia as running south from the Aleutian Islands to Japan, to the Ryukyu Islands, and then to the Philippines. This delineation raised a question about Taiwan and Korea, which lay outside the line. These areas were not completely disregarded. Secretary Acheson pointed out that if they were attacked, ". . . the initial reliance must be on the people attacked to resist it and then upon the commitments of the entire world under the Charter of the United Nations." The question was whether the Communist bloc would construe this statement as a definite American commitment to help defend Taiwan and Korea if they came under attack.

In the case of Korea, the question would be answered in June 1950 following the armed invasion of the Republic of Korea by forces of the Soviet satellite above the 38th parallel. Until then, with the emergence of a bipolar world, the USSR and its satellites on one side, the United States and its allies on the other, the United States had responded with a policy of containing the political ambitions of the Communist bloc with the objective of deterring an outbreak of war. But by mid-1950 the United States had not yet backed that policy with a matching military establishment.

CHAPTER 25

The Korean War, 1950–1953

After the USSR installed a Communist government in North Korea in
September 1948, that government promoted and supported an insurgency in
South Korea in an attempt to bring down the recognized government and gain
jurisdiction over the entire Korean peninsula. Not quite two years later, after
the insurgency showed signs of failing, the northern government undertook a
direct attack, sending the North Korea People's Army south across the 38th
parallel before daylight on Sunday, June 25, 1950. The invasion, in a narrow
sense, marked the beginning of a civil war between peoples of a divided country.
In a larger sense, the cold war between the Great Power blocs had erupted in
open hostilities.

The Decision for War

The western bloc, especially the United States, was surprised by the North
Korean decision. Although intelligence information of a possible June invasion
had reached Washington, the reporting agencies judged an early summer attack
unlikely. The North Koreans, they estimated, had not yet exhausted the possibilities of the insurgency and would continue that strategy only.

The North Koreans, however, seem to have taken encouragement from the
U.S. policy which left Korea outside the U.S. "defense line" in Asia and from
relatively public discussions of the economies placed on U.S. armed forces. They
evidently accepted these as reasons to discount American counteraction, or their
sponsor, the USSR, may have made that calculation for them. The Soviets also
appear to have been certain the United Nations would not intervene, for in
protest against Nationalist China's membership in the U.N. Security Council
and against the U.N.'s refusal to seat Communist China, the USSR member
had boycotted council meetings since January 1950 and did not return in June
to veto any council move against North Korea.

Moreover, Kim Il Sung, the North Korean Premier, could be confident that
his army, a modest force of 135,000, was superior to that of South Korea. Koreans
who had served in Chinese and Soviet World War II armies made up a large
part of his force. He had 8 full divisions, each including a regiment of artillery;
2 divisions at half strength; 2 separate regiments; an armored brigade with 120

Soviet T34 medium tanks; and 5 border constabulary brigades. He also had 180 Soviet aircraft, mostly fighters and attack bombers, and a few naval patrol craft.

The Republic of Korea (ROK) Army had just 95,000 men and was far less fit. Raised as a constabulary during occupation, it had not in its later combat training under a U.S. Military Advisor Group progressed much beyond company-level exercises. Of its eight divisions, only four approached full strength. It had no tanks and its artillery totaled eighty-nine 105-mm. howitzers. The ROK Navy matched its North Korean counterpart, but the ROK Air Force had only a few trainers and liaison aircraft. U.S. equipment, war-worn when furnished to South Korean forces, had deteriorated further, and supplies on hand could sustain combat operations no longer than fifteen days. Whereas almost $11 million in matériel assistance had been allocated to South Korea in fiscal year 1950 under the Mutual Defense Assistance Program, Congressional review of the allocation so delayed the measure that only a trickle of supplies had reached the country by June 25, 1950.

The North Koreans quickly crushed South Korean defenses at the 38th parallel. The main North Korean attack force next moved down the west side of the peninsula toward Seoul, the South Korean capital, thirty-five miles below the parallel, and entered the city on June 28. (*Map 45*) Secondary thrusts down the peninsula's center and down the east coast kept pace with the main drive. The South Koreans withdrew in disorder, those troops driven out of Seoul forced to abandon most of their equipment because the bridges over the Han River at the south edge of the city were prematurely demolished. The North Koreans halted after capturing Seoul, but only briefly to regroup before crossing the Han.

In Washington, where a 14-hour time difference made it June 24 when the North Koreans crossed the parallel, the first report of the invasion arrived that night. Early on the 25th, the United States requested a meeting of the U.N. Security Council. The council adopted a resolution that afternoon demanding an immediate cessation of hostilities and a withdrawal of North Korean forces to the 38th parallel.

In independent actions on the night of the 25th, President Truman relayed orders to General of the Army Douglas MacArthur at MacArthur's Far East Command headquarters in Tokyo, Japan, to supply ROK forces with ammunition and equipment, evacuate American dependents from Korea, and survey conditions on the peninsula to determine how best to assist the republic further. The President also ordered the U.S. Seventh Fleet from its current location in Philippine and Ryukyu waters to Japan. On the 26th, in a broad interpretation of a U.N. Security Council request for "every assistance" in supporting the June 25

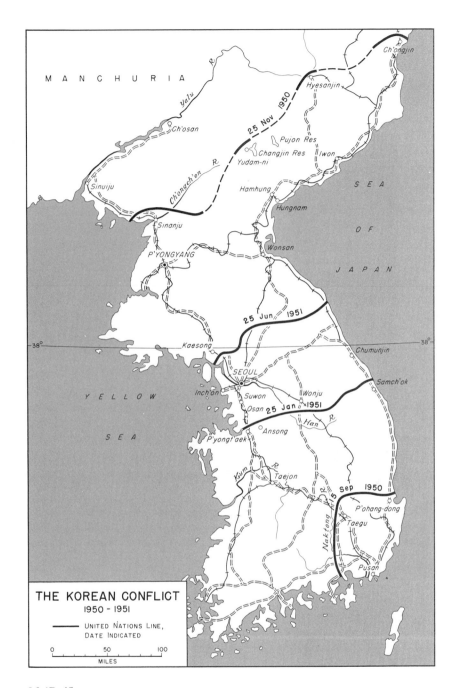

MANCHURIA

Yalu R.

Ch'osan

Ch'ongjin

25 Nov 1950

Hyesanjin

Pujon Res

Changjin Res   Iwon

Yudam-ni

Sinuiju

Chŏngch'ŏn R.

SEA

Hamhung

Sinanju

Hungnam

OF

P'YONGYANG

Wonsan

JAPAN

25 Jun 1951

38°   38°

Kaesong

Chumunjin

SEOUL

Samch'ok

YELLOW

Inch'on   Suwon   Wonju

Osan 25 Jan 1951

SEA

Han R.

Ansong

P'yongt'aek

Kum R.

Taejon

15 Sep 1950

Naktong R.

P'ohang-dong

Taegu

Pusan

THE KOREAN CONFLICT
1950 - 1951

—— UNITED NATIONS LINE,
DATE INDICATED

0   50   100

MILES

MAP 45

resolution, President Truman authorized General MacArthur to use air and naval strength against North Korean targets below the 38th parallel. The President also redirected the bulk of the Seventh Fleet to Taiwan, where by standing between the Chinese Communists on the mainland and the Nationalists on the island it could discourage either one from attacking the other and thus prevent a widening of hostilities.

When it became clear on June 27 that North Korea would ignore the U.N. demands, the U.N. Security Council, again at the urging of the United States, asked U.N. members to furnish military assistance to help South Korea repel the invasion. President Truman immediately broadened the range of U.S. air and naval operations to include North Korea and authorized the use of U.S. Army troops to protect Pusan, Korea's major port at the southeastern tip of the peninsula. MacArthur meanwhile had flown to Korea and, after witnessing failing ROK Army efforts in defenses south of the Han River, recommended to Washington that a U.S. Army regiment be committed in the Seoul area at once and that this force be built up to two divisions. President Truman's answer on June 30 authorized MacArthur to use all forces available to him.

Thus the United Nations for the first time since its founding reacted to aggression with a decision to use armed force. The United States would accept the largest share of the obligation in Korea but, still deeply tired of war, would do so reluctantly. President Truman later described his decision to enter the war as the hardest of his days in office. But he believed that if South Korea was left to its own defense and fell, no other small nation would have the will to resist aggression, and Communist leaders would be encouraged to override nations closer to U.S. shores. The American people, conditioned by World War II to battle on a grand scale and to complete victory, would experience a deepening frustration over the Korean conflict, brought on in the beginning by embarrassing reversals on the battlefield.

South to the Naktong

Ground forces available to MacArthur included the 1st Cavalry Division and the 7th, 24th, and 25th Infantry Divisions, all under the Eighth U.S. Army in Japan, and the 29th Regimental Combat Team on Okinawa. All the postwar depreciations had affected them. Their maneuverability and firepower were sharply reduced by a shortage of organic units and by a general understrength among existing units. Some weapons, medium tanks in particular, could scarcely be found in the Far East, and ammunition reserves amounted to only a 45-day supply. By any measurement, MacArthur's ground forces were unprepared for battle. His air arm, Far East Air Forces (FEAF), moreover, was organized for air defense, not tactical air support. Most FEAF planes were short-range jet interceptors not meant to be flown at low altitudes in support of ground operations. Some F–51's in storage in Japan and more of these World War II planes in the United States would prove instrumental in meeting close air support needs. Naval Forces, Far East, MacArthur's sea arm, controlled only five combat ships and a skeleton amphibious force, although reinforcement was near in the Seventh Fleet.

When MacArthur received word to commit ground units, the main North Korean force already had crossed the Han River. By July 3, a westward enemy attack had captured a major airfield at Kimpo and the Yellow Sea port of Inch'on. Troops attacking south repaired a bridge so that tanks could cross the Han and moved into the town of Suwon, twenty-five miles below Seoul, on the 4th.

The speed of the North Korean drive coupled with the unreadiness of American forces compelled MacArthur to disregard the principle of mass and commit units piecemeal to trade space for time. Where to open a delaying action was clear, for there were few good roads in the profusion of mountains making up the Korean peninsula, and the best of these below Seoul, running on a gentle diagonal through Suwon, Osan, Taejon, and Taegu to the port of Pusan in the southeast, was the obvious main axis of North Korean advance. At MacArthur's order, two rifle companies, an artillery battery, and a few other supporting units of the 24th Division moved into a defensive position astride the main road near Osan, ten miles below Suwon, by dawn on July 5. MacArthur later referred to this 540-man force, called Task Force Smith, as an "arrogant display of strength." Another kind of arrogance to be found at Osan was a belief that the North Koreans might ". . . turn around and go back when they found out who was fighting."

Coming out of Suwon in a heavy rain, a North Korean division supported by thirty-three tanks reached and with barely a pause attacked the Americans around 8:00 a.m. on the 5th. The North Koreans lost 4 tanks, 42 men killed, and 85 wounded. But the American force lacked antitank mines, the fire of its recoilless rifles and 2.36-inch rocket launchers failed to penetrate the T34 armor, and its artillery quickly expended the little antitank ammunition that did prove effective. The rain canceled air support, communications broke down, and the task force was, under any circumstances, too small to prevent North Korean infantry from flowing around both its flanks. By midafternoon, Task Force Smith was pushed into a disorganized retreat with over 150 casualties and the loss of all equipment save small arms. Another casualty was American morale as word of the defeat reached other units of the 24th Division then moving into delaying positions below Osan.

The next three delaying actions, though fought by larger forces, had similar results. In each case, North Korean armor or infantry assaults against the front of the American position were accompanied by an infantry double envelopment. By July 13, the 24th Division was forced back on Taejon, sixty miles below Osan, where it initially took position along the Kum River above the town. Clumps of South Korean troops by then were strung out west and east of the division to help delay the North Koreans.

Fifty-three U.N. members meanwhile signified support of the Security Council's June 27 action and twenty-nine of these made specific offers of assistance. Ground, air, and naval forces eventually sent to assist South Korea would represent twenty U.N. members and one nonmember nation. The United States, Great Britain, Australia, New Zealand, Canada, Turkey, Greece, France, Belgium, Luxembourg, the Netherlands, Thailand, the Philippines, Colombia and Ethiopa would furnish ground combat troops. India, Sweden, Norway, Denmark, and Italy (the non-United Nations country) would furnish medical units. Air forces would arrive from the United States, Australia, Canada, and the Union of South Africa; naval forces would come from the United States, Great Britain, Australia, Canada, and New Zealand.

The wide response to the council's call pointed out the need for a unified command. Acknowledging the United States as the major contributor, the U.N. Security Council on July 7 asked it to form a command into which all forces would be integrated and to appoint a commander. In the evolving command structure, President Truman became executive agent for the U.N. Security Council. The National Security Council, Department of State, and Joint Chiefs of Staff participated in developing the grand concepts of operations in Korea. In the strictly military channel, the Joint Chiefs issued instructions through the Army member to the unified command in the field, designated the United Nations Command (UNC) and established under General MacArthur.

MacArthur superimposed the headquarters of his new command over that of his existing Far East Command. Air and naval units from other countries joined the Far East Air Forces and Naval Forces, Far East, respectively. MacArthur assigned command of ground troops in Korea to the Eighth Army under Lt. Gen. Walton H. Walker, who established headquarters at Taegu on July 13, assuming command of all American ground troops on the peninsula and, at the request of South Korean President Syngman Rhee, of the ROK Army. When ground forces from other nations reached Korea, they too passed to Walker's command.

U.S. MEDIUM TANK M4A3 *on a South Korean village road.*

Between July 14 and 18, MacArthur moved the 25th and 1st Cavalry Divisions to Korea after cannibalizing the 7th Division to strengthen those two units. By then, the battle for Taejon had opened. New 3.5-inch rocket launchers hurriedly airlifted from the United States proved effective against the T34 tanks, but the 24th Division lost Taejon on July 20 after two North Korean divisions established bridgeheads over the Kum River and encircled the town. In running enemy roadblocks during the final withdrawal from town, Maj. Gen. William F. Dean, the division commander, took a wrong turn and was captured some days later in the mountains to the south. When repatriated some three years later, he would learn that for his exploits at Taejon he was one of 131 servicemen awarded the Medal of Honor during the war (Army 78, Marine Corps 42, Navy 7, and Air Force 4).

While pushing the 24th Division below Taejon, the main North Korean force split, one division moving south to the coast, then turning east along the lower coast line. The remainder of the force continued southeast beyond Taejon toward Taegu. Southward advances by the secondary attack forces in the central and eastern sectors matched the main thrust, all clearly aimed to converge on Pusan. North Korean supply lines grew long in the advance, and less and less tenable under heavy UNC air attacks. FEAF meanwhile achieved air superiority, indeed air supremacy, and UNC warships wiped out North Korean naval

Troops Keeping a Lookout *as phosphorous shells fall on enemy-held territory.*

opposition and clamped a tight blockade on the Korean coast. These achievements and the arrival of the 29th Regimental Combat Team from Okinawa on July 26 notwithstanding, American and South Korean troops steadily gave way. American casualties rose above 6,000 and South Korean losses reached 70,000. By the beginning of August, General Walker's forces held only a small portion of southeastern Korea.

Alarmed by the rapid loss of ground, Walker ordered a stand along a 140-mile line arching from the Korea Strait to the Sea of Japan west and north of Pusan. His U.S. divisions occupied the western arc, basing their position on the Naktong River. South Korean forces, reorganized by American military advisers into two corps headquarters and five divisions, defended the northern segment. A long line and few troops kept positions thin in this "Pusan Perimeter." But replacements and additional units now entering or on the way to Korea would help relieve the problem, and fair interior lines of communications radiating from Pusan allowed Walker to move troops and supplies with facility.

Raising brigades to division status and conscripting large numbers of recruits, many from overrun regions of South Korea, the North Koreans over the next month and a half committed thirteen infantry divisions and an armored division against Walker's perimeter. But the additional strength failed to compensate for the loss of some 58,000 trained men and much armor suffered in the advance to the Naktong. Nor in meeting the connected defenses of the perimeter did enemy commanders recognize the value of massing forces for decisive penetration at one point. They dissipated their strength instead in piecemeal attacks at various points along the Eighth Army line.

Close air support played a large role in the defense of the perimeter. But the Eighth Army's defense really hinged on a shuttling of scarce reserves to block a gap, reinforce a position, or counterattack wherever the threat appeared greatest at a given moment. Timing was the key, and General Walker proved a master of it. His brilliant responses prevented serious enemy penetrations and inflicted telling losses that steadily drew off North Korean offensive power. His own strength meanwhile was on the rise. By mid-September, he had over 500 medium tanks. Replacements arrived in a steady flow and additional units came in: the 5th Regimental Combat Team from Hawaii, the 2d Infantry Division and 1st Provisional Marine Brigade from the United States, and a British infantry brigade from Hong Kong. Thus, as the North Koreans lost irreplaceable men and equipment, UNC forces acquired an offensive capability.

North to the Parallel

Against the gloomy prospect of trading space for time, General MacArthur, at the entry of U.S. forces into Korea, had perceived that the deeper the North Koreans drove, the more vulnerable they would become to an amphibious envelopment. He began work on plans for such a blow almost at the start of hostilities, favoring Inch'on, the Yellow Sea port halfway up the west coast, as the landing site. Just twenty-five miles east lay Seoul where Korea's main roads and rail lines converged. A force landing at Inch'on would have to move inland only a short distance to cut North Korean supply routes, and the recapture of the capital city also could have a helpful psychological impact. Combined with a general northward advance by the Eighth Army, a landing at Inch'on could produce decisive results. Enemy troops retiring before the Eighth Army would be cut off by the amphibious force behind them or be forced to make a slow and difficult withdrawal through the mountains farther east.

Though pressed in meeting Eighth Army troop requirements, MacArthur was able to shape a two-division landing force. He formed the headquarters

THE INCH'ON LANDING

of the X Corps from members of his own staff, naming his chief of staff, Maj. Gen. Edward M. Almond, as corps commander. He rebuilt the 7th Division by giving it high priority on replacements from the United States and by assigning it 8,600 South Korean recruits. The latter measure was part of a larger program, called the Korean Augmentation to the United States Army, in which South Korean troops were placed among almost all American units. At the same time, he acquired from the United States the greater part of the 1st Marine Division, which he planned to fill out with the Marine brigade currently in the Pusan Perimeter. The X Corps, with these two divisions, was to make its landing as a separate force, not as part of the Eighth Army.

MacArthur's superiors and the Navy judged the Inch'on plan dangerous. Naval officers considered the extreme Yellow Sea tides, which range as much as thirty feet, and narrow channel approaches to Inch'on as big risks to shipping. Marine officers saw danger in landing in the middle of a built-up area and in having to scale high sea walls to get ashore. The Joint Chiefs of Staff anticipated serious consequences if Inch'on were strongly defended since MacArthur would be committing his last major reserves at a time when no more General Reserve units in the United States were available for shipment to the

Far East. Four National Guard divisions had been federalized on September 1, but none of these was yet ready for combat duty; and, while the draft and call-ups of members of the Organized Reserve Corps were substantially increasing the size of the Army, they offered MacArthur no prospect of immediate reinforcement. But MacArthur was willing to accept the risks.

In light of the uncertainties MacArthur's decision was a remarkable gamble, but if results are what count his action was one of exemplary boldness. The X Corps swept into Inch'on on September 15 against light resistance and, though opposition stiffened, steadily pushed inland over the next two weeks. One arm struck south and seized Suwon while the remainder of the corps cleared Kimpo Airfield, crossed the Han, and fought through Seoul. MacArthur, with dramatic ceremony, returned the capital city to President Rhee on September 29.

General Walker meanwhile attacked out of the Pusan Perimeter on September 16. His forces gained slowly at first; but on September 23, after the portent of Almond's envelopment and Walker's frontal attack became clear, the North Korean forces broke. The Eighth Army, by then organized as four corps, two U.S. and two ROK, rolled forward in pursuit, linking with the X Corps on September 26. About 30,000 North Korean troops escaped above the 38th parallel through the eastern mountains. Several thousand more bypassed in the pursuit hid in the mountains of South Korea to fight as guerrillas. But by the end of September the North Korea People's Army ceased to exist as an organized force anywhere in the southern republic.

North to the Yalu

President Truman, to this point, frequently had described the American-led effort in Korea as a "police action," a euphemism for war that produced both criticism and amusement. But the President's term was an honest reach for perspective. Determined to halt the aggression, he was equally determined to limit hostilities to the peninsula and to avoid taking steps that would prompt Soviet or Chinese participation. By western estimates, Europe with its highly developed industrial resources, not Asia, held the high place on the Communist schedule of expansion; hence, the North Atlantic Treaty Organization (NATO) alliance needed the deterrent strength that otherwise would be drawn off by a heavier involvement in the Far East.

On this and other bases, a case could be made for halting MacArthur's forces at the 38th parallel. In re-establishing the old border, the UNC had met the U.N. call for assistance in repelling the attack on South Korea. In an early statement, Secretary of State Acheson had said the United Nations was intervening ". . . solely for the purpose of restoring the Republic of Korea to its status prior to the invasion from the north." A halt, furthermore, would be consistent with the U.S. policy of containment.

There was, on the other hand, substantial military reason to carry the war into North Korea. Failure to destroy the 30,000 North Korean troops who had escaped above the parallel and an estimated 30,000 more in northern training camps, all told the equivalent of six divisions, could leave South Korea in little better position than before the start of hostilities. Complete military victory, by all appearances within easy grasp, also would achieve the longstanding U.S. and U.N. objective of reunifying Korea. Against these incentives had to be balanced warnings of sorts against a UNC entry into North Korea from both Communist China and the USSR in August and September. But these were counted as attempts to discourage the UNC, not as genuine threats to enter the war, and on September 27 President Truman authorized MacArthur to send his forces north, provided that by the scheduled time there had been no major Chinese or Soviet entry into North Korea and no announcement of intended entry. As a further safeguard, MacArthur was to use only Korean forces in extreme northern territory abutting the Yalu River boundary with Manchuria and that in the far northeast along the Tumen River boundary with the USSR. Ten days later, the U.N. General Assembly voted for the restoration of peace and security throughout Korea, thereby giving tacit approval to the UNC's entry into North Korea.

On the east coast, Walker's ROK I Corps crossed the parallel on October 1 and rushed far north to capture Wonsan, North Korea's major seaport, on the 10th. The ROK II Corps at nearly the same time opened an advance through central North Korea; and on October 9, after the United Nations sanctioned crossing the parallel, Walker's U.S. I Corps moved north in the west. Against slight resistance, the U.S. I Corps cleared P'yongyang, the North Korean capital city, on October 19 and in five days advanced to the Ch'ongch'on River within fifty miles of the Manchurian border. The ROK II Corps veered northwest to come alongside. To the east, past the unoccupied spine of the axial Taebaek Mountains, the ROK I Corps by October 24 moved above Wonsan, entering Iwon on the coast and approaching the huge Changjin Reservoir in the Taebaeks.

The outlook for the UNC in the last week of October was distinctly optimistic, despite further warnings emanating from Communist China. Convinced by all reports, including one from MacArthur during a personal conference at Wake Island on October 15, that the latest Chinese warnings were more saber-rattling bluffs, President Truman revised his instructions to MacArthur only to the extent that if Chinese forces should appear in Korea MacArthur should continue his advance if he believed his forces had a reasonable chance of success.

In hopes of ending operations before the onset of winter, MacArthur on October 24 ordered his ground commanders to advance to the northern border as rapidly as possible and with all forces available. In the west, the Eighth Army sent several columns toward the Yalu, each free to advance as fast and as far as possible without regard for the progress of the others. The separate X Corps earlier had prepared a second amphibious assault at Wonsan but needed only to walk ashore since the ROK I Corps had captured the landing area. General Almond, adding the ROK I Corps to his command upon landing, proceeded to clear northeastern Korea, sending columns up the coast and through the mountains toward the Yalu and the Changjin Reservoir. In the United States, a leading newspaper expressed the prevailing optimism with the editorial comment that "Except for unexpected developments . . . we can now be easy in our minds as to the military outcome."

UNC forces moved steadily along both coasts, and one interior ROK regiment in the Eighth Army zone sent reconnaissance troops to the Yalu at the town of Ch'osan on October 26. But almost everywhere else the UNC columns encountered stout resistance and, on October 25, discovered they were being opposed by Chinese. "Unexpected developments" had occurred.

In the X Corps zone, Chinese stopped a ROK column on the mountain road leading to the Changjin Reservoir. American marines relieved the South Koreans and by November 6 pushed through the resistance within a few miles of the reservoir, whereupon the Chinese broke contact. In the Eighth Army zone, the first Chinese soldier was discovered among captives taken on October 25 by South Koreans near Unsan northwest of the Ch'ongch'on River. In the next eight days, Chinese forces dispersed the ROK regiment whose troops had reached the Yalu, severely punished a regiment of the 1st Cavalry Division when it came forward near Unsan, and forced the ROK II Corps into retreat on the Eighth Army right. As General Walker fell back to regroup along the Ch'ongch'on, Chinese forces continued to attack until November 6, then, as in the X Corps sector, abruptly broke contact.

At first it appeared that individual Chinese soldiers, possibly volunteers, had reinforced the North Koreans. By November 6, three divisions (10,000 men each) were believed to be in the Eighth Army sector and two divisions in the X Corps area. The estimate rose higher by November 24, but not to a point denying UNC forces a numerical superiority nor to a figure indicating full-scale Chinese intervention.

Some apprehension over a massive Chinese intervention grew out of knowledge that a huge Chinese force was assembled in Manchuria. The interrogation of captives, however, did not convince the UNC that there had been a large Chinese commitment; neither did aerial observation of the Yalu and the ground below the river; and the voluntary withdrawal from contact on 6 November seemed no logical part of a full Chinese effort. General MacArthur felt that the auspicious time for intervention in force had long passed; the Chinese would hardly enter when North Korean forces were ineffective rather than earlier when only a little help might have enabled the North Koreans to conquer all of South Korea. He appeared convinced, furthermore, that the United States would respond with all power available to a massive intervention and that this certainty would deter Chinese leaders who could not help but be aware of it. In an early November report to Washington, he acknowledged the possibility of full intervention, but pointed out that ". . . there are many fundamental logical reasons against it and sufficient evidence has not yet come to hand to warrant its immediate acceptance." His reports by the last week of the month indicated no change of mind.

Intelligence evaluations from other sources were similar. As of November 24, the general view in Washington was that ". . . the Chinese objective was to obtain U.N. withdrawal by intimidation and diplomatic means, but in case of failure of these means there would be increasing intervention. Available evidence was not considered conclusive as to whether the Chinese Communists were committed to a full-scale offensive effort." In the theater, the general belief was that future Chinese operations would be defensive only, that the Chinese units in Korea were not strong enough to block a UNC advance, and that UNC airpower could prevent any substantial Chinese reinforcement from crossing the Yalu. UNC forces hence resumed their offensive. There was, in any event MacArthur said, no other way to obtain ". . . an accurate measure of enemy strength. . . ."

In northeastern Korea, the X Corps, now strengthened by the arrival of the 3d Infantry Division from the United States, resumed its advance on November 11. In the west, General Walker waited until the 24th to move the Eighth Army forward from the Ch'ongch'on while he strengthened his attack force and improved his logistical support. Both commands made gains. Part of the U.S. 7th Division, in the X Corps zone, actually reached the Yalu at the town of Hyesanjin. But during the night of November 25 strong Chinese attacks hit the Eighth Army's center and right; on the 27th the attacks engulfed the leftmost forces of the X Corps at the Changjin Reservoir; and by the 28th UNC positions began to crumble.

U.S. Troops Entering Hyesanjin

MacArthur now had a measure of Chinese strength. Around 200,000 Chinese of the XIII Army Group stood opposite the Eighth Army. With unexcelled march and bivouac discipline, this group, with eighteen divisions plus artillery and cavalry units, had entered Korea undetected during the last half of October. The IX Army Group with twelve divisions next entered Korea, moving into the area north of the Changjin Reservoir opposite the X Corps. Hence, by November 24 more than 300,000 Chinese combat troops were in Korea.

"We face an entirely new war," MacArthur notified Washington on November 28. On the following day he instructed General Walker to make whatever withdrawals were necessary to escape being enveloped by Chinese pushing hard and deep through the Eighth Army's eastern sector, and ordered the X Corps to pull into a beachhead around the east coast port of Hungnam, north of Wonsan.

The New War

In the Eighth Army's withdrawal from the Ch'ongch'on, a strong road-block set below the town of Kunu-ri by Chinese attempting to envelop Walker's forces from the east caught and severely punished the U.S. 2d Division, last away from the river. Thereafter, at each reported approach of enemy forces, General Walker ordered another withdrawal before any solid contact could be made. He abandoned P'yongyang on December 5, leaving 8,000 to 10,000 tons of supplies and equipment broken up or burning inside the city. By December 15, he was completely out of contact with the Chinese and was back at the 38th parallel where he began to develop a coast-to-coast defense line.

In the X Corps' withdrawal to Hungnam, the center and rightmost units experienced little difficulty. But the 1st Marine Division and two battalions of the 7th Division retiring from the Changjin Reservoir encountered Chinese positions overlooking the mountain road leading to the sea. After General Almond sent Army troops inland to help open the road, the Marine-Army force completed its move to the coast on December 11. General MacArthur briefly visualized the X Corps beachhead at Hungnam as a "geographic threat" that could deter Chinese to the west from deepening their advance. Later, with prompting from the Joint Chiefs, he ordered the X Corps to withdraw by sea and proceed to Pusan, where it would become part of the Eighth Army. Almond started the evacuation on the 11th, contracting his Hungnam perimeter as he loaded troops and matériel aboard ships in the harbor. With little interference from enemy forces, he completed the evacuation and set sail for Pusan on Christmas Eve.

On the day before, General Walker was killed in a motor vehicle accident while traveling north from Seoul toward the front. Lt. Gen. Matthew B. Ridgway hurriedly flew from Washington to assume command of the Eighth Army. After conferring in Tokyo with MacArthur, who instructed General Ridgway to hold a position as far north as possible but in any case to maintain the Eighth Army intact, the new army commander reached Korea on the 26th.

Ridgway himself wanted at least to hold the Eighth Army in its position along the 38th parallel and if possible to attack. But his initial inspection of the front raised serious doubts. The Eighth Army, he learned, was clearly a dispirited command, a result of the hard Chinese attacks and the successive withdrawals of the past month. He also discovered much of the defense line to be thin and weak. The Chinese XIII Army Group meanwhile appeared to be massing in the west for a push on Seoul, and twelve reconstituted North Korean divisions seemed to be concentrating for an attack in the central region. From all evidence available, the New Year holiday seemed a logical date on which to expect the enemy's opening assault.

Holding the current line, Ridgway judged, rested both on the early commitment of reserves and on restoring the Eighth Army's confidence. The latter, he believed, depended mainly on improving leadership throughout the command. But it was not his intention to start "lopping off heads." Before he would relieve any commander, he wanted personally to see the man in action, to know that the relief would not adversely affect the unit involved, and indeed to be sure he had a better commander available. For the time being, he intended to correct deficiencies in leadership by working "on and through" the incumbent corps and division commanders.

To strengthen the line, he committed the 2d Division to the central sector where positions were weakest, even though that unit had not fully recovered from losses in the Kunu-ri roadblock, and pressed General Almond to quicken the preparation of the X Corps whose forces needed refurbishing before moving to the front. Realizing that time probably was against him, he also ordered his western units to organize a bridgehead above Seoul, one deep enough to protect the Han River bridges, from which to cover a withdrawal below the city should an enemy offensive compel a general retirement.

Enemy forces opened attacks on New Year's Eve, directing their major effort toward Seoul. When the offensive gained momentum, Ridgway ordered his western forces back to the Seoul bridgehead and pulled the rest of the Eighth Army to positions roughly on line to the east. After strong Chinese units assaulted the bridgehead, he withdrew to a line forty miles below Seoul. In the west, the last troops pulled out of Seoul on January 4, 1951, demolishing the Han bridges on the way out, as Chinese entered the city from the north.

Only light Chinese forces pushed south of the city and enemy attacks in the west diminished. In central and eastern Korea, North Korean forces pushed an attack until mid-January. When pressure finally ended all along the front, reconnaissance patrols ordered north by Ridgway to maintain contact encountered only light screening forces, and intelligence sources reported that most enemy units had withdrawn to refit. It became clear to Ridgway that a primitive logistical system permitted enemy forces to undertake offensive operations for no more than a week or two before they had to pause for replacements and new supplies, a pattern he exploited when he assigned his troops their next objective. Land gains, he pointed out, would have only incidental importance. Primarily, Eighth Army forces were to inflict maximum casualties on the enemy with minimum casualties to themselves. "To do this," Ridgway instructed, "we must wage a war of maneuver—slashing at the enemy when he withdraws and fighting delaying actions when he attacks."

Whereas Ridgway was now certain his forces could achieve that objective, General MacArthur was far less optimistic. Earlier, in acknowledging the Chinese intervention, he had notified Washington that the Chinese could drive the UNC out of Korea unless he received major reinforcement. At the time, however, there was still only a slim reserve of combat units in the United States. Four more National Guard divisions were being brought into federal service to build up the General Reserve, but not with commitment in Korea in mind. The main concern in Washington was the possibility that the Chinese entry into Korea was only one part of a USSR move toward global war, a concern great enough to lead President Truman to declare a state of national emergency on December 16. Washington officials, in any event, considered Korea no place to become involved in a major war. For all of these reasons, the Joint Chiefs of Staff notified MacArthur that a major build-up of UNC forces was out of the question. MacArthur was to stay in Korea if he could, but should the Chinese drive UNC forces back on Pusan, the Joint Chiefs would order a withdrawal to Japan.

Contrary to the reasoning in Washington, MacArthur meanwhile proposed four retaliatory measures against the Chinese: blockade the China coast, destroy China's war industries through naval and air attacks, reinforce the troops in Korea with Chinese Nationalist forces, and allow diversionary operations by Nationalist troops against the China mainland. These proposals for escalation received serious study in Washington but were eventually discarded in favor of sustaining the policy of confining the fighting to Korea.

Interchanges between Washington and Tokyo next centered on the timing of a withdrawal from Korea. MacArthur believed Washington should establish all the criteria of an evacuation, whereas Washington wanted MacArthur first to provide the military guidelines on timing. The whole issue was finally settled after General J. Lawton Collins, Army Chief of Staff, visited Korea, saw that the Eighth Army was improving under Ridgway's leadership, and became as confident as Ridgway that the Chinese would be unable to drive the Eighth Army off the peninsula. "As of now," General Collins announced on January 15, "we are going to stay and fight."

Ten days later, Ridgway opened a cautious offensive, beginning with attacks in the west and gradually widening them to the east. The Eighth Army advanced slowly and methodically, ridge by ridge, phase line by phase line, wiping out each pocket of resistance before moving farther north. Enemy forces fought back vigorously and in February struck back in the central region. During that counterattack, the 23d Regiment of the 2d Division successfully defended the town of Chipyong-ni against a much larger Chinese force, a victory that to Ridgway symbolized the Eighth Army's complete recovery of its fighting spirit. After defeating the enemy's February effort, the Eighth Army again advanced steadily, recaptured Seoul by mid-March, and by the first day of spring stood just below the 38th parallel.

Intelligence agencies meanwhile uncovered evidence of rear area offensive preparations by the enemy. In an attempt to spoil those preparations, Ridgway opened an attack on April 5 toward an objective line, designated Kansas, roughly ten miles above the 38th parallel. After the Eighth Army reached Line Kansas, he sent a force toward an enemy supply area just above Kansas in the west-central zone known as the Iron Triangle. Evidence of an imminent enemy offensive continued to mount as these troops advanced. As a precaution, Ridgway on April 12 published a plan for orderly delaying actions to be fought when and if the enemy attacked, an act, events proved, that was one of his last as commander of the Eighth Army.

Plans being written in Washington in March, had they been carried out, well might have kept the Eighth Army from moving above the 38th parallel toward Line Kansas. For as a gradual development since the Chinese intervention, the United States and other members of the UNC coalition by that time were willing, as they had not been the past autumn, to accept the clearance of enemy troops from South Korea as a suitable final result of their effort. On March 20, the Joint Chiefs notified MacArthur that a Presidential announcement was being drafted which would indicate a willingness to negotiate with the Chinese and North Koreans to make "satisfactory arrangements for concluding the fighting," and which would be issued "before any advance with major forces north of 38th Parallel." Before the President's announcement could be made, however, MacArthur issued his own offer to enemy commanders to discuss an end to the fighting, but it was an offer that placed the UNC in the role of victor and which indeed sounded like an ultimatum. "The enemy . . . must by now be painfully aware," MacArthur said in part, "that a decision of the United Nations to depart from its tolerant effort to contain the war to the area of Korea, through an expansion of our military operations to its coastal areas and interior bases, would doom Red China to the risk of imminent military collapse." President Truman considered the statement at cross-purposes with the one he was to have issued and so canceled his own. Hoping the enemy might sue for an armistice if kept under pressure, he permitted the question of crossing the 38th parallel to be settled on the basis of tactical considerations. Thus it became Ridgway's decision; and the parallel would not again assume political significance.

President Truman had in mind, after the March episode, to relieve MacArthur but had yet to make a final decision when the next incident occurred. On April 5, Joseph W. Martin, Republican leader in the House of Representatives, rose and read MacArthur's response to a request for comment on an address Martin had made suggesting the use of Nationalist Chinese forces to open a second front. In that response, MacArthur said he believed in "meeting force with maximum counterforce," and that the use of Nationalist Chinese forces fitted that belief. Convinced, also, that ". . . if we lose this war to Communism in Asia the fall of Europe is inevitable, win it and Europe most probably would avoid war . . . ," he added that there could be " . . . no substitute for victory . . ." in Korea.

President Truman could not accept MacArthur's open disagreement with and challenge of national policy. There were also grounds for a charge of insubordination, since MacArthur had not cleared his March 24 statement or his response to Representative Martin with Washington, contrary to a Presidential directive issued in December requiring prior clearance of all releases touching on national policy. Concluding that MacArthur was ". . . unable to give his wholehearted support to the policies of the United States government and of the United Nations in matters pertaining to his official duties," President Truman recalled MacArthur on April 11 and named General Ridgway as successor. MacArthur returned to the United States to receive the plaudits of a nation shocked by the relief of one of its greatest military heroes. Before the Congress and the public he defended his own views against those of the Truman Administration. The controversy stirred up was to endure for many months, but in the end the nation accepted the fact that, whatever the merit of MacArthur's arguments, the President as Commander in Chief had a right to relieve him.

Before transferring from Korea to Tokyo, General Ridgway on April 14 turned over the Eighth Army to Lt. Gen. James A. Van Fleet. Eight days later twenty-one Chinese and nine North Korean divisions launched strong attacks in western Korea and lighter attacks in the east, with the major effort aimed at Seoul. General Van Fleet withdrew through successive delaying positions to previously established defenses a few miles north of Seoul where he finally contained the enemy advance. When enemy forces withdrew to refurbish, Van Fleet laid plans for a return to Line Kansas but then postponed the countermove when his intelligence sources indicated he had stopped only the first effort of the enemy offensive.

Enemy forces renewed their attack after darkness on May 15. Whereas Van Fleet had expected the major assault again to be directed against Seoul, enemy forces this time drove hardest in the east central region. Adjusting units to place more troops in the path of the enemy advance and laying down tremendous amounts of artillery fire, Van Fleet halted the attack by May 20 after the enemy had penetrated thirty miles. Determined to prevent the enemy from assembling strength for another attack, he immediately ordered the Eighth Army forward. The Chinese and North Koreans, disorganized after their own attacks, resisted only where their supply installations were threatened. Else-where, the Eighth Army advanced with almost surprising ease and by May 31 was just short of Line Kansas. The next day Van Fleet sent part of his force toward Line Wyoming whose seizure would give him control of the lower portion of the Iron Triangle. The Eighth Army occupied both Line Kansas and the Wyoming bulge by mid-June.

Since the Kansas-Wyoming line traced ground suitable for a strong defense, it was the decision in Washington to hold that line and wait for a bid for armistice negotiations from the Chinese and North Koreans, to whom it should be clear by this time that their committed forces lacked the ability to conquer South Korea. In line with this decision, Van Fleet began to fortify his positions. Enemy forces meanwhile used the respite from attack to recoup heavy losses and to develop defenses opposite the Eighth Army. The fighting lapsed into patrolling and small local clashes.

The Static War

On June 23, 1951, Jacob Malik, the USSR delegate to the United Nations, announced in New York during a broadcast of the U.N. radio program, "The Price of Peace," that the USSR believed the war in Korea could be settled. "Discussions," he said, "should be started between the belligerents for a cease-fire and an armistice. . . ." When Communist China endorsed Malik's proposal over Peiping radio, President Truman authorized General Ridgway to arrange armistice talks with his enemy counterpart. Through an exchange of radio messages both sides agreed to open negotiations on July 10 at the town of Kaesong, in territory which was then no-man's-land in the west but which would become a neutral area.

At the first armistice conference the two delegations agreed that hostilities would continue until an armistice agreement was signed. Except for brief, violent episodes, however, action along the front would never regain the momentum of the first year. By July 26, the two armistice delegations fixed the points to be settled in order to achieve an armistice. But then the enemy dele-gates began to delay negotiations, to gain time, it seemed, in which to strengthen their military forces, and thus also to strengthen their bargaining position. In any case, the enemy delegation continued to delay and finally broke off negotiations on August 22.

General Van Fleet, at that juncture, opened limited-objective attacks. In east-central Korea, he sent forces toward terrain objectives five to seven miles above Line Kansas—among them places named the Punchbowl, Bloody Ridge, and

Heartbreak Ridge—to drive enemy forces from positions that favored an attack on Line Kansas. These objectives were won by the last week of October. In the west, Van Fleet's forces struck northwest on a forty-mile front to secure a new line three to four miles beyond the Wyoming line in order to protect important supply roads that lay only a short distance behind the existing western front. The new line was reached by October 12.

These successes may have had an influence on the enemy, who agreed to return to the armistice conference table. Negotiations resumed on October 25, this time at Panmunjom, a tiny settlement seven miles southeast of Kaesong. Hope for an early armistice grew on November 27 when the two delegations agreed that a line of demarcation during an armistice would be the existing line of contact provided an armistice agreement was reached within thirty days. Hence, while both sides awaited the outcome of negotiations, fighting during the remainder of 1951 tapered off to patrol clashes, raids, and small battles for possession of outposts in no-man's-land. The first tactical use of helicopters by U.S. forces occurred about this time when almost a thousand marines were lifted to a front-line position and a like number returned to the rear.

Discord over several issues, including the exchange of prisoners of war, prevented an armistice agreement within the stipulated thirty days. The prisoner of war quarrel heightened in January 1952 after UNC delegates proposed to give captives a choice in repatriation proceedings, maintaining that those prisoners who did not wish to return to their homelands could be simply "set at liberty" according to the Geneva Conventions of 1949. The enemy representatives protested vigorously. While argument continued, both sides tacitly extended the November 27 provisions for a line of demarcation. This had the effect of holding battle action to the pattern of the thirty-day waiting period.

By May 1952 the two delegations were completely deadlocked on the repatriation issue. On the 7th of that month inmates of UNC Prison Camp No. 1 on Koje-do, an island off the southern coast, on orders smuggled to them from North Korea managed to entice the U.S. camp commander to a compound gate, drag him inside, and keep him captive. The strategy, which became clear in subsequent prisoner demands, was to trade the U.S. officer's life and release for UNC admissions of inhumane treatment of captives, including alleged cruelties during previous screenings of prisoners in which a large number of prisoners refused repatriation. The obvious objective was to discredit the voluntary repatriation stand taken by the UNC delegation at Panmunjom.

Although a new camp commander obtained his predecessor's release, in the process he signed a damaging statement including an admission that ". . . there have been instances of bloodshed where many prisoners of war have been killed and wounded by U.N. Forces." There was no change in the UNC stand on repatriation but the statement was widely exploited by the Communists at Panmunjom and elsewhere for its propaganda value.

Amid the Koje-do trouble, General Ridgway received transfer orders placing him in command of NATO forces in Europe. General Mark W. Clark became the new commander in the Far East, with one less responsibility than Mac-Arthur and Ridgway had carried. On April 28 a peace treaty with Japan had gone into effect, restoring Japan's sovereignty and thus ending the occupation. Faced immediately with the Koje-do affair, General Clark had the impression of walking ". . . into something that felt remarkably like a swinging door. . . ." He immediately repudiated the prison camp commander's statement. Moving swiftly, he placed Brig. Gen. Haydon L. Boatner in charge of the camp with instructions to move the prisoners into smaller, more manageable compounds and to institute other measures that would eliminate the likelihood of another uprising. General Boatner completed the task on June 10.

While argument over repatriation went on at Panmunjom, action at the front continued as a series of artillery duels, patrols, ambushes, raids, and bitter contests for outpost positions. But for all the furious and costly small-scale battles that took place, the lines remained substantially unchanged at the end of 1952. The armistice conference meanwhile went into an indefinite recess in October with the repatriation issue still unresolved.

In November, the American people elected a Republican President, Dwight D. Eisenhower. An issue in the campaign had been the war in Korea, over which there was a growing popular discontent, in particular with the lack of progress toward an armistice. In a campaign pledge to "go to Korea," Eisenhower implied that if elected he would attempt to end the war quickly. Consequently, when the President-elect in early December fulfilled his promise to visit Korea, there was indeed some expectation of a dramatic change in the conduct of the war. General Clark went so far as to prepare detailed estimates of measures necessary to obtain a military victory. But it quickly became clear that Eisenhower, like President Truman, preferred to seek an honorable armistice. As he would write later, however, the President-elect did decide to let Communist authorities know that if satisfactory progress toward an armistice was not forthcoming, ". . . we intended to move decisively without inhibition in our use of weapons, and would no longer be responsible for confining hostilities to the Korean peninsula." Immediately after taking office, President Eisenhower made sure this word reached Moscow, Peiping, and P'yongyang.

In the hope of prompting a resumption of armistice negotiations, General Clark in February 1953 proposed to his enemy counterpart that the two sides exchange sick and wounded prisoners. But there was no response and no break in the deadlock at Panmunjom by spring. At the front, where in February Lt. Gen. Maxwell D. Taylor had replaced General Van Fleet as the Eighth Army commander, the battle action continued in the mold of the previous year. The break finally came near the end of March, about three weeks after the death of Josef Stalin, when enemy armistice delegates not only replied favorably to General Clark's proposal that sick and wounded captives be exchanged but also suggested that this exchange perhaps could ".   .   . lead to the smooth settlement of the entire question of prisoners of war." With that, the armistice conference resumed in April. An exchange of sick and wounded prisoners was carried out that same month; and before the middle of June, the prisoner repatriation problem was settled through agreement that each side would have an opportunity to persuade those captives refusing return to their homelands to change their minds.

The pace of battle quickened in May when Chinese forces launched regimental attacks against outposts guarding approaches to the Eighth Army's main line in the west. A large battle flared on June 10 when three Chinese divisions penetrated two miles through a South Korean position in central Korea before being contained. That engagement could have been the last of the war since the terms of an armistice by then were all but complete. But on June 18 ROK President Rhee, who from the beginning had objected to any armistice that left Korea divided, ordered the release of North Korean prisoners who had refused repatriation. Within a few days most of these North Korean captives "broke out" of prison camp and disappeared among a co-operative South Korean populace. Since the captives had been guarded by South Korean troops, UNC officials disclaimed responsibility for the break, but the enemy armistice delegates denounced the action as a serious breach of faith. It took more than a month to repair the damage done by Rhee's order.

Enemy forces used this delay to wrest more ground from UNC control, attacking on July 13 and driving a wedge eight miles deep in the Eighth Army's central sector. General Taylor deployed units to contain the shoulders and point of the wedge, then counterattacked. But he halted his attack force on July 20 short of the original line since by that date the armistice delegations had come to a new accord and needed only to work out a few small details. Taylor's order to halt ended the last major battle of the war.

After a week of dealing with administrative matters, each chief delegate signed the military armistice agreement at Panmunjom at 10:00 a.m. on July 27. General Clark and the enemy commanders later affixed their signatures at their respective headquarters. As stipulated in the agreement, all fighting stopped twelve hours after the first signing, at 10:00 p.m., July 27, 1953. When the final casualty report for the thirty-seven months of fighting was prepared, total UNC casualties reached over 550,000, including almost 95,000 dead. U.S. losses numbered 142,091, of whom 33,629 were killed, 103,284 wounded, and 5,178 missing or captured. U.S. Army casualties alone totaled 27,704 dead, 77,596 wounded, and 4,658 missing or captured. The bulk of these casualties occurred during the first year of the fighting. The estimate of enemy casualties, including prisoners, exceeded 1,500,000, of which 900,000, almost two-thirds, were Chinese.

The Aftermath

By the terms of the armistice, the line of demarcation between North and South Korea closely approximated the front line as it existed at the final hour. (*Map 46*) Slanting as the line did from a point on the west coast fifteen miles below the 38th parallel northeastward to an east coast anchor forty miles above the parallel, the demarcation represented a relatively small adjustment of the

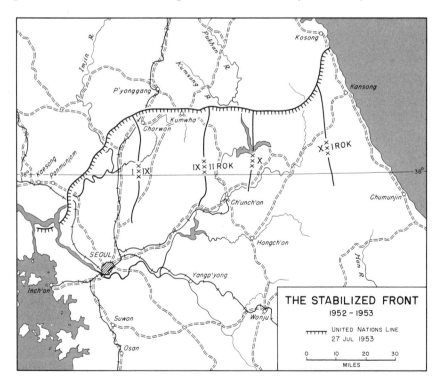

MAP 46

prewar division. Within three days of the signing of the armistice, each opposing force withdrew two kilometers from this line to establish a demilitarized zone that was not to be trespassed.

The armistice provisions forbade either force to bring additional troops or new weapons into Korea, although replacement one for one and in kind was permissible. To oversee the enforcement of all armistice terms and to negotiate settlements of any violations of them, a Military Armistice Commission composed of an equal number of officers from each side was established. This body was assisted by a Neutral Nations Supervisory Commission whose members came from Sweden, Switzerland, Czechoslovakia, and Poland. Representatives of those same countries, with India furnishing an umpire and custodial forces, formed a Neutral Nations Repatriation Commission to handle the disposition of prisoners refusing repatriation. Finally, a provision of the armistice recommended that the belligerent governments convene a political conference to negotiate a final settlement of the whole Korean question.

By September 6, all prisoners wishing to be repatriated had been exchanged. From the UNC returnees came full details of brutally harsh treatment in enemy prison camps and of an extensive Communist indoctrination program, of "brainwashing" techniques, designed to produce prisoner collaboration. Several hundred U.S. returnees were investigated on charges of collaborating with the enemy, but few were convicted.

The transfer of nonrepatriates to the Neutral Nations Repatriation Commission was undertaken next. In the drawn out and troublesome procedure that followed, few of the prisoners changed their minds as officials from both sides attempted to convince former members of their respective commands that they should return home. Of twenty-three Americans who at first refused repatriation, two decided to return. On February 1, 1954, the Neutral Nations Repatriation Commission dissolved itself after releasing the last of the nonrepatriates as civilians free to decide their own destinations.

The main scene then shifted to Geneva, Switzerland, where the political conference recommended in the armistice agreement convened on April 26. There was a complete impasse from the beginning: the representatives of UNC member nations wanted to reunify Korea through elections supervised by the United Nations; the Communist delegation refused to recognize the U.N.'s authority to deal with the matter. The conference on Korea closed June 15, 1954, with the country still divided and with opposing forces, although their guns remained silent, still facing each other across the demilitarized zone. The prognosis was that this situation would continue for some time to come.

The Geneva impasse leaving Korea divided essentially along the prewar line could scarcely be viewed as merely re-establishing the land's *status quo ante bellum*. For by the end of the war, the ROK Army had grown to a well-organized force of sixteen divisions and was scheduled to raise four more divisions, a force North Korea's resources would be strained to match. Within days of the armistice, moreover, South Korea had a mutual security pact with the United States and a first installment, $200 million, of promised American economic aid.

The war's impact reached far beyond Korea. Despite criticism of the armistice by those who agreed with General MacArthur that there was "no substitute for victory," the UNC had upheld the U.N. principle of suppressing armed aggression. True, the U.N. Security Council had been able to enlist forces under the U.N. banner in June 1950 only in the absence of the USSR veto. Nevertheless, the UNC success strengthened the possibility of keeping or restoring peace through the U.N. machinery.

More far reaching was the war's impact on the two Great Power blocs. The primary result for the western bloc was a decided strengthening of the NATO alliance. Virtually without military power in June 1950, NATO could call on fifty divisions and strong air and naval contingents by 1953, a build-up directly attributable to the increased threat of general war seen in the outbreak of hostilities in Korea. With further reinforcement in the NATO forecast at the end of the Korean War, USSR armed aggression in western Europe became unlikely. For the east, the major result was the emergence of Communist China as a Great Power. A steady improvement in the Chinese army and air force during the war gave China a more powerful military posture at war's end than when it had intervened; and its performance in Korea, despite vast losses, won China respect as a nation to be reckoned with not only in Asian but in world affairs.

Outside these direct impacts of the war, the relative positions of west and east also had been affected during the war years by the development of thermonuclear devices. The United States exploded its first such device in 1952, the USSR in August 1953. The exact consequences of all these changes were incalculable. But it was certain that the cold war would continue and that both power blocs would face new challenges and new responses.

CHAPTER 26

The Army and the New Look

Conditioned to the military decisiveness of World Wars I and II, Americans of the twentieth century found the frustration of fighting three years for a stalemate a new experience. Yet most were relieved to see the end of Korean hostilities despite the realization that the signing of the armistice merely marked the transition back to the cold war. The shooting and killing stopped, but the tension continued.

The war had clearly demonstrated that the United States was the only nation in a position to offer determined resistance to Communist expansion. The old era of reliance upon allies to bear the first brunt of battle while the country prepared for war had passed. If the United States intended to continue its policy of Communist containment, it was evident that it would have to depend increasingly upon American forces in being to meet the challenges. The cost in manpower and resources of maintaining large, well-prepared military forces in peacetime promised to be high, since there was little prospect in 1953 of attaining U.S. foreign policy objectives through diplomacy alone.

Acceptance of military power as an indispensable and open partner in the conduct of foreign relations represented a basic change in the American approach to international affairs. Previously the nation had mobilized its latent military strength only under the threat of conflict. For the most part, its wars had been fought as crusades, with overtones of strong emotional and moral support. The post-Korean situation demanded a different response—the sustained and disciplined use of military power against Communist opponents who had always regarded the use of force as a logical and necessary extension of politics. Yet, with remarkably little debate, the American people accepted the new military role and revealed a willingness to shoulder the heavy responsibilities that attended leadership of the free world.

Massive Retaliation and the New Look

With the end of hostilities, the Eisenhower administration could devote more attention to the task of determining the nation's future strategy and the military forces necessary to carry it out. The President and his advisers, torn between pressures generated by worldwide commitments and the desire to cut back defense spending, came up with a policy that placed major emphasis on nuclear air power. The Korean War was to be regarded as an aberration and American land forces would not be committed again to fight conventional battles with the Communist hordes in Asia unless it became necessary in the national interest.

As Secretary of State John Foster Dulles put it:

> The basic decision was to depend primarily upon a great capacity to retaliate, instantly, by means and at places of our choosing. Now the Department of Defense and the Joint Chiefs of Staff can shape our military establishment to fit what is our policy, instead of having to try to be ready to meet the enemy's many choices. That permits of a selection of military means instead of a multiplication of means. As a result, it is now possible to get, and share, more basic security at less cost.

In an effort to regain the strategic initiative through the use of strong and selective responses, Mr. Dulles had sought to raise the threshold of war to a higher level. Since the responses relied heavily upon American nuclear superiority, the doctrine soon came to be known as massive retaliation.

Unlike previous postwar periods, no drastic dismantling of the defense industrial mobilization base took place. The ever-present Russian threat made rearmament a continuous process dependent upon a mobilization base that could be rapidly expanded if the deterrent failed. With the new stress on nuclear capabilities, the armed forces took on a "new look" in the mid-fifties. The Air Force increased its strategic bombing forces, the Navy concentrated its efforts on development of the Polaris nuclear missile, which could be launched from submarines or other ships, and the Army sought to perfect tactical nuclear weapons to support the soldier on the battlefield.

In the absence of experience in waging nuclear war, strategic planning had to evolve in a historical vacuum. National security policy guidance in the post-Korean period, therefore, was issued in general terms, and disputes quickly arose over the types and numbers of the forces required to carry out the policy. Frequently the Secretary of Defense found it difficult to reconcile the differences of opinion among the military chiefs. The end result was hardly surprising. A House Appropriations Committee report noted: "Each service, it would seem, is striving to develop and acquire an arsenal of weapons complete in itself to carry out any and all possible missions."

Since the military budget was divided vertically by service rather than on a functional basis, the annual allocation of funds was attended by some bitterness. As the Air Force's share of the budget increased in the mid-fifties to procure expensive bombers and missiles and as the United States' capability to wage less than general nuclear war decreased, opposition to the massive retaliation policy mounted. The Army Chief of Staff, General Ridgway, upon his retirement in June 1955, expressed his doubts cogently. As Soviet nuclear strength grew, General Ridgway maintained, a situation of nuclear parity would come into being, where neither side would have an advantage. Soviet strategy could then be directed toward creating situations that would preclude the use of nuclear weapons on a worldwide basis. If this should happen, the American military forces then in being would not be strong enough to meet the lesser Soviet challenge. General Ridgway put the case bluntly: "The present United States preoccupation with preparations for general war has limited the military means available for cold war to those which are essentially by-products or leftovers from the means available for general war."

Ridgway's plea for balanced forces capable of coping with general or limited war was supported by his successor, General Maxwell D. Taylor, and taken up by a number of prominent scholars. During the remainder of the decade the debates over general versus limited war, nuclear versus conventional war, and various combinations thereof were waged in Congress, in the universities, and in printed media. Not until the latter part of the decade, when the Soviet Union's nuclear parity with the United States had become clear, did some of the leading supporters of the use of nuclear weapons begin to concede that such a war would result in mutual extermination and that a resort to nuclear weapons should become "the *last* and not the only recourse" of the nation.

The NATO Build-up

While the word battles raged, the strategy of nuclear war had profoundly affected the conduct of American foreign policy and the posture of the U.S. armed forces. Even during the latter stages of the Korean War, the major American build-up had taken place in Europe rather than in the Far East. Fears that the Soviet Union might take advantage of American involvement in Korea to launch an offensive on the Continent had spurred the United States to increase its lone Army division to five divisions by the end of the war. Through the Mutual Defense Assistance Program, the United States had also helped strengthen the NATO ground, air, and naval forces. During this period NATO adopted a "forward defense" strategy which contemplated defending Germany as far east of the Rhine as possible.

The conclusion of the Korean War, the death of Stalin, and the launching of another Soviet peace movement shortly thereafter, all combined to alter conditions in Europe. With tensions temporarily lessened, the NATO build-up slowed down to ease the economic drain upon the United States and its allies and the main effort shifted to the development of the infrastructure—the construction of roads, airfields, and depot areas and the improvement of communications. At the same time the United States began to press its allies to integrate the NATO forces and to rearm the West Germans. Despite strong Communist opposition to the revival of West German military forces, the NATO nations in 1954 approved the formation of an army of twelve divisions.

To redress further the imbalance between Communist and NATO ground forces, American nuclear scientists had produced a growing variety of tactical nuclear warheads that could be fitted to artillery shells and missiles. As these weapons became available, NATO planning was based on the assumption that a Soviet attack would be met by tactical nuclear weapons.

Control of all nuclear devices and weapons remained with the United States political leadership, and America's refusal to share this exclusive control by consultation with its allies occasioned some discontent within the alliance, especially on the part of the French and the British. Both of these allies decided to develop their own nuclear weapons and delivery systems to lessen their dependence upon the United States.

Continental Defense

In the meantime, the Soviet Union developed an intercontinental jet bomber and hydrogen bombs that could be carried in planes. It began to arm its ground forces with tactical nuclear weapons and pushed ahead with the production of long-range missiles. By 1955 the fierce Soviet-American competition and the growth of nuclear stockpiles that could obliterate cities and industrial complexes were causing mounting concern. At a summit conference at Geneva during the summer, the American and Soviet representatives made clear that they fully recognized that a full-scale nuclear war could lead only to mutual suicide. Although the arms race went on unabated, there was a slight relaxation of tension and a growing feeling that neither the United States nor the Soviet Union would resort to general nuclear war unless its own survival was threatened.

Early in 1956 the Russian premier, Nikita Khrushchev, gave an even clearer sign that the Soviet Union was shifting its tactics again. Qualifying to some extent Lenin's thesis that war between Communists and capitalists was inevitable, he indicated that the two worlds could coexist on a competitive basis. However, he made clear that the Soviet Union would still take part in or sponsor wars against the United States and other free world nations. Lest the western nations misunderstand the new peaceful coexistence, Khrushchev warned that the Communists still supported "wars of liberation" to free peoples from colonialism and imperialism and that the ceaseless struggle with capitalism would still be carried on by means other than full-scale warfare between the two countries.

Despite the symptoms of a possible thaw in East-West relations, the United States speeded its efforts to protect the American people in the event of another sudden freeze. Construction of a defensive perimeter in the form of a series of radar warning stations was completed in 1957. In co-operation with the Canadian Government, the distant early warning (DEW) radar net was built across northern Canada and Alaska, supplementing other radar lines in central and southern Canada. Radar outposts in the Aleutians, radar towers and picket boats in the Atlantic, and airborne early warning craft provided additional protection.

Operational responsibility for the direction of the overall air defense fell under the Continental Air Defense Command with the Air Force acting as executive agent for the Secretary of Defense. To assist the interceptor squadrons, the Army contributed ground antiaircraft defense support and developed the first operational antiaircraft missile—the Nike Ajax—with greater range and accuracy than conventional shells. Later and more sophisticated members of the Nike family were fitted with nuclear warheads for greater destructive power, and the Army also developed the Hawk missile to defend against low-flying aircraft. Antiaircraft missile sites grew up around vital defense areas across the nation, and complex control centers had to be established to co-ordinate the missile defense system.

The Missile Era

Although the United States had keyed its efforts to the strategic bomber, the development of missiles for offense proceeded apace. Gradually, the range and efficiency of the missiles increased as new designs and improved fuels emerged. The Army was developing its Jupiter and the Air Force its Thor—both intermediate-range, 1,500-mile missiles—during the mid-fifties, and the Air Force was working on the Atlas and Titan 5,000-mile intercontinental ballistic missiles (ICBM's).

Since, under the roles and missions agreement, the Army was responsible for point defense and the Air Force for area defense, the Army development of intermediate-range missiles eventually led to a jurisdictional dispute. In 1956 the Secretary of Defense ruled that the Air Force should take charge of all land-based intermediate- and long-range missiles, but the Army was allowed to finish the development and testing of the Jupiter. Progress on missiles was steady, but the sense of urgency had lessened somewhat by 1957.

Fresh impetus came from the Soviet Union. The Russians sent aloft an operational ICBM and then followed with a spectacular launching of the first Sputnik satellite in October 1957, revealing a rocket thrust far in excess of anything the United States could then produce. The Soviet feat caused the United States to review its missile programs in order to narrow the rocket-booster gap. To sustain morale, several small American satellites using the Jupiter and Vanguard boosters were launched in 1958, but it would take considerable time to construct engines equaling those already developed by the Russians.

The beginning of the ICBM era and the attendant exploration of space by unmanned and manned vehicles had serious military implications. As soon as the developmental problems could be overcome, the United States and the Soviet Union could build up stockpiles on land and in the future could also arm space stations. The threat of giant, nuclear weapons poised and then irretrievably launched at the nervous touch of a button thousands of miles from the target was a frightening prospect. If the two nations were to act like "two scorpions in a bottle," each certain that the other wished to destroy him, the inclination to push the button first might, in a period of crisis, become overwhelming. Later on, during the Kennedy Administration, the United States sense of responsibility was emphasized by the careful avoidance of a first-strike policy.

Since every new weapon evoked an antiweapon, the Army became responsible for the development of an anti-ICBM and pushed the research and testing of the Nike series for this role. A running debate quickly broke out over the capabilities of the Nike or any missile to protect the United States against a saturation ICBM attack. The technical difficulties and the tremendous expense of attempting to devise an absolute defense against nuclear attack were bound, however, to have a deterrent effect on both sides; as long as neither could be sure of warding off major disaster, there would be little inclination to risk a direct confrontation.

Another part of the ICBM controversy centered about a continued need for American military bases and garrisons in various overseas areas. Under defense agreements with friendly nations, the United States had put airfields and missile sites within striking range of the Soviet Union and Communist China during the decade following World War II. The costs of maintaining these overseas bases and the troops to man them had begun to concern officials in the Congress and the Executive Branch. The advent of long-range missiles that could be launched from the continental United States or from submarines offered some new alternatives, but it would take time to test and put them into operation.

Challenges and Responses

The domination of the fifties by the nuclear threat tended to cast a shadow over developments in other areas. Although the United States did not want to become involved in limited war and was wary of the risks inherent in nuclear confrontation, international challenges arose and had to be met—some by the provision of military and economic aid and others by the dispatch of combat forces.

In an effort to strengthen the military capabilities of friendly and neutral nations in Latin America, the Middle East, Asia, and Europe to resist aggression and subversion, the United States continued the military assistance programs (MAP's) initiated under President Truman before the Korean War. American commitments to provide military aid, advisory groups, and military missions around the world burgeoned despite the concomitant drive to curtail military expenditures.

In such places as Korea, two Army divisions continued to man positions south of the demilitarized zone and the United States provided substantial military assistance to build up South Korean armed forces. Although the Communists broke the uneasy truce many times during the fifties, none of the violations generated renewed hostilities.

Prudence underlined the American approach to the crisis in Indochina in 1954. The United States was willing to give military supplies and equipment and economic aid to the French, but in the absence of support from its allies refused to commit American troops or to carry out bombings to support the French in their battle at Dien Bien Phu. The American leadership and people were reluctant to become embroiled again on the Asian continent so soon after the Korean experience.

After the Geneva Conference of 1954 set up the two Vietnams, the United States was a chief sponsor of the Southeast Asia Treaty Organization, which was launched in early 1955 with Australia, France, New Zealand, Pakistan, the Philippines, Thailand, the United Kingdom, and the United States as charter members. The treaty was a collective defense arrangement calling for mutual help and consultation to resist overt Communist aggression or other acts threatening internal security.

Taiwan and Southeast Asia became the chief trouble spots in 1954. Heavy Chinese Communist bombardment of Nationalist garrison positions on the tiny offshore islands of Quemoy and Matsu seemed to presage a move to take over those outposts. Since the loss of the islands could have opened the way for an invasion of Taiwan, the United States through a Congressional Joint Resolution in 1955 empowered the President to act if the Communists sought to seize the outposts.

In the summer of 1958 the bombardments of Quemoy and Matsu again became severe and the Communist Chinese interdicted the Nationalist supply service to the islands. To defeat the artillery blockade, U.S. ships convoyed the supply vessels and Nationalist aircraft were armed with American missiles. As the tension mounted, a U.S. Composite Air Strike Force moved to Taiwan to strengthen the Nationalist defenses in the event of a Communist invasion. But the Communist Chinese evidently were not prepared to risk war at that time and again slackened their artillery fire. By the end of the year the crisis had passed but the two islands remained vulnerable to a renewed attack.

In Southeast Asia Communist pressure abated yet did not cease after the Geneva settlement in 1954. In the small state of Laos the Communist Pathet Lao in the post-Geneva period had established control of several border provinces abutting North Vietnam and China in order to resist attempts of the government to unite the country. In 1956 the government and the Pathet Lao signed a peaceful coexistence agreement, but efforts to integrate the two forces failed.

Since the United States provided total support for the 25,000-man Laotian Army, the differences between the government and the Pathet Lao became a small part of the larger quarrel between East and West. Open warfare broke out in 1959 in Laos, but neither side could gain the upper hand, despite the military aid given by the Soviet Union and North Vietnam and by the United States.

The serious concern of other nations over the escalation of the Soviet and American assistance programs and the possibility of a direct confrontation in Laos led to behind-the-scenes attempts to convene a conference to consider neutralizing the country. The warring factions in Laos also seemed in early 1961 to be more favorably disposed to this kind of solution. But until the new U.S. administration took office, the likelihood of an immediate settlement was rather remote, and in the meantime both American and Soviet aid and advisory efforts continued.

While the tension in the Far East persisted along the Communist periphery and could be traced, for the most part, to basic East-West conflicts, the problems that arose in the Middle East during the fifties stemmed mainly from resurgent nationalism and Arab hostility toward the Jewish state of Israel. To shore up the West's defenses in the area, the United States sponsored but did not sign the Baghdad Pact of 1955, although it did become a member of several of the pact's major committees in 1956 and 1957. The signatories of the pact included the United Kingdom, Turkey, Iran, Iraq, and Pakistan, all pledging co-operation for their mutual security and defense, and the United States continued to provide military assistance to members of the pact.

Although the United States did not become militarily involved in the Suez crisis of 1956, Congress, at the President's request, adopted in January 1957 a Joint Resolution that came to be known as the Eisenhower Doctrine. It pledged American military assistance to nations in the Middle East that were endangered by Communist aggression and empowered the President to use the armed forces for this purpose.

American action in the Middle East came in the following year. In early 1958 factions favoring Egyptian leader Gamal Abdel Nasser became active in Lebanon, Jordan, and Iraq. Rebellion broke out in Lebanon and in mid-July the King of Iraq was assassinated and an Iraqi Republic under pro-Nasser leadership was set up. The President of Lebanon and the King of Jordan quickly requested assistance for their own governments.

Less than twenty-four hours later, naval units from the U.S. Sixth Fleet arrived offshore and a battalion of marines landed near Beirut, the Lebanese capital. Within two days additional marines were sent by land and sea and the Army began to move airborne, tank, and combat engineer troops to Lebanon to stabilize the situation. By early August the U.S. forces had reached a total of over 5,800 marines and 8,500 soldiers. Navy warships stood off the Lebanese coast and a U.S. composite Air Strike Force moved into Turkey in support of the ground forces. Meanwhile, the British had responded to Jordan's request for help and had dispatched airborne troops to bolster Jordan's armed forces. U.S. aircraft airlifted supplies to the British forces and the Jordanian population. The prompt U.S. and British actions having enabled the Lebanese and Jordanian Governments to restore order, all American forces were withdrawn by October. Both Lebanon and Jordan received special U.S. military assistance to help build up their defense forces and prevent internal outbreaks.

The Iraqi revolt had other repercussions. After Iraq withdrew from the Baghdad Pact in early 1959, a new arrangement became mandatory. When the Central Treaty Organization (CENTO) was established in August, the United States accepted membership on the economic, military, and antisubversion committees along with other acts of participation such as the attendance by the American Secretary of State at the meetings of the CENTO foreign ministers and the attendance of the United States Ambassador to Turkey at other important CENTO meetings in Ankara; it had already concluded separate defense treaties with Turkey, Iran, and Pakistan earlier in the year.

Closer to home, the United States did not intervene in the Cuban rebellion that had broken out in 1958. The United States watched the revolt of Fidel Castro and his followers carefully, and when the Batista government was overthrown the next year, recognized the Castro regime. During the remaining two years of the Eisenhower administration, Castro moved steadily into the Communist camp and U.S.-Cuba relations deteriorated. American military and economic assistance to Cuba was cut off in 1960 to be replaced by arms and other aid from the Soviet Union and Communist China. The situation had so worsened on the eve of the Kennedy inauguration that diplomatic relations were severed completely. Cuba openly charged that the United States was preparing to commit aggression against the island republic to overthrow Castro's government.

The Military Budget

As American commitments reached around the globe and U.S. forces and assistance were dispatched to comply with the agreements concluded during the fifties, it appeared that the nation was more likely to become involved in local wars than in a general conflict. Yet the military budgets following the Korean War had emphasized, for the most part, deterrence of a general nuclear war rather than the contingencies of brush-fire operations.

It was hardly surprising that the Eisenhower administration should seek to cut defense spending after the high outlays during the Korean War, but to some critics it appeared that military policy was being determined by the fixed budget ceilings adopted by the President and his advisers rather than by the requirements of national defense. In any event, the decision to rely heavily upon strategic air power rather than on ground forces soon created an imbalance in the military budget and in the distribution of military forces. In 1953 the Army had a strength of over a million and a half men and had 20 combat divisions—8 in the Far East, 5 in Europe, and 7 in the United States. Of the over $34 billion in military funds voted by Congress for fiscal year 1954, the Army was allocated close to $13 billion.

The lower postwar defense ceilings adopted by the National Security Council in 1953 envisioned sharp manpower cuts, and the Joint Chiefs of Staff came up with a long-range program to trim over 600,000 men from the armed forces over the next four years. While most of the reduction would be absorbed by the ground forces, the air and naval forces would also experience personnel cuts.

By 1958 the manpower adjustments had taken place. The Army had shrunk to 15 divisions and less than 900,000 men. Only 2 reduced-strength divisions remained in Korea and 1 in Hawaii; the deployment of divisions in Europe and the United States held firm at 5 and 7, respectively, but several of the latter were also at reduced strength. New obligational funds for the Army for fiscal year 1959 were slightly more than $9 billion, about 22 percent of the total military budget for one year.

The high costs of deterring nuclear war were evident. Despite administration efforts to hold down military spending, the defense budget climbed from $34 billion in fiscal year 1954 to over $41 billion for fiscal year 1959. Much of the expense could be traced to the intricate air and missile weapons systems needed to carry out and defend against nuclear attack. Not only were the systems costly to procure, but they also became obsolescent almost overnight as the fast pace of technology produced newer and better models. In addition, the complex mechanisms required highly trained personnel who had to be given costlier schooling, training equipment, and higher pay. Under the circumstances, much of the military procurement budget was devoted to the nuclear threat with relatively little allocated to provide for the possibility of limited, conventional war.

Defense Reorganization

The perennial service disputes over strategy, force levels, and funds did little to promote the effective unification and rapid decision-making that the United States required. In response to Congressional criticism the President decided in 1958 to strengthen further the authority of the Secretary of Defense, to lessen the autonomy of the military departments, and to provide a more direct chain of command from the President to the unified commands. The reorganization was approved by the Congress in August, bringing with it a number of sweeping changes.

Henceforth the system of using the military departments as executive agents for operations was abolished. Almost all of the active combat forces were to be placed under unified commands with the chain of command to them running from the President and the Secretary of Defense through the Joint Chiefs of Staff. The Secretary of Defense also received greater freedom to transfer functions within the services, and a Defense Directorate of Research and Development was set up to supervise the research and development programs of all the services. At the JCS level, the Joint Staff was enlarged but specifically directed not to operate or to organize as an over-all armed forces general staff. An effort was also made to free the members of the JCS themselves from some of their routine service duties by permitting them to delegate more authority and duties to their Vice Chiefs.

Under the reorganization the services remained in control of training, equipping, and organizing the forces for unified commands and of developing, under the general supervision of the Secretary of Defense, the weapons and equipment they would need. The services also retained control of all units and individuals not assigned to unified commands and provided logistical support to all their troops, whether in unified commands or not.

The act of 1958 marked the end of one major aspect of the traditional role of the military departments, since they no longer had any part in the direction of combat operations. The JCS and the unified commands were to occupy stage center, while the Secretary of Defense and his assistants were to exercise tighter control of service functions through increasing budgetary and management supervision.

Within the services internal reorganizations had already been carried out by 1958 to improve efficiency of operations and to adjust to the changes necessitated by the threat of nuclear war. In 1955, the Army had replaced the Army Field Forces with the Continental Army Command (CONARC) in an effort to cut down the number of commands reporting directly to the Chief of Staff. CONARC was given responsibility for the six U.S. armies and the Military District of Washington, as well as for certain other units, activities, and installations. Among the chief functions assigned CONARC were supervising the training of the active Army and Reserves, planning for development of the future Army and its equipment, and planning and conducting the ground defenses of the United States.

The Dual Capability Army

The need to adjust to the nuclear threat had a deep impact upon the Army, since it had to be prepared for both conventional and nuclear war. Although the old tactical organization seemed inadequate to meet a nuclear attack, no historical experience factors existed around which to develop a new organization. The tremendous destructive power of nuclear weapons argued that military forces could no longer be massed for offensives of great duration. Since nuclear battlefields would presumably be of great breadth and depth, there would be no point in attempting to hold a solid front; the enemy could easily penetrate the line with nuclear weapons and inflict heavy casualties upon the defenders.

One recourse was to establish a checkerboard pattern with mobile, well-armed units in alternate squares. In the event of attack, either on offense or defense, the mobile units could quickly concentrate, carry out their missions, and just as rapidly disperse before a nuclear counterattack might be launched. The key to success would lie in highly trained troops, equipped with weapons providing a high ratio of firepower and carried by fast and reliable ground and air vehicles. Other essential items would be first-class communications, dependable intelligence on the enemy's dispositions, and an efficient logistics system for resupply of the combat forces. The development of these capabilities, it was hoped, would enable the Army to produce units that could cope with both nuclear and conventional war.

The major tactical reorganization to meet the new conditions began in 1956 when the first pentomic divisions and missiles commands were set up to furnish the mobile units and fire support deemed necessary for nuclear war. The old triangular infantry and airborne divisions were replaced by an organization consisting of five battle groups, each a self-contained force capable of independent operations. Manned by 13,500 men instead of about 17,000, the pentomic divisions were directly supported by artillery and missiles that could employ conventional or nuclear warheads, while the heavier long-range missiles were concentrated in the missile commands. The armored divisions required less drastic overhauling, since they were better adapted to the requisite pattern of mobility and dispersion. By 1958 all of the Regular Army divisions had been reorganized; the National Guard and Reserve divisions did not complete their change-over until 1960.

The seven divisions stationed in the United States constituted the strategic reserve. Four of these—two airborne and two infantry—were designated in 1957 the Strategic Army Corps (STRAC) and were maintained in a high state of readiness for quick deployment in event of an emergency. The other three were earmarked as STRAC reinforcements and as a training base for expansion of Army forces should the crisis become prolonged or develop into a full-scale war.

To provide the weapons and equipment for the nuclear Army, scientists, engineers, and designers, among others, combined to produce a steady stream of new or improved items. From rifles, mortars, semiautomatic and automatic weapons, and recoilless rifles at the company level to powerful rockets, missiles, and artillery in the support commands, more efficient instruments of war were fashioned to increase the firepower of the combat forces. Whole new families of surface-to-surface and surface-to-air missiles emerged, with both short- and long-range capabilities. With the emphasis on mobility, even the larger and heavier weapons and equipment were designed to be air-transportable.

A program to produce ground and air vehicles with the necessary battlefield mobility led to the development of armored personnel carriers, such as the M113 with aluminum armor, that could move troops rapidly to the scene of operations while providing greater protection for the individual soldier. Since

GUIDED MISSILES AT SELFRIDGE AIR FORCE BASE

highways and bridges might be damaged or destroyed, dual-capability amphibious vehicles that could travel on rough terrain and swim across rivers and swamps freed the fighting units from total dependence upon roads. Also, transportable bridges and bridge-laying equipment were designed to help speed movement of land-bound vehicles like the new, diesel-powered M60 battle tank that became operational in 1960. The M60 weighed over fifty-two tons, had a cruising range of 300 miles, and mounted a 105-mm. turret gun.

Perhaps the most dramatic efforts to increase the Army's mobility occurred in the field of aviation. To secure both firepower and maneuverability, the Army pushed its development of helicopters and low-speed fixed-wing aircraft. The versatile helicopter had already been used in Korea to move troops and supplies, conduct reconnaissance, and evacuate casualties. Some of the new fixed-wing planes were designed for short take-off and landing to increase their value in forward areas and to carry pay loads of over three tons; others were to conduct visual, photographic, and electronic surveillance missions over the battlefield and behind enemy lines. Experiments were also initiated on vertical take-off and landing aircraft that would combine the advantages of the helicopter's small operating area requirements with the greater speed of the fixed-wing plane.

In co-ordinating the employment of increased mobility and firepower, the role of communications mounted in importance. Whether the pentomic units operated independently over large areas or quickly concentrated for a major attack, light but reliable radio equipment was essential. The advent of the space age spurred communications research, since the space capsules required that a large number of intricate recording and transmitting instruments be fitted into an extremely limited area. A dramatic breakthrough in miniaturization of component parts helped solve the problem. With tiny transistors replacing bulky tubes, radio equipment became lighter, smaller, and more reliable. Sets could be redesigned to be carried by the individual soldier, in light vehicles, or in aircraft, to ease the command problems involved in exercising control in fluid situations.

Tactical communications was only one facet of the technological advances of the fifties stemming from miniaturization. The ponderous early computers began to give way to smaller versions capable of storing more information and retrieving it more swiftly. In time, the Army found more and more areas where computers could be usefully employed. From the co-ordination of information on approaching air targets and the direction of weapons fire to the storage and retrieval of personnel and logistics data, computers assumed an ever-growing number of functions throughout the Army.

The storage and quick retrieval of information made the computer a valuable intelligence tool as well. To secure the data needed to feed the machines required developing new families of surveillance equipment that could detect the presence of enemy forces, weapons, and supply concentrations. More sophisticated radar and sonar instruments emerged for picking up and identifying objects on land, at sea, and in the air. To aid ground-based and airborne surveillance, infrared, acoustic, and seismic devices were put into use to supplement improved and highly accurate cameras and the side-looking radar carried by planes to locate enemy concentrations by day and night under all weather conditions.

Once the foe had been spotted and operations got under way, the Army logistics system would have to have methods and means for furnishing supplies and equipment to the troops on the nuclear battlefield. Since nuclear wars would, it was expected, be short, the armed forces would have to rely upon munitions in being rather than on future production, leaving no time for the American war machine to gear up and outstrip its enemies a year or two after the outbreak of hostilities. Instead the United States would have to prestock depots at home and in vital overseas areas while at the same time avoiding large concentration of war matériel in ports or other ideal targets for nuclear weapons.

Support for combat troops would have to be keyed to minimum essential requirements. Furnishing the minimum essential requirements in itself presented
problems that were by no means completely solved. By rapidly processing
requisitions in electronic computers, using fast naval vessels and air transport,
delivering over the beaches by means of roll-on-roll-off ships and aerial tramways
instead of through ports, and employing cross-country vehicles to steer clear
of reliance on road nets, the logistics planners hoped to provide adequate support
to the front-line troops.

Despite the influx of new weapons, tactics, machines, and equipment, the
basic strength of the American armed forces remained dependent upon the
caliber of the personnel. With the reductions after the conclusion of the Korean
armistice enabling the bulk of the Reserves called into service for the war to
return to civilian life, the military services again contained a high proportion of
career officers and men.

Just as the logistics planners had to contend with the concept that a nuclear
war would have to be fought with current stocks, the personnel planners soon
decided that it would have to be fought with forces in being. Mobilizing and
training civilians for a year or two as in past wars would no longer be practicable; they would not become available in time to influence military operations
in a nuclear war. Only military forces in being and a well-trained, ready reserve
could be expected to participate in the fighting.

Retaining the more capable officers and enlisted men became of greater
importance as the technological advances of the fifties gave the armed services
a growing inventory of complex weapons and equipment. Developing, operating, and maintaining the new items demanded administrators with scientific
or engineering backgrounds and skilled technicians with considerable schooling.
If the services were going to allocate funds for long and expensive training
courses, they wanted to assure that the graduates would remain in uniform at
least until the investment paid off. Since the graduates would be qualified to
fill well-paid positions in rapidly expanding occupational areas, the services
had to compete with attractive civilian offers.

Yet the situation was not without hope, for the advantages of a military
career were many. The twenty-year retirement option was a strong inducement
to many who had already served ten years or more. Among fringe benefits that
made military life more attractive were free family medical care, and post
exchange, commissary, and recreational and educational facilities. In most
places the pre-World War II cleavage between the civilian and military communities had begun to disappear and military careers had gained more prestige,
both because large numbers of civilians had served in World War II and in

Korea and because many areas had become dependent upon military spending for subsistence. The large post-Korea military establishment thus cut across social lines, while the large defense budgets affected every walk of American economic life.

In one respect, however, a military career had become less attractive. As a steady inflation set in after Korea, military pay had not kept pace with civilian salaries. With more and more talented military personnel shedding their uniforms to take on more lucrative civilian jobs, Congress in 1958 brought military salaries into closer correlation with civilian positions of similar responsibilities and also enabled the services to award proficiency pay for highly skilled personnel. Increased retirement benefits, approved at the same time, added to Social Security benefits, which had become available in early 1957, enabled the services to improve their competitive position considerably and to retain a higher percentage of the best-qualified officers and men.

The Reserve Forces

Despite the progress made in retention, the Army could not rely entirely upon a voluntary recruitment to fill its manpower requirements. During the Korean War, Congress had passed legislation placing a theoretical "military obligation" on all physically and mentally qualified males between the ages of 18½ and 26 for a total of 8 years of combined active and Reserve military duty. The Reserve was divided into two categories, the Ready Reserve, which could be ordered to duty on declaration of an emergency by the President and in numbers authorized by Congress, and the Standby Reserve, which could be ordered to duty only in war or emergency declared by Congress. To fulfill his military obligation, a young eligible male had several alternatives. By spending 5 years of his 8-year obligation on active duty or in a combination of active duty and membership in the Ready Reserve, he could transfer to the Standby Reserve for his last 3 years. Or he might join the National Guard at 18 and by rendering satisfactory service for 10 years avoid active duty unless his Guard unit was called into federal service. For college students there was also the alternative of enrolling in an ROTC course, spending 2 or 3 years on active duty and the remainder of the 8 years as a Reserve officer.

This system had many weaknesses. There was really no compulsory military obligation beyond existing selective service arrangements, and draft quotas dwindled rapidly after the end of the Korean War. Similarly, the armed services found it impossible to accommodate all ROTC graduates for their required active duty. The obligation to remain in the Reserve carried with it no compulsion either to enlist in a Reserve unit or to participate in continued training. Since enlistees in the National Guard required no prior training, Guard units had to spend most of their time drilling recruits. Thus the Reserve, while strong enough numerically, fulfilled none of the requisites for rapid mobilization in case of need, and there was no assurance that it would be kept up to strength by a steady input of young Reservists.

To remedy these faults, Congress, at the urging of the President, passed new Reserve legislation in 1955. While this act reduced the term of obligatory service for enlistees from 8 to 6 years, it imposed a requirement for active participation in Reserve training on those passing out of the armed services with an unexpired obligation. It also authorized voluntary enlistment of young men between the ages of 17 and 18½ in the Reserve up to a total of 250,000 per year. These youths would receive 6 months on active duty followed by 7½ years in the Reserve instead of a 2- or 3-year tour within a 6-year military obligation. The President was authorized, without further Congressional action, to call up to a million Ready Reservists to duty in an emergency proclaimed by him. He could also recall selected members of the Standby Reserve in the event of a national emergency declared by Congress.

It was difficult to eliminate all the weaknesses of Reserve legislation in one swoop, however, and even with a perfect bill circumstances would still have played a role in determining the outcome. In a period of irregular voluntary enlistments and restricted funds, many of the Reserve units soon fell below authorized strength. The main effort was placed upon training those units that could be mobilized and deployed in the early stages of a conflict. To fill the high priority units, Reservists were often assigned without regard to their military specialties, and imbalances that could seriously affect readiness dates increased. Many Reservists failed to keep their parent organization informed of changes in address or in Reserve status and this was especially true of members of the Ready Reserve Mobilization Reinforcement Pool which contained Reservists who did not belong to organized units. Failure to screen out the ineligibles promptly and on a regular basis caused the reinforcement pool to become clogged with deadwood that could only serve to delay a quick and efficient mobilization.

As budget cuts forced the active Army to lower its manpower ceiling, efforts were made to strengthen the Reserves. In the Reserve Forces Act of 1955 provisions were set up for a total Ready Reserve of 2,900,000 by 1970. The Army's share reached about a million and a half men in 1957—over a million in the Army Reserve and over 440,000 in the National Guard, with paid drill strengths reaching 305,000 and 422,000, respectively. At the same time, the number of

Army Reserve divisions was cut from 25 to 10 and manning levels were increased substantially to give these units a higher readiness capability, while the National Guard divisions rose from 26 to 27. Since the active Army could support only a force of 18 divisions on a manpower base of about one million men in 1957, it was evident that the Reserve forces could not come close to supporting adequately a total of 37 divisions on a paid drill strength of only 727,000. With the Reserve divisions heavily involved in training activities and suffering from equipment shortages as well, their capability to attain combat readiness quickly was open to serious question.

The Army's efforts to secure increases to correct these deficiencies, therefore, ran into mounting opposition in the late fifties from the President and his advisers. Convinced that the United States was spending about $80 million a year on sustaining Reserve units that were of little or no military value, President Eisenhower tried to cut the paid drill strength. But it proved to be extremely difficult to persuade Congress of the necessity or desirability of thoroughly reorganizing and reducing the many Reserve units scattered in Congressional districts throughout the country. The political significance of the Reserve forces could not be discounted and Congress in 1959 voted a mandatory 700,000 figure to assure that no further reductions would be made without its approval. Actually, when President Eisenhower left office two years later, the paid drill strength had climbed to over 750,000 men.

During the Eisenhower period the American public had accepted the need for large military forces in being despite its long history of antimilitarism and had shown itself willing to allocate money and troops to insure U.S. security. In assuming the responsibility and loneliness of leadership of the free world, the people had revealed a growing maturity.

CHAPTER 27

Global Pressures and the Flexible Response

When President John F. Kennedy assumed office in the opening days of 1961, the prospects for peace were not encouraging. Premier Khrushchev had been cool since an American U2 plane gathering intelligence had been shot down over Russia in the spring of 1960. Although the possibility of a general nuclear war had receded, Soviet support of wars of national liberation had increased.

Despite the unfavorable signs President Kennedy was quite willing to renew the quest for peace. As he pointed out in his budget message of March 1961, the United States would make "efforts to explore all possibilities and to take every step to lessen tensions, to attain peaceful solutions, and to secure arms limitation." To Mr. Kennedy, diplomacy and defense were not distinct alternatives, but complemented each other.

Yet the President, well aware that the search for peace might be long, determined to give the United States a more flexible defense posture that would enable the nation to back its diplomacy with appropriate military action. The country should be strong enough to survive and retaliate after an enemy attack, on the one hand, and to prevent the erosion of the free world through limited war, on the other, the President informed Congress. "Any potential aggressor contemplating an attack on any part of the free world with any kind of weapons, conventional or nuclear, must know that our response will be suitable, selective, swift, and effective."

The Changing Face of the Cold War

As President Kennedy ushered in the era of flexible response, massive retaliation was officially de-emphasized. The shift in military policy was long overdue, stressing the need for ready non-nuclear forces as a deterrent to limited war. Besides, other changes under way indicated that America would need a more flexible position of strength in the days ahead.

By 1961 the tight bipolar system that had arisen after World War II and under which the United States and the Soviet Union were the only truly great powers was on the wane. No longer could the Russians claim to speak for all Communists without challenge. In eastern Europe the satellite nations were pressing for more freedom of action and were eager to increase trade with the West. The Chinese Communists, on the other hand, were becoming impatient with Russian conservatism and strongly opposed peaceful coexistence. And, in the New World, Fidel Castro was pursuing his own program of intrigue and subversion in Latin America. The Communist monolith, therefore, was in the process of splintering, with groups favoring the Russian, Chinese, or Cuban brand of Communism emerging in many countries.

Dissent was also mounting in the West. With the success of the Marshall plan and the return of economic prosperity to western Europe during the fifties, nations like France and West Germany became creditor countries and were less and less dependent for the maintenance of their economies upon the United States. The return of Charles de Gaulle to power in France under a new and strong executive type of government in 1958 produced growing dissidence within the NATO alliance as he sought to recapture some of France's former glory by taking an increasingly independent role.

Outside the Soviet and American circles the presence of a third force began to make itself felt during the fifties and early sixties. Most of the former colonial possessions in the Middle East, Asia, and Africa were granted independence in the fifteen years following World War II, and although many of them retained economic and cultural ties with the mother country, they were generally reluctant to become politically involved in the East-West struggle. Since the new nonaligned nations contained about one-third of the world's population and controlled much of the earth's oil and mineral resources, they were courted by both sides. Many suffered, however, from basic political instability and economic weakness that made them fertile fields, first for Communist propaganda and subversion and then for "wars of national liberation."

In May 1961 President Kennedy, touching on such revolutionary wars, pointed out to Congress that the great battleground of the sixties would be the whole southern half of the globe, "the lands of the rising peoples." As the revolts to end injustice, tyranny, and exploitation broke out, he noted, the Communists had sent in arms, agitators, technicians, and propaganda to capture the rebel movements. Working behind the scenes with terrorists, assassins, and saboteurs, the Communists had extended their control over large areas since World War II and had even broader ambitions. In such conflicts, the President had affirmed, "It is a contest of will and purpose as well as force and violence—a battle for minds and souls as well as lives and territory." The United States could not, Kennedy concluded, stand aside and passively let this fight be won by the Communists.

With half of the world still in the balance, the prospects for peaceful coexistence between the United States and the Soviet Union dimmed in 1961. Insurgent movements were already disrupting Laos, Vietnam, the Congo, and Algeria and the threat of revolutionary outbreaks hung over several other countries in South America, Africa, and Asia. In most instances, the Communists were abetting the insurgents and the United States was providing aid to the government forces. It was ironic, under the circumstances, that President Kennedy's first brush with the Communists should result from American support of an insurgent group.

Cuba and Berlin

During the closing days of the Eisenhower administration the United States had severed diplomatic relations with Cuba, but the presence of a Communist satellite almost within sight of the mainland remained a constant source of irritation. The effort to remove this annoyance, however, proved to be disastrous. In April 1961 a band of Cuban exiles launched a poorly conceived invasion of the island at the Bay of Pigs with limited air and no naval support. When the people failed to rise and join the invaders, the operation collapsed and most of the exiles were taken prisoner. Since the United States had sponsored the exiles, their utter failure damaged American prestige and enhanced Fidel Castro's stature. The invasion had also brought offers of Soviet help from Premier Khrushchev and dark hints that he was ready to employ Russian missile power to aid Castro.

The timing of the Cuban fiasco was particularly unfortunate, since President Kennedy was scheduled to hold a summit meeting with Khrushchev in Vienna in early June on the delicate subject of Berlin. In that divided and isolated city the growing prosperity of West Berlin contrasted sharply with the poverty and drabness of the Soviet sector and had become as great an irritation to the Communists as Cuba was to the United States. In 1958 Khrushchev had demanded that Berlin be made a free city and threatened that unless western troops were withdrawn in six months, he would conclude a separate treaty with East Germany. Although Khrushchev later backed off on this threat and even showed signs of a conciliatory attitude on Berlin, the Vienna meeting produced a complete about-face.

Once again Khrushchev became adamant and informed Kennedy that unless the West accepted the Russian position, he would take unilateral action to solve the Berlin impasse. If the Soviet premier hoped to intimidate the new President in the wake of the Cuban setback, he was unsuccessful. Instead, Mr. Kennedy in July requested and received additional defense funds from Congress as well as authority to call up to 250,000 members of the Ready Reserve to active duty.

The President refrained from declaring a national emergency which would have permitted him to bring up to a million Reserve members back to federal service, since he did not wish to panic either the American public or the Soviet Union by a huge mobilization. On the other hand, he determined to strengthen the conventional armed forces in the event that the Russian pressure at Berlin demanded a gradual commitment of American military power.

During August tension heightened as thousands of refugees crossed from East to West Berlin, and the Communists took the drastic step of constructing a high wall about their sector to block further losses. As the situation grew worse, the President decided in September to increase American troops in Europe and to call up some Reserve personnel and units to strengthen the continental U.S. forces. By October almost 120,000 Reserve troops, including two National Guard divisions, and over 80,000 Regular spaces had been added to the active Army.

The partial American mobilization and the quick reinforcement of Europe with U.S. ground, air, and naval units were accompanied by strong efforts to bring the military personnel and equipment remaining in the United States to a high degree of readiness. Accelerated training and production prepared and outfitted the new and the Reserve troops as quickly as possible. In the event that an emergency should break out in Europe, extra equipment was shipped there to be held in storage for units that might have to be air-transported from the United States in a hurry.

As the Soviet Union became aware that the Berlin challenge would be met swiftly and firmly, it began to ease the pressure again. The new administration had passed its first test. By mid-1962 the Reserve forces called up were returned to civil life, but the Regular increases were retained.

The next Russian ploy was less direct but more dangerous than the Berlin threat. After the Bay of Pigs invasion, the Soviet Union had dispatched military advisers and equipment to the Castro forces, ostensibly to help them repel any future attacks. In the summer of 1962, however, rumors increased that the Russian assistance might include offensive weapons, such as medium-range bombers and possibly medium-range ballistic missiles as well. Not until mid-

October could the conclusive photographic proof of the presence of the missiles in Cuba be obtained and the President quickly took steps aimed at getting these offensive weapons removed from the island.

Mr. Kennedy made it clear that the United States would retaliate against Soviet Russia with nuclear weapons if any Cuban missiles were used against an American nation. The Strategic Air Command's heavy bombers went on a 15-minute alert status with some aircraft aloft at all times. To buttress the defense of the southeastern states closest to Cuba, fighter-interceptor squadrons and Hawk and Nike missile battalions moved in to supplement the local air defense forces. At sea Polaris-equipped submarines left for preassigned stations in case the Soviet Union decided to use the occasion for a nuclear showdown.

On 22 October President Kennedy announced that he would seek the endorsement of the Organization of American States (OAS) for a quarantine on all offensive military equipment being shipped to Cuba, would tighten surveillance of the island, and would reinforce the U.S. naval base at Guantánamo. With OAS approval, the quarantine went into effect two days later. In the meantime, dependents had been removed from Guantánamo and marines had been lifted by air and sea to defend the base. The Army began to move over 30,000 troops, including the 1st Armored Division, and over 100,000 tons of equipment into the southeastern states to meet the emergency.

As the Navy's Second Fleet started to enforce the quarantine on 25 October, hundreds of Air Force and Navy planes conducted surveillance missions over the Atlantic and Caribbean to locate and track ships that might be carrying offensive weapons to Cuba. The continued activity at missile construction sites in Cuba had now placed the world on the brink of its first nuclear war.

The possibility of a clash between American warships and Soviet merchantmen carrying offensive war items to Cuba added to existing tensions. As the crisis mounted in intensity, the Russians, however, ordered such ships to return home and no incidents occurred. In the meantime a dramatic series of messages passed between Mr. Kennedy and Premier Khrushchev, and the Russians finally agreed on the 28th to dismantle and remove the offensive weapons from Cuba. During the next three weeks the sites were gradually evacuated and the missile systems and technicians were loaded on Soviet ships. Negotiations for the removal of the Russian bombers were completed in November and they were shipped out of Cuba in early December. Although the quarantine ended on 20 November, many air units remained on duty stations to continue surveillance missions in the area to insure that the sites remained inactive. Army forces deployed during the crisis did not return to their home bases until shortly before Christmas.

For the second time in two years the Soviet Union had demonstrated that it was unwilling to risk nuclear war. With the ending of the Cuban missile crisis, Soviet attempts to challenge the United States directly began to subside and Russian interest centered increasingly upon support of "wars of liberation." For the United States, Berlin and Cuba marked the beginning of the flexible response era, as the American reaction ranged from limited and conventional measures to the threat of general war.

Detente in Europe

The aftermath of Berlin and Cuba produced several unexpected developments. Evidently convinced that further testing of the American leadership might be unwise, the Russians adopted a more conciliatory attitude in their propaganda and indicated that at long last they might be willing to conclude a nuclear test ban treaty. In view of the long history of fruitless negotiation over nuclear controls, the Soviet move was a promising breakthrough.

Under the provisions of the accord ratified in the fall of 1963, the Soviet Union, the United Kingdom, and the United States agreed not to conduct nuclear explosions in space, in the atmosphere, or underwater; underground explosions were permissible as long as no radioactive material reached the surface. Although the treaty was weakened by the failure of France to adhere to it, it marked the first major agreement between Russia and the United States since the Austrian peace treaty of 1955.

The explanation for Soviet co-operation with the West in the mid-sixties, however limited, may have resulted from the growing independence of Communist China along with other factors and motives. The Chinese had never embraced the concept of peaceful coexistence with the capitalist countries and their criticism of what their leaders claimed was too soft a line by Moscow to the West had mounted. As the Sino-Soviet split widened, the Russians adopted a less-threatening role in Europe, and the shift had far-reaching effects upon the carefully built-up alliance system designed to guard western Europe against Russian aggression.

The NATO defense system had been constructed around the American strategic deterrent, but the credibility of the U.S. determination to defend western Europe in the face of a growing Russian capability to devastate the United States had come under serious question. Under President Kennedy and, after his assassination in November 1963, under President Lyndon B. Johnson, the United States made several efforts to reassure its NATO allies of American good faith. The reinforcement of U.S. conventional forces in Europe at the time of the Berlin crisis provided NATO with more options in responding to Communist pressure. In 1963 the United States assigned three Polaris submarines to the U.S. European Command and suggested that a multilateral naval force be established, but the idea was dropped in 1965.

By that time it was becoming clear that General de Gaulle intended to disengage France militarily from NATO. The French cut the ties gradually by participating less and less in NATO exercises, while the French nuclear strike force slowly expanded. In early 1966 de Gaulle served notice that all NATO troops in the country would have to depart. All remaining French forces would be relieved from NATO command during 1966, de Gaulle stated, but France would not quit the Alliance. The French President maintained that conditions in Europe had changed since 1949 and the threat to the West from the Soviet Union had lessened.

The military disassociation of France from NATO was unfortunate, since the chief headquarters and many of the elaborate lines of communications supporting the forward military forces were in France. When representation to the French proved fruitless, however, the exodus of NATO troops got under way in mid-1966. Supplies and equipment were relocated at bases in the United Kingdom, Belgium, Germany, and the Netherlands. In early 1967, Supreme Headquarters, Allied Powers Europe (SHAPE), moved to Belgium, the U.S. European Command shifted its headquarters to Germany, and the Ground Central European Command was transferred to the Netherlands.

Changes within the alliance had been slow. Despite the fact that the concept of massive retaliation had been discredited except as a last resort, it was not until 1967 that a strategy of flexible response was officially adopted.

The Growing Commitment in Underdeveloped Areas

The American policy of containment met its most serious challenge in southeast Asia as the Communist revolutionary wars to take over Laos and South Vietnam picked up momentum in the early sixties. Taking advantage of the political instability in these countries, the Communists had built up their political and military organizations and gradually brought large segments of the rural areas under their control. Efforts by the governments to regain these areas through military operations had been largely unsuccessful despite the presence of American advisers and the provision of military equipment and supplies.

In the struggle to keep Laos and South Vietnam out of the Communist camp, American diplomats and advisers soon discovered that the task of winning men's minds and hearts was difficult and elusive. After decades under French rule, many Indochinese leaders were willing to accept American assistance but unenthusiastic about instituting political and economic reforms that might lessen their newly won power.

The situation in Laos mirrored the American frustration. Until 1961 the United States supported the pro-West military leaders with aid and advice, but the efforts to unify the country by force had failed and three different factions controlled segments of the country. As conditions steadily worsened, President Kennedy decided to accept a coalition government in a neutralized Laos.

Fourteen nations signed a declaration in July 1962 confirming the independence and neutrality of Laos, which pledged itself to enter into no military alliance as well as to clear all foreign troops from the country. While the future of Laos remained clouded, a coalition government was preferable to a Communist takeover. By the end of 1962 over 600 American advisers and technicians stationed in Laos had left the country.

The concern over Communist activity in Laos and Vietnam also involved Thailand in mid-1962. To deter Communist expansion and to protect the territorial integrity of Thailand under the SEATO obligations, the United States set up a U.S. Military Assistance Command, Thailand, at the request of the Thai Government. As Communist troops maneuvered not far from the Thai border, a reinforced battalion of marines was quickly transported to that country, followed by a battle group of the 25th Infantry Division. Army signal, engineer, transportation, and other service troops moved in to support the U.S. combat forces and to provide training and advice for Thai units. The quick response so strengthened the Thai Government's position that the Communist threat abated during the remainder of the year, enabling first the marines and then the Army troops to withdraw. Many of the American service support forces, however, remained to assist in Thai training and logistics programs. As the war in Vietnam intensified, the roads, airfields, depots, and communications constructed and maintained by these service forces in Thailand became extremely valuable in supporting the American effort in Vietnam.

Trouble in the Caribbean

Although Europe and Asia remained the critical areas in the policy of Communist containment, American interest in Caribbean developments increased sharply after Cuba's defection from the West. When a military revolt in April 1965 to oust the civilian junta in the Dominican Republic was followed by a military counterrevolution, the United States monitored the situation closely.

As both factions sought to gain control of the government machinery, the capital city of Santo Domingo became a bloody battleground and all semblance of law and order vanished. Concern over the immediate threat to American lives rose as diplomatic efforts to restore peace failed. First to provide protection for U.S. nationals and subsequently to insure that the Communists did not get another foothold in the Caribbean, President Johnson sent marines and then Army airborne troops to Santo Domingo to stabilize the situation.

Less than seventy-two hours after alert, two battalions of the 82d Airborne Division from Fort Bragg, North Carolina, air-landed at a field east of Santo Domingo and fanned out toward the city. They were soon reinforced by four additional airborne battalions with support units. In the meantime, Marine troops consolidated their hold on the western portion of Santo Domingo. Since the forces of one side, the so-called Constitutionalists, were concentrated in the southern part of town, Lt. Gen. Bruce Palmer, Jr., the American ground force commander, carried out a night operation to link up the Army and Marine units. Using three airborne battalions for the action, Palmer had the first move into the easternmost sector, then passed the other two through the first to secure a corridor. With surprising ease and speed, the 82d Airborne's troops crossed the city and joined forces with the marines, separating the warring factions.

By the end of the first week in May all nine battalions of the 82d Airborne Division and four battalions of marines were in the Dominican Republic. With supporting forces the total number of American troops soon reached a peak of about 23,000. They patrolled the streets of Santo Domingo, maintained law and order, and distributed food, water, and medical supplies to both sides. The quick landings in force and the establishment of a buffer zone made further fighting on a large scale impossible. With stalemate the alternative, the adversaries began a series of negotiations that lasted until September.

The U.S. intervention in the Dominican Republic became the subject of spirited discussion in the United States and abroad. Despite the unfavorable public reaction in some Latin American countries to the intervention, the Organization of American States did ask its members to send contingents to the Dominican Republic to help restore order. Six members—Brazil, Costa Rica, El Salvador, Honduras, Nicaragua, and Paraguay—eventually dispatched forces and joined the United States in forming the first inter-American force ever established in the Western Hemisphere. Although American troops constituted the largest contingent of the force, a Brazilian commander, Lt. Gen. Hugo Panasco Alvim, with General Palmer as his deputy, was named in late May to emphasize the international composition of the force. Some U.S. troop withdrawals began almost immediately after the Latin American units arrived on the scene.

The acceptance of a provisional government by both sides in early September relieved much of the tension in the Dominican Republic, and by the end of 1965 all but three battalions of the 82d had returned to the United States. After elections in mid-1966, the last American and Latin American elements pulled out in September, ending the 16-month intervention. Although the legality and the unilateral nature of the U.S. action have been challenged, there is little doubt but that the intervention saved lives and restored law and order in the Dominican Republic.

Civil Rights and Civil Disturbances

Within the United States itself, meanwhile, racial tensions growing out of the civil rights movement dictated the use of troops in civil disturbances on a scale reminiscent of the labor troubles of the late nineteenth century. The first and most dramatic use of federal troops in such an affair came in September 1957 when President Eisenhower dispatched a battle group of the 101st Airborne Division to Little Rock and federalized the entire Arkansas National Guard to enforce a court order permitting nine Negro students to attend Central High School. The paratroopers successfully dispersed the mob that had gathered at the school and stabilized the situation. Some weeks later they turned over the task of protecting the Negro students to the Arkansas National Guard, which kept about 400 members on federal duty at Little Rock until the end of the school year. The incident marked the first time a President had exercised his power to call the "militia" into federal service to control a domestic disturbance since 1867, and it was one of the few times in American history that a Chief Executive had used either Regular troops or the National Guard in the face of opposition of a state's governor.

It was followed by other instances of the same sort in the administrations of Presidents Kennedy and Johnson. When, in September 1962, the governor of Mississippi attempted to block the court-ordered registration of a Negro at the University of Mississippi at Oxford, President Kennedy first sought to enforce the law by using federal marshals, but riots broke out on the campus during the night following the registration of the Negro, and the marshals were unable to control the mob. President Kennedy then federalized the Mississippi

TROOPS GUARDING A RIOT-TORN AREA OF DETROIT

National Guard and ordered active Army troops, some already standing by at Memphis, Tennessee, to Oxford. Eventually about 20,000 active Army troops and 10,000 federalized Guardsmen were deployed during the crisis, with about 12,000 men in the immediate area and the remainder standing by at other stations. With the military forces in firm control the tension rapidly subsided and the number of troops was scaled down, although, as at Little Rock, some federal protection had to be provided throughout the school year.

President Kennedy was forced again to deploy active Army forces and call up a state's National Guard to overcome the opposition of a governor to desegregation orders in Alabama in 1963, and in 1965 President Johnson employed both types of forces to protect a civil rights march from Selma to Montgomery. By 1965, however, the focus of civil rights disturbances was shifting from the south to the large urban centers in the north. Negroes concentrated in slum areas began to protest violently against existing conditions, the protest finding its most violent expression in rioting, looting, and burning. The summer of 1965 witnessed such a massive disturbance at Watts in Los Angeles, where the governor of California had to call up over 13,400 National Guardsmen to aid the Los Angeles police in restoring order.

The rash of racial disturbances showed little sign of abatement in the next two years, and in the summer of 1967 outbreaks occurred in over a dozen places, the most serious disturbance in Detroit. Looting and burning spread through much of the city in almost a week of violence. The governor of Michigan called in about 8,000 National Guardsmen to assist the police and, when this proved to be insufficient, asked President Johnson for federal troops—the first time in twenty-four years that such a request had been made by a governor. Elements of the 82d and 101st Airborne Divisions were moved to Michigan, the Michigan National Guard was federalized and placed under a common command, and law and order were re-established with a minimum of force.

In the wake of the 1967 riots, the President appointed a high-level commission to investigate the causes and possible cures for the disorders, while popular magazines carried provocative articles about "guerrilla warfare in cities," and even spoke of a "second Civil War." Indeed the prospects for relieving the conditions basically responsible for the riots are at best long term. It was reasonable, therefore, to conjecture that both the National Guard and active Army might be called on again to maintain law and order in the nation's cities.

Secretary McNamara and the New Management System

The operational activities of the armed forces during the Kennedy and Johnson administrations reflected but one portion of the wide range of problems confronting the nation's civilian and military leaders. At the same time, changes of far-reaching importance were being carried out in less publicized areas.

For the fixed-wing aircraft the sixties represented the completion of the cycle begun in Korea. The primacy of the heavy manned bomber as the nation's main instrument of nuclear deterrence appeared to be over as Mr. Kennedy and his Secretary of Defense, Robert S. McNamara, continued the phase-down begun during the Eisenhower period. Missiles gradually replaced some of the strategic bombers.

For the ground forces Vietnam also represented the end of a cycle and a reaffirmation that in conventional and limited wars the ground units bore the brunt of battle. The steady decline of the Eisenhower years was dramatically reversed in 1961 as the Army increased both in its numbers and its portion of the defense budget.

Meanwhile within the Department of Defense, exercise of the more extensive authority granted the Secretary of Defense by the reorganization act of 1958 had begun. When Mr. McNamara became Secretary in 1961, he accelerated the process.

President Kennedy gave Mr. McNamara two instructions: develop the force structure necessary to meet American military requirements, without regard to arbitrary or predetermined budget ceilings; and procure and operate the necessary force structure at the lowest possible cost. In accordance with Mr. McNamara's concept of centralized planning, the Joint Chiefs of Staff, assisted by the services, continued to establish the military plans and force requirements deemed necessary to support U.S. national security policies. The forces, however, were now separated according to function, such as strategic retaliation, general purpose, and reserves, and placed in what was called a program package. When Mr. McNamara received these packages, he considered whether each one contained balanced forces and resources to accomplish its function, correlated the costs and the effectiveness of the weapon systems involved, and then forwarded the approved packages in the annual budget for Presidential and Congressional action. To provide assistance in long-range planning, a 5-year projection of all forces, weapon systems, and other activities described in physical terms, together with the costs, was also drawn up yearly for Mr. McNamara's endorsement.

Initially the Kennedy administration had three basic defense goals: to strengthen the strategic retaliatory forces; to build up the conventional forces so that a flexible response could be made to lesser challenges; and to improve the overall effectiveness and efficiency of the defense effort. To attain the first objective, addition of intercontinental ballistic missiles in hardened sites and Polaris nuclear-equipped submarines provided the United States with the capability to retaliate in force in the event of a Soviet nuclear attack.

The second goal gained quick impetus from the Berlin crisis as Army strength alone rose from 860,000 to over 1,060,000 in 1961 and the Navy and the Air Force conventional forces also registered modest gains. Although the National Guard units called up for the crisis were released in mid-1962, the Army was authorized in the meantime to activate two Regular divisions, for a total of sixteen, and to retain a permanent strength of about 970,000 men. The influx of personnel allowed many units to remedy understrengths, and the additional funds allocated during the build-up permitted the procurement of new equipment and weapons to modernize the Army. As the Army budget rose from $10.1 billion to $12.4 billion in fiscal years 1961 and 1962, almost half of the increase was allocated to the purchase of new vehicles, aircraft, missiles, and other equipment.

Seeking greater efficiency and reduced costs for the defense effort, Secretary McNamara instituted changes in organization and procedures utilizing the latest management techniques and computer systems. He established firm control over the services through close budget supervision, and gradually centralized under the Office of the Secretary of Defense many activities formerly administered separately by one of the services. Since a great number of supply items and related services were in common use throughout the Defense Department, he established the Defense Supply Agency (DSA) in 1961. The agency assumed control of the five old and three new commodity single managerships, and of the Defense Traffic Management Service, as well as functions relating to cataloging and standardization. To DSA fell the management, purchase, and distribution of items such as food, petroleum products, and medical, automotive, and construction supplies at the wholesale level. Centralization permitted mass buying at competitive prices, the establishment of tighter inventory controls through the use of computers, the standardization of items to eliminate duplication, and the consolidation of supply installations.

Tied in closely with the objectives in setting up the Defense Supply Agency was the launching of a 5-year defense cost reduction program in 1962. Designed to cut procurement and logistics costs throughout the Defense Department, the program had three main goals: to buy only what was needed, with no frills; to purchase at the lowest sound price after competitive bidding whenever possible; and to decrease operating costs.

Cost reduction was not the prime aim in setting up the Defense Intelligence Agency in 1961. Mr. McNamara had directed that all defense intelligence operations should be co-ordinated at a higher level and that one office should prepare his intelligence estimates. To many critics, however, the centralization of intelligence activities was but a first step toward the elimination of the individual services which were gradually being shorn of their autonomy.

The effects of the 1958 reorganization were most noticeable in the decision-making process. By maintaining close watch over such matters as budget and finance, manpower, logistics, and research and engineering, the Secretary tightened civilian control over the services and carried unification much further than any of his predecessors.

One of the McNamara moves designed to improve unified action was the creation of the U.S. Strike Command, in 1961. By combining the Army's Strategic Army Corps with the Air Force's Tactical Air Command, the new command had combat-ready ground and air support forces that could be deployed quickly to meet contingencies or to reinforce overseas units. The Army and Air Force components of Strike Command remained under the control of their own services until an emergency arose, then passed to the operational control of Strike Command.

Army Reorganization

In view of the changes in organization and procedures at the Defense Department level, it was not surprising that the Secretary should also direct a thorough review of the Army's organization in 1961. A broad reorganization plan, approved by the President in early 1962 under the authority of the Reorganization Act of 1958, called for major shifts in the tasks performed by the Department of the Army Staff and the technical services. The Army Staff became primarily responsible for planning and policy, leaving the carrying out of decisions to the field commands. In an effort to organize the Army along more functional lines, centralize such matters as personnel, training, and research and development activities, and integrate supply operations, most of the technical services were abolished. The statutory offices of the Chief Chemical Officer, the Chief of Ordnance, and The Quartermaster General were completely eliminated. The Chief Signal Officer and the Chief of Transportation continued to perform their duties as special staff officers rather than as chiefs of services. The Chief of Engineers retained his special status only with respect to civil functions; his military functions were placed under the general supervision of the Deputy Chief of Staff for Logistics. Among the technical services, The Surgeon General emerged as the only technical service after the reorganization, because of its unique medical function.

In the administrative services, The Adjutant General and the Chief of Finance also lost their statutory status and became special staff officers. A new Office of Personnel Operations (OPO) was established on the special staff level to provide central control for the career development and assignment of all military personnel. Officers of the technical and administrative services retained their branch designations, but the management of their careers, with certain exceptions, was taken over by OPO. Although many of the most important Quartermaster functions were given to the Defense Supply Agency, a new Chief of Support Services assumed responsibility for such matters as graves registration and burials, commissaries, and clothing and laundry facilities.

Most of the operating functions lost by the Army Staff and the technical services were allocated to the U.S. Continental Army Command and to two new commands—the U.S. Army Materiel Command (USAMC) and the U.S. Army Combat Developments Command (USACDC). USCONARC became responsible for almost all of the Army schools and for the training of all individuals and units in the United States, but lost its test and evaluation mission to USAMC and turned over combat development activities to USACDC.

The Army Materiel Command took over many of the tasks formerly assigned to the technical services and set up subcommands to handle them. It assumed operating responsibility for research, development, testing, production, procurement, storage, maintenance, and distribution of matériel on a wholesale basis.

To the U.S. Combat Developments Command went the mission of developing organizational and operational doctrine, matériel objectives and qualitative requirements, war gaming and field experimentation, and cost effectiveness studies. It was to provide answers to questions as to how the Army was to be organized and equipped and how it should fight in the field.

The transfer of functions began in the spring of 1962 and the new commands became operational in the summer. During the following year other major changes affecting staff responsibilities took place. In January 1963 the Office of Reserve Components (ORC) was established to exercise general supervision over all plans, policies, and programs concerning the National Guard and Reserve forces. The statutory responsibility of the Chief, National Guard Bureau, to advise the Chief of Staff on National Guard affairs and to serve as the channel of communications between the Army and the states adjutants general was not altered by the creation of the new agency. The Chief of the Army Reserve, however, did lose his control of the Reserve officers training program which was transferred to ORC in February and later to the Deputy Chief of Staff, Personnel in 1966.

Since the Deputy Chief of Staff for Military Operations (DCSOPS) had become heavily involved in planning for joint operations, the Army in the spring of 1963 created an Assistant Chief of Staff for Force Development to assure adequate attention to primarily Army affairs. To prepare the Army force plans and structures in consonance with requirements developed by DCSOPS and with manpower and budget limitations as well became the main task of the new office; DCSOPS remained the principal adviser to the Chief of Staff on all joint matters and also retained responsibility for strategic planning and the employment of combat-ready Army troops.

Tactical Readjustment for Flexible Response

The reorganization of the Army staff was accompanied by a major overhauling of the tactical organization. In practice, the pentomic division had proved to be weak in staying power and needed more men to be capable of sustained combat. In 1961, the Army revised the divisional structure to provide a better balance between mobility and firepower and to insure greater flexibility.

Under the Reorganization Objective Army Division (ROAD) concept the Army began in early 1962 to form four types of divisions—infantry, armor, airborne, and mechanized—each with a common base and three brigade headquarters. The base contained a headquarters company, a military police company, a reconnaissance squadron, four artillery battalions, and a battalion of each of the following: engineer, signal, medical, supply and transportation, and maintenance troops. In the combat mix of the ROAD division the Army attained flexibility, since the numbers and types of battalions could be varied at will to carry out the different missions of the theater commanders. An infantry division might ordinarily have eight infantry and two armor battalions with a total strength of 16,000 men, but could control up to fifteen battalions if the need arose. When terrain permitted, more armor or mechanized elements could be added; in the swamps or jungles, the accent could be placed upon the infantry battalions.

The first ROAD divisions were the newly reactivated 1st Armored and 5th Infantry (Mechanized) Divisions, and they were tested during 1962. When the concept worked out well, the Army began to convert the remaining fourteen active divisions in 1963 and to reorganize the National Guard and Army Reserve divisions under ROAD. The active and Reserve reorganizations were completed in mid-1964.

The search for mobility sparked another tactical innovation in 1962 when an Army board compared ground and air vehicles in terms of cost and efficiency. The board recommended that new air combat and transport units be formed. The concept of an air assault division employing air-transportable weapons and aircraft-mounted rockets to replace artillery deeply involved the delicate question of Air Force and Army missions, but Mr. McNamara decided to give it a thorough test.

Organized in February 1963, the 11th Air Assault Division was tested for two years. By the spring of 1965 the situation in Vietnam offered an opportunity to test its capabilities for mobility in rough terrain. In July the division was inactivated and the personnel and equipment used to reorganize the 1st Cavalry Division under the airmobile concept at Fort Benning, Georgia. The 2d Infantry Division took over the personnel and equipment left by the 1st Cavalry Division in Korea; an exchange of divisional colors and the repainting of divisional insignia accomplished the switch. The new airmobile division had an authorized strength of 15,787 men, 428 helicopters, and 1,600 road vehicles (half the number of an infantry division). Although the number of rifles and automatic weapons in the division was the same as in an infantry division, the supporting weapons were lighter. The direct support artillery was moved by helicopters and had no vehicular prime movers. Instead of a general support artillery battalion, the airmobile division used an aerial rocket artillery battalion. Since all equipment was designed to move by air, the division total weight was only 10,000 tons, less than a third of an infantry division's.

The development of the air assault division provided fresh impetus to the dramatic growth of Army aviation. Although Army-Air Force agreements and decisions at Defense Department level during the fifties had generally been designed to restrict the size and weight of Army aircraft and their area of operations, the Army had pushed ahead vigorously in its research and development program. Concentrating heavily in the rotary-wing field, the Army by 1960 had built up its inventory to over 5,500 aircraft, almost half of them helicopters.

The versatility of rotary-wing aircraft made them ideal for observation and reconnaissance, medical evacuation, and command and control missions. Under the service roles and missions agreement all of these activities were permissible for the Army when conducted in the battlefield area. But the Army expansion into the development of larger craft that could be used for transporting large loads of troops and supplies and the subsequent arming of helicopters raised new questions concerning the proper role to be played by the two services.

A reassessment of missions and roles in 1966 placed the larger transports that the Army had developed with the Air Force. Insofar as helicopters were concerned, however, the Army maintained primacy, due in part to the demonstrated ability of rotary-wing aircraft to support land combat operations and to its farsighted research and development effort. Although the Army inventory of fixed-wing aircraft slipped slightly, the number of helicopters, spurred by the demands of the war in Vietnam, had soared from about 2,700 in 1960 to over 7,000 by mid-1967.

The Vietnam war had also accelerated the development and introduction of many improved and new Army aircraft models. Among the new additions were Hueycobra, a gunship armed with combinations of rockets, 7.62-mm. miniguns, and machine guns, and the Cayuse observation helicopter. The Cheyenne, first helicopter designed as a weapon system to provide fire support to ground troops, went into procurement in 1968. Later versions of the Mohawk fixed-wing observation plane, the Chinook medium transport helicopter, and the Iroquois light transport helicopter, among others, incorporated technological advances and tactical adaptations that greatly improved their value in field operations.

New weapon systems, vehicles, and equipment and new organizations to provide better support and greater flexibility for the fighting forces continued to emerge in bewildering rapidity during the sixties. The technological developments in air and ground vehicles promoted mobility, while the advances in communications facilitated the exercise of command and control and the gathering of intelligence. To handle the huge number of personnel and to keep track of the countless items of supply, complex and efficient computer systems were put into operation. Along with sophistication of equipment came highly qualified personnel to operate and maintain the machines and weapons and the development of an elaborate and responsive logistics system to provide the parts, fuel, and ammunition to keep them in action.

The Army school system furnished the bulk of the basic technical training, although civilian manufacturers frequently supplied personnel to demonstrate and instruct military units in the operation and maintenance of new products. Army schools had to keep abreast of the latest technological developments, therefore, and to turn out soldiers who would be able to use new items to the best advantage. The man behind the gun or machine became all the more important as the weapons and engines grew deadlier and more efficient.

In the environment of the sixties professional skills had to be resharpened continually, but the expanding role of the soldier required other talents as well. In the struggle for men's minds which highlighted insurgency in the underdeveloped areas of the world, battlefield proficiency was only part of the task. Military victories gained real estate, but if they failed to win the subsequent support of the local population they were of little consequence. In counterinsurgency operations the important objective was to deprive the insurgents of their base of support—sympathetic villagers and farmers for the most part. To convince the people in the countryside of the central government's interest and concern for their safety and welfare and to earn their loyalty and confidence represented the only victory with any permanent meaning.

Civic action and counterinsurgency operations were not new to the Army for they had played a dominant role in the opening of the American West and the pacification of the Philippines. During the occupation of Germany and Japan after World War II civic action programs had done much to improve the relations between the American military and the peoples of those countries; broad economic assistance plus political and educational reorientation, combined with the willingness to co-operate on the part of the German and Japanese people and their leaders, along with other factors, had simplified the problem of reconstituting civil authority. In underdeveloped countries the task was usually much more difficult since communications were poor and the bonds between the central authority and the rural areas were seldom strong. Special forces, capable of operating independently and of reaching to the grass roots, were required to counter insurgency in such places.

330–505 O—69——40

Although the Army had trained small units in psychological warfare, unconventional warfare, and counterinsurgency operations during the fifties, President Kennedy's personal interest in the field gave the program a significant boost in 1961. The Special Warfare Forces expanded sharply from 1,500 to 9,000 men in a year and continued to grow thereafter. Even more important, new emphasis in Army schools and camps provided all soldiers with basic instruction in counterinsurgency techniques.

The Special Warfare Forces helped train local forces to fight guerrillas and taught them skills essential to strengthening the nation internally. Special Forces Groups were oriented toward specific geographic areas and given language training to facilitate their operations in the field. Each group was augmented with aviation, engineer, medical, civil affairs, intelligence, communications, psychological warfare, military police, or other elements that could be tailored for an assignment. Individual members of each team sent out were cross-trained in other skills to increase their versatility. Working on a people-to-people basis, the Special Action Forces strove to improve the image of the government armed forces and to foster co-operative attitudes among the rural population.

Special warfare training was also given to the Reserve forces to keep them current with counterinsurgency developments and the measures necessary to counteract internal aggression and subversion. One phase of this training—crowd and riot control tactics—became of particular importance because of the growing threat of civil disturbance.

The Reserve Forces

Concerned over the expenditure of defense funds for Reserves that were long on numbers but short on readiness, Mr. McNamara ordered a thorough analysis of the status and functions of the Reserve forces during the early sixties. Maintaining a force of 400,000 National Guardsmen and 300,000 Army Reserves on a paid drill status, for instance, made little sense unless these backup forces could step in quickly in a crisis and replace the regular strategic reserve. The performance of the National Guard and Army Reserve units called up for the Berlin Crisis in 1961 had demonstrated that the Reserve forces could not, at that time, become ready for combat in less than four to nine months. In light of current military requirements, the time lag was excessive. Consequently, a concerted effort was made toward improving the quality of the Reserve forces and raising their combat readiness.

In the spring of 1962 Mr. McNamara announced a plan which the Army had developed to reduce and realign the National Guard and the paid drill strength of the Army Reserve. Considerable opposition from Congress and many state officials led him to defer action on the reduction, but he carried out the realignment the following year, eliminating in the process four National Guard and four Reserve divisions, as well as hundreds of smaller units.

The realignment proved to be but a stopgap measure. At the close of 1964 the Secretary of Defense proposed a far more drastic reorganization of the Reserves to bring them into balance with contingency war plans. Since his office had long been concerned over the duplication existing under the dual National Guard-Army Reserve system, the reorganization plan would place all units under the National Guard; only individuals would be carried in the U.S. Army Reserve. By consolidating units, the paid drill strength could be trimmed from 700,000 to 550,000, and 15 National Guard and 6 Reserve divisions for which there were no military requirements would be eliminated under the Secretary's proposal.

The storm of protest from Congress, the states, and the Reserve associations was quick and long-lived. While the debate went on, Mr. McNamara approved the inactivation of Army Reserve units that were no longer required; all 6 combat divisions were eliminated in the summer of 1965. To improve further the Reserve readiness status, a Selected Reserve Force (SRF) was set up in August, using elements of 9 National Guard divisions and some backup units from the Army Reserve. The SRF contained over 150,000 men—about 119,000 National Guardsmen and 31,000 Army Reservists—and consisted of 3 divisions and 6 separate brigades with combat and service support units. All SRF units were maintained at 100 percent strength, received extra training, and were given priority in equipment allocation.

When the reorganization was finally approved in the fall of 1967, concessions had been made by both sides. The Army Reserve retained organized units, but its paid drill strength was reduced from 300,000 to 260,000. Only 3 USAR combat brigades were included; the remainder were training and support units. Although the National Guard strength remained at slightly over 400,000 men, the division total was lowered from 23 to 8, while the number of brigades was raised to 18. All of the Reserve units not in the Selected Reserve Force were to be maintained at 90 percent of authorized strength and were to be fully supported with equipment, technicians, repair parts, and other essentials.

To help obtain the personnel to fill the Reserve units, legislation had been passed in September 1963 revising the Reserve Forces Act of 1955. Provision had been made for direct enlistment—an optional feature of the 1955 act—and the term of obligated service was reduced from eight to six years. The length of the initial tour became more flexible, generally ranging from four to seven months depending upon the particular military skill involved. Under this Reserve enlistment program, recruits could be given longer periods of initial active duty to train them to fill the requirements for more highly skilled specialists and enlistments could be increased appreciably.

The ROTC program was also revised in 1964 to improve the flow of qualified Reserve officers. The four-year senior program at colleges and universities was strengthened by the addition of scholarship provisions, and a two-year program was added for students who had been unable to complete the first two years of ROTC and who had undergone at least six weeks of field or cruise training to qualify them for entrance into the advanced course (last two years). Congress also authorized the military departments to establish a junior ROTC program at qualified public and private secondary schools, beginning in 1966 and reaching a total of 1,200 units by fiscal year 1971.

Although the Army build-up for the war in Vietnam increased the pressures for a Reserve call-up to replace the Regular troops sent overseas in 1965–67, the Johnson administration decided in July 1965 to rely for the time being upon Selective Service to meet the Army's needs for additional manpower. The President may have been influenced by dissatisfaction caused by the Berlin call-up, the restrictions usually set on the length of the Reserve tour of active duty by the Congress, and the desire to retain the Reserves as an emergency force. At any rate, increased draft calls and voluntary enlistments rather than a resort to the Reserves, swelled the Army strength from about 970,000 in mid-1965 to over 1,460,000 in January 1968. The Army's divisions increased from sixteen to nineteen during this period, and Army appropriations rose from $12 billion in fiscal year 1965 to $23.5 billion in fiscal year 1968 to cover the costs of the war.

Reliance upon Selective Service to meet the growing requirements of the Army, when large Reserve forces were available, drew critical comments from both Congress and the public. This would have been true whether the choice was made by draft board or a lottery, or based on physical, marital, or educational status. The nub of the matter was that some were selected while others stayed home. On the other hand, there was no practicable way to change this state of affairs, since the armed forces could not use nor did they need all those young men eligible for military service. The 4-year extension of the draft law in 1967 attempted to eliminate some of the imbalance but could not solve the basic problem. Nor did the unpopularity of the war in Vietnam among certain members of the draft-age group improve the situation. Such a climate was not calculated to bring forth enough volunteers to make the draft unnecessary.

On the positive side, however, the leavening provided by Selective Service made the Army more truly representative of the nation than any purely volunteer system possibly could. As in World War II and Korea, the Army fighting in Vietnam was a blend of professionals and citizen soldiers from every walk of life.

CHAPTER 28

The U.S. Army in Vietnam

In an effort to prevent French Indochina from falling under Communist domination, the United States in 1950 began to grant military aid to French forces in Southeast Asia, including those in Vietnam. This American military commitment was at the outset minor, only a fragment of the worldwide Military Assistance Program, but over the years it was destined to grow in size and complexity until it tended to overshadow other commitments and to become a test of American resolve.

In the case of Vietnam, the United States acted at first to help the French regain military control over a nationalist movement that, encouraged by outside aid from China and the Soviet Union, had entered the Communist camp. A climate for true self-determination achieved, it was hoped that France would grant the nation independence.

Before U.S. commitment increased, the conflict in Vietnam lost the complexion of colonial war and emerged as a struggle for the survival of a small nation in the face of Communist aggression in the pattern of what the Communists called "wars of national liberation." It was complicated by similar but less well-organized Communist aggression against the neighboring countries of Laos and Cambodia, by an ideological split in the Sino-Soviet Communist bloc, and by a possibility that as a testing ground between Communist and non-Communist resolve it might explode into broader war and bring direct confrontation of the world powers.

Role of the United States Through the Geneva Accords

Since the conflict from the start involved primarily ground operations, officers and men of the U.S. Army made up the bulk of the U.S. military forces committed. Only a few Americans were involved at first, their task limited to administering financial and military aid to the French and those Vietnamese forces loyal to the French-sponsored government of the emperor, Bao Dai.

That situation prevailed for almost four years as the French continued a long-term effort to wrest control of the countryside from Communist forces known as the Viet Minh under a veteran Communist leader, Ho Chi Minh.

The Viet Minh early had proclaimed a separate government professing juris-diction over the entire country, a self-styled Democratic Republic of Vietnam. Provided extensive military assistance from China and the Soviet Union, including advisers and technicians, the Communists had established control over most of the northern and central provinces, leaving to the French and the Bao Dai government little more than the principal cities and a few provinces adjoining the city of Saigon in the south.

Unwilling to grant the Vietnamese full independence, the French were never able to rally widespread support from the populace. Beset by opposition in France to a colonial war and lacking air power and sufficient ground strength to dominate a people with strong nationalist ambitions, while at the same time meeting Communist insurrections in Laos and Cambodia, the French in 1954 agreed to an international conference to be convened at Geneva to negotiate a settlement in all of Indochina.

The discussions at Geneva involved nine nations, including the United States, France, Great Britain, the Soviet Union, Communist China, and rep-resentatives of the Indochinese countries, Laos, Cambodia, and separate delegates for the Democratic Republic of Vietnam (Ho Chi Minh) and the State of Vietnam (Bao Dai). Since the French had yet to grant independence to the Bao Dai government, the delegate from the State of Vietnam had little authority.

The conference produced what became known as the Geneva Accords, a signed cease-fire agreement and an unsigned Final Declaration, with separate documents covering Laos and Cambodia. For Vietnam, the Geneva Accords directed a military disengagement based on a temporary demarcation line across the narrow waist of the country at the 17th parallel. (*Map 47*) The territory north of the line was to be administered by the Viet Minh, that south of the line by the French. Military forces were to regroup on either side of a demilitarized zone ten kilometers wide, while civilians were to be free to choose between the two zones. No increase in foreign military aid was to be made. To reunite the country, general elections were to be held two years later.

Objecting—as did Ho Chi Minh's government—to any division of the country and convinced that free elections were impossible in the north, the Vietnamese government in the south refused to accept these two aspects of the decisions as binding. The United States in turn declined to endorse the decisions but agreed to abide by them and forgo use of force to disturb them so long as others did the same. In regard to elections, the United States noted its long commitment to achieving unity in divided countries through elections supervised by the United Nations.

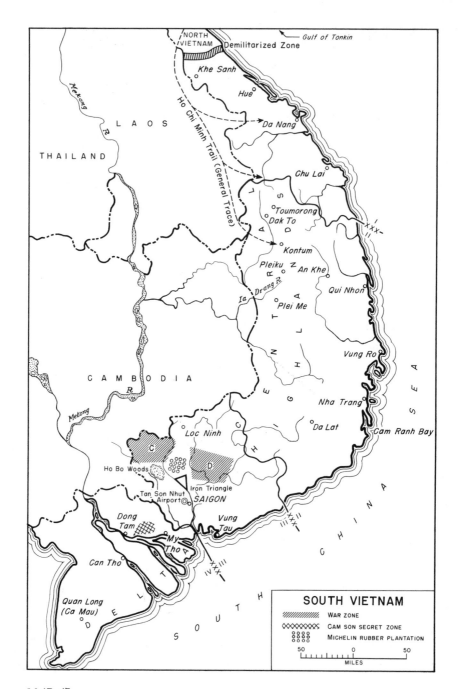

MAP 47

Early Growth of the Insurgency

As an armistice settled over what became, unintentionally but actually, two Vietnams—North and South—over 800,000 North Vietnamese moved to the south. Approximately 100,000 South Vietnamese moved north, most of them active Viet Minh insurgents, while Ho Chi Minh called on a political cadre of the Viet Minh to remain in the south in preparation for what he expected would be a sure Communist victory in the elections. The Viet Minh also retained control of base areas or secret zones they had established in the south.

The United States, meanwhile, acted to create a bulwark against further Communist expansion in Southeast Asia by preserving the southern half of Vietnam outside the Communist sphere. Approximately 400 American advisers, already present in Saigon at the time of the Geneva Accords, remained to assist the South Vietnamese government. Through them the United States worked to improve a South Vietnamese Army of some 200,000 men who had fought with the French and to provide extensive economic aid to the government, which with promise at last of full independence had gained a strong premier in Ngo Dinh Diem. Convinced that a large majority of Vietnamese yearned for a free nation outside the bonds of totalitarian Communism and that by the example of successful resistance to Communism in Vietnam other free Asian peoples would be encouraged to resist, the United States under three successive presidents—Eisenhower, Kennedy, and Johnson—would work to make the institutions of a free society available to that half of the nation to which circumstances afforded access.

Among the first obstacles was the inevitable stigma attached to a government originally sponsored by a colonial power, plus the problem of convincing a people exploited by foreigners through much of their history that the United States had no colonial designs. In a country where a majority of the people were Buddhists, resentment was strong against heavy representation in the government of a Catholic minority, many of whom were refugees from North Vietnam. Two relatively small but powerful religious sects, the Cao Dai and the Hoa Hao, exerted strong political pressures even after the South Vietnamese Army succeeded in establishing authority over autonomous military forces the two sects had long maintained. In the sparsely populated plateaus and mountains of the interior—the Central Highlands—tribal groups known as Montagnards continued a long resistance to governmental authority. A basically agrarian economy, lacking the industry and minerals of the north, was near chaos, much of the country long under Viet Minh control devoid of government services, corruption that had flourished under colonial rule still rampant. The emperor, Bao Dai, was of no assistance, having deserted his country to reside abroad.

Ruling autocratically, Premier Diem managed to bring a measure of order to the country, and the economy improved. Late in 1955 he deposed the absent emperor. After submitting his action to a referendum, he proclaimed a republic with himself as President. He outmaneuvered dissident Army officers seeking to seize power, defeated a strong band of Saigon gangsters, the Binh Xuyen, resettled refugees from the north, and made a start on a program of land reform.

Early in 1956, shortly before the time designated by the Geneva Accords for general elections, the French pulled the last of their forces out of Vietnam. President Diem then reiterated South Vietnamese objection to elections, again declaring that free expression was impossible in the north under a totalitarian regime. The United States backed this position with the notice that "there must first be conditions which preclude intimidation or coercion of the electorate."

Since the Viet Minh anticipated some support in the south and were sure of their controlled electorate in the more populous north, they had allowed the Communist insurgency in the south to lie quiescent while awaiting triumph in the elections. They were preoccupied for the moment in any case with asserting their authority in the north, crushing a popular revolt, and conducting a reign of terror to bring agricultural lands under state control. When the elections failed to come off, it took time for the Viet Minh to reactivate the insurgency, since the resources they had left behind in the south had to be rebuilt, reorganized, and strengthened.

Called by the South Vietnamese the Viet Cong, a contraction meaning Vietnamese Communists, a disparaging term, the insurgents in the south gradually expanded their numbers through a campaign of propaganda and coercion. At the same time the North Vietnamese government made the decision to bring down the South Vietnamese government by aggression, and in 1958 began to infiltrate political cadres and military reinforcements from the north. Terror, assassinations, sabotage, abductions, and attacks on civil guard and local defense units mounted. In late 1960 North Vietnam sponsored a National Front for the Liberation of South Vietnam, designed to attract other nationalists in addition to Communists, a device practiced by the Viet Minh in earlier days with considerable success.

Because of a legacy of conventional French training and equipment, the South Vietnamese Army (ARVN—pronounced *Arvin*—for Army of the Republic of Vietnam) was ill prepared to deal with insurgency, and the limited numbers of U.S. advisers were hard put to provide the comprehensive assistance needed. Upon the departure of French troops, the United States introduced some 350 more Americans to take over the task of recovering and repairing U.S. equipment for ARVN, but the total American strength was still less than 750, mainly U.S. Army personnel. In 1956 the equipment and advisory functions were combined within the Military Assistance Advisory Group (MAAG), Vietnam.

The few U.S. Army advisers were concentrated in Saigon, helping the Vietnamese with high-level planning, training, and logistical organization. Only in early 1960, as the insurgency continued to increase and it became apparent that ARVN capability to combat it had to be drastically improved, did President Diem agree to assigning U.S. advisers to field units down to battalion level. Even then, because of the limited numbers of advisers, assignments had to be selective and temporary.

The deliberate expansion of the Viet Cong insurgency coincided with an increasing separation of President Diem from the needs and desires of his people, as he fell more and more under the influence of members of his family whom he had placed in high positions. Many South Vietnamese were alienated because Diem continued to rule autocratically, failed to involve the people in government at the local level, moved slowly in land reform, and employed arbitrary policies in military and civil administration, along with oppressive police methods. Although Diem rationalized his methods either as necessary for defeating the insurgency or correctable only after national security was achieved, dissatisfaction with his rule spread.

Limited Increase in U.S. Commitment

During 1961 the Viet Cong campaign of murder and abduction continued to increase, directed not only at local officials but often at their families and at the civilian population in general. With such means was awe of the Viet Cong induced, and a belief spread that the government was incapable of protecting the people. By the fall of the year the Viet Cong had achieved enough power to threaten the existence of the Diem regime.

Seriously perturbed by these developments, President Kennedy reviewed in detail the reports and recommendations of a number of special missions sent to study the extent of the crisis. Conscious of the violence already done the Geneva Accords by North Vietnamese infiltration and support of the Viet Cong, he decided finally to increase U.S. support but to stop short of committing combat troops. With this decision, the U.S. commitment grew in 1962 to more than 11,000 men, two-thirds of them U.S. Army.

In February 1962, the U.S. Military Assistance Command, Vietnam (USMACV) was established in Saigon with General Paul D. Harkins as commander. This new command was a subordinate unified command under the operational command of the Commander in Chief, Pacific, who was in turn responsible to the Secretary of Defense through the Joint Chiefs of Staff. General Harkins also directly commanded the Army component.

During 1962 the increase in U.S. strength more than tripled the number of officers and men directly engaged in the advisory effort, and for the first time made possible attaching advisers to almost all ARVN units in the field. Men of the U.S. Army Special Forces also were introduced to train Civilian Irregular Defense Groups, formed among the Montagnard tribesmen in the highlands and other South Vietnamese.

The Communist threat to the highlands had been growing fast in conjunction with a strong Communist movement, supported by the North Vietnamese, in neighboring Laos. In establishing at least some sort of loose control over large portions of Laos, the Communists had firmly secured a wide strip along the South Vietnamese frontier through which they built trails and roads leading from North Vietnam around the flank of the demilitarized zone into South Vietnam. Known collectively as the Ho Chi Minh Trail, these supply routes contained logistical bases and relay stations adequate for a sustained war effort by large forces and linked with a network of trails in South Vietnam.

Manning fortified outposts and patrolling extensively, the Civilian Irregular Defense Groups with their Special Forces advisers sought to disrupt a growing infiltration of North Vietnamese from Laos into South Vietnam and prevent a Communist takeover in the highlands. Even though interested world powers achieved a semblance of peace in Laos with another Geneva conference in mid-1962, the Communists retained possession of the border zone and maintained their build-up. Some 60,000 South Vietnamese trained during 1962 and 1963 by the U.S. Army Special Forces nevertheless held on in the highlands and elsewhere along the frontier.

The role of the advisers throughout Vietnam was difficult and challenging. These were men charged with developing leadership among a people whose colonial rulers had for long years discouraged leadership. These were men who had to adapt swiftly to social, political, and economic conditions foreign to their experience, to communicate their ideas and military acumen to Vietnamese counterparts separated from them by a substantial language and cultural barrier, to entrust their own welfare and safety to foreign troops often unproven and sometimes infiltrated by an enemy almost impossible to detect, and to achieve all goals in an advisory rather than a command role.

When U.S. strength increased in 1962, the bulk of the American effort went into a new task of operational support for ARVN forces, with special attention to mobility, communications, intelligence, and logistics. Easily the most dramatic and portentous development was the introduction of the helicopter to provide ARVN units, heretofore mainly roadbound and thus highly vulnerable to ambush, a new mobility.

The first helicopter to fly in large numbers in South Vietnam was the CH–21, the Flying Banana, followed in 1963 by the faster and more versatile UH–1, the Huey. The helicopter became the symbol of a new kind of war, a checkerboard campaign in which units might be picked up and set down swiftly almost anywhere from the forested highlands to the fertile, densely populated river bottoms along the coast and the largely inundated rice paddies of the Mekong Delta region in the south. An original assignment of one helicopter company to each of four ARVN corps gradually grew to one per division. As the enemy reacted by increasing his antiaircraft capability, gunships— heavily armed versions of the Huey—were added.

By the spring of 1963 considerable progress seemed apparent in the military struggle, but the political situation worsened. In South Vietnam continuing governmental repression, coercion, favoritism, and corruption alienated more and more of the population. The ambassador and other U.S. representatives pressed for reforms, but to little avail. After the government's serious mishandling of a nationwide demonstration by Buddhists in mid-1963, the United States withheld subsidies for imports and for the ARVN Special Forces, which the South Vietnamese President had used to attack Buddhist pagodas.

On November 1, 1963, a military junta of senior South Vietnamese officers staged a *coup d'état,* in which President Diem and his brother Nhu were killed. There followed a year and a half of political instability, uncertainty, and disintegration of government control, which the Viet Cong exploited to the fullest. Despite a gradual American build-up to approximately 23,000 men (not quite two-thirds Army) that afforded additional operational support and provided many more advisory teams for provinces and districts to strengthen the rural pacification program, the Viet Cong increased their strength to approximately a hundred thousand, of which about one-third were "main force" troops (first-line combat soldiers organized in battalions and regiments). The added strength included infiltrated North Vietnamese Army regulars.

In much of South Vietnam the Viet Cong were sufficiently in control to levy taxes in rural regions, and even though government troops might control many areas in daylight, it was generally accepted in much of the countryside that "the night belongs to the VC." A government program to relocate people

ARMED HELICOPTERS BOMBARDING THE ENEMY *in the Central Highlands.*

in supposedly secure "strategic hamlets" all but collapsed. For the first time Viet Cong units were launching numerous daylight attacks, and South Vietnamese casualties increased sharply. Although U.S. troops continued only in advisory and support roles, U.S. losses also rose: 42 U.S. Army troops were killed, for example, in 1963; in 1964, 118 died.

Communist attacks against U.S. facilities were also mounting. In August 1964 North Vietnamese patrol boats attacked U.S. destroyers in the Gulf of Tonkin. In retaliation, President Johnson ordered air strikes against North Vietnamese patrol boats, their bases, and supporting facilities in North Vietnam. U.S. Navy planes carried out these strikes successfully. The Congress at this point passed a resolution authorizing the President to take necessary measures to repel attack against U.S. forces and to prevent further aggression in Southeast Asia.

Growing U.S. Commitment

Beginning early in 1965, the Viet Cong, reinforced by North Vietnamese Army units, opened a series of savage assaults. Under attacks that destroyed on an average a battalion a week, the South Vietnamese Army began to crumble. Leadership failed. Desertions increased. In the Delta and Central Highlands the Communists demonstrated their strength by seizing and temporarily holding some district and provincial capitals. A Communist push from the highlands to the sea to cut South Vietnam in half and isolate Saigon appeared in the offing. The morale of the people dropped sharply, and some observers gave the nation six months to live.

Having reaffirmed U.S. commitment to South Vietnam upon taking office after the death of President Kennedy, President Johnson viewed these developments with grave concern. When in February 1965 the Viet Cong attacked a U.S. compound and helicopter base in the Central Highlands, killing eight Americans, the President ordered retaliatory air strikes against selected military targets in North Vietnam. The President also directed dependents of U.S. military and government personnel evacuated from South Vietnam and deployed to the country a Hawk air defense battalion. Amid continuing terrorism against U.S. installations, including the explosion of a 250-pound bomb in front of the U.S. Embassy in Saigon, and mounting evidence of North Vietnamese support of the Viet Cong, the President ordered sustained bombing of military targets in North Vietnam in hope of bolstering South Vietnamese morale, reducing, or increasing the cost of, North Vietnamese infiltration into the south, and making North Vietnam pay a higher price for its aggression.

As the situation continued to deteriorate, the President concluded that only by introducing U.S. combat troops could Communist domination of the Republic of Vietnam be prevented. In response to a specific request from the South Vietnamese government, increased U.S. commitment began on March 6, 1965, as two battalions of U.S. marines went ashore in the northern part of the country to defend American installations at South Vietnam's second largest city, the port of Da Nang. A U.S. Army military police battalion arrived in Saigon two weeks later, followed in May by the 173d Airborne Brigade. The U.S. Air Force also began to build its strength in South Vietnam, while the U.S. Navy's Seventh Fleet assisted the South Vietnamese Navy on coastal patrol to cut infiltration of North Vietnamese men and supplies by sea and conducted air strikes with carrier planes against North Vietnam. It was the beginning of a truly joint effort by all the U.S. armed services to provide a climate in which the South Vietnamese might build a free and viable nation.

As the U.S. build-up began, from the chaos in Saigon a government had at last emerged that was destined to provide a measure of stability unseen since Diem's overthrow. It was a military government with an Army general, Nguyen Van Thieu, as Chief of State, and an Air Force marshal, Nguyen Cao Ky, as premier, but one that gave promise of an eventual return to representative rule. The new government halved the pay of high officials, doubled that of the soldiers, and offered a program of austerity and reform. The government also put new emphasis on training cadres to help organize village defenses, stimulate self-help projects, and ferret out the clandestine Viet Cong political infrastructure in hamlets and villages.

Logistical Build-up

The U.S. combat troops arriving in South Vietnam moved at first to occupy and secure key positions and existing U.S. installations and begin preparing a logistical base for whatever additional troops might be needed later. Creating a logistical base was particularly difficult in a country where the only major port, Saigon, was already clogged with shipping, where only Tan Son Nhut airport outside Saigon could handle jet traffic, where the only major railroad had ceased to function, and where use of roads was at best minimal. Ports, warehouses, cantonments, airfields, maintenance facilities, communications— all had to be built where there was at the beginning almost nothing.

The logistics system expanded swiftly until at the end of 1967 the Army was supporting more than 1.3 million men, including South Vietnamese armed forces, troops of other free world nations, and a number of U.S. civilian agencies. An average of 850,000 short tons of supplies arrived each month. Troops consumed 10 million field rations each month, expended 80,000 tons of ammunition and 80 million gallons of petroleum products. Manning a highly sophisticated military machine, the individual American soldier in Vietnam received about 96 pounds of supply per day, more than twice the amount per man in the Pacific theaters of World War II.

The engineer construction program in particular provided tangible and dramatic evidence of the extent of the logistical effort. The United States built completely new ports or vastly expanded existing facilities at Cam Ranh Bay, Qui Nhon, Nha Trang, Vung Tau, Vung Ro, and Saigon, thereby making possible discharge and ready supply to all portions of the country in which U.S. Army units operated. Engineers paved 4 million square yards for airfields and heliports, lacing the country with these facilities in a density seldom found elsewhere in the world. They constructed 20 million square feet of covered and open storage facilities, plus half a million cubic feet of refrigerated storage, the latter immensely important in a country with a year-round hot and humid climate. They built 1,700 miles of roads, 15,000 feet of bridges, and vast, fortified base camps. At one camp site, Dong Tam, in the Delta region, millions of cubic yards of sand had first to be dredged from the bottom of an arm of the Mekong River to create a 600-acre island among the rice paddies.

Maintenance in the environment of tropical heat, humidity, and monsoon rains posed an ever-present problem. It was solved at first by improvisation, long hours of extra maintenance work, adaptation of the Red Ball Express concept of World War II to speed critical items from the United States by air, and redirection of general support maintenance units to augment the forward echelon work of direct support units. In the end new techniques of maintenance management, including use of complex electronic computers housed in air-conditioned buildings, and new inspection methods enabled a return to more normal maintenance procedures.

Never before had an army been served by more comprehensive and effective medical support than was the U.S. Army in Vietnam. A casualty was seldom more than half an hour by air from a hospital, and the mortality rate among wounded receiving hospital attention was cut to less than 1 percent, lowest in the history of warfare. The old bane of tropical climates, malaria and intestinal diseases, nevertheless continued to plague the Army, despite modern advances in preventive medicine. Medical assistance to the Vietnamese, woefully short of doctors, nurses, and hospitals, was freely administered.

The organization for logistical support embraced five principal commands, four of them to handle specialized support for aviation, engineers (primarily construction), Hawk missiles, and hospitals, and the fifth, the 1st Logistical Command, to provide all other support. The last operated on an area basis keyed to four corps tactical zones as established early by ARVN. Operating in the chain of command of the United States Army, Pacific, the Army in Vietnam obtained additional logistical support from U.S. bases in Japan and Okinawa.

Early U.S. Operations

As the immense logistical effort grew, the increase of U.S. combat troops proceeded apace and led to early U.S. confrontation with the Viet Cong and with regular units of the North Vietnamese Army. The latter began to appear early in 1965 in regimental and later divisional formations in an apparent effort to help the Viet Cong win the war before American power could be applied in force.

The strategy adopted by the U.S. commander, General William C. Westmoreland, who had succeeded General Harkins in the summer of 1964, was holding action combined with spoiling attacks to keep the enemy off balance and gain the time needed to build base camps and logistical facilities. This accomplished, U.S. units with assistance from ARVN were to engage in search and destroy operations designed to eliminate Communist main force units and their base areas rather than to seize and hold territory permanently. These operations were to provide a shield behind which other ARVN forces could operate against the local guerrillas in support of the rural pacification program. ARVN also was to be responsible for defending government centers, including the cities and the provincial and district capitals.

It was early agreed that U.S. support in the I Corps tactical zone, composed of the five northernmost provinces, was to be primarily a Marine Corps responsibility; the U.S. Army was to operate mainly in the II and III Corps zones, which embraced the Central Highlands, adjacent coastal regions, and the area around Saigon; and ARVN troops were to retain primary responsibility for the Delta region of the IV Corps. The U.S. Air Force was to provide tactical air support and airlift while continuing, along with Navy carrier-based planes, strategic bombardment of North Vietnam. The Air Force was also assigned the mission of striking at troop concentrations with big B–52 bombers based on Guam, and later also in Thailand.

U.S. resources still were meager when in late summer of 1965 the enemy build-up in the Central Highlands began to reach alarming proportions, apparently presaging the long-expected attempt to push through to the sea and cut South Vietnam in two. With only three U.S. Army brigades available at the time, General Westmoreland nevertheless thought it better to risk a setback at the start than to allow the concentration in the highlands to go unchecked. Leaving two brigades to protect Saigon, he sent a third to An Khe, midway between Qui Nhon on the coast and Pleiku in the heart of the highlands, to stake out and secure a site for a base camp for the 1st Cavalry Division (Airmobile), scheduled to arrive in September. When the division reached Qui Nhon, its combat troops within hours vaulted to An Khe in their helicopters.

The airmobile concept faced a battlefield trial a few weeks after the 1st Cavalry Division arrived at An Khe. After South Vietnamese reinforcements had broken a siege of a Special Forces camp at Plei Me near the entrance to the Ia Drang valley southwest of Pleiku, intelligence revealed that three North Vietnamese regiments were regrouping in the vicinity for renewed attack. General Westmoreland ordered the American division into the fight to search out and destroy the enemy regiments.

The operation lasted for over a month. The enemy stood and fought in defense of his bases in densely wooded mountainous country close to the Cambodian border, using every tactic at his disposal: ambush, attack and counterattack, night infiltration, "hugging" (sticking in close contact with U.S. troops to forestall air and artillery strikes), and human wave assaults. In the end, American troops killed more than 1,300 North Vietnamese and sent the survivors fleeing to safe havens across the border. The 1st Cavalry Division lost 300 men killed.

ARMY OF THE REPUBLIC OF VIETNAM TROOPS *landing in a field.*

Although it had proved impossible to encircle and destroy the entire enemy force—something that was destined to frustrate many a U.S. unit in the months to come—what became known as the Ia Drang valley campaign thwarted the enemy's build-up in the highlands, proved the validity of the airmobile concept under conditions existing in Vietnam, and confirmed the ability of U.S. troops to defeat the best of the North Vietnamese even in inhospitable jungle terrain. The Communists relied on surprise, mobility, and mass, but these they could achieve only by carefully planned movements that took weeks to execute, whereas an entire brigade of the airmobile division could move into battle hours after an alert.

As foreshadowed by earlier ARVN operations with U.S. helicopter support, the airmobile concept had opened a new chapter in the history of land warfare, the helicopter providing for the first time a flexible third dimension to the battlefield. In the continuing U.S. build-up, the Army placed heavy emphasis on providing enough helicopter companies to assure an airmobile capability for all infantry units. The concept involved not only long-distance moves but also maneuvers during an engagement over short or long distances, superior firepower either from gunships or from artillery lifted by helicopter, superior logistical, medical, and intelligence support, and flexibility in command and control through aerial command posts.

The Ia Drang valley campaign was a milestone in another way as well. As the first major defeat inflicted on the Communists in many a long, dreary month, the campaign provided a strong psychological boost for ARVN forces. They themselves had broken the siege at Plei Me and then had seen their allies soundly defeat the foe.

The Nature of the War

Within three years, military strength gradually built up in South Vietnam from less than 25,000 to over 500,000. U.S. Army forces grew to include 2 corps headquarters, 7 divisions, 2 separate infantry brigades, an airborne brigade, and an armored cavalry regiment. U.S. Marine forces increased to two divisions and a separate regiment.

Regular ARVN forces meanwhile grew to over 340,000 men, plus regional and popular forces of 300,000. The Republic of Korea furnished 48,000 men, including two divisions and a Marine brigade; Australia, a regiment; and Thailand, the Philippines, and New Zealand, smaller units. Some form of nonmilitary aid was provided by more than thirty other nations.

Despite nearly 180,000 Communists reported killed during these three years and nearly 70,000 captured or detained, the Communists still managed to build their strength to nearly 240,000, including main force units, local guerrillas, and supporting troops. This feat they accomplished by stepping up recruitment through terror and intimidation and by sharply increasing the numbers of North Vietnamese regulars. As casualties rose, Viet Cong main force units often were kept up to strength only by incorporating North Vietnamese replacements.

While not foreign to American experience, the nature of the war in Vietnam was by any standards unusual. It was a war without clearly defined front lines. The enemy could be anywhere and everywhere and often indistinguishable from the native population. Without the usual standards for measuring success or failure, substitutes had to be devised—how many Communists killed by "body count," how many hamlets and villages "pacified," how many miles of essential highways open to travel. These provided some but no certain indication of developments.

It was a war with no shot fired at Fort Sumter, no sinking of the *Maine*, no Zimmermann telegram, no Pearl Harbor, no massed armies crossing the 38th parallel to afford a clear call for American involvement. Toward this war some Americans developed a new form of isolationism, a fear of becoming mired in war on the Asian mainland, reinforced by Communist success in picturing an aggressive North Vietnam as a "Little Belgium"—these and other factors—produced loud dissent from a vocal minority of Americans.

ARMORED PERSONNEL CARRIER

It was the first war that Americans viewed in their homes on television; and in base camps in Vietnam U.S. troops also had television. Many men flew to war by commercial aircraft. U.S. civilians of the State Department, the U.S. Information Agency, the Central Intelligence Agency, and the Agency for International Development were involved close alongside the soldiers. There was no censorship of the soldier's mail nor any involuntary censorship of the American press. Tourists were free to visit the war zone. The Army contracted some of its construction work with U.S. civilian firms. The American commander, General Westmoreland, had no command authority over ARVN or allied troops. As in Korea, the United States imposed a number of restraints on its forces lest the war spread.

How the U.S. Army fought the war was also unusual. All U.S. divisions and separate brigades had fortified base camps. From these they might operate in neighboring districts on security and pacification missions. At other times, leaving a security and housekeeping cadre behind, they might shift far afield, there to construct a temporary base camp and forward fire support bases from which divisional artillery could support far-ranging search and destroy operations. On many of these missions, particularly in the thick jungles of the highlands, companies and battalions would be far from any road or trail and wholly dependent upon the helicopter for resupply and evacuation. If fire support bases came under attack, artillerymen often had to employ their pieces in point-blank fire. Long-distance patrols on which small groups of men might be away for several days were common. Ambush and counterambush were familiar tactics on both sides.

The helicopter and radio communications were the two essential ingredients that made it possible for the U.S. Army to engage in this kind of combat successfully. There were, too, sophisticated weapons and items of equipment—C-130's and CV-2 Caribous capable of carrying large loads of men and equipment; the light, automatic M16 rifle; recoilless rifles; a one-shot antitank rocket; the Claymore mine that was activated electrically and spewed hundreds of dartlike projectiles; an armored personnel carrier modified to serve as a fighting vehicle; the Patton (M48A3) tank; chemical defoliants and the Rome plow, the latter a bulldozer equipped with a special blade capable of demolishing all but the biggest giants of the forest, the two employed to deny the enemy and his base camps the concealment of the jungle; a powerful grenade launcher firing a 40-mm. projectile; and highly complex electronic fire control and infrared surveillance devices. In sharp contrast to the sophistication of other items, barbed wire and the sandbag came back into use to a degree rivaling that of their use in World War I.

The enemy also had excellent weapons, mainly Chinese Communist copies of Soviet models. In the automatic AK47 rifle he had an admired individual weapon. The enemy had ample mortars and heavy rockets, but other than along the demilitarized zone, he employed no artillery and, except in defense against U.S. air strikes on North Vietnam, no aircraft. He also had recoilless rifles and a Chinese version of the Claymore mine, and he was a master of the booby trap, including sharpened bamboo spikes called "punji stakes." In the antiaircraft defense of North Vietnam, he employed Soviet-supplied surface-to-air missiles.

The ability and morale of the American soldier were remarkable. Better educated than the soldier of earlier generations, both in civilian schooling and military training, he was conscious of the excellent medical, logistical, and fire support available to him. Although individual fights might be as fierce and as harrowing as any ever fought in any war, there were sometimes long intervals between engagements, and, except along the demilitarized zone, the constant, nagging dread of enemy shelling was less pronounced than in earlier years. Then too the knowledge that his tour would end in a year was a strong morale factor. Fully integrated with white troops, Negro soldiers proved their worth and, in retrospect, revealed the illogic of earlier segregation practices, however reflective of the nation's social system.

The Communist soldier, too, was accomplished. He had infinite patience and stamina, and he could subsist for long periods on a diet that to a westerner would have been debilitating. During 1967 there was a cautious hope that the Communist soldier's morale and resolve were cracking as the numbers who defected to the South Vietnamese side under a government-sponsored "Chieu Hoi" (open arms, or amnesty) program sharply increased. The number of defectors rose from 11,000 in 1965 to 27,000 in 1967, but continued recruitment and North Vietnamese reinforcement apparently more than made up for these as well as for the enemy's other losses.

The Military Campaign

After the U.S. victory in the Ia Drang valley campaign, General West-moreland for the remainder of 1965 and well into 1966 proceeded with his plan to keep the enemy off balance while building base camps and logistical resources. This involved search and destroy operations covering the logistical bases under construction along the coast and base camps for incoming U.S. units in the provinces near Saigon. It also involved another campaign in the highlands that began with the enemy hitting a Vietnamese outpost named Toumorong and a brigade of the 101st Airborne Division moving to the relief. By midyear of 1966 progress was such that the enemy had become reluctant to mass for large-scale attacks and Ho Chi Minh proclaimed a strategy of protracted war, thus tacitly admitting that a quick military victory had eluded him.

U.S. forces at this point entered a new phase of operations aimed at finding and annihilating the enemy's main force units and invading and destroying his long-established base areas or secret zones. ARVN units turned increasingly to securing the countryside in support of the rural pacification program.

In the II Corps zone, largest but least populous of the four tactical zones, U.S. operations had two basic objectives. One was to eradicate main force units from the rice-rich river bottoms along the coast, denying the enemy this source of food and, by a sustained presence, providing a shield for pacification. The other was to maintain mobile forces in the sparsely populated Central Highlands that, by shifting here and there as the enemy was found, could prevent him from establishing control over the region as a base for operations against the northern provinces and the coastal plain. The troops in the highlands also afforded a reaction force to thwart the enemy's strikes against the Special Forces camps and other outposts along the frontier, from which the South Vietnamese harassed North Vietnamese infiltration routes into the country.

As presaged by the attack on Toumorong, sizable enemy units were by early summer of 1966 returning to the highlands, with indications of another attack forming to hit the Special Forces camp at Plei Me. When contingents of the 25th Infantry Division and the 1st Cavalry Division established contact, the enemy stood and fought, oftentimes from sturdy bunkers located on advantageous hilltops. Only after fighting that lasted through much of August did the enemy finally withdraw across the border, leaving behind over 800 dead.

As additional U.S. forces arrived in Vietnam, the 4th Infantry Division constructed a base camp in a central location in the highlands near Pleiku and built a road deep into the western highlands to within a few miles of

PARAPET CONCEALING GUN EMPLACEMENTS, *Special Forces camp.*

the frontier. This provoked a sharp enemy reaction, primarily against the 4th Division's fire support bases, in which the Communists lost approximately 700 killed; but in general the enemy avoided prolonged contact, constantly falling back behind the border whenever seriously threatened.

With the 4th Division present in the highlands, the 1st Cavalry Division and a brigade of the 101st Airborne Division were free to concentrate on sustained operations in the coastal provinces. By late fall of 1966 they had broken the enemy's hold on this agriculturally rich region. One operation of the 1st Cavalry Division in conjunction with Korean and ARVN units ended in a classic encirclement maneuver in which more than 2,000 Communists were killed. Shattered remnants of a North Vietnamese division fled into mountains to the northwest.

U.S. strength in the provinces near Saigon meanwhile had been increasing to the point where operations other than those designed to secure new base camps might begin. Here American base camps were located near major population centers in order to afford greater emphasis than in the highlands on maintaining control of strategic areas and lines of communication. Although search and destroy operations were as common as elsewhere, they were oriented more toward the local pacification effort, and operations to clear and secure

A Typical Viet Cong Tunnel System

hamlets and villages were frequent. Operations in this III Corps zone also were aimed at driving the enemy away from the environs of Saigon into his secret zones, then destroying them.

The first of the operations against the secret zones began in January 1966, when the 1st Infantry Division struck to eliminate a Viet Cong regional headquarters in the Ho Bo woods, about 25 miles northwest of Saigon, a portion of an enemy stronghold known as the Iron Triangle. As was so often to be the case, the enemy escaped, in this instance through an elaborate underground tunnel system. Beginning in February, the 1st Division and contingents of the 25th invaded the enemy's War Zone C, 75 miles northwest of Saigon close to the Cambodian border, and War Zone D, 40 miles north of the capital. Contacts again were sporadic as the Viet Cong fled across the frontier, but U.S. troops found and destroyed large underground supply caches and logistical and training installations.

Possibly in reaction to these sweeps or in an effort to open up infiltration routes, the enemy massed to hit a Special Forces camp at Loc Ninh, close along the Cambodian border seventy-five miles north of Saigon. In reacting quickly, the 1st Division forestalled the Viet Cong attack and overran a regiment in well-fortified positions in a nearby rubber plantation.

Another sweep in the fall into a big rubber plantation in War Zone C by the 196th Light Infantry Brigade provoked a counterthrust by a Viet Cong division, leading to quick commitment of elements of three U.S. divisions, the 173d Airborne Brigade, and the 11th Armored Cavalry Regiment in the first U.S. operation of the war to be controlled directly by a corps headquarters. Yet despite the large numbers of troops engaged, the fighting remained, as it was everywhere, a small-unit war with almost all contacts with the enemy made at the squad and platoon level. Over a thousand of the elusive enemy eventually were killed, but the Viet Cong's ability to fade away when confronted with American strength and firepower made campaigning against them here and elsewhere tedious and often exasperating.

As 1966 drew to an end, failure to find the enemy in large numbers in the ARVN II and III Corps zones, while frustrating, was at the same time encouraging, for U.S. and ARVN units had dealt the Communists telling blows. That the blows were hurting would be reflected early in 1967 in a North Vietnamese build-up of several divisions, in and just south of the demilitarized zone, in an apparent effort to draw U.S. strength from the south. Heavy artillery fire against U.S. Marine Corps postitions accompanied the build-up.

The Pacification Program

Since U.S. and ARVN forces were limited and thus unable to do everything at once, the build-up in the north, which the North Vietnamese could achieve readily by violating the demilitarized zone, was a clever stratagem, much like the periodic massing against outposts to pull U.S. forces away from conducting search and destroy operations and from securing villages in what was known as the rural pacification program. In that search and destroy was a shield for pacification, doing violence to either hurt pacification, a program that had to succeed if the insurgency ever was to be suppressed.

Communist political cadres composed of an estimated 40,000 men, backed by regular and local units, secretly controlled vast numbers of communities outside the cities by means ranging from propaganda and cajolery to intimidation and murder. This Viet Cong government exacted taxes, drafted young men for its military ranks, and bent the population to its ends. It was this grip that had to be broken if the secret infrastructure providing the guerrilla his sustenance was to be eliminated.

The history of pacification was often a history of frustration and failure. Several programs under President Diem had failed, primarily because they were based on forced resettlement in presumably secure communities that proved to be insecure. After Diem, a new program oriented more toward economic assistance also foundered in the face of the defeats the Viet Cong inflicted on ARVN. At the start of 1966 a new concept called Revolutionary Development displayed early indications of progress, but how lasting it would prove to be remained to be seen.

The core of the new program was a growing group of specially trained 59-man South Vietnamese Revolutionary Development teams. Moving into a hamlet, a team worked to identify and eliminate the underground Viet Cong, remove corrupt officials, build a spirit of co-operation, organize democratic institutions, and create a hamlet defense force. These objectives accomplished, the team moved on to the next hamlet, leaving the first to the South Vietnamese government ministries to develop programs in education, health, land reform, and financial credit.

Supplementing these teams, U.S. civilian agencies worked at various levels in information, agriculture, and public health programs.These were at first supervised by the U.S. Embassy, but in mid-1967, to promote better co-ordination with South Vietnamese provincial officials, who were mainly military men, General Westmoreland was accorded responsibility for the entire task of U.S. support of pacification, with a civilian deputy to assist.

The U.S. Army's role in pacification was widespread, and included both combat units and advisers to the ARVN. The opening and securing of roads directly benefited pacification. U.S. units also provided medical assistance and helped dig wells and build schools, hospitals, bridges. In conjunction with ARVN, U.S. units conducted "County Fair" operations, in which assembled villagers were provided entertainment, medical help, and information on government programs while troops searched the environs for local guerrillas. Both the marines and the Army formed special teams to live with, train, and fight with local Vietnamese defense forces. To many knowledgeable Vietnamese it was also apparent that the nation eventually would inherit the U.S.-built ports, airfields, cantonments, and other facilities.

A great combined effort was under way with encouraging signs of local success, including an increase in previously almost nonexistent intelligence passed by civilians to the ARVN and the U.S. Army. Yet too often civilians remained wary of co-operating lest departure of the military forces to other assignments leave them exposed to the Viet Cong. In the long run, pacification of the countryside would depend as before upon the ability of the South Vietnamese government to protect the people and enlist their support.

The Thieu-Ky government moved closer to identification with the people by calling an election for a constituent assembly in September 1966. Despite disruptive efforts of the Viet Cong, the electorate turned out in impressive numbers. Hamlet and village elections and then national assembly and presidential elections followed the next year. One of several candidates, Thieu failed to gain a majority of the vote, but he achieved a clear plurality to provide his government at last with a base of popular support.

The Military Campaign in 1967

Some U.S. reaction to the North Vietnamese build-up along the demilitarized zone, which looked at times like a prelude to a conventional invasion, was imperative; but because the great mobility of U.S. units permitted quick shifts whenever required, General Westmoreland was able to limit the reaction to a few units that took responsibility for the southernmost provinces of the I Corps zone, thereby enabling Marine troops to achieve greater concentration farther north. Among the relocated units, the 196th and 198th Light Infantry Brigades subsequently formed the nucleus for a new division, the 23d (Americal), the parenthetical designation dating back to a division that had been organized during World War II on New Caledonia.

In the Central Highlands, alert intelligence and quick U.S. reaction thwarted enemy attempts during the summer of 1967 to converge against the Special Forces camps. Meanwhile, in the provinces near Saigon, the campaign continued against the Viet Cong base areas.

Early in the year combined U.S. and ARVN forces totaling the equivalent of more than two divisions sealed off the Iron Triangle and systematically swept that tangle of woods, caves, and bunkers north of Saigon; but the enemy proved as elusive as ever and returned to his hideouts once U.S. and ARVN troops departed. Making a second sweep in the spring, U.S. units this time leveled much of the Iron Triangle with Rome plows.

In late February, American forces, including the 173d Airborne Brigade, making the first combat parachute jump of the war, formed a giant horseshoe-shaped cordon around War Zone C, whereupon airmobile and mechanized units swept up the open end of the horseshoe. One objective was to find and destroy the Central Office South Vietnam, the North Vietnamese-controlled military and political headquarters for all South Vietnam. In this, the operation failed, probably because of the proximity of the Cambodian border, but over a period of three months, more than 2,000 of the enemy were killed. Thousands of fortifications and other installations were destroyed and tons of supplies, equipment, and documents either captured or destroyed. Here and in other operations the feasibility of the tailoring principle of the U.S. Army division under the ROAD concept was convincingly demonstrated.

The ratio of enemy to U.S. troops killed was in most operations disproportionately high. In search and destroy operations, a ratio of 10 to 1 was common, and in enemy assaults against prepared U.S. positions the ratio was far higher. In one 2-day assault against a fire support position in War Zone C, for example, 609 Viet Cong died as against 10 Americans.

With completion early in 1967 of the Dong Tam base among the rice paddies of the Delta, a brigade of the 9th Division initiated the first U.S. operations in that lowland, crisscrossed by canals and rivers. Employing barracks ships, U.S. Navy armored troop carrier and fire support boats, and artillery mounted on firing barges, this brigade extended the principles of land fighting to inland waterways in a modern adaptation of river warfare. One of the first operations was against a heretofore sacrosanct base called the Can Son Secret Zone. By the end of the year, the riverine force had killed approximately 1,500 Viet Cong.

For all the success of U.S. and ARVN operations and the large numbers of Viet Cong and North Vietnamese killed, indications began to develop in the fall of 1967 of increasing enemy build-up, particularly in areas close to Communist havens in Laos and Cambodia. In late October the Viet Cong struck again at the Special Forces camp at Loc Ninh, but intensive air and artillery support plus quick arrival of American and South Vietnamese reinforcements saved the camp. The enemy nevertheless continued to give battle. He finally left the field ten days later after losing 800 dead in exchange for 50 killed in U.S. and ARVN units. The success was in no small part attributable to preponderance of U.S. firepower—30,000 rounds of artillery fire, 450 close support air sorties, and 8 bombardments by B–52's.

At the same time, the Communists again increased their strength in the Central Highlands, concentrating approximately 12,000 men around a Special Forces camp at Dak To, in the northern part of Kontum Province where the borders of Laos, Cambodia, and South Vietnam meet. As the enemy probed, U.S. and ARVN reinforcements brought a total commitment to the defense of sixteen battalions. After repulsing a Communist assault, American and South Vietnamese units moved out from their fire support bases to dislodge an enemy apparently determined to hold onto surrounding hills. Only after two battalions of the 173d Airborne Brigade on November 17th finally carried a strategic hill overlooking a road leading to the border did the Communists desist and withdraw, leaving behind 1,400 dead in the largest and most costly fight in the highlands since the Ia Drang valley campaign two years before.

The enemy resurgence here and at Loc Ninh and another heavy concentration in the vicinity of a Marine base at Khe Sanh, in the northwestern corner of the country equidistant from Laotian and North Vietnamese frontiers, were disturbing developments. Discovery of enemy documents pointing to a major offensive to follow the start of the lunar new year fed U.S. and ARVN apprehension. Coming as these developments did after long months of mounting successes, heavy Communist losses, and relentless air attacks against North Vietnam, they underscored the frustration that was always much a part of this strange war.

In Vietnam through 1967, the United States Army had fought a war of contrasts. On the one hand, it had been more sophisticated than any war in history, introducing amid a mélange of complex weapons and equipment a kind of third dimension that the airborne attacks of World War II and Korea had only foreshadowed. On the other hand, it had been a return to the primitive, often pitting man against man in a conflict and an environment where wile and stamina might determine who would prevail. It had been in another way two wars, a military campaign involving a compendium of all the Army had learned from the Revolution through Korea and at the same time a vast civic action project, using the men and tools of war in the task of winning the hearts and minds of a people. It had been a limited war in the classic sense of the American Revolution, the War of 1812, the Indian wars, the wars with Mexico and Spain, and Korea. In the same way that history cannot prophesy, only illuminate, so through 1967 this war of contrasts had produced no clear pattern for the warfare of the future.

As the year 1967 came to an end, the war in Vietnam had cost the United States almost 16,000 killed and 100,000 wounded, of which roughly 60 percent had been U.S. Army losses—numbers that would be substantially increased in the hard fighting still to come.

Suggested Additional Reading

The literature of American military history is voluminous and constantly growing. This bibliography cites only the most important and most useful titles. It is intended for the convenience of students, instructors, and others who desire a wider knowledge of the topics discussed in the chapters of this book. To assist the reader further the list is preceded by citation of general works.

GENERAL BIBLIOGRAPHY

Bibliographical and Reference Aids

Oscar Handlin, Arthur M. Schlesinger, Samuel Eliot Morison, Frederick Merk, and Arthur Schlesinger, Jr., *Harvard Guide to American History* (Cambridge: Belknap Press of Harvard University Press, 1955), remains a basic tool for any student of the American past. Dated but still useful is Robert G. Albion, *Introduction to Military History* (New York: Appleton-Century-Crofts, 1929). Newer and central to the study of American military history is Department of the Army, *The Writing of American Military History: A Guide,* DA Pamphlet 20–200 (Washington: Government Printing Office, 1956), which contains an extensive bibliography.

Francis B. Heitman, *Historical Register and Dictionary of the United States Army* (Facsimile Reprint, Champaign: University of Illinois Press, 1965), presents varied information on the strength of the Army and its organization from 1789 to 1903, and a listing of wars, battles, and campaigns. Newer reference works include *The Army Almanac: A Book of Facts Concerning the United States Army,* in two editions varying rather widely in coverage (Washington: Government Printing Office, 1950) and (Harrisburg: Stackpole, 1959); Hardin Craig, Jr. (comp.), *A Bibliography of Encyclopedias and Dictionaries Dealing with Military, Naval and Maritime Affairs, 1577–1965* (Houston: Rice University Library, 1965); and Robert D. Heinl, *Dictionary of Military and Naval Quotations* (Annapolis: U.S. Naval Institute, 1966), a collection of quotations dealing with war and related subjects and ideas from Biblical years to Vietnam.

Military Periodicals

A wealth of useful information relating to Army history, activities, policies, development, administration, and operations appears in various journals. Articles, documents, and book reviews on military history can often be located in standard civilian professional journals such as *The American Historical Review, Journal of American History* (formerly *Mississippi Valley Historical Review*), and especially the numerous state historical quarterlies. *Military Affairs* (formerly *Journal of the American Military History Foundation* and *Journal of the American Military Institute*) is currently the sole scholarly journal devoted to military history with emphasis on American affairs. *Military Collector and Historian* is more antiquarian in nature. Also useful are the *U.S. Naval Institute Proceedings,* the *Marine Corps Gazette,* and the *Air University Review.*

Various service journals provide a storehouse of information. See for instance *Air Force Journal* (formerly *Air Corps Newsletter, Air Force,* and *Official Journal of the U.S. Air Force*); *Army Navy Air Force Journal* (formerly *Army Navy Journal*); *Army Navy Air Force Register* (formerly *Army Navy Register*); *Journal of the Military Service Institution of the United States; The Military Review* (formerly *Review of Current Military Writing*); *Army Digest* (formerly *Army Information Digest*); *Armed Forces Management, Armed Forces Communication Journal* (formerly *Signal Magazine*). Some service journals contain historical studies of importance to the arm or service concerned. Most significant are *Army* (formerly *U.S. Combat Forces Journal*), which combined *Infantry Journal, Field Artillery Journal,* and *Antiaircraft Journal* (formerly *Journal of United States Artillery,* and *Coast Artillery Journal*); *Armor* (formerly *Cavalry Journal* and *Armored Cavalry Journal*); *Military Engineer* (formerly *Occasional Papers* and *Memoirs*); *Quartermaster Review; Military Chaplain;* and *Ordnance* (formerly *Army Ordnance*).

Background of War

Oliver L. Spaulding, Hoffman Nickerson, and John W. Wright, *Warfare: A Study of Military Methods from the Earliest Times* (Washington: Combat Forces Press, 1939), offers a good summary of world military history to the mid-eighteenth century. J.F.C. Fuller, *War and Western Civilization, 1832–1932: A Study of War as a Political Instrument and Expression of Mass Democracy* (London: Duckworth, 1932), carries the story past World War I.

Lynn Montross, *War Through the Ages* (New York: Harper, 1946), surveys the art and science of war as developed between 490 B.C. and 1944 A.D. Theodore Ropp, *War in the Modern World* (Durham: Duke University Press, 1959), is a short and vivid study of the wars of Western civilization from 1415 through the 1950's. J.F.C. Fuller, *The Conduct of War 1789–1961: A Study of the Impact of the French, Industrial, and Russian Revolutions on War and Its Conduct* (New Brunswick: Rutgers University Press, 1961), is a brief review of "conduct of war" in Western society from the opening of the Age of Revolution to multi-megaton deterrence, as is Cyril Falls, *The Art of War from the Age of Napoleon to the Present Day* (Oxford: Oxford University Press, 1961). Michael Howard (ed.), *The Theory and Practice of War; Essays Presented to B. H. Liddell Hart on His Seventieth Birthday* (New York: Frederick A. Praeger, 1966), contains fifteen essays which range from Jomini to American doctrine and problems of alliance. Other important works which should be consulted include: Quincy Wright, *A Study of War* (Chicago: University of Chicago Press, 1942, 2 volumes), which discusses the relationship between international law and military history. Edward Meade Earle (ed.), *Makers of Modern Strategy: Military Thought from Machiavelli to Hitler* (Princeton: Princeton University Press, 1943), contains a history of strategic thinking, mainly European, by twenty historians and analysts of military affairs. Gordon B. Turner (ed.), *A History of Military Affairs Since the 18th Century* (New York: Harcourt, Brace, 1956), is a compilation of readings showing the relationship between war and society as well as different persuasions that have arisen in some major controversial issues. R. A. Preston, Sidney F. Wise, and Hermon O. Werner, *Men in Arms: A History of Warfare and Its Interrelationships with Western Society* (New York: Frederick A. Praeger, 1962), places emphasis on war as a social institution, an expression of political, social, and economic organization of society in each age.

On specific aspects of military history, J. F. C. Fuller, *The Decisive Battles of the Western World, and their Influence Upon History* (London: Eyre and Spottiswoode, 1954), focuses upon the results of combat in the past. Franklin Mark Osanka (ed.), *Modern Guerrilla Warfare* (New York: Free Press of Glencoe, 1962), is an almost up-to-date anthology of unconventional warfare garnered from the written and unwritten accounts of past insurgence. James D. Hittle, *The Military Staff* (Harrisburg: Military Service Publishing Co., 1949), deals with the history and development of the general staffs of the armies of the United States, Great Britain, France, Germany, and Russia.

American Military Policy and History

The foundation study remains Emory Upton, *The Military Policy of the United States from 1775* (Washington: Government Printing Office, 1904), although something of a polemic against unpreparedness and a plea for a strong Regular Army. Another analysis, one which advocates a well-organized militia, is John McAuley Palmer, *America in Arms: The Experience of the United States with Military Organization* (New Haven: Yale University Press, 1941). More recent works include: R. Ernest and Trevor N. Dupuy, *Military Heritage of America* (New York: McGraw-Hill, 1956), a survey of the art of war as practiced by Americans, and Walter Millis, *Arms and Men: A Study in American Military History* (New York: Putnam, 1956). Millis describes the evolution of American military institutions and relates institutional developments to parallel social and economic forces in national life. An all too short, yet provocative book of essays examining topics of military organization and strategic decision making is T. Harry Williams, *Americans at War: The Development of the American Military System* (Baton Rouge: Louisiana State University, 1956). Somewhat similar to Millis' *Arms and Men,* but less analytical than Williams' *Americans at War,* is C. Joseph Bernardo and Eugene H. Bacon, *American Military Policy: Its Development Since 1775* (Harrisburg: Stackpole, 1955). Robert Leckie, *The Wars of America* (New York: Harper and Row, 1968), is a readable popular history. Two recent books of readings are "musts" for the student of military history. Raymond G. O'Connor (ed.), *American Defense Policy in Perspective: From Colonial Times to the Present* (New York: John Wiley, 1965), is a useful collection of articles, excerpts from books, officials documents, and speeches designed to reveal the historical nature of defense problems in general. Walter Millis (ed.), *American Military Thought* (Indianapolis: Bobbs-Merrill, 1966), is similar in focus to the O'Connor volume but is more of an anthology of original sources that demonstrate how Americans "have tended to think about war, military policy, and the military factor in their free society." Walter Millis, Harvey C. Mansfield, and Harold Stein, *Arms and the State: Civil Military Elements in National Policy* (New York: The Twentieth Century Fund, 1958), provides an excellent, well-written, general survey of American military policy from 1930 to 1953. Samuel Huntington, *The Common Defense: Strategic Programs in National Politics* (New York: Columbia University Press, 1961), continues the survey of military policy from the onset of the cold war to 1960.

Two standard histories of the United States Army are both dated but still informative: William A. Ganoe, *History of the United States Army* (New York:

Appleton-Century, 1936); and Oliver L. Spaulding, *The United States Army in War and Peace* (New York: Putnam, 1937). Russell F. Weigley, *History of the United States Army* (New York: Macmillan, 1967), the first in a series entitled "The Wars of the United States," is an excellent institutional history of the Army. Weigley has also contributed *Towards an American Army: Military Thought From Washington to Marshall* (New York: Columbia University Press, 1962), in which he examines certain key contributors to the evolution of American military thought.

On battle history, the student should consult the classic Matthew Forney Steele, *American Campaigns* (Washington: Byron S. Adams, 1909, 2 volumes), which long served as a standard textbook in the military schools of America. An indispensable updated version of Steele is Vincent Esposito (ed.), *et al., The West Point Atlas of American Wars, Volume I, 1689–1900; Volume II, 1900–1953* (New York: Frederick A. Praeger, 1959). J. F. C. Fuller, *Decisive Battles of the U.S.A.* (New York: Harper, 1942), examines twenty-two battles since the Revolution. O. K. Armstrong, *Fifteen Decisive Battles of the United States* (New York: Longmans, Green, 1961), is a well-written though undocumented account of selected battles from 1742 to 1945.

On key issues involving military manpower, Marvin A. Kreidberg and Merton G. Henry, *History of Military Mobilization in the United States Army, 1775–1945* (Washington: Government Printing Office, 1955), examines "the assembling and organizing of troops, materiel, and equipment for active military service in time of war or other emergency." Leonard L. Lerwill, *History of the U.S. Army Replacement System* (Washington: Government Printing Office, 1954) and John C. Sparrow, *History of Personnel Demobilization* (Washington: Government Printing Office, 1951), treat the history of the raising and demobilization of the armies of the United States during the various wars. Finally, George G. Lewis and John Mewha, *History of Prisoner of War Utilization by the United States Army* (Washington: Government Printing Office, 1955), examines another facet of manpower utilization from the Revolution through World War II.

Military organization has also prompted extensive treatment. Otto L. Nelson, Jr., *National Security and the General Staff* (Washington: Combat Forces Press, 1946), deals with the development of the general staff concept in the United States. Paul Y. Hammond, *Organizing For Defense: The American Military Establishment in the Twentieth Century* (Princeton: Princeton University Press, 1961), is a study of defense planning and management from 1903 to 1957. John C. Ries, *The Management of Defense* (Baltimore: Johns Hopkins University Press, 1964), is a narrative of changes which have taken place in the basic patterns of the War Department and other defense agencies during the past quarter of a century. On the evolution of Presidential war powers see Clarence A. Berdahl, *War Powers of the Executive in the United States* (Urbana: University of Illinois Press, 1921); Howard White, *Executive Influence in Determining Military Policy in the United States* (Urbana: University of Illinois Press, 1924); and Ernest R. May (ed.), *The Ultimate Decision: The President as Commander in Chief* (New York: Braziller, 1960).

On the problem of civil-military relations, Louis Smith, *American Democracy and Military Power: A Study of Civil Control of the Military Power in the United States* (Chicago: University of Chicago Press, 1951), is a comprehensive analysis. Jerome G. Kerwin (ed.), *Civil-Military Relationships in American Life* (Chicago: University of Chicago Press, 1948), is a collection of lectures by prominent national figures soon after World War II. A later work, Samuel P. Huntington, *The Soldier and the State: The Theory and Politics of Civil-Military Relations* (Cambridge: Belknap Press of Harvard University Press, 1957), is a most original and thought-provoking argument for development of an intellectual climate more favorable to the existence of military professionalism and achievement of objective civilian control. The American antimilitarist tradition is examined by Merle Curti, *Peace or War: The American Struggle, 1636–1936* (New York: Norton, 1936) and Arthur A. Ekirch, *The Civilian and the Military* (New York: Oxford University Press, 1956). On civilian components of the Army, William H. Riker, *Soldiers of the States: The Role of the National Guard in American Democracy* (Washington: Public Affairs Press, 1957), is a good but short institutional history of the National Guard, federalism, and political influence of reserves. Jim Dan Hill, *The Minute Man in Peace and War: A History of the National Guard* (Harrisburg: Stackpole, 1964), is a more recent overview of the subject. On the history of the ROTC, see Gene M. Lyons and John W. Masland, *Education and Military Leadership: A Study of the ROTC* (Princeton: Princeton University Press, 1959).

Approaches to analysis of the American fighting man can profitably begin with Morris Janowitz, *The Professional Soldier* (Glencoe, Ill.: The Free Press, 1960), which is an attempt to describe the professional life, organizational setting, and leadership of the American military as they evolved during the first half of this century. Earlier works include Ben Ames Williams (ed.), *Amateurs at War: The American Soldier in Action* (Boston: Houghton Mifflin, 1943), which portrays the common soldiers of the nation's wars through their own words. James Merrill, *Uncommon Valour* (Chicago: Rand McNally, 1965), is a recent addition in the same vein as Williams' work.

Specialized Phases of Army Development

Useful on certain phases of Army history are the following books:

1. *Branches:* Theophilus F. Rodenbaugh and William L. Haskin (eds.), *The Army of the United States: Historical Sketches of Staff and Line* (New York: Merrill, 1896), is invaluable for histories of the old regiments of the Army, as is Bruce Jacobs, *Soldiers: The Fighting Divisions of the Regular Army* (New York: Norton, 1958), for larger units. The oldest arm, the infantry, has never received adequate treatment, but John K. Mahon's introductory sketch in *The Army Lineage Book, Volume II: Infantry* (Washington: Department of the Army, Office, Chief of Military History, 1953), makes a good beginning. A good short introduction to artillery is Albert Mauncy, *Artillery Through the Ages* (Washington: Government Printing Office, 1949). The cavalry-armor heritage is given in the introduction by Mary L. Stubbs and Stanley R. Connor to *The Army Lineage Book: Armor-Cavalry* (Washington: Department of the Army, Office, Chief of Military History, 1969). On cavalry alone John K. Herr and Edward S. Wallace, *The Story of the U.S. Cavalry, 1775-1942* (Boston: Little, Brown, 1953); James M. Merrill, *Spurs to Glory: The Story of the United States Cavalry* (Chicago: Rand McNally, 1966); and Richard C. Wormser, *The Yellowlegs: The Story of the United States Cavalry* (Garden City: Doubleday, 1966), are recent popular treatments. On armor, see: Mildred Gillie, *Forging the Thunderbolt: A History of the Development of the Armored Forces* (Harrisburg: Military Service Publishing Co., 1947) and Richard M. Ogorkiewicz, *Armor: A History of Mechanized Forces* (New York: Frederick A. Praeger, 1960). For the services the reader should begin with James A. Huston, *The Sinews of War: Army Logistics, 1775-1953* (Washington: Government Printing Office, 1966), a clear and comprehensive history of all aspects of U.S. Army logistics: supply, transportation, evacuation and hospitalization, and service from the Revolution through Korea. Erna Risch, *Quartermaster Support of the Army: A History of the Corps, 1775-1939* (Washington: Government Printing Office, 1962), is something of a textbook on the evolution of supply operations in the Army. No really good treatment of the Signal Corps exists, but Army Times (eds.), *A History of the U.S. Army Signal Corps* (New York: Putnam, 1961) and Max L. Marshall, *The Story of the U.S. Army Signal Corps* (New York: Franklin Watts, 1965), are available. On the Corps of Engineers, G. A. Youngberg, *History of Engineer Troops in the United States Army, 1775-1901* (Washington: Engineer School Press, 1910) and Engineer School, U.S. Army, *History and Traditions of the Corps,* Engineer School Special Text St. 25-1 (Ft. Belvoir: Engineer School, 1953), are older accounts. Newer works

include L. Sprague DeCamp, *The Ancient Engineers* (Garden City: Doubleday, 1963); Forest G. Hill, *Roads, Rails, and Waterways: The Army Engineers and Early Transportation* (Norman: University of Oklahoma Press, 1957); and Franklin M. Davis and Thomas T. Jones, *The U.S. Army Engineers-Fighting Elite* (New York: Franklin Watts, 1967). On the Medical Service, see P. M. Ashburn, *A History of the Medical Department of the United States Army* (Boston: Houghton Mifflin, 1929). The Chaplains Corps is covered in Roy T. Honeywell, *Chaplains of the United States Army* (Washington: Government Printing Office, 1958). Aviation and the U.S. Army can be approached through Alfred Goldberg (ed.), *A History of the United States Air Force, 1907–1957* (Princeton: Van Nostrand, 1957) and Richard Tierney, *The Army Aviation Story* (Northport, Ala.: Colonial Press, 1963).

2. *Weapons:* Harold L. Peterson (ed.), *Encyclopedia of Firearms* (New York: E. P. Dutton, 1964), is a good one-volume, illustrated encyclopedia. Edwin Tunis, *Weapons: A Pictorial History* (Cleveland: The World, 1953), provides an illustrated guide. Marvin L. Worley, Jr., *New Developments in Army Weapons, Tactics, Organization, and Equipment* (Harrisburg: Military Service Publishing Co., 1958), is a digest of all important new developments as of the late 1950's. John S. Tompkins, *The Weapons of World War III: The Long Road Back from the Bomb* (Garden City: Doubleday, 1966), carries the discussion into the 1960's.

3. *Army and Education:* This area has lacked adequate treatment, and West Point has attracted much of the attention. Older works include: R. Ernest Dupuy, *Where They Have Trod: The West Point Tradition in American Life* (New York: Stokes, 1940) and *Men of West Point: The First 150 Years of the United States Military Academy* (New York: Sloane, 1951), and Sidney Foreman, *West Point: A History of the United States Military Academy* (New York: Columbia University Press, 1950). These works have recently been supplemented by Stephen E. Ambrose, *Duty, Honor, Country: A History of West Point* (Baltimore: Johns Hopkins University Press, 1966). Other aspects of the Army's role in education can be followed in John W. Masland and Lawrence I. Radway, *Soldiers and Scholars: Military Education and National Policy* (Princeton: Princeton University Press, 1957); Harold F. Clark and Harold S. Sloan, *Classroom in the Military* (New York: Teachers College, Columbia University, 1964); and George S. Pappas, *Prudens Futuri! The U.S. Army War College, 1901–1967* (Carlisle: Army War College Alumni Association, 1968).

4. *The Army Through Customs and Art:* Army traditions and customs can be traced in such works as Elbridge Colby, *Army Talk: A Familiar Dictionary of Soldier Speech* (Princeton: Princeton University Press, 1943); Mark

M. Boatner, *Military Customs and Traditions* (New York: David McKay, 1956); Gheradi Davis, *The Colors of the United States Army 1789–1912* (New York: Gillis Press, 1912); and Milo M. Quaife, Melvin J. Weig, and Roy Appleman, *The History of the United States Flag* (New York: Harper, 1961). The Library of Congress, *An Album of American Battle Art, 1775–1918* (Washington: Government Printing Office, 1947), is a superb collection of drawings, etchings, and photographs with accompanying text, which goes through World War I. Roy Meredith, *The American Wars, 1775–1953: A Pictorial History from Quebec to Korea* (Cleveland and New York: World, 1955), not only portrays American warfare through the eyes of witnessing artists, but also provides a history of American combat artists themselves. William H. Nelson and Frank K. Vandiver, *Fields of Glory: An Illustrated Narrative of American Land Warfare* (New York: E. P. Dutton, 1961), have deftly molded picture and text into a comprehensive one-volume, illustrated narrative of American land warfare. Gene Guerney, *A Pictorial History of the United States Army in War and Peace From Colonial Times to Vietnam* (New York: Crown, 1966), carries the treatment into the present period. For those readers seeking illustrated guides to individual equipment and uniforms, Jack Coggins, *The Fighting Man: An Illustrated History of the World's Greatest Fighting Forces Through the Ages* (Garden City: Doubleday, 1966), provides a good beginning.

    5. *Biographies and Memoirs:* Biography can be one of the most delightful ways to approach any sort of history. While the listing below is not intended to be exhaustive, it is designed to show students that a wealth of material exists in this area of American military history. Readers should be aware of the indispensable George W. Cullum, *Biographical Register of the Officers and Graduates of the United States Military Academy* (Boston: Houghton Mifflin, 1891, 3 volumes), as well as Heitman, *Historical Register and Dictionary,* already noted. On civilian secretaries the following should be investigated: Charles M. Wiltse, *John C. Calhoun, Nationalist, 1782–1828* (Indianapolis: Bobbs-Merrill, 1944) [Monroe]; J. Fred Rippy, *Joel R. Poinsett, Versatile American* (Durham: Duke University Press, 1933) [Van Buren]; Hudson Strode, *Jefferson Davis: American Patriot, 1808–1861* (New York: Harcourt, Brace, 1955) [Pierce]; Benjamin P. Thomas and Harold M. Hyman, *Stanton: The Life and Times of Lincoln's Secretary of War* (New York: Knopf, 1962) [Lincoln and Johnson]; Philip C. Jessup, *Elihu Root* (New York: Dodd, Mead, 1938, 2 volumes) [McKinley and Theodore Roosevelt]; Henry F. Pringle, *The Life and Times of William Howard Taft* (New York: Farrar and Rinehart, 1939, 2 volumes) [T. Roosevelt]; Henry L. Stimson and McGeorge Bundy, *On Active Service in Peace and War* (New York: Harper, 1947), and Elting E.

Morison, *Turmoil and Tradition: A Study of the Life and Times of Henry L. Stimson* (Boston: Houghton Mifflin, 1960), [Taft and Franklin Roosevelt]; and Frederick Palmer, *Newton D. Baker: America at War* (New York: Dodd, Mead, 1931, 2 volumes) [Wilson].

On senior officers, commanding generals, and chiefs of staff of the Army, the following are useful: for the early period, Douglas Southall Freeman, *George Washington* (New York: Scribner, 1948–57, 7 volumes); North Callahan, *Henry Knox: General Washington's General* (New York: Rinehart, 1958); Richard C. Knopf, *Anthony Wayne, A Name in Arms: The Wayne-Knox-Pickney-McHenry Correspondence* (Pittsburgh: Univerity of Pittsburgh Press, 1960); and Fletcher Pratt, *Eleven Generals: Studies in American Command* (New York: Sloan, 1949) [Maj. Gen. Jacob Brown as well as ten other "unknowns"], all offer insights into the careers of senior officers. Prominent commanding generals of the Army are covered in: Charles Winslow Elliott, *Winfield Scott, the Soldier and the Man* (New York: Macmillan, 1937); Warren W. Hassler, *General George B. McClellan: Shield of the Union* (Baton Rouge: Louisiana State University Press, 1957); Stephen E. Ambrose, *Halleck: Lincoln's Chief of Staff* (Baton Rouge: Louisiana State University Press, 1960); Ulysses S. Grant, *Personal Memoirs of U. S. Grant* (New York: C. L. Webster, 1885–86, 2 volumes); William T. Sherman, *Personal Memoirs of William T. Sherman* (New York: Appleton, 1931 ed., 2 volumes); John M. Schofield, *Forty-Six Years in the Army* (New York: Century, 1897); and Virginia Weisel Johnson, *The Unregimented General: A Biography of Nelson A. Miles* (Boston: Houghton Mifflin, 1962). For the chiefs of staff, good biographies are as follows: Hermann Hagedorn, *Leonard Wood: A Biography* (New York: Harper, 1931, 2 volumes); Frederick Palmer, *Bliss, Peacemaker: The Life and Letters of General Tasker Howard Bliss* (New York: Dodd, Mead, 1934); Edward M. Coffman, *The Hilt of the Sword: The Career of Peyton C. March* (Madison: University of Wisconsin Press, 1966); Frederick Palmer, *John J. Pershing, General of the Armies* (Harrisburg: Military Service Publishing Co., 1948); Douglas MacArthur, *Reminiscences* (New York: McGraw-Hill, 1964); Forrest C. Pogue, *George C. Marshall: Education of a General, 1880–1939* (New York: Viking, 1963) and *George C. Marshall: Ordeal and Hope, 1939–1942* (New York: Viking, 1966); Matthew B. Ridgway, *Soldier: The Memoirs of Matthew B. Ridgway* (New York: Harper, 1960); and Maxwell D. Taylor, *The Uncertain Trumpet* (New York: Harper, 1959). Literature on fighting generals is voluminous. For the Revolutionary period, see: George A. Billias (ed.), *George Washington's Generals* (New York: Morrow, 1964); Thomas Boyd, *Mad Anthony Wayne* (New York: Scribner, 1929); Louis Gottschalk, *Lafayette Joins the American*

Army (Chicago: University of Chicago Press, 1937); Samuel W. Patterson, *Horatio Gates, Defender of American Liberties* (New York: Columbia University Press, 1941); John R. Alden, *General Charles Lee: Traitor or Patriot* (Baton Rouge: Louisiana State University Press, 1951); John M. Palmer, *General Von Steuben* (New Haven: Yale University Press, 1937); Theodore Thayer, *Nathanael Greene: Strategist of the American Revolution* (New York: Twayne, 1960); and Don Higgenbotham, *Daniel Morgan: Revolutionary Rifleman* (Chapel Hill: University of North Carolina Press, 1961).

On the early national period the following will prove helpful: Marquis James, *Andrew Jackson, The Border Captain* (Indianapolis: Bobbs-Merrill, 1933) and Dwight L. Clarke, *Stephen Watts Kearny: Soldier of the West* (Norman: University of Oklahoma Press, 1961). For the Mexican War period, see: Holman Hamilton, Edward Nichols, and Brainerd Dyer, *Zachary Taylor* (Baton Rouge: Louisiana State University Press, 1946) and Lloyd Lewis, *Captain Sam Grant* (Boston: Little, Brown, 1950).

No other period in American military history has provoked as much biographical treatment as the Civil War. Only a fraction of existing works can be cited. On the Federal side, the following should be consulted: T. Harry Williams, *Lincoln and His Generals* (New York: Knopf, 1952); Bruce Catton, *U.S. Grant and the American Military Tradition* (Boston: Little, Brown, 1954); Lloyd Lewis, *Sherman, Fighting Prophet* (New York: Harcourt, Brace, 1958); B. H. Liddell Hart, *Sherman: Soldier, Realist, American* (New York: Frederick A. Praeger, 1958); Richard G. O'Connor, *Sheridan: The Inevitable* (Indianapolis: Bobbs-Merrill, 1953); William M. Lamers, *The Edge of Glory: A Biography of General William S. Rosecrans, U.S.A.* (New York: Harcourt, Brace, 1961); Francis F. McKinney, *Education in Violence: The Life of George H. Thomas and the History of the Army of the Cumberland* (Detroit: Wayne State University Press, 1961); Richard S. West, *Lincoln's Scapegoat General: A Life of Benjamin F. Butler, 1818–1893* (Boston, Houghton Mifflin, 1965); Jay Monaghan, *Custer: General George Custer* (Boston: Little, Brown, 1959); and Freeman Cleaves, *Meade of Gettysburg* (Norman: University of Oklahoma Press, 1960). For the Confederacy, useful volumes include: S. I. Neiman, *Judah P. Benjamin* (Indianapolis: Bobbs-Merrill, 1961); D. S. Freeman, *R. E. Lee* (New York: Scribner, 1935, 4 volumes); Charles P. Roland, *Albert Sidney Johnston: Soldier of Three Republics* (Austin: University of Texas, 1964); T. Harry Williams, *P. G. T. Beauregard: Napoleon in Gray* (Baton Rouge: Louisiana State University Press, 1955); John P. Dyer, *The Gallant Hood* (Indianapolis: Bobbs-Merrill, 1950); Joseph H. Parks, *General Edmund Kirby Smith, C. S. A.* (Baton Rouge: Louisiana State University Press, 1952); D. B.

Sanger and T. R. Hay, *James Longstreet: Soldier and Politician* (Baton Rouge: Louisiana State University Press, 1952); G. F. R. Henderson, *Stonewall Jackson and the American Civil War* (London: Longmans, Green, 1949); Burke Davis, *Jeb Stuart: The Last Cavalier* (New York: Rinehart, 1957); Ralph Selph Henry, *"First With the Most" Forrest* (Indianapolis: Bobbs-Merrill, 1944).

For the Spanish-American War and World War I, see: John P. Dyer, *From Shiloh to San Juan: Fighting Joe Wheeler* (Baton Rouge: Louisiana State University Press, 1961); and Richard G. O'Connor, *Black Jack Pershing* (Garden City: Doubleday, 1961).

For biographies of personalities in World War II and Korea, see: Dwight D. Eisenhower, *Crusade in Europe* (Garden City: Doubleday, 1948); Omar N. Bradley, *A Soldier's Story* (New York: Holt, 1951); Harry H. Semmes, *Portrait of Patton* (New York: Appleton-Century-Crofts, 1955); Mark W. Clark, *From the Danube to the Yalu* (New York: Harper, 1954); William F. Dean, *General Dean's Story* (New York: Viking, 1954); and James M. Gavin, *War and Peace in the Space Age* (New York: Harper, 1958).

CHAPTER BIBLIOGRAPHIES

Note: Recommended Readings are designed to provide specific references for the reader. Other References include more detailed treatments of various topics. (Pb) indicates paperback edition.

Chapter 1: Introduction

Recommended Readings

Albion, Robert G., *Introduction to Military History* (New York: D. Appleton-Century Co., 1929), Chapter VI.
Burr, John G., *The Framework of Battle* (New York: Lippincott, 1943), Chapters 1 and 2.
Craven, W. Frank, *Why Military History?* [The Harmon Memorial Lectures in Military History, Number One] (United States Air Force Academy, Colorado, 1959).
Dupuy, R. Ernest, and Dupuy, Trevor N., *Military Heritage of America* (New York: McGraw-Hill, 1956), Chapters 1 and 2.
Howard, Michael, "The Use and Abuse of Military History," *Journal of the Royal United Service Institution* (February 1962), Vol. CVII, No. 625, pp. 4–10.
The Writing of American Military History: A Guide [Department of the Army Pamphlet No. 20–200] (Washington: Government Printing Office, 1956), Chapter I.

Other References

Earle, Edward M. (ed.), *Makers of Modern Strategy* (Princeton: Princeton University Press, 1943), Chapters 4 and 5 (Pb).
Herring, Pendleton, *The Impact of War: Our American Democracy Under Arms* (New York: Farrar & Rinehart, 1941), Chapters I–III and X.

Howard, Michael (ed.), *The Theory and Practice of War*. (Essays presented to Captain B. H. Liddell Hart on his seventieth birthday) (New York: Frederick A. Praeger, 1966).

Huntington, Samuel P., *The Soldier and the State: The Theory and Politics of Civil-Military Relations* (Cambridge: Belknap Press, 1959) (Pb).

Millis, Walter, *Arms and Men: A Study in American Military History* (New York: Putnam, 1956) (Pb).

Ropp, Theodore, *War in the Modern World* (New York: Collier Books, 1962) (Pb).

Smith, Louis, *American Democracy and Military Power: A Study of Civil Control of the Military Power in the United States* (Chicago: University of Chicago Press, 1951).

Williams, T. Harry, *Americans at War: The Development of the American Military System* (New York: Collier Books, 1962).

Chapter 2: The Beginnings

Recommended Readings

Fortescue, Sir John W., *History of the British Army* (London: Macmillan, 1897–1930), 14 vols., Vol. II, pp. 247–408 and 571–601.

Peckham, Howard H., *The Colonial Wars, 1689–1763* (Chicago: University of Chicago Press, 1964) (Pb), pp. 1–221.

Preston, Richard A., Wise, Sydney F., and Werner, Hermon O., *Men in Arms* (New York: Frederick A. Praeger, 1956) (Pb), pp. 1–175.

Shy, John W., *Toward Lexington: The Role of the British Army in the Coming of the American Revolution* (Princeton: Princeton University Press, 1965), pp. 3–44.

Spaulding, Oliver L., Nickerson, Hoffman, and Wright, John W., *Warfare* (Washington: Infantry Journal Press, 1937), pp. 464–572.

Weigley, Russell F., *History of the United States Army* (New York: Macmillan, 1967), pp. 3–28.

Other References

Boorstin, Daniel J., *The Americans: The Colonial Experience* (New York: Random House, 1958).

Crane, Verner W., *The Southern Frontier, 1670–1732* (Durham: Duke University Press, 1928) (Pb).

Hunt, George T., *The Wars of the Iroquois* (Madison: University of Wisconsin Press, 1940) (Pb).

Leach, Douglas E., *Flintlock and Tomahawk: New England in King Philip's War* (New York: Macmillan, 1958) (Pb).

Osgood, Herbert L., *The American Colonies in the Eighteenth Century* (New York: Macmillan, 1924), 4 vols.

Pargellis, Stanley, *Lord Loudoun in North America* (New Haven: Yale University Press, 1933).

Stacey, Col. C. P., *Quebec 1759: The Siege and the Battle* (New York: St. Martin's Press, 1959).

Chapter 3: The American Revolution: First Phase

Recommended Readings

Alden, John R., *The American Revolution, 1775–1783* (New York: Harper, 1954), pp. 1–111 (Pb).

Freeman, Douglas S., *George Washington: A Biography*, 7 vols. (New York: Scribner, 1948–57), Vol. III: *Planter and Patriot*.

Huston, James A., *Sinews of War: Army Logistics, 1775–1953*, "Army Historical Series" (Washington, Government Printing Office, 1966), pp. 3–85.

Mackesy, Piers, *The War for America, 1775–1783* (Cambridge: Harvard University Press, 1964), pp. 1–102.

Montross, Lynn, *Rag-Tag and Bobtail, The Story of the Continental Army, 1775–1783* (New York: Harper, 1952), pp. 3–140.

Ward, Christopher, *The War of the Revolution*, 2 vols. (New York: Macmillan, 1952), Vol. I, pp. 3–318.

Weigley, Russell F., *History of the United States Army* (New York: Macmillan, 1967), pp. 29–73.

Other References

Alden, John R., *General Gage in America* (Baton Rouge: Louisiana State University Press, 1948).

Anderson, Troyer S., *The Command of the Howe Brothers during the American Revolution* (Oxford: Oxford University Press, 1936).

Cunliffe, Marcus, *George Washington: Man and Monument* (Boston: Little, Brown, 1958) (Pb).

French, Allen, *The First Year of the Revolution* (Boston: Houghton Mifflin, 1934).

Nelson, William H., *The American Tory: A Study of the Loyalists in the American Revolution* (Oxford: Oxford University Press, 1961) (Pb).

Robson, Eric, *The American Revolution in its Political and Military Aspects, 1763–1783* (London: Batchworth Press, 1955) (Pb).

Wallace, Willard M., *Appeal to Arms—A Military History of the American Revolution* (New York: Harper, 1951) (Pb).

Chapter 4: The Winning of Independence, 1777–1783

Recommended Readings

Billias, George Athan, ed., *George Washington's Generals* (New York: William Morrow, 1964) (Pb).

Freeman, Douglas S., *George Washington: A Biography* (New York: Scribner, 1948–57), Vol. IV: *Leader of the Revolution* and Vol. V: *Victory with the Aid of France*. See particularly Vol. V, pp. 478–501.

Mackesy, Piers, *The War for America, 1775–1783* (Cambridge: Harvard University Press, 1964), pp. 103 to end. See particularly pp. 510–516.

Millis, Walter, *Arms and Men: A Study in American Military History* (New York: Putnam, 1956), Chapter I, "The Democratization of War" (Pb).

Robson, Eric, *The American Revolution in its Political and Military Aspects* (London: Batchworth Press, 1955), pp. 93–174 (Pb).

Ward, Christopher, *The War of the Revolution* (New York: Macmillan, 1952), Vol. I, pp. 319 to end and Vol. II.

Willcox, William B., "The British Road to Yorktown: A Study in Divided Command," *American Historical Review*, Vol. LII, No. 1 (October 1946), pp. 1–35.

Other References

Alden, John R., *General Charles Lee, Traitor or Patriot* (Baton Rouge: Louisiana State University Press, 1951).

Higginbotham, Don, *Daniel Morgan, Revolutionary Rifleman* (Chapel Hill: University of
    North Carolina Press, 1961).
Knollenberg, Bernhard, *Washington and the Revolution: A Reappraisal* (New York: Mac-
    millan, 1940).
Nickerson, Hoffman, *Turning Point of the Revolution* (Boston: Houghton Mifflin, 1928).
Palmer, John M., *General Von Steuben* (New Haven: Yale University Press, 1937).
Thayer, Theodore, *Nathanael Greene, Strategist of the Revolution* (New York: Twayne
    Publishers, 1960).
Wallace, Willard M., *Traitorous Hero: The Life and Fortunes of Benedict Arnold* (New
    York: Harper, 1954).

Chapter 5: The Formative Years, 1783–1812

Recommended Readings

May, Ernest R. (ed.), *The Ultimate Decision: The President as Commander in Chief* (New
    York: George Braziller, 1960), Chapter I.
Risch, Erna, *Quartermaster Support of the Army: A History of the Corps, 1775–1939* (Wash-
    ington: Government Printing Office, 1962), Chapters III–IV.
Weigley, Russell F., *History of the United States Army* (New York: Macmillan, 1967),
    Chapters V–VI.
White, Leonard D., *The Federalists: A Study in Administrative History, 1789–1801* (New
    York: Macmillan, 1948), Chapters XII and XXIX (Pb).

Other References

Adams, Henry. Edited and condensed by Herbert Agar, *The Formative Years* (Boston:
    Houghton Mifflin, 1947).
Callahan, North, *Henry Knox: General Washington's General* (New York: Rinehart, 1958).
Cleaves, Freeman, *Old Tippecanoe: William Henry Harrison* (New York: Scribner, 1939).
DeVoto, Bernard (ed.), *Journals of Lewis and Clark* (Boston: Houghton Mifflin, 1953).
Jacobs, James R., *The Beginnings of the US Army* (Princeton: Princeton University Press,
    1947).
Knopf, Richard C. (ed.), *Anthony Wayne, A Name in Arms: The Wayne-Knox-Pickering-
    McHenry Correspondence* (Pittsburgh: University of Pittsburgh Press, 1960).
Van Every, Dale, *Final Challenge: The American Frontier, 1804–1845* (New York: William
    Morrow, 1965).

Chapter 6: The War of 1812

Recommended Readings

Brandt, Irving, *James Madison: Commander in Chief, 1812–1836* (Indianapolis: Bobbs-
    Merrill, 1961), Chapters IX–XXVIII.
Gilpin, Alex R., *The War of 1812 in the Old Northwest* (East Lansing: Michigan State Uni-
    versity Press, 1958), especially Chapters III–VII and X–XI.
James, Marquis, *Andrew Jackson: The Border Captain* (Indianapolis: Bobbs-Merrill, 1933),
    Chapters IX–XX (Pb).
May, Ernest (ed.), *The Ultimate Decision: The President as Commander in Chief* (New
    York: George Braziller, 1960), Chapter II.
Risch, Erna, *Quartermaster Support of the Army: A History of the Corps, 1775–1939* (Wash-
    ington: Government Printing Office, 1962), Chapter V.
White, Leonard D., *The Jeffersonians: A Study in Administrative History, 1801–1829* (New
    York: Macmillan, 1951), Chapters XV–XVIII and XXXIV (Pb).

Other References

Adams, Henry. Edited by H. A. DeWeerd, *The War of 1812* (Washington: Infantry Journal Press, 1944).
Brooks, Charles B., *The Siege of New Orleans* (Seattle: University of Washington Press, 1961).
Coles, Harry L., *The War of 1812* (Chicago: University of Chicago Press, 1965) (Pb).
Hitsman, J. MacKay, *The Incredible War of 1812* (Toronto: University of Toronto Press, 1965) (Pb).
Mahan, Alfred T., *Sea Power in its Relation to the War of 1812* (New York: Scribner, 1903).
Mason, Philip (ed.), *After Tippecanoe: Some Aspects of the War of 1812* (East Lansing: Michigan State University Press, 1963).
Muller, Charles, *The Darkest Day, 1814: The Washington-Baltimore Campaign* (Philadelphia: Lippincott, 1963).

Chapter 7: The Thirty Years' Peace

Recommended Readings

Elliott, Charles Winslow, *Winfield Scott: The Soldier and the Man* (New York: Macmillan, 1937), Chapters XXIV–XXVII.
Falk, Stanley L., "Artillery for the Land Service: The Development of a System," *Military Affairs,* Vol. XXVIII, No. 3 (Fall 1964), pp. 97–110.
James, Marquis, *The Life of Andrew Jackson* (Indianapolis and New York: Bobbs-Merrill, 1938), Chapter XVIII (Pb).
Mahon, John K., *History of the Second Seminole War, 1839–1842* (Gainesville: University of Florida Press, 1967).
Rippy, J. Fred, *Joel R. Poinsett, Versatile American* (Durham: Duke University Press, 1935), Chapters XII and XIII.
Risch, Erna, *Quartermaster Support of the Army: A History of the Corps, 1775–1939* (Washington: Government Printing Office, 1962), Chapter VI.
Weigley, Russell F., *History of the United States Army* (New York: Macmillan, 1967), Chapters VII and VIII.
White, Leonard D., *The Jeffersonians: A Study in Administrative History, 1801–1829* (New York: Macmillan, 1951), Chapters XVII, XVIII, and XXXIV (Pb).

Other References

Beers, Henry P., *The Western Military Frontier, 1815–1846* (Philadelphia: n.p., 1935).
Forman, Sidney, *West Point* (New York: Columbia University Press, 1950).
Sprague, John T., *The Origin, Progress, and Conclusion of the Florida War* (Gainesville, Fla.: University of Florida Press, 1964), quadricentennial edition.
Thian, Raphael P., *Legislative History of the General Staff of the Army of the United States* (Washington: Government Printing Office, 1901).

Chapter 8: The Mexican War and After

Recommended Readings

Elliott, Charles Winslow, *Winfield Scott: The Soldier and the Man* (New York: Macmillan, 1937), Chapters XXXV–XLI.

Risch, Erna, *Quartermaster Support of the Army: A History of the Corps, 1775–1939* (Washington: Government Printing Office, 1962), Chapters VII and VIII.
Strode, Hudson, *Jefferson Davis, American Patriot* (New York: Harcourt, 1955), Chapters XI, XII, XVI, and XVII.

Other References

Bill, Alfred Hoyt, *Rehearsal for Conflict: The War With Mexico, 1846–1848* (New York: Knopf, 1947).
Goetzmann, William H., *Army Exploration in the American West, 1803–1863* (New Haven: Yale University Press, 1959) (Pb).
Hamilton, Holman, *Zachary Taylor* (Indianapolis and New York: Bobbs-Merrill, 1941).
Henry, Robert Selph, *The Story of the Mexican War* (Indianapolis and New York: Bobbs-Merrill, 1950).
Lavender, David, *Climax at Buena Vista* (Philadelphia: Lippincott, 1966).
Singletary, Otis A., *The Mexican War* (Chicago: University of Chicago Press, 1960) (Pb).
Smith, Justin H., *The War With Mexico* (New York: Macmillan, 1919).

Chapter 9: The Civil War, 1861

Recommended Readings

Alexander, Edward P., *Military Memoirs of A Confederate* (Bloomington: Indiana University Press, 1962 Reprint), Chapters 1–3.
Freeman, Douglas Southall, "Lee's Lieutenants: A Study in Command" (New York: Scribner, 1942), Vol. I, *Manassas to Malvern Hill,* Chapters I–X.
Kreidberg, Marvin A., and Merton G. Henry, *History of Military Mobilization in the United States Army, 1775–1945* (Washington: Government Printing Office, 1955), Chapter IV.
Longstreet, James, *From Manassas to Appomattox, Memoirs of the Civil War in America* (Bloomington: Indiana University Press, 1960 Reprint), Chapters 1–4.
Randall, J. G., and David Donald, *The Divided Union* (Boston: Little, Brown, 1961), Chapters I–X.
Risch, Erna, *Quartermaster Support of the Army: A History of the Corps, 1775–1939* (Washington: Government Printing Office, 1962), Chapters IX and X.
United States Military Academy, Department of Military Art and Engineering, *The West Point Atlas of American Wars, Vol. I, 1689–1900* (New York: Frederick A. Praeger, 1959), Maps 17–24.
Wilshin, Francis F., *Manassas (Bull Run) National Battlefield Park, Virginia* (Washington: Government Printing Office, 1957 Rev.), U.S. National Park Service Historical Handbook Series No. 15. The reader should be aware of other useful handbooks in this series pertaining to the Civil War including: *Antietam, Chickamauga and Chattanooga, Custis-Lee Mansion, Fort Pulaski, Fredericksburg Battlefields, Gettysburg, The Lincoln Museum and the House Where Lincoln Died, Petersburg Battlefields, Richmond Battlefields, Shiloh, Vicksburg.*

Other References

Catton, Bruce, *The Coming Fury,* "The Centennial History of the Civil War," Vol. I (Garden City: Doubleday, 1963) (Pb).
Lord, Francis, *They Fought for the Union* (Harrisburg: Stackpole, 1960).
Nevins, Allan, "The War for the Union" (New York: Scribner, 1959), 2 vols., Vol. 1: *The Improvised War, 1861–1862.*
Rozwenc, Edwin C. (ed.), *The Causes of the American Civil War* (Boston: Heath, 1961) (Pb).

Chapter 10: The Civil War, 1862

Recommended Readings

Catton Bruce, *This Hallowed Ground: The Story of the Union Side of the Civil War* (Garden City: Doubleday, 1956), Chapters 3–7 (Pb).

Commager, Henry Steele (ed.), *The Blue and the Gray: The Story of the Civil War as Told by Participants* (Indianapolis: Bobbs-Merrill, 1950), Chapters IV–XIII.

Freeman, Douglas Southall, "Lee's Lieutenants: A Study in Command" (New York: Scribner, 1942–44), Vol. I, *Manassas to Malvern Hill,* Chapters X–XLIII and Vol. II, *Cedar Mountain to Chancellorsville,* Chapters I–XXIII.

Monaghan, James, *Civil War on the Western Border, 1854–1865* (Boston: Little, Brown, 1955), Chapters XX–XXIII.

Nevins, Allan, "The War for the Union," Vol. II: *War Becomes Revolution* (New York: Scribner, 1960), Chapters I–XIV.

Randall, James G., and David Donald, *The Divided Union* (Boston: Little, Brown, 1961), Chapters 10 and 11.

Williams, Kenneth P., *Lincoln Finds a General: A Military Study of the Civil War* (New York: Macmillan, 1949–1959), 5 vols.; Vol. I, Chapters IV–XIII; Vol. II, Chapters XIV–XVI; Vol. III, Chapters V–XV; and Vol. IV, Chapters I–IX.

Williams, T. Harry, *Lincoln and His Generals* (New York: Knopf, 1952), Chapters IV–VIII.

Other References

Colton, Raymond C., *The Civil War in the Western Territories: Arizona, Colorado, New Mexico, and Utah* (Norman: University of Oklahoma Press, 1959).

Mitchell, Joseph B., *Decisive Battles of the Civil War* (New York: Putnam, 1955).

Quarles, Benjamin, *The Negro in the Civil War* (Boston: Little, Brown, 1953).

United States Military Academy, Department of Military Art and Engineering, *The West Point Atlas of American Wars, Vol. I, 1689–1900* (New York: Frederick A. Praeger, 1959), Maps 25–83.

Vandiver, Frank E., *Rebel Brass: The Confederate Command System* (Baton Rouge: Louisiana State University Press, 1956).

Chapter 11: The Civil War, 1863

Recommended Readings

Catton, Bruce, *This Hallowed Ground: The Story of the Union Side of the Civil War* (Garden City: Doubleday, 1956), Chapters 7–11 (Pb).

Commager, Henry Steele (ed.), *The Blue and the Grey: The Story of the Civil War as Told by Participants* (Indianapolis: Bobbs-Merrill, 1950), Chapters XV, XVII, and XVIII.

Cullen, Joseph P., *Where a Hundred Thousand Fell: The Battles of Fredericksburg, Chancellorsville, the Wilderness and Spotsylvania Court House* (Washington: Government Printing Office, 1966), U.S. Park Service Handbook 39.

Freeman, Douglas Southall, "Lee's Lieutenants: A Study in Command" (New York: Scribner, 1942–44), Vol. II, *Cedar Mountain to Chancellorsville,* Chapters XXV–XXXVII and Vol. III, *Gettysburg to Appomattox,* Chapters I–XVII.

Randall, James G., and David Donald, *The Divided Union* (Boston: Little, Brown, 1961), Chapter 23.

United States Military Academy, Department of Military Art and Engineering, *The West Point Atlas of American Wars, Vol. I, 1689–1900* (New York: Frederick A. Praeger, 1959), Maps 84–116.

Williams, Kenneth P., *Lincoln Finds a General: A Military Study of the Civil War* (New York: Macmillan, 1949–1959), 5 vols., Vol. IV, Chapters X–XIII and Vol. V.

Williams, T. Harry, *Lincoln and His Generals* (New York: Knopf, 1952), Chapters IX–XII.

Other References

Catton, Bruce, *Glory Road: The Bloody Route from Fredericksburg to Gettysburg* (Garden City: Doubleday, 1952) (Pb).

Downey, Fairfax, *Storming of the Gateway: Chattanooga, 1863* (New York: D. McKay, 1960).

Miers, Earl Schenk, *The Web of Victory: Grant at Vicksburg* (New York: Knopf, 1955).

Mitchell, Joseph B., *Decisive Battles of the Civil War* (New York: Putnam, 1955).

Wiley, Bell I., *The Life of Billy Yank: The Common Soldier of the Union* (Indianapolis: Bobbs-Merrill, 1952) (Pb).

———, *The Life of Johnny Reb: The Common Soldier of the Confederacy* (Indianapolis: Bobbs-Merrill, 1952) (Pb).

Chapter 12: The Civil War, 1864–1865

Recommended Readings

Catton, Bruce, *This Hallowed Ground: The Story of the Union Side of the Civil War* (Garden City: Doubleday, 1954), Chapters 11–13 (Pb).

Freeman, Douglass Southall, "Lee's Lieutenants: A Study in Command" (New York: Scribner, 1942–44), 3 vols.; Vol. III, *Gettysburg to Appomattox,* Chapters XVIII–XXXVII.

Randall, James G., and David Donald, *The Divided Union* (Boston: Little, Brown, 1961), Chapters 24–30.

United States Military Academy, Department of Military Art and Engineering, *The West Point Atlas of American Wars, Vol. I, 1689–1900* (New York: Frederick A. Praeger, 1959), Maps 117–154.

Williams, T. Harry, *Lincoln and His Generals* (New York: Knopf, 1952), Chapters XII–XIV.

Other References

Davis, Burke, *To Appomattox: Nine April Days, 1865* (New York: Rinehart, 1959) (Pb).

Horn, Stanley, *The Decisive Battle of Nashville* (Baton Rouge: Louisiana State University Press, 1956).

Jones, Virgil Carrington, *Ranger Mosby* (Chapel Hill: University of North Carolina Press, 1944).

Livermore, Thomas L., *Numbers and Losses in the Civil War in America, 1861–65* (Bloomington: Indiana University Press, 1957 Reprint).

Luvaas, Jay, *The Military Legacy of the Civil War: The European Inheritance* (Chicago: University of Chicago Press, 1959).

Miers, Earl S., *The General Who Marched to Hell: William Tecumseh Sherman and His March to Fame and Infamy* (New York: Knopf, 1951) (Pb).

Steere, Edward, *The Wilderness Campaign* (Harrisburg: The Stackpole Co., 1960).

Chapter 13: Darkness and Light: The Interwar Years, 1865–1898

Recommended Readings

Dupree, A. Hunter, *Science in the Federal Government: A History of Policies and Activities to 1940* (Cambridge: The Belknap Press of Harvard University Press, 1957), pp. 129, 184–194, and 256–270.

Eggert, Gerald G., *Railroad Labor Disputes: The Beginnings of Federal Strike Policy* (Ann Arbor: The University of Michigan Press, 1967), pp. 1–57, 136–146, and 152–202.

Gluckman, Arcadi, *United States Muskets, Rifles and Carbines* (Harrisburg: The Stackpole Co., 1959), pp. 227–333, 405–409, and 438–444.

Huntington, Samuel P., *The Soldier and the State: The Theory and Politics of Civil-Military Relations* (Cambridge: The Belknap Press of Harvard University Press, 1957), pp. 222–269 (Pb).

Risch, Erna, *Quartermaster Support of the Army: A History of the Corps, 1775–1939* (Washington: Government Printing Office, 1962), pp. 453–514.

Weigley, Russell F., *History of the United States Army* (New York: Macmillan, 1967), pp. 255–292.

Wilson, Frederick T., *Federal Aid in Domestic Disturbances, 1787–1903*, 57th Congress, 2d Session, Senate Document 209 (Washington: Government Printing Office, 1903), Serial 4430, pp. 107–239.

Other References

Ambrose, Stephen E., *Upton and the Army* (Baton Rouge: Louisiana State University Press, 1964).

Bailey, Thomas A., *A Diplomatic History of the American People* (New York: Appleton-Century-Crofts, 7th ed., 1964), pp. 348–464.

Bentley, George R., *A History of the Freedmen's Bureau* (Philadelphia: University of Pennsylvania Press, 1955).

Bruce, Robert V., *1877: Year of Violence* (Indianapolis: Bobbs-Merrill, 1959).

Caswell, John E., *Arctic Frontiers: United States Explorations in the Far North* (Norman: University of Oklahoma Press, 1956), pp. 42–122 and *passim*.

Fuller, Claud E., *The Breech-Loader in the Service, 1816–1917: A History of All Standard and Experimental U.S. Breechloading and Magazine Shoulder Arms* (New Milford, Conn., 1965), pp. 225–363.

Hill, Jim Dan, *The Minute Man in Peace and War: A History of the National Guard* (Harrisburg: The Stackpole Co., 1964), pp. 99–137.

Hume, Edgar Erskine, *Victories of Army Medicine: Scientific Accomplishments of the Medical Department of the United States Army* (Philadelphia: Lippincott, 1943), pp. 22–30 and 45–57.

Rich, Bennett M., *The Presidents and Civil Disorder* (Washington: The Brookings Institution, 1941), pp. 72–113.

Sefton, James E., *The United States Army and Reconstruction, 1865–1877* (Baton Rouge: Louisiana State University Press, 1967).

Singletary, Otis A., *Negro Militia and Reconstruction* (Austin: University of Texas Press, 1957).

Thomas, Benjamin P., and Harold M. Hyman, *Stanton: The Life and Times of Lincoln's Secretary of War* (New York: Knopf, 1962), pp. 402–640.

Whitnah, Donald R., *A History of the United States Weather Bureau* (Urbana: University of Illinois Press, 1961), pp. 1–60 (Pb).

Chapter 14: Winning the West: The Army in the Indian Wars, 1865–1890

Recommended Readings

Andrist, Ralph K., *The Long Death: The Last Days of the Plains Indians* (New York: Macmillan, 1962), Chapters IV–IX.
Downey, Fairfax, *Indian-Fighting Army* (New York: Scribner, 1944), Chapters III–V and VII–XVI (Pb).
Dunn, J. P., *Massacres of the Mountains* (New York: Harper, 1886. Facsimile edition, New York: Archer House, circa 1959), Chapters XIII–XXI.
Potomac Corral of The Westerners, *Great Western Indian Fights* (New York: Doubleday, 1960), Chapters 10–25 (Pb).
Tebbel, John, and Keith Jennison, *The American Indian Wars* (New York: Harper, 1960), Chapters 14–16).
National Park Service, *Soldier and Brave: Military and Indian Affairs in the Trans-Mississippi West, Including a Guide to Historic Sites and Landmarks* (New York: Harper and Row, 1963), pp. 1–89.

Other References

Brown, Dee, *Fort Phil Kearny: An American Saga* (New York: Putnam, 1962).
Brimlow, George F., *The Bannock Indian War of 1878* (Caldwell: Caxton Press, 1938).
Carter, Robert G., *On the Border With Mackenzie* (New York: Antiquarian Press, 1959).
Graham, W. A., *The Story of the Little Big Horn* (Harrisburg: Military Service Publishing Co., 1941) (Pb).
Grinnell, George Bird, *The Fighting Cheyennes* (New York: Scribner, 1915).
Josephy, Alvin M., Jr., *The Nez Perces and the Opening of the Northwest* (New Haven: Yale University Press, 1965).
Lockwood, Frank C., *The Apache Indians* (New York: Macmillan, 1938).
Murray, Keith A., *The Modocs and Their War* (Norman: University of Oklahoma Press, 1953).
Schmidt, Martin F., and Dee Brown, *Fighting Indians of the West* (New York: Scribner, 1948).
Sprague, Marshall, *Massacre: The Tragedy at White River* (Boston: Little, Brown, 1958).
Utley, Robert M., *The Last Days of the Sioux Nation* (New Haven: Yale University Press, 1963) (Pb).

Chapter 15: Emergence to World Power, 1898–1902

Recommended Readings

Grenville, John A. S., and George Berkeley Young, *Politics, Strategy, and American Diplomacy: Studies in Foreign Policy, 1873–1917* (New Haven: Yale University Press, 1966), Chapters 7–10.
Morgan, H. Wayne, *America's Road to Empire: The War With Spain and Overseas Expansion*, America in Crisis series edited by Robert A. Divine (New York: John Wiley, 1965), especially Chapters 4 and 5 (Pb).
Purcell, Victor, *The Boxer Uprising: A Background Study* (Cambridge: University Press, 1963), especially Chapter 12.
Risch, Erna, *Quartermaster Support of the Army: A History of the Corps, 1775–1939* (Washington: Government Printing Office, 1962), Chapter XII.

Other References

Alger, Russell A., *The Spanish-American War* (New York: Harper, 1901).
Baclagon, Uldarico S., *Philippine Campaigns* (Manila: Graphic House, 1952).
Freidel, Frank, *The Splendid Little War* (Boston: Little, Brown, 1958).
Millis, Walter, *The Martial Spirit: A Study of Our War with Spain* (Cambridge: Harvard
    University Press, 1931) (Pb).
Pratt, Julius, *The Expansionists of 1898* (Baltimore: Johns Hopkins Press, 1936) (Pb).
Sexton, William T., *Soldiers in the Sun* (Harrisburg, Pa.: Military Service Publishing Co.,
    1939). (A second edition appeared in 1944 under a new title: *Soldiers in the Philippines:
    A History of the Insurrection.*)
Tan, Chester C., *The Boxer Catastrophe* (New York: Columbia University Press, 1955).
Wolff, Leon, *Little Brown Brother: How the United States Purchased and Pacified the
    Philippine Islands at the Century's Turn* (Garden City: Doubleday, 1961).

Chapter 16: Transition and Change, 1902–1917

Recommended Readings

Huntington, Samuel P., *The Soldier and the State: The Theory and Politics of Civil-Military
    Relations* (Cambridge: Harvard University Press, 1957), pp. 237–42, 270–74, and
    279–82 (Pb).
Leopold, Richard W., *Elihu Root and the Conservative Tradition* (Boston: Little, Brown,
    1954), Chapter 2 (Pb).
Millis, Walter, ed., *American Military Thought* (Indianapolis: Bobbs-Merrill, 1966), pp.
    xxxii–xxxix and 240–350 (Pb).
Nelson, Otto L., Jr., *National Security and the General Staff* (Washington: Infantry Journal
    Press, 1946), Chapters 1–4 and especially pp. 73–186.
Stimson, Henry L., and McGeorge Bundy, *On Active Service in Peace and War* (New York:
    Harper, 1947), Chapters 2 and 4.

Other References

Beale, Howard K., *Theodore Roosevelt and the Rise of America to World Power* (Balti-
    more: Johns Hopkins Press, 1956) (Pb).
Cline, Howard F., *The United States and Mexico* (Cambridge: Harvard University Press,
    1953).
Hagedorn, Herman, *Leonard Wood,* 2 vols. (New York: Harper, 1931).
Jones, Chester Lloyd, *The Caribbean Since 1900* (New York: Prentice-Hall, 1936).
Mansergh, Nicholas, *The Coming of the First World War: A Study in the European Bal-
    ance, 1878–1914* (London: Longmans, Green, 1949).
Padelford, Norman, *The Panama Canal in Peace and War* (New York: Macmillan, 1942).
Pringle, Henry F., *The Life and Times of William Howard Taft,* 2 vols. (New York: Farrar
    and Rinehart, 1939).
Tompkins, Frank, *Chasing Villa: The Story Behind the Story of Pershing's Expedition into
    Mexico* (Harrisburg, Pa.: Military Service Publishing Co., 1934).

Chapter 17: World War I: The First Three Years

Recommended Readings

Huston, James A., *The Sinews of War: Army Logistics, 1775–1953,* "Army Historical
    Series" (Washington: Government Printing Office, 1966), pp. 308–87.

Kreidberg, Marvin A., and Merton G. Henry, *History of Military Mobilization in the United States Army* (Washington: Department of the Army, DA Pamphlet 20–212, 1955), pp. 189–376.

Ropp, Theodore, *War in the Modern World* (Durham: Duke University Press, 1959), pp. 204–47 (Pb).

Spaulding, Oliver Lyman, *The United States Army in War and Peace* (New York: Putnam, 1937), pp. 406–20.

Weigley, Russell F., *History of the United States Army* (New York: Macmillan, 1967), pp. 342–94.

Other References

Asprey, Robert B., *The First Battle of the Marne* (Philadelphia: Lippincott, 1962).

Coffman, Edward M., *The Hilt of the Sword—The Career of Peyton C. March* (Madison: University of Wisconsin Press, 1966).

Fay, Sidney Bradshaw, *The Origins of the World War* (New York: Macmillan, 1939) (Pb).

Horne, Alistair, *The Price of Glory: Verdun, 1916* (New York: St. Martin's Press, 1963) (Pb).

Marshall, S. L. A., and the editors of *American Heritage, The American Heritage History of World War I* (New York: American Heritage Publishing Co., 1964).

Tuchman, Barbara W., *The Zimmermann Telegram* (New York: Viking, 1958) (Pb).

———, *The Guns of August* (New York: Macmillan, 1962) (Pb).

Watt, Richard M., *Dare Call It Treason* (New York: Simon and Schuster, 1963).

Wolff, Leon, *In Flanders Field: The 1917 Campaign* (New York: Viking, 1958) (Pb).

Chapter 18: World War I: The U.S. Army Overseas

Recommended Readings

Historical Division, Department of the Army, *Organization of the American Expeditionary Forces, I,* "United States Army in the World War, 1917–1919" (Washington: Government Printing Office, 1948), pp. 3–52.

Ropp, Theodore, *War in the Modern World* (Durham: Duke University Press, 1959), pp. 247–55 (Pb).

Spaulding, Oliver Lyman, *The United States Army in War and Peace* (New York: Putnam, 1937), pp. 421–450.

Other References

Harbord, James G., *The American Army in France* (Boston: Little, Brown, 1936).

O'Connor, Richard, *Black Jack Pershing* (Garden City: Doubleday, 1961).

Pershing, John J., *My Experiences in the World War* (New York: Stokes, 1931), 2 vols.

Pitt, Barrie, *1918—The Last Act* (New York: Norton, 1963).

Stallings, Laurence, *The Doughboys: The Story of the AEF, 1917–1918* (New York: Harper, 1963).

Chapter 19: Between World Wars

Recommended Readings

Goldberg, Alfred (ed.), *A History of the United States Air Force, 1907–1957* (Princeton: Nostrand, 1957), pp. 29–55.

Greenfield, Kent Roberts (ed.), *Command Decisions* (Washington: Government Printing Office, 1960), Chapters I, III, and IV.

Huston, James A., *The Sinews of War: Army Logistics, 1775–1953,* "Army Historical Series" (Washington: Government Printing Office, 1967), Chapters XXIV–XXVIII.

Millis, Walter, *American Military Thought* (New York: Bobbs-Merrill, 1966), pp. 362–435 (Pb).

O'Connor, Raymond G., *American Defense Policy in Perspective* (New York: John Wiley, 1965), pp. 185–240 (Pb).

Weigley, Russell F., *History of the United States Army* (New York: Macmillan, 1967), Chapters 17 and 18.

Other References

Bernardo, C. Joseph, and Eugene H. Bacon, *American Military Policy: Its Development Since 1775* (Harrisburg: Military Service Publishing Co., 1955), Chapters 17 and 18.

Conn, Stetson, and Byron Fairchild, *The Framework of Hemisphere Defense,* "U.S. Army in World War II" (Washington: Government Printing Office, 1960).

Greenfield, Kent Roberts, "Origins of the Army Ground Forces: General Headquarters United States Army, 1940–1942," in Greenfield, Robert R. Palmer, and Bell I. Wiley, *The Organization of Ground Combat Troops,* "U.S. Army in World War II" (Washington: Government Printing Office, 1947).

Killigrew, John W., "The Army and the Bonus Incident," in *Military Affairs* (Summer 1962), Vol. XXVI, No. 2, pp. 59–65.

Matloff, Maurice, and Edwin M. Snell, *Strategic Planning for Coalition Warfare, 1941–1942,* "U.S. Army in World War II" (Washington: Government Printing Office, 1953).

Millis, Walter, *Arms and Men: A Study in American Military History* (New York: Putnam, 1956), Chapters IV and V (Pb).

Weigley, Russell F., *Towards an American Army: Military Thought from Washington to Marshall* (New York: Columbia University Press, 1962), Chapter 12.

Chapter 20: World War II: The Defensive Phase

Recommended Readings

Cline, Ray S., *Washington Command Post: The Operations Division,* "U.S. Army in World War II" (Washington: Government Printing Office, 1951), Chapters V–VII.

Conn, Stetson, and Byron Fairchild, *The Framework of Hemisphere Defense,* "U.S. Army in World War II" (Washington: Government Printing Office, 1960), Chapter VII.

Greenfield, Kent Roberts (ed.), *Command Decisions* (Washington: Government Printing Office, 1960), Chapters VI and VII.

Leighton, Richard M., and Robert W. Coakley, *Global Logistics and Strategy, 1940–1943,* "U.S. Army in World War II" (Washington: Government Printing Office, 1956), Chapters VI–VII and XIV–XV.

Matloff, Maurice, and Edwin M. Snell, *Strategic Planning for Coalition Warfare, 1941–1942,* "U.S. Army in World War II" (Washington: Government Printing Office, 1953), Chapters VIII, XII, and XVI–XVII.

Millett, John D., *The Organization and Role of the Army Service Forces,* "U.S. Army in World War II" (Washington: Government Printing Office, 1954), Chapter II.

Watson, Mark S., *Chief of Staff: Prewar Plans and Preparations,* "U.S. Army in World War II" (Washington: Government Printing Office, 1950), Chapter XV.

Other References

Churchill, Winston S., *The Second World War: The Grand Alliance* (Boston: Houghton Mifflin Company, 1950); *The Hinge of Fate* (Boston: Houghton Mifflin, 1950) (both Pb).
Conn, Stetson, Rose C. Engelman, and Byron Fairchild, *Guarding the United States and Its Outposts*, "U.S. Army in World War II" (Washington: Government Printing Office, 1964).
Craven, Wesley F., and James L. Cate (eds.), Vol. I, *Plans and Early Operations*, "The Army Air Forces in World War II" (Chicago: University of Chicago Press, 1948).
Green, Constance M., Harry C. Thomson, and Peter C. Roots, *The Ordnance Department: Planning Munitions for War*, "U.S. Army in World War II" (Washington: Government Printing Office, 1955).
Gwyer, J. M. A., and J. R. M. Butler, *Grand Strategy*, Vol. III in "History of the Second World War, United Kingdom Military Series," edited by J. R. M. Butler (London: H. M. Stationery Office, 1964).
Lord, Walter H., *Day of Infamy* (New York: Henry Holt, 1957) (Pb).
Morison, Samuel E., *The Battle of the Atlantic, September 1939–May 1943; The Rising Sun in the Pacific, 1931–April 1942; Coral Sea, Midway and Submarine Actions, May 1942–August 1942.* All in "History of U.S. Naval Operations in World War II" (Boston: Little, Brown, 1947–1962), 15 vols.
Morton, Louis, *The Fall of the Philippines*, "U.S. Army in World War II" (Washington: Government Printing Office, 1952).
Pogue, Forrest C., *George C. Marshall: Ordeal and Hope, 1939–1942* (New York: Viking, 1966).
Romanus, Charles F., and Riley Sunderland, *Stilwell's Mission to China*, "U.S. Army in World War II" (Washington: Government Printing Office, 1953). (See also bibliography of Chapter 21.)

Chapter 21: Grand Strategy and the Washington High Command

Recommended Readings

Cline, Ray S., *Washington Command Post: The Operations Division*, "U.S. Army in World War II" (Washington: Government Printing Office, 1951), Chapters XII–XIII and XV–XVI.
Coakley, Robert W., and Richard M. Leighton, *Global Logistics and Strategy, 1943–1945* "U.S. Army in World War II" (Washington: Government Printing Office, 1968), Chapters XI, XXII, XXV, and XXXII.
Greenfield, Kent Roberts (ed.), *Command Decisions* (Washington: Government Printing Office, 1960), Chapters X, XV, XVI, and XXII.
Huston, James A., *The Sinews of War: Army Logistics, 1775–1953*, "Army Historical Series" (Washington: Government Printing Office, 1966), Chapter XXVI.
Leighton, Richard M., and Robert W. Coakley, *Global Logistics and Strategy, 1940–1943*, "U.S. Army in World War II" (Washington: Government Printing Office, 1956), Chapters XXV–XXVII.
Matloff, Maurice, *Strategic Planning for Coalition Warfare, 1943–1944*, "U.S. Army in World War II" (Washington: Government Printing Office, 1959), Chapters I, XVI, XXII, and XXIII.
———, *Mr. Roosevelt's Three Wars: FDR as War Leader* (The Harmon Memorial Lectures in Military History, Number 6) (United States Air Force Academy, Colorado, 1964).

——, "The American Approach to War, 1919–1945," in Michael Howard, ed., *The Theory and Practice of War*. (Essays presented to Captain B. H. Liddell Hart on his seventieth birthday) (New York: Frederick A. Praeger, 1966).

Millett, John D., *The Organization and Role of the Army Service Forces,* "U.S. Army in World War II" (Washington: Government Printing Office, 1954), Chapters III–V.

Other References

Bureau of the Budget, *The United States at War* (Washington: Government Printing Office, 1946).

Churchill, Winston S., *The Second World War* (Boston: Houghton Mifflin, 1948–53), 6 vols. See particularly *The Hinge of Fate* (1950), *Closing the Ring* (1951), and *Triumph and Tragedy* (1953).

Ehrman, John, *Grand Strategy,* Vols. V and VI in "History of the Second World War, United Kingdom Military Series," edited by J. R. M. Butler (London: H. M. Stationery Office, 1956).

Feis, Herbert, *Churchill, Roosevelt, Stalin: The War They Waged and the Peace They Sought* (Princeton: Princeton University Press, 1957) (Pb).

Greenfield, Kent Roberts, *American Strategy in World War II: A Reconsideration* (Baltimore: Johns Hopkins Press, 1963).

Greenfield, Kent Roberts, Robert P. Palmer, and Bell I. Wiley, *The Organization of Ground Combat Troops,* "U.S. Army in World War II" (Washington: Government Printing Office, 1947).

Morison, Samuel E., *Strategy and Compromise* (Boston: Little, Brown, 1958) (Pb).

Sherwood, Robert, *Roosevelt and Hopkins: An Intimate History* (New York: Harper, rev. ed., 1950).

Stimson, Henry L., and McGeorge Bundy, *On Active Service in Peace and War* (New York: Harper, 1948).

Chapter 22: World War II: The War Against Germany and Italy

Recommended Readings

Blumenson, Martin, *Breakout and Pursuit,* "U.S. Army in World War II" (Washington: Government Printing Office, 1961), Chapters IV, XI, XII, and XIII.

Cole, Hugh M., *The Ardennes: Battle of the Bulge,* "U.S. Army in World War II" (Washington: Government Printing Office, 1964), Chapters I, V, XIX, and XXV.

Greenfield, Kent Roberts (ed.), *Command Decisions* (Washington: Government Printing Office, 1960), Chapters XII, XIII, XIV, XVII, XVIII, XIX, XX, and XXII.

Harrison, Gordon, *Cross-Channel Attack,* "U.S. Army in World War II" (Washington: Government Printing Office, 1951), Chapters VI and VIII.

Howe, George F., *Northwest Africa: Seizing the Initiative in the West,* "U.S. Army in World War II" (Washington: Government Printing Office, 1957), Chapters XIV, XXIII, and XXIV.

Huston, James A., *The Sinews of War: Army Logistics 1775–1953,* "Army Historical Series" (Washington: Government Printing Office, 1966), Chapter XXX.

MacDonald, Charles B., *The Siegfried Line Campaign,* "U.S. Army in World War II" (Washington: Government Printing Office, 1963), Chapters XIV and XV.

Smyth, Howard McGaw, and Albert N. Garland, *Sicily and the Surrender of Italy,* "U.S. Army in World War II" (Washington: Government Printing Office, 1965), Chapters VI, VII, and IX.

Other References

Blumenson, Martin, *Anzio: The Gamble That Failed* (Philadelphia: Lippincott, 1963).
Cole, Hugh M., *The Lorraine Campaign,* "U.S. Army in World War II" (Washington: Government Printing Office, 1950).
Hechler, Ken, *The Bridge at Remagen* (New York: Ballantine Books, 1957) (Pb).
MacDonald, Charles B., *Company Commander* (New York: Ballantine Books, 1966) (Pb).
———, and Sidney T. Mathews, *Three Battles: Arnaville, Altuzzo, and Schmidt,* "U.S. Army in World War II" (Washington: Government Printing Office, 1954).
Pogue, Forrest C., *The Supreme Command,* "U.S. Army in World War II" (Washington: Government Printing Office, 1954).
Ruppenthal, Roland P., *Logistical Support of the Armies,* Vols. I and II, "U.S. Army in World War II" (Washington: Government Printing Office, 1953, 1959).
Toland, John, *The Last 100 Days* (New York: Random House, 1965) (Pb).
Wilmot, Chester, *The Struggle for Europe* (New York: Harper, 1952) (Pb).

Chapter 23: World War II: The War Against Japan

Recommended Readings

Greenfield, Kent Roberts (ed.), *Command Decisions* (Washington: Government Printing Office, 1953), Chapters XI and XXI.
Morison, Samuel Eliot, *New Guinea and the Marianas,* "History of U.S. Naval Operations in World War II," Vol. VIII (Boston: Little, Brown, 1953), Chapters XIV–XVI.
Morton, Louis, *Strategy and Command: The First Two Years,* "U.S. Army in World War II" (Washington: Government Printing Office, 1961), Chapters VI and XI–XXIX.
———, *Pacific Command: A Study in Interservice Relations* (Harmon Memorial Lectures in Military History No. 3) (USAF Academy, Colorado, 1961).
Smith, Robert Ross, *The Approach to the Philippines,* "U.S. Army in World War II" (Washington: Government Printing Office, 1953), Chapters XII–XIV.
Stamps, T. Dodson, and Esposito, Vincent J., eds., *A Military History of World War II* (New York: U.S. Military Academy, 1956), Vol. II, Part III.

Other References

Craven, Wesley F., and Cate, James L., eds., *Matterhorn to Nagasaki,* "The Army Air Forces in World War II," Vol. V (Chicago: University of Chicago Press, 1953).
Crowl, Philip A., *Campaign in the Marianas,* "U.S. Army in World War II" (Washington: Government Printing Office, 1959).
———, and Iseley, Jeter A., *The U.S. Marines and Amphibious War* (Princeton: Princeton University Press, 1951).
Falk, Stanley, *Decision at Leyte* (New York: Norton, 1966) (Pb).
Miller, John, jr., *Guadalcanal: The First Offensive,* "U.S. Army in World War II" (Washington: Government Printing Office, 1949).
Morison, Samuel Eliot, *Aleutians, Gilberts and Marshalls* and *Victory in the Pacific,* "History of U.S. Naval Operations in World War II," Vols. VII and XIV (Boston: Little, Brown, 1951–60).
Romanus, Charles F., and Sunderland, Riley, *Stilwell's Command Problems,* "U.S. Army in World War II" (Washington: Government Printing Office, 1956).

Smith, Robert Ross, *Triumph in the Philippines,* "U.S. Army in World War II" (Washington: Government Printing Office, 1963).

(In addition, see other volumes in the "U.S. Army in World War II," the "History of U.S. Naval Operations in World War II" and the "Army Air Forces in World War II" series dealing with operations in the war against Japan.)

Chapter 24: Peace Becomes Cold War, 1945–1950

Recommended Readings

Finletter, Thomas K., *Foreign Policy: The Next Phase* (New York: Harper, 1958), Chapter III.
Kennan, George F., "Is War with Russia Inevitable?", *Department of State Bulletin,* February 20, 1950, Vol. XXII, pp. 267–71, 303.
Millis, Walter, *Arms and the State* (New York: The Twentieth Century Fund, 1958), Chapters 4, 5, and 6.
Morgenthau, Hans J., "The Policy of the U. S. A.," *The Political Quarterly,* January–March 1951, Vol. XXII, pp. 43–56.
Schlesinger, Arthur, Jr., "Origins of the Cold War," *Foreign Affairs,* October 1967, Vol. 46, No. 1, pp. 22–52.
Weigley, Russell F., *History of the United States Army* (New York: Macmillan, 1967), Chapter 20.

Other References

Bernardo, Maj. C. Joseph, and Eugene H. Bacon, *American Military Policy, Its Development Since 1775* (Harrisburg: Military Service Publishing Co., 1955), Chapters 20 and 21.
Clay, Lucius D., *Decision in Germany* (New York: Doubleday, Inc., 1950).
The Conflict in Korea, Events Prior to the Attack on June 25, 1950, Department of State Publication 4266, Far Eastern Series 45 (Washington, October 1951).
Huntington, Samuel P., *The Common Defense* (New York: Columbia University Press, 1961) (Pb).
Ismay, Lord, *NATO, The First Five Years, 1949–1954* (Netherlands: Bosch-Utrecht, 1954), Chapters I and II.
Sparrow, Maj. John C., *History of Personnel Demobilization in the United States Army,* Department of the Army Pamphlet No. 20–210 (Washington: Department of the Army, 1952).

Chapter 25: The Korean War, 1950–1953

Recommended Readings

Bernardo, Maj. C. Joseph, and Eugene H. Bacon, *American Military Policy, Its Development Since 1775* (Harrisburg: Military Publishing Co., 1955), Chapter 22.
Dupuy, R. Ernest, and Trevor N. Dupuy, *Military Heritage of America* (New York: McGraw-Hill, 1956), Chapter 20.
Millis, Walter, *Arms and the State* (New York: The Twentieth Century Fund, 1958), Chapter 7.
Sawyer, Maj. Robert K., *Military Advisors in Korea: KMAG in Peace and War,* "Army Historical Series" (Washington: Government Printing Office, 1962), Chapter V.
Truman, Harry S., *Memoirs,* Vol. 2, *Years of Trial and Hope* (New York: Doubleday, 1956), Chapter 22 (Pb).

Weigley, Russell F., *History of the United States Army* (New York: Macmillan, 1967), Chapter 21.
Whiting, Allen S., *China Crosses the Yalu* (New York: Macmillan, 1960), Chapters III, IV, V, VI, and VII.

Other References

Appleman, Roy E., *South to the Naktong, North to the Yalu,* "U.S. Army in the Korean War" (Washington: Government Printing Office, 1961).
Clark, Mark W., *From the Danube to the Yalu* (New York: Harper, 1954).
Gugeler, Russell A., *Combat Actions in Korea* (Washington: Combat Forces Press, 1954).
Hermes, Walter G., *Truce Tent and Fighting Front,* "U.S. Army in the Korean War" (Washington: Government Printing Office, 1966).
MacArthur, Douglas, *Reminiscences* (New York: McGraw-Hill, 1964) (Pb).
Rees, David, *Korea: The Limited War* (New York: St. Martin's Press, 1964).
Ridgeway, Matthew B., *The Korean War* (New York: Doubleday, 1967).

Chapter 26: The Army and the New Look

Recommended Readings

Gavin, James M., *War and Peace in the Space Age* (New York: Harper, 1958), Chapters 5J, 5K, and 7.
Kaufmann, William W., ed., *Military Policy and National Security* (Princeton: Princeton University Press, 1956), Chapters 1, 4, and 8.
Kissinger, Henry A., *Nuclear Weapons and Foreign Policy* (New York: Harper, 1957), Chapters 2 and 12.
O'Connor, Raymond G., ed., *American Defense Policy in Perspective: From Colonial Times to the Present* (New York: John Wiley, 1965), Chapter 20.
Osgood, Robert E., *Limited War: The Challenge to American Strategy* (Chicago: University of Chicago Press, 1957), Chapters I, IX, and X.
Ridgway, Matthew B., *Soldier: The Memoirs of Matthew B. Ridgway* (New York: Harper, 1956), Chapters 30–38.
Taylor, Maxwell D., *The Uncertain Trumpet* (New York: Harper, 1959), Chapters III, IV, and VIII.
Weigley, Russell J., *History of the United States Army* (New York: Macmillan, 1967), Chapter 21.

Other References

Acheson, Dean, *Power and Diplomacy* (Cambridge: Harvard University Press, 1958).
Finletter, Thomas K., *Foreign Policy: The Next Phase* (New York: Harper, 1958).
Garthoff, Raymond L., *Soviet Strategy in the Nuclear Age* (New York: Frederick A. Praeger, 1958).
Kahn, Herman, *On Thermonuclear War* (Princeton: Princeton University Press, 1960).
Knorr, Klaus, ed., *NATO and American Security* (Princeton: Princeton University Press, 1959).
Millis, Walter, *Arms and Men: A Study in American Military History* (New York: Putnam, 1956), Chapter VII.
Stanley, Timothy W., *American Defense and National Security* (Washington: Public Affairs Press, 1956).

Chapter 27: Global Pressures and the Flexible Response

Recommended Readings

Halle, Louis J., *The Cold War as History* (New York: Harper and Row, 1967), Chapters
    XXXVII and XXXVIII.
Kaufmann, William W., *The McNamara Strategy* (New York: Harper and Row, 1964),
    Chapters 1, 2, and 5.
Kissinger, Henry A., *The Troubled Partnership: A Re-appraisal of the Atlantic Alliance*
    (New York: McGraw-Hill, 1965), Chapters 1–3.
O'Connor, Raymond G., ed., *American Defense Policy in Perspective: From Colonial Times
    to the Present* (New York: John Wiley, 1965), Chapter 21.
Schlesinger, Arthur W. Jr., *A Thousand Days: John F. Kennedy in the White House*
    (Boston: Houghton Mifflin, 1965), Chapters X, XV, and XXX.
Taylor, Maxwell D., *Responsibility and Response* (New York: Harper and Row, 1967),
    Chapters I–IV.
Weigley, Russell F., *History of the United States Army* (New York: Macmillan, 1967),
    Chapter 22.

Other References

Deitchman, Seymour J., *Limited War and American Defense Policy* (Cambridge: M.I.T.
    Press, 1964).
Donnelly, Charles H., *U.S. Defense Policies in 1961*, 87th Congress, 2d Session, House Docu-
    ment No. 502 (Washington: Government Printing Office, 1962).
——, *U.S. Defense Policies in 1962*, 88th Congress, 1st Session, House Document No. 155
    (Washington: Government Printing Office, 1963).
——, *U.S. Defense Policies in 1963*, 88th Congress, 2d Session, House Document No. 335
    (Washington: Government Printing Office, 1964).
——, *U.S. Defense Policies in 1964*, 89th Congress, 1st Session, House Document No. 285
    (Washington: Government Printing Office, 1965).
——, *U.S. Defense Policies in 1965*, 89th Congress, 2d Session, House Document No. 344
    (Washington: Government Printing Office, 1966).
Heaps, Willard A., *Riots, U.S.A.: 1765–1965* (New York: The Seeburg Press, 1966).
Heller, Deane, and David, *The Berlin Wall* (New York: Walker and Co., 1962).
Sorenson, Theodore C., *Kennedy* (New York: Harper and Row, 1965).

Chapter 28: The U.S. Army in Vietnam

Recommended Readings

"1965 Green Book, 1965 Status Reports," *Army*, Vol. 15, No. 16 (November 1965).
"1966 Green Book, 1966 Status Reports," *Army*, Vol. 16, No. 10 (October 1966).
"1967 Green Book, 1967 Status Reports," *Army*, Vol. 10, No. 10 (October 1967).
The Military Assistance Institute, The Department of Defense, *Country Study: The Re-
    public of Vietnam* (Washington: Department of Defense, 1965), Chapters I–IV.
Senate Committee on Foreign Relations, U.S. Senate, *Background Information Relating to
    Southeast Asia and Vietnam* (Washington: Government Printing Office, March 1966,
    2d ed.)

Special Operations Research Office, The American University, *Casebook on Insurgency and Revolutionary Warfare: 23 Summary Accounts, Section I, Revolution in Vietnam: 1946–1954* (Washington: Special Operations Research Office, 1962), pp. 25–43.

Young, Kenneth T., "The Stakes in Vietnam," *Current History,* Vol. 54, No. 317 (January (1968), pp. 22–28.

Other References

Bain, Chester A., *Vietnam: The Roots of Conflict* (Englewood Cliffs: Prentice Hall, 1967).

Buttinger, Joseph, *Vietnam: A Dragon Embattled,* 2 vols. (New York: Frederick A. Praeger, 1966).

Fall, Bernard B., *The Two Vietnams: A Political and Military Analysis,* 2d ed. rev. (New York: Frederick A. Praeger, 1967).

Giap, Vo Nguyen, *Big Victory Great Task* (New York: Frederick A. Praeger, 1968).

Kahin, George M., and Lewis, John W., *The United States in Vietnam* (New York: Dial Press, 1966) (Pb).

Marshall, S. L. A., *Battles in the Monsoon: Campaigning in the Central Highlands, Vietnam, Summer 1966* (New York: William Morrow, 1967).

Pike, Douglas, *Viet Cong: The Organization and Techniques of the National Liberation Front of South Vietnam* (Cambridge: M.I.T. Press, 1966).

Trager, Frank N., *Why Vietnam* (New York: Frederick A. Praeger, 1966).

Index

Wilhelm II of Germany, 359, 396, 400, 402–03
Wilkinson, Brig. Gen. James, 118–21, 135, 140
Williamsburg, Va., 96, 221
Wilmington, N.C., 93, 203, 276
Wilson, Field Marshal Henry M., 482
Wilson, Woodrow, 354–59, 364–70, 373, 383–84, 400–402, 407, 529
Wilson's Creek, Mo., 203
Winchester, Va., 199, 221–22, 270
Winchester, Brig. Gen. James, 130
Winnsboro, S.C., 90
Winter Line, 481–82
Wisconsin, 157–59
Wolf Mountains, 316
Wolfe, Maj. Gen. James, 37–38, 51
Womens Army Corps, 463, 541
Wonsan, 556–57
Wood, Maj. Gen. Leonard, 349, 352, 364, 366
Woodlark Island, 508
Wool, Maj. Gen. John E., 166, 170–72, 179, 185
World War I, 8, 13
  Allied offensives, 393–94, 396–403
  casualties, periodic, 362, 368, 371–72, 387–90, 394, 398, 403
  causes, 358–59
  critical periods, 370–72
  demobilization, 405–06
  early campaigns, 359–64, 368–69
  German offensives, 384–94
  impact on United States, 364–66
  mobilization for, 372–78, 403–04
  neutrality policy, 369–70
  troop requirements, 374–75
World War II, 8–9, 13
  beginnings, 417–18
  casualties, periodic, 423–24, 465, 497
  demobilization, 530–31

World War II—Continued
  mobilization of manpower, 416–17, 419, 426, 455–56, 459–60, 462–63
  neutrality policy, 418, 420–22
  preparedness program, 418–20, 422
  strategic planning, 425–28, 431, 439–72, 506–10, 514–16
  U.S. contribution, 497–98
Worth, Brig. Gen. William J., 7, 161, 176
Wounded Knee Creek, 318
Wright brothers, 350
Wyoming, 179, 315
Wyoming Valley, 85

Yakima Indians, 304
Yalta Conference, 458, 526, 533
Yalu River, 556–58
Yamamoto, Admiral Isoroku, 528
Yamashita, General Tomoyuki, 518–19
Yap Island, 515–16
Yazoo River, 237, 240
Yellow Tavern, Va., 268
Yellowstone River and Valley, 315–16
York, Pfc. Alvin C., 401
York (Toronto), Canada, 131–32, 141
York, Pa., 75, 80, 248
York River, 94–98, 223
Yorktown, Va., 8, 93–99, 220–21
Yugoslavia, 424, 536
Yukon, 296
Yunnan Province, 523–24

Zamboanga, 520
Zapata, Emiliano, 354
Zimmermann, telegram, 369–70
Zone of the Interior, 464
Zorndorf, battle of, 24
Zuider Zee, 492